AF765286

Using SUPERCALC®
The Next Generation

A SELF-TEACHING GUIDE

WILLIAM J. DOYLE, JR.

A WILEY PRESS BOOK
JOHN WILEY & SONS, INC.
New York • Chichester • Brisbane • Toronto • Singapore

Wiley Press books are available at quantity discounts when used to promote products or services. For information, please write to the Special Sales Department, John Wiley & Sons.

Copyright © 1985 by John Wiley & Sons, Inc.

All rights reserved. Published simultaneously in Canada.

Reproduction or translation of any part of this work beyond that permitted by Section 107 or 108 of the 1976 United States Copyright Act without the permission of the copyright owner is unlawful. Requests for permission or further information should be addressed to the Permissions Department, John Wiley & Sons, Inc.

Library of Congress Cataloging in Publication Data

Doyle, William J., 1946-
Using SuperCalc.

Includes index.
1. SuperCalc (Computer program) 2. Business—Data processing. I. Title.
HF5548.4.S85D69 1984 001.64'25 84-25752
ISBN 0-471-80828-8

Printed in the United States of America

85 86 10 9 8 7 6 5 4 3 2 1

SuperCalc®, SuperCalc2®, and SuperCalc3® are registered trademarks of Sorcim/IUS Micro Software.
SuperWriter™ and EasyWriterII™ System are trademarks of Sorcim/IUS Micro Software.
dBase II® is a registered trademark of Ashton-Tate.
DataStar® is a registered trademark of MicroPro International.
VisiCalc® is a registered trademark of VisiCorp.
1-2-3™ and Lotus™ are trademarks of Lotus Development Corporation.
Sperry PC is referred to courtesy of Sperry Corporation.
IBM® PC is a registered trademark of International Business Machines Corp.
Z-150 PC is a Zenith Data Systems Product; Zenith Data Systems is a wholly owned subsidiary of Zenith Electronics Corporation.
Columbia refers to any of the personal computers of Columbia Data Products, Inc.
Compaq-Plus™ is a trademark of Compaq Computer Corporation.
Apple® is a registered trademark of Apple Computer, Inc.
Microsoft® is a registered trademark of Microsoft Corporation.
GWBASIC™ is a trademark of Microsoft Corporation.

To my wife, Connie, and children, Sean and Lauren.

Acknowledgments

My thanks for their support and advice about this book's prospectus and manuscript go to Connie Doyle; Jeff Brown, Anne Christ, Paul Driehaus, Jean Prickett, and Ken Schreiber of Sperry Information Systems; Peggy McManus of La Salle University; Jim Archibald, Rick Wooten, and Rich Lobron of the Southeastern Pennsylvania Transportation Authority; Rosemary Driehaus of Comquest, Inc.; and Shirley-Ann Ericksson.

Special thanks are due to the following wonderful people who helped me when my aging Apple II died midway through the manuscript: Connie Doyle, who drove many miles to purchase replacement parts; Luie Aynat of Tseng Labs, Incorporated, who repaired the Apple; and Bill and Mary Powell, who lent me their Apple while mine was being repaired.

A very special acknowledgment goes to Sorcim/IUS Micro Software for their support and cooperation throughout this project. They provided the following software: SuperCalc², SuperCalc³, Super³ Release 2, and SuperWriter. Special thanks go to Richard Goodhue, the SuperCalc product manager, and the following members of the Customer Support staff: Dave Kesterson, Keith Sturdivant, and Paul Thatcher.

Contents

Preface

Using SuperCalc: The Next Generation addresses the needs of the beginning microcomputer user. It is recommended for business professionals and hobbyists who want an introductory text on how to use the SuperCalc^3 integrated electronic spreadsheet. It presents a logical, pragmatic approach to electronic spreadsheets, covering SuperCalc^3 features in the sequence a person, particularly a novice, would most likely use them.

It specifically addresses SuperCalc^3 Release 2, supplementing the reference manuals with explanations easily understandable by the layperson. Simple examples are built on from chapter to chapter. The organization, examples, and end of chapter review exercises make this book well suited as a text for an introductory course in electronic spreadsheets.

The book is divided into four main sections. Section One, An Introduction, contains Chapters 1 and 2. Chapter 1 presents an overview of electronic spreadsheets. Chapter 2 summarizes key attributes of the two most popular operating systems used on the IBM PC class of microcomputers: PC-DOS and MS-DOS. SuperCalc^3 has been specifically designed to run under these operating systems.

Section Two, Basic Features of SuperCalc^3, contains Chapters 3 through 9. Chapter 3 covers entering and exiting SuperCalc and moving around the spreadsheet. Chapter 4 covers entering text and formulas. Detailed emphasis is placed on arithmetic operations and expressions.

Spreadsheet sizing, calculation control, movement control, and display modes are introduced in Chapter 5 as /Global command options. Spreadsheet formats, both standard and user-defined, are covered in Chapter 6. Chapter 7 covers duplicating, manipulating, and editing your spreadsheet. Various input and output commands and techniques are taught in Chapter 8. Chapter 9 covers arithmetic, date, business, and special functions as well as logical operators.

Section Three, Advanced SuperCalc^3 Features, includes Chapters 10 through 15. Chapter 10 covers screen partitioning and title locking. Chapter 11 deals with table lookups and sorting. Chapter 12 introduces SuperCalc^3 graphics. Database management is introduced in Chapter 13. Chapter 14 introduces creating "canned" command streams to increase processing speed. Chapter 15 illustrates interfacing SuperCalc files with BASIC, using SuperData Interchange (SDI).

Section Four, Business Applications, consists of Chapter 16, which presents guidelines and examples for designing SuperCalc^3 templates and applications.

This book is designed to be read while you are using SuperCalc^3 on your microcomputer. How you use the book will depend on your experience with SuperCalc^3. Novices should read Chapters 1 and 2 in conjunction with the SuperCalc^3 installation instructions. Then they should sequentially read Chapters 3 through 9. Only when they are thoroughly comfortable with the preceding material should they go to Chapters 10 through 16. The exercises at the end of each chapter will give beginners feedback about how well they understand the material. Readers can skip Chapter 12 if their system does not have graphics capability.

Although more experienced users may want to skip around the book, it is suggested they verify their understanding of the subject matter by completing the review exercises at the end of each chapter before proceeding to more advanced subjects. Also, more experienced users will find that spreadsheets created under SuperCalc, SuperCalc^2, and SuperCalc^3 (Release 1) are upwardly compatible with SuperCalc^3, Release 2.

SECTION ONE

An Introduction

CHAPTER 1

What Is an Electronic Spreadsheet?

Setting the Stage

Collecting and processing data that eventually results in reporting information is an important consideration for business and financial professionals and government administrators. Managers and administrators are regularly involved with budgetary planning and control.

Historically, these people did most of their work with pencils, erasers, calculators, and the infamous columnar pads. They would tediously write entries of one kind or another onto these pads, then add across each row to calculate a total to enter at the end of the row. Next, they'd add down each column, calculating a total for the bottom of the column. Finally, they'd add down the last column, representing row totals, then add across the last row, representing column totals.

Holding their breath, they'd invoke a deity and hope their column and row totals cross-footed—that is, the total at the bottom of the last column equalled the total at the end of the last row. When the totals did not cross-foot, the rows and columns had to be added again. Hopefully, the mistake would be found and corrected. The time it took to do this varied with how many rows and columns were being used.

Consider the labor budgeting worksheet shown in Figure 1.1, parts A and B. It represents planned salaries for the fiscal year. It also assumes an average annual salary increase of 10%.

Figure 1.1 uses the following calculations:

Old Biweekly Salary = Old Annual Salary divided by 26.

New Biweekly Salary = Old Biweekly Salary increased by the "raise" percentage.

New Annual Salary = New Biweekly Salary times 26.

Employee Monthly Labor = Biweekly Salary times the number of pay periods, occurs 12 times.

Department Monthly Labor = Sum of Employee Monthly Labor.

Total Labor = Sum of Employee Monthly Labor plus Sum of Department Monthly Labor.

Figure 1.1A Salary Budget: Manual Worksheet 1

	Initials	Date
Prepared By		
Approved By		

INFORMATION SYSTEMS DEPARTMENT FISCAL YEAR 1985 SALARY BUDGET – WORKSHEET # 1

EMPLOYEE NAME	ANNUAL PAY BEFORE RAISE	BIWEEKLY PAY BEFORE RAISE	PAY INCREASE PERCENT	BIWEEKLY PAY AFTER RAISE	ANNUAL PAY AFTER RAISE
ARTHUR	48048	1848	12	2070	53820
BERNADETTE	28028	1078	10	1186	30836
CYNTHIA	32500	1250	9	1363	35438
DAVID	27300	1050	9	1145	29770
EDWARD	18512	712	10	783	20358
TOTAL	154388		* 10	6547	170222

* AVERAGE PERCENT INCREASE

Figure 1.1B Salary Budget: Manual Worksheet 2

	Initials	Date
Prepared By		
Approved By		

INFORMATION SYSTEMS DEPARTMENT FISCAL YEAR 1985 SALARY BUDGET – WORKSHEET #2

EMPLOYEE NAME	JULY 1984 (4)	AUGUST 1984 (5)	SEPTEMBER 1984 (4)	OCTOBER 1984 (4)	NOVEMBER 1984 (5)	DECEMBER 1984 (4)	JANUARY 1985 (4)	FEBRUARY 1985 (4)	MARCH 1985 (5)	APRIL 1985 (4)	MAY 1985 (5)	JUNE 1985 (4)	FY1985 TOTAL (52)
ARTHUR	3696	4620	3696	3696	4620	3696	3696	3696	5175	4140	5175	4140	50046
BERNADETTE	2156	2695	2156	2156	2695	2156	2156	2156	2695	2156	2695	2156	28028
CYNTHIA	2500	3125	2500	2500	3408	2726	2726	2726	3408	2726	3408	2726	34478
DAVID	2100	2625	2100	2100	2625	2100	2100	2100	2625	2100	2625	2290	27490
EDWARD	1424	1780	1424	1424	1780	1424	1424	1424	1780	1424	1780	1424	18512
TOTAL	11876	14845	11876	11876	15128	12102	12102	12102	15683	12546	15683	12736	158554

(There are two pay periods in four-week months and two-and-a-half pay periods in five-week months. Selection of the Old or New Biweekly Salary depends on whether or not the employee has received a raise yet.)

No single calculation on this worksheet is very complicated. However, 15 calculations per employee, prior to cross-footing, can result in quite a few computations as the number of employees increases. That's a lot to recalculate if things don't cross-foot correctly.

Of course, getting their columnar pads to cross-foot isn't necessarily the end of the accountants' problem. How about those times when the boss says, "I wonder what would happen to the budget if the average salary increase were restricted to 7%?" In the past, these people knew exactly what would happen: they'd be reworking that columnar pad trying to get answers to those dreaded and time-consuming "What if . . .?" questions. Can you imagine reworking Figure 1.1 to reflect What if . . .? And remember, Figure 1.1 is a very small worksheet. Think about a department with a hundred or more people.

Preparing charts and graphs is another problem that plagues managers, analysts, and administrators. Consider making a pie chart to represent each employee's share of the departmental salary dollar. First, you'd have to calculate each person's salary as a percentage of the department total. Next, you'd have to draw a big circle and carve out each person's slice based on their relative salary. Hopefully, you're a good artist and you won't have to redraw the pie too many times because of What if . . .? Maybe you'll end up with something like Figure 1.2.

Figure 1.2 Salary Budget: Manually Drawn Pie Chart

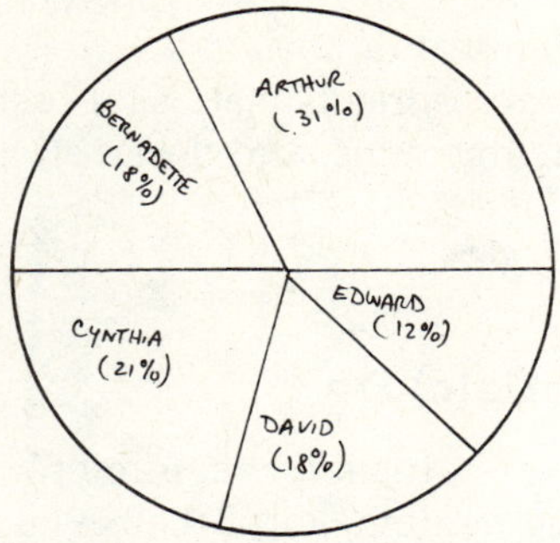

How Can SuperCalc³ Help?

Things don't have to be that way now. The SuperCalc³ electronic spreadsheet doesn't make mistakes summing rows and columns, unless you make a mistake entering the addition instructions. But once you've gotten the instructions right—and the instructions are very easy—you don't have to worry about addition errors. You also don't have to worry about that previously fearsome "What if . . .?" question. SuperCalc³ has an automatic calculation feature that recalculates the entire spreadsheet whenever you change a number. SuperCalc³ also has capabilities for graphics video display and plotted graphics output. Figures 1.3 and 1.4 illustrate the SuperCalc³ spreadsheet with some of its graphics capabilities.

Figure 1.3 Salary Budget: Electronic Spreadsheet

	A	B	C	D	E	F	G	H	I	J	K	L	M	N	O	P	Q	R	S	T
1	Information Systems Department																			
2	Fiscal Year 1985																			
3	Salary Budget																			
4																				
5		Annual	Biweekly		Biweekly	Annual														
6		Salary	Salary	Salary	Salary	Salary	Jul 84	Aug 84	Sep 84	Oct 84	Nov 84	Dec 84	Jan 85	Feb 85	Mar 85	Apr 85	May 85	Jun 85		
7	Employee	Before	Before	Increase	After	After	Weeks =	Weeks =	Weeks =	Weeks =	Weeks =	Weeks =	Weeks =	Weeks =	Weeks =	Weeks =	Weeks =	Weeks =	Total	
8	Name	Raise	Raise	Percent	Raise	Raise	4	5	4	4	5	4	4	4	5	4	5	4	52	
9																				
10	Arthur	48,048	1,848	12	2,070	53,820	3,696	4,620	3,696	3,696	4,620	3,696	3,696	3,696	5,175	4,140	5,175	4,140	50,046	
11	Bernadette	28,028	1,078	10	1,186	30,836	2,156	2,695	2,156	2,156	2,695	2,156	2,156	2,156	2,695	2,156	2,695	2,156	28,028	
12	Cynthia	32,500	1,250	9	1,363	35,438	2,500	3,125	2,500	2,500	3,408	2,726	2,726	2,726	3,408	2,726	3,408	2,726	34,478	
13	David	27,300	1,050	9	1,145	29,770	2,100	2,625	2,100	2,100	2,625	2,100	2,100	2,100	2,625	2,100	2,625	2,290	27,490	
14	Edward	18,512	712	10	783	20,358	1,424	1,780	1,424	1,424	1,780	1,424	1,424	1,424	1,780	1,424	1,780	1,424	18,512	
15																				
16	Total	154,388	5,938	10	6,547	170,222	11,876	14,845	11,876	11,876	15,128	12,102	12,102	12,102	15,683	12,546	15,683	12,736	158,554	

Figure 1.4 SuperCalc³ Pie Chart

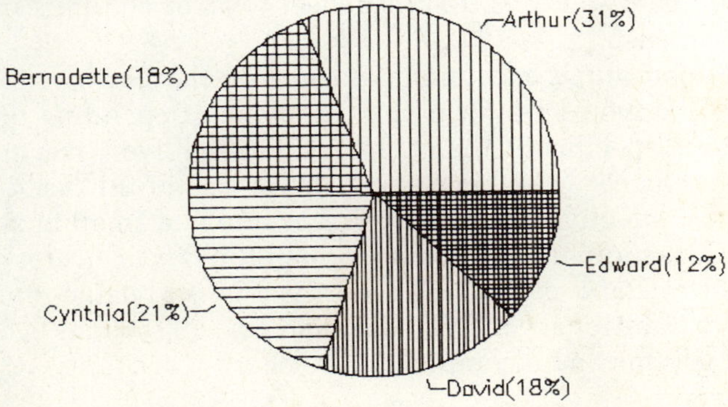

Contrast the electronic spreadsheet in Figure 1.3 with the manual worksheet in Figure 1.1. Also compare the hand-drawn pie chart in Figure 1.2 with the computer-plotted pie in Figure 1.4.

The SuperCalc^3 electronic spreadsheet, as illustrated in Figure 1.3, can contain numbers, algebraic formulas, and descriptive text.

What Else Can SuperCalc^3 Do?

SuperCalc^3 applications are probably as numerous as SuperCalc^3 owners. Because SuperCalc^3 is very flexible, and because good software for microcomputers is very expensive, people have used SuperCalc^3 for almost every imaginable financial and administrative problem. Some uses of SuperCalc^3 are:

Forecasting sales, market growth, and income.
Analyzing breakeven points and rates of return.
Preparing financial statements such as balance sheets and income statements.
Accounting journals for payables, receivables, cash receipts, and cash disbursements.
Estimating materials.
Maintaining checkbook registers.
Calculating mortgage payments and amortization schedules.
Projecting cash flows and discounted cash flow analyses.
Performing capital budgeting analyses.
Preparing organizational operating budgets.
Calculating contract bids and price estimates.
Calculating asset depreciation schedules.
Maintaining bowler, team, and league statistics.
Maintaining student test scores and calculating course grades.

SuperCalc^3 allows consolidation of spreadsheets. For example, consider a situation where three Profit & Loss statement spreadsheets represent Divisions A, B, and C. Using very simple commands, these three spreadsheets could be consolidated into one spreadsheet to make a Profit & Loss statement for the entire company. SuperCalc^3 also allows you to define your own formats for displaying numbers and to sort spreadsheet rows or columns in ascending or descending sequence.

Although SuperCalc^3 is exceptionally versatile and flexible, don't assume it's a panacea for the world's information problems. Depending on the scope of your application, specifically the volume of data involved, you may find that an electronic spreadsheet, whether SuperCalc^3 or one of the "calc-alikes," is not always the most effective alternative. For example, a small business may find that SuperCalc^3 is more than adequate for handling its needs for general ledger, financial reporting, and payroll. Conversely, a larger business may find that it needs the more traditional general ledger and payroll systems because of a large transactional volume and a comprehensive chart of accounts.

What Is an Electronic Spreadsheet?

The SuperCalc³ electronic spreadsheet is a two-dimensional array of rows and columns that resides in your microcomputer's memory. Rows are identified by numbers, columns by letters. The point at which a particular row and column intersect is called a *cell*. Cells are identified by the letter and number of the intersecting row and column.[1] For example, the cell at the intersection of column B and row 5 is called B5. This technique of *cell referencing* is the basis of SuperCalc³. You cannot become proficient at SuperCalc³ without understanding it. Cell referencing is sometimes called *cell addressing*.

The SuperCalc³ spreadsheet can have up to 9,999 rows and 127 columns. The rows are referenced by the numbers 1 through 9,999. Columns are addressed by the following letters:

A through Z for the first 26 columns
AA through AZ for the second 26 columns
BA through BZ for the third 26 columns
CA through CZ for the fourth 26 columns
DA through DW for the last 23 columns

The size of the spreadsheet available to you is determined by your computer's memory capacity. Refer to Figure 1.5 for an illustration of the SuperCalc³ spreadsheet's rows and columns.

Figure 1.5 The SuperCalc³ Spreadsheet's Rows and Columns

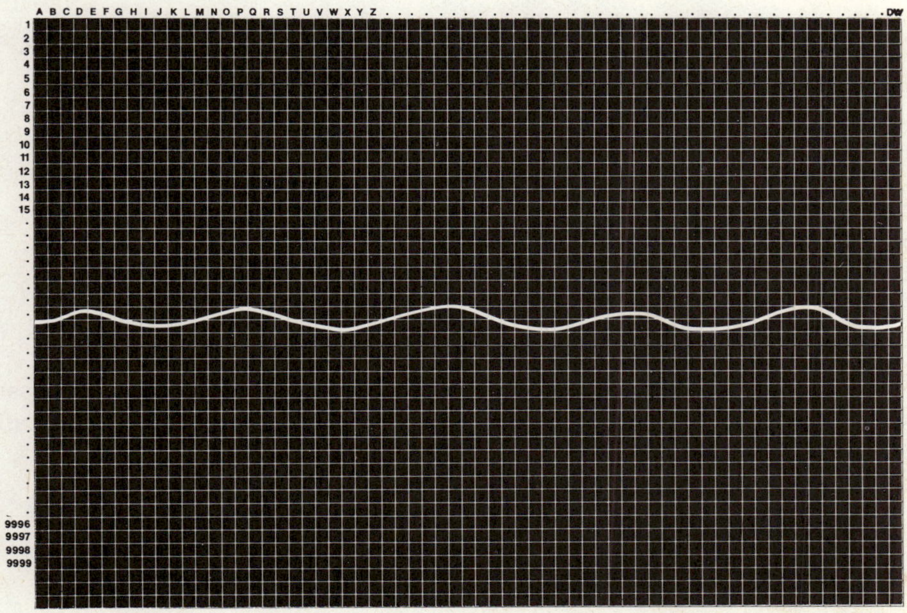

1. Contrast this with programming languages such as BASIC, FORTRAN, Pascal, and COBOL, where the row indicator is always shown before the column indicator.

Depending on how you intend to use SuperCalc³, you may find it necessary to upgrade your memory capacity. Many systems in the IBM PC class of microcomputers come standard with 128K memories that can be expanded to 640K in increments of 64K.

K means thousands of characters or kilobytes. A byte is one character, a kilobyte approximately 1,000 characters. Technically, one kilobyte represents 1,024 characters. So a 128K system has a memory capacity of 131,072 characters (128 × 1,024) rather than 128,000 characters.

How Much Do You Need to Know About Computers?

There is a fundamental difference between using your computer to write your own programs and using it to run an application package like SuperCalc³. Novice users sometimes feel they must know how to program a computer to use it. False. No programming is involved when you use SuperCalc³; the programming has already been done.

SuperCalc³ itself is a program that has built-in features you can use by giving English-like commands. If you aren't sure what command to use or what other information should be passed with the command, just ask for HELP. SuperCalc³, one of the most friendly electronic spreadsheets, will display an AnswerScreen telling you what it's expecting next. You don't have to know very much about computers. This book will teach you all you must know to use SuperCalc³ effectively.

Which Computers Are Covered?

SuperCalc³ was developed for the class of IBM PC-compatible microcomputers that run under the MS-DOS and PC-DOS operating systems.[2] Examples of these computers are:

IBM PC
Sperry PC
Texas Instruments Professional
Zenith Data Systems Z-150

The next chapter surveys MS-DOS and PC-DOS. Read it if you haven't used these operating systems before. If you intend to follow the exercises of this book on your computer, install SuperCalc³ before starting Chapter 3.

---

2. MS-DOS is an acronym for Microsoft Disk Operating System. It is used by IBM-compatible PCs. PC-DOS is an acronym for Personal Computer Disk Operating System. It is used by the IBM PC.

CHAPTER 2

The Environment of SuperCalc^3

Chapter Overview and Objectives

- General Systems Concepts for Microcomputers
- MS-DOS and PC-DOS Operating Systems
- Suggestions for Installing SuperCalc^3 on Your System
- Security and Housekeeping on Your Personal Computer

This chapter introduces the environment in which SuperCalc^3 is used. The section on general systems concepts provides information about disk drive identifiers, filenaming conventions, and file referencing techniques.

The next section surveys common commands for the MS-DOS and PC-DOS operating systems.

The remaining sections deal with security and housekeeping techniques to help you protect your software investment, and how to get SuperCalc^3 up and running on your system.

When you complete this chapter you will have a fundamental understanding of your computer's operating system and the environment in which you'll be using SuperCalc^3.

General Systems Concepts for Microcomputers

The floppy disk concepts in this section are applicable to all personal computers. The remaining concepts apply to MS-DOS and PC-DOS operating systems.

FLOPPY DISKS

Floppy disks are your data storage media. They are available in 5.25-inch and 8-inch sizes. Only 5.25-inch disks are dealt with since they are the most popular size for personal computers.

Manufacturers' labels identify disks as single-sided, single-density; single-sided, double-density; or double-sided, double-density. Most floppy disk drives used by the IBM PC class of personal computers are double-sided, double-density. Your dealer can advise you about the kind of floppy your system requires.

Figure 2.1 shows two disks. The first illustration (Part A) shows a *write-enable notch* near the upper-right corner of the disk. When this notch is exposed, data can be written onto the disk. The second illustration (Part B) shows the notch covered by a small piece of tape. The disk is *write-protected* whenever the notch is covered.

Figure 2.1A
Write-enabled 5.25-inch Disk

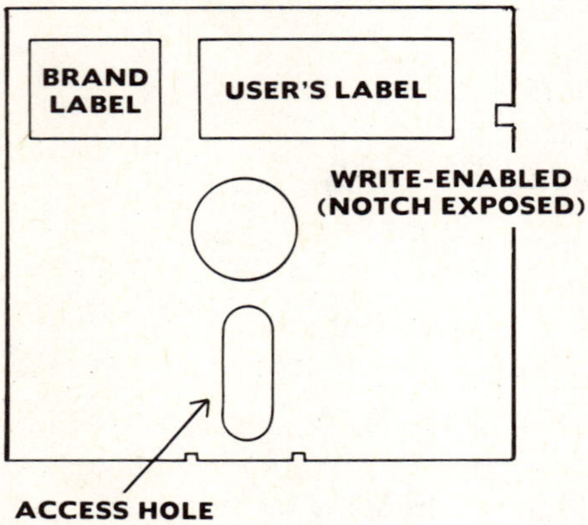

Figure 2.1B
Write-protected 5.25-inch Disk

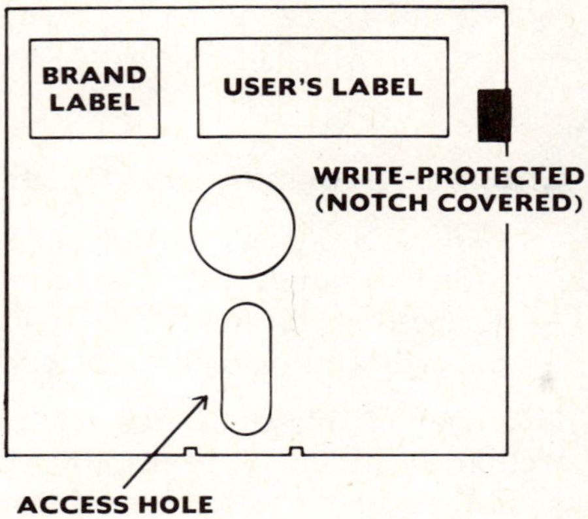

The *access hole* shown in Figure 2.1 is the area where the disk drive's read/write mechanism makes contact with the surface of the disk. *Do not touch the access hole. You risk damaging your disk!*

The user's *label* shown in Figure 2.1 does not come attached to the disk. Generally, a supply of blank labels is in the box of disks. It's a good habit to fill out the label before you put it on the disk so you don't risk warping the disk. If it's necessary to write on a label once it has been affixed to the disk, use a felt-tipped pen. Do not use pencils or ballpoint pens. You don't want to warp the disk or make handwriting impressions on the celluloid.

Disk Drive Identifiers

Most systems in the IBM PC class of microcomputers are configured with two disk drives. The drives are identified by the letters A and B. The primary drive is the A drive; the secondary drive is the B drive. Your system's operations manual will identify the location of drives A and B.

The process of turning on your system is called booting. When you first boot your system, the default disk drive is the A drive. This means that all disk references are to drive A, unless you specify otherwise.

If you want to access a file on a disk in drive B, you must precede the filename by a letter identifying the drive. So that the operating system can determine when the letter B refers to a disk drive or when it's part of a filename, enter a colon (:) after the drive letter. For example:

B:FILENAME.EXT

Your operating system always indicates the default drive via the prompt **drive identifier>**. For example, when drive A is the default drive, it is shown as

A>

The default drive can be changed from A to B by entering

B:

then pressing the ENTER key. When this entry is made, all file references that do not contain an explicit disk drive identifier will default to drive B. The default drive can be reset to A by entering

A:

then pressing the ENTER key.

Current drive, active drive, and currently logged drive are synonyms for the default drive.

Filenames and Extensions

Files are referenced by a filename and a file extension. Filenames are one to eight characters long. The following characters are invalid in filenames since they have special meanings to the operating system:

< > . , ; : = ? * [ ]

The file extension is a three-character item separated from the filename by a period. It usually provides an indication of the file's use, either to the user or to the system.

The following file extensions are used by SuperCalc^3:

.CAL This identifies the file as a spreadsheet. Files with this extension are created by SuperCalc^3's /Save command. Although they can be copied by certain operating system commands, they are readable only via SuperCalc^3's /Load command and the SuperData Interchange utility.

.PRN Files with this extension have been created by SuperCalc^3's /Output command using the D(isk) option. They may be listed from disk using the TYPE command at operating system level.

.BAK The previous version of a file is backed up under this extension when the /Save and /Output commands are used with the B(ackup) option.

.XQT Files with this extension are created via the /Output command using the D(isk) option. Any files to be used by SuperCalc^3's /eXecute command must have this extension. Files with this extension may be listed by the TYPE command.

.COM	Files with this extension are called external commands. They are directly executable. One SuperCalc^3 program that uses this extension is SC3.COM (SuperCalc^3 main program).
.OVL	Identifies the file to SC3.COM as containing a series of overlays used for the SuperCalc^3 "slash" commands.
.HLP	Identifies the file to SC3.COM as containing a series of help messages for the SuperCalc^3 AnswerScreens.

Filenaming Conventions

Establish an organized naming method so you can tell from the filename what kind of data is in the file and the approximate age or creation date. For example:

SPRDSHTx	where x represents a sequentially numbered spreadsheet—for example, **SPRDSHT1.**
BUDFYyy	where yy represents the fiscal year for a budget file—for example, **BUDFY85.**
ACCTmmyy	where mmyy represents an accounting period's two-digit month and two-digit year—for example, **ACCT0385.**
GRADEtyy	where tyy represents an academic term and year for a file of student grades (F = Fall and S = Spring)—for example, **GRADEF83.**

Whatever naming convention you select, use it consistently so that the file's name will identify its intended purpose. Avoid randomly assigning names to files.

The file extensions .CAL, .PRN, and .XQT must be appended to the filename when using most operating system commands. These extensions may, however, be omitted in some SuperCalc^3 commands that access files. The /Save, /Load, and /Delete commands use a default file extension of .CAL, while the /Output command uses a default file extension of .PRN. The /eXecute command uses a default file extension of .XQT.

File References

Files may be referenced in two ways. A *specific file reference* uses a unique name; in other words, the name applies to only one file. Examples of specific file references are:

B:ACCT1084.CAL
B:ACCT1184.CAL
B:ACCT1284.CAL
B:ACCT0185.PRN
B:ACCT0285.PRN
B:ACCT0385.PRN

Each of the previous filenames specifically references only one file.

The second method of file referencing is called *global file referencing*. This technique uses asterisks (*) or question marks (?) as *wild card characters*. The asterisk represents any number or combination of characters, while each question mark represents one "wild" character. The resulting global name may be applicable to many files.

For example, assume the disk in drive B contains only those files shown before as specific filenames. The global reference B:*.* would match all files on drive B. In effect it references

B:ACCT1084.CAL
B:ACCT1184.CAL
B:ACCT1284.CAL
B:ACCT0185.PRN
B:ACCT0285.PRN
B:ACCT0385.PRN

The global reference B:*.CAL would match all files with an extension of .CAL on drive B. It would refer to

B:ACCT1084.CAL
B:ACCT1184.CAL
B:ACCT1284.CAL

The global reference B:ACCT??84.CAL matches filenames beginning with ACCT and ending with 84 and having an extension of .CAL on drive B. The files referenced are

B:ACCT1084.CAL
B:ACCT1184.CAL
B:ACCT1284.CAL

MS-DOS and PC-DOS Commands

System level commands are typed immediately following the prompt:

drive-identifier>

There are two types of DOS commands,[1] *internal* and *external*. *DOS internal commands* are loaded into memory when you boot your system and remain there until shutdown time. *DOS external commands* are loaded by DOS from disk as part of the execution. Only one external command may be in memory at a given time. External commands are really nothing more than files containing programs. All DOS external program files have an extension of .COM.

---

1. Ruth Ashley and Judi N. Fernandez. *PC DOS: Using the IBM PC Operating System.* New York: John Wiley & Sons, 1983. See this book for a detailed treatment of DOS that is easily understandable by novices.

DOS Internal Commands

The internal commands shown below will satisfy your needs when using SuperCalc[3].

COPY Copies global or specific files from one disk to another. See your documentation for other uses of this command.

COPY B:*.CAL A: Copies all spreadsheet files from drive B to drive A.

COPY A:*.* B: Copies all files from drive A to drive B.

COPY A:SC3.* B: Copies all SuperCalc[3] program files from drive A to drive B.

DATE Allows you to set or change the system date.[2] Valid date formats are:

mm–dd–yy
mm–dd–yyyy
mm/dd/yy
mm/dd/yyyy

where mm represents month, dd represents day, yy represents year in two-digit format, e.g., 85, and yyyy represents year in four-digit format, e.g., 1985.

Note: Period (.) may be substituted for dash (–) and slash (/) in MS-DOS.

DATE Displays the current system date, then prompts for the new date.

DATE 12–18–1984 Suppresses date display and prompts. Replaces the current system date with 12-18-1984.

DIR Displays a listing of filenames contained on a disk. When no options are used, DIR shows the filename, file extension, file size in bytes, date and time of creation or last change. There is one file entry per video screen line. If more than 24 files are on your disk, the directory listing will scroll off the top of your screen. Two options[3] are available:

/P Provides one entry per line, but pauses when 23 filenames have been displayed. Pressing any key releases the hold, displaying 23 more lines.

/W Displays only the filename and extension. There are five filename entries per line on your video screen.

The option can be specified anywhere after DIR. Some examples:

DIR Displays a long-form listing of all filenames on the currently logged drive.

---

2. It is advisable to set the current date each time you boot the system because new files are "date-stamped" in the disk's directory.

3. The /P and /W options are available only with DOS versions greater than 1.10.

DIR/P B: Displays a full directory of all files on drive B, pausing after every 23 files.
DIR *.CAL/W Displays a short-form listing of all SuperCalc³ spreadsheet files on the currently logged drive.
DIR B:*.PRN/P Displays a directory of all .PRN files on drive B, pausing every 23 lines.

ERASE Erases the designated global or specific files.
ERASE B:DUDFILE.CAL Erases the specified spreadsheet file from drive B.
Although DOS will allow it, *never* use global filenames with the ERASE command. You may destroy more files than you intended. Play it safe! Always use specific filenames with ERASE.

RENAME Changes the name of a specific file on disk.
RENAME B:OLDNAME.CAL B:NEWNAME.CAL Renames OLDNAME.CAL as NEWNAME.CAL.
OLDNAME.CAL must already exist on the disk in drive B. NEWNAME.CAL must not exist on the disk in drive B. Errors result if either condition is violated. Global file references may not be used with the RENAME command.

TIME Allows you to set or change the system time.[4] Valid time formats are:

hh
hh:mm
hh:mm:ss
hh:mm:ss.dd

where hh represents hours in military time, mm represents minutes, ss represents seconds, dd represents fractions of seconds up to two places of precision.
Note: Period (.) may be substituted for colon (:) in MS-DOS.
TIME Displays the current system time, then prompts for the new time.
TIME 21:35:33.2 Suppresses time display and prompts. Replaces the current system time with 21:35:33.2.

TYPE Lists the contents of a specific text file from disk.
TYPE B:BUDGET.PRN Lists the contents of the file BUDGET.PRN onto your video display. One way to print spreadsheets is to put them into a .PRN file using the SuperCalc³ /O(utput) command. The .PRN file can then be printed using the TYPE command.

---

4. It is advisable to set the current time each time you boot the system because new files are "time-stamped" in the disk's directory.

DOS External Commands

The external commands shown next are typical of what you need to use SuperCalc³ in the DOS environment. When invoking external commands, omit the .COM file extension. This extension is used only if you were taking some action on the file containing the external command, such as copying or deleting it.

CHKDSK Provides information about the space available on the specified disk drive. Also indicates how much memory is currently free.

DISKCOPY Formats, then makes a complete copy of a disk.
DISKCOPY A: B: Formats the disk in drive B, then copies the source disk in drive A to the destination disk in drive B.

FORMAT Initializes a blank disk into MS-DOS or PC-DOS format. The /S option will copy the operating system in addition to formatting the disk. Some examples:
FORMAT B: Formats the disk in drive B.
FORMAT B: /S Formats the disk in drive B and copies the operating system.
Formatting can also be used to "clean up" old disks, wiping out obsolete data. Be careful not to accidentally destroy data on good disks with the FORMAT command.

SC3 Loads the SuperCalc³ program into your computer.

SYS Copies the system files from the default drive to the destination disk in the target drive. This is a nondestructive alternative to FORMAT x: /S. For example, assume that drive A is the default drive and that the disk in drive A contains the system files. The entry **SYS B:** will copy the system files onto the disk in drive B.

Suggestions for Installing SuperCalc³ on Your System

This is the process of preparing your SuperCalc³ package to run on your own microcomputer. You must not go beyond this point until you have successfully completed the installation procedures that came with your package. Follow these procedures as carefully as you can. Thoroughness at installation time will help make your association with SuperCalc³ productive and enjoyable. Check your SuperCalc³ licensing agreement to determine how many copies you may have in existence at a given time.

The following steps summarize the installation procedure. They are not intended to replace the instructions contained in the User's Guide and Reference Manual.

1. Format an even number of blank disks. Use new disks of good quality for the installation process since you want a dependable master disk with a

long life. Use the /S option on the FORMAT command to copy the operating system during the formatting process.

2. Copy the contents of the "SuperCalc³ PROD" disk you received with your SuperCalc³ package onto one of the new disks from step 1.
3. Copy the contents of the "SuperCalc³ UTIL" disk you received with your SuperCalc³ package onto one of the new disks from step 1. *Warning:* There may not be enough space to copy the entire UTIL disk onto a disk that has been formatted with the /S option. If you encounter problems, just reformat without the /S.
4. Repeat steps 2 and 3 until all disks from step 1 have been used.

Refer to the SuperCalc³ User's Guide and Reference Manual for more information. If you need further assistance, contact your dealer or a Customer Support Representative at Sorcim/IUS Micro Software.

Security and Housekeeping on Your Personal Computer

When you finish making your backup copies, put a strip of tape on the write-enable notch of the original SuperCalc³ PROD disk and the original SuperCalc³ UTIL disk. These tape strips are usually included with each box of disks. If you've misplaced them, strips of electrical tape work just as well. As you learned earlier in this chapter, the tape will prevent you from accidentally writing over your disks.

Take one of the SuperCalc³ PROD disks just copied and use it as your "working master disk." Put the remaining disks in a safe place; an empty disk box is an inexpensive storage container. It is a good idea to store your original SuperCalc³ PROD and UTIL disks with your backup disks. Don't leave them in the binder flap of your SuperCalc³ documentation manual where they could become warped.

Do not try to run SuperCalc³ using the original PROD disk that came with your package. Always use a copy. If you inadvertently damage or destroy the copy, you can always recreate it from your original SuperCalc³ PROD disk. However, if you damage your original disk, it may be necessary to buy another one.

Separate your disks into those that contain data and those that contain programs. Also, do not mix different kinds of data on the same disk. For example, if you are using SuperCalc³ for spreadsheet processing and SuperWriter for word processing, you will have better control of your data if you maintain your spreadsheets on one set of disks and word processing documents on another set.

Although more disks are used by putting each classification on a separate disk, you have much better organization and control over individual data files. Also, with fewer files per disk the effect of a disk going bad is less catastrophic. Any disks containing critical data files should be copied onto a backup disk to eliminate the chance of data loss due to a disk failure.

This concludes Chapter 2. Complete the Review Exercises before attempting to install SuperCalc³ on your computer system.

Review Exercises

This section reviews the disk concepts and DOS commands you learned in Chapter 2. The exercises address items you must understand to install SuperCalc³ and to properly back up your disk files. The exercises are designed for pencil and paper; exercises in other chapters can be done using SuperCalc³.

1. Given the following disk operations:
   read files
   write files
   erase files
   rename files
   a. Which ones can be executed when the disk is write-protected?
   b. Which ones can be executed when the disk is write-enabled?
2. Given a system with two disk drives:
   a. What are the disk drive identifiers?
   b. Which disk drive is the default drive when the system is booted?
   c. How would you switch the default drive?
3. What command would be used to:
   a. Find out what files are on a disk?
   b. Find out how much space is available on a disk?
   c. Delete a file from a disk?
   d. Change the name of a file?
   e. Set or change the current date?
   f. List the contents of a file?
   g. Initialize and format a disk and put the operating system on it?
   h. Copy files from one disk to another?
   i. Completely copy one disk to another?
4. Assume that a disk contains the following files:

NPV1AMT.BAS	SORTDEMO.BAS	SC3.COM	SDI.COM
NPV2AMT.CAL	LOOPDEMO.BAS	SC3.OVL	SDI.OVL
NPV3AMT.PRN	BADSHEET.CAL	SC3.HLP	DISKCOPY.COM

   a. Provide the command to identify all files with an extension of .BAS.
   b. Provide the command to identify all filenames that begin with NPV and end with AMT.
   c. Provide the command to delete BADSHEET.CAL.
   d. Provide the command to list the contents of NPV3AMT.PRN.
   e. Provide the command that will change the name of SC3.COM to GOODSTUF.COM.
   f. Can you change the name of BUBLSORT.BAS to SORTDEMO.BAS?
   g. Given that this disk is in drive B, how would you copy all the SC3 files to a disk in drive A?
   h. Given that this disk is in drive B, how would you copy the entire disk to drive A?

Answers to Review Exercises

1. Allowable disk operations:
   a. When the disk is write-protected, only *read operations* may be executed.
   b. When the disk is write-enabled, all the following operations may be executed:
      read files
      write files
      erase files
      rename files
2. Given a system with two disk drives:
   a. The disk drive identifiers are A and B.
   b. Drive A is the default drive when the system is booted.
   c. Entering B: switches the default drive from A to B.
3. Command identification:
   a. DIR one filename per line; scrolls off screen if more than 23 files on disk.
      DIR/P same as above, but pauses after every 23 lines.
      DIR/W displays five filenames per line.
   b. CHKDSK
   c. ERASE
   d. RENAME
   e. DATE
   f. TYPE
   g. FORMAT /S
   h. COPY
   i. DISKCOPY
4. Command exercises:
   a. DIR *.BAS
   b. DIR NPV?AMT.*
   c. ERASE BADSHEET.CAL
   d. TYPE NPV3AMT.PRN
   e. RENAME SC3.COM GOODSTUF.COM
   f. No, the old filename must already exist and the new filename must not exist. In this exercise, the old filename BUBLSORT.BAS does not exist. Furthermore, the new filename SORTDEMO.BAS already exists. An error would result if you tried to execute this rename operation.
   g. COPY B:SC3.* A:
   h. B:DISKCOPY B: A: or COPY B:*.* A:

SECTION TWO

Basic Features of SuperCalc^3

CHAPTER 3

SuperCalc³ Spreadsheet Fundamentals

Chapter Overview and Objectives

- Entering SuperCalc³
- The SuperCalc³ Screen Display
- Moving Around the Spreadsheet
- The HELP Function
- Exiting SuperCalc³

This chapter covers the fundamentals of the SuperCalc³ spreadsheet. When you've completed the chapter, you'll be able to enter SuperCalc³, move around the spreadsheet, get a disk directory from within SuperCalc³, ask for help from the SuperCalc³ AnswerScreen, and exit SuperCalc³. Data entry and the associated instructions on saving spreadsheets are covered in Chapter 4, so don't put any important data into the spreadsheet during the exercises in this chapter.

Entering SuperCalc³

If your computer is turned off, insert the SuperCalc³ working master disk you created in Chapter 2 into disk drive A. Turn on your computer and boot your system. If your computer is already turned on, insert your SuperCalc³ working master into drive A.

The next task is to call the SuperCalc³ program. Enter **SC3** after the **A>** prompt, then press the RETURN key. When your SuperCalc³ program is called, the access lamp on drive A will light up to indicate that SuperCalc³ is being loaded. After a few seconds the SuperCalc³ logo will appear on your screen. The logo identifies the version of SuperCalc³ and the product serial number, and the computer and operating system your package has been configured for. If you have to contact the developers of SuperCalc³, always indicate the product serial number of your package.

As you can see from Figure 3.1, you have the option of pressing the ? key, the F1 key, or the RETURN key.

Figure 3.1 SuperCalc^3 Initial Sign-on Screen

```
                    SuperCalc3(tm)
                    Version  2.00
                    I B M    P C
                   (8087 not present)
                  S/N-000540 , IBM DOS

                    Copyright 1984

                SORCIM/IUS MICRO SOFTWARE
                     A division of
           Computer Associates International Inc.




Enter "?" for HELP or (RETURN) to start.
F1 = Help; F2 = Cancel; F9 = Plot; F10 = View
```

Pressing the RETURN key takes you directly to an empty spreadsheet, while the ? and F1 keys[1] call the HELP function. You will find this function particularly useful since it can be called at any point in a SuperCalc^3 session.

The Help screen displayed will vary depending on what you are doing at the time you ask for help. Throughout the documentation manuals, the display returned by the HELP function is referred to as the *AnswerScreen* and F1 is called the *AnswerKey*.

Since this is your first entry into SuperCalc^3, press the F1 key. Your monitor will display the first half of an initial Help screen. This screen contains a brief description of SuperCalc^3's features and functions. When you have read the display, press any key to continue to the second half of this initial Help screen.

If your system only has floppy disk drives, don't be concerned with the "PATH=" frame. It applies only to hard disks. Press any key and an empty spreadsheet will be displayed as in Figure 3.2.

It is very important that your SuperCalc^3 working master disk remain in the drive it was loaded from for the duration of your session. Each time you issue a command or call the HELP function, SuperCalc^3 checks a special command area in memory to see if your command is resident there. If it is, it's immediately executed. However, if the command you specified is not currently resident in this area, it's loaded from your working master disk into the command area and then executed.

1. The F1 and ? keys have equivalent functions. F1 is unique to the IBM PC class of personal computers and will refer to the HELP function throughout the rest of this book. If you have another kind of computer, you should substitute ? for F1.

Figure 3.2 Empty SuperCalc^3 Spreadsheet

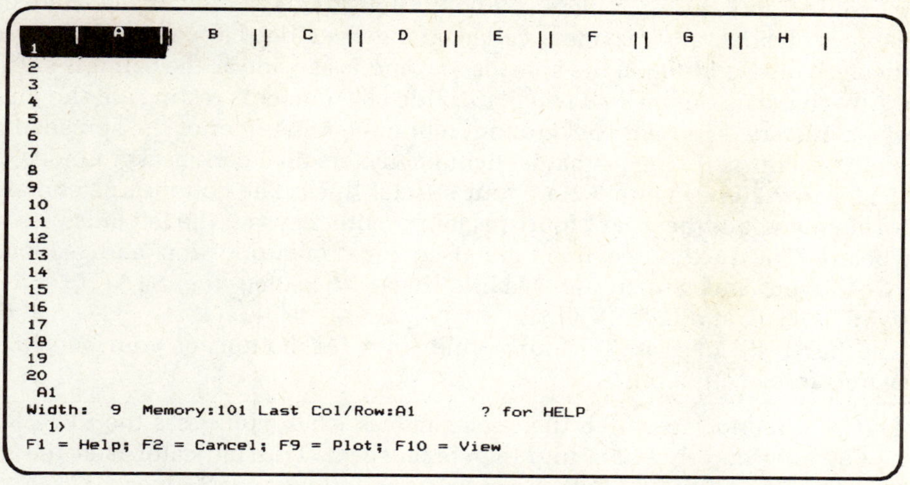

The SuperCalc^3 Screen Display

Although SuperCalc^3 can handle a maximum spreadsheet size of 9,999 rows and 127 columns, it automatically sets the spreadsheet boundary based on the memory capacity of your computer with speed pre-empting data storage capacity. These default settings are:

2,000 rows by 127 columns for memories of 192K or larger.
254 rows by 63 columns for memories less than 192K.

The defaults can be changed 1) so that data-space takes precedence over speed, and 2) to let you select a spreadsheet boundary consistent with your needs.

The number of available cells in a given boundary is determined from the product of the number of rows and the number of columns. For example:

Number of Rows	Number of Columns	Available Cells
9,999	127	1,269,873
2,000	127	254,000
254	63	16,002

Do not equate the number of available cells with the number of cells that can hold data. They are not the same. While all cells can be accessed when the spreadsheet is empty, the maximum number of data cells in a completed spreadsheet depends on the physical memory capacity of your system.

Looking at the empty spreadsheet in Figure 3.2, notice that it contains columns A through H and rows 1 through 20. Assuming that your computer monitor has the standard capacity of 25 lines, SuperCalc^3 will display 20 rows of a spreadsheet at a time. The number of columns displayed varies depending on individual column widths. The default column width for SuperCalc^3 is nine positions. At this width, the spreadsheet will display eight columns at a time.

At cell A1 in Figure 3.2 there is a box of light. This is the *cursor.* There are two types of cursors.[2] This one is called an *inverse video bar* cursor. The cursor indicates your position on the spreadsheet and is as wide as the cell it is sitting on. Any characters in the cell where the video bar cursor is resting are shown as dark characters on a light background, while the remainder of the spreadsheet is shown in normal video—that is, light characters on a dark background.

Under row 20 in Figure 3.2 are four special lines. The bottom line contains information about the use of four special function keys on the left side of your keyboard. The next three lines are used for communication and feedback between you and SuperCalc³. These lines are called the STATUS LINE, PROMPT LINE, and ENTRY LINE.

The *STATUS LINE* is the fourth line from the bottom of your screen. It provides information on:

1. The direction in which the cursor moves when you press the RETURN[3] key after entering data into the spreadsheet. This indicator is at the left end of the STATUS LINE. It can have the following meanings:
   ↑ Move to the cell above the current cell.
   ↓ Move to the cell below the current cell.
   ← Move to the cell on the left of the current cell.
   → Move to the cell on the right of the current cell.
2. The name of the cell where the cursor is currently sitting. This cell is also called the *active cell.* Figure 3.2 shows the cursor sitting on cell A1; the STATUS LINE identifies A1 as the current cell.
3. The contents of the current cell and a description of its attributes:
   Protected, indicated by P
   Text, indicated by Text = "actual cell text.
   Numeric formula, indicated by Form = numeric value or expression.
   Repeating text, indicated by Rtxt = 'repeating character(s).

The *PROMPT LINE* is the third line from the bottom of the screen. It provides information about the width of the active cell, the amount of spreadsheet memory remaining, and the highest cell used by the spreadsheet. This line also displays SuperCalc³ command prompts and error messages; its importance will become apparent as you go through the book.

The *ENTRY LINE* is the line above the last line on the screen. All data is entered and all commands are issued from this line. The ENTRY LINE contains its own cursor, usually a flashing underline character. At the left end of the line is a number followed by a right-angle bracket, >. The angle bracket points to the beginning of the user data entry area; the number indicates the position of the cursor.

---

2. The other is an *angle-bracket* cursor. There is an < in the leftmost cell position and an > in the rightmost cell position. This cursor type obscures any characters in the extreme right and left positions.

3. The RETURN key is usually an L-shaped key, which some PCs call the ↩ key. Also, some PCs have an ENTER key at the extreme bottom right of the keyboard that is interchangeable with the RETURN key.

Moving Around the Spreadsheet

Now that you've seen the structure of the SuperCalc³ spreadsheet, how do you get from one cell to another? There are three methods: scrolling, paging, and jumping. All use a series of special keys to move around the spreadsheet. Most of these keys are on the right side of the keyboard in the vicinity of the numeric keypad.

On the top row is a NUM LCK key, which usually has a lamp built into it. This is a toggle key. Pressing it engages and disengages the NUM LCK key. The key lamp is lit when this key is engaged, and **NUM** is displayed at the bottom of the screen. Many of the special movement keys require the NUM LCK key to be disengaged. If you have NUM LCK engaged when it shouldn't be, numbers will appear in the ENTRY LINE. This is easy to correct. Press the F2 key to clear the ENTRY LINE, then disengage the NUM LCK key. (Use the CTRL Z key combination if your computer doesn't have function keys.)

Scrolling is moving around contiguous cells. The arrows on the numeric keypad cause movement from the current cell in the direction of the arrowhead. Continuous pressure on an arrow key causes repeated movement in the same direction until a spreadsheet boundary is reached. The NUM LCK key must be disengaged to use the directional arrows.

Another way to do contiguous movement is to use a special key called the CONTROL key. Many keyboards have it as CTRL.

This key is pressed simultaneously with the E, X, S, and D keys. It doesn't matter whether or not the NUM LCK key is engaged when you use this method of scrolling:

CTRL E	Move to the cell above the current cell.
CTRL X	Move to the cell below the current cell.
CTRL S	Move to the cell on the left of the current cell.
CTRL D	Move to the cell on the right of the current cell.

Notice on your keyboard that the E, X, S, and D keys are arranged in a diamond pattern. An easy way to remember the directional movement caused by each letter when used with the CONTROL key is to think of each letter's position within the diamond on the keyboard. You can also relate them to the directional arrows on the numeric keypad:

```
  E           ↑           up
 S D        ←   →     left    right
  X           ↓          down
```

As with the arrows, continuous pressure on these keys causes repeated movement in the same direction until a spreadsheet boundary is reached. Although the directional arrows and the CTRL E, X, S, and D keys can be used interchangeably, you'll probably use the directional arrows because less keystroking is involved.

The SCROLL LCK key, located at the upper right corner of your keyboard, is a toggle key. Pressing the key engages and disengages it. When the SCROLL LCK is engaged, **SCROLL** is displayed on the bottom line of your screen. Engaging this key locks the spreadsheet cursor at the current cell. The directional arrows move the rest of the screen relative to this cell. This lock is overridden at spreadsheet boundaries and when the locked cell is scrolled off the screen. In these situations, the scroll lock is transferred to an adjacent row or column depending on the movement direction.

Paging is the horizontal and vertical movement from one screen to the next. Depending on how far you need to move, paging can be more efficient than scrolling. There are four paging keys located on the numeric keypad:

PGUP	Moves the screen up 20 lines.
PGDN	Moves the screen down 20 lines.
CTRL ←	Moves a full screen width to the left.
CTRL →	Moves a full screen width to the right.

The number of columns to a screen width varies depending on the width of the individual columns. The default column width puts the screen capacity at eight columns. Consequently, each horizontal page command moves your screen eight columns.

When you are paging, the spreadsheet cursor retains its relative position on the screen. For example, if you press the PGDN key while the cursor is at cell E10, the screen will move down 20 rows and the cursor will now be at cell E30. Before paging down, the cursor was on the tenth row, fifth column of the first screen. After paging down, the cursor is still on the tenth row, fifth column of the current screen. The cursor has stayed in the same relative position.

Jumping is the direct and immediate movement to specific cells or to extreme cells within the spreadsheet. Most of the jumping keys are located on or near the keypad.

HOME	Moves to cell A1.
END HOME	Moves to the last cell in the spreadsheet that contains data. If the spreadsheet is empty, the cursor moves to cell A1.
END ↑	Moves the cursor to the top of the current column.
END →	Moves the cursor to the end of the current row.
END ←	Moves the cursor to the beginning of the current row.
END ↓	Moves the cursor to the bottom of the current column.
=cell	Moves the cursor to the specified cell.
=RETURN	Shifts the screen so the current cell is displayed in the upper left corner.

Whenever you press the END key, SuperCalc[3] displays **END** on the last line of your screen and waits for you to enter the rest of the jump command.

Now try some moving around. The cursor should be sitting at cell A1 and the NUM LCK key should be disengaged. SuperCalc[3] highlights the cursor's position in the row and column borders of the screen display. This supplements the STATUS LINE information.

Press ←. Nothing happened? That's because you're at the left edge of the spreadsheet and further leftward movement is impossible.

Now try →. The cursor has moved to cell B1. Hold down the → key until the cursor is at cell H1. You have moved across the entire screen. Press → one more time and the screen changes. Although your screen still shows rows 1 through 20, it now displays columns B through I. The cursor is at cell I1.

Press HOME and you have columns A through H on your screen with the cursor at cell A1. Now press CTRL → and you have columns I through P on display, with the cursor at cell I1.

Press CTRL ←, and you're back to cell A1. The vertical movement enabled by ↑ and ↓ is like the horizontal movement of ← and →. Now press ↑. Nothing happens. No upward movement is allowed beyond row 1 in the spreadsheet. Hold down ↓ until the cursor is at cell A10.

Now press =. SuperCalc³ responds with **Enter cell to jump to** on the PROMPT LINE. Enter **E10** and press the RETURN key. The cursor is now in the center of the screen at cell E10. Press PGDN twice. The cursor is still in the center of the screen, but is now at cell E50. Press = RETURN. Cell E50 is now in the upper left corner of the display screen.

The HELP Function

Earlier in this chapter you saw that pressing the F1 key called the HELP function. The initial call for "help" was made just after entering SuperCalc³. You were at the system logo and received a two-screen Help message. Pressing the F1 key now gives you two screens of Initial Character Meanings. These screens contain information on scrolling, paging, jumping, and other initial entry characters covered in later chapters.

Since many SuperCalc³ spreadsheet commands are preceded by a slash, "/", they are called "Slash" commands. Pressing / displays the following in the PROMPT LINE:

Enter A,B,C,D,E,F,G,I,L,M,O,P,Q,R,S,T,U,W,X,Z,/,?

This prompt contains all the valid SuperCalc³ "Slash" commands. However, at this point you may not have the slightest idea what any of these commands mean. If that's true, press F1 or ? to see AnswerScreens about the "Slash" commands. The first AnswerScreen briefly defines each "Slash" command, while the second gives examples on how to use them.

The F1 key represents one of the most important features of SuperCalc³. You can press it any time while entering a command and it will display an AnswerScreen explaining what SuperCalc³ is expecting next. This feature is especially useful for novices since it eliminates many time-consuming searches through the reference manual.

Exiting SuperCalc³

When you've completed your spreadsheet session, use the /Q(uit) command to terminate SuperCalc³. Enter **/Q.** The PROMPT LINE responds with

EXIT SuperCalc3? Y(es), N(o), or T(o)

The ENTRY LINE awaits your response, displaying

7>/Quit,

Your possible responses:

F1	Displays a Help screen explaining the options for /Quit.
Y	Immediately exits SuperCalc³. If you didn't save your spreadsheet, it is destroyed, with no way of recovery other than re-entering it from the very beginning. Since you haven't entered any data into your spreadsheet, this isn't a problem. We will cover the /Save command later, so don't worry about not knowing how to save a spreadsheet.
N	Returns you to your spreadsheet. This response gives you a second chance to save your work in case you forgot to save it the first time. Pressing the F2 key produces the same result.
T	Exits SuperCalc³ as in the "Y" option, but also lets you specify a .COM file to be executed as soon as you are out of SuperCalc³. *Do not try to use a .CAL file.* Some possible filenames to use with this option are: **BASIC** If you want to work in BASIC after leaving SuperCalc³. **SW** If you want to get into SuperWriter, the word processing companion to SuperCalc³. **SC3** If you just want to test the "T" option, you can exit SuperCalc³ and have it call itself back. The spreadsheet you had in memory when you quit would be lost if you didn't save it. This technique could also be used to restart SuperCalc³ after customizing it via the K(eep) option of the /G(lobal) command.[4]

Don't forget to include the disk drive identifier if the file does not reside on the default disk drive.

Enter **N** as your first response to /Quit. You are now back at your spreadsheet. Enter **/Q** again. When you are prompted with

Exit SuperCalc3? Y(es), N(o), or T(o)

press T and the PROMPT LINE will respond with

Enter File Name (or <RETURN> for directory)

For now, disregard the option of just pressing RETURN to get a directory. (The directory options are covered by the /S(ave) and /L(oad) commands.) Enter **SC3,** then press RETURN. The screen will go blank for a moment, then you'll see the SuperCalc³ logo screen. Press any key to get to an empty spreadsheet.

Now enter **/Q** and then **Y.** The screen will clear and the system prompt will be displayed. You have just completed your first session with SuperCalc³.

---

4. Although /G(lobal),K(eep) is covered in a later chapter, you should have been exposed to it during the initial installation process.

Review Exercises

1. You have just entered SuperCalc³. Is it all right to remove your master disk from the drive?
2. Your spreadsheet cursor is at cell A1. How would you get to cell B3?
3. How would you get to cell A21 from cell A1?
4. Your spreadsheet cursor is at cell H20. What is the fastest way to reposition the spreadsheet cursor to cell A1?
5. Which spreadsheet line tells you the location and contents of the active cell?
6. How do you know which way your spreadsheet cursor will move when you press RETURN after entering data?
7. Which spreadsheet line displays command prompts and error messages?
8. Which spreadsheet line is used to enter commands and data?
9. You're in a spreadsheet and the ENTRY LINE is empty. What three options do you have?
10. You accidentally pressed /Q. What do you do next?
11. Since you accidentally pressed /Q, you decide to respond with N; however, your finger slips and you press T. Is there anything you can do, or are you forced to leave?
12. Which line on your screen indicates whether the NUM LCK key is engaged?

Answers to Review Exercises

1. No, the master disk must remain in the drive because it is periodically accessed by SuperCalc³ to load commands and Help screens.
2. There are several ways:
   a. scrolling via directional arrows:
      ↓, ↓, → or →, ↓, ↓
   b. scrolling via CONTROL keys:
      CTRL X, CTRL X, CTRL D or CTRL D, CTRL X, CTRL X
   c. jumping:
      =B3
3. There are several ways:
   a. scrolling via directional arrows:
      pressing ↓ 20 times or holding key down
   b. scrolling via CONTROL keys:
      pressing CTRL X 20 times or holding keys down
   c. jumping:
      =A21
   d. paging:
      pressing PGDN key
4. Pressing the HOME key.
   Jumping via =A1 is the next fastest way.
5. The STATUS LINE, which is the fourth line from the bottom of your screen.

6. The STATUS LINE uses directional indicators ↑, ↓, ←, →.
7. The PROMPT LINE, which is the third line from the bottom of your screen.
8. The ENTRY LINE, which is immediately above the bottom line on your screen.
9. Once you've gotten into a spreadsheet, you have three choices:
   a. You can move around it via scrolling, paging, or jumping.
   b. You can enter data.
   c. You can issue a command.

   If you called for Help from an empty ENTRY LINE, you'd get information about items 9a and 9b. If you called for Help after a "/", you'd get information about item 9c.
10. Any time /Q is entered, the PROMPT LINE displays

    EXIT SuperCalc3? Y(es), N(o), or T(o)

    Since you accidentally entered /Q, your response should be N to get back to your spreadsheet. F2 would have the same effect.
11. F2 will cancel the /Q(uit) command and return you to the spreadsheet.
12. The bottom line. This line also displays:

    F1 = Help; F2 = Cancel; F9 = Plot; F10 = View

CHAPTER 4

Getting Data into Your Spreadsheet

Chapter Overview and Objectives

- Basic Types of Spreadsheet Entries
- Normal Text Entries
- Repeating Text Entries
- Simple Formula Entries:
    - Numeric Constants
    - Cell Names
    - Expressions
    - Textual Values

This chapter summarizes the various inputs to the ENTRY LINE and differentiates command entries from data entries. The chapter provides in-depth coverage of text and formula entries, and will enable you to

- Enter normal text
- Enter repeating text
- Enter formulas
- Edit the ENTRY LINE
- Edit previously entered data
- Build an accounting worksheet—the P&L Statement
- Save a spreadsheet onto diskette
- Load a spreadsheet from diskette

If you've had previous exposure to SuperCalc or SuperCalc^2, you may first want to complete the exercises at the end of the chapter and then review any areas of difficulty before proceeding to Chapter 5. The P&L Statement will be used as a demonstration vehicle in a number of chapters, so you should start building it in Chapter 4.

Basic Types of Spreadsheet Entries

Throughout a SuperCalc^3 session you have three types of entries from which to select your next action for the ENTRY LINE. You can scroll, issue a command, or enter data.

Scrolling, as you saw in Chapter 3, moves the spreadsheet cursor via the four directional arrows or the CTRL E, X, S, and D keys. Once an entry is started on the ENTRY LINE, these keys move the entry line cursor rather than the spreadsheet cursor.

Commands specify some action to be taken with one or more cells, rows, columns, or the entire spreadsheet. Commands always involve special purpose keys, some of which you saw in Chapter 3:

F1	Calls the HELP function or AnswerScreen.
F2	Cancels the ENTRY LINE and returns you to the spreadsheet.
=	Moves the spreadsheet cursor to the specified cell.
/	Followed by an alphabetic character, calls one of the "Slash" commands. You saw /Q in Chapter 3.
↑↓←→	Used for editing the ENTRY LINE. You saw how these directional arrows moved the spreadsheet cursor when the ENTRY LINE was empty. You'll learn in this chapter to use them to move the entry line cursor. The CTRL E, X, S, and D keys also have this dual usage feature.
!	Initiates manual recalculation. The default spreadsheet setting is automatic recalculation each time an entry is made to a cell. As you'll learn in this chapter, there are times to suppress automatic recalculation.
;	Moves the spreadsheet cursor to the other window of a split screen. This command is used with the /W(indow).
&	Returns to the "execute file." This is covered with the /X(Execute) command.

Pressing any key other than those above, or the paging and jumping keys from Chapter 3, is interpreted by SuperCalc³ as an entry of data into the active cell.

There are two general types of entries into a cell: text and formula. An entry is classified as text in SuperCalc³ when one of the following situations exists:

The first initial character is " (double quotes), which indicates normal text.
The first initial character is ' (apostrophe), which indicates repeating text.
The entry does not meet the criteria for a formula.[1]

An entry is classified as formula in SuperCalc³ when both of the following situations exist:

The first initial character is neither " nor '.
The entry contains a number, formula, function, cell reference, or textual value. These characteristics are covered in this chapter.

---

1. SuperCalc³ assumes your entry is normal text and enters the " for you. While this saves some keystrokes, it's possible that formulas with mistakes will go in as text. Be careful and be alert. This feature can be turned off.

Normal Text Entries

These entries are generally used for column headings and row captions. Traditional business reports are structured this way. Consider a Profit & Loss Statement. The column headings represent time periods; the row captions describe revenue and expense items. Each item in the P&L Statement illustrated in Figure 4.1 represents one normal text entry.

The text in a normal text entry can be preceded by a double quotation mark ("). In most cases, the double quotes can be omitted and the entry will still be interpreted as text. The " must be used when the text has leading spaces or when SuperCalc³ would interpret the text as a formula entry or as a command.

Figure 4.1 P&L Statement Layout

```
                          QTR #1    QTR #2    QTR #3    QTR #4    TOTAL

SALES
COST OF GOODS SOLD
                          ------    ------    ------    ------    ------
GROSS MARGIN

OPERATING EXPENSES
  MARKETING
  ADMINISTRATIVE
                          ------    ------    ------    ------    ------
     TOTAL

PRE-TAX PROFIT
INCOME TAX
                          ------    ------    ------    ------    ------
NET INCOME
                          ======    ======    ======    ======    ======
```

Now enter the structure of Figure 4.1 into an empty spreadsheet, so get into SuperCalc³ if you aren't already there. Don't forget to use the SHIFT key and CAPS LCK where appropriate. The CAPS LCK key is a toggle key. It works like the NUM LCK key.

Position the spreadsheet cursor at cell B1 and enter

"QTR #1

You'll see this appear in the ENTRY LINE. Now press RETURN. The ENTRY LINE will clear itself and cell B1 will display **QTR #1.** Scroll back to cell B1 and notice in the STATUS LINE that the cell is identified as a text cell:

Text = "QTR #1

Position the spreadsheet cursor at cell C1 and enter

QTR #2

Press RETURN and cell C1 displays **QTR #2.** The entry is treated as normal text even though the double quotes were omitted.

Position the spreadsheet cursor at cell D1 and enter

QTR #3

Press RETURN and cell D1 will display **QTR #3.**

Position the spreadsheet cursor at cell E1 and enter

QTR #4

Press RETURN and cell E1 will display **QTR #4.**

Position the spreadsheet cursor at cell F1 and enter

"TOTAL

Press RETURN and cell F1 will display **TOTAL.**

Looking at Figure 4.1 you'll see a series of dashes (–) and equal signs (=); accountants use these to represent breaks for subtotals and grand totals, respectively. The next step is to get them into the spreadsheet.

Position the spreadsheet cursor at cell B5 and enter

Press RETURN and cell B5 will display **------.** Repeat this entry for cells C5, D5, E5, F5, B11, C11, D11, E11, F11, B16, C16, D16, E16, and F16.

Position the spreadsheet cursor at cell B18 and enter

"= = = = = =

Press RETURN and cell B18 displays = = = = = =. The double quotation marks must precede the equal signs because = is a jump command. If you omit " you'll see the message **Range ERROR.** Repeat this entry for cells C18, D18, E18, and F18.

Next, enter the row captions for rows 3, 4, 6, 8, 9, 10, 12, 14, 15, and 17.

Position the spreadsheet cursor at cell A3 and enter

SALES

Press RETURN and cell A3 will display **SALES.**

Position the spreadsheet cursor at cell A4 and enter

CPST OF GOODS SOLD

Don't press the RETURN key yet. If you look at your ENTRY LINE, you'll notice that **COST** has been incorrectly spelled as **CPST.** This is a common error; correcting it is quite easy.

Make sure the NUM LCK key is disengaged, then press ←. Notice that the entry line cursor moved one position to the left. Hold down the ← key until the entry line cursor is positioned on the P in **CPST,** then type **O.** Now press RETURN. Cell A4 will display **COST OF GOODS SOLD.**

Position the spreadsheet cursor at cell A6 and enter

"GROOSSS MARGIN

Don't press RETURN yet. If you look at your ENTRY LINE, you'll notice that **GROSS** has been incorrectly spelled **GROOSSS.** Another typing error. This time it's two characters too many. Again, correcting it is quite simple. Press the TAB key. Notice that the entry line cursor jumped to the start of the entry. Now press → until the entry line cursor is positioned on either **O** in **GROOSSS.** Press ↓, and the excess **O** is now deleted from the ENTRY LINE. From this point each character is shifted one position to the left. Now press →. The ENTRY LINE cursor moves one character to the right. Press ↓, and the excess **S** is deleted. Press RETURN and cell A6 now displays **GROSS MARGIN.**

Position the spreadsheet cursor at cell A8 and enter

OPERATINGEXPENSES

Don't press RETURN yet. If you look at your ENTRY LINE, you'll notice the space that should separate the words **OPERATING** and **EXPENSES** has been omitted. To correct this, hold down the ← key until the ENTRY LINE cursor is positioned on the **E** that begins the word **EXPENSES,** then press ↑. The missing space is inserted in the ENTRY LINE, and the word **EXPENSES** is shifted one position to the right. Press RETURN and cell A7 now displays **OPERATING EXPENSES.**

Now finish inputting the row captions:

Enter " **MARKETING** into cell A9
Enter " **ADMINISTRATIVE** into cell A10
Enter " **TOTAL** into cell A12

The leading spaces in the preceding three items necessitates using the ".

Enter **PRE-TAXPROFIT** into cell A14
Enter **INCOME TAX** into cell A15
Enter **NET INCOME** into cell A17

Mission successful? Well, not quite. Look at cell A14. Notice it displays **PRE-TAXPROFIT. PRE-TAX** and **PROFIT** should be separated by a space. Since you didn't notice this error prior to pressing RETURN, here's how to fix it.

Use an =A14 to jump the spreadsheet cursor to cell A14; then press /E. SuperCalc³ responds with

From? Enter cell (on PROMPT LINE)
/Edit(into current cell), (on ENTRY LINE)

Just press RETURN and the contents of cell A14 will be displayed on the ENTRY LINE. Now you can correct **PRE-TAXPROFIT** using the directional arrows exactly as you did to correct **OPERATINGEXPENSES.** Press RETURN and **PRE-TAX PROFIT** will be properly entered into cell A14.

You have completed making your normal text entries into the P&L spreadsheet. If you've been concurrently making entries into your own spreadsheet, your spreadsheet should match the one illustrated in Figure 4.2.

Figure 4.2 P&L Spreadsheet with Normal Text Entries

```
   |  A   ||  B    ||  C    ||  D    ||  E    ||  F    ||  G  ||  H  |
1          QTR #1   QTR #2   QTR #3   QTR #4   TOTAL
2
3   SALES
4   COST OF GOODS SOLD
5          ------   ------   ------   ------   ------
6   GROSS MARGIN
7
8   OPERATING EXPENSES
9     MARKETING
10    ADMINISTRATIVE
11         ------   ------   ------   ------   ------
12       TOTAL
13
14  PRE-TAX PROFIT
15  INCOME TAX
16         ------   ------   ------   ------   ------
17  NET INCOME
18         ======   ======   ======   ======   ======
19
20
 A14          Text="PRE-TAX PROFIT
Width:  9  Memory:100 Last Col/Row:F18      ? for HELP
  1>
F1 = Help; F2 = Cancel; F9 = Plot; F10 = View
```

As you look at your spreadsheet, notice that each text entry starts on the left side of a cell. This is known as *left justification;* it's the standard data processing default for placing and displaying text. It means the text is aligned at the left end of the cell and any text overflowing the width of the cell will be truncated (chopped off) on the right.

At this point you don't see any truncation, but its potential is there nonetheless. Remember that the default column width is nine positions. Also note that cells A4, A6, A8, A9, A10, A12, A14, A15, and A17 have entries that exceed nine characters. How do you know this? One way is to count the number of characters in each entry. An easier and faster way is to observe in the spreadsheet display that these entries drift into column B. As long as the right adjacent cell is empty, SuperCalc³ permits text overflow into that adjacent cell. If the adjacent cell is not blank, then for display purposes any characters that extend beyond the defined column width are truncated.

It's important to note that the actual cell contents are not truncated; only the cell display shows the effect of truncation.

As your P&L Statement spreadsheet evolves, you'll see that your text entered as column headings might be better displayed with *right justification*. As you've probably guessed, right justification is exactly the opposite of left justification. With right justification, alignment takes place at the right end of the cell. If any characters overflow the cell, they will be truncated on the left when the left adjacent cell is not blank.

Before leaving this section, take a moment to look at some features of the /E(dit) command. As you just saw, this command is quite helpful for correcting or otherwise changing the contents previously placed into a cell. When you enter /E, you have two options:

1. Simply pressing RETURN pulls the contents of the current cell into the ENTRY LINE. When you've finished making your changes, press RETURN and the edited results of the ENTRY LINE are placed in the current cell. This is how you corrected cell A14.
2. Specify a cell, then press RETURN. The contents of the specified cell are brought into the ENTRY LINE. When you've finished making your changes, press RETURN and the edited results of the ENTRY LINE are placed in the current cell. The contents of the originally specified cell are unchanged. This technique is useful for duplicating cells that are similar but not identical; it saves the time of having to enter each cell completely.

Repeating Text Entries

A common use of these entries is to place dashes across an entire row as either an underline or a dividing line in a business report. Many other possibilities for using repeating text entries exist. They are limited only by the scope of your imagination or the problem you are solving with SuperCalc³.

The text in a repeating entry must be preceded by an apostrophe ('). If this is omitted, the entry will be interpreted as a regular text entry or as a command. When repeating text is entered, the actual entry is contained in the cell in which the entry is made. The display, however, repeats across the entire row, stopping at the first non-blank cell. If the row contains only empty cells, the repetitious display will continue through the last cell in that row. This will be column BK or DW, depending on the memory capacity of your system and on how you have optimized SuperCalc³ at installation time.

To contrast the use of repeating text with the use of normal text, consider the following illustration. You want to put dashes across row 2 of the P&L spreadsheet, starting at column B. Based on what you learned about normal text entries, you could certainly enter **---------** in cells B2, C2, D2, E2, and F2. This takes four normal text entries. A similar effect can be achieved by a single repeating text entry. At cell B2, enter **'-** and press RETURN. You now have a series of hyphens starting at B2 and displaying continuously across the rest of row 2. If you reposition the spreadsheet cursor to cell B2, you'll see it identified in the STATUS LINE as a repeating text cell:

Rtxt='-

You should recognize that these results using repeating text are not identical with the results that would have been obtained by the four normal text entries, since the repeating text continues beyond cell F2. However, this lack of identity can be very quickly corrected.

Position your spreadsheet cursor at cell G2, enter " and press RETURN. The repeating text stopped at the end of cell F2. As you learned earlier, repeating text continues until a cell that is not empty is encountered. Cell G2 is not empty; it contains a single space. While emptiness and a space may be the same to the human eye, the two are totally dissimilar to the computer.

Before going on to the next section, you must learn two new "Slash" commands, /S(ave) and /Z(ap). As the command names imply, one is constructive, the other destructive.

Since you need an empty spreadsheet for the first part of the next section, you're going to "save" the spreadsheet you've been building so you can retrieve it later.

First, make sure you have a properly formatted disk in your data drive. To transfer the P&L spreadsheet from your computer's memory onto disk, enter **/S.** SuperCalc³ responds with:

Enter File Name (or <RETURN> for directory)

on the PROMPT LINE and

/Save,

on the ENTRY LINE. Now enter

PALDEMO

and press RETURN. *Note:* PALDEMO represents Profit & Loss Statement Demonstration. If you prefer some other name, insert it instead of PALDEMO. Don't forget to precede PALDEMO with the drive identifier of the data drive.

SuperCalc³'s next prompt is

A(ll), V(alues), or P(art)?

So you enter **A,** because you want the entire spreadsheet saved. SuperCalc³'s last display on the PROMPT LINE is

Saving . . .

At this point you can either terminate your SuperCalc³ session by the /Q(uit) command or continue on to the next section. If you intend to continue, you must do one more thing before moving on—create an empty spreadsheet.

With what you have learned so far you could get an empty spreadsheet via the /Q(uit) command with SC3 specified as the filename under the T(o) option. Such an action would take you out of SuperCalc³ and bring you back with an empty spreadsheet.

An easier alternative is to use the /Z(ap) command. On entering **/Z,** the PROMPT LINE displays

Y(es), N(o),C(ontents)

while the ENTRY LINE displays

/Zap-ENTIRE-Worksheet?

The options on the PROMPT LINE mean:

Y(es) Erases the ENTIRE spreadsheet, including all formats, definitions, and global settings. The current data disk drive setting is not changed.

N(o) Cancels the /Z(ap) command and returns to the current spreadsheet. F2 produces the same effect.

C(ontents) Erases the contents and formats of the spreadsheet but leaves the User-Defined Format Table and the current data disk drive settings intact.

Enter **Y** to erase everything.

Simple Formula Entries

There are several types of formula entries, all numeric, so they can be used in arithmetic and logical operations:

Numeric Constants
Cell Names
Expressions
Textual Values

The numeric constant represents a formula entry in its most elementary form. Entering a numeric constant is done by keystroking a number, then pressing the RETURN key. As you enter the number you'll see it on the ENTRY LINE. When you press RETURN, the number you keyed will be placed in the current cell. The number may not, however, be displayed on the spreadsheet in exactly the way you entered it.

Spreadsheet representation is controlled by the /F(ormat) command. Even though you haven't used this command yet, there are certain defaults set by SuperCalc³. These remain in effect until you change them. You've seen some of the defaults in the previous section:

- Column width of nine positions
- Left justification of text entries

Two additional defaults you'll see in this section are

- Right justification of formula entries
- Revised representation of formula entries to obtain the best fit within the defined width of the cell

Numeric Constants

Mathematically, numeric constants have three representations:

1. Integer representation, which has no positions to the right of the implied decimal point. Integer numbers are popularly called whole numbers. Examples: 1, 32, 256, 1024, 4096.
2. Fixed point representation, which has some positions to the right of an actual decimal point. Examples: 1.98, 0.022, 499.95, 4.3125
3. Floating point representation, which is based on multiplication of a number by 10 raised to some power. Although this sounds like scientific notation, it's called exponential notation, or *E-notation* for short.

If you haven't left SuperCalc³ at the end of the previous section, you should be looking at an empty spreadsheet. If you quit after the last section, now is a good time to boot SuperCalc³ into your system and get into an empty spreadsheet. When you're ready, you'll enter a series of numbers so you can see how their display is adjusted to get the best fit to the cell width.

Position your spreadsheet cursor at cell A1. Enter **123** into cell A1. After pressing RETURN you see **123** displayed right justified at cell A1 on the spreadsheet.

Enter **123.4** into cell A2. After pressing RETURN you see **123.4** displayed right justified at cell A2 on the spreadsheet.

So far, each value you've entered has been displayed right justified with digits identical to those keystroked.

Enter **1234.5678** into cell A3. After pressing RETURN you see **1234.568** displayed right justified at cell A3 on the spreadsheet. Look at the positions to the right of the decimal point. You entered **.5678** but **.568** is displayed. SuperCalc³ rounded the entry to one less decimal position so it would fit within the default cell width of nine digits.

Counting the number of digits in 1234.5678, you get exactly nine. Did SuperCalc³ make a mistake? No, it always allows a leading space so that the numeric entry in a given cell doesn't touch the entry in the left adjacent cell. If the actual numbers in adjacent cells were contiguous, two groups of numbers would be perceived as one big number.

You can see what is displayed at cell A3. However, you might wonder what is actually stored in cell A3. This is easily determined. Move your spreadsheet cursor back to cell A3 and look at the STATUS LINE. You'll see **Form = 1234.5678.** Your actual entry hasn't been lost. The only change that has taken place is the way the number is displayed.

Enter **123456.78901** into cell A4. After pressing RETURN you see **123456.8** displayed right justified at cell A4 on the spreadsheet. This entry has been rounded for the same reasons that the entry at A3 was rounded. The only difference is that the rounding operation changed five decimal places of precision to one decimal place.

Enter **1234567890.1234** into cell A5. After pressing RETURN you see **1.2346e9** displayed right justified at cell A5 on the spreadsheet. This is the *E-notation* mentioned earlier. Since SuperCalc³ can fit only eight digits, including algebraic sign and decimal point, in a cell nine positions wide, it looks for the best way to fit the number into the cell. The number you entered at cell A5 has ten digits to the left of the decimal point and four digits to the right of the decimal point. Even if SuperCalc³ rounded the number to an integer, the 10 significant digits are still too many for the cell width. E-notation is the only way to fit the number into cell A5.

The displayed number, **1.2346e9,** should be interpreted as 1.2346 times the 9th power of 10 or 1.2346 × 1000000000. The display is approximately equal to the original entry 1234567890.1234. E-notation is not generally used for business and administrative computations, but you should be familiar with it in case a spreadsheet calculates some large number and SuperCalc³ converts it to E-notation.

Enter **123456789** into cell A6. After pressing RETURN you see **1.2346e8** displayed right justified at cell A6 on the spreadsheet. Again, the conversion to E-notation occurred because the nine-digit number entered couldn't fit into the eight *available* positions of cell A6.

Enter **12345678** into cell A7. After pressing RETURN you see **12345678** displayed at cell A7 on the spreadsheet. Since the entered number exactly fit the eight available positions of cell A7, no conversion was made for display purposes.

Enter **−12345678** into cell A8. After pressing RETURN you see **−1.235e7** displayed right justified at cell A8 on the spreadsheet. Although the entered number contained only eight digits, it also contained a negative sign. In effect, the entry consisted of nine positions. Since the eight usable numeric positions must also accommodate the *minus sign and decimal point,* the nine-position entry was converted to E-notation. If your computer supports color and you have a color monitor connected to your system, you'll notice that −1.235e7 is displayed in *red.* SuperCalc³ is capable of displaying all negative values in red. Whether it does or not depends on your hardware configuration.

All numbers are limited to a maximum of 16 positions. Any attempt to enter a number containing more than 16 positions produces one of the following results:

1. When the double quotation is optional for normal text, numbers greater than 16 positions are accepted as normal text entries.
2. When the double quotation is required for normal text, numbers greater than 16 positions are rejected as formula errors.

As proof, try to enter **12345678901234567.** Under the default settings the entry goes into cell A9 as normal text. If you scroll back to A9, the STATUS LINE shows

Text="12345678901234567

Now, what happens when the double quotation mark is required for normal text? First, enter **/G"** to toggle off the optional setting for ". Next, try to enter **12345678901234567.** You got the **Formula ERROR** message as soon as you pressed RETURN, right? And your entry line cursor is still sitting to the right of the rejected number 12345678901234567, right? Now that you've proved the point, you can kill the entry with an F2. Also, enter **/G"** to toggle back on the optional setting for ". Next, position your spreadsheet cursor at cell A9, then enter **/B** to erase the cell.

This concludes your exercise using numeric constants. If you've been doing this exercise concurrently on your own system, your spreadsheet should look like the one illustrated in Figure 4.3.

Figure 4.3 Numeric Constants as Formula Entries

```
     |  A   ||   B   ||   C   ||   D   ||   E   ||   F   ||   G   ||   H   |
1          123
2          123.4
3     1234.568
4     123456.8
5     1.2346e9
6     1.2346e8
7     12345678
8     -1.235e7
9
10
11
12
13
14
15
16
17
18
19
20
 A9
Width:  9  Memory:101 Last Col/Row:A8        ? for HELP
  1>
F1 = Help; F2 = Cancel; F9 = Plot; F10 = View
```

Cell Names

The name of another cell can be entered into the current cell, and the current cell will display the value of the first cell. If the contents of the first cell are changed, any cells that reference the first cell will use the new value of the first cell.

To demonstrate this, position your spreadsheet cursor at cell B1. Enter **A1** and press RETURN. Scroll down to cell B2 and enter **A1.** Now move to B3 and enter **A1** one more time. Your spreadsheet will display **123** in cells A1, B1, B2, and B3.

To further demonstrate the concept of cell referencing, jump to cell A1. Enter **456** and press RETURN. Now your spreadsheet displays **456** in cells A1, B1, B2, and B3.

This SuperCalc^3 feature has been illustrated by very simple cell references. Its value is enhanced when cells are referenced from within complex expressions. The previous examples used cell A1 as the keystone cell since cells B1, B2, and B3 depended on its value. Practical examples of cell A1 include interest rates, tax rates, production rates, and market expansion rates. Changing the keystone cell can result in a radically different spreadsheet when references to that cell pervade the entire spreadsheet. An important business application of this feature is "What if . . .?" analysis. Here you may be interested in the effect of changes on certain key factors in product profitability or budgetary planning.

Expressions

If you understand numeric constants and cell references, you already understand half of the concept of expressions. An *arithmetic expression* is simply a collection of numeric constants and cell references linked together by special symbols called *arithmetic operators*.

The *arithmetic operators* are shown here in order of precedence:

Hierarchy of Arithmetic Operators

Level	Operator	Operation
1	( )	Override Hierarchy
2	^ or **	Exponentiation
3	*	Multiplication
3	/	Division
3	%	Percentage
4	+	Addition
4	−	Subtraction

The hierarchy determines the order operators and their associated operands are evaluated in when an expression contains multiple operators. When operators of the same precedence level appear in the same expression, the operator on the left is evaluated first.

Every expression, no matter how large, is broken into segments. Each segment consists of three pieces: an arithmetic operator and two arithmetic operands—e.g., 2 + 2. The operator is simply a special symbol that describes the kind of arithmetic to be performed.

An operand is something acted on by the arithmetic operator. It's one of the following:

- A numeric constant
- A numeric variable that's a cell name
- A result from a previously evaluated expression segment

These concepts are illustrated in the examples that follow.

EXAMPLE NO. 1: 2+6*2

Since multiplication [*] comes before addition [+] in the hierarchy, 6 is multiplied by 2. The product of 12 is then added to 2, for a result of 14.

To prove the answer in SuperCalc³, scroll to cell C1 and enter **2+6*2.** After you press RETURN, **14** is displayed at C1 and your spreadsheet cursor is now at C2 or D1, depending on which way your directional indicator was pointing. Move back to cell C1. You should see **Form=2+6*2** on the STATUS LINE.

EXAMPLE NO. 2: (2+6)*2

Since parentheses [()] override the hierarchy, their contents are evaluated first. Inside a set of parentheses the normal rules of the hierarchy are followed. In the example, 2 is added to 6. The result of 8 is then multiplied by 2, giving a product of 16.

To prove your answer in SuperCalc^3, scroll to cell C2 and enter **(2+6)*2.** After you press RETURN, **16** is displayed at C2. Move back to cell C2. You should see **Form=(2+6)*2** on the STATUS LINE.

EXAMPLE NO. 3: 6*3+6*2

Since multiplication [*] comes before addition [+] in the hierarchy, a multiplication operation will execute first. But which one? When arithmetic operators of the same hierarchical level are in an expression, the operator on the left executes first. Note that the operators themselves need not be identical. Only the level has to be the same. In this example, 6 is multiplied by 3, giving a product of 18. Next is the second multiplication with operands of 6 and 2. This multiplication gives a product of 12. The two products are then added, for a result of 30.

To prove your answer in SuperCalc^3, scroll to cell C3 and enter **6*3+6*2.** After you press RETURN, **30** is displayed at C3. Now move back to cell C3. You should see **Form=6*3+6*2** on the STATUS LINE.

EXAMPLE NO. 4: 2^8

Here, 2 is exponentiated by 8. In other words, 2 is raised to the eighth power. Exponentiation is a more concise way of multiplying 2 by itself eight times. The result of this process is 256.

To prove the answer, enter **2^8** or **2****8** into cell C4. The STATUS LINE for cell C4 shows **Form=2^8** or **Form=2**8,** depending on how you made the entry.

EXAMPLE NO. 5: 2^4^2

This example contains two exponentiation operations. Again, when an expression contains operations of the same level of precedence, the one on the left is evaluated first. Here, 2 is exponentiated by 4, giving a result of 16, which is then squared. The final result is 256.

For proof, enter **2^4^2** into cell C5. After you press RETURN, **256** is displayed at C5. Looking into cell C5 you see **Form=2^4^2** on the STATUS LINE.

EXAMPLE NO. 6: 2^4^2*2

This example contains two exponentiation operations plus a multiplication operation. The exponentiation operations are exactly as in Example No. 5, giving an interim result of 256. The interim result is an operand in the next operation, where it is multiplied by 2, giving a final result of 512.

For proof, enter **2^4^2*2** into cell C6. After you press RETURN, **512** is displayed on the spreadsheet at C6. Looking into cell C6 you see **Form=2^4^2*2** on the STATUS LINE.

EXAMPLE NO. 7: A1+A2

This example performs an addition operation on the contents of cells A1 and A2. Assuming your spreadsheet cursor is positioned at location cell C7 when you enter the example, the result, 579.4, is stored in cell C7. Looking into cell C7 you see **Form=A1+A2.** This is particularly important because if the contents of either A1 or A2 are changed, the value displayed by cell C7 will also change.

EXAMPLE NO. 8: (B1+44)/2

As in Example No. 2, the parentheses override the hierarchy. Here, 44 is added to the current contents of cell B1 (456), giving an interim result of 500, which is subsequently divided by 2. If you make this entry at C8, the final result of **250** will be displayed at cell C8. If the result displayed on your spreadsheet is **478,** you forgot to enter the parentheses.

If you forget to enter a left [(] or right [)] parenthesis and /G" is toggled off, the message **"Formula ERROR"** will be displayed on your STATUS LINE. SuperCalc³ validates formula entries to ensure that the count of left parentheses equals the count of right parentheses. Viewing the STATUS LINE for C8 you'll find **Form=(B1+44)/2.**

EXAMPLE NO. 9: 20%240

This example is read as "take 20% of 240"—equivalent to .2 * 240. The result is 48. Make this entry at cell C9. Viewing the STATUS LINE for C9 you'll find **Form=20%240.**

At this point your spreadsheet should match the one illustrated in Figure 4.4.

Figure 4.4 Expressions as Formula Entries: Example 1

```
     |    A    ||    B    ||    C    ||  D  ||  E  ||  F  ||  G  ||  H  |
1          456        456         14
2        123.4        456         16
3     1234.568        456         30
4     123456.8                   256
5     1.2346e9                   256
6     1.2346e8                   512
7     12345678                 579.4
8     -1.235e7                   250
9                                 48
10
11
12
13
14
15
16
17
18
19
20
 C10
Width:  9  Memory:100 Last Col/Row:C9        ? for HELP
  1)
F1 = Help; F2 = Cancel; F9 = Plot; F10 = View
```

Reviewing your spreadsheet, you should find that cells B1, B2, B3, C7, and C8 all reference cell A1. Consequently, if a change is made to cell A1, the contents of cells B1, B2, B3, C7, and C8 will also change.

To demonstrate this feature, first jump to cell A1. Into cell A1 enter **200.** Cells A1, B1, B2, B3, C7, and C8 have changed. Your spreadsheet should match the one shown in Figure 4.5

Figure 4.5 Expressions as Formula Entries: Example 2

```
    |    A    ||    B    ||    C    ||    D    ||    E    ||    F    ||    G    ||    H    |
1         200       200        14
2       123.4       200        16
3    1234.568       200        30
4    123456.8                 256
5    1.2346e9                 256
6    1.2346e8                 512
7    12345678               323.4
8   -1.235e7                  122
9                              48
10
11
12
13
14
15
16
17
18
19
20
 C9          Form=20%240
Width:  9  Memory:100 Last Col/Row:C9       ? for HELP
  1>
F1 = Help; F2 = Cancel; F9 = Plot; F10 = View
```

It's a good idea to /S(ave) this spreadsheet onto disk for future reference. As you did earlier in this chapter, enter **/S.** When SuperCalc^3 prompts you for a filename, enter **B:FORMDEMO,** then press RETURN. When SuperCalc^3 prompts you for **A(ll), V(alues), or P(art)?,** enter **A** (indicating you want to save all of the spreadsheet), then press RETURN.

Your next step is to retrieve the skeleton spreadsheet of the Profit & Loss Statement you put onto disk at the end of the previous section. Since your P&L should be loaded into an empty spreadsheet, you must erase the current spreadsheet. So, enter **/ZY.** As you learned previously, this entry calls the /Z(ap) command. Give a **Y** response to the **/Zap-ENTIRE-Worksheet?** prompt.

To retrieve your P&L, enter **/L.** This is the call for the /L(oad) command. The PROMPT LINE displays

Enter File Name (or <RETURN> for directory)

While the ENTRY LINE waits for you to specify a filename, it displays

/Load,

Enter **B:PALDEMO,** then press RETURN. If you used a different filename when you saved the P&L at the end of the section on text entries, use that name instead of PALDEMO.

When your PROMPT LINE displays

A(ll), P(art), C(onsolidate) or * for graphs only

it means SuperCalc^3 has found the file, so enter **A** to indicate that the entire spreadsheet should be loaded. The PROMPT LINE will then respond with

Loading . . .

When loading is completed, the P&L spreadsheet will be in memory. The spreadsheet cursor will be positioned wherever it was when you saved the spreadsheet. Use a jump command to reposition the cursor to cell A1.

Entering Formulas on the P&L

The Profit & Loss Statement displayed on your screen should look just as it did prior to saving it. You are going to enter a series of formulas into your P&L.

Before starting the data entry process you may want to turn off automatic recalculation by entering **/GM.** If you don't do this, SuperCalc³ will recalculate the entire spreadsheet each time you make an entry.

The SALES amounts and their associated cells are

Cell	Sales
B3	**5000**
C3	**4000**
D3	**4500**
E3	**7500**

Position your spreadsheet cursor at cell B3 and make the indicated entries to cells B3, C3, D3, and E3. If you make any mistakes before pressing RETURN, use the directional arrows to make the necessary corrections in the entry line. If you see a mistake after pressing RETURN, scroll back to the cell and re-enter the amount. You could also use **/E(dit),** but for relatively small numeric constants, such as these, a simple re-entry is faster.

As you are entering these SALES amounts, you'll notice that they don't align very nicely with the column headings in row 1. This is due to the default left justification of text entries and the default right justification of formula entries. Don't concern yourself with it now. You'll learn how to fix it later.

After you've completed the SALES amount entries, position your spreadsheet cursor at cell F3. Since you need a SALES total for the four quarters, enter **B3+C3+D3+E3** and press RETURN.

The COST OF GOODS SOLD is computed as 30% of SALES. Position your cursor at cell B4 and make the following entries (note that 30% can be expressed as a decimal amount or a percent):

Cell	Entry
B4	**30%B3**
C4	**30%C3**
D4	**D3*.30**
E4	**E3*.30**
F4	**B4+C4+D4+E4**

GROSS MARGIN is computed as the difference between SALES and COST OF GOODS SOLD. Position your cursor at cell B6 and make the following entries:

Cell	Entry
B6	**B3-B4**
C6	**C3-C4**
D6	**D3-D4**
E6	**E3-E4**
F6	**B6+C6+D6+E6**

MARKETING EXPENSES are constant at 1000, so enter **1000** into cells B9, C9, D9, and E9. At cell F9, enter **B9+C9+D9+E9** to calculate TOTAL MARKETING EXPENSE.

ADMINISTRATIVE EXPENSE is computed as 10% of SALES. Position your cursor at cell B10 and make the entries below (note that 10% can be expressed as a decimal amount or a percent):

Cell	Entry
B10	**10%B3**
C10	**10%C3**
D10	**D3*.10**
E10	**E3*.10**
F10	**B10+C10+D10+E10**

TOTAL Operating Expenses is calculated as the sum of MARKETING Expense and ADMINISTRATIVE Expense. Position your cursor at cell B12 and make the following entries:

Cell	Entry
B12	**B9+B10**
C12	**C9+C10**
D12	**D9+D10**
E12	**E9+E10**
F12	**B12+C12+D12+E12**

PRE-TAX PROFIT is calculated as the difference between GROSS MARGIN and TOTAL Operating Expense. Position your cursor at cell B14 and make the following entries:

Cell	Entry
B14	**B6-B12**
C14	**C6-C12**
D14	**D6-D12**
E14	**E6-E12**
F14	**B14+C14+D14+E14**

INCOME TAX is computed as 50% of PRE-TAX PROFIT. Position your cursor at cell B15 and make the entries shown on the next page (note that 50% can be expressed as a decimal amount or a percent):

Cell	Entry
B15	**50%B14**
C15	**50%C14**
D15	**D14*.50**
E15	**E14*.50**
F15	**B15+C15+D15+E15**

NET INCOME is calculated as the difference between PRE-TAX PROFIT and INCOME TAX. Position your cursor at cell B17 and make the following entries:

Cell	Entry
B17	**B14-B15**
C17	**C14-C15**
D17	**D14-D15**
E17	**E14-E15**
F17	**B17+C17+D17+E17**

You have now completed the entry of numeric constants and expressions into your Profit & Loss Statement spreadsheet. Press ! so that SuperCalc³ recalculates the spreadsheet. The P&L displayed on your screen should match the one illustrated in Figure 4.6.

Figure 4.6 P&L Spreadsheet with Text and Formula Entries

```
   |    A    ||    B    ||    C    ||    D    ||    E    ||    F    ||    G    ||    H    |
1            QTR #1     QTR #2     QTR #3     QTR #4     TOTAL
2            ------------------------------------------------------
3   SALES         5000       4000       4500       7500      21000
4   COST OF G     1500       1200       1350       2250       6300
5            ------     ------     ------     ------     ------
6   GROSS MAR     3500       2800       3150       5250      14700
7
8   OPERATING EXPENSES
9     MARKETI     1000       1000       1000       1000       4000
10    ADMINIS      500        400        450        750       2100
11           ------     ------     ------     ------     ------
12       TOTA     1500       1400       1450       1750       6100
13
14  PRE-TAX P     2000       1400       1700       3500       8600
15  INCOME TA     1000        700        850       1750       4300
16           ------     ------     ------     ------     ------
17  NET INCOM     1000        700        850       1750       4300
18           ======     ======     ======     ======     ======
19
20
 F17              Form=B17+C17+D17+E17
Width:   9   Memory: 99 Last Col/Row:G18        ? for HELP
  1>
F1 = Help; F2 = Cancel; F9 = Plot; F10 = View
```

When you have made any necessary corrections and are satisfied with your P&L, save it onto disk because you'll need it in the next chapter. To save it, enter **/SB:PALDEMO** and press RETURN. The PROMPT LINE will display

File Already Exists: C(hange name), B(ackup) or O(verwrite)?

You should enter **O** so that SuperCalc³ saves the latest version of your P&L on top of the previous version. When you are prompted for **A(ll), Values, or P(art)?**, enter **A.**

Textual Values

This type of formula entry has the outward appearance of simple text but is treated by SuperCalc³ as though it were numeric. Textual values are used primarily with logical functions and table lookups. Both of these features require numeric components. They are covered in later chapters. The textual value consists of up to nine characters of text enclosed in a set of double quotation marks, then enclosed in a set of parentheses. The general format is ("text").

Review Exercises

1. Your ENTRY LINE displays **"TOOTALSELAS;** it should display **"TOTAL SALES.** How do you correct the ENTRY LINE?
2. Cell A3 contains **"TOOTALSELAS;** it should contain **"TOTAL SALES.** How do you correct cell A3? Use a "Slash" command; do not re-enter the text.
3. Show the text entry to get repeating asterisks (*), starting at cell B3 and ending at cell G3.
4. Evaluate the following expressions:
   a. 2+4^2
   b. 2+4^2/2
   c. 2+4^2/2+2*5
   d. (2+4)^2/2-2*4
   e. (2+4)^2/(4+2)*4
5. Given the expression B3*4-C3*2:
   a. What is the result when cell B3 contains 10 and cell C3 contains 15?
   b. What is the result when cell B3 is changed to 5?
6. Which "Slash" command would you use to retrieve a spreadsheet from disk?
7. Which "Slash" command would you use to erase your spreadsheet? Enter this command before proceeding to Exercise No. 10.
8. Which "Slash" command would you use to turn off automatic recalculation?
9. Which command would you use to force a manual recalculation?
10. From the layout on the following page, create a spreadsheet that represents monthly interest charges on credit cards:
    Other requirements:
    a. Calculate a monthly total at the end of each row.
    b. Calculate a credit card total and a grand total at the bottom of the appropriate columns.

	VISA	MASTER CHARGE	SEARS	TOTAL
JAN	9.05	8.96	9.74	
FEB	12.06	8.84	9.98	
MAR	13.31	8.23	9.62	
APR	14.88	7.67	9.29	
MAY	33.49	7.74	8.89	
JUN	20.75	8.06	9.05	
JUL	23.1	8.04	9.37	
AUG	24.95	7.31	10.64	
SEP	26.71	7.45	11.59	
OCT	27.38	8.44	12.64	
NOV	27.89	7.96	12.48	
DEC	26.7	7.4	12.3	
TOTAL				

11. When you have completed Exercise No. 10, enter the proper "Slash" command to put your spreadsheet onto disk.

Answers to Review Exercises

1. Procedure to edit ENTRY LINE:
   a. Hold down the ← key until the entry line cursor is positioned over the first **O** in **"TOOTALSELAS.**
   b. Press the ↓ key to delete **O.**
   c. Hold down the → key until the entry line cursor is positioned over the first **S** in **"TOTALSELAS.**
   d. Press the ↑ key to insert a space.
   e. Press the → key twice to position the entry line cursor over the **E** in **"TOTAL SELAS.**
   f. Press **A** to correct the first misplaced character.
   g. Press the → key twice to position the entry line cursor over the next **A** in **"TOTAL SALAS.**
   h. Press **E** to correct the second misplaced character.
   i. Press RETURN to enter the text **"TOTAL SALES** into the cell.
2. Position your spreadsheet cursor at the cell to be corrected. Enter /**E,** then press RETURN. Follow the procedures in the solution to Exercise No. 1.
3. Position your spreadsheet cursor at cell B3. Enter **'*,** then press RETURN. Position your spreadsheet cursor at cell H3. Enter " then press RETURN.
4. Expression Evaluation:
   First solve these evaluations manually. Afterward you may want to enter the expressions into a spreadsheet so SuperCalc³ can solve them.

a. 18
Proof: 4 is exponentiated by 2, resulting in 16.
2 is added to 16, giving 18.

b. 10
Proof: 4 is exponentiated by 2, resulting in 16.
16 is divided by 2, giving 8.
2 is added to 8, giving 10.

c. 20
Proof: 4 is exponentiated by 2, resulting in 16.
16 is divided by 2, giving 8.
2 is multiplied by 5, giving 10.
2 is added to 8, giving 10.
10 is added to 10, giving 20.

d. 10
Proof: Within the parentheses, 2 is added to 4, giving 6.
6 is exponentiated by 2, resulting in 36.
36 is divided by 2, giving 18.
2 is multiplied by 4, giving 8.
8 is subtracted from 18, giving 10.

e. 24
Proof: Within the first set of parentheses, 2 is added to 4, giving 6.
Within the second set of parentheses, 4 is added to 2, giving 6.
6 is exponentiated by 2, resulting in 36.
36 is divided by 6, giving 6.
6 is multiplied by 4, giving 24.

5. Expression evaluation with cell references.

a. 10
Proof: 10 (contents of cell B3) is multiplied by 4, giving 40.
15 (contents of cell C3) is multiplied by 2, giving 30.
30 is subtracted from 40, giving 10.

b. −10 (displayed in red if you have a color system).
Proof: 5 (contents of cell B3) is multiplied by 4, giving 20.
15 (contents of cell C3) is multiplied by 2, giving 30.
30 is subtracted from 20, giving −10.

6. /L(oad)
7. /Z(ap)
To erase your current spreadsheet, enter /**ZY**.
8. /GM
9. !
10. Formulas are required for the following cells:

a. row total formulas:

Cell	Formula
E4	B4+C4+D4
E5	B5+C5+D5
E6	B6+C6+D6
E7	B7+C7+D7

(continued on next page)

E8	B8 + C8 + D8
E9	B9 + C9 + D9
E10	B10 + C10 + D10
E11	B11 + C11 + D11
E12	B12 + C12 + D12
E13	B13 + C13 + D13
E14	B14 + C14 + D14
E15	B15 + C15 + D15

b. column total formulas:

Cell	Formula
B17	B4 + B5 + B6 + B7 + B8 + B9 + B10 + B11 + B12 + B13 + B14 + B15
C17	C4 + C5 + C6 + C7 + C8 + C9 + C10 + C11 + C12 + C13 + C14 + C15
D17	D4 + D5 + D6 + D7 + D8 + D9 + D10 + D11 + D12 + D13 + D14 + D15
E17	E4 + E5 + E6 + E7 + E8 + E9 + E10 + E11 + E12 + E13 + E14 + E15

c. See Figure 4.7 for the final product.

Figure 4.7 Credit Interest Spreadsheet: Exercise 4-10

```
     |   A    ||   B    ||   C    ||   D    ||   E    ||   F    ||   G    ||   H    |
 1                           MASTER
 2                  VISA     CHARGE     SEARS      TOTAL
 3                  ------------------------------------
 4   JAN             9.05      8.96      9.74     27.75
 5   FEB            12.06      8.84      9.98     30.88
 6   MAR            13.31      8.23      9.62     31.16
 7   APR            14.88      7.67      9.29     31.84
 8   MAY            33.49      7.74      8.89     50.12
 9   JUN            20.75      8.06      9.05     37.86
10   JUL             23.1      8.04      9.37     40.51
11   AUG            24.95      7.31     10.64      42.9
12   SEP            26.71      7.45     11.59     45.75
13   OCT            27.38      8.44     12.64     48.46
14   NOV            27.89      7.96     12.48     48.33
15   DEC             26.7       7.4      12.3      46.4
16                 ------    ------    ------    ------
17   TOTAL         260.27      96.1    125.59    481.96
18                 ======    ======    ======    ======
19
20
 B17               Form=B4+B5+B6+B7+B8+B9+B10+B11+B12+B13+B14+B15
Width:  9   Memory: 99 Last Col/Row:F18       ? for HELP
 1>
F1 = Help; F2 = Cancel; F9 = Plot; F10 = View
```

11. /S to call the /S(ave) command. Then enter **B:EX4-10** for the filename and press A to save the entire spreadsheet.

CHAPTER 5

Global Control of Your Spreadsheet

Chapter Overview and Objectives

- Setting Global Menu Options
- Setting On/Off Toggles
- Setting Calculation Options

When you've completed Chapter 5, you'll have a basic understanding of how to set size and memory constraints for your spreadsheets. You'll be able to update selected menu settings into the SuperCalc³ program so that they become your customized defaults. You'll be able to control what is displayed on your video screen: whether or not the column letters and row numbers are displayed and whether the actual cell formulas or the computed values are displayed. You'll also be able to control both the timing and the sequence of spreadsheet calculations.

Setting Options for the Entire Spreadsheet

SuperCalc³ has a /G(lobal) command that lets you set and control processing and display options for the entire spreadsheet. In preparation for the /G(lobal) command, either boot SuperCalc³ or /Zap whatever spreadsheet is in memory. Next, /Load the P&L spreadsheet. If you forgot, it's **/LB:PALDEMO,A.**

When the /G(lobal) command is invoked via /G, the PROMPT LINE displays[1]

Optimum,Keep,Graphics,Form,",Next,Border,Tab,Row/Col/Dep,IterS, Man/Auto?

Current selections are displayed in high intensity. The ENTRY LINE displays

9>/Global,

Press one of the characters O, K, G, F, ", N, B, T, R, C, D, I, M, or A. It's not

1. Please note that your screen will display this on one line. Due to the limited size of our book page, we are not always able to show a complete line exactly as it would appear on your screen.

necessary to press the RETURN key. SuperCalc[3] will either prompt you for additional information or immediately implement the global option you specified.

These global options can be split into three categories:

- Global Menu Options (use full screen menus): Optimum, Keep, and Graphics.
- On/Off Toggles: Form, ", Next, Border, Tab, Prot.
- Calculation Options: Row/Col/Dep, Iter, Man/Auto.

Global Menu Options

OPTIMUM SPREADSHEET CONDITIONS MENU

This menu is called by entering /**GO.** It covers three processing conditions:

Memory Allows you to choose between speed and data-space for spreadsheet entries.

F Selects speed over spreadsheet data-space. This is the default setting.

D Selects spreadsheet data-space over speed.

Spreadsheet Boundary Allows you to choose between several sizes of spreadsheets.

S Selects a small spreadsheet boundary, 63 columns by 254 rows. The highest cell address is BK254. This option provides the most data-space in memory.

M Selects a medium spreadsheet boundary, 127 columns by 2,000 rows. The highest cell address is DW2000. This option provides about 4K less data-space than option S.

L Selects a large spreadsheet boundary, 127 columns by 9,999 rows. The highest cell address is DW9999. This option provides about 20K less data-space than option S.

A Allows SuperCalc[3] to automatically select the boundary based on the memory capacity of your system: *Small* (63 columns × 254 rows) for systems with less than 192K memories. *Medium* (127 columns × 2,000 rows) for systems with at least 192K memories.

Scroll Allows you to choose the best scroll for your type of computer.

I Selects scrolling for the IBM PC class of personal computers.

C Selects scrolling for the COMPAQ class of personal computers.

The TAB, ↑, ↓, and SPACE keys will scroll you around this menu. RETURN makes your entry, then moves you to the next menu item. F2 takes you back to the spreadsheet. Pressing F1 provides an AnswerScreen that tells you how to move around this menu.

Any selections made are not applicable during the current session. They are for future sessions only after being updated into the SuperCalc³ program by the Keep option. See the Global Keep option in the next section for more information.

Global Keep

This command allows you to update various menu settings into SuperCalc³ as program defaults. To invoke this option enter **/GK.** The PROMPT and ENTRY lines will display

Save all current MENU settings as program defaults? Y(es) or N(o)?
14>/Global,Keep,

Pressing Y updates SuperCalc³ to reflect settings from the following menus:

Menu Name	Setting Commands & Options
Graphics Colors	/Global,Graphics,Colors
Graphics Fonts	/Global,Graphics,Fonts
Graphics Layouts	/Global,Graphics,Layouts
Graphics Options	/Global,Graphics,Options
Graphics Device Selections	/Global,Graphics,Device
Directory Options	/Load
	/Save
	/Output . . . Disk
	/Delete,File
	/Quit,To
	/eXecute
Optimum Spreadsheet Conditions	/Global,Optimum
Setup Printer	/Output . . . Setup

Pressing N cancels /Global,Keep. Pressing F2 has the same result.

Global Graphics

This command allows you to call a series of menus for the selection of various graphics options. To invoke it, enter **/GG.** The PROMPT and ENTRY lines will display

C(olors), F(onts), L(ayout), O(ptions) or D(evice)?
18>/Global,Graphics,

C Select the colors to be used when graphing to a color printer or plotter.

F Select the type style to be used for all plotted labels and headings.

L Select the size of your graph and its position on the page of plotted output.

O Select optional graph features and alter the graphics printer and plotter settings.

D Select the model of your graphics printer or plotter from a list of supported devices.

The TAB, ↑, ↓, and SPACE keys will scroll you around these menus. RETURN makes your entry, then moves you to the next selection item. F2 takes you back to the spreadsheet. Pressing F1 provides an AnswerScreen that tells you how to move around the menu.

Chapter 12 on graphics gives an in-depth treatment of the specific items on the preceding menus.

On/Off Toggles

These options provide control of the way your spreadsheet is displayed and how you scroll around it. They work on a toggle principle similar to the NUM LCK key. The following toggle options are available with SuperCalc³:

Form Controls the display of the actual formulas versus the values computed from the formulas. The default setting is formulas off.

/GF toggles on display of your formulas if computed values are currently shown.

/GF toggles back to a display of computed values if formulas are currently shown.

You toggle on formulas whenever you want to see the actual contents of cells with numeric or formula entries. Using your Profit & Loss Statement spreadsheet, enter **/GF.** Your display will match Figure 5.1.

Re-enter **/GF** to toggle your formulas off. When formulas exceed a cell's width and the right adjacent contains data, the formula is truncated, just like text.

" Controls whether the double quote (") must be specifically entered as the first character in a normal text entry. The default setting is when the double quote is off—i.e., not required as the first character. Under the default, SuperCalc³ implicitly inserts " when you enter normal text. Even with the double quote requirement toggled off, the " must be explicitly keyed when the text has leading spaces or an initial character such as /, =, !, ", ;, ?, or '.

The entry **/G"** toggles the double quote on and off.

Figure 5.1 P&L Spreadsheet with Formulas Toggled On

```
     |  A   ||   B   ||   C   ||   D   ||   E   ||   F   ||  G  ||  H  |
1              QTR #1   QTR #2   QTR #3   QTR #4   TOTAL
2            --------------------------------------------
3    SALES     5000     4000     4500     7500     B3+C3+D3+E3
4    COST OF G 30%B3    30%C3    D3*.30   E3*.30   B4+C4+D4+E4
5              ------   ------   ------   ------   ------
6    GROSS MAR B3-B4    C3-C4    D3-D4    E3-E4    B6+C6+D6+E6
7
8    OPERATING EXPENSES
9      MARKETI 1000     1000     1000     1000     B9+C9+D9+E9
10     ADMINIS 10%B3    10%C3    D3*.10   E3*.10   B10+C10+D10+E10
11             ------   ------   ------   ------   ------
12        TOTA B9+B10   C9+C10   D9+D10   E9+E10   B12+C12+D12+E12
13
14   PRE-TAX P B6-B12   C6-C12   D6-D12   E6-E12   B14+C14+D14+E14
15   INCOME TA 50%B14   50%C14   D14*.50  E14*.50  B15+C15+D15+E15
16             ------   ------   ------   ------   ------
17   NET INCOM B14-B15  C14-C15  D14-D15  E14-E15  B17+C17+D17+E17
18             ======   ======   ======   ======   ======
19
20
 F17             Form=B17+C17+D17+E17
Width:  9  Memory: 99 Last Col/Row:G18       ? for HELP
  1>
F1 = Help; F2 = Cancel; F9 = Plot; F10 = View
```

Next Controls whether you move to the adjacent cell after entering data. When Next is on, you move to the adjacent cell based on the previous direction moved. If the last movement was to the left, then the next move is to the left adjacent cell. If the last movement was downward, then the next move is to the below adjacent cell.

When Next is off, pressing RETURN to enter data does not automatically move you to the next cell. You must make the move. The default setting is Next on. It is the ideal setting for initial data entry.

The entry **/GN** toggles Next on and off.

Border Controls the display of borders. These are the row numbers on the left edge of your screen and the column letters across the top line of your screen. The default setting is Borders on.

/GB toggles off display of your borders if they are currently visible.

/GB toggles on display of your borders if they are not currently visible. You toggle off borders whenever you want presentation-quality reports.

If you previously loaded the Profit & Loss Statement, enter **/GB.** Your display will match Figure 5.2.

Reenter **/GB** to toggle your borders back on.

Tab Controls whether empty or protected cells are bypassed during movement to the next cell. The default is Tab off—i.e., empty and protected cells are not bypassed. The Tab on option is useful for editing situations where you are only interested in cells with entries. During initial data entry, you want Tab turned off.

/GT turns Tab on and off.

Figure 5.2 P&L Spreadsheet with Borders Toggled Off

```
                QTR #1    QTR #2    QTR #3    QTR #4    TOTAL
                ---------------------------------------------
SALES             5000      4000      4500      7500     21000
COST OF G         1500      1200      1350      2250      6300
                ------    ------    ------    ------    ------
GROSS MAR         3500      2800      3150      5250     14700

OPERATING EXPENSES
  MARKETI         1000      1000      1000      1000      4000
  ADMINIS          500       400       450       750      2100
                ------    ------    ------    ------    ------
     TOTA         1500      1400      1450      1750      6100

PRE-TAX P         2000      1400      1700      3500      8600
INCOME TA         1000       700       850      1750      4300
                ------    ------    ------    ------    ------
NET INCOM         1000       700       850      1750      4300
                ======    ======    ======    ======    ======


 F17               Form=B17+C17+D17+E17
Width:  9   Memory: 99 Last Col/Row:G18        ? for HELP
  1>
F1 = Help; F2 = Cancel; F9 = Plot; F10 = View
```

Prot Controls whether protected cells can be edited or have data entered into them. The default is Protect on—i.e., the contents of protected cells cannot be changed. The Protect off option is useful for situations where large groups of cells have already been protected. This feature allows you to lower the protective shield so you can make changes to your spreadsheet. Once you've made the changes, you should raise the shield—i.e., toggle protection back on.

This Global option cannot give protection where none exists. You must have previously issued the /P(rotect) command for a range of cells. It does, however, save you from having to remove protection from a group of cells via the U(nprotect) command.

The entry **/GP** turns Protect on and off.

Calculation Options

Six global options provide control over calculations. It's much easier to understand these options if they're broken into three categories.

The first category controls the time at which calculation occurs. The two options in this category are mutually exclusive.

Auto The entire spreadsheet is automatically recalculated each time one of the following actions occurs:

Entry of data
Execution of /A(rrange) command
Execution of /B(lank) command
Execution of /C(opy) command
Execution of /D(elete) command
Execution of /L(oad) command

Execution of /M(ove) command
Execution of /R(eplicate) command
Automatic recalculation is the default setting. It is inefficient, however, when making initial data entry into a spreadsheet, especially a large spreadsheet. In such a situation, the entire spreadsheet would be recalculated each time an entry is made into a cell.

The automatic recalculation feature is useful if you'd like to see the effect of changes on an existing spreadsheet.

The entry /**GA** turns off a previous entry of /**GM.**

Man The spreadsheet is not recalculated until an entry of ! is made. Manual recalculation is particularly useful during the initial entry of data into a spreadsheet, especially a large spreadsheet.

The entry of /**GM** turns off a previous entry of /**GA.**

The second category of options controls the order in which calculation occurs. The three options in this category are mutually exclusive.

Row Row-wise calculation. The entire spreadsheet is calculated one cell at a time, moving left to right across a row before going down to the next row. This calculation order may produce incomplete results for forward and circular references.[2]

The entry /**GR** turns off a previous entry of /**GC** or /**GD.**

Col Column-wise calculation. The entire spreadsheet is calculated one cell at a time, moving from top to bottom down a column before starting at the top of the next column. This sequence of calculation can be used when a formula in a given row references a calculation in a subsequent row. For example, cell C2 contains the expression **B5*3.** With the column-wise calculation sequence, cell B5 would be calculated before cell C2.

Although this calculation order can correct one type of forward reference problem, it may still produce incomplete results for others.

The entry /**GC** turns off a previous entry of /**GR** or /**GD.**

Dep Dependency calculation. This is the default setting. The spreadsheet is calculated in an order that resolves forward references and, as much as possible, circular references. The computational passes through the spreadsheet, after the first

2. Forward references are references to cells in subsequent rows or columns whose formulas have not yet been evaluated. For example, cell A1 has the formula A10 + 5. Circular references involve two or more cells that refer to each other in a circular loop. Not all circular references are solvable. For example, cell A1 contains A10 + 1 and cell A10 contains A1 + 1.

complete calculation, address only those cells involved with circular references. The number of computational passes is controlled by the /Global,Iter option.

Selection of this calculation option usually causes substantial reductions in computation times for the resolution of circular reference problems.

The entry /**GD** turns off a previous entry of /**GR** or /**GC.**

The last category has only one option. It controls the maximum number of computational passes, called iterations, allowed for the resolution of circular references.

Iter Iteration control. The entry /**GI** produces the following display on the PROMPT and ENTRY lines:

Enter S(olve) or <1-99> for fixed iteration count

27>/Global,Iteration Control,

1-99 Allows you to specify a fixed iteration count—i.e., n times. If the calculation order is row-wise or column-wise, the entire spreadsheet is recalculated the n times, as set by the fixed iteration count.

If the calculation order is dependent, the entire spreadsheet is recalculated once. Then, the cells involved in the circular reference are recalculated n-1 times, as set by the fixed iteration count. Under the fixed iteration option, it's not necessary to press RETURN unless the specified iteration count is less than ten.

After indicating the number of iterations, you are automatically returned to your spreadsheet.

S Allows SuperCalc³ to make however many iterations are necessary to solve the circular reference problem. SuperCalc³ recalculates the spreadsheet until the values in the circular loop stop changing. When this option is used with unresolvable circular loops, the recalculation process will continue infinitely. If this occurs, press F2 to abort the iterative process. Pressing S displays the following on your PROMPT and ENTRY lines:

D(elta) or R(ange)?

33>/Global,Iteration Control,Solve,

RETURN Uses the resolution tolerance, also called the delta value, as it was last set. The default delta value is 0.01.

Returns you to your spreadsheet, which is then recalculated as follows: If the calculation order is row-wise or column-wise, the entire spreadsheet is recalculated until the change in each circular reference, from one iteration to the next, falls below delta. If there are no circular references, only one recalculation occurs.

If the calculation order is dependent, the entire spreadsheet is recalculated once. Then the cells involved in the circular reference are recalculated until the amount of iterative change falls below delta.

D Allows you to set the amount of the delta value by specifying the cell name that contains it. Recalculation will occur until the amount of iterative change falls below the value contained in the specified cell. An entry of – sets delta to the default value of 0.01.

Pressing D displays the following on your PROMPT and ENTRY lines:

Enter cell, containing Delta value, or < – > for .01 (Now –)
39>/Global,Iteration Control,Solve,Delta

After making an entry for delta, you are again prompted with:

D(elta) or R(ange)?

Press RETURN to get back to your spreadsheet, or R to make a range entry.

R Allows you to control which cells are to be tested for convergence—i.e., comparing the amount of iterative change against the delta value. This option is useful when there is a combination of converging and non-converging cells—i.e., circular references with no resolution in the same spreadsheet. It accelerates recalculation by iterating only the specified range of cells.

Pressing R displays the following on your PROMPT and ENTRY lines:

Enter range to converge (now A1:DW2000)
39>/Global,Iteration Control,Solve,Range

After making a range entry, you are again prompted with:

D(elta) or R(ange)?

Press RETURN to get back to your spreadsheet, or D to set delta.

When circular references exist in your spreadsheet, SuperCalc^3 displays **CIRC** in the upper left corner of your screen at the apex of the row and column borders.

Since the screen display is updated during the iterative recalculation process, there is a reduction in the recalculation speed. You can improve performance by paging to a spreadsheet area that is not impacted by the successive iterations, prior to starting the computational process. You shouldn't do this unless you're sure there are no unresolvable circular loops. You don't want to risk being blindly thrown into an infinite series of iterations.

Take time now to experiment with these computation settings. First, /Zap whatever spreadsheet is in memory. Next, set your spreadsheet for formula display by entering **/GF.** Set row-wise calculation order by entering **/GR,** then set the number of fixed interations to 1 by entering **/GI1** and pressing RETURN. Last, make the entries to columns A, B, and C as shown by Figure 5.3.

Figure 5.3 SuperCalc³'s Iterative Process: Illustration 1

```
    |    A    ||    B    ||    C    ||    D    ||    E    ||    F    ||    G    ||    H    |
1    5          2*A10      2*B10
2    10         2*A9       2*B9
3    15         2*A8       2*B8
4    20         2*A7       2*B7
5    25         2*A6       2*B6
6    30         2*A5       2*B5
7    35         2*A4       2*B4
8    40         2*A3       2*B3
9    45         2*A2       2*B2
10   50         2*A1       2*B1
11
12
13
14
15
16
17
18
19
20
 A1                Form=5
Width:  9  Memory:100 Last Col/Row:C10       ? for HELP
 1>
F1 = Help; F2 = Cancel; F9 = Plot; F10 = View
```

Toggle off the display of formulas by entering **/GF** again and your spreadsheet should look like Figure 5.4.

Figure 5.4 SuperCalc³'s Iterative Process: Illustration 2

```
    |    A    ||    B    ||    C    ||    D    ||    E    ||    F    ||    G    ||    H    |
1             5      100       20
2            10       90       40
3            15       80       60
4            20       70       80
5            25       60      100
6            30       50      120
7            35       40      140
8            40       30      160
9            45       20      180
10           50       10      200
11
12
13
14
15
16
17
18
19
20
 A1                Form=5
Width:  9  Memory:100 Last Col/Row:C10       ? for HELP
 1>
F1 = Help; F2 = Cancel; F9 = Plot; F10 = View
```

Now change cell A1 to 6. Remember, an automatic recalculation takes place at each data entry, as long as **/GA** is in effect.

Having changed A1, you can expect cell B10 to display 12, based on the formula 2*A1. Also expect cell C1 to display 24, based on the formula 2*B10. Looking at Figure 5.5, you see that cell C1 has not changed. This is a forward referencing problem caused by the row-wise calculation sequence and only one fixed iteration. Cell C1 is calculated based on the previously calculated value of cell B10. Cell B10 is calculated based on the value of cell A1.

Theoretically, if cell A1 changes, so should cells B10 and C1. However, with row-wise calculation and limited iterations, cell C1 is calculated before cell B10. Consequently, cell C1 is incorrect. See Figure 5.5.

Figure 5.5 SuperCalc³'s Iterative Process: Illustration 3

```
     |   A   ||   B   ||   C   ||   D   ||   E   ||   F   ||   G   ||   H   |
1            6      100       20
2           10       90       40
3           15       80       60
4           20       70       80
5           25       60      100
6           30       50      120
7           35       40      140
8           40       30      160
9           45       20      180
10          50       12      200
11
12
13
14
15
16
17
18
19
20
 A1             Form=6
Width:  9  Memory:100 Last Col/Row:C10       ? for HELP
  1>
F1 = Help; F2 = Cancel; F9 = Plot; F10 = View
```

You could press ! once to force a manual recalculation and your forward referencing problem would be eliminated. A much better technique is to set the Iter option back to Solve, so SuperCalc³ can automatically resolve the forward referencing problem. Further efficiencies are obtained when recalculation is applied only to the affected areas of the spreadsheet. To do this, enter /**GIS** and press RETURN, then enter /**GD.**

To prove the point, reset the spreadsheet by entering **5** in cell A1 and pressing RETURN. Cell B10 contains 10 and cell C1 contains 20. The forward reference problem is resolved. The spreadsheet should match Figure 5.6.

Figure 5.6 SuperCalc³'s Iterative Process: Illustration 4

```
     |   A   ||   B   ||   C   ||   D   ||   E   ||   F   ||   G   ||   H   |
1            5      100       20
2           10       90       40
3           15       80       60
4           20       70       80
5           25       60      100
6           30       50      120
7           35       40      140
8           40       30      160
9           45       20      180
10          50       10      200
11
12
13
14
15
16
17
18
19
20
 A1             Form=5
Width:  9  Memory:100 Last Col/Row:C10       ? for HELP
  1>
F1 = Help; F2 = Cancel; F9 = Plot; F10 = View
```

The next example illustrates circular loops. Enter **/ZY** to erase your spreadsheet. Now, make the following entries in the order shown:

Cell	Entry
A1	**1**
A2	**2**
A3	**3**
A4	**4**
A5	**5**
A6	**'–**
A7	**A1 + A2 + A3 + A4 + A5**
B1	**3**
B7	**B1 + B5**
B5	**A7-B7**

When you make the entry into cell B5, **CIRC** appears in the upper left corner of your screen and your PROMPT LINE displays

Solving . . . Iteration n (F2 to stop)

You have just created an unresolvable circular loop. Cells B5 and B7 are continuously incrementing. Press F2. The recalculation stops and **User abort** is displayed inversely at the right end of your STATUS LINE.

Other than aborting it, is there a way to control this infinite recalculation loop? Yes, by entering **/GI1,** then pressing RETURN. Next, enter **0** in cell B5 to clear out the incorrect accumulations from the loop. Now, enter **A7-B7** and press RETURN. If you press ! several times, cells B5 and B7 will alternate between the results displayed.

Which result is correct? That depends on how you want to use cell B5. The intent in this example is to make the sum of column B, cell B7, equal to the sum of column A, cell A7. This simple example has applicability to many accounting operations. The formula in cell B5 represents the "plug" amount to close out account balances and subsequently determine profit or loss.

Caution. When building a circular loop, first set your spreadsheet to manual calculation mode by entering **/GM.** This will synchronize all calculations to start at the same time.

This completes the material on global spreadsheet options. You are now ready for the Review Exercises. Enter **/ZY** to erase your spreadsheet before starting the exercises.

Review Exercises

Exercises 5.5 through 5.8 use the Credit Card Interest Spreadsheet from Exercise 4.10.

1. Provide the command to give you a medium-size spreadsheet. What are its boundaries?
2. Provide the command to save the menu settings as program defaults.

3. Identify the on/off toggle options and their default settings.
4. Identify the calculation options and to what extent they are mutually exclusive. Also indicate their default settings.
5. Provide the command to load the spreadsheet from Exercise 4.10.
6. Provide commands to do the following:
   a. Turn off automatic recalculation.
   b. Turn on formula display.
   c. Change cell B4 to 5.95, then force a manual recalculation of the spreadsheet.
   d. Turn off formula display.
7. Display the spreadsheet without row numbers and column letters.
8. Provide the commands to:
   a. Save the spreadsheet as EX5-8.
   b. Erase the spreadsheet.

Answers to Review Exercises

1. /GO, then tab to the Spreadsheet Boundary menu item and enter **M.** The boundaries for a medium-size spreadsheet are cells A1 through DW2000.
2. /GKY
3. On/off toggle options:

Command	Description	Default
/GF	Formula display	Off
/G"	Required leading " for text	Off
/GN	Cursor advance to next cell	On
/GB	Border display	On
/GT	Skip empty and protected cells	Off
/GP	Enable shield on protected cells	On

4. Calculation options:

   Category 1: Order of calculation. /GR, /GC, and /GD are mutually exclusive. /GD is the default.

Command	Description
/GR	Row-wise calculation
/GC	Column-wise calculation
/GD	Dependency

   Category 2: Recalculation control. /GM and /GA are mutually exclusive. /GA is the default.

Command	Description
/GM	Manual recalculation
/GA	Automatic recalculation

Category 3: Iteration control. /GIS is the default with delta equal to 0.01.

5. /LB:EXER4-10.CAL,A
6. a. /GM
   b. /GF
   c. =B4, then press RETURN. Enter **5.95,** then press RETURN. Press !.
   d. /GF
7. /GB
   See Figure 5.7.

Figure 5.7 Credit Interest Spreadsheet: Exercise 5-7

```
                         MASTER
              VISA       CHARGE     SEARS      TOTAL
              -------------------------------------
  JAN              5.95      8.96      9.74     24.65
  FEB             12.06      8.84      9.98     30.88
  MAR             13.31      8.23      9.62     31.16
  APR             14.88      7.67      9.29     31.84
  MAY             33.49      7.74      8.89     50.12
  JUN             20.75      8.06      9.05     37.86
  JUL              23.1      8.04      9.37     40.51
  AUG             24.95      7.31     10.64      42.9
  SEP             26.71      7.45     11.59     45.75
  OCT             27.38      8.44     12.64     48.46
  NOV             27.89      7.96     12.48     48.33
  DEC              26.7       7.4      12.3      46.4
              ------    ------    ------    ------
  TOTAL          257.17      96.1    125.59    478.86
              ======    ======    ======    ======

A4             Text="JAN
Width:  9  Memory: 99 Last Col/Row:F18        ? for HELP
 1>
F1 = Help; F2 = Cancel; F9 = Plot; F10 = View
```

8. a. /SB:EX5-8,A
   b. /ZY

CHAPTER 6

Controlling Your Spreadsheet's Display

Chapter Overview and Objectives

- Standard Format Settings
- User-Defined Format Table

When you've completed Chapter 6, you'll have an understanding of how to format a spreadsheet into a professional-looking report. You'll be able to control what's displayed on your video screen using both standardized and customized format settings.

Getting Ready

Before proceeding, boot SuperCalc^3 if you haven't already done so. When you get the empty spreadsheet, load the Profit & Loss Statement you saved in Chapter 4. Enter **/LB:PALDEMO,** then press RETURN. When you are prompted for:

A(ll), P(art), or C(onsolidate)?

enter **A** for A(ll). This /L(oad) option will bring the entire P&L spreadsheet into your computer's memory. After the /L(oad) command finishes, you should have a screen display that looks like Figure 4.6 on page 52.

Examining your display, you'll see that truncation has occurred on the leftmost characters in cells A4, A6, A9, A10, A12, A14, A15, and A17. Column A has a width of nine positions, while the above cells all have entries of more than nine characters. The truncation is due to the presence of entries in the contiguous cells of column B.

Also notice the misalignment between the formula entries and the text entries in columns B through F. Remember from Chapter 4 that this misalignment is caused by the default right justification of formulas and the default left justification of text. Although at present the P&L Statement does not look very pretty, it can be fixed easily by the /F(ormat) command.

Scope of the /F(ormat) Command

The /F(ormat) command defines display representations for either the entire spreadsheet or just a portion of it. To invoke the /F(ormat) command, enter **/F.** SuperCalc³ responds with the following on your PROMPT and ENTRY lines:

Enter Level: G(lobal), C(olumn), R(ow), E(ntry), or D(efine)

9>/Format,

You must pick the level at which your spreadsheet is to be formatted:

G The selected format is applicable to the entire spreadsheet, except where formats have been previously set for entries, rows, or columns.

C The selected format is applicable to the specified column or range of columns. This format level takes precedence over the global format level.

R The selected format is applicable to the specified row or range of rows. This format level takes precedence over the global and column format levels.

E The selected format is applicable to the specified cell or range of cells. This format level takes precedence over all other format levels.

D Displays the *User-Defined Format Table* for review or update. This is covered later in the chapter.

After specifying C, R, or E, you'll be prompted for a range. The concept of ranges is very important. It's used in many more "Slash" commands than just /F(ormat). Some of these commands permit only row or column ranges, others allow row, column, or cell ranges.

In any range, the beginning item is entered, followed by a delimiter, which is followed by the ending item in the range. Valid delimiters are the colon (:) and the period (.). They are necessary so that SuperCalc³ can distinguish the beginning item from the ending item. Although the colon and the period can be used interchangeably, you may prefer the period. It can be entered without pressing the SHIFT key.

If you want to specify a column range, enter:

beginning column letter . ending column letter

The spaces are for illustration only; they are not used in actual situations. Some column examples are:

A:E The range includes 5 columns: A, B, C, D, E.

AA.AZ The range includes 26 columns: AA, AB, AC, AD, AE, AF, AG, AH, AI, AJ, AK, AL, AM, AN, AO, AP, AQ, AR, AS, AT, AU, AV, AW, AX, AY, AZ.

If you want to specify a row range, enter:

beginning row number : ending row number

Again, the spaces are for illustration only; they are not used in actual situations. Some row examples are:

1.5 The range includes 5 rows: 1, 2, 3, 4, 5.

10:37 The range includes 28 rows: 10, 11, 12, 13, 14, 15, 16, 17, 18, 19, 20, 21, 22, 23, 24, 25, 26, 27, 28, 29, 30, 31, 32, 33, 34, 35, 36, 37.

If you want to specify a cell range, enter

beginning cell . ending cell

As in the previous examples, the spaces are for illustration only; they are not used in actual situations. Some cell examples are:

A1:A5 The range includes A1, A2, A3, A4, A5—i.e., the first 5 rows within column A.

A1.E1 The range includes A1, B1, C1, D1, E1—i.e., the first 5 columns within row 1.

A1:E5 The range includes the *block* of 25 cells in columns A through E and rows 1 through 5—

i.e., A1, B1, C1, D1, E1
A2, B2, C2, D2, E2
A3, B3, C3, D3, E3
A4, B4, C4, D4, E4
A5, B5, C5, D5, E5.

Cell blocking is an important concept used quite frequently with many "Slash" commands. The example below illustrates how to determine which cells would be included in a block of cells. Observe that the block in the example involves a diagonal line between the beginning cell and the ending cell.

```
A1--B1--C1--D1--E1
|  \             |
|                |
A2   B2   C2   D2   E2
|      \             |
|                    |
A3   B3   C3   D3   E3
|           \        |
|                    |
A4   B4   C4   D4   E4
|                \   |
|                    |
A5--B5--C5--D5--E5
```

The diagonal line is then flushed out to a rectangle. Visualize on both sides of the diagonal line how the rows and columns are extended from the beginning cell to form a block terminating at the row and column coordinates of the ending cell.

The following examples illustrate the range prompts you'll see on the PROMPT and ENTRY lines:

EXAMPLE NO. 1

Enter Column Range

16>/Format,Column,

You could confine your format to a single column—for example:

/Format,Column,A, then press RETURN
or you could apply a format to a range of columns, such as
/Format,Column,B:F, then press RETURN
In the first illustration, only column A will be subject to whatever format is subsequently defined. In the second illustration, all columns from B through F are affected by the subsequently defined format.

Both illustrations override any global formats.

EXAMPLE NO. 2

Enter row range of 1 to 254 or R for Remaining rows (255 to 9999)
13>/Format,Row,
You could confine your format to a single row—for example:
/Format,Row,1, then press RETURN
or you could apply a format to a range of rows—for example:
/Format,Row,1:10, then press RETURN
or
/Format,Row,R, then press RETURN
When the Remaining row option is used, all rows in the range 255 through 9999 are formatted as a unit.

In the first illustration, only row 1 will be subject to whatever format is subsequently defined. In the second illustration, all rows from 1 through 10 are affected by the subsequently defined format. In the third illustration, all rows from 255 through 9999 are affected by the subsequently defined format.

All three illustrations override any global or column formats.

EXAMPLE NO. 3

Enter Range
15>/Format,Entry,
You could confine your format to a single cell—for example:
/Format,Entry,B2, then press RETURN
or you could apply a format to a range of cells, such as
/Format,Entry,A1:F1, then press RETURN
In the first illustration, only cell A1 will be subject to whatever format is subsequently defined. In the second illustration, all cells from A1 to F1 are affected by the subsequently defined format. Both illustrations would override any global, column, or row formats.

You may have noticed an order to the formatting levels in which one level overrides another. This is called a *hierarchy of format precedence*. It's summarized here:

Hierarchy of Format Levels

Override Priority	Format Level
1	Entry
2	Row
3	Column
4	Global

Format Options

As soon as you enter **G, C, R,** or **E,** and press RETURN, the PROMPT LINE displays:

Define Formats:(I,G,E,$,R,L,TR,TL,TC,*,U(1-8),H,D,column width)

You now enter the kind of format to be applied. The preceding format options have the following meanings:

Option	Meaning
I	Integer representation. Applicable only to cells with formula or numeric value entries. The cell contents are rounded to whole numbers for display purposes.
G	General representation. Applicable only to cells with formula or numeric value entries. For display purposes, the cell contents are put into the format that best fits the cell width. This is one of the default formats.
E	Exponential representation. Applicable only to cells with formula or numeric value entries. The cell contents are put into E-notation for display purposes. This format is typically found in scientific and engineering applications.
$	Dollar and cents representation. Applicable only to cells with formula or numeric value entries. The cell contents are put into a fixed point representation with two decimal places for display purposes. The currency symbol ($) is not displayed.
R	Right justification. Applicable only to cells with formula or numeric value entries. The cell contents are aligned on the right side of the cell for display purposes. This is one of the default formats.
L	Left justification. Applicable only to cells with formula or numeric value entries. The cell contents are aligned on the left side of the cell for display purposes.
TR	Right justification of text. Applicable only to cells with text entries. The cell contents are aligned on the right side of the cell for display purposes. This is an easy way to set proper columnar alignment when both text and formula entries are in the same column.
TL	Left justification of text. Applicable only to cells with text entries. The cell contents are aligned on the left side of the cell for display purposes. This is one of the default formats.
TC	Centering of text. Applicable only to cells with text entries. The cell contents are positioned in the center of the cell for display purposes.
*	Histogram or bar chart representation. Applicable only to cells with formula or numeric value entries. The cell con-

tents are converted to a series of asterisks (*) based on their value. For example,

****** would be displayed if the cell had a value of 6.

*** would be displayed if the cell had a value of 3.

U(1-8) Calls one of the eight user-defined formats from the User-Defined Format Table. Applicable only to cells with formula or numeric value entries. Refer to the section in this chapter covering the table for more information (p. 83).

H Hides the specified range of cells, rows, or columns. This format can be used to provide security on sensitive information such as executive salaries in a payroll spreadsheet. The Hide can be removed by selecting one of the following display characteristics:
I, G, E, $, *, or U(1-8).

D Resets the specified range of cells, rows, or columns to the D(efault) format:

G General or best fit
R Right justification of formulas
TL Left justification of text
9 Column width

column width Sets the width of a column or range of columns. Valid entries for column are the range of integer numbers 0 through 127. Although a given column may have a maximum width of 127 positions, the contents of a given cell are subject to the following limitations:
Maximum text width: 115 positions
Maximum formula width: 116 positions
Maximum number width: 16 positions

Reformatting the P&L Spreadsheet

You are now ready to fix your P&L. First, you want to eliminate the truncation problem in column A. When you enter **/F**, you see the following on the PROMPT and ENTRY lines:

Enter Level: G(lobal), C(olumn), R(ow), E(ntry) or D(efine)
9>/Format,

Since you are interested in a column, press C. SuperCalc³ responds with

Enter Column Range
16>/Format,Column,

Now press A and either the RETURN or (,) keys. Note that the RETURN or comma keys may be used interchangeably in most "Slash" commands that are expecting additional parameters from the ENTRY LINE. The bottom two lines of your screen now show:

Define Formats:(I,G,E,$,R,L,TR,TL,TC,*,U(1-8),H,D,column width)
18>/Format,Column,A,

You need to extend the width of column A from 9 positions to the number of positions that can display the largest entry. Since the longest text entries are **"COST OF GOODS SOLD** and **"OPERATING EXPENSES**, both having a length of 18, you need a column width of at least 18 positions. Unless columnar space is exceptionally tight, you should always throw in a few extra positions for good measure. These extras protect you from miscounting and also allow for later inclusion of longer items.

So, use a new width of 20, based on the length of the longest entry in column A, plus an extra two positions. Since a number by itself is interpreted as a column width, enter **20** and press RETURN.

Your next task is to correct the alignment problem in columns B through F. The easiest way to fix this is to have both the text entries and the formula entries justified at the same edge of the column. This means that the formula entries can be changed to left justification so they match the default alignment of the text.

Another alternative is to change the text entries to right justification so they match the alignment of the formulas. Since columns of numbers are easier to read when they are right justified, switch the text entries from left justification to right justification. Pressing /F, you are presented with

Enter Level:G(lobal), C(olumn), R(ow), E(ntry) or D(efine)

9>/Format,

Since our problem is still of a columnar nature, press C again and receive the following display:

Enter Column Range

16>/Format,Column,

Since the alignment problem is in columns B through F, enter **B:F**, then press either RETURN or (,). Do not include column A in this range; column A should remain left justified. SuperCalc³'s response is

Define Formats:(I,G,E,$,R,L,TR,TL,TC,*,U(1-8),H,D,column width)

18>/Format,Column,B:F,

Now specify **TR** for right justification of text. As you make this entry, notice how the ENTRY LINE spells out the format.

30>/Format,Column,B:F,TextRight,

Press RETURN.

You probably think you've finished with your P&L since you fixed the two problems. That's not entirely true. While you did, indeed, fix the truncation and columnar alignment problems, you also introduced another problem.

Take a close look at your screen, observing the dash (–) under the **1** in **QTR #1** of cell B2. Wasn't there previously repeating text starting at cell B2 and ending at cell F2? What happened to it?

For repeating text to function properly, it must be left justified. When the /F(ormat) command set all text in column as right justified, it disabled the repeating text entry at cell B2. Are you, as the naval cliche goes, "dead in the water"? No, simply override the problem with a cell format that left justifies B2.

Entering **/F** you'll see the PROMPT and ENTRY lines display:

Enter Level:G(lobal), C(olumn), R(ow), E(ntry) or D(efine)

9>/Format,

Since the problem is in a cell, enter **E.** SuperCalc³ responds with

Enter Range

15>/Format,Entry,

Enter **B2,** and press either RETURN or (,) since there is only one cell to fix. SuperCalc³ displays

Define Formats:(I,G,E,$,R,L,TR,TL,TC,*,U(1-8),H,D,column width)

18>/Format,Entry,B2,

Now specify **TL** for left justification of text. Again, notice how the ENTRY LINE spells out the format

27>/Format,Entry,B2,TextLeft,

Press RETURN and you'll see the repeating text enabled in your P&L.

While this spreadsheet is still on display, make one more format change. The P&L you've been using to this point has contained integer representation for all formula entries. Now change this to dollar & cents representation. Set the level of formatting applicable to columns B through F. Your PROMPT and ENTRY lines should show the following:

Define Formats:(I,G,E,$,R,L,TR,TL,TC,*,U(1-8),H,D,column width)

18>/Format,Column,B:F,

Now enter **$** and press RETURN. Compare your screen with Figure 6.1. They should look the same. Notice that no dollar signs ($) are displayed. If you want the currency symbols to appear, you'll need to use the User-Defined Format Table.

Figure 6.1 P&L Spreadsheet

```
   |         A          ||   B   ||   C   ||   D   ||   E   ||   F   ||  G  |
1                            QTR #1   QTR #2   QTR #3   QTR #4    TOTAL
2                         ----------------------------------------------------
3   SALES                 5000.00  4000.00  4500.00  7500.00 21000.00
4   COST OF GOODS SOLD    1500.00  1200.00  1350.00  2250.00  6300.00
5                          ------   ------   ------   ------   ------
6   GROSS MARGIN          3500.00  2800.00  3150.00  5250.00 14700.00
7
8   OPERATING EXPENSES
9     MARKETING           1000.00  1000.00  1000.00  1000.00  4000.00
10    ADMINISTRATIVE       500.00   400.00   450.00   750.00  2100.00
11                         ------   ------   ------   ------   ------
12         TOTAL          1500.00  1400.00  1450.00  1750.00  6100.00
13
14  PRE-TAX PROFIT        2000.00  1400.00  1700.00  3500.00  8600.00
15  INCOME TAX            1000.00   700.00   850.00  1750.00  4300.00
16                         ------   ------   ------   ------   ------
17  NET INCOME            1000.00   700.00   850.00  1750.00  4300.00
18                         ======   ======   ======   ======   ======
19
20
 A1
Width: 20  Memory: 99 Last Col/Row:G18      ? for HELP
  1>
F1 = Help; F2 = Cancel; F9 = Plot; F10 = View
```

You're finished with the P&L for the moment, so put it on disk where it will be safe. As a refresher, enter **/SB:PALDEMO** and press RETURN. You'll be prompted with

File already exists: C(hange name), B(ackup) or O(verwrite)?

Press O. It's not necessary to press RETURN. Now you'll be prompted with

A(ll), V(alues), or P(art)?

Press A. It's not necessary to press RETURN.

Demonstrating Other Format Definitions

There are some other format definitions to be experienced. First, erase the existing spreadsheet from memory with an entry of **/ZY.** Second, load the spreadsheet created in Chapter 4 that demonstrated expressions and formulas. Enter **/LB:FORMDEMO.** When you are prompted with

A(ll), P(art), or C(onsolidate)?

enter A. Do not press RETURN. When loading is completed, your spreadsheet will reflect the default settings used by SuperCalc³. See the D(efault) entry and resulting settings in the Format Options section at the beginning of this chapter if you need more information.

The first demonstration involves global formatting of formula entries. Enter **/FGL.** The resulting PROMPT and ENTRY lines are

Define Formats:(I,G,E,$,R,L,TR,TL,TC,*,U(1-8),H,D,column width)
21>/Format,Global,Left,

You have just globally set the spreadsheet to left justification for formulas and expressions. When you press RETURN, you'll get a display similar to Figure 6.2.

Figure 6.2 Expressions Globally Left Justified

```
      |  A    ||   B    ||   C    ||   D    ||   E    ||   F    ||   G    ||   H    |
 1     200       200       14
 2     123.4     200       16
 3     1234.568  200       30
 4     123456.8            256
 5     1.2346e9            256
 6     1.2346e8            512
 7     12345678            323.4
 8     -1.235e7            122
 9                         48
10
11
12
13
14
15
16
17
18
19
20
 C9               Form=20%240
Width:  9   Memory:100 Last Col/Row:C9        ? for HELP
   1>
F1 = Help; F2 = Cancel; F9 = Plot; F10 = View
```

The second demonstration involves multiple global format parameters. Enter **/FGER.** The resulting PROMPT and ENTRY lines are

Define Formats:(I,G,E,$,R,L,TR,TL,TC,*,U(1-8),H,D,column width)
31>/Format,Global,Exponent,Right,

You have now globally set the spreadsheet to be right justified with exponential notation. When you press RETURN, you'll get a display that matches Figure 6.3.

The third demonstration involves an attempt to globally format the displayed spreadsheet to integer representation. Enter **/FGI.** The resulting PROMPT and ENTRY lines are shown on the following page.

Figure 6.3 **Expressions Globally Right Justified with Exponential Representation**

```
     |    A    ||    B    ||    C    ||    D    ||    E    ||    F    ||    G    ||    H    |
1          2e2        2e2      1.4e1
2     1.234e2         2e2      1.6e1
3    1.2346e3         2e2        3e1
4    1.2346e5                 2.56e2
5    1.2346e9                 2.56e2
6    1.2346e8                 5.12e2
7    1.2346e7                3.234e2
8    -1.235e7                 1.22e2
9                              4.8e1
10
11
12
13
14
15
16
17
18
19
20
 C9                    Form=20*240
Width:  9  Memory:100 Last Col/Row:C9        ? for HELP
  1>
F1 = Help; F2 = Cancel; F9 = Plot; F10 = View
```

Define Formats:(I,G,E,$,R,L,TR,TL,*,U(1-8),H,D,column width)
24>/Format,Global,Integer,

After pressing RETURN, notice that both your display and Figure 6.4 show >>>>>>>> in cells A5, A6, and A8. You are looking at an *overflow error.*

Figure 6.4 **Expressions Globally Set to Integer Representation with Overflow Errors**

```
     |    A    ||    B    ||    C    ||    D    ||    E    ||    F    ||    G    ||    H    |
1          200        200         14
2          123        200         16
3         1235        200         30
4       123457                   256
5    >>>>>>>>                    256
6    >>>>>>>>                    512
7    12345678                    323
8    >>>>>>>>                    122
9                                 48
10
11
12
13
14
15
16
17
18
19
20
 A5                    Form=1234567890.1234
Width:  9  Memory:100 Last Col/Row:C9        ? for HELP
  1>
F1 = Help; F2 = Cancel; F9 = Plot; F10 = View
```

If you check the STATUS lines for these cells, you'll find their contents are

Cell A5	Form = 1234567890.1234
Cell A6	Form = 123456789
Cell A8	Form = −12345678

Under the G(eneral), or best fit, representation, the contents for each of these cells are displayed in E-notation. However, when formats other than G(eneral) or E(xponent) are used, the column width must be wide enough to accommodate the cell contents; otherwise an overflow error results.

Figure 6.5 shows that overflow errors can easily be eliminated simply by increasing the column width. The entry for this is **/FG16.**

Before you press RETURN, your PROMPT and ENTRY lines should look like this:

Define Formats:(I,G,E,$,R,L,TR,TL,TC,*,U(1-8),H,D,column width)
19>/Format,Global,16,

Figure 6.5 **Expressions Globally Set to Integer Representation and Column Width of 16**

```
      |          A      ||       B     ||       C     ||       D      |
1                      200           200              14
2                      123           200              16
3                     1235           200              30
4                   123457                           256
5               1234567890                           256
6                123456789                           512
7                 12345678                           323
8                -12345678                           122
9                                                     48
10
11
12
13
14
15
16
17
18
19
20
 A8             Form=-12345678
Width: 16   Memory:100 Last Col/Row:C9        ? for HELP
 1>
F1 = Help; F2 = Cancel; F9 = Plot; F10 = View
```

The column width entry of 16 has been used because numbers may not exceed 16 positions. A column width of 17 could also have been specified. Enter **/S B:FORMDEMO,OA** to save this spreadsheet onto disk.

You can easily return to the format of your spreadsheet prior to these examples simply by entering /FGD. Before pressing RETURN, your PROMPT and ENTRY lines appear as

Define Formats:(I,G,E,$,R,L,TR,TL,TC,*,U(1-8),H,D,column width)
24>/Format,Global,Default,

After pressing RETURN, you'll get a display like Figure 6.6.

Since you're finished with this spreadsheet for the moment, you can zap it. Remember how? **/ZY.**

Now you're going to make a new spreadsheet to demonstrate the histogram format. The basis of the model is a frequency distribution of student letter grades. For those not previously exposed to statistics, a frequency distribution is nothing more than a list of categories accompanied by the number of

Figure 6.6 Expressions Using Default Format

```
     |    A    ||    B    ||    C    ||    D    ||    E    ||    F    ||    G    ||    H    |
1           200       200         14
2         123.4       200         16
3      1234.568       200         30
4      123456.8                  256
5      1.2346e9                  256
6      1.2346e8                  512
7      12345678                323.4
8      -1.235e7                  122
9                                 48
10
11
12
13
14
15
16
17
18
19
20
 A8                  Form=-12345678
Width:   9   Memory:100 Last Col/Row:C9           ? for HELP
  1>
F1 = Help; F2 = Cancel; F9 = Plot; F10 = View
```

occurrences within each category. For example, letter grade ("A"), as shown at cell A1, is a category with five occurrences, based on the entry at cell B1.

Please make the following entries into your spreadsheet to establish the grade frequency distribution:

Cell	Entry	Cell	Entry
A1	**("A")**	B1	**5**
A2	**("B")**	B2	**9**
A3	**("C")**	B3	**6**
A4	**("D")**	B4	**2**
A5	**("F")**	B5	**1**
A6	**("W")**	B6	**3**

The entries to column A are *textual values*. Looking at your own screen, you'll see that they are right justified as though they were numeric.

Many times, pictorial displays can provide more information at a glance than numeric displays. A histogram can provide a snapshot of the grade distribution. To get this picture, use the * format.

First, enter /**FCB,*.** This will display PROMPT and ENTRY lines like those shown below:

Define Formats:(I,G,E,$,R,L,TR,TL,TC,*,U(1-8),H,D,column width)
20>/Format,Column,B,*,

Now press RETURN and your screen will display a histogram similar to the one shown in Figure 6.7.

Zap this spreadsheet and reload **B:FORMDEMO** before going to the next section.

Figure 6.7 Grade Frequency Distribution Using * Format

```
   |   A   ||   B    ||   C   ||   D   ||   E   ||   F   ||   G   ||   H   |
1          A *****
2          B ********
3          C ******
4          D **
5          F *
6          W ***
7
8
9
10
11
12
13
14
15
16
17
18
19
20
 B7
Width:  9  Memory:101 Last Col/Row:B6       ? for HELP
  1>
F1 = Help; F2 = Cancel; F9 = Plot; F10 = View
```

User-Defined Format Table

SuperCalc[3] has a feature that lets you define your own formats, up to eight, and later call them as U1 through U8. Before using this feature, review the default definitions for formats U1 through U8. You can change any or all of them at any time. To display this table, enter **/F.** The PROMPT and ENTRY lines display

Enter Level: G(lobal), C(olumn), R(ow), E(ntry) or D(efine)

8>/Format,

Now press D. A shorthand entry is **/FD.** In either case, the format table will be displayed on your screen. Figure 6.8 shows the default settings for this table.

Figure 6.8 User-Defined Format Table: Default Settings

```
                     User-defined formats
                     1  2  3  4  5  6  7  8

Floating $           Y  Y  Y  Y  Y  Y  Y  Y

Embedded Commas      Y  Y  Y  Y  Y  Y  Y  Y

Minus in ( )         N  N  N  N  N  N  N  N

Zero as Blank        N  N  N  N  N  N  N  N

%                    N  N  N  N  N  N  N  N

Decimal Places       2  2  2  2  2  2  2  2

Scaling factor       0  0  0  0  0  0  0  0


F2 to return to spreadsheet.


 A1
Y(es) or N(o) ?
 15>/Format,Define
F1 = Help; F2 = Cancel; F9 = Plot; F10 = View
```

The directional arrows are used to move around this table. When scrolling through the table, it's advisable to scroll and edit completely through one format before moving on to the next. In other words, scroll down a given column, scroll across to the next column, then scroll up that column.

Looking at the table, observe that it contains a series of columns numbered 1 through 8. Column 1 is format U1, column 2 is format U2, . . . column 8 is format U8. In the leftmost column are the format categories. Here are their definitions and possible settings:

Format	Entry	Definition
Floating $	Y	A dollar sign ($) immediately precedes the most significant digit in a numeric value. Y is the default setting. For example, if this format were used for a cell containing 1234, the spreadsheet displays **$1234.** If the cell had a value of 1, then **$1** would be displayed.
	N	No dollar sign is used. Most financial reports do not have each entry preceded by $.
Embedded Commas	Y	A comma (,) is displayed in front of every third digit, moving to the left of the decimal point, either actual or implied. Y is the default setting. For example, if this format were used for a cell containing 1234567, the spreadsheet would display **1,234,567.** If the cell had a value of 12, then **12** would be displayed.
	N	No embedded commas are used. Many financial reports do not use embedded commas unless the typical number has a magnitude greater than five positions.
Minus In ( )	Y	The leading minus sign, −, is eliminated and the entire number is enclosed in ( ). Most financial and accounting reports use this convention. N is the default setting. For example, if this format were used for a cell containing −1234, the spreadsheet would display **(1234).** If the cell had a value of 1234, then **1234** is displayed, except that it is shifted one position to the left to maintain columnar alignment.
	N	The minus sign, −, continues to precede negative numbers.
Zero As Blank	Y	Blanks are displayed instead of zeroes for any cells having a value of zero. N is the default setting.
	N	Displays zero when the cell value is zero.
%	Y	Multiplies numeric cell contents by 100 and

		displays the result with a percent sign (%). N is the default setting. For example, if this format is used for a cell containing 0.043125, the spreadsheet displays **4.3125%.** If the cell had a value of 1.5, then **150%** would be displayed.
	N	The numeric value is displayed as it exists in the cell, subject to other formats.
Decimal Places	**0-7**	An entry between 0 and 7 specifies how many positions are to be displayed to the right of the decimal point. The default is 2, which is the same as using the dollar & cents ($) option of the /F(ormat) command.
Scaling Factor	**0-7**	An entry between 0 and 7 specifies the power of 10 by which a numeric cell is divided or scaled down. The default is 0, which means that a numeric cell would be divided by 10^0. Since 10^0 equals 1, there is no downward scaling. If the table entry had been 4, the numeric cell would have been scaled down by 10,000 or 10^4.

Defining Your Own Formats

You are now going to learn to define and use the format table.

First, you need to define your formats, so enter **/FD** if you haven't already done so, then scroll through the table. As you scroll, change User-Defined Formats 1 through 5 to match the definitions in Figure 6.9.

Figure 6.9 User-Defined Format Table: Customized Settings

```
                     User-defined formats
                     1  2  3  4  5  6  7  8

Floating $           Y  Y  N  N  N  Y  Y  Y

Embedded Commas      Y  Y  N  N  N  Y  Y  Y

Minus in ( )         Y  Y  Y  N  N  N  N  N

Zero as Blank        Y  Y  N  N  Y  N  N  N

%                    N  N  N  Y  N  N  N  N

Decimal Places       2  1  1  4  2  2  2  2

Scaling factor       0  3  4  0  4  0  0  0

F2 to return to spreadsheet.


 A8            Form=-12345678
Enter number from (0 - 7)
 15) /Format,Define
F1 = Help; F2 = Cancel; F9 = Plot; F10 = View
```

It's important to understand that all attributes of a given definition are applied to the area of the spreadsheet being formatted. Consequently, you may want to turn off some attributes.

After making your changes to the table, return to your spreadsheet and enter **0.043125** in cell A9. Now enter **/FEA9,U4** and press RETURN. In Figure 6.10 the entry to cell A9 is shown as **4.3125%.** Looking at User-Defined Format No. 4, you'll see that Floating $, Embedded Commas, Minus In ( ), and Zero As Blank have been turned off *(i.e., set to N)*. The Scaling Factor is also turned off *(set to zero)*. The only attributes still turned on are % *(set to Y)* and Decimal Places *(set to 4)*.

Figure 6.10 **Display with User-Defined Formats: Example 1**

```
   |    A    ||    B    ||    C    ||    D    ||    E    ||    F    ||    G    ||    H    |
1         200       200         14
2       123.4       200         16
3    1234.568       200         30
4    123456.8                  256
5    1.2346e9                  256
6    1.2346e8                  512
7    12345678                323.4
8   -1.235e7                   122
9     4.3125%                   48
10
11
12
13
14
15
16
17
18
19
20
  A10
Width:  9  Memory:100 Last Col/Row:C9        ? for HELP
  1>
F1 = Help; F2 = Cancel; F9 = Plot; F10 = View
```

For the second demonstration, enter **/FCA,U1** and press RETURN. Your screen should have a display similar to Figure 6.11. Notice that cells A1, A2, A3, A4, and A7 display a dollar sign next to the most significant digit. Calls A3, A4, and A7 also have embedded commas. Cell A9 is not changed since formats directed at an entry level take precedence over formats directed at column level. Cells A5, A6, and A8 display >>>>>>>>>>>>>>>, indicating overflow errors.

Cell A5 has a width of 16 positions, of which 15 are available for a numeric entry. The current value of cell A5 is 1234567890.1234. Using format U1, the expected display is **$1,234,567,890.12,** shifted one position to the left [Minus In ( ) set to Y]. This format involves a total of 18 characters, which exceeds the 15 available positions and results in an overflow error.

Cell A6 also has a width of 16 positions. Again, 15 positions are available for use with a numeric entry. The current value of cell A6 is 123456789. From format U1, the expected display would be **$123,456,789.00,** shifted one position to the left because of the Minus In ( ) set to Y. This expected format involves a total of 16 characters, which exceeds the 15 available positions and results in an overflow error.

Figure 6.11 Display with User-Defined Formats: Example 2

```
   |         A       ||       B       ||      C       ||  D  ||  E  ||  F  |
1           $200.00          200             14
2           $123.40          200             16
3         $1,234.57          200             30
4       $123,456.79                         256
5    >>>>>>>>>>>>>>>>                       256
6    >>>>>>>>>>>>>>>>                       512
7    $12,345,678.00                       323.4
8    >>>>>>>>>>>>>>>>                       122
9           4.3125%                          48
10
11
12
13
14
15
16
17
18
19
20
 A10
Width: 16   Memory:100 Last Col/Row:C9        ? for HELP
 1>
F1 = Help; F2 = Cancel; F9 = Plot; F10 = View
```

Cell A8, like cells A5 and A6, has a width of 16 positions, with 15 positions available for numeric display. The current value of cell A8 is −12345678. The expected display from format U1 is **($12,345,678.00)** because of the Minus In ( ) set to Y. This expected format requires a total of 16 characters, exceeding the 15 available positions and resulting in an overflow error.

For the third demonstration, enter **/FCA,U2** and press RETURN. Your screen should have a display similar to Figure 6.12. Notice that all cells except A9 display a dollar sign next to the most significant digit. Cells A5, A6, A7, and A8 also have embedded commas. Cell A9 is not changed since entry level formats take precedence over column level formats. This time there are no overflow errors.

Format U2 is similar to format U1. The differences are in the Decimal Places and Scaling Factor. With a Scaling Factor of 3, each entry in cells A1 through A8 is divided by 1000 (i.e., 10^3) and rounded to one decimal place as specified in the format U2.

For the next demonstration, enter **/FCA:C,U3** and press RETURN. Your screen will have a display similar to Figure 6.13. The floating dollar signs and embedded commas are not displayed since they have been turned off in format U3 (i.e., set to N). All cells in columns A through C, except A9, have been scaled down by 10^4. Cell A9 is not changed since entry level formats take precedence over column level formats. Some cells display **.0,** caused by rounding to one decimal place where the scaled down value is greater than 0 but less than 0.05.

For the last demonstration, enter **/FR1:3,U5** and press RETURN. Your screen will have a display like Figure 6.14. This level of format is applicable to rows 1

Figure 6.12 Display with User-Defined Formats: Example 3

```
     |         A      ||        B       ||       C        ||       D       |
1                  $.2            200              14
2                  $.1            200              16
3                 $1.2            200              30
4               $123.5                            256
5         $1,234,567.9                            256
6           $123,456.8                            512
7            $12,345.7                            323
8      (     $12,345.7)                           122
9              4.3125%                             48
10
11
12
13
14
15
16
17
18
19
20
 A8               Form=-12345678
Width: 16   Memory:100 Last Col/Row:C9        ? for HELP
 1>
F1 = Help; F2 = Cancel; F9 = Plot; F10 = View
```

Figure 6.13 Display with User-Defined Formats: Example 4

```
     |         A      ||        B       ||       C        ||       D       |
1                   .0             .0              .0
2                   .0             .0              .0
3                   .1             .0              .0
4                 12.3                             .0
5             123456.8                             .0
6              12345.7                             .1
7               1234.6                             .0
8      (        1234.6)                            .0
9              4.3125%                             .0
10
11
12
13
14
15
16
17
18
19
20
 A8               Form=-12345678
Width: 16   Memory:100 Last Col/Row:C9        ? for HELP
 1>
F1 = Help; F2 = Cancel; F9 = Plot; F10 = View
```

through 3. As in all previous examples, the PROMPT and ENTRY lines are shown in the figure.

Now contrast Figure 6.13 with Figure 6.14. Notice that the block of cells B1 through C3 displays **.0** under format U3 in Figure 6.13. Using format U5 in Figure 6.14, cells B1 through B3 display **.02,** and cells C1 through C3 display blanks. Both formats U3 and U5 use a scaling factor of 4, but format U5 calls for two decimal places while format U3 calls for only one decimal place. In Figure 6.13, zeroes are shown for any scaled down values less than 0.05, the minimum value necessary to round to 0.1. Format U5 replaces zeroes with blanks. Figure 6.14 displays blanks in the cell range C1 through C3, since these cells have

Figure 6.14 Display with User-Defined Formats: Example 5

```
        |      A       ||      B       ||      C       ||      D       |
1                 .02           .02
2                 .01           .02
3                 .12           .02
4                12.3                               .0
5            123456.8                               .0
6             12345.7                               .1
7              1234.6                               .0
8       (      1234.6)                              .0
9              4.3125%                              .0
10
11
12
13
14
15
16
17
18
19
20
 A1             Form=200
Width: 16   Memory:100 Last Col/Row:C9        ? for HELP
  1>
F1 = Help; F2 = Cancel; F9 = Plot; F10 = View
```

scaled down values less than 0.005, the minimum value necessary to round to 0.01.

This concludes the material for the /F(ormat). You should be able to generate some very professional-looking spreadsheets at this point. You are now ready for the Review Exercises. Enter **/ZY** to erase your spreadsheet before starting the exercises.

Review Exercises

These exercises use the Credit Card Interest Spreadsheet from Exercise 5.8.

1. Provide the command to load the spreadsheet from Exercise 5.8.
2. Make the necessary entry to display the spreadsheet with row numbers and column numbers.
3. Make the necessary entry to right justify the text in columns B through E.
4. Correct any problems with repeating text.
5. Make all interest charges and totals display as whole numbers.
6. Make all interest charges and totals display with two decimal places.
7. Suppress the display of the totals in column E and row 17.
8. Restore the display of the totals in column E and row 17.
9. Provide the commands to:
   a. Save the spreadsheet as EX6-9.
   b. Erase the spreadsheet.

Answers to Review Exercises

1. /LB:EX5-8.CAL,A
2. **/GB**
3. **/FCB:E,TR**, then press RETURN.
4. **/FEB3,TL**, then press RETURN.
5. **/FCB:E,I**, then press RETURN. See Figure 6.15.

Figure 6.15 Credit Interest Spreadsheet: Exercise 6-5

```
      |  A   ||   B   ||   C   ||   D   ||   E   ||   F   ||   G   ||   H   |
1                           MASTER
2                     VISA  CHARGE      SEARS     TOTAL
3               ------------------------------------
4     JAN                6        9        10        25
5     FEB               12        9        10        31
6     MAR               13        8        10        31
7     APR               15        8         9        32
8     MAY               33        8         9        50
9     JUN               21        8         9        38
10    JUL               23        8         9        41
11    AUG               25        7        11        43
12    SEP               27        7        12        46
13    OCT               27        8        13        48
14    NOV               28        8        12        48
15    DEC               27        7        12        46
16              ------   ------    ------    ------
17    TOTAL            257       96       126       479
18              ======   ======    ======    ======
19
20
B3        TL        Rtxt='-
Width:   9   Memory: 99 Last Col/Row:F18        ? for HELP
  1>
F1 = Help; F2 = Cancel; F9 = Plot; F10 = View
```

6. **/FCB:E,$**, then press RETURN. See Figure 6.16.

Figure 6.16 Credit Interest Spreadsheet: Exercise 6-6

```
      |  A   ||   B   ||   C   ||   D   ||   E   ||   F   ||   G   ||   H   |
1                           MASTER
2                     VISA  CHARGE      SEARS     TOTAL
3               ------------------------------------
4     JAN             5.95     8.96      9.74     24.65
5     FEB            12.06     8.84      9.98     30.88
6     MAR            13.31     8.23      9.62     31.16
7     APR            14.88     7.67      9.29     31.84
8     MAY            33.49     7.74      8.89     50.12
9     JUN            20.75     8.06      9.05     37.86
10    JUL            23.10     8.04      9.37     40.51
11    AUG            24.95     7.31     10.64     42.90
12    SEP            26.71     7.45     11.59     45.75
13    OCT            27.38     8.44     12.64     48.46
14    NOV            27.89     7.96     12.48     48.33
15    DEC            26.70     7.40     12.30     46.40
16              ------   ------    ------    ------
17    TOTAL         257.17    96.10    125.59    478.86
18              ======   ======    ======    ======
19
20
B3        TL        Rtxt='-
Width:   9   Memory: 99 Last Col/Row:F18        ? for HELP
  1>
F1 = Help; F2 = Cancel; F9 = Plot; F10 = View
```

7. **/FCE,H**, then press RETURN. **/FR17,H**, then press RETURN.
8. **/FCE,$**, then press RETURN. **/FR17,$**, then press RETURN. Your screen should match the solution screen for Exercise 6.
9. a. /SEX6-9,A
   b. /ZY

CHAPTER 7

Manipulating Your Spreadsheet

Chapter Overview and Objectives

- Inserting and Deleting Rows or Columns
- Copying, Moving, and Replicating Cells
- Blanking and Editing Cells
- Protecting and Unprotecting Cells

When you've completed Chapter 7, you'll have an understanding of how to build spreadsheets using /Replicate and /Copy. You'll see how to revise your spreadsheet via /Insert, /Delete, and /Move as well as /Blank and /Edit. Finally, you'll learn how to incorporate security into your spreadsheets with /Protect and to remove it with /Unprotect.

"Slash" Commands to Modify Your Spreadsheet

SuperCalc^3 has a series of commands that allow you to easily change, expand, or contract your spreadsheet. To get ready for a demonstration of these commands, either boot SuperCalc^3 or /Zap whatever spreadsheet is in memory. Next /Load the P&L spreadsheet.

The Blank Command

The Blank command clears out one or more unprotected cells, replacing the contents with null characters. This command is invoked by /B, whereupon the PROMPT and ENTRY lines display

Enter range, or *graph-range

8>/Blank,

You now have three options:

1. Press RETURN. This will blank the current cell, assuming it's not protected. If you attempt to blank a protected cell, the STATUS LINE displays the error message

   Protected Entry

2. Enter a cell or cell range and press RETURN. This blanks all unprotected cells in the specified range. If one or more cells in the range are protected, the STATUS LINE displays the error message
   Protected Entry
3. Enter a graph number or graph range preceded by * and press RETURN. This deletes the specified graphs, setting the graph formats back to the defaults. The graph numbers are not resequenced. See Chapter 12 on graphics for additional information.

If it's necessary to blank a protected cell, either unprotect it by the /Unprotect command or lower the protective shield by the /Global,Protect toggle.

Now practice blanking cells. First, position your spreadsheet cursor at cell F3. Next, enter **/B** and press the RETURN key. For an instant, the PROMPT and ENTRY lines will display

Blanking . . .

10/Blank,F3

and then the value of 21000 will disappear from your screen. If you are in automatic recalculation mode, the PROMPT LINE will then display

Calculating . . .

The next /Blank command will destroy most of your Profit & Loss Statement; but don't worry, you'll quickly learn to rebuild it. As a matter of fact, the rebuilding process will be much faster than the time it took to create the spreadsheet initially. Enter **/BB4:F18** and press RETURN. For an instant, the PROMPT and ENTRY lines will display

Blanking . . .

14/Blank,B4:F18

and all entries from cell B4 through F18 will disappear from your screen. Your spreadsheet should resemble the one shown in Figure 7.1.

Figure 7.1 P&L Spreadsheet: Cell Range B4.F18 Blanked

```
   |          A           ||    B    ||    C    ||    D    ||    E    ||    F    ||    G    |
1                             QTR #1     QTR #2     QTR #3     QTR #4     TOTAL
2                          --------------------------------------------------------
3   SALES                    5000.00    4000.00    4500.00    7500.00
4   COST OF GOODS SOLD
5
6   GROSS MARGIN
7
8   OPERATING EXPENSES
9     MARKETING
10    ADMINISTRATIVE
11
12       TOTAL
13
14  PRE-TAX PROFIT
15  INCOME TAX
16
17  NET INCOME
18
19
20
 A5
Width: 20   Memory:100 Last Col/Row:G17      ? for HELP
  1>
F1 = Help; F2 = Cancel; F9 = Plot; F10 = View
```

You'll need this spreadsheet as it currently stands toward the end of the next section, so save it now.

The Replicate and Copy Commands

The Replicate command duplicates a cell or cell range into one or more groups of cells. The Copy command duplicates a cell or cell range into another cell or group of cells. Users often confuse the Replicate command with the Copy command. Although there is a similarity between the two, /Replicate allows multiple copies (one-to-many copy), whereas /Copy allows only single copies (a one-to-one copy).

Replicating Cells

The Replicate command is invoked by /R, causing the PROMPT and ENTRY lines to display

From? (Enter Range)

12>/Replicate,

Your *From* range can be

A single cell
A partial column
A partial row

After entering the *From Range,* you are prompted

To? (Enter Range), then Return; or "," for Options

Your *To* or *Destination* range can be:

A partial column, given that your *From Range* was a single cell. For example, the entry

/RA1,A2:A5

replicates the contents of cell A1 into the partial column composed of cells A2 through A5.

A partial row, given that your *From Range* was a single cell. For example, the entry

/RB1,C1:E1

replicates the contents of cell B1 into the partial row composed of cells C1 through E1.

A group of partial columns, given that your *From Range* was a partial column. The entry

/RA1:A5,B1:E1

replicates the contents of the partial column A1 through A5 into a group of partial columns composed of cells B1 through B5, C1 through C5, D1 through D5, and E1 through E5.

A group of partial rows, given that your *From Range* was a partial row. For example, the entry

/RB5:E5,B6:B9

replicates the contents of the partial row B5 through E5 into a group of partial rows composed of cells B6 through E6, B7 through E7, B8 through E8, and B9 through E9.

If you want to enter the demonstration exercises that follow, make certain you have saved your P&L spreadsheet because you'll need it shortly. You can zap the spreadsheet once it's been saved.

The following options are available for /Replicate:

RETURN Causes automatic adjustment of formulas. For example, assume that cell A1 contains the number 2 and cell B1 contains the formula 2*A1. If you entered **/GF** to toggle on formula display, then entered

/RB1,C1.H1

and pressed RETURN, you'd see the formulas shown next. Another entry of **/GF** would display the values shown next:

	Formulas	Values
cell A1:	2	2
cell B1:	2*A1	4
cell C1:	2*B1	8
cell D1:	2*C1	16
cell E1:	2*D1	32
cell F1:	2*E1	64
cell G1:	2*F1	128
cell H1:	2*G1	256

Note that the references of the replicated cells are adjusted to duplicate the reference in the source cell, but relative to their own positions in the spreadsheet.

The source cell, B1, refers to the cell on its left, A1. The first replicated cell, C1, refers to the cell on its left, B1. The eighth replicated cell, H1, refers to the cell on its left, G1.

N Suppresses adjustment of formulas. Using the above example, enter **/GF** to toggle on formula display and then enter

/RB1,C1:H1,N

You'll see the formulas shown next. Another entry of **/GF** will display the values shown next.

	Formulas	Values
cell A1:	2	2
cell B1:	2*A1	4
cell C1:	2*A1	4
cell D1:	2*A1	4
cell E1:	2*A1	4
cell F1:	2*A1	4
cell G1:	2*A1	4
cell H1:	2*A1	4

Notice that the formula in cell B1 has been exactly duplicated in cells C1 through H1. Suppression of formula adjustment would be applicable when you need a consistent reference to a cell by a series of other cells. Consider a situation where cell A1 contains an interest rate used by a series of other formulas for discounting and compounding.

A Prompts for formula adjustment for each cell to be copied. Using the previous example, an entry of

/RB1,C1.H1,A

gives the following displays on the STATUS, PROMPT, and ENTRY lines:

Source cell B1. Adjust A1 (Y or N)?
Replicating . . . 1
22>2***A1**

The entry **Y** gives the same results as bypassing the options and pressing RETURN. The entry **N** gives the same results as selecting the **N** option.

When the source cell references more than one cell, you are queried on each of the referenced cells. Assuming cell B1 contains the formula A1*A2, the entry of

/RB1,C1:H1,A

displays

Source cell B1. Adjust A1 (Y or N)?
Replicating . . . 1
22>A1*A2

After an entry is made, SuperCalc³ displays

Source cell B1. Adjust A2 (Y or N)?
Replicating . . . 1
22>A1***A2**

The replication completes after you specify Yes or No. Your decisions to adjust or not adjust are independent of one another, so you can enter **Y** on some and **N** on others. However, if you specify **Y** on all, it would be more efficient to use RETURN instead of the A option. Likewise, if you enter **N** on all, it would be faster just to use the N option.

V Copies the value of the source cell's contents into the destination cell as a numeric constant. Using the same example as above, enter /**GF** to toggle on formula display and then enter

/RB1,C1.H1,V

The results are shown next. Notice that the only true formula is in cell B1. All other entries are constants.

	Formulas	Values
cell A1:	2	2
cell B1:	2*A1	4
cell C1:	4	4

(continued on next page)

	Formulas	Values
cell D1:	4	4
cell E1:	4	4
cell F1:	4	4
cell G1:	4	4
cell H1:	4	4

The next series of options are known as *Consolidation Options*. They are applicable in situations where "across the board changes" are necessary. Examples are wage and tax changes as well as certain kinds of "What if . . .?" analyses.

+ Adds the value of the source cell's contents to the destination cell's contents. The sum is stored in the destination cell as a numeric constant. Assuming that cells C1 through H1 have contents of 1 through 6, respectively, enter **/GF** to toggle on formula display. Now enter

/RB1,C1:H1,+

The results are shown next.

	Before	After
cell A1:	2	2
cell B1:	2*A1	2*A1
cell C1:	1	5
cell D1:	2	6
cell E1:	3	7
cell F1:	4	8
cell G1:	5	9
cell H1:	6	10

– Subtracts the value of the source cell's contents from the destination cell's contents. The difference is stored in the destination as a numeric constant. Assuming that cells C1 through H1 have contents of 5 through 10, respectively, enter **/GF** to toggle on formula display. Now enter

/RB1,C1.H1,–

The results are shown next.

	Before	After
cell A1:	2	2
cell B1:	2*A1	2*A1
cell C1:	5	1
cell D1:	6	2
cell E1:	7	3
cell F1:	8	4
cell G1:	9	5
cell H1:	10	6

* Multiplies the value of the source cell's contents by the destination cell's contents. The product is stored in the destination cell as a numeric constant. Assuming that cells C1 through H1 have contents of 1 through 6, respectively, enter **/GF** to toggle on formula display. Now enter

/RB1,C1:H1,*

The results are shown next.

	Before	After
cell A1:	2	2
cell B1:	2*A1	2*A1
cell C1:	1	4
cell D1:	2	8
cell E1:	3	12
cell F1:	4	16
cell G1:	5	20
cell H1:	6	24

/ Divides the value of the source cell's contents into the destination cell's contents. The quotient is stored in the destination cell as a numeric constant. Assuming that cells C1 through H1 have contents of 4 through 24, respectively incremented by 4, enter **/GF** to toggle on formula display. Now enter

/RB1,C1:H1,/

The results are shown next.

	Before	After
cell A1:	2	2
cell B1:	2*A1	2*A1
cell C1:	4	1
cell D1:	8	2
cell E1:	12	3
cell F1:	16	4
cell G1:	20	5
cell H1:	24	6

Copying Cells

The Copy command is invoked by /C, causing the PROMPT and ENTRY lines to display

From? Enter range or *graph-number

7>/Copy,

Your *From* range can be

A single cell
A partial column
A partial row

A block of cells
A graph

After entering the *From Range*, you are prompted for the target or destination cell:

To? (Enter Cell), then <Return> or <,> for Options

The *To* or *Destination* cell becomes the upper left cell in the duplicated range of cells. This block copying capability is a key feature of /Copy. The Replicate command cannot duplicate a block. Here are some examples of copying:

Single Cell The entry **/CA1,B1** copies the contents of cell A1 into cell B1.

Partial Row The entry **/CA1:H1,A3** copies the contents of cells A1 through H1 into cells A3 through H3.

Partial Column The entry **/CA1:A5,E1** copies the contents of cells A1 through A5 into cells E1 through E5.

Cell Block The entry **/CA1:E3,A10** copies the contents of cells A1 through E3 into cells A10 through E12.

When you enter a graph number in response to

From? Enter range or *graph-number

7>/Copy,

you are prompted:

To? Enter graph number

Graph numbers must be in the range of 1 through 9. Refer to Chapter 12 on graphics for additional information.

If you want to do the following demonstration exercises, be sure to save your P&L spreadsheet. If you already did this in the /Replicate command section, ignore this.

The following options are available for /Copy. They are equivalent to the Replicate options.

RETURN Causes automatic adjustment of formulas. For example, assume that cell A1 contains the number 2 and cell B1 contains the formula 2*A1. Enter **/GF** to toggle on formula display, if it's not already on. Now enter

/CB1,C1

and press RETURN. You'll see the formulas shown next. Another entry of **/GF** displays the values shown next.

	Formulas	Values
cell A1:	2	2
cell B1:	2*A1	4
cell C1:	2*B1	8

Note that the references of the copied cell are adjusted to duplicate the reference in the source cell, but relative to its own position in the spreadsheet. The source cell, B1, refers to the cell on its left, A1. The copied cell, C1, refers to the cell on its left, B1.

N Suppresses adjustment of formulas. Using the last example, enter **/GF** to toggle on formula display and enter
/CB1,C1,N
You'll see the formulas shown next. Another entry of **/GF** will display the values shown next.

	Formulas	Values
cell A1:	2	2
cell B1:	2*A1	4
cell C1:	2*A1	4

Notice that the formula in cell B1 has been exactly duplicated in cell C1. Suppression of formula adjustment is useful when you want to repeatedly reference the same cell.

A Prompts for formula adjustment for each cell to be copied. Using the previous example, the entry
/CB1,C1,A
gives the following displays on the STATUS, PROMPT, and ENTRY lines:
Source cell B1. Adjust A1 (Y or N)?
Copying . . .
14>2***A1**
The entry **Y** gives the same results as pressing RETURN. The entry **N** gives the same results as selecting the **N** option.

When the source cell references more than one cell, you are queried on each of the referenced cells. Assuming cell B1 contains the formula A1*A2, the entry
/CB1,C1,A
displays
Source cell B1. Adjust A1 (Y or N)?
Copying . . .
14>**A1***A2
After an entry is made, SuperCalc[3] displays
Source cell B1. Adjust A2 (Y or N)?
Copying . . .
14>A1***A2**
The copy completes after you specify Yes or No. Your decisions to adjust or not adjust are independent of one another, so you can enter **Y** on some and **N** on others. However, if you specify **Y** on all, it would be more efficient to use RETURN instead of the A option.

Likewise, if you enter **N** on all, it will be faster to just use the N option.

V Copies the value of the source cell's contents into the destination cell as a numeric constant. Using the same example as before, enter **/GF** to toggle on formula display and then enter

/CB1,C1,V

The results are shown next. Notice that B1 is the only cell with a formula. The other entries are constants.

	Formulas	Values
cell A1:	2	2
cell B1:	2*A1	4
cell C1:	4	4

The next series of options are known as *Consolidation* options:

\+ Adds the value of the source cell's contents to the destination cell's contents. The sum is stored in the destination cell as a numeric constant. See the next table for the initial contents of cells A1 through H1. Enter

/CA1.D1,E1,+

As the copy executes, the following addition occurs:

cell A1 + cell E1, results stored in cell E1
cell B1 + cell F1, results stored in cell F1
cell C1 + cell G1, results stored in cell G1
cell D1 + cell H1, results stored in cell H1

The results are shown next.

	Before	After
cell A1:	2	2
cell B1:	4	4
cell C1:	5	5
cell D1:	6	6
cell E1:	1	3
cell F1:	2	6
cell G1:	3	8
cell H1:	4	10

– Subtracts the value of the source cell's contents from the destination cell's contents. The difference is stored in the destination as a numeric constant. See the next table for the initial contents of cells A1 through H1. Enter

/CA1:D1,E1,–

As the copy executes, the following subtraction occurs:

cell E1 – cell A1, results stored in cell E1
cell F1 – cell B1, results stored in cell F1
cell G1 – cell C1, results stored in cell G1
cell H1 – cell D1, results stored in cell H1

The results are shown next.

	Before	After
cell A1:	2	2
cell B1:	4	4
cell C1:	5	5
cell D1:	6	6
cell E1:	3	1
cell F1:	6	2
cell G1:	8	3
cell H1:	10	4

* Multiplies the value of the source cell's contents by the destination cell's contents. The product is stored in the destination cell as a numeric constant. See the next table for the initial contents of cells A1 through H1. Enter

/CA1.D1,E1,*

As the copy executes, the following multiplication occurs:

cell A1 * cell E1, results stored in cell E1
cell B1 * cell F1, results stored in cell F1
cell C1 * cell G1, results stored in cell G1
cell D1 * cell H1, results stored in cell H1

The results are shown next.

	Before	After
cell A1:	2	2
cell B1:	4	4
cell C1:	5	5
cell D1:	6	6
cell E1:	1	2
cell F1:	2	8
cell G1:	3	15
cell H1:	4	24

/ Divides the value of the source cell's contents into the destination cell's contents. The quotient is stored in the destination cell as a numeric constant. See the next table for the initial contents of cells A1 through H1. Enter

/CA1:D1,E1,/

As the copy executes, the following division occurs:

cell E1 / cell A1, results stored in cell E1
cell F1 / cell B1, results stored in cell F1
cell G1 / cell C1, results stored in cell G1
cell H1 / cell D1, results stored in cell H1

The results are shown next.

	Before	After
cell A1:	2	2
cell B1:	4	4
cell C1:	5	5
cell D1:	6	6
cell E1:	2	1
cell F1:	8	2
cell G1:	15	3
cell H1:	24	4

Recreating the P&L Via /R and /C

Now you're going to apply your newly acquired knowledge of the Replicate and Copy commands to recreate your Profit & Loss spreadsheet.

First, zap the current spreadsheet, then load your P&L into SuperCalc^3. It should resemble the spreadsheet in Figure 7.1 with the block of cells from B4 through F18 blanked out.

Next, toggle on formula display by **/GF**, set column F to a width of 16 by **/FCF,16**, and turn on manual recalculation mode by **/GM.** This action makes it easier to see what you're doing. It also speeds things up by suppressing automatic recalculation.

Position your spreadsheet cursor at cell B4 to input the first quarter's Cost of Goods Sold formula. Enter **30%B3** and press RETURN. In Chapter 4 you made similar entries in cells C4, D4, and E4. You're now going to take a shortcut by entering

/RB4,C4.E4

then pressing RETURN. Your Cost of Goods Sold formulas are now replicated into the second, third, and fourth quarters.

Position your spreadsheet cursor at cell B6 and input **B3-B4** as the first quarter's Gross Margin formula. Now replicate this formula into the second, third, and fourth quarters by entering

/RB6,C6:E6

then pressing RETURN.

Position your spreadsheet cursor at cell B9 and input **1000** as the first quarter's Marketing Expense amount. Replicate this value into the second, third, and fourth quarters by entering

/RB9,C9.E9

then pressing RETURN.

Position your spreadsheet cursor at cell B10 and input **10%B3** as the first quarter's Administrative Expense formula. Replicate this formula into the second, third, and fourth quarters with the entry

/RB10,C10:E10

then press RETURN.

Position your spreadsheet cursor at cell B12 and input **B9+B10** as the first quarter's Total Operating Expense formula. Replicate this formula into the second, third, and fourth quarters with the entry

/RB12,C12.E12

then press RETURN.

Position your spreadsheet cursor at cell B14 and input **B6-B12** as the first quarter's Pre-Tax Profit formula. Replicate this formula into the second, third, and fourth quarters with the entry

/RB14,C14:E14

then press RETURN.

Position your spreadsheet cursor at cell B15 and input **50%B14** as the first quarter's Income Tax formula. Replicate this formula into the second, third, and fourth quarters with the entry

/RB15,C15:E15

then press RETURN.

Isn't this a lot faster than the way you did it in Chapter 4? Watch closely; it gets better. Position your spreadsheet cursor at cell B17 and input **B14-B15** as the first quarter's Net Income formula. Now, position your spreadsheet cursor at cell C17. You're still going to replicate Qtr #1 Net Income into Qtr #2, Qtr #3, and Qtr #4 but with a slightly different twist.

First, enter **/R.** Now press the ESC key. **C17** appears on your ENTRY LINE as the From Cell. Also, **POINT** displays on the bottom line of your screen. Now press the ← key to position the cursor at cell B17, then press either the RETURN or comma (,) keys. You get prompted for the **To Range**; the cursor has also moved back to cell C17.

Press either the period (.) or colon (:) keys and the **To Range** is shown as **C17:C17**. Now press the → key. The cursor moves to cell D17; the **To Range** is shown as **C17:D17**. There is also an inverse video bar covering cells C17 and D17. Press the C one more time and the **To Range** is now shown as **C17:E17**. The inverse video bar now covers cells C17 through E17. The purpose of this bar is to indicate the range you're going to replicate into. You can now press the RETURN key to make the replication.

This procedure has the same effect as entering

/RB17,C17.E17

then pressing RETURN. It's useful for people who have difficulty seeing a straight line and who would therefore tend to make errors on the row and column coordinates.

You've nearly finished fixing your spreadsheet. You have to put totals in column F as well as underlines in rows 5, 11, 16, and 18.

Position your spreadsheet cursor at cell F3. Enter the formula **B3+C3+D3+E3** in this cell to calculate Total Sales. Since you need totals for Cost of Goods Sold, Gross Margin, Operating Expenses, Pre-Tax Profit, Income Tax, and Net Income, enter

/RF3,F4:F17

then press RETURN. Looking at column F, you can see some unwanted formulas in F5, F7, F8, F11, F13, and F16. These are easily corrected.

First, fix the problem in F7 and F8 by entering

/BF7.F8

then pressing RETURN. You might want to try using the ESC key to point at these cells.

Next, fix the problem in F13 with the entry

/BF13

then press RETURN.

The remaining unwanted formulas will take care of themselves when you put in your underlines. Position your spreadsheet cursor at cell B5. Make the text entry **--------**, then enter

/RB5,C5:F5

and press RETURN.

The Copy command can be used to get underlines into rows 11 and 16. This is done by the following entries:

/CB5:F5,B11, then press RETURN

and

/CB5:F5,B16, then press RETURN

Revisiting the Edit Command

Your last task is to get the double underlines into row 18. As in the previous illustrations, you could position your spreadsheet cursor at cell B18 and make a text entry of **"========.** Also as before, you could enter

/RB18,C18:F18, then press RETURN

Although the above process would work quite well, you're going to take an alternate path using the /Edit command.

You used Edit in Chapter 4. You'll now see another application. Position your spreadsheet cursor at cell B18 and enter **/E.** When the PROMPT and ENTRY lines display

From? Enter Cell

26>/Edit(into current cell),

enter B16, press RETURN, and the ENTRY LINE now displays

10>"--------

Press the TAB key and the entry line cursor moves to the beginning of the text string. Press the → key to position your cursor on the leftmost hyphen. Now type an = over each **-.** Press RETURN and the first set of double underlines is in cell B18.

Position your spreadsheet cursor at cell C18 and enter **/E.** When the PROMPT and ENTRY lines display

From? Enter Cell

26>/Edit(into current cell),

enter B18, press RETURN, and the ENTRY LINE now displays

10>"========

Press RETURN and the underlines are copied from cell B18 into cell C18. Now enter

/RC18,D18.F18

and press RETURN.

You have now restored your spreadsheet. It should match Figure 7.2.

Figure 7.2 **P&L Spreadsheet: Cell Range B4.F18 Restored, Formulas Toggled On**

```
    |          A          ||    B    ||    C    ||    D    ||    E    ||        F        |
1                               QTR #1    QTR #2    QTR #3    QTR #4              TOTAL
2                         ----------------------------------------------------------------
3     SALES                       5000      4000      4500      7500       B3+C3+D3+E3
4     COST OF GOODS SOLD         30%B3     30%C3     30%D3     30%E3       B4+C4+D4+E4
5                             --------  --------  --------  --------          --------
6     GROSS MARGIN               B3-B4     C3-C4     D3-D4     E3-E4       B6+C6+D6+E6
7
8     OPERATING EXPENSES
9       MARKETING                 1000      1000      1000      1000       B9+C9+D9+E9
10      ADMINISTRATIVE           10%B3     10%C3     10%D3     10%E3   B10+C10+D10+E10
11                            --------  --------  --------  --------          --------
12          TOTAL               B9+B10    C9+C10    D9+D10    E9+E10   B12+C12+D12+E12
13
14    PRE-TAX PROFIT           B6-B12    C6-C12    D6-D12    E6-E12   B14+C14+D14+E14
15    INCOME TAX              50%B14    50%C14    50%D14    50%E14   B15+C15+D15+E15
16                            --------  --------  --------  --------          --------
17    NET INCOME              B14-B15   C14-C15   D14-D15   E14-E15   B17+C17+D17+E17
18                            ========  ========  ========  ========          ========
19
20
 A5                                                                             TEXT
Width: 20   Memory: 99 Last Col/Row:G18       ? for HELP
  1>
F1 = Help; F2 = Cancel; F9 = Plot; F10 = View                    CAPS
```

Set the width of column F back to nine positions via /**FCF,9,** then toggle off the display of formulas via /**GF,** and force a manual recalculation by entering **!** to make your spreadsheet look like Figure 7.3.

Figure 7.3 **P&L Spreadsheet: Cell Range B4.F18 Restored, Formulas Toggled Off**

```
    |          A          ||    B    ||    C    ||    D    ||    E    ||        F        |
1                               QTR #1    QTR #2    QTR #3    QTR #4              TOTAL
2                         ----------------------------------------------------------------
3     SALES                    5000.00   4000.00   4500.00   7500.00          21000.00
4     COST OF GOODS SOLD       1500.00   1200.00   1350.00   2250.00           6300.00
5                             --------  --------  --------  --------          --------
6     GROSS MARGIN             3500.00   2800.00   3150.00   5250.00          14700.00
7
8     OPERATING EXPENSES
9       MARKETING              1000.00   1000.00   1000.00   1000.00           4000.00
10      ADMINISTRATIVE          500.00    400.00    450.00    750.00           2100.00
11                            --------  --------  --------  --------          --------
12          TOTAL              1500.00   1400.00   1450.00   1750.00           6100.00
13
14    PRE-TAX PROFIT           2000.00   1400.00   1700.00   3500.00           8600.00
15    INCOME TAX               1000.00    700.00    850.00   1750.00           4300.00
16                            --------  --------  --------  --------          --------
17    NET INCOME               1000.00    700.00    850.00   1750.00           4300.00
18                            ========  ========  ========  ========          ========
19
20
 A5
Width: 20   Memory: 99 Last Col/Row:G18       ? for HELP
  1>
F1 = Help; F2 = Cancel; F9 = Plot; F10 = View                    CAPS
```

Save your spreadsheet before proceeding to the next section.

Inserting, Deleting, and Moving

The Insert command adds rows or columns to a spreadsheet. The Delete command eliminates rows or columns from a spreadsheet and can also delete files from disk. The Move command shifts row or columns from one point in a spreadsheet to another; it is a destructive copy. SuperCalc³ allows row and column ranges to be specified with the Insert, Delete, and Move commands.

To start this exercise, load the Profit & Loss Statement you rebuilt in the previous section, if it's not currently in memory.

The Insert command is called by /I. The PROMPT and ENTRY lines respond with

R(ow) or C(olumn)?

9>/Insert,

Specify whether you want to insert a row or column. Enter **R** to insert a row. Now the PROMPT and ENTRY lines respond with

Enter Row Range

13/Insert,Row,

You've selected row insertion because you need to put two more heading lines on the P&L. These lines will identify the business entity filing the report and the fiscal year covered by the report. Since you can't use the existing rows without destroying what's already there, insert two additional rows.

Enter **2:3** and press RETURN. For an instant the PROMPT LINE will display

Inserting . . . 2

Inserting . . . 3

followed by an equally brief

Adjusting . . . 2

Adjusting . . . 3

The numbers after **Inserting . . .** and **Adjusting . . .** identify each row as it is inserted and the associated cell references are adjusted. If you're in automatic calculation mode, you'll also see

Calculating . . .

The spreadsheet on your video screen should match the one shown in Figure 7.4. Looking at the P&L, you'll notice that the empty lines have been inserted in the wrong place. They should be at rows 1 and 2. There are two ways to correct this.

The first way is to delete the lines and reinsert them at the proper place. To implement the fix this way, call the Delete command by /D. When the PROMPT and ENTRY lines display

R(ow), C(olumn) or F(ile)?

9>/Delete,

enter **R** for row deletion. Now the PROMPT and ENTRY lines display

Enter Row Range

13/Delete,Row,

Enter **2.3** and press RETURN. For an instant the PROMPT LINE will display

Deleting . . . 2

Deleting . . . 3

followed by an equally brief

Figure 7.4 P&L Spreadsheet: Erroneous Insert of Two Rows

```
   |          A           ||    B    ||    C    ||    D    ||    E    ||    F    ||    G    |
1                              QTR #1     QTR #2     QTR #3     QTR #4     TOTAL
2
3
4                           --------------------------------------------------------
5    SALES                   5000.00   4000.00   4500.00   7500.00  21000.00
6    Cost of Goods Sold      1500.00   1200.00   1350.00   2250.00   6300.00
7                           --------  --------  --------  --------  --------
8    GROSS MARGIN            3500.00   2800.00   3150.00   5250.00  14700.00
9
10   OPERATING EXPENSES
11     MARKETING             1000.00   1000.00   1000.00   1000.00   4000.00
12     ADMINISTRATIVE         500.00    400.00    450.00    750.00   2100.00
13                          --------  --------  --------  --------  --------
14        TOTAL              1500.00   1400.00   1450.00   1750.00   6100.00
15
16   PRE-TAX PROFIT          2000.00   1400.00   1700.00   3500.00   8600.00
17   INCOME TAX              1000.00    700.00    850.00   1750.00   4300.00
18                          --------  --------  --------  --------  --------
19   NET INCOME              1000.00    700.00    850.00   1750.00   4300.00
20                          ========  ========  ========  ========  ========
 C18           Text="--------
Width:  9  Memory: 99 Last Col/Row:G20       ? for HELP
   1>
F1 = Help; F2 = Cancel; F9 = Plot; F10 = View                 CAPS
```

Adjusting . . . 2
Adjusting . . . 3

The numbers after **Deleting . . .** and **Adjusting . . .** identify each row as it is deleted and the associated cell references are adjusted. If you're in automatic calculation mode, you'll also see

Calculating . . .

Now properly insert the lines at rows 1 and 2 by entering

/IR1.2

The second way to fix the problem is via the Move command. Enter **/M.** When the PROMPT and ENTRY lines display

R(ow) or C(olumn)?
7>/Move,

enter **R** to indicate a row move. Now the PROMPT and ENTRY lines display

From? Enter row range.
11/Move,Row,

Enter **2.3** to identify the rows to be moved and press RETURN. Next the PROMPT and ENTRY lines show

To? Enter row number.
15/Move,Row,2.3,

Enter **1** to identify the first destination row and press RETURN. For an instant the PROMPT LINE will display

Moving . . . 2

followed by an equally brief

Moving . . . 3

The numbers after **Moving . . .** identify each row as it's moved, just as they did for /Insert and /Delete. If you're in automatic calculation mode, you'll also see

Calculating . . .

Although the /Move approach is the faster of the two methods, the outcome is the same regardless of the approach taken.

Now that the lines have been inserted, it's time to make the heading entries. First, position your cursor at cell C1 and enter

/FEC1:C2,TL, then press RETURN

to enable left justification of text in cells C1 and C2. This entry allows overflow into empty right-adjacent cells. Next, enter "   **BILL'S P & L STATEMENT** into cell C1 and scroll to cell C2, entering "   **FISCAL YEAR 1984.** There are three spaces separating " from **BILL'S** and six spaces separating " from **FISCAL.**

Your Profit & Loss Statement should look the same as the one in Figure 7.5.

Figure 7.5 P&L Spreadsheet: Headings Inserted

```
   |         A          ||   B    ||   C   ||   D   ||   E    ||   F    ||   G   |
1                                   Bill's P & L Statement
2                                      Fiscal Year 1984
3                              QTR #1   QTR #2   QTR #3   QTR #4    TOTAL
4                            --------------------------------------------
5    SALES                   5000.00  4000.00  4500.00  7500.00 21000.00
6    Cost of Goods Sold      1500.00  1200.00  1350.00  2250.00  6300.00
7                            -------- -------- -------- -------- --------
8    GROSS MARGIN            3500.00  2800.00  3150.00  5250.00 14700.00
9
10   OPERATING EXPENSES
11     MARKETING             1000.00  1000.00  1000.00  1000.00  4000.00
12     ADMINISTRATIVE         500.00   400.00   450.00   750.00  2100.00
13                           -------- -------- -------- -------- --------
14        TOTAL              1500.00  1400.00  1450.00  1750.00  6100.00
15
16   PRE-TAX PROFIT          2000.00  1400.00  1700.00  3500.00  8600.00
17   INCOME TAX              1000.00   700.00   850.00  1750.00  4300.00
18                           -------- -------- -------- -------- --------
19   NET INCOME              1000.00   700.00   850.00  1750.00  4300.00
20                           ======== ======== ======== ======== ========
 C3           Text="QTR #2
Width:  9  Memory: 99 Last Col/Row:G20      ? for HELP
  1>
F1 = Help; F2 = Cancel; F9 = Plot; F10 = View                  CAPS
```

Save this spreadsheet before going to the next section.

Security within Your Spreadsheet

In the previous section, a /Blank command cleared cell F6 and the block of cells from B6 through F20. These are the cell references from Figure 7.5, after inserting the two new rows. This destructive command was issued for demonstration purposes, but it could just as easily have happened accidentally.

The Protect command prevents alteration to the contents of non-blank cells. It is invoked by /P, causing the PROMPT and ENTRY lines to display

Enter Range

10>/Protect,

You have two options here:

1. Press RETURN. This will protect the current cell if it is not empty. The command has no effect if the current cell is empty or if it is already protected.
2. Enter a cell or cell range and press RETURN. This protects all cells in the specified range that are not empty or not already protected.

The STATUS LINE displays a **P** in front of the cell type to indicate the cell is protected. Color monitors display protected cells in yellow, while monochrome monitors use a lower video intensity to display protected cells.

The following entries would be typical for protecting a business report:

/PA1:A20	Protects the P&L classifications in column A.
/PB1:F4	Protects the headings in rows 1 through 4.

You could have entered **/PA1:F20** to protect the entire spreadsheet. On the surface, this may seem to complicate subsequent amount changes or "What if . . .?" analyses. This apparent problem can easily be eliminated by using /GP to toggle the protective shield on and off.

The following examples demonstrate the effectiveness of your protection.

Try to blank **OPERATING EXPENSES** out of cell A10 by entering **/BA10** and pressing RETURN. The right end of the STATUS LINE displays **Protected Entry,** and cell A10 remains intact.

Scroll to cell A8 and try to edit that cell. As soon as you press /E, the right end of the STATUS LINE displays **Protected Entry,** and your ENTRY LINE is cleared.

Try to delete rows 6 through 10 by entering **/DR6:10** and pressing RETURN. The right end of the STATUS LINE displays **Protected Entry,** rows 6 through 10 remain intact, and you're hung up on the ENTRY LINE. Press F2 to cancel the command. Similarly, an attempt to delete column D would fail because cells D1, D2, and D3 are protected.

Three commands override cell protection. The first is the /ZY command, which you saw in Chapter 4 and have used many times since.

The second is the /GP command, which you saw in Chapter 5. This command is used to temporarily lift protection from the entire spreadsheet to allow mass changes.

The third command that overrides cell protection is the Unprotect command. This command removes protection from a specified range of cells. It's invoked by /U, which causes the PROMPT and ENTRY lines to display

Enter Range

12>/UnProtect,

The options of the /Unprotect command are:

1. Press RETURN. This removes protection from the current cell. The command has no effect if the current cell is empty or not protected.
2. Enter a cell or cell range and press RETURN. This action removes protection from all cells in the specified range. The command has no effect on cells that are empty or not protected.

This concludes the material about manipulating your spreadsheet. You now know how to use the /R and /C commands to greatly accelerate building new spreadsheets. You can also use the /E, /I, /D, and /M commands to modify existing spreadsheets, as well as the /P and /U commands to set security. You're now ready for the Review Exercises. Enter **/ZY** to erase your spreadsheet before starting the exercises.

Review Exercises

These exercises use the Credit Card Interest Spreadsheet from Exercise 6.9.

1. Provide the command to load the spreadsheet from Exercise 6.9.
2. Provide commands to do the following:
   a. Turn off automatic recalculation.
   b. Turn on formula display.
   c. Clear out the Monthly Totals in column E.
   d. Clear out the Annual Totals in row 17 for MASTER CHARGE, SEARS, and Monthly.
   e. Re-enter the Monthly Total for January as the sum of the interest expense for VISA, MASTER CHARGE, and SEARS.
   f. Expand the width of column E to 15 positions.
   g. Duplicate January's total, with proper cell adjustment, for February through December.
   h. Duplicate VISA's annual total, with proper cell adjustment, for the MASTER CHARGE, SEARS, and TOTAL columns.
   i. Turn off formula display.
   j. Force a manual recalculation of the spreadsheet.
3. Provide the commands to do the following:
   a. Add two empty rows at the top of the spreadsheet.
   b. Enter the following headings in these new rows and display them approximately centered over the interest columns:

      BILL & CONNIE'S CREDIT CARD INTEREST FOR CALENDAR YEAR 1984
4. Issue a command to protect the entire spreadsheet.
5. What commands could be used to remove security?
6. Provide the commands to
   a. Save the spreadsheet at EX7-6.
   b. Erase the spreadsheet.

Answers to Review Exercises

1. /LB:EX6-9.CAL,A
2. a. /GM
   b. /GF
   c. /BE4.E15 and press RETURN.
   d. /BC17:E17 and press RETURN.
      See Figure 7.6 on page 112.
   e. In cell E4, enter **B4 + C4 + D4** and press RETURN.
   f. /FCE,15 and press RETURN.
   g. /RE4,E5:E15 and press RETURN.
   h. /RB17,C17:E17 and press RETURN.
      See Figure 7.7 on page 112.
   i. /GF
   j. !

Figure 7.6 Credit Interest Spreadsheet: Exercise 7-2d

```
    |  A    ||   B    ||   C    ||   D    ||   E    ||   F    ||   G    ||   H    |
 1                          MASTER
 2                 VISA     CHARGE     SEARS     TOTAL
 3            ----------------------------------------
 4    JAN          5.95       8.96      9.74
 5    FEB         12.06       8.84      9.98
 6    MAR         13.31       8.23      9.62
 7    APR         14.88       7.67      9.29
 8    MAY         33.49       7.74      8.89
 9    JUN         20.75       8.06      9.05
10    JUL          23.1       8.04      9.37
11    AUG         24.95       7.31     10.64
12    SEP         26.71       7.45     11.59
13    OCT         27.38       8.44     12.64
14    NOV         27.89       7.96     12.48
15    DEC          26.7        7.4      12.3
16               ------     ------    ------    ------
17    TOTAL   3+B14+B15
18               ======     ======    ======    ======
19
20
B17             Form=B4+B5+B6+B7+B8+B9+B10+B11+B12+B13+B14+B15
Width:  9   Memory: 99 Last Col/Row:F18      ? for HELP
  1>
F1 = Help; F2 = Cancel; F9 = Plot; F10 = View                 CAPS
```

Figure 7.7 Credit Interest Spreadsheet: Exercise 7-2h

```
    |  A    ||   B    ||   C    ||   D    ||       E       ||   F    ||   G    |
 1                          MASTER
 2                 VISA     CHARGE     SEARS           TOTAL
 3            -------------------------------------------------
 4    JAN          5.95       8.96      9.74        B4+C4+D4
 5    FEB         12.06       8.84      9.98        B5+C5+D5
 6    MAR         13.31       8.23      9.62        B6+C6+D6
 7    APR         14.88       7.67      9.29        B7+C7+D7
 8    MAY         33.49       7.74      8.89        B8+C8+D8
 9    JUN         20.75       8.06      9.05        B9+C9+D9
10    JUL          23.1       8.04      9.37     B10+C10+D10
11    AUG         24.95       7.31     10.64     B11+C11+D11
12    SEP         26.71       7.45     11.59     B12+C12+D12
13    OCT         27.38       8.44     12.64     B13+C13+D13
14    NOV         27.89       7.96     12.48     B14+C14+D14
15    DEC          26.7        7.4      12.3     B15+C15+D15
16               ------     ------    ------          ------
17    TOTAL   3+B14+B153+C14+C153+D14+D15E12+E13+E14+E15
18               ======     ======    ======          ======
19
20
B17             Form=B4+B5+B6+B7+B8+B9+B10+B11+B12+B13+B14+B15
Width:  9   Memory: 99 Last Col/Row:F18      ? for HELP
  1>
F1 = Help; F2 = Cancel; F9 = Plot; F10 = View                 CAPS
```

3. a. /IR1:2
   b. /FR1:2,TL and press RETURN.
   In cell B1, enter **"BILL & CONNIE'S CREDIT CARD INTEREST**
   In cell B2, enter "   **FOR CALENDAR YEAR 1984**
   See Figure 7.8.

Figure 7.8 Credit Interest Spreadsheet: Exercise 7-3

```
   |  A     ||  B   ||  C   ||  D   ||     E      ||  F  ||  G  |
1            BILL & CONNIE'S CREDIT CARD INTEREST
2                   FOR CALENDAR YEAR 1984
3                          MASTER
4                   VISA   CHARGE    SEARS         TOTAL
5            -------------------------------------------
6   JAN             5.95     8.96     9.74         24.65
7   FEB            12.06     8.84     9.98         30.88
8   MAR            13.31     8.23     9.62         31.16
9   APR            14.88     7.67     9.29         31.84
10  MAY            33.49     7.74     8.89         50.12
11  JUN            20.75     8.06     9.05         37.86
12  JUL            23.10     8.04     9.37         40.51
13  AUG            24.95     7.31    10.64         42.90
14  SEP            26.71     7.45    11.59         45.75
15  OCT            27.38     8.44    12.64         48.46
16  NOV            27.89     7.96    12.48         48.33
17  DEC            26.70     7.40    12.30         46.40
18                ------   ------   ------        ------
19  TOTAL         257.17    96.10   125.59        478.86
20                ======   ======   ======        ======
A2
Width:   9   Memory: 99 Last Col/Row:F20      ? for HELP
  1>
F1 = Help; F2 = Cancel; F9 = Plot; F10 = View              CAPS
```

4. /PA1:E20 and press RETURN.
5. /GP to temporarily lift the protective shield. /UA1:E20 to actually remove the protection.
6. a. /SEX7-6,A
   b. /ZY

CHAPTER 8

Spreadsheet Input and Output

Chapter Overview and Objectives

- Saving Your Spreadsheet onto Disk
- Loading Your Spreadsheet from Disk
- Generating Other Spreadsheet Outputs
    - to your Printer
    - to your Console
    - to your Disk
- Deleting Disk Files from within SuperCalc^3

After completing Chapter 8 you'll know how to handle most types of SuperCalc^3 disk input and output. The most common use is the loading and saving of spreadsheets.

You'll learn how to construct a spreadsheet template from a series of partial loads. A template is a skeleton from which other spreadsheets are built. For example, a template for the Profit & Loss Statement would eliminate creating that kind of a spreadsheet from scratch at the start of each fiscal year.

You'll also learn how to generate printed output of the spreadsheet's display and contents.

Saving Spreadsheets onto Disk

By now you have used the /Save command several times to put your Profit & Loss spreadsheet onto a disk. Since these previous "saves" have been somewhat mechanical, you'll now learn the full structure and options of the /Save command.

Before going any further, make certain that your P&L spreadsheet has been loaded into memory.

Now invoke the /Save command by entering **/S.** The STATUS and ENTRY lines will display

Enter File Name (or <RETURN> for directory)

7>/Save,

You have the option of either specifying the filename under which you want the spreadsheet saved or requesting a directory of the files on disk.

After you've built a few spreadsheet files, you'll remember enough of the names to enter them immediately after /S. For the moment, however, press RETURN. You'll receive the display shown in Figure 8.1.

Figure 8.1 SuperCalc³ Directory Options Menu

```
SUPERCALC3 DIRECTORY OPTIONS MENU

Program drive:\directory is
    A:\
Data drive:\directory is
    B:\
Current spreadsheet file is : fig8-1.CAL

DATA DRIVE & DIRECTORY OPTIONS
    C(hange) data drive
    N(ew) to change or make directory
    D(isplay) all filenames
    S(ee) .CAL filenames & graph names

OTHER OPTIONS
    E(nter) filename
    G(raphs) - current spreadsheet

F2 to abort command or return to spreadsheet.



Enter C(hange), N(ew), D(isplay), S(ee), E(nter) or G(raphs)
  7>/Save,
F1 = Help; F2 = Cancel; F9 = Plot; F10 = View
```

It's called the SuperCalc³ Directory Options Menu and is also accessed via the /D(elete), /L(oad), /O(utput), /X(eXecute), and /Q(uit) commands. Its settings are defined as follows:

Program drive:\directory is Identifies the drive where the SuperCalc³ program files reside. This setting is made automatically when you boot SuperCalc³. It cannot be changed during a SuperCalc³ session.

Data drive:\directory is Identifies the drive to be accessed if no drive identifier is specified with a filename. This setting initially matches the Program drive setting. It can be changed at any time during a SuperCalc³ session via the C option.

Current spreadsheet file is : Identifies the last spreadsheet, .CAL file, brought into SuperCalc³ by the /L(oad) command. Prior to the first spreadsheet load in a given session, it is set to "NONE".

The Data Drive and Directory options are defined as follows:

C Changes the setting of the Data Drive. Make this change as soon as you finish booting SuperCalc³. This selection can be permanently set via the /Global,Keep command.

N Allows you to establish a new subdirectory or to change the existing subdirectory. This feature is available for DOS versions 2.0 and later.

Subdirectories are primarily used in multi-user situations, particularly for fixed disks. They minimize the potential for different people to accidentally damage each another's files by using the same naming conventions. Access by users would be restricted to a collection of files in their respective subdirectories. Novices working on single-user systems do not need this option. Refer to your DOS manual for more information on subdirectories.

D Provides a list of all files on the data drive. The format of this list is similar to the DOS command DIR /W. Pressing the SPACE BAR shows additional filenames then returns you to the Directory Options Menu.

S Provides the following detailed information about each spreadsheet (.CAL) file on the data drive:
Spreadsheet name and the version of SuperCalc that created it
Contents of cell A1
Each active graph and the associated graph type

Other available options:

E Prompts you to enter the filename. The default file extension is .CAL.

G Provides a list of active graphs for the current spreadsheet. The associated graph types are also listed.

The next step in the saving process is to set the data drive to the drive containing your data disk. Enter **C.** The PROMPT LINE will show

Enter drive or < – > for original program default:

Pressing B sets your data drive to drive B; all default file references will now go there. As soon as the setting is changed, the PROMPT LINE displays

Enter C(hange), N(ew), D(isplay), S(ee), E(nter) or G(raphs)

Now press D. SuperCalc displays a list of all files in your directory. The exact files shown will vary depending on what you have on the disk in drive B. Figure 8.2 illustrates the display. Press the SPACE BAR to return to the Directory Options Menu.

Again, the PROMPT LINE displays

Enter C(hange), N(ew), D(isplay), S(ee), E(nter) or G(raphs)

You are now ready to pick a filename to be saved, so enter E. You will be returned to the spreadsheet and the PROMPT and ENTRY lines will show

Enter File Name (or <RETURN> for directory)

7>/Save,

Now enter your filename; you should be using PALDEMO. You can enter the filename either with or without the file extension. SuperCalc³ will assume a file extension of .CAL, if you don't provide one. If you have any questions about filenames, refer to Chapter 2 or press F1 to get the AnswerScreen on filenames.

When you key the filename and press RETURN, SuperCalc³ checks the

Figure 8.2 Directory of Drive B Using the D Option

```
Files on            B:\
   COMMAND .com   A082684 .cal   FIG4-3   .cal   FIG4-2   .cal   FIG4-4   .cal
   FIG4-5  .cal   FIG4-6  .cal   FIG4-7   .cal   FIG4-8   .cal   FORMDEMO.cal
   FIG4-9  .cal   PALDEMO .cal   FIG4-12  .cal   EX4-10   .cal   FIG4-11  .cal
   FIG5-1  .cal   FIG5-2  .cal   FIG5-3   .cal   FIG5-4   .cal   FIG5-5   .cal
   TST5-7  .cal   FIG5-6  .cal   FIG5-7   .cal   FIG5-8   .cal   FIG5-9   .cal
   FIG5-10 .cal   EX5-8   .cal   FIG6-2   .cal   FIG6-3   .cal   FIG6-4   .cal
   FIG6-5  .cal   FIG6-6  .cal   FIG6-7   .cal   FIG6-8   .cal   FIG6-9   .cal
   FIG6-10 .cal   FIG6-11 .cal   FIG6-12  .cal   FIG6-15  .cal   FIG6-16  .cal
   FIG6-17 .cal   FIG6-18 .cal   FIG6-19  .cal   FIG6-20  .cal   FIG6-21  .cal
   FIG6-22 .cal   FIG6-24 .cal   FIG7-1   .cal   FIG7-2   .cal   FIG7-3   .cal
   FIG7-4  .cal   FIG7-5  .cal   FIG7-6   .cal   EX6-9    .cal   FIG7-8   .cal
   FIG7-7  .cal   FIG7-9  .cal   FIG7-10  .cal   EX7-6    .cal   CC053-A  .cal
   FIG1-3  .cal   PALDEMO .prn   PALDEMO  .bak   FIG8-3   .cal   FIG8-4   .cal
   FIG8-5  .cal   FIG8-6  .cal   FIG8-7   .cal   FIG8-8   .cal   FIG8-9   .cal
   FIG8-10 .cal   FIG8-25 .cal   FIG8-26  .cal   FIG8-27  .cal   EX8-9    .prn
   FIG1-3  .prn   FIG6-14 .cal   FIG6-16  .bak

Sub-directories on B:\
NONE


(F2)=abort,  (SP)=more...
  7>/Save,
F1 = Help; F2 = Cancel; F9 = Plot; F10 = View
```

directory of the disk on drive B to see if the file exists. If it does, the PROMPT LINE displays

File already exists: C(hange name), B(ackup) or O(verwrite)?

Your choices are defined as follows:

C Redisplays the original PROMPT and ENTRY lines so you can change the filename:

Enter File Name (or <RETURN> for directory)
7>/Save,

The save process continues if the new filename does not exist, otherwise the **File already exists** message is repeated.

B Renames the original disk file with a file extension of .BAK, then saves your spreadsheet with an extension of .CAL. Both files can be accessed later. For example, assume there was a file named SPRDSHT.CAL on drive B. Also assume that you wanted to save your current spreadsheet as SPRDSHT.CAL. If you specify the B option, B:SPRDSHT.CAL is renamed to B:SPRDSHT.BAK on disk. Your spreadsheet in memory is saved as B:SPRDSHT.CAL. If a .BAK file already exists when you enter the B option, it is deleted before the original .CAL file is renamed to a .BAK file.

O Writes the spreadsheet from memory over the file on disk. The previous contents of your disk file are destroyed. Use this option when you are correcting or updating a spreadsheet file. Once used, this option is irrevocable, so be careful! When in doubt, use the B option.

If the file is not currently on disk or if you have resolved the "file already exists" message, the next PROMPT LINE display is

A(ll), V(alues), or P(art)?

These options are defined as follows:

A Saves the entire spreadsheet. This includes cell contents, cell values, display formats, global settings, graph specifications, and current cell location. Also saved are any locked titles and split windows.

V Saves text as it is displayed. Also saves the displayed numeric cell values as numeric constants. These constants become the cell contents of the newly saved file. Formulas are not saved.

P Saves the specified range of cells from your spreadsheet. On specifying P(art), you will be prompted for
A(ll) or V(alues)?
These prompts mean the same as **A** and **V**, as defined above, except that their scope applies only to the cell range requested by the next prompt:
From? (Enter Range)

Demonstrations of Saving Spreadsheets

Try the following examples to increase your knowledge of saving files.

SAVE EXAMPLE NO. 1

Save the entire P&L under a new name PLDEMO2.CAL on your data drive. Your entry of **/S** results in PROMPT and ENTRY lines of
Enter File Name (or <RETURN> for directory)
7>/Save,
Key the filename on the ENTRY LINE and press RETURN. Now the PROMPT and ENTRY lines show
A(ll), V(alues), or P(art)?
19>/Save,PLDEMO2.CAL,
So enter **A.** The PROMPT LINE responds with
Saving . . .
When an empty ENTRY LINE is displayed, the save process has been completed.

SAVE EXAMPLE NO. 2

Save the entire P&L under the original name PALDEMO.CAL on your data drive. As before, your entry of **/S** results in PROMPT and ENTRY lines of
Enter File Name (or <RETURN> for directory)
7>/Save,

Since the filename to be used is the same filename under which the spreadsheet was loaded, just press the ESC key. Notice how the *current spreadsheet file* appears in your ENTRY LINE.

18>/Save,PALDEMO.CAL

Now press RETURN and the PROMPT LINE displays

File already exists: C(hange name), B(ackup) or O(verwrite)?

Enter C and the following is displayed:

Enter File Name (or <RETURN> for directory)

18>/Save,PALDEMO.CAL

You can use the directional arrows to move the entry line cursor so you can change the filename. For this time, just press RETURN. Again the PROMPT LINE displays

File already exists: C(hange name), B(ackup) or O(verwrite)?

Enter B and the PROMPT LINE shows:

A(ll), V(alues), or P(art)?

Press A. The PROMPT LINE responds with

Saving . . .

When an empty ENTRY LINE is displayed, the original spreadsheet has been renamed as PALDEMO.BAK and the spreadsheet in memory has been saved as PALDEMO.CAL.

SAVE EXAMPLE NO. 3

Save part of the P&L under the name PLDEMO2.CAL on your data drive. The entry of **/S** results in PROMPT and ENTRY lines of

Enter File Name (or <RETURN> for directory)

7>/Save,

Enter the filename PLDEMO2 and press RETURN. Now the PROMPT LINE displays

File already exists: C(hange name), B(ackup) or O(verwrite)?

Enter **O** and the following is displayed:

A(ll), V(alues), or P(art)?

Enter **P** and the PROMPT LINE responds with

A(ll) or V(alues)?

Enter **V** and you are prompted with

From? (Enter Range)

Enter A1:A19, then press RETURN and SuperCalc^3 responds with

Saving . . .

When an empty ENTRY LINE is displayed, the cell range A1 through A19 has overwritten PLDEMO2.CAL, destroying the previous contents of that file.

Save Errors

The following error messages may be encountered when using the /Save command:

Command aborted due to disk error

There are two possible reasons for this error message:

1. Either the drive door has been left open or there is no disk in the drive. Insert a disk, close the drive door, then try again.
2. The disk in your drive is write-protected—i.e., the write-enable notch is covered. Either put in the correct disk or remove the protective tape strip. Try again when ready.

Disk FULL, command aborted.
There is insufficient space available on disk to save the spreadsheet; the Save command is terminated. Insert a fresh disk with enough available space and repeat the save procedure.

Filename ERROR
The filename you entered is not in the proper format. Check your ENTRY LINE and make the necessary corrections. Repeat the save procedure by pressing RETURN.

File NOT on specified drive or directory
A nonexistent disk drive has been specified. SuperCalc[3] allows you to correct the error or cancel the /Save.

Loading Spreadsheets from Disk

By now you have used the /Load command a few times to bring your P&L spreadsheet into memory from disk. Since these previous "loads" have been somewhat mechanical, you will now learn the complete syntax of the /Load command.

Before proceeding further, clear memory via the /Zap command. This action is necessary because /Load only overlays those spreadsheet cells that have non-blank counterparts on the disk file. Cells in memory that don't have a non-blank match on the disk file are left intact. As you can guess, failure to use a /Zap when loading unrelated spreadsheets may result in a mixture of "apples and oranges." There will be times when you'll want to merge related spreadsheets and consequently would not use /Zap. Merging of spreadsheets will be covered later under the Consolidation option (p. 122).

Now invoke the /Load command by entering **/L**. The STATUS and ENTRY lines will display

Enter File Name (or <RETURN> for directory)
7>/Load,

You have the option of specifying either the spreadsheet filename to be loaded or requesting a directory of the files on disk. The procedure for obtaining a disk directory under the /Load command is identical to the directory procedure described for the /Save command in the previous section.

The next step in the loading process is to specify a filename. If you loaded PALDEMO.CAL at the beginning of the section on /Save and have not /Quit SuperCalc[3] in the interim, you can press ESC to capture the filename, otherwise you must key the filename into the ENTRY LINE. In either case, your spreadsheet PROMPT and ENTRY lines display

Enter File Name (or <RETURN> for directory)
18>/Load,PALDEMO.CAL

Don't forget to precede the filename by a disk drive identifier or use the Directory Options Menu to set the data drive. If you omit the file extension, SuperCalc³ will assume a file extension of .CAL. Refer to Chapter 2 or press F1 for more information on filenames.

After you press RETURN, SuperCalc³ checks the disk directory of the data drive to see if the file exists. Whether the file exists or not, the *current spreadsheet file* on the Directory Options Menu is updated to reflect the filename specified with the /Load command. If the filename is not found in the disk directory, the PROMPT LINE displays the error message

File NOT on specified drive or directory

For recovery action, see the section on /Load command error messages (p. 128).

If the filename is found in the disk's directory, the PROMPT LINE displays

A(ll), P(art), C(onsolidate) or * for graphs only

These options are defined as follows:

A Loads the entire spreadsheet exactly as it existed at the time it was last saved. This includes formats, global settings, and the current cell location.

C Algebraically adds corresponding non-blank cells of the disk file with the spreadsheet in memory. The Consolidate option is useful for merging P&L spreadsheets of several company divisions or subsidiaries into a spreadsheet for the parent company. When using this option, be careful to consolidate only spreadsheets that have identical layouts, albeit different numeric data. A consolidation of unrelated layouts would create meaningless information.

***graph number range** Loads one or more graph descriptions from a spreadsheet on disk. The specified graphs must be in the range 1 through 9.

P Loads the specified range of cells into your spreadsheet at the indicated point. Any settings that have been made via /Global,Keep are unaffected. On specifying P(art), you will be prompted for

From? (Enter Range)

After designating the cell range to be loaded from disk, you are prompted for

To? (Enter Cell)

A series of partial loads could be used to build a spreadsheet template. This technique is shown in the /Load command examples that follow this section.

P(ARTIAL LOAD) OPTIONS

There are two groups of options available for a partial load:

Formula Adjustment Options

These options have the same meanings as their /Replicate counterparts:

RETURN Causes automatic adjustment of all formulas.

N Suppresses adjustment of all formulas.

A Prompts for adjustment of cell references in each formula. An entry of **Y** to each prompt is the same as pressing RETURN for the automatic adjustment option. An entry of **N** to each prompt is the same as pressing N to suppress adjustment option.

V Loads the numeric value of the cell on the disk file into the spreadsheet as a numeric constant. Any text entries on the disk file are transferred intact.

Consolidation Arithmetic Options

These options have the same meanings as their /Replicate counterparts. The outcome of an arithmetic consolidation is dependent on whether the corresponding disk file cells and spreadsheet cells are blank or contain formulas. The following consolidation algorithm applies:

1. If the disk file cell is blank and the spreadsheet cell is blank, the consolidated cell is blank.
2. If the disk file cell is not blank and the spreadsheet cell is blank, the consolidated cell is blank.
3. If the disk file cell is blank and the spreadsheet cell is not blank, the consolidated cell has the contents of the spreadsheet cell.
4. If the disk file cell is numeric and the spreadsheet cell is numeric, the consolidated cell has contents resulting from the arithmetic operation.

The following arithmetic operations may be used for consolidation, subject to the above constraints:

+ Adds the value of the disk file cell to the value of the spreadsheet cell. The sum is stored in the spreadsheet cell as a numeric constant.

− Subtracts the value of the disk file cell from the value of the spreadsheet cell. The difference is stored in the spreadsheet cell as a numeric constant.

* Multiplies the value of the disk file cell by the value of the spreadsheet cell. The product is stored in the spreadsheet cell as a numeric constant.

/ Divides the value of the disk file cell into the value of the spreadsheet cell. The quotient is stored in the spreadsheet cell as a numeric constant.

Demonstrations of Loading Spreadsheets

Try the following examples to practice loading spreadsheet files.

LOAD EXAMPLE NO. 1

Clear memory and load the entire P&L spreadsheet. An entry of /**ZY** zaps everything that was in memory and /**L** produces the following PROMPT and ENTRY lines:

Enter File Name (or <RETURN> for directory)

7>/Load,

Key the filename on the ENTRY LINE and press RETURN. You may also press ESC and then press RETURN to use the current spreadsheet file. Whichever method you used, the ENTRY LINE should display

18>/Load,PALDEMO.CAL

After pressing RETURN the PROMPT LINE shows

A(ll), P(art) or C(onsolidate)?

Enter **A.** The PROMPT LINE responds with

Loading . . .

22>/Load,PALDEMO.CAL,All

When the loading process is completed, your screen will display a P&L spreadsheet similar to Figure 7.5 on page 109.

LOAD EXAMPLE NO. 2

Load an unrelated spreadsheet, FORMDEMO.CAL, on top of the P&L. This example demonstrates what happens when you forget to clear memory prior to a load. Enter /**L** to invoke the /Load command. Now key **FORMDEMO** and press RETURN. The PROMPT and ENTRY lines will display

A(ll), P(art) or C(onsolidate)?

16>/Load,FORMDEMO

Enter **A** and SuperCalc^3 responds with

Loading . . .

23>/Load,FORMDEMO.CAL,All

When the loading process is completed, your screen displays a garbled P&L spreadsheet similar to Figure 8.3.

You should also notice that the width of column A has changed from 20 positions to 9 positions. This is because the All option brings in all formats from the spreadsheet on disk. Such a load produces a meaningless screen display. Zap the entire spreadsheet in memory.

Figure 8.3 Garbage Load: FORMDEMO.CAL Overlaying PALDEMO.CAL

```
   |        A      ||       B      ||       C      ||       D       |
1             200            200   Bill's P & L Statement
2             123            200      Fiscal Year 1984
3            1235QTR #1           QTR #2           QTR #3
4          123457----------------            256
5    SALES                  5000             256             4500
6    COST OF GOODS SO       1500             512             1350
7            12345678--------                323--------
8    GROSS MARGIN           3500             122             3150
9                                             48
10   OPERATING EXPENSES
11     MARKETING            1000            1000             1000
12     ADMINISTRATIVE        500              26              450
13                 --------        --------        --------
14        TOTAL             1500            1026             1450
15
16   PRE-TAX PROFIT         2000            -904             1700
17   INCOME TAX             1000            -452              850
18                 --------        --------        --------
19   NET INCOME             1000            -452              850
20                 ========        ========        ========
 A8         P Text="GROSS MARGIN                          Protected Entry
Width: 16  Memory: 98 Last Col/Row:G20     ? for HELP
  1>
F1 = Help; F2 = Cancel; F9 = Plot; F10 = View
```

LOAD EXAMPLE NO. 3

This example demonstrates the Consolidation option using the P&L spreadsheet, PALDEMO.CAL. The P&L will be loaded three times to simulate the consolidation of subsidiaries A, B, and C into a Profit & Loss Statement for the parent company. To simplify these procedures, the instructions will be given without showing the prompts.

Step No. 1—Load Subsidiary A into the Consolidation
Enter **/LPALDEMO,A.** The entry of the comma has the same effect as pressing RETURN. When the load process for this step is completed, your screen will display a P&L spreadsheet similar to Figure 7.5. Note the following amounts in the P&L at the end of this first consolidation step:

Total Sales in cell F5 = $21,000
Total Net Income in cell F19 = $4,300

Step No. 2—Load Subsidiary B into the Consolidation
Enter **/LPALDEMO,C.** When the load process for this step is completed, your screen will display a P&L spreadsheet with all the dollar values doubled. Note the following amounts in the P&L at the end of this second consolidation step:

Total Sales in cell F5 = $42,000
Total Net Income in cell F19 = $8,600

Step No. 3—Load Subsidiary C into the Consolidation
Enter **/LPALDEMO,C.** When the load process for this step is completed, your screen will display a P&L spreadsheet similar to Figure 8.4.

Figure 8.4 P&L Spreadsheet: Consolidation Load

```
   |          A          ||    B    ||    C    ||    D    ||    E    ||    F    ||    G    |
1                                           Bill's P & L Statement
2                                              Fiscal Year 1984
3                             QTR #1    QTR #2    QTR #3    QTR #4     TOTAL
4                           --------------------------------------------------
5    SALES                  15000.00  12000.00  13500.00  22500.00  63000.00
6    COST OF GOODS SOLD      4500.00   3600.00   4050.00   6750.00  18900.00
7                           --------  --------  --------  --------  --------
8    GROSS MARGIN           10500.00   8400.00   9450.00  15750.00  44100.00
9
10   OPERATING EXPENSES
11     MARKETING             3000.00   3000.00   3000.00   3000.00  12000.00
12     ADMINISTRATIVE        1500.00   1200.00   1350.00   2250.00   6300.00
13                          --------  --------  --------  --------  --------
14        TOTAL              4500.00   4200.00   4350.00   5250.00  18300.00
15
16   PRE-TAX PROFIT          6000.00   4200.00   5100.00  10500.00  25800.00
17   INCOME TAX              3000.00   2100.00   2550.00   5250.00  12900.00
18                          --------  --------  --------  --------  --------
19   NET INCOME              3000.00   2100.00   2550.00   5250.00  12900.00
20                          ========  ========  ========  ========  ========
A1
Width: 20  Memory: 99 Last Col/Row:G20      ? for HELP
  1>
F1 = Help; F2 = Cancel; F9 = Plot; F10 = View               CAPS
```

Note the following amounts in the P&L at the end of this third consolidation step:

Total Sales in cell F5 = $63,000
Total Net Income in cell F19 = $12,900

All amounts have been tripled compared to the original P&L in Figure 7.5.

LOAD EXAMPLE NO. 4

This example demonstrates the Part option using consolidation arithmetic to "back out" a subsidiary from the Consolidated P&L. It is assumed that the Consolidated P&L from Load Example No. 3 is still in memory. Enter **/L** to invoke the /Load command. Now key the file name on the ENTRY LINE and press RETURN. The PROMPT and ENTRY lines will display

A(ll), P(art) or C(onsolidate)?
19>/Load,PALDEMO.CAL

Enter **P.** The PROMPT LINE responds with

From? (Enter Range)

Enter **B5:F19** and press RETURN since these cells are the block of cells to be subtracted from the consolidated P&L. Next, you are prompted with

To? (Enter Cell),then <Return> or <,> for Options
31>/Load,PALDEMO.CAL,Part,B5:F19,

Enter **B5,** to indicate the destination for the block of cells being loaded. The comma indicates that more options are needed. Now you are prompted for

N(o Adjust), A(sk for Adjust), V(alues), +, −, *, /
34>/Load,PALDEMO.CAL,Part,B5:F19,B5,

Enter **−** to indicate that the cell range being loaded is to be subtracted from the destination block starting at cell B5. When the load process is completed, your screen will display a P&L spreadsheet similar to Figure 8.5. Note the following amounts in the P&L after the consolidation arithmetic has taken place:

Total Sales in cell F5 = $42,000
Total Net Income in cell F19 = $8,600

Figure 8.5 P&L Spreadsheet: Partial Load Using Consolidation Arithmetic to Backout a Division

```
    |          A          ||    B    ||    C    ||    D    ||    E    ||    F    ||    G    |
1                                       Bill's P & L Statement
2                                            Fiscal Year 1984
3                              QTR #1    QTR #2    QTR #3    QTR #4     TOTAL
4                            --------------------------------------------------
5    SALES                    10000.00   8000.00   9000.00  15000.00  42000.00
6    COST OF GOODS SOLD        3000.00   2400.00   2700.00   4500.00  12600.00
7                             --------  --------  --------  --------  --------
8    GROSS MARGIN              7000.00   5600.00   6300.00  10500.00  29400.00
9
10   OPERATING EXPENSES
11     MARKETING               2000.00   2000.00   2000.00   2000.00   8000.00
12     ADMINISTRATIVE          1000.00    800.00    900.00   1500.00   4200.00
13                            --------  --------  --------  --------  --------
14         TOTAL               3000.00   2800.00   2900.00   3500.00  12200.00
15
16   PRE-TAX PROFIT            4000.00   2800.00   3400.00   7000.00  17200.00
17   INCOME TAX                2000.00   1400.00   1700.00   3500.00   8600.00
18                            --------  --------  --------  --------  --------
19   NET INCOME                2000.00   1400.00   1700.00   3500.00   8600.00
20                            ========  ========  ========  ========  ========
 A7
Width: 20   Memory: 99 Last Col/Row:G20       ? for HELP
  1>
F1 = Help; F2 = Cancel; F9 = Plot; F10 = View                    CAPS
```

The spreadsheet in memory now has amounts that are only twice those of the original P&L spreadsheet.

LOAD EXAMPLE NO. 5

This example demonstrates how to build a spreadsheet template via a series of partial loads. The template will be built from PALDEMO.CAL.

Step No. 1—Loading the Headings

First, zap the spreadsheet in memory via /ZY, then enter **/LPALDEMO,P.** The PROMPT LINE responds with

From? (Enter Range)

24>/Load,PALDEMO.CAL,Part,

Enter **A1:G4** and press RETURN. This identifies the cells containing the heading lines. Looking at the P&L, you might think the cell range A1 through H4 should have been used. Remember, however, that cell G4 contains a space to shut off the repeating text that started in cell B4. Next, you are prompted for

To? (Enter Cell),then <Return> or <,> for Options

30>/Load,PALDEMO.CAL,Part,A1:G4,

Enter **A1** and press RETURN to indicate the destination for the block of cells being loaded. The RETURN specifies that no options are needed.

Step No. 2—Loading the Line Captions

Enter **/LPALDEMO,P.** You are prompted for

From? (Enter Range)

24>/Load,PALDEMO.CAL,Part,

Enter **A5.A20** and press RETURN. This identifies the cells containing the line captions for column A. Next, you are prompted for

To? (Enter Cell),then <Return> or <,> for Options

31>/Load,PALDEMO.CAL,Part,A5.A20,

Enter **A5** and press RETURN to indicate the destination for the block of cells being loaded. The RETURN specifies that no options are needed.

Step No. 3—Loading the Total Column Formulas

Enter **/LPALDEMO,P.** Now you are prompted for

From? (Enter Range)

24>/Load,PALDEMO.CAL,Part,

Enter **F5.F20** and press RETURN. This identifies the cells containing the line total formulas for column F. Next, you are prompted for

To? (Enter Cell),then <Return> or <,> for Options

31>/Load,PALDEMO.CAL,Part,F5.F20,

Enter **F5** and press RETURN to indicate the destination for the block of cells being loaded. The RETURN specifies that no options are needed.

When you review the display, you'll notice that it doesn't have exactly the same format as the original P&L spreadsheet. This is because the formats of the **From** spreadsheet are not brought over with a partial load. If you want to fix up the display, enter the following commands:

/FCA,20	Expands column A width to 20 positions.
/FCB.F,TR	Right justifies text in columns B through F.
/RF7,B7.E7	Replicates the underlines in cell F7 to cells B7 through E7.
/CB7.E7,B13	Copies the underlines in cells B7 through E7 to cells B13 through E13.
/CB7.E7,B18	Copies the underlines in cells B7 through E7 to cells B18 through E18.
/RF20,B20.E20	Replicates the double underlines in cell F20 to cells B20 through E20.
/FCF,16	Expands column F width to 16 positions. This is done so the displayed formulas won't be truncated.
/GF	Toggles on formula display.

When you've finished the above patches, your template should look like Figure 8.6.

Figure 8.6 P&L Spreadsheet: Finished Template

```
   |         A          ||   B    ||   C    ||   D    ||   E    ||        F        |
1                                        Bill's P & L Statement
2                                           Fiscal Year 1984
3                              QTR #1    QTR #2    QTR #3    QTR #4             TOTAL
4                     -------------------------------------------------------------
5    SALES                                                              B5+C5+D5+E5
6    COST OF GOODS SOLD                                                 B6+C6+D6+E6
7                       --------  --------  --------  --------             --------
8    GROSS MARGIN                                                       B8+C8+D8+E8
9
10   OPERATING EXPENSES
11     MARKETING                                                    B11+C11+D11+E11
12     ADMINISTRATIVE                                               B12+C12+D12+E12
13                      --------  --------  --------  --------             --------
14        TOTAL                                                     B14+C14+D14+E14
15
16   PRE-TAX PROFIT                                                 B16+C16+D16+E16
17   INCOME TAX                                                     B17+C17+D17+E17
18                      --------  --------  --------  --------             --------
19   NET INCOME                                                     B19+C19+D19+E19
20                      ========  ========  ========  ========             ========
 A1
Width: 20   Memory: 99 Last Col/Row:G20      ? for HELP
  1>
F1 = Help; F2 = Cancel; F9 = Plot; F10 = View                   CAPS
```

Load Errors

The following error messages could be encountered when using the /Load command:

Command aborted due to disk error

There are two possible reasons for this error message. Either the drive door has been left open or there is no disk in the drive. Insert a disk and close the drive door, then try again.

Filename ERROR

The filename you entered is not in the proper format. Check your ENTRY LINE and make the necessary corrections. Repeat the load procedure by pressing RETURN.

File not loadable

The filename specified exists on disk, but it is not in SuperCalc³ format. Try doing a directory of SuperCalc³ files to see if that's really the filename you should be using.

File NOT on specified drive or directory

The filename specified does not exist on the specified disk drive. Some possible causes for this error are:

1. The disk drive identifier has been omitted from either the /Load command or from the /Save command when the file was created. Try doing a disk directory on both drives.
2. The filename has been spelled wrong on either the current /Load command or on the /Save command when the file was created. Try doing a disk directory of the SuperCalc³ files on the data drive.
3. A nonexistent disk drive has been specified. SuperCalc³ allows you to correct the error or cancel the /Load.

Deleting Spreadsheets from Disk

Sometimes it's necessary to remove a spreadsheet from disk. You should periodically delete obsolete or erroneous files to free up disk space. Although the ERASE command can do this at operating system level, SuperCalc³ also has the capability with the /Delete command.

When deleting files, by whatever command, it's very important that the filename specified is really the file you want deleted. Once a file has been deleted, it can't be recovered unless you have it backed up under another name or on another disk.

The contents of memory are not affected by the /Delete command. This command is invoked by entering **/D.** The STATUS and ENTRY lines display

R(ow), C(olumn) or F(ile)
9>/Delete,

Press F to indicate that a file is to be deleted. Now the STATUS and ENTRY lines display

Enter File Name (or <RETURN> for directory)
14>/Delete, File,

Like the /Save and /Load commands, you have the option of either specifying the filename or requesting a directory of the files on disk.

Since /Delete is a destructive command, you can't be too careful. First, press RETURN to get the directory menu. Next, set the data drive and use the D option to get a directory listing of all files on disk.

From the directory display, choose the file to be deleted. In this demonstration, use B:PLDEMO2.CAL. Now press the space bar to return to the Directory Display Menu. When you're ready to input the name, press E. You are prompted with

Enter File Name (or <RETURN> for directory)
14>/Delete,File,

Now enter your filename. Precede it by the drive identifier if you want to access a drive other than the data drive. If you omit the file extension, SuperCalc³ will assume a file extension of .CAL. Since the /Delete command can erase any kind of file, an extension must be provided for files other than .CAL files—e.g., .BAK, .PRN, and .XQT.

Refer to Chapter 2 for more information on filenames and file extensions. You can also press F1 to get the AnswerScreen on filenames.

When you've finished entering your filename, the PROMPT and ENTRY lines should look like this:

Enter File Name (or <RETURN> for directory)
21>/Delete,File,PLDEMO2

After you press RETURN, SuperCalc³ checks the directory of the data drive to see if the file exists. If it does, the file is deleted and an empty ENTRY LINE is displayed. If the file does not exist, the PROMPT displays the error message

File NOT on specified drive or directory

For recovery action on this error, see the section on /Delete command error messages, which follows.

Delete Errors

The following error messages could be encountered when using the /Delete command:

Command aborted due to disk error

There are two possible reasons for this error message:

1. Either the drive door has been left open or there is no disk in the drive. Insert a disk and close the drive door, then try again.
2. The disk in your drive is write-protected—i.e., the write-enable notch is covered. Either put in the correct disk or remove the protective tape strip. Try again when ready.

Filename ERROR

The filename you entered is not in the proper format. Check your ENTRY LINE and make the necessary corrections. Repeat the delete procedure by pressing RETURN.

File NOT on specified drive or directory

The filename you entered is not on the specified disk drive. Some possible reasons for this error are:

1. The disk drive identifier has been omitted from either the /Delete command or from the /Save command when the file was created. Try doing a disk directory on both drives.
2. The filename has been spelled wrong on either the current /Delete command or on the /Save command when the file was created. Try doing a disk directory of the SuperCalc³ files on the data drive.

Generating Output from Spreadsheets

This section shows you how to create different types of output from your spreadsheet. Here are some examples of output:

- *Printed output, also known as "hard copy"*. Generally, you can't give your boss a handful of disks containing the monthly reports. Printed reports can be copied and distributed without requiring the recipient to have access to a personal computer.
- *Disk output*. This type of output generates .PRN files in ASCII format and has several uses.

  You can generate .PRN files for extremely wide spreadsheets. These files can be printed at operating system level using the SIDEWAYS command. This capability eliminates "cutting and pasting."

  If you don't have a printer, you can use this option to generate your reports on disk. Later, you can print them on another personal computer, same class as yours, that has a printer. To do this, use the operating system's PRINT command.

  The generated .PRN files can be merged with other reports on a word processor. For example, this option allows you to merge a Profit & Loss spreadsheet created by SuperCalc³ with a P&L analysis created in SuperWriter, EasyWriter I, and EasyWriter II.

You can use this option to generate .XQT files containing "Slash" commands. These files save you from keying in repetitive commands. They are used by the /eXecute command.

- *Output to your console.* Sometimes you need to see how your output looks before you print it or write it to disk. This option is helpful when you don't have a printer. You can use it to verify that your report is correct. Next, you would put the report on disk. Then, when you have a chance, you could print it on a friend's printer. The Console option avoids surprises when you finally get a printed copy.

The above examples of output are all generated by the /Output command.

Entering **/O** invokes the /Output command. The STATUS and ENTRY lines display

D(isplay) or C(ontents) report?

9>/Output,

This first option prompt pertains to the output mode:

D	Outputs the spreadsheet exactly as it is displayed on your video screen. This includes all formats and global settings. This option would be used to generate a formal report from your spreadsheet.
C	Outputs a list of cell contents. This list displays one cell per line. It includes such information as: the actual contents; an indication if the cell is protected; the display format if one has been set at cell level. Global, row, and column formats are not shown. This option would be used to generate a "dump" of your spreadsheet for back-up purposes. You could use it to rebuild the spreadsheet if your disk was destroyed.

When you select an output mode and press either D or C, you are prompted for the cell range to be output. You can enter a cell, a block of cells, or **ALL** if the entire spreadsheet is to be output.

If you are using the D option output and your spreadsheet's rightmost column has cell overflow for left justified text, include an extra column in your cell range. For example, assume that column G is nine positions wide. Assume that there are some cells with left justified text entries longer than nine positions. Also assume that this hypothetical spreadsheet contains entries in cell A1 through G20. If you enter **ALL** as the output cell range, truncation will occur on those entries that overflow into column H. Truncation will also happen if you enter an output cell range of **A1:G20.** This output truncation problem can be eliminated by using the cell range **A1:H20.**

Once you specify an output cell and press either "," or RETURN, you are prompted for output device options:

P(rinter), S(etup), C(onsole), or D(isk)?

These options are defined as follows:

P Sends your output to your printer. See the S option for information about page dimensions. SuperCalc³ prints as many whole columns as will fit on one page. Any columns that exceed the page width are printed on the next page.

S Allows you to set printing parameters. You can make these settings applicable to the current session only, or you can update them into the SuperCalc³ program by /Global,Keep. After being updated into SuperCalc³, they apply to all future sessions until you change them.

C Sends your output to your console's video screen. This option enables you to preview your reports prior to printing them. As indicated previously, the C option is particularly useful for reviewing reports before they are written to disk.

D Generates an ASCII output file using .PRN as the default file extension. As with the /Save command, the ESC key can be pressed to specify the name of the last file that was load-ed. If you use the ESC feature to get the name of the current spreadsheet file, erase the .CAL file extension or change it to .PRN.

When prompted for a filename, you can press RETURN to get a disk directory. The procedure is the same as that described for /Load, /Save, /Delete with the File option, and /Quit with the To option.

If the output filename currently exists, you get the following prompt:

File already exists: C(hange name), B(ackup) or O(verwrite)?

which allows you to

- Change the name on the ENTRY LINE, or
- Rename the file on disk as a .BAK file and create an output file using the name specified in the ENTRY LINE, or
- Create an output file that overwrites the matching filename on disk, destroying its contents.

Refer to the section on the /Save command for additional information on the C, B, and O options. Files that have been created as .PRN files cannot be /Load-ed into a spreadsheet since they are in an ASCII format rather than the compressed binary format of .CAL files. Attempts to do this result in a *File not loadable* error message.

When you select the /Output Setup option, you are presented with a setup menu. You can specify the following:

L Sets the page length. The default setting is 66 lines per page. The valid range of entries is 0 through 255. An entry of 0 prints continuously with no top or bottom page margins. This entry would be used for printers using rolled paper instead of fan-fold paper.

A recommendation is to set your page length at 60. Also, each time you power up your printer set your Top Of Forms (TOF) 3 lines down from the top of the page. This gives you a three-line margin at the top and bottom of each page. It results in nicely framed output reports when full page printed output is done.

W Sets the line width. The default setting is 132 characters per line. The valid range of entries is 0 through 255. The width specified here is for output only; it has no effect on the line width displayed on your screen display.

If you want to direct output to a disk file, the line width for the disk output can be specified via this option. However, since there is no provision for starting disk output from this menu level, press F2 after setting the width. This will return you to the spreadsheet where you can re-issue the /Output command and specify the Disk option.

N This option allows you to select a new border character. The default border character is the vertical rule (|). You would use this option if your printer couldn't print |. In this situation, the colon (:) is suggested as a border character.

A This is a toggle switch for automatic form feed. The default setting is off. When auto form feed is toggled off, the space bar must be pressed after each page is printed to continue the printing operation. When auto form feed is toggled on, the print operation is done start to finish without interruption.

B This is a toggle switch to control printing of borders. There are three settings; pressing B rolls you through them.

Now matches display Prints borders if they are toggled on by /GB. Does not print borders if they are toggled off by /GB. This is the default setting.

On Always prints borders, regardless of the /GB setting.

Off Never prints borders, regardless of the /GB setting.

D This is a toggle switch for single or double line spacing. When double spacing is toggled on, there is a blank line between each printed row.

When double spacing is toggled off, single spacing is used. This means the spreadsheet rows print consecutively with no intervening blank lines. The default setting is off for single spacing.

E This is a toggle switch for generating end-of-line control characters.

On A line feed and a carriage return are sent to the printer. This is the default setting.

Off Only a carriage return is sent to the printer.

The setting to be used is determined by your printer. If you make the wrong setting, you'll know as soon as you try to print:

- Double spacing when the D option is set to off means option E is toggled on when it should be toggled off.
- Over-printing with no line advance means option E is toggled off when it should be toggled on.

S Allows you to set up a control sequence to use some of your printer's special functions such as:

Compressed print Shift from a character density of 10 characters per inch (cpi) to 17 cpi. You would use this feature to print 132 characters on an 8.5-inch physical line width.

Boldface print Print style where characters are thicker and darker. You would generally use boldface for spreadsheet headings. It could also be used to do an entire spreadsheet if you wanted to make overhead transparencies from the printed output.

Elongated print Print style where characters are twice their normal width for the character density. You would probably use elongated print only for spreadsheet headings. When using this feature, be sure to position your heading text an extra word width to the left to allow for proper centering.

When using the boldface and elongated print features for headings, you should use the following procedure:

1. Toggle off automatic form feed.
2. Toggle off border print.
3. Set the control sequence for boldface or elongated printing.
4. Output only the cell range for printing the report headings.
5. Turn off the control sequence for boldface or elongated printing.
6. Output the cell range for printing the body of the report.
7. Toggle on automatic form feed.

The control sequences used in the setup procedure vary from printer to printer. Also, older printers may not have all or any of the above features.

The demonstrations provided later in this section use a C. ITOH model 8510A PROWRITER. The control sequences can be entered using either the actual ASCII character or the associated ASCII decimal value preceded by a backslash (\ ). For example, compressed print mode on the C.ITOH 8510 is set by ESC Q. This setting can be entered in either of two ways:

1. Pressing ESC Q, then pressing RETURN.
2. \ 27 \ 81, then pressing RETURN.

P Prints your report on the printer using the setup parameters established above.

R Retains the control character sequence for the entire session. When the control sequence is retained, it can also be updated into SuperCalc³ by /GK so that it applies to all future sessions.

Demonstrations of Outputting Spreadsheets

The following examples generate output from your P&L spreadsheet, so make sure it's loaded before you go any further.

OUTPUT EXAMPLE NO. 1

This example prints the entire P&L spreadsheet. Enter **/O** and the PROMPT and ENTRY lines respond with

D(isplay) or C(ontents) report?

9>/Output,

Enter **D** to select the report as displayed on your screen. The PROMPT and ENTRY lines respond with

Enter Range

17>/Output,Display,

Enter **ALL** to specify that the entire spreadsheet is to be output, then press either the RETURN or comma (,) keys. The PROMPT and ENTRY lines respond with

P(rinter), S(etup), C(onsole), or D(isk)?

21>/Output,Display,ALL,

Press P to send the spreadsheet directly to your printer. While the spreadsheet is printing, the following message is displayed near the bottom of your screen:

Enter F2 to STOP print

When the printing is complete, another message is displayed:

End of Report . . . Press a key to continue

Since the key pressed terminates the /Output, it's a good habit to press the SPACE bar. If you try to start another "Slash" command at this point, the / will be interpreted as the continuation character and will be lost. You'll get meaningless characters on your ENTRY LINE.

Now follow whatever procedures are necessary to advance the paper in your printer and tear off the printed page. It should look like Figure 8.7.

Figure 8.7 P&L Spreadsheet: Output Display of Cells A1.F20 to Printer

```
  |        A         ||    B    ||    C    ||    D    ||    E    ||    F    |
1                                     Bill's P & L Statement
2                                        Fiscal Year 1984
3                          QTR #1     QTR #2     QTR #3     QTR #4      TOTAL
4                        -------------------------------------------------
5    SALES                5000.00    4000.00    4500.00    7500.00  21000.00
6    COST OF GOODS SOLD   1500.00    1200.00    1350.00    2250.00   6300.00
7                        --------   --------   --------   --------  --------
8    GROSS MARGIN         3500.00    2800.00    3150.00    5250.00  14700.00
9
10   OPERATING EXPENSES
11     MARKETING          1000.00    1000.00    1000.00    1000.00   4000.00
12     ADMINISTRATIVE      500.00     400.00     450.00     750.00   2100.00
13                       --------   --------   --------   --------  --------
14        TOTAL           1500.00    1400.00    1450.00    1750.00   6100.00
15
16   PRE-TAX PROFIT       2000.00    1400.00    1700.00    3500.00   8600.00
17   INCOME TAX           1000.00     700.00     850.00    1750.00   4300.00
18                       --------   --------   --------   --------  --------
19   NET INCOME           1000.00     700.00     850.00    1750.00   4300.00
20                       ========   ========   ========   ========  ========
```

OUTPUT EXAMPLE NO. 2

This example outputs the entire P&L spreadsheet to your console. First, get to the Setup Printer Menu by entering **/ODALL,S.** The PROMPT and ENTRY lines will show:

Length,Width,New,Border,Auto FF,Double Space,End LF,Set,Retain, or Print?
27>/Output,Display,ALL,Setup

Press B to toggle the borders to OFF. Since you can't use the console option from the Printer Setup Menu, press F2 to cancel the /Output command. Next, enter **/ODALL,C.** The output will be displayed on your console a full screen at a time. The last line of the screen displays the message:

End of Report . . . Press a key to continue

Your console output should look like Figure 8.8.

Figure 8.8 P&L Spreadsheet: Output Display of Cells A1.F20 to Console

```
                                   Bill's P & L Statement
                                      Fiscal Year 1984
                        QTR #1     QTR #2     QTR #3     QTR #4      TOTAL
                      -------------------------------------------------
SALES                  5000.00    4000.00    4500.00    7500.00  21000.00
COST OF GOODS SOLD     1500.00    1200.00    1350.00    2250.00   6300.00
                      --------   --------   --------   --------  --------
GROSS MARGIN           3500.00    2800.00    3150.00    5250.00  14700.00

OPERATING EXPENSES
  MARKETING            1000.00    1000.00    1000.00    1000.00   4000.00
  ADMINISTRATIVE        500.00     400.00     450.00     750.00   2100.00
                      --------   --------   --------   --------  --------
     TOTAL             1500.00    1400.00    1450.00    1750.00   6100.00

PRE-TAX PROFIT         2000.00    1400.00    1700.00    3500.00   8600.00
INCOME TAX             1000.00     700.00     850.00    1750.00   4300.00
                      --------   --------   --------   --------  --------
NET INCOME             1000.00     700.00     850.00    1750.00   4300.00
                      ========   ========   ========   ========  ========

End of Report...Press a key to continue

F1 = Help; F2 = Cancel; F9 = Plot; F10 = View                    CAPS
```

Press the SPACE bar to return to the spreadsheet. You can reset the Setup Printer Menu so the border output matches the display by entering **/ODALL,SBB**, then pressing F2.

OUTPUT EXAMPLE NO. 3

This example outputs a contents listing for cells A1 through F10 of your P&L spreadsheet to the printer. It outputs the cell contents regardless of the current display format. Enter **/OC** and the PROMPT and ENTRY lines respond with

Enter range

18>/Output, Contents,

Enter **A1.F10** to specify a contents list for the first half of the spreadsheet, then press either the RETURN or comma (,) keys. The PROMPT and ENTRY lines display:

P(rinter), S(etup), C(onsole), or D(isk)?

25>/Output,Contents,A1:F10,

Press P to output the contents list to your printer. While the spreadsheet is printing, the following message is displayed near the bottom of your screen:

Enter F2 to STOP print

When the printing completes, SuperCalc^3 displays

End of Report . . . Press a key to continue

Press the SPACE bar to return to the spreadsheet and remove the output page from your printer. It should look like Figure 8.9. Notice that the output is sequenced as column within row. This means that all non-blank columns for a given row are printed before moving onto the next row. Wherever P precedes the =, it indicates that the cell is Protected. The TL shown for cells C1, C2, and B4 means those cells have an entry level format of left justified text.

Figure 8.9 P&L Spreadsheet: Output Contents of Cells A1.F10 to Printer

```
SuperCalc ver.  2.00

C1 ITL   P= "   Bill's P & L Statement
C2 ITL   P= "       Fiscal Year 1984
B3       P= "QTR #1
C3       P= "QTR #2
D3       P= "QTR #3
E3       P= "QTR #4
F3       P= "TOTAL
B4 TL     = '-
A5       P= "SALES
B5        = 5000
C5        = 4000
D5        = 4500
E5        = 7500
F5        = B5+C5+D5+E5
A6       P= "COST OF GOODS SOLD
B6        = 30%B5
C6        = 30%C5
D6        = 30%D5
E6        = 30%E5
F6        = B6+C6+D6+E6
B7        = "--------
C7        = "--------
D7        = "--------
E7        = "--------
F7        = "--------
A8       P= "GROSS MARGIN
B8        = B5-B6
C8        = C5-C6
D8        = D5-D6
E8        = E5-E6
F8        = B8+C8+D8+E8
A10       P= "OPERATING EXPENSES
```

OUTPUT EXAMPLE NO. 4

This example demonstrates the effects of trying to print a report with a width of 128 positions on an 80 position line. Enter the following preliminary commands:

/GF	To toggle on formula display.
/FCB.F,17	To set the column width to 17 positions for columns B through F.

Access the Printer Setup Menu by entering **/ODALL,S.** The PROMPT and ENTRY lines display

Length,Width,New,Border,Auto FF,Double Space,End LF,Set,Retain, or Print?
27>/Output,Display,ALL,Setup

This example requires the following menu settings:

Length of page: 60
Width of page: 80
Automatic form feed: On

If your menu is not set accordingly, the steps below will show you how to do it.

1. Set page length to 60. Press L. When you are prompted with
   Enter number (0-255), then return.
   Enter 60 and press RETURN. You will see the new page length updated into the menu.
2. Set page width to 80. Press W. When you are prompted with
   Enter number (0-255), then return.
   Enter 80 and press RETURN. You will see the new page width updated into the menu.
3. Set automatic form feed. Press A to toggle ON automatic form feed.

The resulting Printer Setup Menu should match Figure 8.10.

Figure 8.10 Setup Printer Menu

```
SETUP PRINTER MENU
L = Length of page [0 = continuous form]
    (now  60 lines)
W = Width of page
    (now  80 chars)
N = New border character
    (now !)
B = toggle Border
    (now matches display)
A = toggle Auto-form-feed
    (now ON )
D = toggle Double space
    (now OFF)
E = toggle End-line-feed
    (now ON )
S = Set printer control codes
Current control codes are:

R = Retain printer control codes for session
P = Print report

A1
Length,Width,New,Border,Auto FF,Double Space,End LF,Set,Retain,or Print?
 27>/Output,Display,ALL,Setup,
F1 = Help; F2 = Cancel; F9 = Plot; F10 = View                  CAPS
```

Press P to start printing your report. While the spreadsheet is printing, the following message is displayed near the bottom of your screen:

Enter F2 to STOP print

When the printing is complete, SuperCalc³ displays

End of Report . . . Press a key to continue

Press the SPACE bar to return to the spreadsheet and remove the output page from your printer. It should look like Figure 8.11, parts A and B.

Figure 8.11A **P&L Spreadsheet: Output Display of Cells A1.F20 with Wrap-around, First Half**

```
    :        A          ::     B      ::    C       ::      D    :
1                                    Bill's P & L Statement
2                                       Fiscal Year 1984
3                                  QTR #1        QTR #2        QTR #3
4                  ---------------------------------------------------
5   SALES                            5000          4000          4500
6   COST OF GOODS SOLD              30%B5         30%C5         30%D5
7                                ---------     ---------     ---------
8   GROSS MARGIN                    B5-B6         C5-C6         D5-D6
9
10  OPERATING EXPENSES
11    MARKETING                      1000          1000          1000
12    ADMINISTRATIVE                10%B5         10%C5         10%D5
13                               ---------     ---------     ---------
14       TOTAL                    B11+B12       C11+C12       D11+D12
15
16  PRE-TAX PROFIT                 B8-B14        C8-C14        D8-D14
17  INCOME TAX                     50%B16        50%C16        50%D16
18                               ---------     ---------     ---------
19  NET INCOME                    B16-B17       C16-C17       D16-D17
20                               ========      ========      ========
```

Figure 8.11B **P&L Spreadsheet: Output Display of Cells A1.F20 with Wrap-around, Second Half**

```
     :      E      ::       F       ::  G  :
1
2
3         QTR #4          TOTAL
4   ---------------------------------
5           7500    B5+C5+D5+E5
6          30%E5    B6+C6+D6+E6
7       ---------     ---------
8          E5-E6    B8+C8+D8+E8
9
10
11          1000  B11+C11+D11+E11
12         10%E5  B12+C12+D12+E12
13      ---------     ---------
14       E11+E12  B14+C14+D14+E14
15
16        E8-E14  B16+C16+D16+E16
17        50%E16  B17+C17+D17+E17
18      ---------     ---------
19       E16-E17  B19+C19+D19+E19
20      ========      ========
```

Notice that page 1 of your report contains columns A through D, while page 2 contains columns E and F. This is the wrap-around feature of SuperCalc³ whereby excess columns are wrapped onto a succeeding page. The Auto Form Feed On setting caused an automatic advance to the top of the next page prior to printing cells E1 through F20.

OUTPUT EXAMPLE NO. 5

This example demonstrates how to use the Setup option to specify compressed print. This enables you to output 132 characters to an 8-inch physical line.

Access the Printer Setup Menu by entering **/ODALL,S.** The PROMPT and ENTRY lines display

Length,Width,New,Border,Auto FF,Double Space,End LF,Set,Retain, or Print?
27>/Output,Display,ALL,Setup

Press W. When you are prompted with

Enter number (0-255), then return.

Enter 132 and press RETURN. You will see the new line width updated into the menu. Press S to specify a control sequence for your printer. When you are prompted with

Use arrow keys to edit, any other character to start fresh.

Enter the control sequence for your printer that selects the compressed print mode (17 cpi) and press RETURN. You will see the control characters appear under the setup line:

Current control codes are:

The control sequence used to generate the demonstration output for a C. ITOH model 8510A printer is ESC Q. No spaces should separate the control characters. Press P to start printing your report. While the spreadsheet is printing, the following message is displayed near the bottom of your screen:

Enter F2 to STOP print

When the printing is complete, SuperCalc³ displays

End of Report . . . Press a key to continue

Press the SPACE bar to return to the spreadsheet and remove the page from your printer. It should look like Figure 8.12. Notice that columns A through F printed on the same page.

Figure 8.12 P&L Spreadsheet: Output Display of Cells A1.F20 Using Compressed Print

	A	B	C	D	E	F	G
1			Bill's P & L Statement				
2			Fiscal Year 1984				
3		QTR #1	QTR #2	QTR #3	QTR #4	TOTAL	
4	------------------------	------------------------	------------------------	------------------------	------------------------	------------------------	
5	SALES	5000	4000	4500	7500	B5+C5+D5+E5	
6	COST OF GOODS SOLD	30%B5	30%C5	30%D5	30%E5	B6+C6+D6+E6	
7		--------	--------	--------	--------	--------	
8	GROSS MARGIN	B5-B6	C5-C6	D5-D6	E5-E6	B8+C8+D8+E8	
9							
10	OPERATING EXPENSES						
11	MARKETING	1000	1000	1000	1000	B11+C11+D11+E11	
12	ADMINISTRATIVE	10%B5	10%C5	10%D5	10%E5	B12+C12+D12+E12	
13		--------	--------	--------	--------	--------	
14	TOTAL	B11+B12	C11+C12	D11+D12	E11+E12	B14+C14+D14+E14	
15							
16	PRE-TAX PROFIT	B8-B14	C8-C14	D8-D14	E8-E14	B16+C16+D16+E16	
17	INCOME TAX	50%B16	50%C16	50%D16	50%E16	B17+C17+D17+E17	
18		--------	--------	--------	--------	--------	
19	NET INCOME	B16-B17	C16-C17	D16-D17	E16-E17	B19+C19+D19+E19	
20		========	========	========	========	========	

OUTPUT EXAMPLE NO. 6

This example demonstrates how to use the Setup option to turn off compressed print and also how to get boldfaced headings. Enter the following preliminary commands:

/GF	To toggle off formula display.
/FCB:F,9	To set the column width to 9 positions for columns B through F.

Access the Printer Setup Menu by entering **/ODA1.F3,S.** The PROMPT and ENTRY lines display

Length,Width,New,Border,Auto FF,Double Space,End LF,Set,Retain, or Print?
29>/Output,Display,A1.F3,Setup,

Press B to toggle off border output. Press A to toggle off automatic form feed. Press W. When you are prompted with

Enter number (0-255), then return.

Enter 80 and press RETURN. Press S to specify a control sequence for your printer. When you are prompted with

Use arrow keys to edit, any other character to start fresh.

Enter the control sequences for your printer that turn off compressed print and select boldfaced print, then press RETURN. You will see the control characters appear under the setup line:

Current control codes are:

The control sequences to generate the demonstration output for a C. ITOH model 8510A printer are ESC N and ESC !. No spaces should separate the characters. Enter the control sequences for your printer, then press RETURN. Press P to start printing your report. While the spreadsheet is printing, the following message is displayed near the bottom of your screen:

Enter F2 to STOP print

When the printing is complete, SuperCalc[3] displays

End of Report . . . Press a key to continue

Press the SPACE bar to return to the spreadsheet. Do not disturb the printed page yet. You still need to generate output for the body of the P&L. Now enter **/ODA4.F20,S.** The PROMPT and ENTRY lines display

Length,Width,New,Border,Auto FF,Double Space,End LF,Set,Retain, or Print?
30>/Output,Display,A4.F20,Setup,

Press A to toggle on automatic form feed. Press S to specify a control sequence for your printer. When you are prompted with

Use arrow keys to edit, any other character to start fresh.

enter the control sequences for your printer that turn off boldfaced print, then press RETURN. You will see the control characters appear under the setup line:

Current control codes are:

The control sequence to generate the demonstration output for a C. ITOH model 8510A printer is ESC ". No spaces should separate the characters. Enter the control sequences for your printer, then press RETURN.

Press P to start printing your report. While the spreadsheet is printing, the following message is displayed near the bottom of your screen:

Enter F2 to STOP print

When the printing is complete, SuperCalc³ displays

End of Report . . . Press a key to continue

Press the SPACE bar to return to the spreadsheet. Now remove the printed page from the printer. Your output should look like Figure 8.13.

Figure 8.13 P&L Spreadsheet: Output Display Using Boldfaced Headings

```
                                  Bill's P & L Statement
                                    Fiscal Year 1984
                           QTR #1   QTR #2   QTR #3   QTR #4     TOTAL
                         -----------------------------------------------
SALES                    5000.00  4000.00  4500.00  7500.00  21000.00
COST OF GOODS SOLD       1500.00  1200.00  1350.00  2250.00   6300.00
                         -------- -------- -------- -------- --------
GROSS MARGIN             3500.00  2800.00  3150.00  5250.00  14700.00

OPERATING EXPENSES
  MARKETING              1000.00  1000.00  1000.00  1000.00   4000.00
  ADMINISTRATIVE          500.00   400.00   450.00   750.00   2100.00
                         -------- -------- -------- -------- --------
     TOTAL               1500.00  1400.00  1450.00  1750.00   6100.00

PRE-TAX PROFIT           2000.00  1400.00  1700.00  3500.00   8600.00
INCOME TAX               1000.00   700.00   850.00  1750.00   4300.00
                         -------- -------- -------- -------- --------
NET INCOME               1000.00   700.00   850.00  1750.00   4300.00
                         ======== ======== ======== ======== ========
```

OUTPUT EXAMPLE NO. 7

This example outputs the entire P&L spreadsheet to disk and also shows you how to use the SIDEWAYS utility. Enter **/ODALL,D.** The PROMPT and ENTRY lines respond with

Enter File Name (or <RETURN> for directory)

26>/Output,Display,ALL,Disk,

Enter a filename, then press RETURN and the spreadsheet display will be output to the data disk as an ASCII formatted file. A suggestion—use the same filename as the original spreadsheet file, omitting the file extension. Pressing the ESC key in this example results in a disk output file that is named PALDEMO.PRN. This file is easily associated with the spreadsheet file PALDEMO.CAL.

After exiting SuperCalc³ you can easily verify that output occurred properly by using the operating system's TYPE command to display the file on your screen:

TYPE B:PALDEMO.PRN

You should get a screen display similar to Figure 8.14.

At operating system level you can send this file to your printer by placing your operating system master disk in drive A and entering

PRINT B:PALDEMO.PRN.

Figure 8.14 P&L Spreadsheet: TYPE of PALDEMO.PRN

```
A>TYPE B:PALDEMO.PRN
                                  Bill's P & L Statement
                                     Fiscal Year 1984
                          QTR #1    QTR #2    QTR #3    QTR #4     TOTAL
                       ---------------------------------------------------
SALES                    5000.00   4000.00   4500.00   7500.00  21000.00
Cost of Goods Sold       1500.00   1200.00   1350.00   2250.00   6300.00
                       --------- --------- --------- --------- ---------
GROSS MARGIN             3500.00   2800.00   3150.00   5250.00  14700.00

OPERATING EXPENSES
  MARKETING              1000.00   1000.00   1000.00   1000.00   4000.00
  ADMINISTRATIVE          500.00    400.00    450.00    750.00   2100.00
                       --------- --------- --------- --------- ---------
     TOTAL               1500.00   1400.00   1450.00   1750.00   6100.00

PRE-TAX PROFIT           2000.00   1400.00   1700.00   3500.00   8600.00
INCOME TAX               1000.00    700.00    850.00   1750.00   4300.00
                       --------- --------- --------- --------- ---------
NET INCOME               1000.00    700.00    850.00   1750.00   4300.00
                       ========= ========= ========= ========= =========

A>
```

Your printed results should match the printed output generated from within SuperCalc³. See Figure 8.8.

You can also use the SIDEWAYS utility (see Appendix B for more information on this utility). This utility is useful for spreadsheets that are wider than 132 positions. SIDEWAYS requires input files to be in ASCII format, so you must have previously generated a disk output file via the /Output command. To execute the utility, place the SC3 Util disk in drive A and enter SIDEWAYS immediately followed by the filename to be printed. Press RETURN. When the print job is completed, press F10 to exit SIDEWAYS. Your printed output should match Figure 8.15.

Figure 8.15 P&L Spreadsheet: PALDEMO.PRN Printed Via SIDEWAYS Utility

```
                                  Bill's P & L Statement
                                     Fiscal Year 1984
                          QTR #1    QTR #2    QTR #3    QTR #4     TOTAL
                       ---------------------------------------------------
SALES                    5000.00   4000.00   4500.00   7500.00  21000.00
Cost of Goods Sold       1500.00   1200.00   1350.00   2250.00   6300.00
                       --------- --------- --------- --------- ---------
GROSS MARGIN             3500.00   2800.00   3150.00   5250.00  14700.00

OPERATING EXPENSES
  MARKETING              1000.00   1000.00   1000.00   1000.00   4000.00
  ADMINISTRATIVE          500.00    400.00    450.00    750.00   2100.00
                       --------- --------- --------- --------- ---------
     TOTAL               1500.00   1400.00   1450.00   1750.00   6100.00

PRE-TAX PROFIT           2000.00   1400.00   1700.00   3500.00   8600.00
INCOME TAX               1000.00    700.00    850.00   1750.00   4300.00
                       --------- --------- --------- --------- ---------
NET INCOME               1000.00    700.00    850.00   1750.00   4300.00
                       ========= ========= ========= ========= =========
```

Disk Output Errors

The following error messages could be encountered when using the Disk option of the /Output command:

Command aborted due to disk error

There are two possible reasons for this error message:

1. Either the drive door has been left open or there is no disk in the drive. Insert a disk and close the drive door, then try again.
2. The disk in your drive is write-protected—i.e., the write-enable notch is covered. Either put in the correct disk or remove the protective tape strip. Try again when ready.

Disk FULL, command aborted.

There is insufficient space available on disk to save the spreadsheet; the Output command is terminated. Insert a fresh disk with enough available space and repeat the save procedure.

Filename ERROR

The filename you entered is not in the proper format. Check your ENTRY LINE and make the necessary corrections. Repeat the save procedure by pressing RETURN.

File NOT on specified drive or directory

A nonexistent disk drive has been specified. SuperCalc³ allows you to correct the error or cancel the /Output.

Review Exercises

These exercises use the Credit Card Interest Spreadsheet from Exercise 7.6.

1. Provide the command to load the entire spreadsheet from Exercise 7.6.
2. Provide the commands to consolidate the .CAL file two times with the credit card interest spreadsheet currently in memory.
3. Provide the commands to back out the data in cells B6 through E19. Do a partial load of the spreadsheet from Exercise 7.6 using consolidation arithmetic.
4. Provide the command to save this spreadsheet with values only into a file named B:DUMMY.CAL.
5. Clear memory, then provide the commands to build a credit interest template. Use a series of partial loads.
6. Delete the file created in Exercise 4.
7. Generate a contents report for the spreadsheet template you built in Exercise 5. Send this report to your printer.
8. Generate a display report for the spreadsheet template you built in Exercise 5. Send this report to your console.
9. Generate a display report for the spreadsheet template you built in Exercise 5. Send this report to a disk file named B:EXER6-9.PRN.
10. Provide an operating system command to list out the file you created in Exercise 9.

Answers to Review Exercises

1. /LEX7-6.CAL,A
   See Figure 7.8.
2. /LEX7-6.CAL,C
   /LEX7-6.CAL,C

Figure 8.16 Credit Interest Spreadsheet: Exercise 8-2

```
     |  A    ||  B   ||  C   ||  D   ||       E          ||  F  ||  G  |
1              BILL & CONNIE'S CREDIT CARD INTEREST
2                      FOR CALENDAR YEAR 1984
3                             MASTER
4                    VISA     CHARGE     SEARS            TOTAL
5              ------------------------------------------------
6    JAN            17.85      26.88     29.22            73.95
7    FEB            36.18      26.52     29.94            92.64
8    MAR            39.93      24.69     28.86            93.48
9    APR            44.64      23.01     27.87            95.52
10   MAY           100.47      23.22     26.67           150.36
11   JUN            62.25      24.18     27.15           113.58
12   JUL            69.30      24.12     28.11           121.53
13   AUG            74.85      21.93     31.92           128.70
14   SEP            80.13      22.35     34.77           137.25
15   OCT            82.14      25.32     37.92           145.38
16   NOV            83.67      23.88     37.44           144.99
17   DEC            80.10      22.20     36.90           139.20
18                 ------     ------    ------           ------
19   TOTAL         771.51     288.30    376.77          1436.58
20                 ======     ======    ======           ======
A2
Width:  9  Memory: 99 Last Col/Row:F20     ? for HELP
  1>
F1 = Help; F2 = Cancel; F9 = Plot; F10 = View                    CAPS
```

3. /LEX7-6.CAL,PB6.E19,B6, –

Figure 8.17 Credit Interest Spreadsheet: Exercise 8-3

```
     |  A    ||  B   ||  C   ||  D   ||       E          ||  F  ||  G  |
1              BILL & CONNIE'S CREDIT CARD INTEREST
2                      FOR CALENDAR YEAR 1984
3                             MASTER
4                    VISA     CHARGE     SEARS            TOTAL
5              ------------------------------------------------
6    JAN            11.90      17.92     19.48            49.30
7    FEB            24.12      17.68     19.96            61.76
8    MAR            26.62      16.46     19.24            62.32
9    APR            29.76      15.34     18.58            63.68
10   MAY            66.98      15.48     17.78           100.24
11   JUN            41.50      16.12     18.10            75.72
12   JUL            46.20      16.08     18.74            81.02
13   AUG            49.90      14.62     21.28            85.80
14   SEP            53.42      14.90     23.18            91.50
15   OCT            54.76      16.88     25.28            96.92
16   NOV            55.78      15.92     24.96            96.66
17   DEC            53.40      14.80     24.60            92.80
18                 ------     ------    ------           ------
19   TOTAL         514.34     192.20    251.18           957.72
20                 ======     ======    ======           ======
A2
Width:  9  Memory: 99 Last Col/Row:F20     ? for HELP
  1>
F1 = Help; F2 = Cancel; F9 = Plot; F10 = View                    CAPS
```

4. /SB:DUMMY,V
5. a. /ZY

b. /LEX7-6.CAL,PA1.E5,A1, then press RETURN.
c. /LEX7-6.CAL,PA6:A20,A6, then press RETURN.
d. /LEX7-6.CAL,PE6.E17,E6, then press RETURN.
e. /LEX7-6.CAL,PB18:E20,B18, then press RETURN.
f. /FCB.E,TR, then press RETURN.
g. /FCB1.B2,TL, then press RETURN.

6. /DFB:DUMMY.CAL, then press RETURN.
7. /OCALL,P

Figure 8.18 Credit Interest Spreadsheet: Exercise 8-7

```
SuperCalc ver.   2.00

B1        = "BILL & CONNIE'S CREDIT CARD INTEREST
B2        = "         FOR CALENDAR YEAR 1984
C3        = "MASTER
B4        = "VISA
C4        = "CHARGE
D4        = "SEARS
E4        = "TOTAL
B5 TL     = '-
F5        = "
A6        = "JAN
E6        = B6+C6+D6
A7        = "FEB
E7        = B7+C7+D7
A8        = "MAR
E8        = B8+C8+D8
A9        = "APR
E9        = B9+C9+D9
A10       = "MAY
E10       = B10+C10+D10
A11       = "JUN
E11       = B11+C11+D11
A12       = "JUL
E12       = B12+C12+D12
A13       = "AUG
E13       = B13+C13+D13
A14       = "SEP
E14       = B14+C14+D14
A15       = "OCT
E15       = B15+C15+D15
A16       = "NOV
E16       = B16+C16+D16
A17       = "DEC
E17       = B17+C17+D17
B18       = "------
C18       = "------
D18       = "------
E18       = "------
A19       = "TOTAL
B19       = B6+B7+B8+B9+B10+B11+B12+B13+B14+B15+B16+B17
C19       = C6+C7+C8+C9+C10+C11+C12+C13+C14+C15+C16+C17
D19       = D6+D7+D8+D9+D10+D11+D12+D13+D14+D15+D16+D17
E19       = E6+E7+E8+E9+E10+E11+E12+E13+E14+E15+E16+E17
B20       = "======
C20       = "======
D20       = "======
E20       = "======
```

8. /ODALL,C

Figure 8.19 Credit Interest Spreadsheet: Exercise 8-8

```
    |  A  ||  B  ||  C  ||  D  ||      E      ||  F  |
1            BILL & CONNIE'S CREDIT CARD INTEREST
2                   FOR CALENDAR YEAR 1984
3                        MASTER
4                VISA    CHARGE     SEARS            TOTAL
5            ----------------------------------------------
6   JAN                                                .00
7   FEB                                                .00
8   MAR                                                .00
9   APR                                                .00
10  MAY                                                .00
11  JUN                                                .00
12  JUL                                                .00
13  AUG                                                .00
14  SEP                                                .00
15  OCT                                                .00
16  NOV                                                .00
17  DEC                                                .00
18                ------    ------    ------         ------
19  TOTAL            .00       .00       .00            .00
20                ======    ======    ======         ======
More...  (<RETURN> to continue or F2 to stop).

F1 = Help; F2 = Cancel; F9 = Plot; F10 = View               CAPS
```

9. /ODALL,D:EX8-9.PRN
10. PRINT B:EX8-9.PRN

Figure 8.20 Credit Interest Spreadsheet: Exercise 8-10

```
    |  A  ||  B  ||  C  ||  D  ||      E      ||  F  |
1            BILL & CONNIE'S CREDIT CARD INTEREST
2                   FOR CALENDAR YEAR 1984
3                        MASTER
4                VISA    CHARGE     SEARS            TOTAL
5            ----------------------------------------------
6   JAN                                                .00
7   FEB                                                .00
8   MAR                                                .00
9   APR                                                .00
10  MAY                                                .00
11  JUN                                                .00
12  JUL                                                .00
13  AUG                                                .00
14  SEP                                                .00
15  OCT                                                .00
16  NOV                                                .00
17  DEC                                                .00
18                ------    ------    ------         ------
19  TOTAL            .00       .00       .00            .00
20                ======    ======    ======         ======
```

CHAPTER 9

Spreadsheet Functions

Chapter Overview and Objectives

- Arithmetic Functions
- Conditional Functions
- Financial Functions
- Calendar Functions

This chapter introduces a series of built-in spreadsheet functions that saves you time and keystrokes. You don't have to develop expressions and formulas to do the tasks of the functions. That's already been done since they are built-in. You just specify the cells or values that the functions are to use in their calculations.

The functions covered have been selected for their usefulness in business, finance, and statistics. After completing this chapter, you will have learned how to use these functions for sales performance analysis, student testing, taxation, capital budgeting, mortgage payment computation, and pension plan analysis. In many cases, the functions are contrasted with the formulas and expressions needed to calculate the task without the function.

Arithmetic Functions

These functions return values resulting from built-in arithmetic calculations. They operate only on formulas. Text entries are ignored if they happen to be in the range of cells used by the arithmetic functions. You need only supply the function name with a set of parentheses containing the data the function is to operate on.

The general format for an arithmetic function is:

function name(one or more arguments separated by commas)

The general format's components are defined as follows:

function name 3 to 7 letters that identify the function. Arithmetic functions covered:

ABS Absolute value function

AVERAGE Arithmetic mean function
COUNT Item count function
INT Integer function
MAX High value function
MIN Low value function
ROUND Round function
SQRT Square root function
SUM Sum function

argument Designates the target the function is to operate on. There are three types of arguments for arithmetic functions.

value May be a numeric constant, a single cell reference, an expression, or another function. Examples:

SQRT(144)
ABS(A1)
INT(A1*144/25-C3)
SQRT(ABS(−144))

range A group of cells identified by the beginning and ending cell separated by a colon or period. Example:

COUNT(A1.A10)

list A group of ranges or values separated by commas. Examples:

COUNT(A1:A10,B1.B10)
SUM(A1.A10,B1:B10,C5,25)

Arithmetic functions are grouped into three categories:

Totals and Averages: AVERAGE, COUNT, and SUM.
Finding Highs and Lows: MAX and MIN.
Truncating and Rounding: INT and ROUND.
Statistical: ABS, SQRT.

Totals and Averages

Consider a spreadsheet that contains 1 in cell A1 and 2, 3, 4, 5 in cells B1 through B4. See Figure 9.1.

Figure 9.1 Summing and Averaging Functions

```
    |   A   ||   B   ||   C   ||   D   ||   E   ||   F   ||   G   ||   H   |
1           1        2
2                    3
3                    4
4                    5
5   Summing                   15                       15
6   Averaging                  3                        3
7                              3                        3
8
9
10
```

SUM Function

If you need a total of cells A1, B1, B2, B3, and B4, you could enter the following formula:

A1 + B1 + B2 + B3 + B4

This formula has been entered at cell C5. It's not a very big expression, but think of all the keystroking if you wanted to get a total of all the cells from B1 through B100 inclusive.

The SUM function presents a much more efficient way to obtain totals. The general format for this function is

SUM(list)

Totals of cells A1 and B1 through B4 can be calculated with the following entry:

SUM(A1,B1:B4)

This formula has been enterd in cell F5. Comparing cells C5 and F5 in Figure 9.1, you'll see identical results.

Averaging

Sometimes it's necessary to calculate an average, more correctly the arithmetic mean, for a data series. Examples of this are bowling averages and student averages. In each case the sum of the data in the series is divided by the number of data items in the series. The data in cells A1, B1, B2, B3, and B4 are used to demonstrate calculation of an average. You could use the formula in cell C6 of Figure 9.1.

(A1 + B1 + B2 + B3 + B4)/5

Entered properly, such a formula will calculate the correct answer, but it's cumbersome. It's also susceptible to logic errors such as miscounting the number of items or forgetting the parentheses. The latter error results in the division of 5 into cell B5 only. The SUM, COUNT, and AVERAGE functions can be used to calculate the arithmetic mean more efficiently.

COUNT Function

The COUNT function returns the number of items in a list. The general format for this function is

COUNT(list)

It can be used with the SUM function to calculate the arithmetic mean:

SUM(A1,B1:B4)/COUNT(A1,B1:B4)

See also cell F6 in Figure 9.1. Comparing cells C6 and F6 in Figure 9.1, you'll see identical results.

AVERAGE Function

The AVERAGE function returns the arithmetic mean of the items specified in the list. The general format for this function is

AVERAGE(list) or **AV(list)**

It's the same as entering

SUM(list)/COUNT(list)

To calculate the arithmetic mean of the data in cells A1, B1, B2, B3, and B4 via this function, enter

AVERAGE(A1,B1:B4) or **AV(A1,B1:B4)**

See also cell F7 in Figure 9.1. Cells C6, C7, F6, and F7 in Figure 9.1 have identical results. When calculating averages, it's more efficient to use the AVERAGE function if the nature of your application doesn't require you to separately store a total.

Finding Highs and Lows

Sometimes it's necessary to identify the extreme values in a series of data. Examples include finding the high and low sales volumes for a group of salespeople or finding the high and low test scores for a group of students. This section uses the data contained in cells A1, B1, B2, B3, and B4 of the spreadsheet illustrated in Figure 9.2.

Figure 9.2 Functions for Finding Highs and Lows

	A	B	C	D	E	F	G	H
1	1	2						
2		3						
3		4						
4		5						
5	Summing		15			15		
6	Averaging		3			3		
7			3			3		
8	High Number					5		
9	Low Number					1		
10								

MAX Function

This function returns the highest numeric value from the specified list. Its general format is

MAX(list)

To find the highest value from the cell list A1 and B1 through B4, enter

MAX(A1,B1:B4)

As you can see in cell F8 of Figure 9.2, the highest value is 5.

MIN Function

This function returns the lowest numeric value from the specified list. Its general format is

MIN(list)

To find the lowest value from the cell list A1 and B1 through B4, enter

MIN(A1,B1:B4)

As you can see in cell F9 of Figure 9.2, the lowest value is 1.

Figure 9.3 displays the formulas used in Figures 9.1 and 9.2.

Figure 9.3 Formulas Display for Summing, Averaging, High, and Low Functions

	A	B	C	D	E	F	G	H
1	1	2						
2		3						
3		4						
4		5						
5	Summing		A1+B1+B2+B3+B4			SUM(A1,B1:B4)		
6	Averaging		(A1+B1+B2+B3+B4)/5			F5/COUNT(A1,B1:B4)		
7			C5/5			AV(A1,B1:B4)		
8	High Number					MAX(A1,B1:B4)		
9	Low Number					MIN(A1,B1:B4)		
10								

Truncating and Rounding

You've seen how to format the spreadsheet. Even though you may have the spreadsheet formatted for dollars and cents, the actual cell contents haven't changed. This can cause a problem when totals are calculated. For example, assume that

Cell A1 contains 10.035, which displays as 10.04 in $ format.
Cell A2 contains 20.066, which displays as 20.07 in $ format.

When **SUM(A1:A2)** is entered into cell A3, which is also formatted as dollars and cents, the resulting display is **30.10.** You would have expected **30.11** since that's the sum of 10.04 and 20.07. It's very important to recognize that formats are applied after formulas or functions have been evaluated. In the preceding case, cells A1 and A2 were summed, giving **30.101,** which was then formatted to **30.10.**

Truncating or rounding the cell contents to the proper number of decimal places prior to summing eliminates this problem. The functions covered in this section demonstrate truncating and rounding algorithms.

This section uses the data contained in cells A1 through A6 and B1 of the spreadsheet illustrated in Figure 9.4.

Figure 9.4 Rounding and Truncating Functions

	A	B	C	D	E	F	G	H
1	12.53452	-1.5	-1					
2	125.3452		12					
3	1253.452		13			13		
4	12534.52		12.5			12.5		
5	125345.2		12.53			12.53		
6	1253452		12.535			12.535		
7			12.5345			12.5345		
8						10		
9						100		
10						1000		
11						10000		
12						100000		
13						1000000		
14								
15								

INT Function

This function truncates all positions to the right of the decimal point on the value passed to it and returns as integer number. The general format of this function is

INT(value)

Regardless of whether the value passed to the function is positive or negative, the decimal positions are truncated and the number to the left of the point is returned as an integer. Refer to cells C1 and C2 in Figure 9.4.

The INT function can be enhanced to do rounding.

Round to a whole number: INT(value +0.5)
See cell C3 in Figure 9.4.
Round to 1 decimal place: INT(value *10 +0.5) / 10
See cell C4 in Figure 9.4.
Round to 2 decimal places: INT(value *100 +0.5) / 100
See cell C5 in Figure 9.4.
Round to 3 decimal places: INT(value *1000 +0.5) / 1000
See cell C6 in Figure 9.4.
Round to 4 decimal places: INT(value *10000 +0.5) / 10000
See cell C7 in Figure 9.4.

ROUND Function

This function returns a rounded number based on the specified number of places. If the specified number of places is positive, rounding takes place to the right of the decimal point. If the specified number of places is negative, rounding takes place to the left of the decimal point. This attribute is particularly useful when rounding to whole hundreds, whole thousands, etc.

The general format of this function is

ROUND(value, number of places)

Since the number of places is a value, a cell reference could be used. This allows the decimal precision of the spreadsheet to be easily changed.

Some examples of rounding:

Round to a whole number: ROUND(value,0)
See cell F3 in Figure 9.4.
Round to 1 decimal place: ROUND(value,1)
See cell F4 in Figure 9.4.
Round to 2 decimal places: ROUND(value,2)
See cell F5 in Figure 9.4.
Round to 3 decimal places: ROUND(value,3)
See cell F6 in Figure 9.4.
Round to 4 decimal places: ROUND(value,4)
See cell F7 in Figure 9.4.
Round to whole tens: ROUND(value, −1)
See cell F8 in Figure 9.4.

Round to whole hundreds: ROUND(value, – 2)
See cell F9 in Figure 9.4.
Round to whole thousands: ROUND(value, – 3)
See cell F10 in Figure 9.4.
Round to whole 10 thousands: ROUND(value, – 4)
See cell F11 in Figure 9.4.
Round to whole 100 thousands: ROUND(value, – 5)
See cell F12 in Figure 9.4.
Round to whole millions: ROUND(value, – 6)
See cell F13 in Figure 9.4.

A Comprehensive Example for Averaging, Highs, Lows, and Rounding

The spreadsheet shown in Figure 9.5 represents academic performance data for students in a computer science course. With minor modification, the concepts shown here could be used in a personnel setting for employee aptitude testing and performance appraisal by group or department.

Figure 9.5 Student Test and Program Data

	A	B	C	D	E	F	G	H	I	J	K	L
1	NAME	TEST #1	TEST #2	TEST #3	TEST #4	PROG #1	PROG #2	PROG #3	PROG #4	TEST AVG	PROG AVG	CRSE AVG
2	-------											
3	ABLE	85	74	65	60	90	80	90	80			
4	BAKER	92	90	86	89	88	90	92	94			
5	CHARLES	89	70	53	0	100	90	0	0			
6	DELTA	77	85	82	71	100	100	90	85			
7	ECHO	83	85	87	80	100	100	96	100			
8	FOX	97	93	94	94	100	100	100	100			
9	GAMMA	66	74	66	74	100	86	86	80			
10	HOTEL	65	63	65	60	70	75	65	80			
11	INCA	97	92	97	92	100	100	100	100			
12	-------	-------	-------	-------	-------	-------	-------	-------	-------	-------	-------	-------
13	AVERAGE											
14	HIGH											
15	LOW											

Each student's name, test scores, and programming assignment scores are shown in columns A through I. Column J represents the average of the four tests. Column K represents the average of the four programming assignment scores. Column L represents the weighted average of test average (75%) and the programming assignment average (25%). Row 13 represents the class average for each of the tests and programming assignments as well as the test, program, and course averages. Row 14 represents the high value in the class for each of the tests and programming assignments as well as the test, program, and course averages. Row 15 represents the low value in the class for each of the tests and programming assignments as well as the test, program, and course averages. Columns A through L have right justified text entries and the recalculation mode has been set to manual.

Given that Figure 9.5 has already been created, the formulas to calculate class statistics can be entered in a very short time.

Step No. 1. Calculate the test average
In cell J3, enter

ROUND(AVERAGE(B3:E3),0)

This is an illustration of a nested function. Earlier you saw that a function could have another function as its argument. This entry calculates the test average for the student named ABLE, then rounds it to an integer. You now need to provide test average computation formulas for the eight remaining students. This can be done very quickly via the /Replicate command. Enter

/RJ3,J4:J11

then press RETURN.

Step No. 2. Calculate the program average
In cell K3, enter

ROUND(AVERAGE(F3:I3),0)

This entry calculates the program average for the student named ABLE, then rounds it to an integer. You now need to provide program average computation formulas for the eight remaining students. Enter

/RK3,K4:K11

then press RETURN.

Step No. 3. Calculate the weighted course average
In cell L3, enter

ROUND(J3*.75+K3*.25,0) or **ROUND(75%J3+25%K3,0)**

This entry calculates the course average based on 75% of the test average and 25% of the program average for the student named ABLE, then rounds it to an integer. You now need to provide course average computation formulas for the eight remaining students. Enter

/RL3,L4:L11

then press RETURN.

Step No. 4. Calculate class averages
In cell B13, enter

ROUND(AVERAGE(B3:B11),0)

This entry calculates the class average for Test 1. You now need to provide class averages for Tests 2 through 4, Programs 1 through 4, test average, program average, and course average. Enter

/RB13,C13:L13

then press RETURN.

Step No. 5. Calculate class high
In cell B14, enter

MAX(B3:B11)

This entry calculates the class high score for Test 1. You now need to provide class highs for Tests 2 through 4, Programs 1 through 4, test average, program average, and course average. Enter

/RB14,C14:L14

then press RETURN.

Step No. 6. Calculate class low

In cell B15, enter

(MIN(B3:B11)

This entry calculates the class low score for Test 1. You now need to provide class lows for Tests 2 through 4, Programs 1 through 4, test average, program average, and course average. Enter

/RB15,C15:L15

then press RETURN.

When you've finished, press ! to force a manual recalculation. Your spreadsheet should look like Figure 9.6. Zap your spreadsheet before continuing to the next section.

Figure 9.6 Calculated Student Averages

	A	B	C	D	E	F	G	H	I	J	K	L
1	NAME	TEST #1	TEST #2	TEST #3	TEST #4	PROG #1	PROG #2	PROG #3	PROG #4	TEST AVG	PROG AVG	CRSE AVG
2	-------	-------	-------	-------	-------	-------	-------	-------	-------	-------	-------	-------
3	ABLE	85	74	65	60	90	80	90	80	71	85	75
4	BAKER	92	90	86	89	88	90	92	94	89	91	90
5	CHARLES	89	70	53	0	100	90	0	0	53	48	52
6	DELTA	77	85	82	71	100	100	90	85	79	94	83
7	ECHO	83	85	87	80	100	100	96	100	84	99	88
8	FOX	97	93	94	94	100	100	100	100	95	100	96
9	GAMMA	66	74	66	74	100	86	86	80	70	88	75
10	HOTEL	65	63	65	60	70	75	65	80	63	73	66
11	INCA	97	92	97	92	100	100	100	100	95	100	96
12	-------	-------	-------	-------	-------	-------	-------	-------	-------	-------	-------	-------
13	AVERAGE	83	81	77	69	94	91	80	80	78	86	80
14	HIGH	97	93	97	94	100	100	100	100	95	100	96
15	LOW	65	63	53	0	70	75	0	0	53	48	52

Arithmetic Functions for Statistical Analysis

ABS FUNCTION

This function removes the negative sign from its argument and returns the absolute value. Its general format is

ABS(value)

AN ABSOLUTE DEVIATION EXAMPLE

The ABS function can be used to determine the absolute deviation. Consider an example where management wants a sales performance analysis showing how much each individual's performance has deviated from the group average. Management is not interested at this point whether a given salesperson was above or below average, just the deviation from the average. Figure 9.7 contains sales data and a group average for nine salespeople.

Figure 9.7 Sales Data

	A	B	C	D	E	F	G	H
1								
2	Name	Sales						
3	-------	-------						
4	Able	4790						
5	Baker	2528						
6	Charles	3516						
7	Delta	6777						
8	Echo	8684						
9	Fox	8182						
10	Gamma	6266						
11	Hotel	5490						
12	Inca	5570						
13	-------	-------						
14	Average	5756						
15								

In cell C4, enter

ABS(B4-B14)

This calculates salesperson Able's absolute deviation from average sales.

Now use /Replicate to create absolute deviation formulas for the remaining eight salespeople. Enter

/RC4,C5:C12,AYN

Since management also wants to know the average deviation, it's necessary to compute the mean of these individual deviations. This can be done in one of two ways: In cell C14, enter

ROUND(AVERAGE(C4:C12),0)

or

/RB14.C14, then press RETURN

Figure 9.8 illustrates the resulting spreadsheet.

Figure 9.8 Sales Data: Absolute Deviation

	A	B	C	D	E	F	G
1			Absolute				
2	Name	Sales	Deviation				
3	-------	-------	-------				
4	Able	4790	966				
5	Baker	2528	3228				
6	Charles	3516	2240				
7	Delta	6777	1021				
8	Echo	8684	2928				
9	Fox	8182	2426				
10	Gamma	6266	510				
11	Hotel	5490	266				
12	Inca	5570	186				
13	-------	-------	-------				
14	Average	5756	1530				
15							

SQRT FUNCTION

This function returns the square root of a positive argument. Its primary statistical use is to calculate the Standard Deviation, a more statistically precise measure of deviation than the absolute deviation. If you're not statistically oriented you should skip this function and accompanying example. The general format of the SQRT function is

SQRT(value)

It's mathematically impossible to compute the square root of a negative number. Any attempt to do so puts ERROR into the cell contents. If there's any possibility that the argument may be negative, nest the ABS function within the SQRT function as follows:

SQRT(ABS(value))

A STANDARD DEVIATION EXAMPLE

This example uses the sales performance analysis from Figure 9.7 as a basis. In cell C4, enter

B4-B14

This calculates salesperson Able's deviation from average sales. Now use /Replicate to create deviation formulas for the remaining eight salespeople. Enter

/RC4,C5:C12

then press RETURN. In cell D4, enter

C4^2

This computes the squared deviation. Statistically, it's a better way of removing negatives than the ABS function. Now use /Replicate to create squared deviation formulas for the remaining eight salespeople. Enter

/RD4,D5:D12

then press RETURN.

Now compute the average squared deviation. Statistically, this is called the Variance. The Variance can be computed in one of two ways: In cell D14, enter

ROUND(AVERAGE(D4:D12),0)

or

/RB14,D15

and press RETURN. Now compute the Standard Deviation. This is the square root of the Variance. In cell D16, enter

ROUND(SQRT(D15),0)

Figure 9.9 illustrates the resulting spreadsheet.

Figure 9.9 Sales Data: Standard Deviation

	A	B	C	D
1				Squared
2	Name	Sales	Deviation	Deviation
3	----------	----------	----------	----------
4	Able	4790	-966	933156
5	Baker	2528	-3228	10419984
6	Charles	3516	-2240	5017600
7	Delta	6777	1021	1042441
8	Echo	8684	2928	8573184
9	Fox	8182	2426	5885476
10	Gamma	6266	510	260100
11	Hotel	5490	-266	70756
12	Inca	5570	-186	34596
13	----------	----------	----------	----------
14	Average	5756		
15	Variance			3581921
16	Standard Deviation			1893

Conditional Functions

These functions are used for decision making in your spreadsheet. They make SuperCalc^3 select from a series of actions based on the results of one or more comparisons. Conditional functions are based on Boolean algebra, which focuses on values that evaluate as true or false. In SuperCalc^3, the conditional functions evaluate a statement like "The number in cell B2 is less than the number in cell C12" and determine whether that statement is true or false. The power of the functions comes not from knowing whether a given statement is true or false, but because you can instruct SuperCalc^3 to take one action if the statement is true and another if it's false.

Comparisons are a critical part of all conditional functions. They are also known as conditional expressions. The general format of a conditional expression is

expression #1 relational operator expression #2

Relational operators are special symbols used to compare expression #1 and expression #2. The relational operators are shown below.

Operator	Meaning	Example
<	less than	B1<C4 means the value of cell B1 is less than the value of cell C4. So if B1 is 2 and C4 is 3, the result is true. If B1 is 3 or 4 or more, the result is false.
<=	less than or equal to	B1<=C4 means the value in B1 is either less than or the same as C4. So if B1 is 1 or 2 and C4 is 2, the result is true. If B1 is 3, the result is false.
>	greater than	B1>C4 means the value in B1 is greater than the value in C4. So if B1 is 3 and C4 is 2, the result is true. If C4 is 3 or 4 or more, the result is false.
>=	greater than or equal to	B1>=C4 means the value in B1 is either greater than or the same as C4. So if B1 is 3, 4, or more and C4 is 3, the result is true. If B1 is 2, the result is false.
=	equal to	B1=C4 means B1 is equal to C4. If B1 and C4 have the same values, the result is true, otherwise the result is false.
< >	not equal to	B1<>C4 means B1 is not equal to C4. If B1 and C4 do not have the same values, the result is true, otherwise the result is false.

IF Function: Simple Conditions

This function specifies a condition and two actions to take, one if the result is true, the other if the result is false. The general format for this function is

IF(expression a,expression b,expression c)

Expression a is the conditional expression. It can be a simple condition or it can be a compound condition using the OR and AND functions. This section covers simple conditions. *Expression b* is the action taken when expression a is true. It can be any numeric expression, function, or cell reference. *Expression c* is the action taken when expression a is false. It can be any numeric expression, function, or cell reference.

Consider an example where you wanted to display cell A1 or cell B1 in cell A2, depending on which was greater. Using the IF function, you would enter the following into cell A2:

IF(A1>=B1,A1,B1)

This entry is read as "If A1 is greater than or equal to B1, then display A1, otherwise display B1."

A Business Example of Simple IF

Consider the professional recruiting example shown in Figure 9.10. The employment agency charges client companies for placements using an algorithm of 1% plus 1% per thousand dollars of annual salary with a rate ceiling of 30%. The annual salaries for two prospective recruits are shown in cells A4 and A5 as $28,000 and $40,000, respectively. The following formulas in cells B1 and B2 represent the agency fee algorithms:

IF(INT(A4/1000)+1<30,(INT(A4/1000)+1)%A4,30%A4)
IF(INT(A5/1000)+1<30,(INT(A5/1000)+1)%A5,30%A5)

The conditional expression determines whether or not the 30% ceiling is applicable. It has the following components:

1. Integral number of thousands in the annual salary plus the base point of 1—i.e., **INT(A4/1000) + 1.**
2. Comparison of the results from step 1 to see if they are less than 30.

The conditional expression is true when the agency rate comes to less than 30, as is the case for cell B4. Here, the agency rate is calculated to be 29 and is then taken as a percent of the annual salary—i.e., **(INT(A4/1000)+1)%A4.**

The conditional expression is false when the agency rate is 30 or greater, as is the case for cell B5. Here, a flat 30% rate is applied to the annual salary—i.e., **30%A5.**

Figure 9.10 Simple IF

	A	B	C	D	E	F	G
1	Annual	Placement					
2	Salary	Fee					
3	------------	------------	------------	------------	------------	------------	------------
4	28000	8120					
5	40000	12000					

An Absolute Deviation Example of Simple IF

Earlier, a sales performance analysis spreadsheet was created using the absolute deviation (see Figure 9.8). This spreadsheet can be enhanced to identify those salespeople whose individual deviation exceeds the average deviation in cell C14. This will save management's time when analyzing the report.

An interesting attribute of this type of analysis is that it identifies both high and low performers. Ideally, the high performers can be rewarded as well as divulge their secret of success to benefit the low and average performers. The low performers can be counselled. The following entries generate this type of analysis. At cell D4, enter

IF(C4>C14,("REVIEW"),NA)

If the individual's deviation from average sales exceeds the average deviation, a textual value flags the individual to be reviewed, otherwise the NA function marks the individual as N/A. *Note:* NA is a special function meaning that data is not available. It only returns the value N/A.

Using /Replicate, you can duplicate the entry in cell D4 for the remaining eight salespeople:

/RD4,D5:D12,AYN

Figure 9.11 illustrates the resulting spreadsheet.

Figure 9.11 Simple IF: Absolute Deviation

	A	B	C	D
1			Absolute	
2	Name	Sales	Deviation	
3	-----------	-----------	-----------	-----------
4	Able	4790	966	N/A
5	Baker	2528	3228	Review
6	Charles	3516	2240	Review
7	Delta	6777	1021	N/A
8	Echo	8684	2928	Review
9	Fox	8182	2426	Review
10	Gamma	6266	510	N/A
11	Hotel	5490	266	N/A
12	Inca	5570	186	N/A
13	-----------	-----------	-----------	-----------
14	Average	5756	1530	

OR Function: Compound Conditions

This function specifies two conditions: if either is true, the result is true. The result is false only when both conditions are false. This is demonstrated below:

Condition #1	Condition #2	Result
True	True	True
True	False	True
False	True	True
False	False	False

The general format of this function is

OR(condition #1,condition #2)

The OR function would most typically be used as **expression a** within the IF function. The general format for this is

IF(OR(condition #1,condition #2),expression b,expression c)

A Compound OR Example

Figure 9.12 presents a payroll spreadsheet. Column B contains monthly gross pay for a group of salespeople. Column C indicates the location code for the city where the salesperson lives. Column D contains the location code for the city where the salesperson works. The municipality identified by location code 10 has imposed a wage tax of 4.3125% on the gross wages of all people who either live or work in that city. Make the following entries to properly calculate the city wage tax: At cell E4, enter

IF(OR(C4=10,D4=10) ,ROUND(B4*0.043125,2),0)

If an individual's residence code is equal to 10 or work code is equal to 10, that person is charged a city wage tax, otherwise the person pays no tax. Using /Replicate, the entry in cell E4 is duplicated for the remaining four people:

/RE4,E5:E7

then press RETURN. Figure 9.12 illustrates the resulting spreadsheet. Figure 9.12 shows that Delta is the only person not paying the city wage tax because Delta neither lives nor works in city code 10.

Figure 9.12 Compound Conditional: IF with OR

	A	B	C	D	E
1	Employee	Gross	Residence	Employment	City Wage
2	Name	Pay	City Code	City Code	Tax
3	----------	----------	----------	----------	----------
4	Able	4790	10	25	206.57
5	Baker	2528	12	10	109.02
6	Charles	3516	10	10	151.63
7	Delta	6777	15	15	0

AND Function: Compound Conditions

This function specifies two conditions: the result is true only when both are true, otherwise the result is false. This is shown here:

Condition #1	Condition #2	Result
True	True	True
True	False	False
False	True	False
False	False	False

The general format of this function is

AND(condition #1,condition #2)

The AND function would most typically be used as **expression a** within the IF function. The general format for this usage is

IF(AND(condition #1,condition #2),expression b,expression c)

A Compound AND Example

Figure 9.13 contains a list of people with their residency codes in column B and their ages in column C. The municipality identified by location code 10 has imposed a per capita tax of $10 on all residents over 18 years of age. Make the following entries to properly calculate the per capita tax: At cell D4, enter

IF(AND(B4=10,C4>=18),10,0)

If an individual's residence code is 10 and he or she is 18 years of age or older, then that person is charged a per capita tax, otherwise the person pays no tax. Using /Replicate, the entry in cell D4 is duplicated for the remaining four people:

/RD4,D5:D7

then press RETURN. Figure 9.13 illustrates the resulting spreadsheet. Figure 9.13 shows that Able is the only person paying the per capita tax because Able is the only resident of city code 10 who is 18 or older.

Figure 9.13 Compound Conditional: IF with AND

	A	B	C	D
1		Residence		Per Capita
2	Name	City Code	Age	Tax
3	------	------	------	------
4	Able	10	25	10.00
5	Baker	12	18	.00
6	Charles	10	2	.00
7	Delta	15	15	.00

IF Function: Complex Conditions

This variation of the IF function nests another IF function where **expression c** is positioned. This inner IF is executed only when the condition associated with the outer IF is false. The general format is

IF(express a,express b,IF(express a, express b,express c))

There may be any number of nested IFs, but the length of the entire formula may not exceed 116 characters.

A Course Grade Example of Nested IF

Figure 9.6 showed course averages for a group of students. The next step in the grading process is to determine the course letter grades for these students. Assume the following grading scheme:

Average	Course Grade
94–100	A
85–93	B
70–84	C
60–69	D
0–59	F

The following entry determines the course letter grades: At cell M3, enter
IF(L3<60,("F"),IF(L3<70,("D"),IF(L3<85,("C"),IF(L3<94,("B"),("A")))))
This formula is evaluated as follows:

If the student's course average in column L is less than 60, the course grade is F.
If the course average is less than 70, the course grade is D.
If the course average is less than 85, the course grade is C.
If the course average is less than 94, the course grade is B.
If none of these, the course grade is A.

The order of these nested IFs is extremely important. When a student's average is less than 85, that student gets a C because the first two conditions are false: the course average is not less than 60 and the course average is not less than 70.

Similarly, when a student gets an A, it's because all of the preceding conditions are false: the course average is not less than 60, it is not less than 70, it is not less than 85, and it is not less than 94.

The letter grades must be expressed as textual values so that they are compatible with the formula comparisons in the IF function.

Using /Replicate, you can duplicate the entry in M3 for the remaining eight students. Refer to column M in Figure 9.14 for the letter grade distribution.

Figure 9.14 Nested IF

	A	B	C	D	E	F	G	H	I	J	K	L	M
1	NAME	TEST #1	TEST #2	TEST #3	TEST #4	PROG #1	PROG #2	PROG #3	PROG #4	TEST AVG	PROG AVG	CRSE AVG	Grade
2	------	------	------	------	------	------	------	------	------	------	------	------	------
3	ABLE	85	74	65	60	90	80	90	80	71	85	75	C
4	BAKER	92	90	86	89	88	90	92	94	89	91	90	B
5	CHARLES	89	70	53	0	100	90	0	0	53	48	52	F
6	DELTA	77	85	82	71	100	100	90	85	79	94	83	C
7	ECHO	83	85	87	80	100	100	96	100	84	99	88	B
8	FOX	97	93	94	94	100	100	100	100	95	100	96	A
9	GAMMA	66	74	66	74	100	86	86	80	70	88	75	C
10	HOTEL	65	63	65	60	70	75	65	80	63	73	66	D
11	INCA	97	92	97	92	100	100	100	100	95	100	96	A
12	------	------	------	------	------	------	------	------	------	------	------	------	
13	AVERAGE	83	81	77	69	94	91	80	80	78	86	80	
14	HIGH	97	93	97	94	100	100	100	100	95	100	96	
15	LOW	65	63	53	0	70	75	0	0	53	48	52	

Financial Functions

This section covers five financial functions that can be used for financial analysis of a capital budgeting nature. All the functions use interest compounding:

Net Present Value (NPV) function
Internal Rate of Return (IRR) function
Payment (PMT) function
Future Value (FV) function
Present Value (PV) function

The equivalent algebraic formulas are provided for each function as a proof.

Net Present Value Function

The NPV function determines the profitability of a capital acquisition, usually equipment. It's based on the following formula:

$$NPV = \sum_{i=0}^{n} (C_i * (1 /((1 + r) ^\wedge i)))$$

where i = Period; n = last period; r = discount rate in decimal format; and C_i = cash flow for period_i.

The general format for the NPV function is

NPV (discount rate, periodic cash flow range) + period 0 cash flow

Its components are defined as follows:

discount rate Must be expressed as a decimal. May be a value or cell reference. Referencing a cell near the top of the spreadsheet allows more flexibility for subsequent analyses using different rates. The rate used might be the current rate of return for cash investments in securities or the current cost of borrowing.

periodic cash flow range Identifies the cell range containing the cash flows for periods 1 through n. These values represent the estimated savings or losses generated in each operating period. Savings are positive values; losses are negative values. The number of periods is determined by the useful life of the asset.

period 0 cash flow Specifies the cost of the proposed asset. It's usually a negative value, since it represents money spent.

There are two decision-making criteria associated with net present value:

1. Accept the proposal when the NPV function returns a value that is zero or positive. A zero value indicates that the discounted future cash flows exactly offset the cost of acquiring the asset in period 0. The rate of return is equal to the discount rate for this investment. A positive value means that the discounted future cash flows have more than offset the cost of acquiring the asset. The rate of return is greater than the discount rate for this investment.
2. Reject the proposal when the NPV function returns a value that is less than zero. A negative value indicates that the discounted future cash flows do not offset the cost of acquiring the asset in period 0. The rate of return is less than the discount rate for this investment.

An NPV Example

Figure 9.15, parts A and B, demonstrates the NPV function with a 12% discount rate and an asset with a cost of $4000 that saves $1000, $1165, $1375, $1800, and $1350 in the respective periods of its five-year useful life.

Cells B6 through B11 and D6 through D13 illustrate the formula on which the NPV function is based. This is a manual proof of the NPV function's results.

The entry at cell D17 uses the NPV function. Its results are rounded to two decimal places:

ROUND(NPV(C2,C7:C11),2) + C6

Contrasting cell D17 with the manual approach shows just how much work the NPV function saves.

The $0.01 difference between the manually computed results of $710.25 and the $710.24 returned by the NPV function is due to rounding. It is an insignificant difference. The positive value returned by these computations suggests that the asset be acquired.

Figure 9.15A NPV Function: Formulas On

```
     :  A  ::                 B              ::   C   ::               D               :
1    NET PRESENT VALUE
2    DECIMAL DISCOUNT RATE                           .12
3                                     DISCOUNT      CASH                       DISCOUNTED
4    PERIODS                           FACTORS     FLOWS                       CASH FLOWS
5    ------------------------------------------------------------------------------------
6     0             ROUND(1/((1+C2)^A6),6)         -4000                   ROUND(B6*C6,2)
7     1             ROUND(1/((1+C2)^A7),6)          1000                   ROUND(B7*C7,2)
8     2             ROUND(1/((1+C2)^A8),6)          1165                   ROUND(B8*C8,2)
9     3             ROUND(1/((1+C2)^A9),6)          1375                   ROUND(B9*C9,2)
10    4            ROUND(1/((1+C2)^A10),6)          1800                 ROUND(B10*C10,2)
11    5            ROUND(1/((1+C2)^A11),6)          1350                 ROUND(B11*C11,2)
12                                                                       ------------
13                MANUALLY COMPUTED NPV                                    SUM(D6:D11)
14                                                                       ============
15
16
17                            NPV FUNCTION                    ROUND(NPV(C2,C7:C11),2)+C6
18                                                                       ============
```

Figure 9.15B NPV Function: Formulas Off

```
     :  A  ::                 B              ::   C   ::               D               :
1    NET PRESENT VALUE
2    DECIMAL DISCOUNT RATE                       .120000
3                                     DISCOUNT      CASH                       DISCOUNTED
4    PERIODS                           FACTORS     FLOWS                       CASH FLOWS
5    ------------------------------------------------------------------------------------
6                0                    1.000000  -4000.00                         -4000.00
7                1                     .892857   1000.00                           892.86
8                2                     .797194   1165.00                           928.73
9                3                     .711780   1375.00                           978.70
10               4                     .635518   1800.00                          1143.93
11               5                     .567427   1350.00                           766.03
12                                                                       ------------
13                MANUALLY COMPUTED NPV                                            710.25
14                                                                       ============
15
16
17                            NPV FUNCTION                                         710.24
18                                                                       ============
```

Internal Rate of Return Function

The IRR function determines the discount rate that sets the value returned by the NPV function to zero. It is based on the same formula as the NPV function.

The IRR is useful in situations of capital rationing where management wants to fund only capital investment projects with the highest returns.

The general format for the IRR function is

IRR(best guess discount rate,cash flow range for all periods)

Its components are defined as follows:

best guess discount rate Must be expressed as a decimal. It may be a value or cell reference. This is an optional argument. If it is omitted, a default value of 0.1 is used.

cash flow range for all periods Identifies the cell range containing the cash outflow for period 0 and the cash flows for periods 1 through n.

Caution:

1. This function uses a looping technique for computation. If a solution within 0.0000001 has not been calculated after 20 passes through this loop, the IRR function aborts with ERROR. Recalculate the function using a different best guess discount rate.
2. The IRR is unreliable for periodic cash flows with negative values in periods 1 through n. In this situation, different best guess discount rates will return different values for the same series of cash flows.

An IRR Example

Figure 9.16, parts A and B, demonstrates the IRR function for a proposed asset with a cost of $4000 that saves $1000, $1165, $1375, $1800, and $1350 over its five-year useful life.

The following entry in cell D20 returns a discount rate of .184019:

ROUND (IRR(0.10,C6:C11),6)

The Net Present Value calculations are used in this illustration as a proof for the Internal Rate of Return. Entering the value returned by the IRR function into cell C2 returns an NPV of 0 in cell D17.

The .01 difference between the manually computed NPV of −.01 and the .00 returned by the NPV function is due to rounding. It is an insignificant difference.

Figure 9.16A IRR Function: Formulas On

```
     !  A  !!                B              !!    C   !!                 D             !
1    NET PRESENT VALUE
2    DECIMAL DISCOUNT RATE                        .184019
3                                   DISCOUNT        CASH                        DISCOUNTED
4    PERIODS                         FACTORS       FLOWS                        CASH FLOWS
5    ------------------------------------------------------------------------------------
6     0          ROUND(1/((1+C2)^A6),6)            -4000                  ROUND(B6*C6,2)
7     1          ROUND(1/((1+C2)^A7),6)             1000                  ROUND(B7*C7,2)
8     2          ROUND(1/((1+C2)^A8),6)             1165                  ROUND(B8*C8,2)
9     3          ROUND(1/((1+C2)^A9),6)             1375                  ROUND(B9*C9,2)
10    4         ROUND(1/((1+C2)^A10),6)             1800                ROUND(B10*C10,2)
11    5         ROUND(1/((1+C2)^A11),6)             1350                ROUND(B11*C11,2)
12                                                                      ------------
13             MANUALLY COMPUTED NPV                                      SUM(D6:D11)
14                                                                      ============
15
16
17                          NPV FUNCTION                   ROUND(NPV(C2,C7:C11),2)+C6
18                                                                      ============
19
20                          IRR FUNCTION                    ROUND(IRR(0.10,C6:C11),6)
21                                                                      ============
```

Figure 9.16B IRR Function: Formulas Off

```
   |  A  ||           B            ||  C  ||               D               |
1   NET PRESENT VALUE
2   DECIMAL DISCOUNT RATE                      .184019
3                              DISCOUNT        CASH                 DISCOUNTED
4   PERIODS                     FACTORS       FLOWS                 CASH FLOWS
5   -------------------------------------------------------------------------
6             0                1.000000 -4000.00                      -4000.00
7             1                 .844581  1000.00                        844.58
8             2                 .713317  1165.00                        831.01
9             3                 .602454  1375.00                        828.37
10            4                 .508821  1800.00                        915.88
11            5                 .429741  1350.00                        580.15
12                                                                ------------
13                 MANUALLY COMPUTED NPV                                  -.01
14                                                                ============
15
16
17                          NPV FUNCTION                                   .00
18                                                                ============
19
20                          IRR FUNCTION                               .184019
21                                                                ============
```

Payment Function

The PMT function calculates periodic payments for a given principal, interest rate, and number of periods. It's most commonly used to calculate monthly payments for mortgages and installment loans. The Payment function is based on the formula:

$$PMT = P * r / (1 - 1 / (1 - (1 + r) ^ n))$$

where P = principal for loan or mortgage; r = interest rate per compounding period; and n = number of periods for the loan or mortgage.

The general format for the PMT function is

PMT (principal,periodic interest rate,number of periods)

Its components are defined as follows:

principal The amount borrowed. It may be a value or cell reference.

periodic interest rate Must be expressed as a decimal. May be a value or cell reference. When computing monthly payments, the annual rate for the loan must be divided by 12 to get a monthly rate.

number of periods Represents the number of repayment periods making up the term of the loan. It may be a value or cell reference. When computing monthly payments, a mortgage term expressed in years must be multiplied by 12 to get the number of repayment periods.

A Mortgage Payment Example

Figure 9.17, parts A and B, demonstrates the PMT function for a mortgage with a principal of $48,100, an annual interest rate of 9%, and a term of 30 years. The following entry in cell B8 returns a monthly payment of $387.02:

ROUND(PMT(B3,B6,B7),2)

The following entry in cell B9:

ROUND((B3*B6)/(1−1/(1+B6)^B7),2)

serves as a proof of the PMT function.

Figure 9.17A PMT Function: Formulas On

```
    !              A              !!    B    !!   C   !!   D   !!   E   !!   F   !
1   MORTGAGE PAYMENTS
2   ---------------------------------------------------------------------------
3   PRINCIPAL                         48100
4   INTEREST:
5      ANNUAL RATE                    0.09
6      MONTHLY RATE                   ROUND(B5/12,4)
7   NUMBER OF PERIODS                 360
8   MONTHLY PAYMENT                   ROUND(PMT(B3,B6,B7),2)
9   MANUALLY COMPUTED PAYMENT         ROUND((B3*B6)/(1-1/(1+B6)^B7),2)
10
```

Figure 9.17B PMT Function: Formulas Off

```
    !              A              !!    B    !!   C   !!   D   !!   E   !!   F   !
1   MORTGAGE PAYMENTS
2   ---------------------------------------------------------------------------
3   PRINCIPAL                            48100
4   INTEREST:
5      ANNUAL RATE                         .09
6      MONTHLY RATE                      .0075
7   NUMBER OF PERIODS                      360
8   MONTHLY PAYMENT                     387.02
9   MANUALLY COMPUTED PAYMENT           387.02
10
```

Future Value Function

The FV function calculates the future value of fixed amount payments at a given interest rate over a specified number of periods. It is typically used to calculate the maturity values of pension plan contributions. The Future Value function is based on the formula:

$$FV = P * ((1 + r)\hat{}\, n - 1) / r$$

where P = periodic contribution; r = interest rate per compounding period; and n = number of contribution periods.

The general format for the FV function is

FV(payment,periodic interest rate,number of periods)

Its components are defined as follows:

payment The amount contributed each period. It is a constant amount and may be a value or cell reference.

periodic interest rate Must be expressed as a decimal. It may be a value or cell reference. When computing the future value of monthly contributions, the annual rate of return must be divided by 12 to get a monthly compounding rate.

number of periods Represents the number of contribution periods. It may be a value or cell reference. If the contribution term is expressed in years, it must be multiplied by 12 to get the number of monthly contribution periods.

An IRA Contribution Example

Figure 9.18, parts A and B, demonstrates the FV function for Individual Retirement Account (IRA) contributions. For 1984 federal tax returns, the IRS allowed qualified taxpayers to exclude from income $2,000 of IRA contributions. With this incentive, a 35-year-old taxpayer decides to make monthly contributions of $166.67 to an IRA with an annual interest rate of 9%. The taxpayer wants to know the worth of this account at time of retirement, 30 years later. The following entry in cell B9 returns a future value of $305,130.02:

ROUND(FV(B4,B7,B8),2)

The following entry in cell B10:

ROUND((B4*((1+B7)^B8−1)/B7),2)

serves as a proof of the FV function.

Figure 9.18A FV Function: Formulas On

```
   :            A                   ::      B      ::  C  ::  D  ::  E  :
 1  FUTURE VALUE
 2  --------------------------------------------------------------------
 3  ANNUAL IRA CONTRIBUTION           2000
 4  MONTHLY IRA CONTRIBUTION          ROUND(B3/12,2)
 5  INTEREST:
 6     ANNUAL RATE                    0.09
 7     MONTHLY RATE                   ROUND(B6/12,4)
 8  NUMBER OF PERIODS                 360
 9  FUTURE VALUE                      ROUND(FV(B4,B7,B8),2)
10  MANUALLY COMPUTED FUTURE VALUE ROUND(B4*((1+B7)^B8-1)/B7,2)
```

Figure 9.18B FV Function: Formulas Off

```
   :            A                   ::      B      ::  C  ::  D  ::  E  :
 1  FUTURE VALUE
 2  --------------------------------------------------------------------
 3  ANNUAL IRA CONTRIBUTION                2000.00
 4  MONTHLY IRA CONTRIBUTION                166.67
 5  INTEREST:
 6     ANNUAL RATE                           .0900
 7     MONTHLY RATE                          .0075
 8  NUMBER OF PERIODS                          360
 9  FUTURE VALUE                       $305,130.02
10  MANUALLY COMPUTED FUTURE VALUE     $305,130.02
```

Present Value Function

The PV function calculates the present value of fixed amount payments at a given interest rate over a specified number of periods. You could use this function to decide whether to take a lump sum distribution from a pension plan or to take a series of payments over some fixed term. The Present Value function is based on the formula:

$$PV = P * (1 - (1 / (1 + r) ^ n)) / r$$

where P = periodic payment; r = interest rate per compounding period; and n = number of contribution periods.

The general format for the PV function is

PV(payment,periodic interest rate,number of periods)

Its components are defined as follows:

payment The amount received each period. It is a constant amount and may be a value or cell reference.

periodic interest rate Must be expressed as a decimal. May be a value or cell reference. When computing the present value of monthly receipts, the annual rate of return must be divided by 12 to get a monthly compounding rate.

number of periods Represents the number of payment periods. It may be a value or cell reference. If the payment term is expressed in years, it must be multiplied by 12 to get the number of monthly payment periods.

A Present Value Example

Figure 9.19, parts A and B, demonstrates the PV function. A retiree has been given a choice between a lump sum distribution of $125,000 or a guaranteed annual income of $20,000, paid monthly over a term of 15 years using an annual rate of 9%. Which choice should the retiree make? The following entry in cell B9 returns a present value of $164,322.68:

ROUND(PV(B4,B7,B8),2)

Unless the retiree does not expect to survive the next 15 years, the most profitable choice is to select the 15-year annuity. The following entry in cell B10:

ROUND(B4*(1−(1/(1+B7)^B8))/B7,2)

serves as a proof of the PV function.

Figure 9.19A PV Function: Formulas On

```
   :             A                    ::     B    ::  C  ::  D  ::  E  :
1   PRESENT VALUE
2   ----------------------------------------------------------------------
3   ANNUAL PENSION AMOUNT              20000
4   MONTHLY PENSION AMOUNT             ROUND(B3/12,2)
5   INTEREST:
6      ANNUAL RATE                     0.09
7      MONTHLY RATE                    ROUND(B6/12,4)
8   NUMBER OF PERIODS                  180
9   PRESENT VALUE                      ROUND(PV(B4,B7,B8),2)
10  MANUALLY COMPUTED PRESENT VALUE    ROUND(B4*(1-(1/(1+B7)^B8))/B7,2)
```

Figure 9.19B PV Function: Formulas Off

```
    :                  A                  ::     B     ::  C  ::  D  ::  E  :
1   PRESENT VALUE
2   ---------------------------------------------------------------------------
3   ANNUAL PENSION AMOUNT                      20000.00
4   MONTHLY PENSION AMOUNT                      1666.67
5   INTEREST:
6       ANNUAL RATE                               .0900
7       MONTHLY RATE                              .0075
8   NUMBER OF PERIODS                               180
9   PRESENT VALUE                           $164,322.68
10  MANUALLY COMPUTED PRESENT VALUE         $164,322.68
```

Calendar Functions

The calendar functions covered in this section are based on an internal calendar with a 200-year range, March 1, 1900, through February 28, 2100. This internal calendar is a Modified Julian Calendar containing 73,049 days. Dates outside this range are invalid and result in a **Formula ERROR.**

There are two types of calendar functions, entry functions and reference functions. There are three functions for entering dates: DATE, TODAY, and DVAL. There are five functions for referencing dates: MONTH, DAY, YEAR, WDAY, and JDATE.

Dates are displayed using the formats mm/dd/yy and mm/dd/yyyy, depending on cell width and how the date was entered.

Date Entry Functions

The values returned by the date entry functions are called date values. These are special values to be used by the date reference functions. These values can also be used with the addition and subtraction operators in limited situations. Date values are treated as text by all other functions.

DATE Function

The general format for this function is

DATE(mm,dd,yy) or DATE(mm,dd,yyyy)

When a 2-digit year is used, the century number is assumed to be 19. For years after 1999, the 4-digit year should be used. Regardless of the function format, date values are displayed as **mm/dd/yy** when the column width is nine or ten positions. Displaying **mm/dd/yyyy** requires a column width of at least eleven positions.

Numbers outside the valid number of days in a month or the valid number of months in a year are converted based on the overflow. Some examples:

DATE(6,33,76) converts to **7/ 3/76**

DATE(20,02,81) converts to **8/ 2/82**

TODAY Function

The general format for this function is

TODAY

This function has no argument. It loads the current system date[1] into the active cell. The system date must have been previously entered. If there is no system date, the function returns **N/A,** not available.

Be careful how you use this function since its returned value changes with your system date. A suggestion: use it for a report date in the heading of your spreadsheet.

DVAL Function

The general format for this function is

DVAL(value)

The argument of this function must be an integer between 1 and 73049. This function is used to convert a Modified Julian Date to a date value in mm/dd/yy format.

Date Value Arithmetic

Numeric values can be added to or subtracted from date values. The numeric value is interpreted in terms of days. The resulting date value is the specified number of days before or after the original depending on whether addition or subtraction occurred. Some examples:

DATE(2,28,84) + 15 results in **3/14/84**

DATE(12,25,84) − 31 results in **11/22/84**

Dates may be subtracted from one another. The difference is the number of days between the two dates. For example:

DATE(9,1,84) − DATE(3,4,84) results in **180 days**

An attempt to subtract a date value from a numeric value results in a **Formula ERROR.**

Figure 9.20, parts A and B, presents a sales discount example to illustrate date value arithmetic. Cells C4 through C9 establish an invoice date of 10/10/84 by the entry

DATE(10,10,84)

Column D represents the percent discount allowed when the invoice is paid within the number of days specified in column E. Column F indicates the latest payment date for which the discount can be taken.

For the customer named Baker, Figure 9.20, part B, shows a due date of 11/4/84 in cell F5. This is based on the date value arithmetic C5 + E5, which is the same as

DATE(10,10,84) + 25

1. Use the DATE command; refer to Chapter 2 for more information.

Figure 9.20A Date Value Arithmetic: Formulas On

	A	B	C	D	E	F	G
1	Customer	Invoice	Invoice	Discount	Discount	Payment	Payment
2	Name	Amount	Date	Rate	Terms	Due Date	Amount Due
3	----------	----------	----------	----------	----------	----------	----------
4	Able	100	DATE(10,10,84)	0	30	C4+E4	B4-ROUND(D4%B4,2)
5	Baker	150	DATE(10,10,84)	1	25	C5+E5	B5-ROUND(D5%B5,2)
6	Charles	175	DATE(10,10,84)	2	20	C6+E6	B6-ROUND(D6%B6,2)
7	Delta	200	DATE(10,10,84)	3	15	C7+E7	B7-ROUND(D7%B7,2)
8	Easy	225	DATE(10,10,84)	4	10	C8+E8	B8-ROUND(D8%B8,2)
9	Fox	250	DATE(10,10,84)	5	5	C9+E9	B9-ROUND(D9%B9,2)

Figure 9.20B Date Value Arithmetic: Formulas Off

	A	B	C	D	E	F	G
1	Customer	Invoice	Invoice	Discount	Discount	Payment	Payment
2	Name	Amount	Date	Rate	Terms	Due Date	Amount Due
3	----------	----------	----------	----------	----------	----------	----------
4	Able	100.00	10/10/1984	0	30	11/ 9/1984	100.00
5	Baker	150.00	10/10/1984	1	25	11/ 4/1984	148.50
6	Charles	175.00	10/10/1984	2	20	10/30/1984	171.50
7	Delta	200.00	10/10/1984	3	15	10/25/1984	194.00
8	Easy	225.00	10/10/1984	4	10	10/20/1984	216.00
9	Fox	250.00	10/10/1984	5	5	10/15/1984	237.50

Date Reference Functions

The values returned by the date reference functions are numeric values. These values can be used with all other functions except the date entry functions. The arguments of the date reference functions must contain date values or reference other cells that contain date values. A **Formula ERROR** results if the argument is not a date value.

MONTH, DAY, and YEAR Functions

Together, these functions can break a date value into its three separate components.

The general format for the MONTH function is

MONTH(date value)

The MONTH function returns a value of **1** through **12**, representing January through December, respectively. For example:

MONTH(DATE(3,4,84)) returns **3** for March

The general format for the DAY function is

DAY(date value)

The DAY function returns a value of **1** through **31.** For example:

DAY(DATE(3,4,84)) returns **4**

The general format for the YEAR function is

YEAR(date value)

The YEAR function returns a value of **1900** through **2100.** For example:

YEAR(DATE(3,4,84)) returns **1984**

Weekday Function

The general format for the Weekday function is
WDAY(date value)
The WDAY function returns a value of **1** through **7**, representing Sunday through Saturday, respectively. This is the day of the week for the specified date value. For example:
WDAY(DATE(3,4,84)) returns **1** for Sunday
WDAY(DATE(2,29,84)) returns **4** for Wednesday

Julian Date Function

The general format for this function is
JDATE(date value)
The JDATE function returns a value of **1** through **73049**, representing the Modified Julian Date. For example:
JDATE(DATE(3,1,00)) returns **1**
JDATE(DATE(2,28,2100)) returns **73049**

Other Functions

The following functions are also available in SuperCalc³. Refer to your User's Guide & Reference Manual for additional information.

Arithmetic Functions

EXP(value) Returns the exponent, base e, of the argument.

LN(value) Returns the natural logarithm, base e, of the argument.

LOG(value) Returns the common logarithm, base 10, of the argument.

MOD(value a, value b) Returns the remainder of value a divided by value b.

PI Returns the constant 3.14592653589793.

RAN Returns a random number.

Trigonometric Functions

ACOS(cosine value) Returns the radian angle of the argument.

ASIN(sine value) Returns the radian angle of the argument.

ATAN(tangent value) Returns the radian angle of the argument.

COS(radian angle value) Returns the cosine of the argument.

SIN(radian angle value) Returns the sine of the argument.

TAN(radian angle value) Returns the tangent of the argument.

Logical Function

NOT(expression a) Returns 1, when expression a is false. Returns 0, when expression a is true.

Special Functions

ERR Displays "ERROR".

ISDATE(value) Checks argument for date value. Returns 1 for true, 0 for false.

ISERROR(value) Checks argument for "ERROR" value. Returns 1 for true, 0 for false.

ISNA(value) Checks argument for "N/A" value. Returns 1 for true, 0 for false.

ISNUM(value) Checks argument for numeric value. Returns 1 for true, 0 for false.

ISTEXT(value) Checks argument for textual value. Returns 1 for true, 0 for false.

ITER Returns the number of iterations that have occurred.

TRUE Checks expression for true—i.e., 1.

FALSE Checks expression for false—i.e., 0.

This concludes the material on functions. You have surveyed the most commonly used functions for business applications. You are now ready for the Review Exercises. Enter /**ZY** to erase your spreadsheet.

Review Exercises

1. Use the Credit Card Interest Spreadsheet from Exercise 7.6 to do the following:
   a. Replace the expressions in column E and row 19 by the SUM function.
   b. Calculate the average monthly payment rounded to two decimal places for each month in column F.
   c. Calculate the average monthly payment rounded to two decimal places for each charge account, columns B through F, in row 21.
   d. Determine the highest monthly payment for each charge account, columns B through F, in row 22.
   e. Determine the lowest monthly payment for each charge account, columns B through F, in row 23.
   f. Provide the additional row and column headings.
2. Given the following extract from an IRS Form 1040:

TAX PER TABLES	3604
LESS TAX CREDITS:	
INVESTMENT CREDIT	385
CHILD & DEPENDENT CARE	250
TOTAL TAX	????
PAYMENTS	
FEDERAL INCOME TAX WITHHELD	5000
EXCESS SOCIAL SECURITY TAX	570
TOTAL PAYMENTS	????
TAXES OVERPAID	????
TAXES DUE	????

a. Calculate Total Tax.
b. Calculate Total Payments.
c. Use the IF function to calculate Taxes Overpaid and Taxes Due:
When Total Tax minus Total Payments is less than zero, Taxes Overpaid is the absolute value of the difference, otherwise Taxes Overpaid is not available.
When Total Tax minus Total Payments is greater than zero, Taxes Due is the difference, otherwise Taxes Due is not available.

3. An asset costing $1000 has been proposed. This asset generates the following cash flows over its five-year life:

Year #1	$100
Year #2	200
Year #3	300
Year #4	400
Year #5	500

a. Calculate the Net Present Value rounded to whole dollars using a discount rate of 10%.
b. Use the IF function to determine whether the proposal should be accepted or rejected.
c. Calculate the Internal Rate of Return rounded to whole dollars.

4. Given the following information about the purchase of a new, fully equipped sports car:

DELIVERED PRICE	24995.00
LESS:	
20% CASH DOWN PAYMENT	???????
TRADE-IN ALLOWANCE	2000.00
AMOUNT TO BE FINANCED	????????

(continued on next page)

INTEREST:	
ANNUAL RATE	.137500
MONTHLY RATE	???????
NUMBER OF YEARS	4
NUMBER OF MONTHS	??
MONTHLY PAYMENT	???????

a. Calculate the down payment rounded to two decimal places.
b. Calculate the amount to be financed.
c. Calculate the monthly interest rate rounded to six decimal places.
d. Calculate the financing term in months.
e. Calculate the monthly payment rounded to two decimal places.

5. Given the following information about an employee's pension plan contributions:

All contributions are a percentage of monthly gross pay.
The given employee is contributing 10%.
The employee's monthly gross pay is $3200.
The employee's age is 25.
When employee contributions are greater than or equal to 4%, the company contributes 2%.
The company has guaranteed an annual interest rate of 12%.

a. Calculate the monthly amounts contributed by the employee and the company.
b. Calculate the total monthly contribution amount.
c. Calculate the monthly interest rate rounded to six decimal places.
d. Calculate the number of months in the contribution term.
e. Calculate the Future Value of total monthly contributions after ten years.
f. Calculate the Future Value of total monthly contributions when the employee retires at age 65.

6. Given the following personnel file information for pension plan eligibility and contributions:

Name	Hire Date	Age	Base Pay	Contrib Percent
ABLE	03/10/83	24	100	2
BAKER	01/01/84	30	200	0
CHARLES	01/01/80	22	300	5
DELTA	08/02/82	28	400	7
ECHO	01/01/84	34	500	10
FOX	07/03/76	38	1000	12

a. Enter the Hire Date using the DATE function.
b. Enter the Current Date in the heading of the spreadsheet using the TODAY function.

c. Calculate the contribution using IF, AND, and OR functions as follows:
IF the contribution percent is greater than zero
AND
(employment longevity is greater than or equal to two years
OR
employee age is greater than or equal to 28) take the contribution percent as a percent of base pay, rounded to whole dollars, otherwise the contribution amount is not available.

Answers to Review Exercises

1. a. **/LEX7-6,A**
   b. At cell E6, enter **SUM(B6.D6)**,
   then enter **/RE6,E7:E17** and press RETURN.
   At cell B19, enter **SUM(B6.B17)**,
   then enter **/RB19,C19:E19** and press RETURN.
   b. At cell F6, enter **ROUND(AV(B6.D6),2)**,
   then enter **/RF6,F7:F17** and press RETURN.
   c. At cell B21, enter **ROUND(AV(B6.B17),2)**
   d. At cell B22 enter **MAX(B6.B17)**
   e. At cell B23 enter **MIN(B6.B17)**
   then enter **/RB21:B23,C21:E21** and press RETURN.
   f. Enter the headings at cells A21, A22, A23, and F4.
   See Figure 9.21.
2. a. At cell B6, enter **B1-SUM(B3.B4)**
   b. At cell B12, enter **SUM(B9.B10)**

Figure 9.21 Credit Interest Spreadsheet: Exercise 9-1

	A	B	C	D	E	F	G
1		BILL & CONNIE'S CREDIT CARD INTEREST					
2			FOR CALENDAR YEAR 1984				
3			MASTER				
4		VISA	CHARGE	SEARS	TOTAL	AVERAGE	
5	--------	--------	--------	--------	--------	--------	
6	JAN	5.95	8.96	9.74	24.65	8.22	
7	FEB	12.06	8.84	9.98	30.88	10.29	
8	MAR	13.31	8.23	9.62	31.16	10.39	
9	APR	14.88	7.67	9.29	31.84	10.61	
10	MAY	33.49	7.74	8.89	50.12	16.71	
11	JUN	20.75	8.06	9.05	37.86	12.62	
12	JUL	23.10	8.04	9.37	40.51	13.50	
13	AUG	24.95	7.31	10.64	42.90	14.30	
14	SEP	26.71	7.45	11.59	45.75	15.25	
15	OCT	27.38	8.44	12.64	48.46	16.15	
16	NOV	27.89	7.96	12.48	48.33	16.11	
17	DEC	26.70	7.40	12.30	46.40	15.47	
18		------	------	------	------		
19	TOTAL	257.17	96.10	125.59	478.86		
20		======	======	======	======		
21	AVERAGE	21.43	8.01	10.47	39.91		
22	HIGH	33.49	8.96	12.64	50.12		
23	LOW	5.95	7.31	8.89	24.65		

c. At cell B14, enter **IF(B6-B12<0,ABS(B6-B12),NA)**
At cell B15, enter **IF(B6-B12)>0,B6-B12,NA)**
See Figure 9.22, parts A and B.

3. Make the following entries, plus the headings, to set up the spreadsheet:
At cell B1, enter **.10**
At cell B5, enter **-1000**
At cell B6, enter **100**
At cell B7, enter **200**
At cell B8, enter **300**
At cell B9, enter **400**
At cell B10, enter **500**
a. At cell B12, enter **ROUND(NPV(B1,B6:B10),0)+B5**
b. At cell B14, enter **IF(B12>=0,("ACCEPT"),("REJECT"))**
c. At cell B16, enter **ROUND(IRR(B1,B5:B10),2)**
See Figure 9.23, parts A and B.

Figure 9.22A Tax Spreadsheet, Formulas On: Exercise 9-2

```
    :                  A                  ::  B    ::   C   ::   D   ::   E   :
1   TAX PER TABLES                           3604
2   LESS TAX CREDITS:
3       INVESTMENT CREDIT                    385
4       CHILD & DEPENDENT CARE               250
5                                           ---------
6   TOTAL TAX                                B1-SUM(B3.B4)
7
8   PAYMENTS
9       FEDERAL INCOME TAX WITHHELD          5000
10      EXCESS SOCIAL SECURITY TAX           570
11                                          ---------
12  TOTAL PAYMENTS                           SUM(B9.B10)
13
14  TAXES OVERPAID                           IF(B6-B12<0, ABS(B6-B12), NA)
15  TAXES DUE                                IF(B6-B12>0, B6-B12, NA)
```

Figure 9.22B Tax Spreadsheet, Formulas Off: Exercise 9-2

```
    :                  A                  ::     B    ::   C   ::   D   ::   E   :
1   TAX PER TABLES                                3604
2   LESS TAX CREDITS:
3       INVESTMENT CREDIT                          385
4       CHILD & DEPENDENT CARE                     250
5                                            ---------
6   TOTAL TAX                                     2969
7
8   PAYMENTS
9       FEDERAL INCOME TAX WITHHELD               5000
10      EXCESS SOCIAL SECURITY TAX                 570
11                                           ---------
12  TOTAL PAYMENTS                                5570
13
14  TAXES OVERPAID                                2601
15  TAXES DUE                                      N/A
```

Figure 9.23A NPV and IRR Spreadsheet, Formulas On: Exercise 9-3

```
    :          A                 ::   B   ::   C   ::   D   ::   E   ::   F   :
1   DISCOUNT RATE                  .10
2                                         CASH
3                           PERIODS     FLOWS
4   ------------------------------------------------------------------------
5    0                             -1000
6    1                             100
7    2                             200
8    3                             300
9    4                             400
10   5                             500
11
12  NET PRESENT VALUE              ROUND(NPV(B1,B6.B10),0)+B5
13
14  RECOMMENDATION:                IF(B12)=0,("ACCEPT"),("REJECT"))
15
16  INTERNAL RATE OF RETURN        ROUND(IRR(B1,B5.B10),2)
```

Figure 9.23B NPV and IRR Spreadsheet, Formulas Off: Exercise 9-3

```
    :          A                 ::   B   ::   C   ::   D   ::   E   ::   F   :
1   DISCOUNT RATE                             .10
2                                            CASH
3                           PERIODS         FLOWS
4   ------------------------------------------------------------------------
5                                  0        -1000
6                                  1          100
7                                  2          200
8                                  3          300
9                                  4          400
10                                 5          500
11
12  NET PRESENT VALUE                          65
13
14  RECOMMENDATION:                        ACCEPT
15
16  INTERNAL RATE OF RETURN                   .12
```

4. Make the following entries, plus the headings, to set up the spreadsheet:
   At cell C3, enter **24995**
   At cell C6, enter **2000**
   At cell B11, enter **.1375**
   At cell B14, enter **4**
   a. At cell C5, enter **ROUND(20%C3,2)**
   b. At cell C8, enter **C3-SUM(C5.C6)**
   c. At cell B12, enter **ROUND(B11/12,6)**
   d. At cell B15, enter **B14*12**
   e. At cell B17, enter **ROUND(PMT(C8,B12,B15),2)**
   See Figure 9.24, parts A and B.

Figure 9.24A Car Payment Spreadsheet, Formulas On: Exercise 9-4

```
     !          A          !!    B    !!    C    !!    D    !!    E    !!    F    !
1    SPORTS CAR FINANCING
2    --------------------
3    DELIVERED PRICE                           24995
4    LESS:
5       20% CASH DOWN PAYMENT                  ROUND(20%C3,2)
6       TRADE-IN ALLOWANCE                     2000
7    ----------------------------------------------------------------------------
8    AMOUNT TO BE FINANCED                     C3-SUM(C5.C6)
9
10   INTEREST:
11      ANNUAL RATE               .1375
12      MONTHLY RATE              ROUND(B11/12,6)
13
14   TERM IN YEARS                4
15   TERM IN MONTHS               B14*12
16
17   MONTHLY PAYMENT              ROUND(PMT(C8,B12,B15),2)
18
19   Note for cells B11 and B12:
20      User-Defined Format: 4 decimal places and % display
```

Figure 9.24B Car Payment Spreadsheet, Formulas Off: Exercise 9-4

```
     !          A          !!    B    !!    C    !!    D    !!    E    !!    F    !
1    SPORTS CAR FINANCING
2    --------------------
3    DELIVERED PRICE                               24995
4    LESS:
5       20% CASH DOWN PAYMENT                       4999
6       TRADE-IN ALLOWANCE                          2000
7    ----------------------------------------------------------------------------
8    AMOUNT TO BE FINANCED                         17996
9
10   INTEREST:
11      ANNUAL RATE                 13.7500%
12      MONTHLY RATE                 1.1458%
13
14   TERM IN YEARS                         4
15   TERM IN MONTHS                       48
16
17   MONTHLY PAYMENT                  489.51
18
19   Note for cells B11 and B12:
20      User-Defined Format: 4 decimal places and % display
```

5. Make the following entries, plus the headings, to set up the spreadsheet:
   At cell B3, enter **3200**
   At cell B6, enter **10**
   At cell B12, enter **.12**
   a. At cell B7, enter **IF(C6>=4,2,0)**
      At cell D6, enter **ROUND(B6%B3,2)**
      At cell D7, enter **ROUND(B7%B3,2)**
   b. At cell D9, enter **SUM(D6.D7)**
   c. At cell B13, enter **ROUND(B12/12,6)**
   d. At cell B16, enter **B15*12**
   e. At cell B15, enter **10**
      At cell B18, enter **ROUND(FV(D9,B13,B16),2)**
      See Figure 9.25, parts A and B.

Figure 9.25A Pension Plan Spreadsheet, Formulas On: Exercise 9-5e

```
     :               A              ::      B     ::  C  ::  D  ::  E  :
1    PENSION PLAN PROJECTIONS
2    ------------------------
3    MONTHLY GROSS PAY                3200
4
5    PENSION PLAN CONTRIBUTIONS          PER CENT              AMOUNT
6       EMPLOYEE                      10                     ROUND(B6%B3,2)
7       COMPANY                       IF(B6)=4,2,0)          ROUND(B7%B3,2)
8    ------------------------------------------------------------------------
9    TOTAL                                                   SUM(D6.D7)
10
11   INTEREST:
12      ANNUAL RATE                   .12
13      MONTHLY RATE                  ROUND(B12/12,6)
14
15   TERM IN YEARS                    10
16   TERM IN MONTHS                   B15*12
17
18   FUTURE VALUE                     ROUND(FV(D9,B13,B16),2)
```

Figure 9.25B Pension Plan Spreadsheet, Formulas Off: Exercise 9-5e

```
     :               A              ::      B     ::  C  ::  D  ::  E  :
1    PENSION PLAN PROJECTIONS
2    ------------------------
3    MONTHLY GROSS PAY                           3200
4
5    PENSION PLAN CONTRIBUTIONS             PER CENT             AMOUNT
6       EMPLOYEE                                  10                320
7       COMPANY                                    2                 64
8    ------------------------------------------------------------------------
9    TOTAL                                                          384
10
11   INTEREST:
12      ANNUAL RATE                         12.0000%
13      MONTHLY RATE                         1.0000%
14
15   TERM IN YEARS                                10
16   TERM IN MONTHS                              120
17
18   FUTURE VALUE                           88334.86
```

f. At cell B15, enter **40**
   See Figure 9.26.

Figure 9.26 Pension Plan Spreadsheet, Formulas On: Exercise 9-5f

```
     :               A              ::      B     ::  C  ::  D  ::  E  :
1    PENSION PLAN PROJECTIONS
2    ------------------------
3    MONTHLY GROSS PAY                           3200
4
5    PENSION PLAN CONTRIBUTIONS             PER CENT             AMOUNT
6       EMPLOYEE                                  10                320
7       COMPANY                                    2                 64
8    ------------------------------------------------------------------------
9    TOTAL                                                          384
10
11   INTEREST:
12      ANNUAL RATE                         12.0000%
13      MONTHLY RATE                         1.0000%
14
15   TERM IN YEARS                                40
16   TERM IN MONTHS                              480
17
18   FUTURE VALUE                         4517672.64
```

6. All employee detail entries are in rows 9 through 14. Columns are used as follows:

   Column A—Name
   Column B—Hire Date
   Column C—Age
   Column D—Base Pay
   Column E—Contribution Percent
   Column F—Contribution Amount

   a. At cell B7, enter **DATE(3,10,83)**
      At cell B8, enter **DATE(1,1,84)**
      At cell B9, enter **DATE(1,1,80)**
      At cell B10, enter **DATE(8,2,82)**
      At cell B11, enter **DATE(1,1,84)**
      At cell B12, enter **DATE(7,3,76)**
   b. At cell B3, enter **TODAY**
      Make sure you have set the current date on your system before entering SuperCalc³.
   c. At cell F7, enter
      IF(AND(OR(B3-B7>=2*365,C7>=28),E7>0),ROUND(E7%D7,0),NA)
      Then enter **/RF7,F8:F12,ANYYYYY**
      See Figure 9.27

Figure 9.27 Pension Plan Eligibility Spreadsheet: Exercise 9-6

```
     :      A      ::     B     ::  C  ::  D  ::   E   ::   F   :
 1   PENSION PLAN ELIGIBILITY ANALYSIS
 2   ---------------------------------
 3   CURRENT DATE:      12/ 9/1984
 4                                                 CONTRIB   CONTRIB
 5   NAME                HIRE DATE      AGE BASE PAY  PERCENT    AMOUNT
 6   ------------------------------------------------------------------
 7   ABLE                3/10/1983       24      100         2       N/A
 8   BAKER               1/ 1/1984       30      200         0       N/A
 9   CHARLES             1/ 1/1980       22      300         5        15
10   DELTA               8/ 2/1982       28      400         7        28
11   ECHO                1/ 1/1984       34      500        10        50
12   FOX                 7/ 3/1976       38     1000        12       120
```

SECTION THREE

Advanced SuperCalc^3 Features

CHAPTER 10

More on Controlling Spreadsheet Screen Displays

Chapter Overview and Objectives

- Screen Splitting
- Title Locking

This chapter introduces two "Slash" commands that provide you with additional screen display controls. The features of these new commands are in addition to the control features of the /Format and /Global commands.

In this chapter you'll learn how to use the /Window command for simultaneously viewing different portions of a spreadsheet and simultaneously displaying the same portion of a spreadsheet in different formats and global settings. You'll also learn how to use the /Title command for locking column headings or row headings or locking both column headings and row headings. You'll find the /Title command useful for scrolling through large spreadsheets.

Screen Splitting

The /Window command allows you to split your screen into two separate windows. The split can be made horizontally, resulting in upper and lower windows, or vertically, resulting in left and right windows.

The point of the split is determined by the position of the spreadsheet cursor. For a horizontal split, window partitioning occurs between the current row and the preceding row. The current row becomes the first row in the bottom window. The preceding row becomes the last row in the top window.

For a vertical split, window partitioning occurs between the current column and the preceding column. The current column becomes the first column in the right window. The preceding column becomes the last column in the left window.

Although the windows do not have to be split into equal portions, horizontal splits may not be attempted from row 1 and vertical splits may not be attempted from column A. If you try to do either of these invalid splits, SuperCalc^3 returns the following error message:

No Room (at edge) to display window

While the spreadsheet can be /Saved with a split screen, the /Output command will not generate a report with a split screen. When the /Output command is used, the generated results will reflect the format and global display settings of the window where the spreadsheet cursor is positioned.

There are two important benefits to using a split screen display. First, you can simultaneously display distant sections of a spreadsheet. This command eliminates the necessity of scrolling back and forth. Consider an Income Statement that contains more than 24 rows. In a single screen it might not be possible to see both Total Revenue and Total Profit at the same time. As an alternative to repetitious scrolling, the screen could be split horizontally so that Revenue falls in the upper window and Profit falls in the lower window.

The second benefit is that the formats and global display settings function independently between the first and second windows. During spreadsheet creation or maintenance, a vertical split allows formulas to be toggled on in one window and toggled off in the other. This allows you to see formulas and their evaluated results simultaneously. Column widths and other formats can be varied between windows. Separate title locks can also be set.

The spreadsheet cursor is moved between windows by pressing the semicolon (;) key.

To split your screen, enter **/W.** Your PROMPT and ENTRY lines display

H(oriz.), V(ert.), C(lear Split), S(ynch.) or U(nsynch.)

9>/Window,

You have the following options:

H Causes a horizontal screen split. The current row is the first row in the lower window. The spreadsheet cursor is positioned at the first (upper left) cell in the lower window. This option can only be used from a full screen, otherwise the following error results:

CLEAR Current Split

V Causes a vertical screen split. The current column is the first column in the right window. The spreadsheet cursor is positioned at the first (upper left) cell in the right window. This option can only be used from a full screen, otherwise the following error results:

CLEAR Current Split

C Clears the current split. If the split is horizontal, the full screen returned starts at the upper window of the split screen; the formats, global settings, and title locks for that window govern the full screen.

If the split is vertical, the full screen returned starts at the left window of the split screen; the formats, global settings, and title locks for that window govern the full screen.

S Synchronizes scrolling for the two windows. When the spreadsheet cursor moves parallel to the split, both windows move concurrently in the same direction. This option is used after a split has been made. It is mutually exclusive of the **U**

option. You would probably use synchronized scrolling for a vertical split with formulas displayed in one window and values displayed in the other. This would insure that you viewed the same cells in each window.

U Unsynchronizes scrolling for the two windows. This option is the default. It allows the windows to scroll independently of one another. It is mutually exclusive of the **S** option. You would need unsynchronized scrolling to view distant sections of a spreadsheet simultaneously.

Screen Splitting Examples

The following examples use the Income Statement Spreadsheet to demonstrate the /Window command. Figure 10.1 shows a full screen display of the spreadsheet PALDEMO. The spreadsheet cursor is positioned at cell C9.

Figure 10.1 P&L Spreadsheet: Full Screen View

```
    |          A          ||    B    ||    C    ||    D    ||    E    ||    F    ||    G    |
1                                          Bill's P & L Statement
2                                               Fiscal Year 1984
3                               QTR #1     QTR #2     QTR #3     QTR #4      TOTAL
4                            --------------------------------------------------------
5    SALES                     5000.00    4000.00    4500.00    7500.00  21000.00
6    COST OF GOODS SOLD        1500.00    1200.00    1350.00    2250.00   6300.00
7                            --------   --------   --------   --------   --------
8    GROSS MARGIN              3500.00    2800.00    3150.00    5250.00  14700.00
9
10   OPERATING EXPENSES
11     MARKETING               1000.00    1000.00    1000.00    1000.00   4000.00
12     ADMINISTRATIVE           500.00     400.00     450.00     750.00   2100.00
13                           --------   --------   --------   --------   --------
14        TOTAL                1500.00    1400.00    1450.00    1750.00   6100.00
15
16   PRE-TAX PROFIT            2000.00    1400.00    1700.00    3500.00   8600.00
17   INCOME TAX                1000.00     700.00     850.00    1750.00   4300.00
18                           --------   --------   --------   --------   --------
19   NET INCOME                1000.00     700.00     850.00    1750.00   4300.00
20                           ========   ========   ========   ========   ========
 C9
Width:  9  Memory: 99 Last Col/Row:G20     ? for HELP
 1>
F1 = Help; F2 = Cancel; F9 = Plot; F10 = View                     CAPS
```

To split the screen horizontally at the current cursor position, enter **/WH.** This results in a display identical to the one shown in Figure 10.2.

Note that each window has its own set of borders. In the lower window the spreadsheet cursor is still sitting at cell C9.

In this example, screen splitting can be used to confine the display to Sales, Cost of Goods Sold, Gross Margin, Pre-Tax Profit, Income Tax, and Net Income. Enter **=A16** and press RETURN to jump to cell A16. Next, enter = and press RETURN. This moves cell A16 to the upper left corner of the bottom window. Figure 10.3 shows the new display.

Figure 10.2 P&L Spreadsheet: Horizontally Split Screen

```
   |          A          ||    B    ||    C    ||    D    ||    E    ||    F    ||    G    |
 1                                       Bill's P & L Statement
 2                                          Fiscal Year 1984
 3                             QTR #1    QTR #2    QTR #3    QTR #4     TOTAL
 4                            --------------------------------------------------
 5  SALES                      5000.00   4000.00   4500.00   7500.00  21000.00
 6  COST OF GOODS SOLD         1500.00   1200.00   1350.00   2250.00   6300.00
 7                            --------  --------  --------  --------  --------
 8  GROSS MARGIN               3500.00   2800.00   3150.00   5250.00  14700.00
   |          A          ||    B    ||    C    ||    D    ||    E    ||    F    ||    G    |
 9
10  OPERATING EXPENSES
11     MARKETING               1000.00   1000.00   1000.00   1000.00   4000.00
12     ADMINISTRATIVE           500.00    400.00    450.00    750.00   2100.00
13                            --------  --------  --------  --------  --------
14          TOTAL              1500.00   1400.00   1450.00   1750.00   6100.00
15
16  PRE-TAX PROFIT             2000.00   1400.00   1700.00   3500.00   8600.00
17  INCOME TAX                 1000.00    700.00    850.00   1750.00   4300.00
18                            --------  --------  --------  --------  --------
19  NET INCOME                 1000.00    700.00    850.00   1750.00   4300.00
 C9
Width:  9   Memory: 99 Last Col/Row:G20       ? for HELP
  1>
F1 = Help; F2 = Cancel; F9 = Plot; F10 = View                    CAPS
```

Figure 10.3 P&L Spreadsheet: Horizontally Split Screen with Unsynchronized Scrolling

```
   |          A          ||    B    ||    C    ||    D    ||    E    ||    F    ||    G    |
 1                                       Bill's P & L Statement
 2                                          Fiscal Year 1984
 3                             QTR #1    QTR #2    QTR #3    QTR #4     TOTAL
 4                            --------------------------------------------------
 5  SALES                      5000.00   4000.00   4500.00   7500.00  21000.00
 6  COST OF GOODS SOLD         1500.00   1200.00   1350.00   2250.00   6300.00
 7                            --------  --------  --------  --------  --------
 8  GROSS MARGIN               3500.00   2800.00   3150.00   5250.00  14700.00
   |          A          ||    B    ||    C    ||    D    ||    E    ||    F    ||    G    |
16  PRE-TAX PROFIT             2000.00   1400.00   1700.00   3500.00   8600.00
17  INCOME TAX                 1000.00    700.00    850.00   1750.00   4300.00
18                            --------  --------  --------  --------  --------
19  NET INCOME                 1000.00    700.00    850.00   1750.00   4300.00
20                            ========  ========  ========  ========  ========
21
22
23
24
25
26
 A16          P Text="PRE-TAX PROFIT
Width: 20   Memory: 99 Last Col/Row:G20       ? for HELP
  1>
F1 = Help; F2 = Cancel; F9 = Plot; F10 = View                    CAPS
```

Press ; then HOME and the spreadsheet cursor jumps to cell A1 in the top window. An entry of **/WC** changes the display to match Figure 10.1.

In full screen display mode you could toggle formulas on and off, but you could never see both at the same time. The next example demonstrates using vertical screen splits to display formulas and values simultaneously. First, position the spreadsheet cursor at cell D1, since it is the approximate center of the spreadsheet. Next, enter **/WV.** As displayed in Figure 10.4, your screen is split into left and right windows. The left window contains columns A, B, and C. The right window contains columns D, E, and F.

Figure 10.4 P&L Spreadsheet: Vertically Split Screen

```
   |          A           ||    B    ||    C    |  |    D    ||    E    ||    F    |
1                                       Bill's 1    P & L Statement
2                                          Fis 2   cal Year 1984
3                               QTR #1    QTR #2 3      QTR #3    QTR #4      TOTAL
4                             ------------------ 4   ----------------------------
5      SALES                   5000.00   4000.00 5     4500.00   7500.00 21000.00
6      COST OF GOODS SOLD      1500.00   1200.00 6     1350.00   2250.00   6300.00
7                             --------  -------- 7    --------  --------  --------
8      GROSS MARGIN            3500.00   2800.00 8     3150.00   5250.00 14700.00
9                                                9
10     OPERATING EXPENSES                        10
11       MARKETING             1000.00   1000.00 11    1000.00   1000.00   4000.00
12       ADMINISTRATIVE         500.00    400.00 12     450.00    750.00   2100.00
13                            --------  -------- 13   --------  --------  --------
14          TOTAL              1500.00   1400.00 14    1450.00   1750.00   6100.00
15                                               15
16     PRE-TAX PROFIT          2000.00   1400.00 16    1700.00   3500.00   8600.00
17     INCOME TAX              1000.00    700.00 17     850.00   1750.00   4300.00
18                            --------  -------- 18   --------  --------  --------
19     NET INCOME              1000.00    700.00 19     850.00   1750.00   4300.00
20                            ========  ======== 20   ========  ========  ========
 D1
Width:  9  Memory: 99 Last Col/Row:G20        ? for HELP
  1>
F1 = Help; F2 = Cancel; F9 = Plot; F10 = View                     CAPS
```

The cursor is in the right window. Now enter **/GF** to toggle on formula display. As shown in Figure 10.5, the left window displays values while the right window shows formulas.

Figure 10.5 P&L Spreadsheet: Vertically Split Screen with Formulas On in Right Window

```
   |          A           ||    B    ||    C    |  |    D    ||    E    ||    F    |
1                                       Bill's 1    P & L Statement
2                                          Fis 2   cal Year 1984
3                               QTR #1    QTR #2 3      QTR #3    QTR #4      TOTAL
4                             ------------------ 4   ----------------------------
5      SALES                   5000.00   4000.00 5        4500        7500+C5+D5+E5
6      COST OF GOODS SOLD      1500.00   1200.00 6       30%D5     30%E5+C6+D6+E6
7                             --------  -------- 7    --------  --------  --------
8      GROSS MARGIN            3500.00   2800.00 8       D5-D6     E5-E6+C8+D8+E8
9                                                9
10     OPERATING EXPENSES                        10
11       MARKETING             1000.00   1000.00 11       1000        10001+D11+E11
12       ADMINISTRATIVE         500.00    400.00 12      10%D5      10%E52+D12+E12
13                            --------  -------- 13   --------  --------  --------
14          TOTAL              1500.00   1400.00 14    D11+D12   E11+E124+D14+E14
15                                               15
16     PRE-TAX PROFIT          2000.00   1400.00 16     D8-D14    E8-E146+D16+E16
17     INCOME TAX              1000.00    700.00 17     50%D16    50%E167+D17+E17
18                            --------  -------- 18   --------  --------  --------
19     NET INCOME              1000.00    700.00 19    D16-D17   E16-E179+D19+E19
20                            ========  ======== 20   ========  ========  ========
 D1
Width:  9  Memory: 99 Last Col/Row:G20        ? for HELP
  1>
F1 = Help; F2 = Cancel; F9 = Plot; F10 = View                     CAPS
```

Since the displayed portions are not the same for each window, an entry of **=B1** changes the display area in the right window to be consistent with the display area in the left window. See Figure 10.6.

Figure 10.6 P&L Spreadsheet: Vertically Split Screen Positioned for Synchronized Scrolling

```
   |          A          ||    B    ||    C    |   |    B    ||    C    ||    D    |
1                                        Bill's 1                Bill's P & L St
2                                           Fis 2                  Fiscal Year
3                             QTR #1    QTR #2 3       QTR #1    QTR #2    QTR #3
4                          ------------------- 4   ----------------------------
5   SALES                  5000.00   4000.00 5         5000      4000      4500
6   COST OF GOODS SOLD     1500.00   1200.00 6        30%B5     30%C5     30%D5
7                          --------  -------- 7    --------  --------  --------
8   GROSS MARGIN           3500.00   2800.00 8        B5-B6     C5-C6     D5-D6
9                                            9
10  OPERATING EXPENSES                       10
11     MARKETING           1000.00   1000.00 11        1000      1000      1000
12     ADMINISTRATIVE       500.00    400.00 12      10%B5     10%C5     10%D5
13                         --------  -------- 13   --------  --------  --------
14        TOTAL            1500.00   1400.00 14    B11+B12   C11+C12   D11+D12
15                                           15
16  PRE-TAX PROFIT         2000.00   1400.00 16     B8-B14    C8-C14    D8-D14
17  INCOME TAX             1000.00    700.00 17     50%B16    50%C16    50%D16
18                         --------  -------- 18   --------  --------  --------
19  NET INCOME             1000.00    700.00 19    B16-B17   C16-C17   D16-D17
20                         ========  ======== 20   ========  ========  ========
 B1
Width:  9  Memory: 99 Last Col/Row:G20      ? for HELP
  1>
F1 = Help; F2 = Cancel; F9 = Plot; F10 = View                    CAPS
```

In a vertical split situation like the current one, it's very important that the values on the left and the formulas on the right are properly aligned by row. As the spreadsheet presently stands, there's no guarantee that it will not be scrolled out of alignment. Remember that the default is unsynchronized scrolling. An entry of **/WS** turns on synchronized scrolling. The following entries illustrate how synchronized movement works:

=**B10** and press RETURN

= and press RETURN

Even though the entries have been made from the window on the right side, Figure 10.7 shows both windows now positioned at row 10.

Figure 10.7 P&L Spreadsheet: Vertically Split Screen with Synchronized Scrolling

```
   |          A          ||    B    ||    C    |   |    B    ||    C    ||    D    |
10  OPERATING EXPENSES                       10
11     MARKETING           1000.00   1000.00 11        1000      1000      1000
12     ADMINISTRATIVE       500.00    400.00 12      10%B5     10%C5     10%D5
13                         --------  -------- 13   --------  --------  --------
14        TOTAL            1500.00   1400.00 14    B11+B12   C11+C12   D11+D12
15                                           15
16  PRE-TAX PROFIT         2000.00   1400.00 16     B8-B14    C8-C14    D8-D14
17  INCOME TAX             1000.00    700.00 17     50%B16    50%C16    50%D16
18                         --------  -------- 18   --------  --------  --------
19  NET INCOME             1000.00    700.00 19    B16-B17   C16-C17   D16-D17
20                         ========  ======== 20   ========  ========  ========
21                                           21
22                                           22
23                                           23
24                                           24
25                                           25
26                                           26
27                                           27
28                                           28
29                                           29
 B10
Width:  9  Memory: 99 Last Col/Row:G20      ? for HELP
  1>
F1 = Help; F2 = Cancel; F9 = Plot; F10 = View                    CAPS
```

Title Locking

The /Title command allows you to lock one or more rows into place at the top of your screen to be used as column headings. It allows you to lock one or more columns into place at the left of your screen to be used as row headings. The /Title command also allows you to lock both rows and columns into place at the upper left vertex of your screen to provide both row and column headings.

The point of the lock is determined by the position of the spreadsheet cursor. For horizontal titles, locking starts at the current row and continues to all rows above the current row. For vertical titles, locking starts at the current column and continues to all columns to the left of the current column. For simultaneous horizontal and vertical titles, locking starts at the current cell and continues to all rows above the current row as well as all columns to the left of the current column.

While the spreadsheet can be /Saved with titles locked, the /Output command will not generate a report showing locked titles. To achieve the effect of horizontal titles with the /Output command, it's necessary to /Copy the heading rows to the appropriate rows in the spreadsheet so they print out at the top of each output page.

To achieve the effect of vertical titles with the /Output command, it's necessary to /Format any unwanted intervening columns to a width of zero prior to using the /Output command.

The primary benefit of title locks is that they facilitate scrolling through large spreadsheets. The frozen headings prevent you from forgetting the description of given rows and columns. Consider using horizontal title locks whenever your spreadsheet exceeds 20 rows. Consider using vertical title locks whenever column A has descriptive headings applicable to all columns in the row and the entire row cannot be displayed on one screen due to either column width or the number of columns. Consider using both horizontal and vertical title locks when the individual guidelines for horizontal and vertical locks are concurrently applicable.

The spreadsheet cursor cannot be moved into locked rows or columns via scrolling commands, but it can be positioned in a locked area by the = command.

To set title locks, enter **/T.** Your PROMPT and ENTRY lines display

H(oriz.), V(ert.), B(oth) or C(lear)?

8>/Title,

You have the following options:

H Sets a horizontal title lock at the current row and extending to all rows above. If a title lock was already in effect, it is cleared and the following message is displayed:

Title Cleared

V Sets a vertical title lock at the current column, extending to all columns on the left. If a title lock was already in effect, it is cleared and the following message is displayed:

Title Cleared

B Sets both horizontal and vertical title locks extending from the current cell to all rows above and to all columns on the left. If a title lock was already in effect, it is cleared and the following message is displayed:

Title Cleared

C Clears the current title lock and displays the following message:

Title Cleared

Title Locking Example

The following example uses a student grade spreadsheet[1] to demonstrate the /Title command. This spreadsheet consists of 13 columns representing student name, four tests, four program assignments, test average, program average, course average, and letter grade. Figure 10.8 shows only the first eight columns due to screen width limitations.

Figure 10.8 Student Grade Spreadsheet: Columns A.H

```
   |  A     ||   B     ||   C     ||   D     ||   E     ||   F     ||   G     ||   H     |
1   NAME      TEST #1    TEST #2    TEST #3    TEST #4    PROG #1    PROG #2    PROG #3
2   -------------------------------------------------------------------------------------
3   ABLE           85         74         65         60         90         80         90
4   BAKER          92         90         86         89         88         90         92
5   CHARLES        89         70         53          0        100         90          0
6   DELTA          77         85         82         71        100        100         90
7   ECHO           83         85         87         80        100        100         96
8   FOX            97         93         94         94        100        100        100
9   GAMMA          66         74         66         74        100         86         86
10  HOTEL          65         63         65         60         70         75         65
11  INCA           97         92         97         92        100        100        100
12  -------   -------    -------    -------    -------    -------    -------    -------
13  AVERAGE        83         81         77         69         94         91         80
14  HIGH           97         93         97         94        100        100        100
15  LOW            65         63         53          0         70         75          0
16
17
18
19
20
A1               Text="NAME
Width:  9  Memory: 95 Last Col/Row:M15      ? for HELP
 1)
F1 = Help; F2 = Cancel; F9 = Plot; F10 = View                  CAPS
```

If you were interested in the averages and course grades, you could scroll to the other half of the spreadsheet. Although this information would now be displayed on your screen, as illustrated in Figure 10.9, you could not see the name of the student it described.

1. See Chapter 9, Figure 9.14, and associated text for more information on this spreadsheet.

Figure 10.9 Student Grade Spreadsheet: Columns F.M

```
     |   F    ||   G    ||   H    ||   I    ||   J    ||   K    ||   L    ||   M    |
1      PROG #1  PROG #2  PROG #3  PROG #4 TEST AVG PROG AVG CRSE AVG    Grade
2    -------------------------------------------------------------------------------
3          90       80       90       80       71       85       75        C
4          88       90       92       94       89       91       90        B
5         100       90        0        0       53       48       52        F
6         100      100       90       85       79       94       83        C
7         100      100       96      100       84       99       88        B
8         100      100      100      100       95      100       96        A
9         100       86       86       80       70       88       75        C
10         70       75       65       80       63       73       66        D
11        100      100      100      100       95      100       96        A
12     -------  -------  -------  -------  -------  -------  -------
13         94       91       80       80       78       86       80
14        100      100      100      100       95      100       96
15         70       75        0        0       53       48       52
16
17
18
19
20
 M1             Text="Grade
Width:   9  Memory: 95 Last Col/Row:M15       ? for HELP
  1>
F1 = Help; F2 = Cancel; F9 = Plot; F10 = View                CAPS
```

Usage of the title locks easily corrects this problem. First, an entry of **=A1** positions the spreadsheet cursor at cell A1. Next, an entry of **/TV** locks the student names in column A. The spreadsheet cursor can be positioned at cell J1 by a jump command or by scrolling. The resulting screen, as shown in Figure 10.10, displays the averages and letter adjacent to the student names locked in column A.

Figure 10.10 Student Grade Spreadsheet: Vertical Title Lock on Column A

```
     |   A    ||   J    ||   K    ||   L    ||   M    ||   N    ||   O    ||   P    |
1    NAME      TEST AVG PROG AVG CRSE AVG   Grade
2    -------------------------------------------------------------------------------
3    ABLE            71       85       75      C
4    BAKER           89       91       90      B
5    CHARLES         53       48       52      F
6    DELTA           79       94       83      C
7    ECHO            84       99       88      B
8    FOX             95      100       96      A
9    GAMMA           70       88       75      C
10   HOTEL           63       73       66      D
11   INCA            95      100       96      A
12   -------    -------  -------  -------
13   AVERAGE         78       86       80
14   HIGH            95      100       96
15   LOW             53       48       52
16
17
18
19
20
 J1             Text="TEST AVG
Width:   9  Memory: 95 Last Col/Row:M15       ? for HELP
  1>
F1 = Help; F2 = Cancel; F9 = Plot; F10 = View                CAPS
```

Review Exercises

These exercises use the spreadsheet created in Exercise 9.1.

1. Split the screen so that the months, VISA, and MASTER CHARGE are in one window, and SEARS, TOTAL, and AVERAGE are in the other.
2. In the left window, lock the names of the months and position the TOTAL and AVERAGE columns adjacent to the months.
3. In the right window, scroll so columns C, D, and E are shown, then toggle on formula display.
4. From the left window, clear both the title and the screen split.

Answers to Review Exercises

1. **=D1**
   /WV

Figure 10.11 Credit Interest Spreadsheet: Exercise 10-1

```
   |  A  ||  B  ||  C   |  |  D  ||     E       ||  F  ||  G  |
1          BILL & CONNIE'S CR 1  EDIT CARD INTEREST
2                FOR CALENDA 2   R YEAR 1984
3                     MASTER 3
4              VISA   CHARGE 4        SEARS          TOTAL   AVERAGE
5         ------------------ 5   ----------------------------------
6   JAN        5.95     8.96 6         9.74          24.65      8.22
7   FEB       12.06     8.84 7         9.98          30.88     10.29
8   MAR       13.31     8.23 8         9.62          31.16     10.39
9   APR       14.88     7.67 9         9.29          31.84     10.61
10  MAY       33.49     7.74 10        8.89          50.12     16.71
11  JUN       20.75     8.06 11        9.05          37.86     12.62
12  JUL       23.10     8.04 12        9.37          40.51     13.50
13  AUG       24.95     7.31 13       10.64          42.90     14.30
14  SEP       26.71     7.45 14       11.59          45.75     15.25
15  OCT       27.38     8.44 15       12.64          48.46     16.15
16  NOV       27.89     7.96 16       12.48          48.33     16.11
17  DEC       26.70     7.40 17       12.30          46.40     15.47
18           ------   ------ 18      ------         ------
19  TOTAL    257.17    96.10 19      125.59         478.86
20           ======   ====== 20      ======         ======
 D1
Width:  9  Memory: 98 Last Col/Row:G23      ? for HELP
  1>
F1 = Help; F2 = Cancel; F9 = Plot; F10 = View              CAPS
```

2. ; to get from right window to left window.
   =A1
   /TV
   =E1

Figure 10.12 Credit Interest Spreadsheet: Exercise 10-2

```
    |  A  ||      E        |      |  D  ||      E       ||   F   ||  G  |
1            INTEREST           1   EDIT CARD INTEREST
2           84                  2   R YEAR 1984
3                               3
4                      TOTAL    4       SEARS        TOTAL   AVERAGE
5           ----------------    5   -------------------------------------
6   JAN                24.65    6        9.74        24.65      8.22
7   FEB                30.88    7        9.98        30.88     10.29
8   MAR                31.16    8        9.62        31.16     10.39
9   APR                31.84    9        9.29        31.84     10.61
10  MAY                50.12    10       8.89        50.12     16.71
11  JUN                37.86    11       9.05        37.86     12.62
12  JUL                40.51    12       9.37        40.51     13.50
13  AUG                42.90    13      10.64        42.90     14.30
14  SEP                45.75    14      11.59        45.75     15.25
15  OCT                48.46    15      12.64        48.46     16.15
16  NOV                48.33    16      12.48        48.33     16.11
17  DEC                46.40    17      12.30        46.40     15.47
18                    ------    18     ------       ------
19  TOTAL             478.86    19     125.59       478.86
20                    ======    20     ======       ======
 E1
Width: 15  Memory: 98 Last Col/Row:G23     ? for HELP
  1>
F1 = Help; F2 = Cancel; F9 = Plot; F10 = View              CAPS
```

3. ; to get from left window to right window.
   ←
   /GF

Figure 10.13 Credit Interest Spreadsheet: Exercise 10-3

```
    |  A  ||      E        |      |  C  ||  D  ||        E          ||   F   |
1            INTEREST           1   NNIE'S CREDIT CARD INTEREST
2           84                  2   R CALENDAR YEAR 1984
3                               3      MASTER
4                      TOTAL    4      CHARGE     SEARS            TOTAL   AVERAGE
5           ----------------    5   ---------------------------------------------
6   JAN                24.65    6        8.96      9.74    SUM(B6.D6)B6.D6),2)
7   FEB                30.88    7        8.84      9.98    SUM(B7.D7)B7.D7),2)
8   MAR                31.16    8        8.23      9.62    SUM(B8.D8)B8.D8),2)
9   APR                31.84    9        7.67      9.29    SUM(B9.D9)B9.D9),2)
10  MAY                50.12    10       7.74      8.89   SUM(B10.D10)0.D10),2)
11  JUN                37.86    11       8.06      9.05   SUM(B11.D11)1.D11),2)
12  JUL                40.51    12       8.04      9.37   SUM(B12.D12)2.D12),2)
13  AUG                42.90    13       7.31     10.64   SUM(B13.D13)3.D13),2)
14  SEP                45.75    14       7.45     11.59   SUM(B14.D14)4.D14),2)
15  OCT                48.46    15       8.44     12.64   SUM(B15.D15)5.D15),2)
16  NOV                48.33    16       7.96     12.48   SUM(B16.D16)6.D16),2)
17  DEC                46.40    17        7.4      12.3   SUM(B17.D17)7.D17),2)
18                    ------    18     ------    ------          ------
19  TOTAL             478.86    19  M(C6.C17)M(D6.D17)     SUM(E6.E17)
20                    ======    20     ======    ======          ======
C1
Width:  9  Memory: 98 Last Col/Row:G23     ? for HELP
  1>
F1 = Help; F2 = Cancel; F9 = Plot; F10 = View              CAPS
```

4. ; to get from right window to left window.
   /TC
   /WC

Figure 10.14 Credit Interest Spreadsheet: Exercise 10-4

```
    |  A   ||  B  ||  C  ||  D  ||    E     ||  F  ||  G  |
1                BILL & CONNIE'S CREDIT CARD INTEREST
2                       FOR CALENDAR YEAR 1984
3                            MASTER
4                     VISA   CHARGE     SEARS          TOTAL  AVERAGE
5                ---------------------------------------------------
6    JAN              5.95     8.96      9.74          24.65     8.22
7    FEB             12.06     8.84      9.98          30.88    10.29
8    MAR             13.31     8.23      9.62          31.16    10.39
9    APR             14.88     7.67      9.29          31.84    10.61
10   MAY             33.49     7.74      8.89          50.12    16.71
11   JUN             20.75     8.06      9.05          37.86    12.62
12   JUL             23.10     8.04      9.37          40.51    13.50
13   AUG             24.95     7.31     10.64          42.90    14.30
14   SEP             26.71     7.45     11.59          45.75    15.25
15   OCT             27.38     8.44     12.64          48.46    16.15
16   NOV             27.89     7.96     12.48          48.33    16.11
17   DEC             26.70     7.40     12.30          46.40    15.47
18                  ------   ------    ------         ------
19   TOTAL          257.17    96.10    125.59         478.86
20                  ======   ======    ======         ======
A1
Width:  9   Memory: 98 Last Col/Row:G23      ? for HELP
  1>
F1 = Help; F2 = Cancel; F9 = Plot; F10 = View                  CAPS
```

CHAPTER 11

Searching and Sorting

Chapter Overview and Objectives

- Concept of Table Searching
- Structure of Tables
- Creating and Searching Tables
- Sorting Spreadsheets

This chapter introduces table lookup concepts and sorting. You will learn how to build tables and how to make the data entry process substantially more flexible and efficient.

The sorting techniques illustrated free you from dependency on the order in which the data was initially entered into the spreadsheet. The examples provided show how to use sorting as an analytical tool.

Concept of Table Searching

This technique uses a value to search a range of cells, called a table, located somewhere else in your spreadsheet. When a value match is found, the contents of an adjacent cell are returned. The process is known as a table lookup and is done using the LOOKUP function. It allows you to enter a one- or two-digit code in the main body of the spreadsheet and subsequently pull numeric or textual values associated with this code from another area of the spreadsheet.

This feature is more powerful than simple cell referencing. It provides more flexibility for your spreadsheets since unlimited searches can be made from various points in your spreadsheet. Here are some practical applications of table searches:

job titles Puts a position code in the employee's master record, then uses the position code to get the employee's job title from the table.

hourly rates Puts a job code in the employee's time record, then uses the job code to get the employee's hourly rate from the table.

currency conversion rates Uses a currency code to get the current exchange rate from a currency conversion table.

Structure of Tables

SuperCalc³ tables consist of paired rows or paired columns. The upper row or left column of a given table contains a series of table location numbers. These numbers are also called location pointers since they point to the table entry in the lower row or right column, depending on how the table is structured. These pointers must be in ascending sequence. All table entries must be formula entries, usually either numeric values or textual values.

Whether a given table uses a row or column approach is a design consideration. Use whichever approach best fits the structure of the main body of your spreadsheet and whichever is preferable to you and any of your users. The columnar approach seems to be the most popular.

Creating and Searching Tables

Cells A1 through B5 in Figure 11.1, parts A and B, illustrate a columnar approach to table organization. Parts A and B show formulas on and off, respectively.

Column A contains the location pointers. Column B contains the list of values returned when a given pointer is referenced. Notice the textual values in column B.

Figure 11.1A Columnar Table Organization: Formulas On

```
    :  A   ::   B   ::   C   ::   D   ::   E   ::   F   ::   G   ::   H   :
1     1        ("first")
2     2        ("second")
3     3        ("third")
4     4        ("fourth")
5     5        ("fifth")
6
7    entry:    1
8    lookup:   LOOKUP(B7,A1.A5)
9
10   entry:    4
11   lookup:   LOOKUP(B10,A1.A5)
12
13   entry:    0
14   lookup:   LOOKUP(B13,A1.A5)
15
16   entry:    10
17   lookup:   LOOKUP(B16,A1.A5)
```

The LOOKUP function is used for the table search. It has the following format:

LOOKUP(pointer value,table pointer cell range)

SuperCalc³ allows a shorthand entry of **LU**, making data entry easier for you.

The function is shown in the spreadsheet as **LOOKUP,** no matter how it was entered.

The pointer value can be specified in the function as a numeric constant, a cell reference, or an expression.

The LOOKUP function uses the pointer value contained in its first argument to find a match in the range of cells specified in the second argument. When a match is found, the adjacent cell value is displayed in the cell containing the LOOKUP function.

If no match is found, one of the following is returned:

1. The contents of the adjacent cell associated with the highest pointer when the pointer value in argument 1 is greater than the highest pointer in the table.
2. N/A when the pointer value in argument 1 is less than the lowest pointer in the table.

Consider some illustrations based on Figure 11.1:

LOOKUP(1,A1.A5) Searches the table pointers in cells A1 through A5 for the pointer value 1 and finds it in cell A1. The contents of cell B1, **FIRST**, are returned.

LOOKUP(4,A1.A5) Searches the table pointers in cells A1 through A5 for the pointer value 4 and finds it in cell A4. The contents of cell B4, **FOURTH**, are returned.

LOOKUP(0,A1.A5) Searches the table pointers in cells A1 through A5 for the pointer value 0, which is not found. Since 0 is less than 1 in A1, **N/A** is returned.

LOOKUP(10,A1.A5) Searches the table pointers in cells A1 through A5 for the pointer value 10, which is not found. Since 10 is greater than 5 in A5, the contents of cell B5, **FIFTH**, are returned.

Figure 11.1, part B, shows the results of the lookups. Cells A7 through B17 confirm the preceding LOOKUP illustrations.

Figure 11.1B Columnar Table Organization: Formulas Off

```
    !   A    !!     B   !!   C   !!   D   !!   E   !!   F   !!   G   !!   H   !
1              1   first
2              2  second
3              3   third
4              4  fourth
5              5   fifth
6
7   entry:             1
8   lookup:        first
9
10  entry:             4
11  lookup:       fourth
12
13  entry:             0
14  lookup:          N/A
15
16  entry:            10
17  lookup:        fifth
```

Figure 11.2, parts A and B, illustrate a row approach to table structure. Parts A and B show formulas on and off, respectively.

Figure 11.2A Row Table Organization: Formulas On

```
    !    A    !!    B     !!    C    !!    D     !!    E    !!  F  !
1    1          2           3           4            5
2    ("first")  ("second")  ("third")   ("fourth")   ("fifth")
3
4
5
6
7   entry:      1
8   lookup:     LOOKUP(B7,A1.E1)
9
10  entry:      4
11  lookup:     LOOKUP(B10,A1.E1)
12
13  entry:      0
14  lookup:     LOOKUP(B13,A1.E1)
15
16  entry:      10
17  lookup:     LOOKUP(B16,A1.E1)
```

Figure 11.2B Row Table Organization: Formulas Off

```
    !   A   !!   B   !!   C   !!   D   !!   E   !!   F  !!  G  !!  H  !
1             1       2        3       4        5
2         first   second   third  fourth    fifth
3
4
5
6
7   entry:              1
8   lookup:         first
9
10  entry:              4
11  lookup:        fourth
12
13  entry:              0
14  lookup:           N/A
15
16  entry:             10
17  lookup:         fifth
```

The rules for the LOOKUP function are the same except that the value returned is from the cell directly beneath the matched table pointer. Consider the following illustrations:

LOOKUP(1,A1.E1) Searches the table pointers in cells A1 through E1 for the pointer value 1 and finds it in cell A1. The contents of cell A2, **FIRST**, are returned.

LOOKUP(4,A1.E1) Searches the table pointers in cells A1 through E1 for the pointer value 4 and finds it in cell D1. The contents of cell D2, **FOURTH**, are returned.

LOOKUP(0,A1.E1) Searches the table pointers in cells A1 through E1 for the pointer value 0, which is not found. Since 0 is less than 1 in A1, **N/A** is returned.

LOOKUP(10,A1.E1) Searches the table pointers in cells A1 through E1 for the pointer value 10, which is not found. Since 10 is greater than 5 in E1, the contents of cell E2, **FIFTH**, are returned.

Examples of Tables

EXAMPLE NO. 1—MONTH AND DAY LOOKUP

Figure 11.3, parts A and B, illustrates this example. Part A displays the formulas, while Part B displays the results.

Figure 11.3A Month and Day Lookup Tables: Formulas On

```
    :  A  ::       B      ::  C  ::  D  ::      E      ::  F  ::  G  :
1   Month Lookup Table              Weekday Lookup Table
2   ------------------              --------------------
3        Code         Month               Code        Month
4   ----------------------          ----------------------
5    1         ("January")          1          ("Sunday")
6    2         ("February")         2          ("Monday")
7    3         ("March")            3          ("Tuesday")
8    4         ("April")            4          ("Wednesday")
9    5         ("May")              5          ("Thursday")
10   6         ("June")             6          ("Friday")
11   7         ("July")             7          ("Saturday")
12   8         ("August")
13   9         ("September")
14   10        ("October")
15   11        ("November")
16   12        ("December")
17
18  Current Date:           TODAY
19  Current Month:          LOOKUP(MONTH(C18),A5.A16)
20  Current Day:            LOOKUP(WDAY(C18),D5.D11)
```

Figure 11.3B Month and Day Lookup Tables: Formulas Off

```
    :  A  ::       B      ::  C  ::  D  ::      E      ::  F  ::  G  :
1   Month Lookup Table              Weekday Lookup Table
2   ------------------              --------------------
3        Code         Month               Code        Month
4   ----------------------          ----------------------
5           1       January                  1       Sunday
6           2      February                  2       Monday
7           3         March                  3      Tuesday
8           4         April                  4    Wednesday
9           5           May                  5     Thursday
10          6          June                  6       Friday
11          7          July                  7     Saturday
12          8        August
13          9     September
14         10       October
15         11      November
16         12      December
17
18  Current Date:          12/10/84
19  Current Month:         December
20  Current Day:             Monday
```

Two tables are used. Cells A5 through B16 represent the Month Lookup Table, while cells D5 through E11 represent the Weekday Lookup Table.

Cell C18 uses the TODAY function to capture the current date, which is subsequently used to compute the LOOKUP function's pointer value argument.

Cells C19 and C20 both contain LOOKUP functions that respectively display the names of the current month and day. The LOOKUP function in C19 uses the MONTH function as its pointer value argument. The value returned by the MONTH function (1 through 12) is matched against the location pointers in cells A5 through A16. Since TODAY is currently 10/10/84, the MONTH function returns **10**, which is passed to the LOOKUP function, which displays **October** in cell C19.

The LOOKUP function in C20 uses the WDAY function as its pointer value argument. The value returned by the WDAY function (1 through 7) is matched against the location pointers in cells D5 through D11. Since TODAY is currently 10/10/84, the WDAY function returns **4**, which is passed to the LOOKUP function, which displays **Wednesday** in cell C20.

Although this is a very simple example, it demonstrates how to use a calculation to determine the pointer value for a search.

EXAMPLE NO. 2—JOB TITLE LOOKUP

This example demonstrates how to use a position code to search a table of job titles. It's useful for making "employee master file" spreadsheets. Its key feature is that a job title doesn't have to be keyed in for each employee. Instead, you need only enter one or two digits representing the position code for a given employee. When a person is promoted or reclassified, it's only necessary to change the position code and the new title is automatically retrieved from the Job Title Table.

Figure 11.4, parts A and B, illustrates this example (see pages 205 and 206). Part A displays the formulas, while Part B displays the results.

Cells A5 through B14 contain the Job Lookup Table, while cells A23 through C37 contain a list of employees and their associated position numbers. The LOOKUP function is entered into cell D23 as

LU(C23,A5.A14)

then replicated as follows:

/RD23,D24.D37,AYNN

As the spreadsheet is calculated, each of the cells in the range C23 through C37 is matched against the location pointers in cells A5 through A14. At each match an associated entry in cells B5 through B14 is displayed in cells D23 through D37.

EXAMPLE NO. 3—HOURLY RATE LOOKUP

This example demonstrates how to use a job code to search a table of hourly rates. It allows usage of "time card" spreadsheets in a situation where the rate of compensation is dependent on the job rather than the individual. Such a situation is usually found in unionized shops. An additional benefit of this approach is the speed with which the table can be updated to reflect new rates after renegotiation of labor contracts. The table eliminates the need for an hourly rate in each person's time record. Figure 11.5 illustrates the example in a /Output display listing.

Since this example is a bit more involved than the previous two, consider the seven steps in the following setup guidelines:

1. The following cells are formatted as TextRight: D5 through K6, A20 through A21, D20, D21, E20, and E21.
2. The hourly rates in cells B23 through B32 are set at four decimal places via the User-Defined Format Table.
3. The tax rates in cells E23 through E26 are entered in a decimal format—i.e., 0.225, 0.067, 0.0245, and 0.043125—but are displayed as percentages via the User-Defined Format Table.
4. Enter the data for cells A8 through E13 as shown in Figure 11.5. Note that cells A8 through C13 are text.
5. Enter the Rate Table and Tax List data to cells A18 through B32 and D18 through E26, respectively.

Figure 11.4A Title Lookup Table: Formulas On

```
    !  A  !!      B    !!  C  !!    D    !!     E    !!  F  !!  G  !
1   Job Table
2   ---------
3      Number        Title
4   ---------------------
5    1           ("President")
6    2           ("Physician")
7    3           ("Detective")
8    4           ("Analyst")
9    5           ("Taximan")
10   6           ("Boss")
11   7           ("Lackey")
12   8           ("Janitor")
13   9           ("Captain")
14   10          ("Lawyer")
15
16
17  Employee Listing
18  ----------------
19                                  Job
20                         ---------------------
21  Name                        Code          Title
22  ----------------       ---------------------
23  Bill Doyle              4          LOOKUP(C23,A5.A14)
24  Louie di Palma          5          LOOKUP(C24,A5.A14)
25  Magnum                  3          LOOKUP(C25,A5.A14)
26  J. R.                   1          LOOKUP(C26,A5.A14)
27  Quincy                  2          LOOKUP(C27,A5.A14)
28  J. D. Hogg              6          LOOKUP(C28,A5.A14)
29  Schneider               8          LOOKUP(C29,A5.A14)
30  Frank Ferillo           9          LOOKUP(C30,A5.A14)
31  Joyce Davenport         10         LOOKUP(C31,A5.A14)
32  Roscoe                  7          LOOKUP(C32,A5.A14)
33  Hawkeye                 2          LOOKUP(C33,A5.A14)
34  Ronald Reagan           1          LOOKUP(C34,A5.A14)
35  Nemo                    9          LOOKUP(C35,A5.A14)
36  C. Darrow               10         LOOKUP(C36,A5.A14)
37  Ahab                    9          LOOKUP(C37,A5.A14)
38
39
40
```

Figure 11.4B Title Lookup Table: Formulas Off

```
    :  A  ::      B      ::  C  ::      D      ::      E      ::  F  ::  G  :
1   Job Table
2   ---------
3        Number        Title
4   ---------------------
5                1   President
6                2   Physician
7                3   Detective
8                4     Analyst
9                5     Taximan
10               6        Boss
11               7      Lackey
12               8     Janitor
13               9     Captain
14              10      Lawyer
15
16
17  Employee Listing
18  ----------------
19                                  Job
20                         ---------------------
21  Name                          Code       Title
22  ----------------       ---------------------
23  Bill Doyle                       4     Analyst
24  Louie di Palma                   5     Taximan
25  Magnum                           3   Detective
26  J. R.                            1   President
27  Quincy                           2   Physician
28  J. D. Hogg                       6        Boss
29  Schneider                        8     Janitor
30  Frank Ferillo                    9     Captain
31  Joyce Davenport                 10      Lawyer
32  Roscoe                           7      Lackey
33  Hawkeye                          2   Physician
34  Ronald Reagan                    1   President
35  Nemo                             9     Captain
36  C. Darrow                       10      Lawyer
37  Ahab                             9     Captain
38
39
40
```

Figure 11.5 Hourly Rate Lookup Table

```
    :  A  ::  B  ::  C  ::  D  ::  E  ::  F  ::  G  ::  H  ::  I  ::  J  ::  K  :
1
2
3   Payroll Report
4   --------------
5   Dept     Employee Employee      Job   Hours    Gross  Federal     Fica    State     City      Net
6   No.      No.      Name         Code  Worked      Pay      Tax      Tax      Tax      Tax      Pay
7   ------------------------------------------------------------------------------------------------
8   053      1011     Alpha          10      40   320.00    72.00    21.44     7.84    13.80   204.92
9   062      1015     Zebra           5      55   390.63    87.89    26.17     9.57    16.85   250.15
10  062      1002     Bravo           2      30   166.73    37.51    11.17     4.08     7.19   106.78
11  053      1014     Yankee          3      20   115.10    25.90     7.71     2.82     4.96    73.71
12  062      2012     Gamma           1      60   350.00    78.75    23.45     8.58    15.09   224.13
13  053      3015     Maryjane        9      55   468.75   105.47    31.41    11.48    20.21   300.18
14  ------------------------------------------------------------------------------------------------
15                                              1811.21   407.52   121.35    44.37    78.10  1159.87
16
17
18      Rate Table             Tax List
19  ------------------     ------------------
20       Job   Hourly            Tax      Tax
21      Code     Rate           Name     Rate
22  ------------------     ------------------
23         1   5.0000      Federal   22.5000%
24         2   5.5575      Fica       6.7000%
25         3   5.7550      State      2.4500%
26         4   6.0000      City       4.3125%
27         5   6.2500
28         6   6.5000
29         7   6.7500
30         8   7.0000
31         9   7.5000
32        10   8.0000
```

6. Enter the formulas in columns F through K as follows:

   F8 **ROUND(IF(E8>40,(E8-40)*1.5*LOOKUP(D8,A23.A32)**
   +40*LOOKUP(D8,A23.A32),E8*LOOKUP(D8,A23.A32)),2)
   G8 **ROUND(F8*E23,2)**
   H8 **ROUND(F8*E24,2)**
   I8 **ROUND(F8*E25,2)**
   J8 **ROUND(F8*E26,2)**
   K8 **F8-SUM(G8.J8)**
   F15 **SUM(F8:F13)**

7. Replicate the above formulas as follows:

   /RF8,F9:F13,AYYYNNYNNYNN
   /RG8,G9:G13,AYN
   /RH8,H9:H13,AYN
   /RI8,I9:I13,AYN
   /RJ8,J9:J13,AYN
   /RK8,K9:K13, then press RETURN
   /RF15,G15:K15, then press RETURN

Considering the number of calculations involved with this spreadsheet, it's advisable to set manual calculation mode so your data entry goes faster.

As the spreadsheet is calculated, each of the cells in the range D8 through D13 is matched against the location pointers in cells A23 through A32. At each match, the associated entry in cells B23 through B32 is multiplied by the hours worked in cells E8 through E13. The product is gross pay, shown in cells F8 through F13.

Looking at cell F8, you'll notice that an overtime premium of 1.5 is applied to all hours worked in excess of 40:

ROUND(IF(E8>40,<u>(E8-40)*1.5*LU(D8,A23:A32)</u>
+40*LU(D8,A23:A32),E8*LU(D8,A23:A32)),2)

This example could be further enhanced to allow variable overtime premiums. An additional table could be put in cells G18 through H27 containing the following:

OT Code	Overtime Premium	Explanation
1	1.0	Straight time
2	1.5	Time and one-half
3	2.0	Double time
4	2.5	Double time and one-half
5	3.0	Triple time

It would also be necessary to insert an OT Code column prior to column E. The entry in cell F8 could be revised as follows:

IF(E8>40,(E8-40)*LU(<u>OT code</u>,G23:G27)*LU(D8,A23:A32)
+40*LU(D8,A23:A32),E8*LU(D8,A23:A32))

Sorting Spreadsheets

There are occasions when it's necessary to get a spreadsheet into an order based on some value called a "key." The order may be ascending or descending. Examples of key usage:

- Ascending sequence based on employee name
- Ascending sequence based on employee number
- Descending sequence based on gross pay

These examples are typical for a payroll application. An accounts payable application would use invoice amount instead of gross pay and replace employee name and number by vendor name and number. In effect, the extent of sorting applications is limited only by your imagination.

The /Arrange Command

The /Arrange command sorts a spreadsheet using the key values of a particular row or column, depending on whether you're doing a row sort or a column sort. This command also allows you to specify the sort sequence, ascending or descending, and whether or not formulas are to be adjusted.

Although sort sequencing may be either ascending or descending, all data is first grouped by cell type before it's arranged into either ascending or descending order. The following types of groupings are used:

- Text cells
- Textual values cells
- Date values cells
- ERROR cells
- N/A cells
- Numerical value cells
- Blank cells

The ordering used for text and textual values is shown next and is technically called the *collating sequence*.

1. SPACE
2. Special ASCII characters in the following order:
   ! " # $ % & ' ( ) * + , − . / :
   ; < = > ? @ [\ ] ^ _ ` { | } ~
3. Alphabetic characters with each lowercase character preceding its uppercase associate. For example:
   aAbBcCdDeEfFgGhHiIjJkKlLmMnNoOpPqQrRsStTuUvVwWxXyYzZ
4. Any numeric characters entered as text or textual values:
   0 1 2 3 4 5 6 7 8 9

Column Sort

Sorting by column rearranges the spreadsheet rows so that the column used as a key is in either ascending or descending order. To do a column sort, enter **/A.** The PROMPT and STATUS lines display

R(ow) or C(olumn)?

10>/Arrange,

Enter **C.** The PROMPT and STATUS lines respond with

Enter Column; then <RETURN>, or <,> for options

17>/Arrange,Column,

Once a column has been specified, pressing RETURN sorts the spreadsheet using the following defaults:

- All rows are included in the sort.
- The spreadsheet is arranged in ascending sequence on the key column.
- None of the spreadsheet formulas is adjusted.

You'll probably find these defaults to be limited for many sorting operations and will consequently use the comma to specify additional options. Assume that you want to use column A as the key to sort rows 5 through 25 into descending sequence. Pressing the comma key results in the following display on the PROMPT and STATUS lines:

Enter Row Range

19>/Arrange,Column,A,

Enter **5.25** and press RETURN. Now the PROMPT and STATUS lines display

A(scending) or D(escending) ?

24>/Arrange,Column,A,5.25,

Enter **D** and press RETURN. The PROMPT and STATUS lines show

Adjust? Y(es) or N(o); then <RETURN> or <,> for options

35>/Arrange,Column,A,5.25,Descending,

The /Arrange command alters the original relationships between cells and may result in an absence of any meaningful relationship between cells. Consequently, in most cases it's best to specify that no formula adjustment be made. A beneficial side effect is that you can later resort to your original sequence and thus restore the original cell relationships. Having decided to suppress formula adjustment, press N.

You have two choices for the next step:

1. Press RETURN to start the sort.
2. Press the comma. You'll be prompted for secondary sort parameters. This option is demonstrated in the next section.

Two precautions are suggested to protect against unexpected sort results. The first is to /Save your spreadsheet prior to entering the /Arrange command.

The second is to enter sequence numbers in an unused column of your spreadsheet. Assume that a hypothetical spreadsheet contains data in rows 1 through 25 and that column H is available for sequence numbers. The following steps will automatically generate sequence numbers in cells H1 through H25:

Enter **1** in cell H1
/RH1,H2.H25, then press RETURN
/CH1.H24,H2,+

If a mistake is made while sorting, the original sequence can be restored by entering
/ACH
then pressing RETURN.

Row Sort

Sorting by row rearranges the spreadsheet columns so that the row used as a key is in either ascending or descending order. To do a row sort, enter **/A.** The PROMPT and STATUS lines display
R(ow) or C(olumn)?
10>/Arrange,
Enter **R.** The PROMPT and STATUS lines respond with
Enter Row; then <Return>, or <,> for options
14>/Arrange,Row,
Once a row has been specified, pressing RETURN sorts the spreadsheet using the following defaults:

- All columns are included in the sort.
- The spreadsheet columns are arranged in ascending sequence on the key row.
- None of the spreadsheet formulas is adjusted.

These defaults provide limited flexibility. As with column sorting, you may want to use the comma to specify additional options. Assume that you want to use row 1 as the key to sort columns A through D into descending sequence. Pressing the comma key results in the following display on the PROMPT and STATUS lines:
Enter Column Range
16>/Arrange,Row,1,
Enter **A:D** and press RETURN. Now the PROMPT and STATUS lines display
A(scending) or D(escending) ?
20>/Arrange,Row,1,A:D,
Enter **D** and press RETURN. The PROMPT and STATUS lines show
Adjust? Y(es) or N(o); then <RETURN> or <,> for options
31>/Arrange,Row,1,A:D,Descending,

As with the column sort, you generally want to suppress formula adjustment, so press N. The sort executes at this point. The same two precautions for insurance against sorting errors suggested for column sorting are also suggested for row sorting. First, /Save your spreadsheet prior to sorting. Second, generate sequence numbers in an unused row of your spreadsheet. Assume that a hypothetical spreadsheet contains data in columns A through G and that row

25 is available for sequence numbers. The following steps will automatically generate sequence numbers in cells A25 through G25:

Enter **1** in cell A25
/RA25,B25.G25<RETURN>
/CA25.F25,B25,+

If a mistake is made while sorting, the original sequence can be restored by entering

/AR25

then pressing RETURN.

Sorting Examples

EXAMPLE NO. 1—A TRIVIAL DEMONSTRATION

This example demonstrates the alphabetic collating sequence and how to use sequence numbers to return to your order prior to the sort. Figure 11.6 contains the names of some popular microcomputers and an operating system. Each name is shown twice, first in uppercase, then in lowercase. Column D contains sequence numbers that were generated as follows:

Cell D1 entry: **1**
/RD1,D2.D20, then press RETURN
/CD1.D19,D2,+

Figure 11.6 Random List of Computer Names

```
    :  A   ::  B  ::  C  ::  D  ::  E  ::  F  ::  G  ::  H  :
 1  LEADING EDGE PC            1
 2  ZENITH Z-100               2
 3  COMPAQ                     3
 4  TI PROFESSIONAL            4
 5  COLUMBIA                   5
 6  IBM PC                     6
 7  SPERRY PC                  7
 8  ZENITH Z-150               8
 9  IBM XT                     9
10  MS-DOS                    10
11  leading edge pc           11
12  zenith z-100              12
13  compaq                    13
14  ti professional           14
15  columbia                  15
16  ibm pc                    16
17  sperry pc                 17
18  zenith z-150              18
19  ibm xt                    19
20  ms-dos                    20
```

Enter /**ACA**, then press RETURN. This entry sorts the spreadsheet into ascending sequence using column A as the sort key. Notice how each lowercase computer name precedes its uppercase counterpart. See Figure 11.7.

Figure 11.7 Alphabetically Sorted List of Computer Names

```
     !  A   !!   B   !!   C   !!   D   !!   E   !!   F   !!   G   !!   H   !
1    columbia                          15
2    COLUMBIA                           5
3    compaq                            13
4    COMPAQ                             3
5    ibm pc                            16
6    IBM PC                             6
7    ibm xt                            19
8    IBM XT                             9
9    leading edge pc                   11
10   LEADING EDGE PC                    1
11   ms-dos                            20
12   MS-DOS                            10
13   sperry pc                         17
14   SPERRY PC                          7
15   ti professional                   14
16   TI PROFESSIONAL                    4
17   zenith z-100                      12
18   ZENITH Z-100                       2
19   zenith z-150                      18
20   ZENITH Z-150                       8
```

In a real situation you should uniformly use upper- and lowercase. If you want mixed case, always show the first letter as uppercase and the remaining letters in lowercase.

The original list of names consisted of an uppercase group followed by a lowercase group. The sequence numbers can be used to restore the case groupings.

An entry of **/ACD,1.20,DN** sorts the spreadsheet into descending sequence using the sequence numbers in column D. Observe in Figure 11.8 that the lowercase group is now at the top and that both groups are in reverse order compared with the original random sequence.

Figure 11.8 List of Computer Names Sorted in Descending Sequence on Column D

```
     !  A   !!   B   !!   C   !!   D   !!   E   !!   F   !!   G   !!   H   !
1    ms-dos                            20
2    ibm xt                            19
3    zenith z-150                      18
4    sperry pc                         17
5    ibm pc                            16
6    columbia                          15
7    ti professional                   14
8    compaq                            13
9    zenith z-100                      12
10   leading edge pc                   11
11   MS-DOS                            10
12   IBM XT                             9
13   ZENITH Z-150                       8
14   SPERRY PC                          7
15   IBM PC                             6
16   COLUMBIA                           5
17   TI PROFESSIONAL                    4
18   COMPAQ                             3
19   ZENITH Z-100                       2
20   LEADING EDGE PC                    1
```

An entry of **/ACD<RETURN>** restores the spreadsheet shown in Figure 11.6.

EXAMPLE NO. 2—A PAYROLL SORT

This example uses the spreadsheet created in Figure 11.5. The only difference is that sequence numbers have been generated into rows 1 through 32 of column M.[1] It demonstrates a series of partial column sorts as well as recovering for sorting disasters. The initial intent was to sort rows 8 through 13 alphabetically on employee name. The entry should have been

/ACC,8.13,AN

However, excessive zeal caused an entry of /**ACC.** When RETURN was pressed, havoc was wreaked upon the spreadsheet, as shown in Figure 11.9.

Figure 11.9 Improperly Sorted Spreadsheet

```
    ¦ A  ¦¦  B  ¦¦  C  ¦¦  D  ¦¦  E  ¦¦  F  ¦¦  G  ¦¦  H  ¦¦  I  ¦¦  J  ¦¦  K  ¦¦  L  ¦¦  M ¦
1   Dept      Employee Employee      Job    Hours   Gross Federal    Fica   State    City     Net              5
2        Job    Hourly               Tax      Tax                                                            20
3   No.       No.     Name          Code   Worked     Pay     Tax     Tax     Tax     Tax     Pay             6
4        Code     Rate              Name     Rate                                                            21
5   062       1002    Bravo            2       30     .00     .00     .00     .00     .00     .00            10
6   053       1011    Alpha           10       40     .00     .00     .00     .00     .00     .00             8
7   053       1014    Yankee           3       20     .00     .00     .00     .00     .00     .00            11
8   062       1015    Zebra            5       55     .00     .00     .00     .00     .00     .00             9
9   062       2012    Gamma            1       60     .00     .00     .00     .00     .00     .00            12
10  053       3015    Maryjane         9       55     .00     .00     .00     .00     .00     .00            13
11               1  5.0000     Federal  22.5000%                                                             23
12               2  5.5575     Fica      6.7000%                                                             24
13               3  5.7550     State     2.4500%                                                             25
14               4  6.0000     City      4.3125%                                                             26
15               5  6.2500                                                                                   27
16               6  6.5000                                                                                   28
17               7  6.7500                                                                                   29
18               8  7.0000                                                                                   30
19               9  7.5000                                                                                   31
20              10  8.0000                                                                                   32
21                                                                                                            1
22                                                                                                            2
23  Payroll Report                                                                                            3
24  ----------------                                                                                          4
25  ------------------------------------------------------------------------------------------------          7
26  ------------------------------------------------------------------------------------------------         14
27                                            .00     .00     .00     .00     .00     .00                    15
28                                                                                                           16
29                                                                                                           17
30      Rate Table            Tax List                                                                       18
31  --------------------   --------------------                                                              19
32  --------------------   --------------------                                                              22
```

Fortunately, the sequence numbers enable an easy recovery. Enter /**ACM**, then press RETURN to restore the spreadsheet, as shown in Figure 11.10.

Rows 8 through 13 of the restored spreadsheet can now be alphabetically sorted on employee name. Enter /**ACC,8.13,AN**, then press RETURN. Refer to Figure 11.11 for the resulting spreadsheet.

---

1. Here are the entries to generate these sequence numbers:
   In cell M1, enter **1**
   /RM1,M2.M32 then press RETURN
   /CM1.M31,M2,+

Figure 11.10 Restored Spreadsheet

```
   :  A  ::  B  ::  C  ::  D  ::  E  ::  F  ::  G  ::  H  ::  I  ::  J  ::  K  ::  L  ::  M  :
1                                                                                              1
2                                                                                              2
3  Payroll Report                                                                              3
4  --------------                                                                              4
5  Dept      Employee Employee        Job   Hours    Gross  Federal     Fica   State    City      Net   5
6  No.       No.      Name           Code  Worked      Pay      Tax      Tax     Tax     Tax      Pay   6
7  ----------------------------------------------------------------------------------------------   7
8  053       1011     Alpha            10      40   320.00    72.00    21.44    7.84   13.80   204.92   8
9  062       1015     Zebra             5      55   390.63    87.89    26.17    9.57   15.85   250.15   9
10 062       1002     Bravo             2      30   166.73    37.51    11.17    4.08    7.19   106.78   10
11 053       1014     Yankee            3      20   115.10    25.90     7.71    2.82    4.96    73.71   11
12 062       2012     Gamma             1      60   350.00    78.75    23.45    8.58   15.09   224.13   12
13 053       3015     Maryjane          9      55   468.75   105.47    31.41   11.48   20.21   300.18   13
14 ----------------------------------------------------------------------------------------------   14
15                                                1811.21   407.52   121.35   44.37   78.10  1159.87   15
16                                                                                             16
17                                                                                             17
18      Rate Table             Tax List                                                       18
19 ----------------      ----------------                                                     19
20       Job  Hourly             Tax      Tax                                                  20
21      Code    Rate            Name     Rate                                                  21
22 ----------------      ----------------                                                     22
23         1  5.0000      Federal  22.5000%                                                    23
24         2  5.5575      Fica      6.7000%                                                    24
25         3  5.7550      State     2.4500%                                                    25
26         4  6.0000      City      4.3125%                                                    26
27         5  6.2500                                                                           27
28         6  6.5000                                                                           28
29         7  6.7500                                                                           29
30         8  7.0000                                                                           30
31         9  7.5000                                                                           31
32        10  8.0000                                                                           32
```

Figure 11.11 Rows 8-13 Sorted Ascending Sequence on Employee Name

```
   :  A  ::  B  ::  C  ::  D  ::  E  ::  F  ::  G  ::  H  ::  I  ::  J  ::  K  ::  L  ::  M  :
1                                                                                              1
2                                                                                              2
3  Payroll Report                                                                              3
4  --------------                                                                              4
5  Dept      Employee Employee        Job   Hours    Gross  Federal     Fica   State    City      Net   5
6  No.       No.      Name           Code  Worked      Pay      Tax      Tax     Tax     Tax      Pay   6
7  ----------------------------------------------------------------------------------------------   7
8  053       1011     Alpha            10      40   320.00    72.00    21.44    7.84   13.80   204.92   8
9  062       1002     Bravo             2      30   166.73    37.51    11.17    4.08    7.19   106.78   10
10 062       2012     Gamma             1      60   350.00    78.75    23.45    8.58   15.09   224.13   12
11 053       3015     Maryjane          9      55   468.75   105.47    31.41   11.48   20.21   300.18   13
12 053       1014     Yankee            3      20   115.10    25.90     7.71    2.82    4.96    73.71   11
13 062       1015     Zebra             5      55   390.63    87.89    26.17    9.57   16.85   250.15   9
14 ----------------------------------------------------------------------------------------------   14
15                                                1811.21   407.52   121.35   44.37   78.10  1159.87   15
16                                                                                             16
17                                                                                             17
18      Rate Table             Tax List                                                       18
19 ----------------      ----------------                                                     19
20       Job  Hourly             Tax      Tax                                                  20
21      Code    Rate            Name     Rate                                                  21
22 ----------------      ----------------                                                     22
23         1  5.0000      Federal  22.5000%                                                    23
24         2  5.5575      Fica      6.7000%                                                    24
25         3  5.7550      State     2.4500%                                                    25
26         4  6.0000      City      4.3125%                                                    26
27         5  6.2500                                                                           27
28         6  6.5000                                                                           28
29         7  6.7500                                                                           29
30         8  7.0000                                                                           30
31         9  7.5000                                                                           31
32        10  8.0000                                                                           32
```

Another sort could be done to have the spreadsheet sequenced in ascending order by employee number. Enter **/ACB,8.13,AN**, then press RETURN. The resulting spreadsheet is illustrated in Figure 11.12.

If management wanted to identify the high and low earners, the same rows of the spreadsheet could be sorted into descending sequence on gross pay. Enter **/ACF,8.13,DN**, then press RETURN. The sorted result is shown in Figure 11.13.

In many instances, management will want employees sorted into employee number sequence within their respective departments. This involves two sorting levels. The primary sort level is department, while the secondary sort level is employee number. Enter **/ACA,8.13,AN**, and you will be prompted with

Enter Secondary sort column

36>/Arrange,Column,A,8.13,Ascending,N,

Enter **B** and press RETURN. Press A when you are prompted with

A(scending) or D(escending) ?

38>/Arrange,Column,A,8.13,Ascending,N,B,

The sorted result is shown in Figure 11.14.

Some users may feel that the presence of sequence numbers detracts from the spreadsheet's appearance. This problem is easily corrected by the Hide option of the /Format command. Enter **/FEM1:M32,H** and press RETURN.

Figure 11.12 Rows 8-13 Sorted Ascending Sequence on Employee Number

	A	B	C	D	E	F	G	H	I	J	K	L	M
1													1
2													2
3	Payroll Report												3
4	------------												4
5	Dept	Employee	Employee	Job	Hours	Gross	Federal	Fica	State	City	Net		5
6	No.	No.	Name	Code	Worked	Pay	Tax	Tax	Tax	Tax	Pay		6
7	------	------	------	------	------	------	------	------	------	------	------		7
8	062	1002	Bravo	2	30	166.73	37.51	11.17	4.08	7.19	106.78		10
9	053	1011	Alpha	10	40	320.00	72.00	21.44	7.84	13.80	204.92		8
10	053	1014	Yankee	3	20	115.10	25.90	7.71	2.82	4.96	73.71		11
11	062	1015	Zebra	5	55	390.63	87.89	26.17	9.57	16.85	250.15		9
12	062	2012	Gamma	1	60	350.00	78.75	23.45	8.58	15.09	224.13		12
13	053	3015	Maryjane	9	55	468.75	105.47	31.41	11.48	20.21	300.18		13
14	------	------	------	------	------	------	------	------	------	------	------		14
15						1811.21	407.52	121.35	44.37	78.10	1159.87		15
16													16
17													17
18	Rate Table			Tax List									18
19	------	------		------	------								19
20	Job	Hourly		Tax	Tax								20
21	Code	Rate		Name	Rate								21
22	------	------		------	------								22
23	1	5.0000		Federal	22.5000%								23
24	2	5.5575		Fica	6.7000%								24
25	3	5.7550		State	2.4500%								25
26	4	6.0000		City	4.3125%								26
27	5	6.2500											27
28	6	6.5000											28
29	7	6.7500											29
30	8	7.0000											30
31	9	7.5000											31
32	10	8.0000											32

Figure 11.13 Rows 8-13 Sorted Descending Sequence on Gross Pay

	A	B	C	D	E	F	G	H	I	J	K	L	M	
1														1
2														2
3	Payroll Report													3
4	--------------													4
5	Dept	Employee	Employee	Job	Hours	Gross	Federal	Fica	State	City	Net			5
6	No.	No.	Name	Code	Worked	Pay	Tax	Tax	Tax	Tax	Pay			6
7	--------	--------	--------	--------	--------	--------	--------	--------	--------	--------	--------			7
8	053	3015	Maryjane	9	55	468.75	105.47	31.41	11.48	20.21	300.18			13
9	062	1015	Zebra	5	55	390.63	87.89	26.17	9.57	16.85	250.15			9
10	062	2012	Gamma	1	60	350.00	78.75	23.45	8.58	15.09	224.13			12
11	053	1011	Alpha	10	40	320.00	72.00	21.44	7.84	13.80	204.92			8
12	062	1002	Bravo	2	30	166.73	37.51	11.17	4.08	7.19	106.78			10
13	053	1014	Yankee	3	20	115.10	25.90	7.71	2.82	4.96	73.71			11
14	--------	--------	--------	--------	--------	--------	--------	--------	--------	--------	--------			14
15						1811.21	407.52	121.35	44.37	78.10	1159.87			15
16														16
17														17
18	Rate Table			Tax List										18
19	--------	--------		--------	--------									19
20	Job	Hourly		Tax	Tax									20
21	Code	Rate		Name	Rate									21
22	--------	--------		--------	--------									22
23	1	5.0000		Federal	22.5000%									23
24	2	5.5575		Fica	6.7000%									24
25	3	5.7550		State	2.4500%									25
26	4	6.0000		City	4.3125%									26
27	5	6.2500												27
28	6	6.5000												28
29	7	6.7500												29
30	8	7.0000												30
31	9	7.5000												31
32	10	8.0000												32

Figure 11.14 Rows 8-13 Sorted Ascending Sequence on Employee Number within Department Number

	A	B	C	D	E	F	G	H	I	J	K	L	M	
1														1
2														2
3	Payroll Report													3
4	--------------													4
5	Dept	Employee	Employee	Job	Hours	Gross	Federal	Fica	State	City	Net			5
6	No.	No.	Name	Code	Worked	Pay	Tax	Tax	Tax	Tax	Pay			6
7	--------	--------	--------	--------	--------	--------	--------	--------	--------	--------	--------			7
8	053	1011	Alpha	10	40	320.00	72.00	21.44	7.84	13.80	204.92			8
9	053	1014	Yankee	3	20	115.10	25.90	7.71	2.82	4.96	73.71			11
10	053	3015	Maryjane	9	55	468.75	105.47	31.41	11.48	20.21	300.18			13
11	062	1002	Bravo	2	30	166.73	37.51	11.17	4.08	7.19	106.78			10
12	062	1015	Zebra	5	55	390.63	87.89	26.17	9.57	16.85	250.15			9
13	062	2012	Gamma	1	60	350.00	78.75	23.45	8.58	15.09	224.13			12
14	--------	--------	--------	--------	--------	--------	--------	--------	--------	--------	--------			14
15						1811.21	407.52	121.35	44.37	78.10	1159.87			15
16														16
17														17
18	Rate Table			Tax List										18
19	--------	--------		--------	--------									19
20	Job	Hourly		Tax	Tax									20
21	Code	Rate		Name	Rate									21
22	--------	--------		--------	--------									22
23	1	5.0000		Federal	22.5000%									23
24	2	5.5575		Fica	6.7000%									24
25	3	5.7550		State	2.4500%									25
26	4	6.0000		City	4.3125%									26
27	5	6.2500												27
28	6	6.5000												28
29	7	6.7500												29
30	8	7.0000												30
31	9	7.5000												31
32	10	8.0000												32

Review Exercises

1. Given the spreadsheet in Figure 11.15, provide the following:
   a. Construct two tables of depreciation rates:

3-Year Table

Recovery Period	Depreciation Factor
1	.25
2	.38
3	.37

5-Year Table

Recovery Period	Depreciation Factor
1	.15
2	.22
3	.21
4	.21
5	.21

   b. Depending on the depreciable life in column C, look up the depreciation factor in either the 3- or 5-year table. Use the recovery period from column D for the lookup value. Enter this formula in cell E4 and use the appropriate duplication command for the remaining cells in column E.
   c. Multiply the depreciation factor by the asset cost to get the depreciation expense, rounded to an integer. Enter this formula in cell F4 and use the appropriate duplication command for the remaining cells in column F.
   d. Calculate the total depreciation expense using the appropriate function.
2. Given the spreadsheet in Figure 11.16, provide the following:
   a. Construct two tables:

Currency Table

Code	Rate
1	0.22000
2	0.01550
3	0.00234
4	0.36500
5	2.12000

Country Table

Code	Name
1	France
2	Belgium
3	Italy
4	Germany
5	England

   b. Show the commands to automatically generate the sequence numbers contained in cells H1 through H20.
   c. Using the foreign currency code, look up the exchange rate and multiply it by the foreign currency amount to calculate U. S. dollars, rounded to two decimal places. Enter this formula in cell D4 and use the appropriate duplication command for the remaining cells in column D.
   d. Using the foreign currency code, look up the country name. Enter this

Figure 11.15 Depreciation Spreadsheet Layout: Exercise 11-1

	A	B	C	D	E	F	G
1	Asset		Depreciable	Recovery	Depreciation		
2	Name	Cost	Life	Period	Factor	Expense	
3	----------	----------	----------	----------	----------	----------	----------
4	Printer	500	5	1			
5	Car	6000	3	2			
6	IBM PC	5000	5	4			
7	Truck	12000	3	3			
8	Color Monitor	350	5	2			
9	----------	----------	----------	----------	----------	----------	----------
10			Total Depreciation Expense				
11							
12							
13							
14							
15							
16							
17							
18							
19							
20							

Figure 11.16 Currency Conversion Spreadsheet Layout: Exercise 11-2

	A	B	C	D	E	F	G	H
1	Foreign Currency							
2	----------	----------	----------	U.S.				
3	Code	Country	Amount	Dollars				
4	3		100					
5	1		200					
6	4		300					
7	2		400					
8	5		500					
9	----------	----------	----------	----------				
10	Total	N/A	N/A					

formula in cell B4 and use the appropriate duplication command for the remaining cells in column B.

e. Provide commands to do the following:

Display U. S. dollars with two decimal places.
Display currency exchange rates with five decimal places.

f. Calculate total U. S. dollars using the appropriate function.

g. Assume you tried to sort this spreadsheet and you ran into problems. Show the sorting command you should use to restore the spreadsheet.

3. Given the spreadsheet in Figure 11.17, provide the following:

a. Construct three product tables:

Code	Product Name	Code	Selling Price	Code	Commission Rate
1	Columbia	1	2995	1	0.245
2	IBM PC	2	3245	2	0.100
3	Sperry PC	3	3119	3	0.150
4	ZDS Z-150	4	2800	4	0.200
5	Compaq +	5	4995	5	0.180

Figure 11.17 Computer Sales Spreadsheet Layout: Exercise 11-3

	A	B	C	D	E	F	G	H	
1		Product	Units			Net	Product		1
2	Seller	Code	Sold	Sales	Commission	Proceeds	Name		2
3	----	----	----	----	----	----	----		3
4	Bravo	2	200						4
5	Alpha	1	600						5
6	Yankee	4	200						6
7	Zebra	3	400						7
8	Gamma	5	450						8
9	----	----	----	----	----	----	----		9
10	Totals	N/A					N/A		10
11									11
12									12
13									13
14									14
15									15
16									16
17									17
18									18
19									19
20									20

b. Using the product code, look up the selling price and multiply it by units sold to get sales. Enter this formula in cell D4 and use the appropriate duplication command for the remaining cells in column D.

c. Using the product code, look up the commission rate and multiply it by sales to calculate the commission amount, rounded to two decimal places. Enter this formula in cell E4 and use the appropriate duplication command for the remaining cells in column E.

d. Calculate net proceeds as sales minus commission. Enter this formula in cell F4 and use the appropriate duplication command for the remaining cells in column F.

e. Using the product code, look up the product name. Enter this formula in cell G4 and use the appropriate duplication command for the remaining cells in column G.

f. Calculate net total units sold using the appropriate function. Enter this formula in cell C10 and use the appropriate duplication command for the remaining cells in row 10.

g. Provide a descending sequence sort on commission amount.

Answers to Review Exercises

1. a. See cells B12 through F19 of Figure 11.18.

   b. In cell E4:

   IF(C4=3,LU(D4,B15.B17),IF(C4=5,LU(D4,E15.E19),NA))
   /RE4,E5.E8,AYYNNYYNN

   c. In cell F4: **ROUND(B4*E4,0)**
   /RF4,F5.F8 then press RETURN.

   d. In cell F10: **SUM(F4:F8)**

Figure 11.18 Depreciation Spreadsheet Solution: Exercise 11-1

	A	B	C	D	E	F	G
1	Asset		Depreciable	Recovery	Depreciation		
2	Name	Cost	Life	Period	Factor	Expense	
3	----------	----------	----------	----------	----------	----------	----------
4	Printer	500	5	1	.15	75	
5	Car	6000	3	2	.38	2280	
6	IBM PC	5000	5	4	.21	1050	
7	Truck	12000	3	3	.37	4440	
8	Color Monitor	350	5	2	.22	77	
9	----------	----------	----------	----------	----------	----------	----------
10			Total Depreciation Expense			7922	
11							
12		3 Year Table			5 Year Table		
13		Year	Rate		Year	Rate	
14		----------	----------		----------	----------	
15		1	.25		1	.15	
16		2	.38		2	.22	
17		3	.37		3	.21	
18					4	.21	
19					5	.21	
20							

2. a. See cells A12 through E18 of Figure 11.19.
   Note that the country names are entered as textual values:
   cell E14: **("France")**
   cell E15: **("Belgium")**
   cell E16: **("Italy")**
   cell E17: **("Germany")**
   cell E18: **("England")**

   b. cell H1: **1**
   /RH1,H2.H20 then press RETURN.
   /CH1.H19,H2,+

   c. cell D4: **ROUND(LU(A4,A14.A18)*C4,2)**
   /RD4,D5.D8,AYNNY

   d. cell B4: **LU(A4,D14.D18)**
   /RB4,B5.B8,AYNN

   e. **/FED4.D10,$** then press RETURN.
   /FD then set decimal places to 5 in User-Defined format 1.

Figure 11.19 Currency Conversion Spreadsheet Solution: Exercise 11-2

	A	B	C	D	E	F	G	H	
1	Foreign Currency								1
2	----------	----------	----------	U.S.					2
3	Code	Country	Amount	Dollars					3
4	3	Italy	100	.23					4
5	1	France	200	44.00					5
6	4	Germany	300	109.50					6
7	2	Belgium	400	6.20					7
8	5	England	500	1060.00					8
9	----------	----------	----------	----------					9
10	Total	N/A	N/A	1219.93					10
11									11
12	Currency Table			Country Table					12
13	Code	Rate		Code	Name				13
14	1	.22000		1	France				14
15	2	.01550		2	Belgium				15
16	3	.00234		3	Italy				16
17	4	.36500		4	Germany				17
18	5	2.12000		5	England				18
19									19
20									20

F2 to exit User-Defined Format Table.
/FEB14.B18,U1 then press RETURN.

f. In cell D10: **SUM(D4:D8)**

g. **/ACH** then press RETURN.

3. a. See cells A12 through G19 of Figure 11.20.
   Note that the product names are entered as textual values:
   - cell A15: **("Columbia")**
   - cell A16: **("IBM PC")**
   - cell A17: **("SPERRY PC")**
   - cell A18: **("ZDS Z-150")**
   - cell A19: **("Compaq +")**

   b. cell D4: **ROUND(LU(B4,D15.D19)*C4,0)**
   /RD4,D5.D8,AYNNY

   c. cell E4: **ROUND(LU(B4,F15.F19)*D4,2)**
   /RE4,E5.E8,AYNNY

   d. cell F4: **D4-E4**
   /RF4,F5.F8 then press RETURN.

   e. cell G4: **LU(B4,A15:A19)**
   /RG4,G5:G8,AYNN

   f. cell C10: **SUM(C4.C8)**
   /RC10,D10.F10 then press RETURN.

   g. **/ACE,4.8,DN** then press RETURN.

Figure 11.20 Computer Sales Spreadsheet Solution: Exercise 11-3

```
   !  A   !!   B   !!  C  !!    D   !!     E    !!    F    !!    G    !!  H  !
1            Product   Units                               Net   Product        1
2  Seller       Code    Sold      Sales Commission  Proceeds      Name        2
3  ---------------------------------------------------------------------        3
4  Alpha           1     600 1,797,000    440,265 1,356,735  Columbia        5
5  Gamma           5     450 2,247,750    404,595 1,843,155  Compaq +        8
6  Zebra           3     400 1,247,600    187,140 1,060,460 Sperry PC        7
7  Yankee          4     200   560,000    112,000   448,000 ZDS Z-150        6
8  Bravo           2     200   649,000     64,900   584,100    IBM PC        4
9  ---------------------------------------------------------------------        9
10 Totals        N/A    1850 6,501,350  1,208,900 5,292,450       N/A       10
11                                                                          11
12 Product Name Table          Product Price Table  Commission Table        12
13      Code     Name                 Code   Price       Code    Rate       13
14 ------------------          -------------------  ----------------        14
15         1  Columbia                   1    2995          1    .245       15
16         2    IBM PC                   2    3245          2    .100       16
17         3 Sperry PC                   3    3119          3    .150       17
18         4 ZDS Z-150                   4    2800          4    .200       18
19         5  Compaq +                   5    4995          5    .180       19
20                                                                          20
```

CHAPTER 12

Integrated Spreadsheet Graphics

Chapter Overview and Objectives

- Graphs and Their Components
- Defining Graphs
- Generating Graphics Output
- Other Graphics Commands
- Graphics Examples

This chapter introduces graphics concepts and techniques. You'll learn how to define seven types of graphs and how to plot them with variable fonts and headings.

Graphs and Their Components

SuperCalc[3] supports seven types of graphs. Their names and a plotted illustration are shown here.

Figure 12.1 Pie Chart

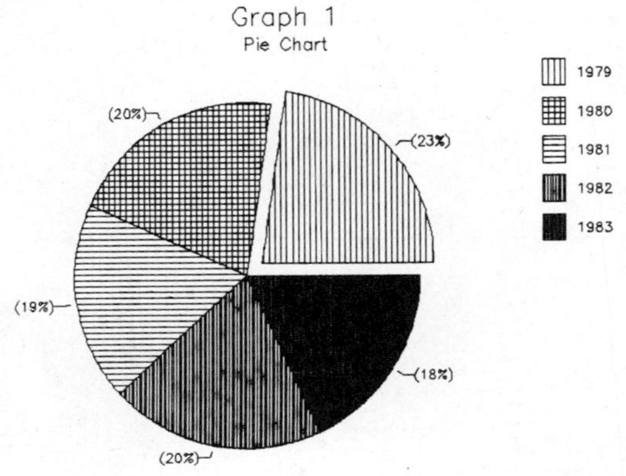

Figure 12.2 Hi-Lo Graph

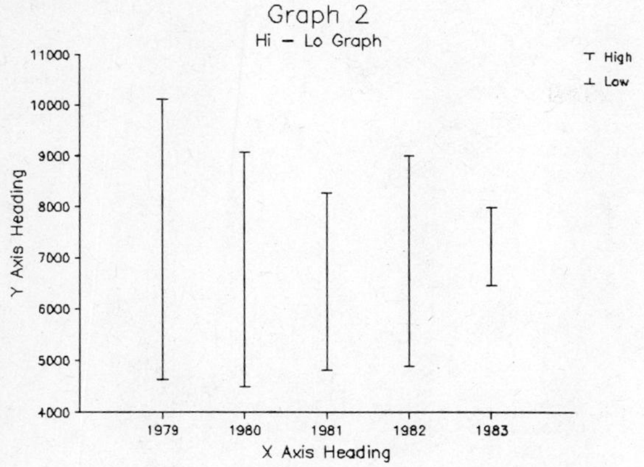

Figure 12.3 Line Graph

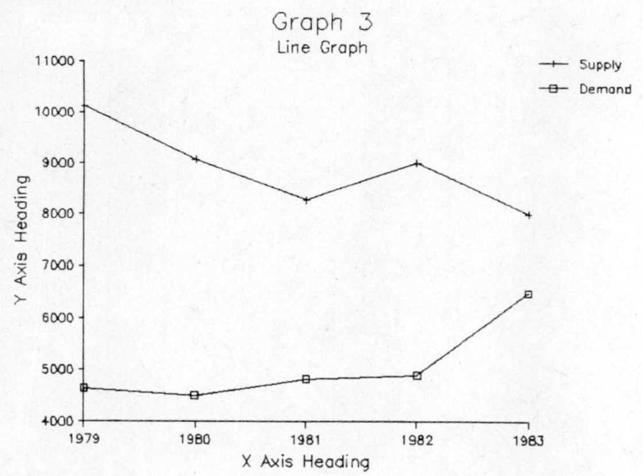

Figure 12.4 Area Graph

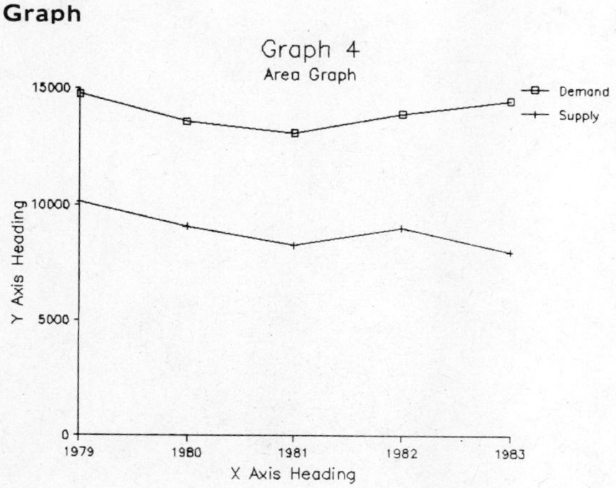

Figure 12.5 Bar Chart

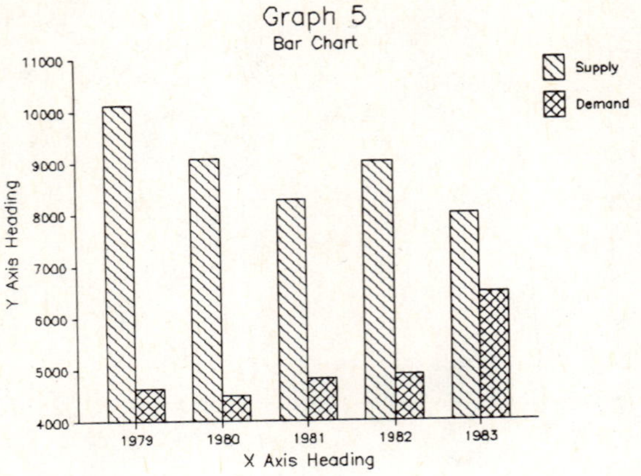

Figure 12.6 Stacked Bar Chart

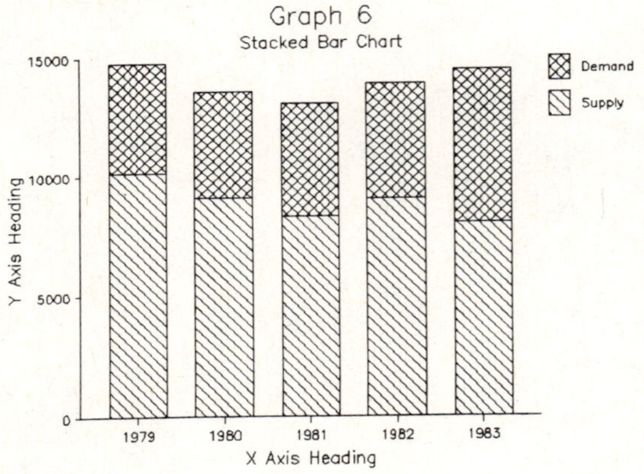

Figure 12.7 X-Y Graph

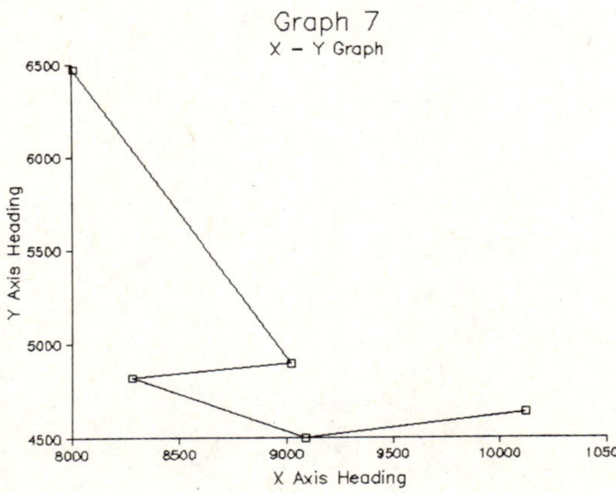

Each of these graph types may contain some of the following components:

Main Heading Primary title of your graph. Centered above the graph in large print.

Sub Heading Secondary title of your graph. Centered directly beneath the main heading in characters smaller than the main heading.

X-Axis Heading Text describing the horizontal axis of your graph. Positioned below the time labels.

Y-Axis Heading Text describing the vertical axis of your graph. Positioned on the left side of the graph.

Y-Axis Labels Numeric labels identifying the ticks on the y-axis. Although they appear by default in all graphs except the pie chart, they can be suppressed. Their values can be formatted.

Time Labels Numbers or text placed on the x-axes of bar, stacked bar, line, area, and hi-lo graphs. Shown as a legend in the upper right corner of pie charts.

Variable Labels Legends on bar, stacked bar, line, area, and hi-lo graphs. They appear in the upper right corner of these graphs. They identify the plotted colors or hatch patterns in the body of the graph.

Point Labels Numbers or text that identify the values of plotted variables. They eliminate the tedium of visually relating plotted points against the y-axis labels.

Ticks Short lines marking points on the horizontal and vertical axes. They connect with time labels and y-axis labels.

Figure 12.8 provides an illustration of where these components appear on a graph.

Figure 12.8 Graph Headings and Labels

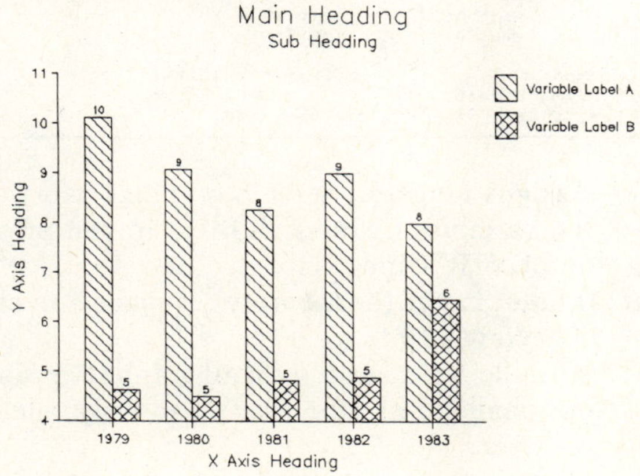

Defining Graphs

The integrated graphics feature of SuperCalc³ uses the /View command to define graphs. Each SuperCalc³ spreadsheet can contain up to nine separate graph definitions. Prior to using the /View command, you must have the spreadsheet to be graphed on display. You can do this via the /Load command or you can create a new spreadsheet. Next, enter **/V.** The PROMPT and ENTRY lines respond with:

#,?,D(ata),G(raph-Type),T(ime-Labs),V(ar-Labs),P(oint-Labs),H(eads) or O(pts)
7>/View,

These graph definition parameters have the following meanings:

Specifies a graph number in the range of 1 through 9. The default is 1 or the number of the last graph accessed. The last graph accessed is called the current graph. Do not enter the #.

? Displays the status screen for the current graph. It contains such information as graph number and type, current graphics device, and the cells used for labels and data. See Figure 12.9 for an illustration of a status screen. Do not use the F1 key because it will produce an AnswerScreen rather than a status screen.

Figure 12.9 Graph Status Screen

```
Current Graph (#8) -> Bar    Current Device -> C.ITOH 8510A Printer

HEADINGS:                    SCALING:
Main:    (A19)               Y-Axis: Auto
Sub:     (B19)               X-Axis: Auto
X-Axis:  (F9)
Y-Axis:  (F10)

TIME LABELS: (A5:A9)

   Data             Pt-Labels       Var-Labels      FORMATS:
A: (B5:B9)          (B5:B9)         (B20)           Axis: U3
B: (C5:C9)          (C5:C9)         (C20)           Time:
C: (empty)          (empty)         (empty)         Var:
D: (empty)          (empty)         (empty)         Point: U3
E: (empty)          (empty)         (empty)         % :
F: (empty)          (empty)         (empty)
G: (empty)          (empty)         (empty)
H: (empty)          (empty)         (empty)
I: (empty)          (empty)         (empty)
J: (empty)          (empty)         (empty)

PIE EXPLOSION: None                 MODE: One Variable (A)
F1 or <?> for AnswerScreen.
F1 = Help; F2 = Cancel; F9 = Plot; F10 = View
```

D Assigns ranges of cells to graphics data variables. There are ten variables, A through J. When you press D, the PROMPT and ENTRY lines display

Var A: Enter range (now empty), <space> to skip, <−> to clear
14>/View,1,Data,

Variable A is required for all graphs. Variables B through J are optional and may be used in any sequence.

Ranges for variable assignment may be blocked or unblocked. For example, cells A5 through D9 could be assigned to data variables in two ways. The first uses an unblocked approach. Each of the following variable entries falls within the same column.

When prompted with

Var A: Enter range (now empty), <space> to skip, <−> to clear

enter **A5.A9**, then press the comma (,) key.

When prompted with

Var B: Enter range (now empty), <space> to skip, <−> to clear

enter **B5.B9**, then press the comma (,) key.

When prompted with

Var C: Enter range (now empty), <space> to skip, <−> to clear

enter **C5.C9**, then press the comma (,) key.

When prompted with

Var D: Enter range (now empty), <space> to skip, <−> to clear

enter **D5.D9**, then press the RETURN key.

The above process can be done in one entry using the blocked approach. When prompted with

Var A: Enter range (now empty), <space> to skip, <−> to clear

enter **A5.D9**, then press the RETURN key.

Here, SuperCalc^3 evaluates the block to make a variable assignment that uses the fewest number of variables. In this example there are fewer columns than rows, so SuperCalc^3 makes the variable assignments based on the number of columns. Where there is an equal number of rows and columns, SuperCalc^3 assigns the variables as follows:

For blocks that do not exceed 10 rows by 10 columns, the assignment is based on row.

For blocks that exceed 10 rows by 10 columns, you are prompted for a row or column preference.

The block approach is useful when you want to get contiguous cell ranges into a graph. You can scroll through the variables by pressing the space bar. You can clear individual variables by pressing the minus (−) key. After you make a variable entry, you can get back to the /View prompt by pressing RETURN. If you want to move to the next variable, press the comma (,) key instead of the RETURN key.

G Allows you to select the type of graph. Pressing G displays the following on the PROMPT and ENTRY lines:

P(ie), B(ar), S(tacked-Bar), L(ine), X(-Y), A(rea), H(i-Lo)?
15>/View,1,Graph,

The current graph type is displayed at high intensity; the remaining types at low intensity. The available graph types are defined as follows:

P (Pie Chart) This graph uses only one variable, it defaults to Variable A. See Figure 12.1 for an illustration of a pie chart.

B (Bar Chart) The horizontal axis of this graph is based on the number of cells in the data variables. For example, if a data variable contained the cell range B5 through B9, there would be five bar clusters on the horizontal axis. The number of bars in a cluster is controlled by the number of data variables that have been assigned. If only variable A has been assigned, there is only one bar per cluster. If variables A and B have been assigned, there are two bars per cluster. If variables A, B, and C have been assigned, there are three bars per cluster, etc.

The bar chart's vertical axis is a numeric value scale against which the cells in each are measured. Time labels can be plotted beneath the horizontal axis for each bar cluster. Points can be plotted above each bar. See Figure 12.5 for an illustration of a bar chart.

S (Stacked Bar Chart) The horizontal axis of this graph is based on the number of cells in the data variables. For example, if each data variable contained five cells, there would be five bars on the horizontal axis. The number of stacks in a bar is controlled by the number of data variables that have been assigned. If variables A and B have been assigned, there are two stacks per bar. If variables A, B, and C have been assigned, there are three stacks per bar, etc.

The cumulative value of a bar is the sum of the individual stacks in a bar. For example, assume that three variables have been assigned. Variable A contains the cell range A1:A3, variable B contains the cell range B1:B3, and variable C contains the cell range C1:C3. Three bars will be plotted. Bar #1 will have a cumulative value based on the sum of A1 + B1 + C1. Bar #2 will have a cumulative value based on the sum of A2 + B2 + C2. Bar #3 will have a cumulative value based on the sum of A3 + B3 + C3.

The stacked bar chart's vertical axis is a numeric value scale against which the cumulative value of each bar is measured.

Time labels can be plotted beneath the horizontal axis for each bar. Point labels, indicating the individual stack's value, can be plotted adjacent to each stack. See Figure 12.6 for an illustration of a stacked bar chart.

L (Line Graph) The horizontal axis of this graph is based on the number of cells in the data variables. For example, if a data variable contained the cell range B5 through B9, there would be five points plotted on the horizontal axis. The number of lines plotted is controlled by the number of data variables that have been assigned. If only variable A has been assigned, only one is line plotted. If variables A and B have been assigned, two lines are plotted. If variables A, B, and C have been assigned, three lines are plotted, etc.

The line graph's vertical axis is a numeric value scale against which the cells in each are measured. Time labels can be plotted beneath the horizontal axis for each line point. Point values can be plotted above each line point. See Figure 12.3 for an illustration of a line graph.

X (X-Y Graph) This graph is also called a scatter graph. At least two variables must be assigned. All variables are plotted against variable A. Time labels and variable labels are not applicable since each plotted point represents two variables. Point labels can be set for variables B through J. See Figure 12.7 for an illustration of an X-Y graph.

A (Area Graph) This graph is the line equivalent of a stacked bar chart. The horizontal axis of this graph is based on the number of cells in the data variables. For example, if each data variable contained five cells, there would be five points on the horizontal axis. The cumulative process for each line is controlled by the number of data variables that have been assigned. For example, assume that three variables have been assigned. Variable A contains the cell range A1:A3, variable B contains the cell range B1:B3, and variable C contains the cell range C1:C3.

Three lines will be plotted. The three points on line #1 will represent the values of cells A1, A2, and A3. The three points on line #2 will represent the cumulative values of A1 + B1, A2 + B2, and A3 + B3. The three points on line #3 will represent the cumulative values of A1 + B1 + C1, A2 + B2 + C2, and A3 + B3 + C3.

Time labels can be plotted beneath the horizontal axis for each point. Point labels, indicating the individual point's value, can be plotted above each point. See Figure 12.4 for an illustration of an area graph.

H (Hi-Lo Graph) This graph shows the spread between two variables. For example, assume that variable A contains the cell range A1:A3 and variable B contains the cell range B1:B3. The plotted results will show the high and low of A1 versus B1, high and low of A2 versus B2, and the high and low of A3 versus B3. If variables C through J were used, they would show as points along each vertical high-low line. See Figure 12.2 for an illustration of a hi-lo graph.

T Assigns a range of cells to identify the tick marks along the x-axis of a graph. The contents of the specified cell range should identify some measurement of time. Examples are days, weeks, months, quarters, and years. Within the cell range, these labels should be sequenced chronologically.

When you press T, the PROMPT and ENTRY lines display

Enter Time-Label range (now empty) or <–> to clear

21>/View,1,Time-Labels,

Assume that cells A1 through A5 contain the years 1980 through 1984, respectively. You would specify the time label range as A1:A5. You can clear time labels by pressing the minus (–) key. Pressing RETURN updates any changes and returns you to the **/View** prompt. If you press RETURN and haven't made any changes, you are simply returned to the **/View** prompt.

V Assigns names to the graphics data variables. You can assign a range of labels for each of the ten variables, A through J. When you press V, the PROMPT and ENTRY lines display

Var A: Var-Label cell or range (now empty), <space> to skip, <–> to clear

25>/View,1,Variable-Labels,

You can scroll through the variables by pressing the space bar. You can clear individual variables by pressing the minus (–) key. After you make a variable entry you can get back to the **/View** prompt by pressing RETURN. If you want to move to the next variable, press the comma (,) key instead of the RETURN key.

Usage of variable labels is an optional feature. These labels can be either text or numeric.

P Assigns labels to the plotted points on your graph. You can assign a range of labels for each of the ten variables, A through J. When you press P, the PROMPT and ENTRY lines display

Var A: Enter Point-Label range (now empty), <space> to skip, <–> to clear

22>/View,1,Point-Labels,

You can scroll through the variables by pressing the space bar. You can clear individual variables by pressing the minus (–) key. After you make a variable entry, you can get back to the **/View** prompt by pressing RETURN. If you want to move to the next variable, press the comma (,) key instead of the RETURN key. Usage of point labels is an optional feature.

H Assigns titles to selected areas of your graph. When you press H, the PROMPT and ENTRY lines display

M(ain),S(ub),X(-axis) or Y(-axis)?

18>/View,1,Headings,

Press M to assign the main heading. The PROMPT and ENTRY lines display

Enter title cell (now empty) or <–> to clear

23>/View,1,Headings,Main,

Enter the appropriate cell. When you press RETURN, the PROMPT and ENTRY lines display

M(ain),S(ub),X(-axis) or Y(-axis)?

18>/View,1,Headings,

A similar procedure is used to assign subheadings and headings for x and y axes. Refer to the beginning of this chapter for definitions of these headings.

You can clear individual headings by pressing the minus (−) key. Headings are limited to one cell per heading; cell ranges are invalid.

O Allows additional formatting to be set for the graph. When you press O, the PROMPT and ENTRY lines display

F(ormat),E(xplosion), P(ie-Mode) or S(caling)?

17>/View,1,Options,

These options are defined as follows:

F Allows you to format the display of labels. Pressing F generates the PROMPT LINE shown below:

A(xis), T(ime), V(ar), P(oint) or % Labels?

Subsequently selecting A, T, V, or P causes the PROMPT LINE to display

Enter: (I,G,E,$,R,L,TR,TL,U(1-8),H,D or label width)

These choices are identical to those of the /Format command, except that:

The * option has been eliminated.

The column width has been changed to label width.

Subsequently selecting % causes the PROMPT LINE to display

Enter <0-9> as width for (xx%) field in Pie, or D(efault)

This parameter applies only to pie charts. It allows you to control the label width for each pie segment, thereby maximizing the size of the displayed pie. The value entered counts all characters, including the parentheses. For example, if a given pie segment represented 25% of the pie, a % width of 5 would display that label as **"(25%)."** A % width of 3 would display that label as **"25%."** Entering a % width of 0, 1, or 2 suppresses display of the % labels. This is equivalent to the Hide option of the /Format command.

E This is the Explosion option. It allows you to explode up to eight segments from the body of the pie. When you press E, the PROMPT LINE displays

Highlight Pie Segments? A(ll), N(one) or <1-8> (segment #)

Segments 1 through 8 address the first eight cells in your data variable range.

P This is the Pie-Mode option. It allows you to specify whether the pie chart is composed of all cells within a single variable or a series of corresponding points across all defined variables. For example, you could choose between all time periods within a given variable or all variables within a given period of time.

SuperCalc³ automatically adjusts your labels, both time and variable, to represent the variable range being graphed. It also automatically displays the appropriate time or variable label as the X-axis label. When you press P, the PROMPT LINE displays

O(ne Variable) or A(ll variables)?

Pressing O prompts you with

Select Variable for Pie Segments: Enter (A-J)

Enter a variable and press RETURN. The graphed pie segments will use time labels in the legend. Pressing A prompts you with

Select any element from all Variables for Pie Segments: Enter (1-9999)

Enter a row number and press RETURN. The graphed pie segments will use variable labels in the legend. Depending on the maximum spreadsheet size set under the O option of the /Global command, the prompt could also display **"Enter (1-254)"** or **"Enter (1-2000)."**

S This option overrides the automatic scaling by SuperCalc³. It enables you to generate your scaling. This feature applies to all graph types, except the pie chart. It generates the numbers associated with the y-axis tick marks. It can also produce numbers for the x-axis ticks on the X-Y graph. Pressing S prompts you with

X(-axis) or Y(-axis)?

In most cases you'll enter **Y.** When an entry is made, you are prompted with

Enter Cell containing Minimum, or <space> for Auto-Scaling.

If you want to create your own scaling, enter the cell with the minimum value, then press RETURN. Next, you will be prompted with

Cell containing Maximum?

Enter the cell with the maximum value, then press RETURN. The PROMPT LINE then displays

Number of divisions for Axis? (1-9)

You now make an entry indicating the number of ticks that you want on the axis. The value from the cell identified as the minimum is used for the first tick mark. The value from the cell identified as the maximum is used for the last tick mark. SuperCalc³ calculates values for the intervening ticks using the number of divisions and the difference between the minimum and maximum values.

Generating Graphics Output

As a preliminary step in producing graphics output, you need to use the Global Graphics Menu. Enter **/GG** to call this menu. The PROMPT LINE will display

C(olors), F(onts), L(ayout), O(ptions), or D(evice)?

Enter a letter to select one of the five sub-menus. The individual sub-menus are defined as follows:

C *Calls the Colors Menu.* The numbers shown correspond with the pen numbers on a graphics plotter. You can vary the numbers to generate multi-colored plotted output. See Figure 12.10 for an illustration of this menu and its default settings.

Figure 12.10 Colors Menu

```
        COLORS MENU: SELECTIONS FOR PLOTTING  [F2 to return to spreadsheet]

        Variables:                          Labels:
        A               1                   Axis                0
        B               2                   Time                0
        C               3                   Vars                V
        D               4                   Point               V
        E               5
        F               6
        G               7
        H               8
        I               9
        J              10

        Headings:                           Field:
        Main            0                   Axes and Box        0
        Sub             0                   Grids               0
        X-Axis          0                   Ticks               0
        Y-Axis          0                   Solid-Fill Outline  0

Color number <0-99> or N(one):
 24>/Global,Graphics,Colors
F1 = Help; F2 = Cancel; F9 = Plot; F10 = View
```

Readers who use a dot-matrix graphics printer should ignore this menu.

F *Calls the Fonts Menu.* This menu allows you to select the typeface for your headings and labels from eight character styles. The default setting is font 1, single-stroke block. The stroke indicates whether the characters are overprinted and, if so, how many times. If you intend to use your plotted output for overhead transparencies, fonts 2, double-stroke block, or 4, triple-stroke Roman, are recommended.

Depending on your spreadsheet, it's possible that there may not be enough memory available to accommodate multiple fonts. If this occurs, the following message will be displayed:

Insufficient memory for alternate font

You have two alternatives to correct this problem:

Set all font selections back to font 1, single-stroke block.

Enter /**GOD** to make more memory available.

See Figure 12.11 for an illustration of this menu and its default settings.

Figure 12.11 Fonts Menu

```
FONTS MENU: SELECTIONS FOR PLOTTING  [F2 to return to spreadsheet]

Headings:                          Labels:
Main          1                    Axis          1
Sub           1                    Time          1
X-Axis        1                    Vars          1
Y-Axis        1                    Point         1

1 = Block,  single-stroke
2 = Block,  double-stroke
3 = Roman,  double-stroke
4 = Roman,  triple-stroke
5 = Italic, double-stroke
6 = Italic, triple-stroke
7 = Script, single-stroke
8 = Script, double-stroke



Font number (1-8):
 23>/Global,Graphics,Fonts
F1 = Help; F2 = Cancel; F9 = Plot; F10 = View
```

L *Calls the Layout Menu.* This allows you to control the page positioning of your plotted output:

Full page. This is the default setting.
Top of page.
Bottom of page.
Quadrant 1: upper left.
Quadrant 2: upper right.
Quadrant 3: lower left.
Quadrant 4: lower right.
Vertical rotation.
Horizontal rotation.

Note: Settings other than F(ull page) require that M(anual) mode be set first.

See Figure 12.12 for an illustration of this menu and its default settings.

Figure 12.12 Layout Menu

```
LAYOUT MENU: SELECTIONS FOR PLOTTING  [F2 to return to spreadsheet]

Page Size:              * "Page Size" describes the physical paper you are using
Paper          1          with your graphics printer or plotter. Page Width is the
Width       8.50          direction along which the paper is normally read.
Length     11.00        * "Graph Size" describes where, how large and in which
                          direction the graph is drawn.
Graph Size:             * Size, Rotation and Offset adjust automatically EXCEPT in
Mode           F          Manual Mode. In Manual Mode you can change graph settings.
Rotation       V        * In Horizontal Rotation the graph is viewed in the normal
                          reading direction of the paper. Vertical Rotation is the
Width      10.00          opposite of Horizontal.
Length      7.50        * Graph Width is approximately 1.3 times Graph Length for
                          most graphics devices. If this "aspect ratio" is changed
Graph/Page Offset:        (allowed only in Manual Mode) your Pie graphs will look
Top         0.50          like watermelons. If you set Graph Width OR Length to 0.00
Left        0.50          SuperCalc3 substitutes an appropriate value using the
                          aspect ratio for your device.
                        * "Graph/Page Offset" tells SuperCalc3 where on the page
                          (measured from the Top and Left) to start the graph.


1 = 8.5" X 11":
 24>/Global,Graphics,Layout
F1 = Help; F2 = Cancel; F9 = Plot; F10 = View
```

O *Calls the Options Menu*. This menu allows you to control the graph appearance and device settings. See Figure 12.13 for an illustration of this menu and its default settings.

Figure 12.13 Options Menu

```
    OPTIONS MENU: GRAPH APPEARANCE & DEVICE SETTINGS  [F2 for spreadsheet]
    For all graphs except Pie:              Plotter Interface:
    Grids           N                       Use               P
    Axes            Y
    Ticks           Y                       Parallel Options:
    Graph Box       N                       Printer number    1

    For Pie, Bar and Stacked-Bar:           Serial Options:
    Fill Type       S                       Com number        1
                                            Baud Rate      4800
    For Line, Hi-Lo, Area and X-Y:          Parity            N
    Point Markers   Y                       Data bits         8
    Lines         . Y                       Stop bits         1

    Color Monitor:                          Two monitors:
    Display         B                       Dual Display      Y
                                            Regraph           A
    Graphics Printers:
    Resolution      S

    Pen Plotters:
    Num. pens       1
H(orizontal), V(ertical), N(either) or B(oth)?
 25>/Global,Graphics,Options
F1 = Help; F2 = Cancel; F9 = Plot; F10 = View
```

The first three options can be previewed on your video monitor prior to plotting. These options with their possible settings follow:

For all graphs except pie

Grids: H(orizontal), V(ertical), N(either), or B(oth)
Axes: Y(es) or N(o)
Ticks: Y(es) or N(o)
Graph Box: Y(es) or N(o)

For Pie, Bar, and Stacked-bar

Fill type S(olid), O(utline), C(rosshatched)

Note: Dot-matrix graphics printers interpret solid as crosshatched.

For Line, Hi-Lo, Area, and X-Y

Point Markers: Y(es) or N(o)
Lines: Y(es) or N(o)

The remaining options are applicable to the monitor, plotter, or graphics printer.

Color Monitor

Display: C(olor) or B(lack and white)

Note: C sets a color monitor to a medium resolution color display, supporting all fill types. B sets a color monitor to a high resolution, black and white display, supporting outline and crosshatched fill types. Any settings for the solid fill type are displayed as crosshatched.

Graphics Printers
Resolution: S(ingle density), D(ouble density), T(riple density), or Q(uad density).

Note: The density determines the number of dots per inch. Single density has the fewest number of dots per inch, while quad density has the most. There is an inverse relationship between density and printing speed. The higher densities should be used for presentation quality graphics.

Pen Plotters
Num. Pens: Plotter Penholders <1-16>

Note: Setting is automatically changed whenever you make a selection through the Device Selection Menu.

Plotter Interface
Use: P(arallel) or S(erial)

Note: Setting is automatically changed whenever you make a selection through the Device Selection Menu.

Parallel Options

Note: Readers using serial printing devices can ignore this section.

Printer number: 1, 2, or 3.

Identifies which parallel printer port is to be used.

Serial Options
Note: Readers using parallel printing devices can ignore this section.

Com number: 1 or 2

Identifies which serial port is to be used.

Baud rate: 110, 150, 300, 600, 1200, 2400, 4800, or 9600.

Identifies the data transmission rate in bits per second. This value must match the capability of your plotting device. A baud rate of 4800 is recommended.

Parity: O(dd), E(ven), or N(one)
Data Bits: 7 or 8
Stop Bits: 1 or 2

The values for these three settings must match the capabilities of your plotting device.

Two monitors
Dual Display: Y(es) or N(o)
Regraph: A(uto) or M(anual)

Note: When Dual Display is set to Y(es), you can simultaneously view spreadsheets on your monochrome monitor and graphics on your color monitor. A setting of N(o) allows viewing of the current display on the primary monitor only.

When Regraph is set to A(uto) and Dual Display is set to Y(es), the current graph display is automatically drawn at each spreadsheet recalculation. Spreadsheet operations are faster when the Regraph option is set to M(anual).

D *Calls the Device Selection Menu.* This menu allows you to select your graphics output device. See Figure 12.14 for an illustration of this menu.

Figure 12.14 Device Selection Menu

```
DEVICE SELECTION MENU  [F2 to return to spreadsheet]

Printers:                                         Plotters:
  IBM Graphics     HP ThinkJet                      AMDEK Amplot II
  ANADEX DP-9725   IDS PRISM 80                     APPLE 410
  ANADEX DP-9625   IDS PRISM 132                    C.ITOH  CX-4800
  ANADEX DP-9620   M.T. MT160                       C.ITOH  CX-6000
  C.ITOH 1550      M.T. MT180                       CALCOMP M84
  C.ITOH 8510A     NEC PinwriterP2                  ENTER Sweet-P 100
  C.ITOH 8600      NEC PinwriterP3                  GOULD DS7
  DIABLO P11       OKIDATA 82A                      GOULD DS10
  DIABLO P32       OKIDATA 83A                      HIPL0T DMP-29
  EPSON FX80       OKIDATA 84                       H/P 7470A
  EPSON FX100      OKIDATA 92                       H/P 7475A
  EPSON JX80       OKIDATA 93                       IBM XY/749
  EPSON LQ1500     OKIDATA 2410                     NICOLET ZETA 8
  EPSON MX80       TI OMNI 850                      ROLAND DG DXY-800
  EPSON MX100      TI OMNI 855                      SANYO PR100
  EPSON RX80                                        STROBE 100
  EPSON RX100                                       STROBE 260
                                                    WATANABE MP1000


 24>/Global,Graphics,Device
F1 = Help; F2 = Cancel; F9 = Plot; F10 = View
```

The Device Selection Menu lists all the graphics output devices supported by SuperCalc[3], Release 2.

You can use the directional arrows to move the menu cursor to the name that describes your device. The device name at the cursor position is shown in inverse video. Press RETURN to select a graphics device. The selected device name is displayed at high intensity. All other device names are shown at low intensity. The default device is the IBM Graphics Printer.

If the name of your printing device isn't shown, then you do not have the capability of generating graphics output. Check your printing device's documentation manual; it may be compatible with one of the devices listed on the menu. Press the F2 function key twice to return to the spreadsheet. You can permanently retain the graphics device selected by entering **/GK.** This selection will not change unless you acquire a new output device.

As soon as you've finished setting your global graphics definitions, you're ready to generate graphics output. You can produce two types of graphics output—*displayed* and *plotted*.

Displayed output is the faster of the two to generate. It is the process of getting a picture of your graph onto the screen of your video monitor. It can be done using any of the following methods:

1. Entering **/V** then pressing RETURN. This method displays the most recently accessed graph or graph 1, which is the default when no graph has been previously accessed.
2. Entering **/V#** then pressing RETURN. This method displays the specified graph. An integer in the range 1 through 9 is entered in place of the # symbol.
3. Pressing the F10 function key. This method displays the most recently accessed graph or graph 1, which is the default when no graph has been previously accessed.
4. Simultaneously pressing the Ctrl and T keys. This method displays the most recently accessed graph or graph 1, which is the default when no graph has been previously accessed. It would be used only if your computer did not have function keys.

Once you've displayed your graph, you can press any key to return to your spreadsheet.

Generating *plotted output* is the process of getting a picture of your graph onto a piece of paper. This process takes longer because printers and plotters are substantially slower than your video monitor.

Plotting can be done by either of the following methods:

1. Pressing the F9 function key. This method plots the most recently accessed graph or graph 1, which is the default when no graph has been previously accessed.
2. Simultaneously pressing the Ctrl and Y keys. This method plots the most recently accessed graph or graph 1, which is the default when no graph has been previously accessed. It would be used only if your computer did not have function keys.

Control is returned to your spreadsheet when the plotting process is completed. If it's necessary to abort the process, press function key F2. If your computer doesn't have function keys, simultaneously press the Ctrl and Z keys.

Other Graphics Commands

The following "Slash" commands have options affecting graphs:

1. Blank allows you to erase one or more graphs.
   e.g., /B*1 Erases graph 1.
   /B*1.9 Erases graphs 1 through 9.
2. /Copy allows you to copy graphs.
   e.g., /C*1,2 Copies graph 1 into graph 2.
3. /Load allows you to load an entire spreadsheet with all its associated graphs or just selected graphs.
   e.g., /LPALDEMO,A Loads the file PALDEMO.CAL and all associated graphs, if any.
   /LPALDEMO,*1,1 Loads graph 1 from the file PALDEMO.CAL into graph 1 of the spreadsheet in memory.

/LPALDEMO,*1.3,4 Loads graphs 1 through 3 from the file PALDEMO.CAL into graphs 4 through 6 of the spreadsheet in memory.

4. /Save allows you to save an entire spreadsheet with all its associated graphs.

   e.g., /SPALDEMO,A Saves the spreadsheet in memory as file PALDEMO.CAL and all associated graphs, if any.

Graphics Examples

EXAMPLE NO. 1

The spreadsheet shown in Figure 12.15 represents the budgeted salaries for five people in an Information Systems department. It will be used to construct a series of Pie Charts. Refer to Appendix A for a contents listing of this spreadsheet.

Figure 12.15 Salary Budget Spreadsheet

	A	B	C	D	E	F	G	H	I	J	K	L	M	N	O	P	Q	R	S	T
1	Information Systems Department																			
2	Fiscal Year 1985																			
3	Salary Budget																			
4																				
5		Annual	Biweekly		Biweekly	Annual														
6		Salary	Salary	Salary	Salary	Salary	Jul 84	Aug 84	Sep 84	Oct 84	Nov 84	Dec 84	Jan 85	Feb 85	Mar 85	Apr 85	May 85	Jun 85		
7	Employee	Before	Before	Increase	After	After	Weeks =	Weeks =	Weeks =	Weeks =	Weeks =	Weeks =	Weeks =	Weeks =	Weeks =	Weeks =	Weeks =	Weeks =	Total	
8	Name	Raise	Raise	Percent	Raise	Raise	4	5	4	4	5	4	4	4	5	4	5	4	52	
9																				
10	Arthur	48,048	1,848	12	2,070	53,820	3,696	4,620	3,696	3,696	4,620	3,696	3,696	3,696	5,175	4,140	5,175	4,140	50,046	
11	Bernadette	28,028	1,078	10	1,186	30,836	2,156	2,695	2,156	2,156	2,695	2,156	2,156	2,156	2,695	2,156	2,695	2,156	28,028	
12	Cynthia	32,500	1,250	9	1,363	35,438	2,500	3,125	2,500	2,500	3,408	2,726	2,726	2,726	3,408	2,726	3,408	2,726	34,478	
13	David	27,300	1,050	9	1,145	29,770	2,100	2,625	2,100	2,100	2,625	2,100	2,100	2,100	2,625	2,100	2,625	2,290	27,490	
14	Edward	18,512	712	10	785	20,358	1,424	1,780	1,424	1,424	1,780	1,424	1,424	1,424	1,780	1,424	1,780	1,424	18,512	
15																				
16	Total	154,388	5,938	10	6,547	170,222	11,876	14,845	11,876	11,876	15,128	12,102	12,102	12,102	15,683	12,546	15,683	12,736	158,554	

An optional first step is to set your graphics printer to a high print resolution. To do this, enter **/GGO.** When SuperCalc³ displays the OPTIONS MENU, use ↓ to move down to the menu item for graphics printer resolution. Press D for double density. Although this setting gives higher quality output from your printer, it will also slow it down. While you're in this menu you should also set the Color Monitor Display. Press C or B, depending on whether you have a color or monochrome monitor. After making these selections, press function key F2 twice to return to your spreadsheet.

You're now ready to define your graph. Enter **/V1GP.** This entry selects graph 1 and sets the graph type as a Pie Chart.

The next step is to specify the data to be used. Press D. The PROMPT and ENTRY lines display

Var A: Enter range (now empty), <space> to skip, <−> to clear
14>/View,1,Data

Use the monthly budgeted salary totals for January through June for the data values. Since these amounts are contained in cells G16 through R16 in Figure 12.15, enter **G16.R16** and press RETURN.

You can press function key F10 to display the resulting graph on your screen, or function key F9 to plot a hardcopy of the graph. Your output should match Figure 12.16.

Figure 12.16 Unlabeled Pie Chart of Total Monthly Salary Expense

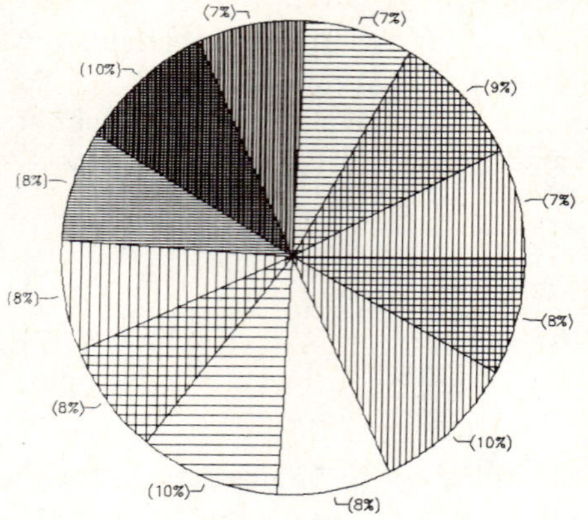

Having built the graph, you know that it represents each month's portion of the total salaries budgeted for Fiscal Year 1985. This would not be apparent to someone else because the graph has no identifying labels. The next few steps illustrate how to put headings and labels on the pie chart.

Enter **/VH.** The PROMPT and ENTRY lines respond with

M(ain),S(ub),X(-axis) or Y(-axis)?

18>/View,1,Headings,

The first step is to specify "Information Systems Department" from cell A1 as the main heading. Press M. You'll be prompted with

Enter title cell (now empty) or <-> to clear

23>/View,1,Headings,Main

Enter A1 and press RETURN. The PROMPT and ENTRY lines redisplay

M(ain),S(ub),X(-axis) or Y(-axis)?

18>/View,1,Headings,

Now press S. When prompted to enter the title cell, enter **A3** and press RETURN. When the PROMPT and ENTRY lines redisplay

M(ain),S(ub),X(-axis) or Y(-axis)?

18>/View,1,Headings,

press X. When prompted to enter the title cell, enter **A2** and press RETURN twice. Your PROMPT and ENTRY lines now display

#,?,D(ata),G(raph-Type),T(ime-labs),V(ar-Labs),P(oint-Labs),H(eads) or O(pts)

7>/View,

The next step is to create a legend to identify the individual pie segments. Press T to specify time labels. The PROMPT and ENTRY lines display

Enter Time-Label range (now empty) or <-> to clear

21>/View,1,Time-Labels,

Enter **G6.R6** and press RETURN. Depending on whether you want displayed or plotted output, press F10 or F9. The resulting graph should match Figure 12.17.

You can produce a summary display of all headings, labels, and data set for graph 1 by entering **/V?.**

Figure 12.17 Labeled Pie Chart of Total Monthly Salary Expense

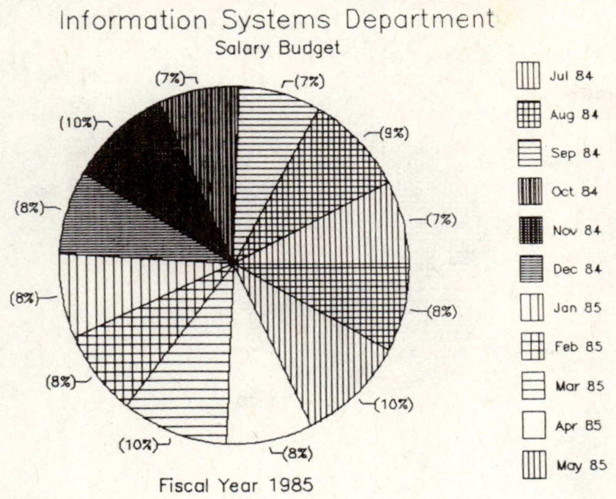

EXAMPLE NO. 2

This example uses a Pie Chart where each segment represents one person's share of the budget, based on annual salary. Since this graph will be similar to the one in Example No. 1, you can copy graph 1 into graph 2 by entering **/C*1,2** and pressing RETURN.

The following series of steps involves changing the data, labels, and headings parameters. To begin, enter **/V2T.** When prompted for the time labels, enter **A10.A14.** This uses the names of the five people on the pie chart legend. Press RETURN after entering the cell range. The PROMPT and ENTRY lines will show

?,D(ata),G(raph-Type),T(ime-labs),V(ar-Labs),P(oint-Labs),H(eads) or O(pts)
9>/View,2,

Next, specify the cells containing the data to be used in the graph by pressing D. This entry generates the following display:

Var A: Enter range (now G16:R16), <space> to skip, <−> to clear
14>/View,2,Data,

Since the graph should address each person's annual salary, enter **F10.F14** and press RETURN.

In Graph 2 in its present form, the pie segments only indicate each employee's relative share. The graph doesn't show the salary dollars associated with each slice. This omission can be corrected via point labels. Press P since you're still in the /View command. The PROMPT and ENTRY lines show

Var A: Enter Point-Label range (now empty), <space> to skip, <−> to clear
22>/View,2,Point-Labels,

Since you want the annual salary plotted for each pie slice, the point label range of cells must match the cell range used for data variable A. Enter **F10.F14** and press RETURN. You can now plot your graph, so press F10 or F9. Your plotted output should match Figure 12.18.

If you look closely at Figure 12.18, you'll notice that the annual salaries are awkward to read. This is because the point labels are not formatted. You can,

Figure 12.18 Pie Chart of Annual Salaries After Pay Raises

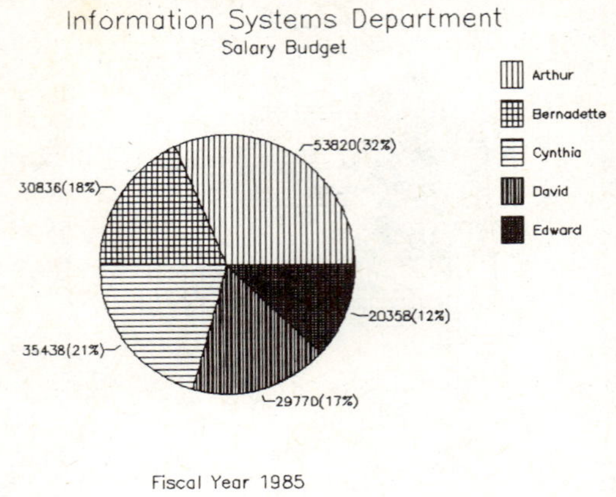

however, use the User-Defined format table to take advantage of its comma insertion and floating dollar sign features.

To do this, first, enter **/FD** to call the table. Next, pick a User-Defined format number and make the following settings:

Feature	Setting
Floating $	Y
Embedded Commas	Y
Minus in ( )	N
Zero as Blank	N
%	N
Decimal Places	0
Scaling factor	0

Press F2 to return to your spreadsheet. Now enter **/V2O.**[1] The PROMPT and ENTRY lines display

F(ormat), E(xplosion), P(ie-Mode) or S(caling)?
17>/View,2,Options,

Press F and SuperCalc³ responds with

A(xis), T(ime), V(ar), P(oint) or % Labels?
24>/View,2,Options,Format

Press P to select point label formatting. The PROMPT and ENTRY lines now show

Enter: (I,G,E,$,R,L,TR,TL,U(1-8),H,D or label width)
30>/View,2,Options,Format,Point,

1. Note that the character following the 2 is an alphabetic letter, not a numeric digit.

Enter **U8,** or whatever format you used on your own system, and press RETURN. The PROMPT and ENTRY lines display

F(ormat), E(xplosion), P(ie-Mode) or S(caling)?

17>/View,2,Options,

From this point in the Options menu, you can also specify whether any slices are to be exploded from the pie. Pressing E displays the explosion menu:

Highlight Pie Segments? A(ll), N(one) or <1-8> (segment #)

27>/View,2,Options,Explosion,

Press A so that all slices are exploded from the pie. To plot the graph, press F10 or F9. Your plotted output should match Figure 12.19.

Figure 12.19 Pie Chart of Annual Salaries After Pay Raises: Exploded Segments

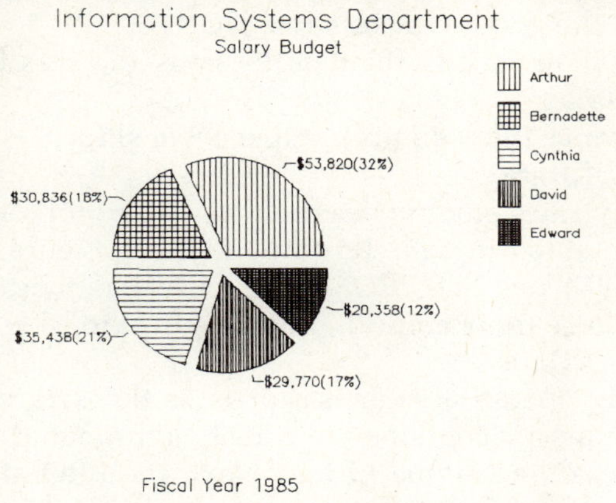

You can produce a summary display of all headings, labels, and data set for graph 2 by entering **/V?.** If you want to make selected explosions for this example, choose one of the following:

Segment Entry	Exploded Employee
1	Arthur
2	Bernadette
3	Cynthia
4	David
5	Edward

You can subsequently suppress pie explosions by entering **/VOEN.**

EXAMPLE NO. 3

The spreadsheet shown in Figure 7.5 on page 109 is the Profit & Loss Statement created earlier. It will be used to construct a series of Bar Charts, Stacked Bar Charts, Line Graphs, and Hi-Lo Graphs.

As a first step, zap the current spreadsheet and load the P&L spreadsheet. Enter **/GGO** to call the OPTIONS MENU. Make the following option selections:

Option	Setting
Grids	H
Graph Box	Y
Resolution	D
Display	B or C, as appropriate

After making these selections, press function key F2 twice to return to your spreadsheet.

You are now ready to define your graph. Enter **/V1GB.** This entry selects graph 1 and sets the graph type as a Bar Chart.

The next step is to specify the data to be used. Press D. The PROMPT and ENTRY lines display

Var A: Enter range (now empty), <space> to skip, < – > to clear
14>/View,1,Data

Use the quarterly sales amounts as the data values for variable A. Since these amounts are contained in cells B5 through E5 in Figure 7.5, enter B5.E5 and press the comma (,) key. The PROMPT and ENTRY lines display

Var B: Enter range (now empty), <space> to skip, < – > to clear
14>/View,1,Data

Use the quarterly operating expense totals as the data values for variable B. Since these amounts are contained in cells B14 through E14 in Figure 7.5, enter **B14.E14** and press the comma (,) key. Next, the PROMPT and ENTRY lines display

Var C: Enter range (now empty), <space> to skip, < – > to clear
14>/View,1,Data

Use the quarterly pre-tax profit amounts as the data values for variable C. Since these amounts are contained in cells B16 through E16 in Figure 7.5, enter **B16.E16** and press RETURN. The PROMPT and ENTRY lines respond with

?,D(ata),G(raph-Type),T(ime-labs),V(ar-Labs),P(oint-Labs),H(eads) or O(pts)
9>/View,1,

The next few steps illustrate how to put headings and labels on the bar chart. Press H. The PROMPT and ENTRY lines respond with

M(ain),S(ub),X(-axis) or Y(-axis)?
18>/View,1,Headings,

The first step is to set "Bill's P & L Statement" as the main heading. Press M. You'll be prompted with

Enter title cell (now empty) or < – > to clear
23>/View,1,Headings,Main

You can enter **C1** and press RETURN or you can press the ESC key, scroll to cell C1, and press RETURN. The PROMPT and ENTRY lines redisplay

M(ain),S(ub),X(-axis) or Y(-axis)?
18>/View,1,Headings,

Now press S. When prompted to enter the title cell, enter **C2** and press

RETURN. When the PROMPT and ENTRY lines redisplay

M(ain),S(ub),X(-axis) or Y(-axis)?

18>/View,1,Headings,

Press X. When prompted to enter the title cell, enter **A2** and press RETURN twice. Your PROMPT and ENTRY lines now display

#,?,D(ata),G(raph-Type),T(ime-labs),V(ar-Labs),P(oint-Labs),H(eads) or O(pts)

7>/View,

The next step is to assign labels to the tick marks along the X-axis of the bar chart. Press T to specify time labels. The PROMPT and ENTRY lines display

Enter Time-Label range (now empty) or <−> to clear

21>/View,1,Time-Labels,

Enter **B3.E3** and press RETURN.

Now you need to create a legend to identify the individual bars. Press V to specify variable labels. The PROMPT and ENTRY lines display

Var A: Var-Label cell or range (now empty), <space> to skip, <−> to clear

25>/View,1,Variable-Labels,

Enter **A5** to capture SALES, and press the comma (,) key. The PROMPT and ENTRY lines show

Var B: Var-Label cell or range (now empty), <space> to skip, <−> to clear

25>/View,1,Variable-Labels,

Enter **A10** to capture OPERATING EXPENSES, and press the comma (,) key. The PROMPT and ENTRY lines show

Var C: Var-Label cell or range (now empty), <space> to skip, <−> to clear

25>/View,1,Variable-Labels,

Enter **A16** to capture PRE-TAX PROFIT, and press RETURN.

Depending on whether you want displayed or plotted output, press F10 or F9. The resulting graph should match Figure 12.20.

Figure 12.20 Bar Chart of P&L Spreadsheet: Three Variables

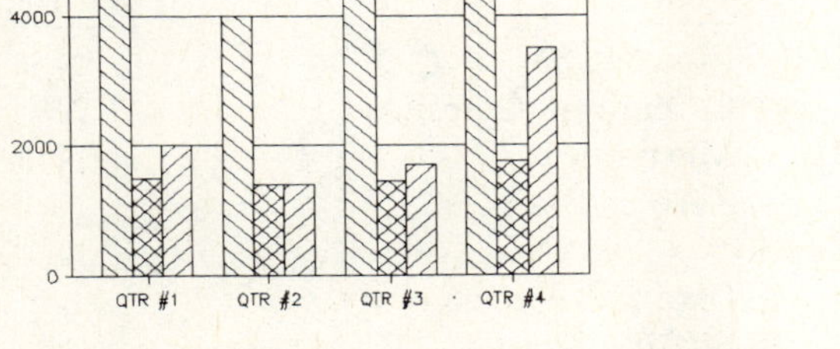

You can produce a summary display of all headings, labels, and data set for graph 1 by entering **/V?**.

EXAMPLE NO. 4

This example is similar to Example No. 3 except that it uses a Stacked Bar Chart. You can save time by copying graph 1 into graph 2. To do this, enter **/C*1,2** and press RETURN.

Next, enter **/GGO** to call the options menu and set Grids to N. Then press F2 twice to return to your spreadsheet.

In cell A1, enter the text string **"Thousands of Dollars,"** which will be used shortly as the Y-axis label. Since this text has meaning only to the graph, it should not be displayed in the body of the spreadsheet. To hide the text entry in cell A1, enter **/FEA1,H** and press RETURN.

You are now ready to change some of the labels and headings parameters in your definition for graph 2. To begin, enter **/V2GS.** This defines graph 2 as a Stacked Bar Chart. Next, press H. When prompted for the heading type, enter **Y.** When prompted for the title cell, enter **A1** and press RETURN twice.

After returning to the main /View command prompt, press P. When prompted with

Var A: Point-Label range (now empty), <space> to skip, < – > to clear
22>/View,2,Point-Labels,

enter **B5.E5** and press the comma (,) key. The PROMPT and ENTRY lines show

Var B: Point-Label range (now empty), <space> to skip, < – > to clear
22>/View,2,Point-Labels,

Enter **B14.E14** and press the comma (,) key. The PROMPT and ENTRY lines show

Var C: Point-Label range (now empty), <space> to skip, < – > to clear
22>/View,2,Point-Labels,

Enter **B16.E16** and press RETURN. The PROMPT and ENTRY lines will show

?,D(ata),G(raph-Type),T(ime-labs),V(ar-Labs),P(oint-Labs),H(eads) or O(pts)
9>/View,2,

Looking at Figure 7.5, you'll notice that each of the cells specified as point labels has four significant digits in its displayed value. They are wider than the gaps between the vertically stacked bars. If SuperCalc^3 tries to plot them using the default format, they will plot in exponential representation. You can, however, use the User-Defined format table to correct the plotting problem. To do this, enter **/FD** to call the table. Next, pick a User-Defined format number and make the following settings:

Feature	Setting
Floating $	N
Embedded Commas	N
Minus in ( )	N
Zero as Blank	N
%	N
Decimal Places	0
Scaling factor	3

Press F2 to return to your spreadsheet. Now enter **/V2O.** The PROMPT and

ENTRY lines display

F(ormat), E(xplosion), P(ie-Mode) or S(caling)?

17>/View,2,Options,

Press F, and SuperCalc[3] responds with

A(xis), T(ime), V(ar), P(oint) or % Labels?

24>/View,2,Options,Format

Press P to select point label formatting. The PROMPT and ENTRY lines now show

Enter: (I,G,E,$,R,L,TR,TL,U(1-8),H,D or label width)

30>/View,2,Options,Format,Point,

Enter U1, or whatever format you used on your own system, and press RETURN. The PROMPT and ENTRY lines display

F(ormat), E(xplosion), P(ie-Mode) or S(caling)?

17>/View,2,Options,

The label formatting process should be repeated so that the axis labels and point labels are scaled consistent with one another. Press F again and SuperCalc[3] displays:

A(xis), T(ime), V(ar), P(oint) or % Labels?

24>/View,2,Options,Format

This time press A to select axis label formatting. The PROMPT and ENTRY lines show

Enter: (I,G,E,$,R,L,TR,TL,U(1-8),H,D or label width)

30>/View,2,Options,Format,Point,

Enter U1, or whatever format you used on your own system, and press RETURN. The PROMPT and ENTRY lines display

F(ormat), E(xplosion), P(ie-Mode) or S(caling)?

17>/View,2,Options,

To plot the graph, press F10 or F9. Your plotted output should match Figure 12.21.

Figure 12.21 Stacked Bar Chart of P&L Spreadsheet

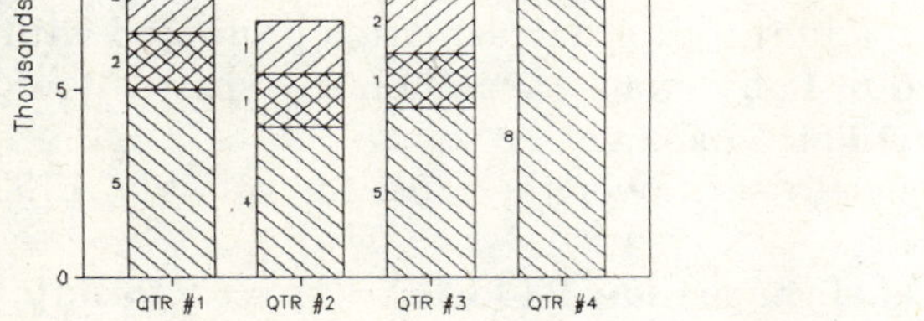

You can produce a summary display of all headings, labels, and data set for graph 2 by entering **/V?**.

EXAMPLE NO. 5

This example uses a Hi-Lo Graph. You can save some time by copying graph 2 into graph 3. To do this, enter **/C*2,3** and press RETURN.

You are now ready to change some of the labels and headings parameters in your definition for graph 3. To begin, enter **/V3GH.** This defines graph 3 as a Hi-Lo Graph.

Next, press H. When prompted for the heading type, enter **Y.** When prompted for the title cell, press – to clear A1 as the Y-axis heading, then press RETURN twice.

After returning to the main /View command prompt, press D. When prompted with

Var A: Enter range (now B5:E5), <space> to skip, < – > to clear
14>/View,3,Data,

Press the space bar. The PROMPT and ENTRY lines show

Var B: Enter range (now B14:E14), <space> to skip, < – > to clear
14>/View,3,Data,

Enter **B19.E19** to select net income data, and press the comma (,) key. The PROMPT and ENTRY lines show

Var C: Enter range (now B16:E16), <space> to skip, < – > to clear
14>/View,3,Data,

Press – to clear variable C. The PROMPT and ENTRY lines show

Var D: Enter range (now empty), <space> to skip, < – > to clear
14>/View,3,Data,

Press RETURN and the main prompt for the /View command will be shown.

Next, press V to edit the variable labels. When prompted with:

Var A: Var-Label cell or range (now A5), <space> to skip, < – > to clear
25>/View,3,Variable-Labels,

Press the space bar to skip over the label for variable A. The PROMPT and ENTRY lines show:

Var B: Var-Label cell or range (now A10), <space> to skip, < – > to clear
25>/View,3,Variable-Labels,

Enter **A19** and press the comma (,) key. The PROMPT and ENTRY lines show

Var C: Var-Label cell or range (now A16), <space> to skip, < – > to clear
25>/View,3,Variable-Labels,

Press – to clear variable label C. The PROMPT and ENTRY lines show

Var D: Var-Label cell or range (now empty), <space> to skip, < – > to clear
25>/View,3,Variable-Labels,

Press RETURN to display the main prompt for the /View command.

Next, press P to edit the point labels. When prompted with

Var A: Enter Point-Label range (now B5:E5), <space> to skip, < – > to clear
22>/View,3,Point-Labels,

Press the space bar to skip over the label for variable A. The PROMPT and ENTRY lines show

Var B: Point-Label range (now B14:E14), <space> to skip, < – > to clear
22>/View,3,Point-Labels,

Enter **B19.E19** and press the comma (,) key. The PROMPT and ENTRY lines show

Var C: Point-Label range (now B16:E16), <space> to skip, <−> to clear
22>/View,3,Point-Labels,

Press − to clear the point label for variable C. The PROMPT and ENTRY lines show

Var D: Point-Label range (now empty), <space> to skip, <−> to clear
22>/View,3,Point-Labels,

Press RETURN to display the main prompt for the /View command.

To plot the graph, press F10 or F9. Your plotted output should match Figure 12.22.

Figure 12.22 Hi-Lo Chart of P&L Spreadsheet

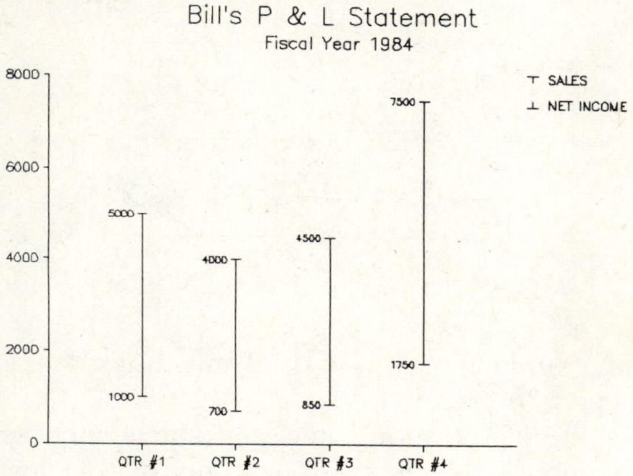

You can produce a summary display of all headings, labels, and data set for graph 3 by entering **/V?.**

EXAMPLE NO. 6

This example uses a Line Graph. You can save some time by copying graph 3 into graph 4. To do this, enter **/C*3,4** and press RETURN.

Next, use the Global Graphics Menu Option to turn on both vertical and horizontal grids. To do this, enter **/GGOB,** then press F2 twice.

You can now edit the parameters for graph 4. To begin, enter **/V4GL**. This sets the graph type to Line Graph. Now press P to edit the point labels. When prompted with

Var A: Enter Point-Label range (now B5:E5), <space> to skip, <−> to clear
22>/View,4,Point-Labels,

Press − to clear the label for variable A. The PROMPT and ENTRY lines show

Var B: Point-Label range (now B19:E19), <space> to skip, <−> to clear
22>/View,4,Point-Labels,

Press − to clear the label for variable B. The PROMPT and ENTRY lines show

Var C: Point-Label range (now empty), <space> to skip, <−> to clear
22>/View,4,Point-Labels,

Press RETURN to display the main prompt for the /View command.

To plot the graph, press F10 or F9. Your plotted output should match Figure 12.23.

Figure 12.23 Line Graph of P&L Spreadsheet

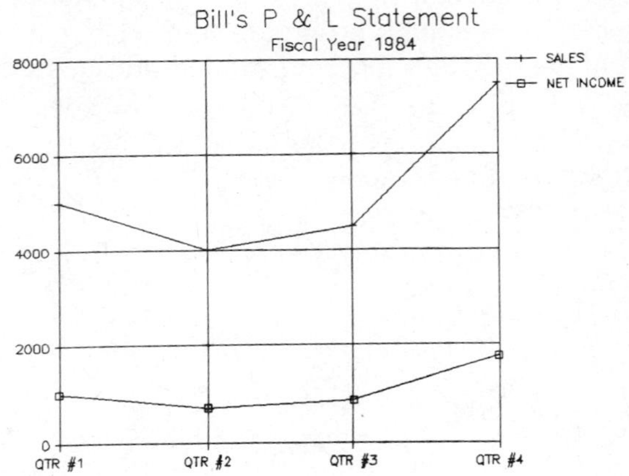

You can produce a summary display of all headings, labels, and data set for graph 4 by entering **/V?**.

This concludes the material on integrated spreadsheet graphics. You have surveyed some common business applications of this feature and are now ready for the Review Exercises.

Review Exercises

These exercises use the Credit Card Interest Spreadsheet from Exercise 9.1. This spreadsheet is illustrated in Figure 9.21 (see p. 179).

1. Define and plot a pie chart, using the following criteria:
   a. *Headings*
      Main: "BILL & CONNIE'S CREDIT CARD INTEREST"
      Sub: "FOR CALENDAR YEAR 1984"
   b. *Data:* Totals in row 19 for VISA, M/C, and SEARS.
   c. *Labels*
      Time: The three credit card names.
      Point: Totals in row 19 for VISA, M/C, and SEARS.
   d. *Options*
      Format: Point labels with floating dollar sign and no decimal places.
      Explosion: Sears only.

2. Define and plot a pie chart, using the following criteria:
   a. *Headings*
      Main: Same as graph 1.
      Sub: Same as graph 1.
      X-axis: "AVERAGE"
   b. *Data:* The average monthly interest expense.
   c. *Labels:*
      Time: The names of the 12 months.
      Point: The average monthly interest expense.
   d. *Options*
      Format: Same as graph 1.
      Explosion: Entire pie.
3. Define and plot a line graph, using the following criteria:
   a. *Headings*
      Main: Same as graph 2.
      Sub: Same as graph 2.
      X-axis: Same as graph 2.
   b. *Data:* Same as graph 2.
   c. *Labels*
      Time: Same as graph 2.
      Point: Same as graph 2.
   d. *Options*
      Format: Same as graph 2, but extended to axis labels.
      Explosion: N/A.
4. Define and plot a line graph, using the following criteria:
   a. *Headings*
      Main: Same as graph 3.
      Sub: Same as graph 3.
      X-axis: N/A.
   b. *Data:* Same as graph 3 for variable A, but extended to include:
      Variable B: VISA interest for each month in the year.
      Variable C: M/C interest for each month in the year.
      Variable D: SEARS interest for each month in the year.
   c. *Labels*
      Time: Same as graph 3.
      Point: N/A.
      Variable:
         Var A: AVERAGE interest for each month in the year.
         Var B: VISA interest for each month in the year.
         Var C: M/C interest for each month in the year.
         Var D: SEARS interest for each month in the year.
   d. *Options*
      Format: Same as graph 3.
      Explosion: Same as graph 3.
5. Define and plot a bar chart, using the following criteria:
   a. *Headings*
      Main: Same as graph 4.

Sub: Same as graph 4.
X-axis: Same as graph 4.

b. *Data*
Variable A: N/A.
Variable B: Same as graph 4.
Variable C: Same as graph 4.
Variable D: Same as graph 4.

c. *Labels*
Time: Same as graph 4.
Point: Same as graph 4.
Variable:
Var A: N/A.
Var B: Same as graph 4.
Var C: Same as graph 4.
Var D: Same as graph 4.

d. *Options*
Format: Same as graph 4.
Explosion: Same as graph 4.

Answers to Review Exercises

1. Enter **/VIGP**
   a. At main /View command prompt, enter **HMB1**
   At Headings prompt, enter **SB2**
   b. At main /View command prompt, enter **D**
   At Variable A prompt, enter **B19.D19** and press RETURN.
   c. At main /View command prompt, enter **T**
   At time label prompt, enter **B4.D4** and press RETURN.
   At main /View command prompt, enter **P**
   At Variable A prompt, enter **B19.D19** and press RETURN.
   d. Enter **/FD,** then set decimal places to 0 in format U1.
   Press F2 to return to your spreadsheet.
   Enter **/V1OFPU1** and press RETURN.
   At Options prompt, enter **E3** and press RETURN.
   e. Press F9 or F10, depending on whether you want plotted or displayed output.

   Your results should match the plotted output shown in Figure 12.24 (see page 253).

2. Enter **/C*1,2**
   Enter **/V2GP**
   a. At main /View command prompt, enter **HXF4** and press RETURN twice.
   b. At main /View command prompt, enter **D**
   At Variable A prompt, enter **F6.F17** and press RETURN.

c. At main /View command prompt, enter **T**
   At time label prompt, enter **A6.A17** and press RETURN.
   At main /View command prompt, enter **P**
   At Variable A prompt, enter **F6.F17** and press RETURN.
d. At main /View command prompt, enter **O**
   At Options prompt, enter **EA** and press RETURN.
e. Press F9 or F10, depending on whether you want plotted or displayed output.

Your results should match the plotted output shown in Figure 12.25.

Figure 12.24 Pie Chart of Credit Card Interest Spreadsheet: Exercise 12-1

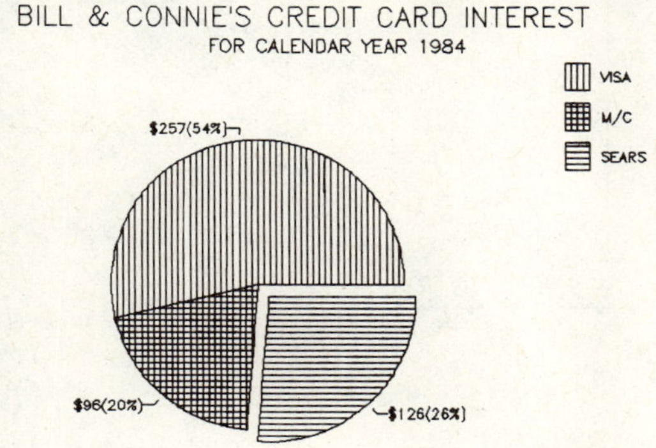

Figure 12.25 Exploded Pie Chart of Credit Card Interest Spreadsheet: Exercise 12-2

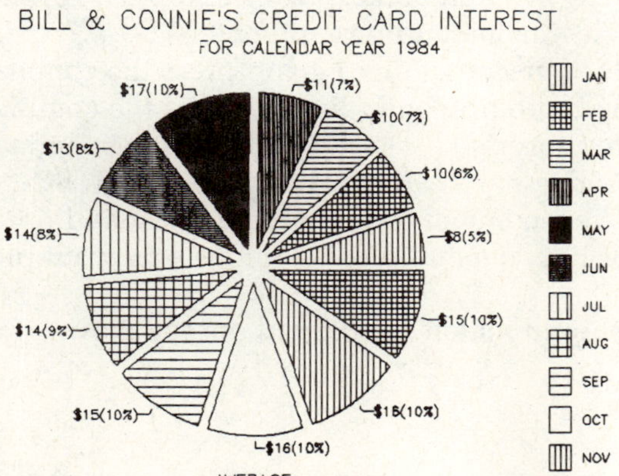

3. Enter **/C*2,3**
   Enter **/V3GL**
   a. At main /View command prompt, enter **O**
      At Options prompt, enter **FAU1** and press RETURN.
   b. Press F9 or F10, depending on whether you want plotted or displayed output.

   Your results should match the plotted output shown in Figure 12.26.

Figure 12.26 **Line Graph of Credit Card Interest Spreadsheet: Exercise 12-3**

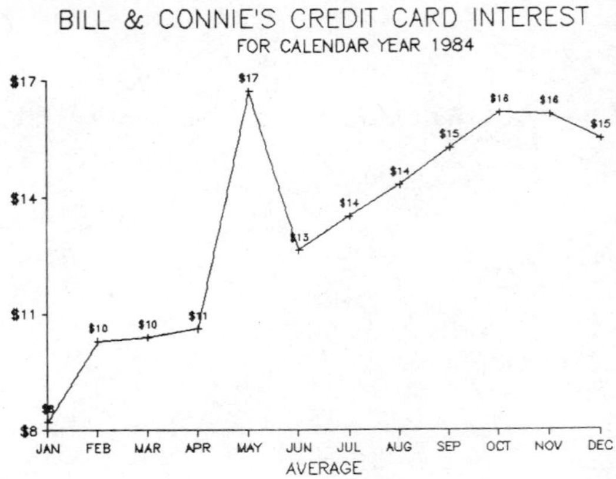

4. Enter **/C*3,4**
   Enter **/V4GL**
   a. At main /View command prompt, enter **HX–** and press RETURN twice.
   b. At main /View command prompt, enter **D**
      At Variable A prompt, press the space bar.
      At Variable B prompt, enter **B6.B17** and press the comma.
      At Variable C prompt, enter **C6.C17** and press the comma.
      At Variable D prompt, enter **D6.D17** and press RETURN.
   c. At main /View command prompt, enter **V**
      At Variable A prompt, enter **F4** and press the comma.
      At Variable B prompt, enter **B4** and press the comma.
      At Variable C prompt, enter **C4** and press the comma.
      At Variable D prompt, enter **D4** and press RETURN.
   d. At main /View command prompt, enter **P–** and press RETURN.
   e. Press F9 or F10, depending on whether you want plotted or displayed output.

   Your results should match the plotted output shown in Figure 12.27.

Figure 12.27 Line Graph of Credit Card Interest Spreadsheet: Exercise 12-4

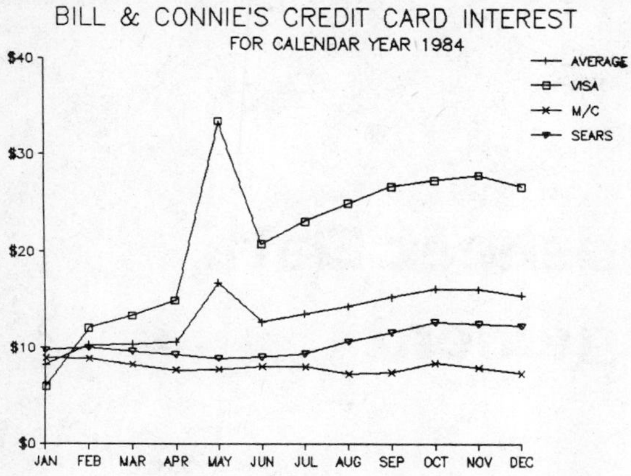

5. Enter /**C*4,5**
   Enter /**V5GB**
   a. At main /View command prompt, enter **D**
      At Variable A prompt, press –.
      At Variable B prompt, press RETURN.
   b. At main /View command prompt, enter **V**
      At Variable A prompt, press –.
      At Variable B prompt, press RETURN.
   c. Press F9 or F10, depending on whether you want plotted or displayed output.

   Your results should match the plotted output shown in Figure 12.28.

Figure 12.28 Bar Chart of Credit Card Interest Spreadsheet: Exercise 12-5

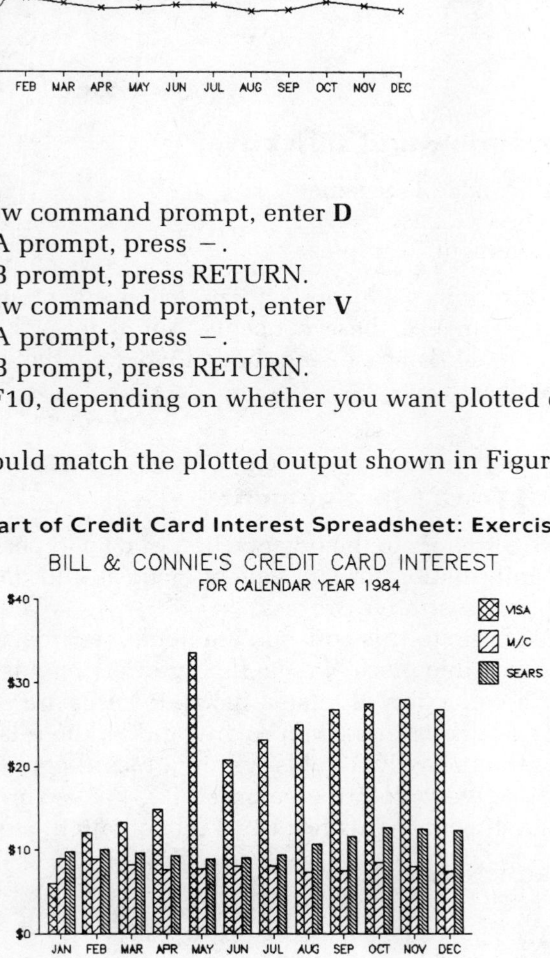

CHAPTER 13

Spreadsheet Data Management

Chapter Overview and Objectives

- Concepts of Data Management
- Defining the Database
- Data Management Examples

This chapter introduces concepts of data management and the related SuperCalc^3 techniques to use these concepts. You'll learn how to organize your spreadsheet into a database and how to define the selection criteria for accessing that base.

Concepts of Data Management

Data management refers to the organization of data to permit the selection and extraction of information for subsequent analysis and decision-making in the business and administrative process.

Three terms, basic to this concept, are fields, records, and files. The field is the smallest accessible piece of data. In SuperCalc^3, fields are called cells.

A record is a collection of related fields. Records are called rows in SuperCalc^3. The various cells in a given row would be the related fields within the record. While the individual fields within a record contain different pieces of data, they collectively describe some entity. For example, consider an employee personnel record. This record might contain the following fields:

Social Security Number
Name
Date of Birth
Date of Hire
Marital Status
Number of Dependents
Job Title
Base Pay
Pay Frequency

Viewed individually, these fields are not very meaningful. For example, a base pay of $1,000 doesn't really convey much information. It leaves some questions unanswered. Whose base pay? Is the pay frequency weekly or monthly? However, when two or more fields are viewed together, the ambiguity is removed. For example, J. Doe has a base pay of $1,000 on a weekly pay frequency. This information quite specifically describes J. Doe's earnings.

A file is a collection of related records. In SuperCalc^3, a file represents the entire spreadsheet. The data records in a file should be homogeneous—there should be no mixing of unlike records. For example, an employee master file should contain only employee information. It should not contain customer or inventory records.

Files should be organized into a predetermined sequence using a specified field in the record as a sort key. A common sequence for employee payroll and personnel master files uses department number as the primary sort key and employee number as the secondary sort key. This groups records in ascending sequence by department. Within department, records are grouped in ascending sequence by employee number. This type of sequencing can be done in SuperCalc^3 via the /Arrange command. Refer to Chapter 11 for more information.

Sorting supplements data management because it allows a smaller area of the database to be searched during an inquiry, reducing the time it takes to do the inquiry. Also, the results of an inquiry can be sorted into a different sequence from that of the actual database.

The sections that follow cover the creation of a database in SuperCalc^3 and how to make inquiries against the database.

Defining the Database

Setting up a database in SuperCalc^3 requires the creation of three areas in the spreadsheet—the input block, the output block, and the criterion block. All inquiries are made against the input block. This area can be the entire spreadsheet or just a portion of it. The output block is a designated open area that receives the results of your inquiries. The criterion block contains the selection logic for the search of your database.

Figure 13.1 contains a spreadsheet of employees and their respective gross pay. It uses textual values to indicate whether they live in the city and work in the city. Column E has conditional logic for calculating the city wage tax:

IF(OR(C4=("Yes"),D4=("Yes")),ROUND(B4*0.043125,2),0)

Figure 13.1 Wage Tax Spreadsheet

```
   :  A    ::   B   ::     C       ::      D       ::      E     :
1  Employee     Gross          City            City    City Wage
2  Name           Pay     Residence      Employment          Tax
3  ---------------------------------------------------------------
4  Able          4790           Yes              No       206.57
5  Baker         2528            No             Yes       109.02
6  Charles       3516           Yes             Yes       151.63
7  Delta         6777            No              No            0
8  ===============================================================
```

The following steps illustrate how to modify this spreadsheet to accommodate data management:

1. Enter **/IR1.3** and press RETURN. This inserts three new rows, starting at row 1.
2. At cell A1, enter **"Criteria:** . This identifies the beginning of the criterion block. The block requires a minimum of two rows. It can be anywhere in the spreadsheet, provided it doesn't overlap the input or output blocks. Since the selection logic in this block will change with each search, you should consider putting it at the top of your spreadsheet.
3. At cell A3, enter **"Input Block** . This identifies the beginning of the input block. For large spreadsheets, consider placing the input block after the output block. The input block could start at row 21 or 41. Since these rows are the tops of the second and third video display screens, respectively, you could use the PGUP and PGDN keys to enter and exit the main database area.
4. At cell A13, enter **"Output Block** . This identifies the beginning of the output block. For large spreadsheets, consider placing the output block before the input block. With the output block immediately following the criterion block, you can simultaneously view the selection logic and the search results.
5. Enter **/CA4.E6,A14** and press RETURN. This copies the column headings from the input block into the output block. This step is optional. You should consider doing it because it provides columnar descriptions of the search results.
6. Enter **/CA11,A22** and press RETURN. This copies the repeating text used as end-of-block markers.

Figure 13.2 illustrates the spreadsheet after it has been customized for data management.

Figure 13.2 Wage Tax Spreadsheet Modified for Data Management

```
    !  A   !!   B  !!      C      !!      D      !!      E     !
1   Criteria:
2
3   Input Block
4   Employee        Gross         City          City     City Wage
5   Name              Pay    Residence    Employment           Tax
6   --------------------------------------------------------------
7   Able             4790          Yes            No        206.57
8   Baker            2528           No           Yes        109.02
9   Charles          3516          Yes           Yes        151.63
10  Delta            6777           No            No             0
11  ==============================================================
12
13  Output Block
14  Employee        Gross         City          City     City Wage
15  Name              Pay    Residence    Employment           Tax
16  --------------------------------------------------------------
17
18
19
20
21
22  ==============================================================
```

The next phase in defining a database is entering the selection criteria. The first row in the criterion block identifies the fields to be searched. The field name is always taken from the last heading line in the input block. When no field name is specified in the criterion block, the entire database is searched. The second and subsequent rows contain the selection criteria, which can be formula or text. If two or more selection criteria are specified, SuperCalc[3] treats them similarly to the logical function "OR." Selection occurs when a match is made against any one of them.

Formula selection criteria use relational operators in conjunction with numeric constants, numeric expressions, and logical functions. The match criteria can be set for exact matching or selective matching. The cell name specified as the starting cell for the search is always in the row preceding the actual data to be searched. The following illustrations are based on Figure 13.2.

Consider three independent sets of selection criteria:

1. **Employees who live in the city**
   The entries to the criterion block are:
   Row 1: Residence — Field name to be searched.
   Row 2: C6 = ("Yes") — Exact match on the textual value ("Yes"), starting in cell C6.
2. **Employees who work in the city**
   Row 1: Employment — Field name to be searched.
   Row 2: D6 = ("Yes") — Exact match on the textual value ("Yes"), starting in cell D6.
3. **Employees who pay between $150 and $200 in city wage tax**
   Row 1: Tax — Field name to be searched.
   Row 2: AND(E6< = 200,E6> = 150) — Selective match on all values in the range of 150 through 200, starting in cell E6.

The preceding illustrations all specify row 6 as the search starting point, even though the actual data fields to be searched begin at row 7. The search would fail if row 7 were used as the starting point.

Text selection criteria simply involves entry of the text string to be used in the search. The match criteria can be set for exact matching or selective matching. Exact matching recognizes spaces as well as upper- and lowercase. For example, "WDoyle" is not the same as "W Doyle." Also, "w. doyle" does not match "W. DOYLE."

Selective text matching is done using the following wildcard characters:

? — The question mark matches any character at the position where the question mark has been entered. Precede the text string with a double quote so that the AnswerScreen is not called. For example, an entry of **"B?ll** would match Ball, Bell, Bill, and Bull.

* — The asterisk matches anything that follows it. This wildcard character should only be at the end of a text string criterion. Any characters following it in the criterion string are ignored. For example, an entry of **"Ba*** matches all text strings beginning with Ba. An entry of "* matches all text strings.

˜ The tilde matches everything except the characters following it. For example, an entry of **"˜A** matches all text strings except those beginning with an uppercase A.
Note: The tilde is entered by holding down the ALT key and pressing 126 on the numeric keypad.

The following illustrations are based on Figure 13.2. Consider three independent sets of selection criteria:

1. **Employees whose names do not begin with A**
   The entries to the criterion block are:
   Row 1: Name Field name to be searched.
   Row 2: ˜A Selective match on all text strings not beginning with uppercase A.
2. **Employees whose names start with Ba***
   Row 1: Name Field name to be searched.
   Row 2: Ba* Selective match on all text strings beginning with Ba.
3. **Employees whose names are Delta or Able**
   The entries to the criterion block are:
   Row 1: Name Field name to be searched.
   Row 2: Delta Exact match on all text strings equal to Delta.
   Row 3: Able Exact match on all text strings equal to Able.

You can now make the following entries to the criterion block:

Cell	Entry
C1	**Residence**
C2	**C6=("Yes")**
D1	**"Employment**
D2	**D6=("Yes")**
E1	**"Tax**
E2	**AND(E6<=200,E6>=150)**
F1	**Name**
F2	**"˜A**
G1	**"Name**
G2	**"Ba***
H1	**"Name**
H2	**"Delta**
H3	**"Able**

Your spreadsheet should match the one shown in Figure 13.3.

The final phase in defining your database involves specifying the locations of the three database blocks. This is done via the //Data management command. This command also searches the database. Enter **//D.** The PROMPT and ENTRY lines respond with

I(nput),C(riterion),O(utput),F(ind),E(xtract),S(elect),R(emain)?
8>//Data,

These data management options are defined as follows:

Figure 13.3 Wage Tax Spreadsheet with Criterion Block Entries

```
     |  A . ||  B ||    C   ||    D    ||    E   ||   F   ||   G   ||   H  |
1    Criteria:          Residence Employment        Tax      Name      Name      Name
2                               0          0          0        ~A       Ba*     Delta
3    Input Block
4    Employee  Gross         City       City  City Wage
5    Name        Pay Residence Employment         Tax
6    ------------------------------------------------------------------------------
7    Able       4790          Yes         No     206.57
8    Baker      2528           No        Yes     109.02
9    Charles    3516          Yes        Yes     151.63
10   Delta      6777           No         No          0
11   ==============================================================================
12
13   Output Block
14   Employee  Gross         City       City  City Wage
15   Name        Pay Residence Employment         Tax
16   ------------------------------------------------------------------------------
17
18
19
20
21
22   ==============================================================================
```

I Identifies the cell range of the input block. Pressing I displays the following prompt:

Input range (now empty), < – > to clear
14>//Data,Input,

The first row in the input range must be either text or blank. This row uses the column headings as field names. When the first row is blank, SuperCalc³ ignores the field names in the criterion block. The second row should also be blank or contain repeating text, otherwise the search will fail.

You must specify an input range before you can use the Find, Extract, or Select options. Using Figure 13.3 as an example, enter **A5.E11.** When you press RETURN, the main //Data prompt is displayed.

C Identifies the cell range for the criterion block. Pressing C displays the following prompt:

Criterion range (now empty), < – > to clear
18>//Data,Criterion,

The criterion range should include all rows in the criterion block. If multiple columns are used in the criterion range, SuperCalc³ treats them like the logical function "AND." Selection occurs when a match is made against the selection criterion in each column.

You must specify a criterion range before you can use the Find, Extract, or Select options. Using Figure 13.3 as an example, consider the following:

1. An entry of **C1.C2** selects all employees who live in the city.
2. An entry of **D1.D2** selects all employees who work in the city.

3. An entry of **C1.D2** selects all employees who both live in the city and work in the city.
4. An entry of **C1.E2** selects all employees who live in the city, work in the city, and pay between $150 and $200 in city wage tax.

Once you make an entry and press RETURN, the main //Data prompt is displayed.

O Identifies the cell range for the output block. Pressing **O** displays the following prompt:

Output range (now empty), < – > to clear
15>//Data,Output,

The output range specifies the cells into which matched records are to be placed. The output block may not overlap either of the other two blocks. If it does, one of the following error messages results:

Output & Criterion range overlap
Output & Input range overlap

The output block must be large enough to receive all extracted records. If it isn't, an error message results:

Output area full

You could make the output block the same size as the input block. This "worst case" approach will work for small spreadsheets but may cause problems with larger ones. When working with large spreadsheets, you should estimate the number of matches and set your output range accordingly. SuperCalc³ will tell you if the output range isn't big enough. You can then increase the size of the output block.

You must specify an output range before you can use the Find, Extract, or Select options. The first row in the output block is used for field names. See row 15 in Figure 13.3. Using this figure as an example, enter **A15.E21.** When you press RETURN, the main //Data prompt is displayed.

F Searches the input block using the selection logic from the criterion block. Any matching records are highlighted on your video screen. Pressing F displays the following prompt:

Next record ↓ or ↑, Next field ← or →, Cancel <RETURN>
12>//Data,Find,

The directional arrows ↓ and ↑ allow you to scroll between matched records. The directional arrows ← and → allow you to scroll between fields in a given matched record.

Before you can use the Find option, you must have specified an input range and a criterion range. The Find option is useful for determining the size needed for the output block.

Using Figure 13.3 as an example, with the criterion block set at C1.C2, the Find option identifies Able and Charles as employees living in the city. When you press RETURN, the

Find option is terminated and the main //Data prompt is displayed.

E Searches the input block using the selection logic from the criterion block. Any matching records are copied to the output block. Pressing E executes the extract and returns you to the main //Data prompt.

The records copied to the output block consist only of text and values. Any formulas encountered in matched records are first converted to values. "What if . . .?" analyses cannot be done on the output block. If you need to do "What if . . .?" do it on the input block, then repeat the extract. Using the city wage tax spreadsheet as an example, with the criterion block set at C1.C2, the Extract option put the records for Able and Charles into the output block. See Figure 13.4 for an illustration of the extracted results.

Figure 13.4 Wage Tax Spreadsheet Using Criteria at C1 and C2 to Extract Output

```
    ¦   A   ¦¦  B ¦¦    C   ¦¦    D    ¦¦     E    ¦¦   F   ¦¦   G   ¦¦   H  ¦
1   Criteria:        Residence Employment        Tax     Name     Name     Name
2                            0          0          0       ~A      Ba*    Delta
3   Input Block                                                            Able
4   Employee  Gross       City       City  City Wage
5   Name        Pay  Residence Employment        Tax
6   ---------------------------------------------------------------------------
7   Able       4790        Yes         No     206.57
8   Baker      2528         No        Yes     109.02
9   Charles    3516        Yes        Yes     151.63
10  Delta      6777         No         No          0
11  ===========================================================================
12
13  Output Block
14  Employee  Gross       City       City  City Wage
15  Name        Pay  Residence Employment        Tax
16  Able       4790        Yes         No     206.57
17  Charles    3516        Yes        Yes     151.63
18
19
20
21
22  ===========================================================================
```

S The Select option functions like the Extract option, except that it allows you to further screen which matched records are written to the output block. Pressing S displays the following prompt:

Extract? Y(es) or N(o), Next field ← or →,Cancel <RETURN>
14>//Data,Select,

Pressing Y accepts the matched record. It is immediately copied into the output block. Pressing N rejects the matched record. It is not copied into the output block. The ← and → directional arrows allow you to review individual fields before making your selection decision for a given matched record.

Using the city wage tax spreadsheet as an example, pressing N rejects Able, while pressing Y copies Charles to the output block. See Figure 13.5 for an illustration of the selected results.

Figure 13.5 Wage Tax Spreadsheet Using Select Option

```
    !  A   !! B !!    C   !!     D    !!     E    !!   F  !!    G  !!    H  !
 1  Criteria:       Residence Employment        Tax      Name      Name     Name
 2                          0          0          0        ~A       Ba*    Delta
 3  Input Block                                                             Able
 4  Employee   Gross      City        City  City Wage
 5  Name         Pay Residence  Employment        Tax
 6  ---------------------------------------------------------------------------
 7  Able        4790       Yes          No     206.57
 8  Baker       2528        No         Yes     109.02
 9  Charles     3516       Yes         Yes     151.63
10  Delta       6777        No          No          0
11  ===========================================================================
12
13  Output Block
14  Employee   Gross      City        City  City Wage
15  Name         Pay Residence  Employment        Tax
16  Charles     3516       Yes         Yes     151.63
17
18
19
20
21
22  ===========================================================================
```

R The Remain option terminates the //Data command, leaving the spreadsheet cursor at its current position. This allows for easy editing of selection criteria as well as found records. The //Data command can also be terminated by pressing RETURN at the main //Data prompt or by pressing F2 at any point. If you use either of these two methods to terminate //Data, the spreadsheet cursor returns to its last position prior to entry of the //Data command.

The next section provides some additional examples of how data management can be used in SuperCalc³.

Data Management Examples

EXAMPLE NO. 1

This example uses the course grade spreadsheet shown in Figure 13.6. Columns B through I are not displayed because they have a column width of 0.

The following steps illustrate how to modify the spreadsheet to accommodate data management:

1. Enter **/IR1.3** and press RETURN.
2. At cell A1, enter **"Criteria:**
3. At cell A3, enter **"Input Block**

4. At cell A21, enter **"Output Block**
5. Enter **/CA4.M5,A22** and press RETURN.
6. Enter **/CA18,A35** and press RETURN.

The resulting spreadsheet should match Figure 13.7.

Figure 13.6 Student Grade Spreadsheet

```
    !  A    !!  J    !!  K    !!  L    !!  M    !!  N    !!  O    !!  P  !
1   Name        Test Avg Prog Avg Crse Avg     Grade
2   -------------------------------------------------------------------------
3   ABLE              71       85       75        C
4   BAKER             89       91       90        B
5   CHARLES           53       48       52        F
6   DELTA             79       94       83        C
7   ECHO              84       99       88        B
8   FOX               95      100       96        A
9   GAMMA             70       88       75        C
10  HOTEL             63       73       66        D
11  INCA              95      100       96        A
12
13
14
15  =========================================================================
16
17
18
19
20
```

Figure 13.7 Student Grade Spreadsheet Modified for Data Management

```
    !  A    !!  J    !!  K    !!  L    !!  M    !!  N    !!  O    !!  P  !
1   Criteria:
2
3   Input Block
4   Name        Test Avg Prog Avg Crse Avg     Grade
5   -------------------------------------------------------------------------
6   ABLE              71       85       75        C
7   BAKER             89       91       90        B
8   CHARLES           53       48       52        F
9   DELTA             79       94       83        C
10  ECHO              84       99       88        B
11  FOX               95      100       96        A
12  GAMMA             70       88       75        C
13  HOTEL             63       73       66        D
14  INCA              95      100       96        A
15
16
17
18  =========================================================================
19
20
21  Output Block
22  Name        Test Avg Prog Avg Crse Avg     Grade
23  -------------------------------------------------------------------------
24
25
26
27
28
29
30
31
32
33
34
35  =========================================================================
36
37
38
39
40
```

The next step illustrates how to establish data selection criteria:

Select all students with satisfactory grades
At cell J1, enter **"Grade**
At cell J2, enter **OR(M5 = ("A"),OR(M5 = ("B"),M5 = ("C")))**

You can now call data management by entering //**D.** The following steps illustrate how to define your database and then generate extracted output:

1. Press I, then enter **A4.M17** and press RETURN.
2. Press C, then enter **J1.J2** and press RETURN.
3. Press O, then enter **A22.M34** and press RETURN.
4. Press E, then press RETURN.

The resulting spreadsheet should match Figure 13.8.

Figure 13.8 **Student Grade Spreadsheet with Extracted Output of All Grades above F**

```
   |  A  ||   J  ||   K   ||   L   ||   M   ||   N   ||   O   ||   P   |
1   Criteria:     Grade
2                     0
3   Input Block
4   Name       Test Avg Prog Avg Crse Avg     Grade
5   ---------------------------------------------------------------------------
6   ABLE             71       85       75         C
7   BAKER            89       91       90         B
8   CHARLES          53       48       52         F
9   DELTA            79       94       83         C
10  ECHO             84       99       88         B
11  FOX              95      100       96         A
12  GAMMA            70       88       75         C
13  HOTEL            63       73       66         D
14  INCA             95      100       96         A
15
16
17
18  ===========================================================================
19
20
21  Output Block
22  Name       Test Avg Prog Avg Crse Avg     Grade
23  ABLE             71       85       75         C
24  BAKER            89       91       90         B
25  DELTA            79       94       83         C
26  ECHO             84       99       88         B
27  FOX              95      100       96         A
28  GAMMA            70       88       75         C
29  INCA             95      100       96         A
30
31
32
33
34
35  ===========================================================================
36
37
38
39
40
```

EXAMPLE NO. 2

This example uses the telephone directory spreadsheet shown in Figure 13.9.

Figure 13.9 Telephone Information Spreadsheet

```
     !     A      !!       B       !!        C        !!     D     !!  E  !!  F  !
1    Name           Telephone          Profession
2    ---------------------------------------------------------------------------
3    Able           (215)555-1212      Rich man
4    Apple          (201)245-2528      Poor man
5    Baker          (609)254-3516      Beggar man
6    Berry          (212)508-6777      Thief
7    Charlie        (215)542-8684      Doctor
8    Cherry         (215)555-8182      Lawyer
9    Date           (214)231-3131      Indian chief
10   Delta          (213)555-5490      Butcher
11   Foxtrot        (215)441-5570      Baker
12   Fruit          (201)245-7778      Candlestick maker
13   Gamma          (609)542-6135      Tinker
14   Grape          (800)915-1234      Tailor
15   Honey          (212)805-6778      Soldier
16   Hotel          (213)924-7177      Spy
17   Inca           (214)742-3026      Indian chief
18   Juliet         (215)461-5843      Doctor
19   Mary           (213)742-3647      Teacher
20
```

The following steps illustrate how to modify the spreadsheet to accommodate data management:

1. Enter **/IR1.41** and press RETURN.
2. At cell A1, enter **"Criteria:**
3. At cell A21, enter **"Output Block**
4. At cell A41, enter **"Input Block**
5. Enter **/CA42.C43,A22** and press RETURN.

The resulting spreadsheet should match Figure 13.10.

The next series of steps illustrates how to establish data selection criteria:

1. **Select all people who are in area code 609**
   At cell B1, enter **"Telephone**
   At cell B2, enter **"(609)***
2. **Select all people who are doctors in area code 215**
   At cell C1, enter **"Telephone**
   At cell C2, enter **"(215)***
   At cell D1, enter **"Profession**
   At cell D2, enter **"Doctor**
3. **Select all people who are tinkers, tailors, soldiers, or spies**
   At cell E1, enter **"Profession**
   At cell E2, enter **"Tinker**
   At cell E3, enter **"Tailor**
   At cell E4, enter **"Soldier**
   At cell E5, enter **"Spy**

Figure 13.10 **Telephone Information Spreadsheet Modified for Data Management**

```
    |   A    ||    B     ||    C    ||    D   ||  E  ||  F  |
1   Criteria:
2
3
4
5
6
7
8
9
10
11
12
13
14
15
16
17
18
19
20
21  Output Block
22  Name          Telephone        Profession
23  ----------------------------------------------------------------
24
25
26
27
28
29
30
31
32
33
34
35
36
37
38
39
40
41  Input Block
42  Name          Telephone        Profession
43  ----------------------------------------------------------------
44  Able          (215)555-1212    Rich man
45  Apple         (201)245-2528    Poor man
46  Baker         (609)254-3516    Beggar man
47  Berry         (212)508-6777    Thief
48  Charlie       (215)542-8684    Doctor
49  Cherry        (215)555-8182    Lawyer
50  Date          (214)231-3131    Indian chief
51  Delta         (213)555-5490    Butcher
52  Foxtrot       (215)441-5570    Baker
53  Fruit         (201)245-7778    Candlestick maker
54  Gamma         (609)542-6135    Tinker
55  Grape         (808)915-1234    Tailor
56  Honey         (212)805-6778    Soldier
57  Hotel         (213)924-7177    Spy
58  Inca          (214)742-3026    Indian chief
59  Juliet        (215)461-5843    Doctor
60  Mary          (213)742-3647    Teacher
```

You can now call data management by entering **//D.** The following steps illustrate how to define your database and generate extracted output:

1. Press I, then enter **A42.C60** and press RETURN.
2. Press O, then enter **A22.C40** and press RETURN.
3. Press C, then enter **B1.B2** and press RETURN.
4. Press E, then press RETURN.
   The resulting spreadsheet should match Figure 13.11.

Figure 13.11 Telephone Information Spreadsheet Extracting All Records for Area Code 609

```
    |    A     ||     B        ||     C      ||    D      ||    E    ||   F   |
1    Criteria:   Telephone       Telephone    Profession  Profession
2                (609)*          (215)*       Doctor      Tinker
3                                                         Tailor
4                                                         Soldier
5                                                         Spy
6
7
8
9
10
11
12
13
14
15
16
17
18
19
20
21   Output Block
22   Name        Telephone       Profession
23   Baker       (609)254-3516   Beggar man
24   Gamma       (609)542-6135   Tinker
25
26
27
28
29
30
31
32
33
34
35
36
37
38
39
40
41   Input Block
42   Name        Telephone       Profession
43   ----------------------------------------------------------------------
44   Able        (215)555-1212   Rich man
45   Apple       (201)245-2528   Poor man
46   Baker       (609)254-3516   Beggar man
47   Berry       (212)508-6777   Thief
48   Charlie     (215)542-8684   Doctor
49   Cherry      (215)555-8182   Lawyer
50   Date        (214)231-3131   Indian chief
51   Delta       (213)555-5490   Butcher
52   Foxtrot     (215)441-5570   Baker
53   Fruit       (201)245-7778   Candlestick maker
54   Gamma       (609)542-6135   Tinker
55   Grape       (800)915-1234   Tailor
56   Honey       (212)805-6778   Soldier
57   Hotel       (213)924-7177   Spy
58   Inca        (214)742-3026   Indian chief
59   Juliet      (215)461-5843   Doctor
60   Mary        (213)742-3647   Teacher
```

5. Press C, then enter **C1.D2** and press RETURN.
6. Press E, then press RETURN.
   The resulting spreadsheet should match Figure 13.12.

Figure 13.12 Telephone Information Spreadsheet Extracting All Records for Doctors in Area Code 215

```
   |    A    ||     B        ||     C       ||     D      ||    E     ||   F   |
1   Criteria:  Telephone       Telephone     Profession   Profession
2              (609)*          (215)*        Doctor       Tinker
3                                                         Tailor
4                                                         Soldier
5                                                         Spy
6
7
8
9
10
11
12
13
14
15
16
17
18
19
20
21  Output Block
22  Name       Telephone       Profession
23  Charlie    (215)542-8684   Doctor
24  Juliet     (215)461-5843   Doctor
25
26
27
28
29
30
31
32
33
34
35
36
37
38
39
40
41  Input Block
42  Name       Telephone       Profession
43  -----------------------------------------------------------------------------
44  Able       (215)555-1212   Rich man
45  Apple      (201)245-2528   Poor man
46  Baker      (609)254-3516   Beggar man
47  Berry      (212)508-6777   Thief
48  Charlie    (215)542-8684   Doctor
49  Cherry     (215)555-8182   Lawyer
50  Date       (214)231-3131   Indian chief
51  Delta      (213)555-5490   Butcher
52  Foxtrot    (215)441-5570   Baker
53  Fruit      (201)245-7778   Candlestick maker
54  Gamma      (609)542-6135   Tinker
55  Grape      (800)915-1234   Tailor
56  Honey      (212)805-6778   Soldier
57  Hotel      (213)924-7177   Spy
58  Inca       (214)742-3026   Indian chief
59  Juliet     (215)461-5843   Doctor
60  Mary       (213)742-3647   Teacher
```

7. Press C, then enter **E1.E5** and press RETURN.
8. Press E, then press RETURN.
   The resulting spreadsheet should match Figure 13.13.

Figure 13.13 Telephone Information Spreadsheet Extracting All Records Matching a List of Professions

	A	B	C	D	E	F
1	Criteria:	Telephone	Telephone	Profession	Profession	
2		(609)*	(215)*	Doctor	Tinker	
3					Tailor	
4					Soldier	
5					Spy	
6						
7						
8						
9						
10						
11						
12						
13						
14						
15						
16						
17						
18						
19						
20						
21	Output Block					
22	Name	Telephone	Profession			
23	Gamma	(609)542-6135	Tinker			
24	Grape	(800)915-1234	Tailor			
25	Honey	(212)805-6778	Soldier			
26	Hotel	(213)924-7177	Spy			
27						
28						
29						
30						
31						
32						
33						
34						
35						
36						
37						
38						
39						
40						
41	Input Block					
42	Name	Telephone	Profession			
43	----------	----------	----------	----------	----------	----------
44	Able	(215)555-1212	Rich man			
45	Apple	(201)245-2528	Poor man			
46	Baker	(609)254-3516	Beggar man			
47	Berry	(212)508-6777	Thief			
48	Charlie	(215)542-8684	Doctor			
49	Cherry	(215)555-8182	Lawyer			
50	Date	(214)231-3131	Indian chief			
51	Delta	(213)555-5490	Butcher			
52	Foxtrot	(215)441-5570	Baker			
53	Fruit	(201)245-7778	Candlestick maker			
54	Gamma	(609)542-6135	Tinker			
55	Grape	(800)915-1234	Tailor			
56	Honey	(212)805-6778	Soldier			
57	Hotel	(213)924-7177	Spy			
58	Inca	(214)742-3026	Indian chief			
59	Juliet	(215)461-5843	Doctor			
60	Mary	(213)742-3647	Teacher			

This concludes the material on data management. You have seen several examples of how this powerful feature can be used and are now ready for the Review Exercises.

Review Exercises

These exercises use the Pension Plan Spreadsheet from Exercise 9.6. Given the spreadsheet shown in Figure 13.14, perform the following:

1. Modify the spreadsheet to accommodate data management.
2. Establish the following criteria:
   a. Select all employees 30 years of age or older.
   b. Select all employees contributing more than 5% to the pension plan.
   c. Select all employees with at least two years on the job and earnings of $300 or more.
3. Define the database and extract three output reports using the above criteria.

Figure 13.14 Pension Plan Spreadsheet

	A	B	C	D	E	F
1	PENSION PLAN ELIGIBILITY ANALYSIS					
2	--------------------------------					
3	CURRENT DATE:	11/24/1984				
4					CONTRIB	CONTRIB
5	NAME	HIRE DATE	AGE	BASE PAY	PERCENT	AMOUNT
6	----------	----------	----------	----------	----------	----------
7	ABLE	3/10/1983	24	100	2	N/A
8	BAKER	1/ 1/1984	30	200	0	N/A
9	CHARLES	1/ 1/1980	22	300	5	15
10	DELTA	8/ 2/1982	28	400	7	28
11	ECHO	1/ 1/1984	34	500	10	50
12	FOX	7/ 3/1976	38	1000	12	120
13						
14						
15						
16						
17						
18						
19						
20						

Answers to Review Exercises

1. Spreadsheet modification:
   a. Enter **/IR4.21** and press RETURN.
   b. At cell A5, enter **"CRITERIA:**
   c. At cell A21, enter **"INPUT BLOCK**
   d. At cell A8, enter **"OUTPUT BLOCK**
   e. Enter **/CA22.F24,A9** and press RETURN.
   Your resulting spreadsheet should match Figure 13.15.
2. Data selection criteria:
   a. At cell B5, enter **"AGE**
   At cell B6, enter **C24>=30**
   b. At cell C5, enter **"PERCENT**
   At cell C6, enter **E24>5**
   c. At cell D5, enter **"HIRE DATE**
   At cell D6, enter **B3-B24>=2*365**
   Note: Cell D6 will display **"ERROR"** because cell B24 does not contain

Figure 13.15 Pension Plan Spreadsheet: Exercise 13-1

```
    |     A      ||     B     ||   C  ||    D    ||   E   ||     F    |
 1  PENSION PLAN ELIGIBILITY ANALYSIS
 2  ----------------------------------
 3  CURRENT DATE:       11/24/1984
 4
 5  CRITERIA:
 6
 7
 8  OUTPUT BLOCK
 9                                                   CONTRIB       CONTRIB
10  NAME                  HIRE DATE      AGE   BASE PAY  PERCENT        AMOUNT
11  ------------------------------------------------------------------------
12
13
14
15
16
17
18
19
20
21  INPUT BLOCK
22                                                   CONTRIB       CONTRIB
23  NAME                  HIRE DATE      AGE   BASE PAY  PERCENT        AMOUNT
24  ------------------------------------------------------------------------
25  ABLE                  3/10/1983       24        100        2           N/A
26  BAKER                 1/ 1/1984       30        200        0           N/A
27  CHARLES               1/ 1/1980       22        300        5            15
28  DELTA                 8/ 2/1982       28        400        7            28
29  ECHO                  1/ 1/1984       34        500       10            50
30  FOX                   7/ 3/1976       38       1000       12           120
31
32
33
34
35
36
37
38
39
40
```

a date function. This message can be ignored, since the proper date representation exists in the cells to be searched.

At cell E5, enter **"BASE PAY**

At cell E6, enter **D24>=300**

3. Database definition and extract generation:
   a. Enter //**D**
      Press I, then enter **A23.F30** and press RETURN.
   b. Press O, then enter **A10.F20** and press RETURN.
   c. Press C, then enter **B5.B6** and press RETURN.
   d. Press E, then press RETURN.

   The resulting spreadsheet should match Figure 13.16.

Figure 13.16 Pension Plan Spreadsheet: Exercise 13-3d

```
    :      A      ::     B     ::   C   ::     D    ::    E   ::     F     :
1   PENSION PLAN ELIGIBILITY ANALYSIS
2   ---------------------------------
3   CURRENT DATE:     11/24/1984
4
5   CRITERIA:                    AGE   PERCENT  HIRE DATE BASE PAY
6                                  0         0      ERROR        0
7
8   OUTPUT BLOCK
9                                                          CONTRIB       CONTRIB
10  NAME                   HIRE DATE        AGE   BASE PAY  PERCENT        AMOUNT
11  BAKER                  1/ 1/1984         30        200        0             0
12  ECHO                   1/ 1/1984         34        500       10            50
13  FOX                    7/ 3/1976         38       1000       12           120
14
15
16
17
18
19
20
21  INPUT BLOCK
22                                                         CONTRIB       CONTRIB
23  NAME                   HIRE DATE        AGE   BASE PAY  PERCENT        AMOUNT
24  ---------------------------------------------------------------------------
25  ABLE                   3/10/1983         24        100        2           N/A
26  BAKER                  1/ 1/1984         30        200        0           N/A
27  CHARLES                1/ 1/1980         22        300        5            15
28  DELTA                  8/ 2/1982         28        400        7            28
29  ECHO                   1/ 1/1984         34        500       10            50
30  FOX                    7/ 3/1976         38       1000       12           120
31
32
33
34
35
36
37
38
39
40
```

e. Press C, then enter **C5.C6** and press RETURN.
f. Press E, then press RETURN.

The resulting spreadsheet should match Figure 13.17.

Figure 13.17 Pension Plan Spreadsheet: Exercise 13-3f

```
    :       A       ::      B     ::   C   ::     D     ::    E    ::      F    :
1   PENSION PLAN ELIGIBILITY ANALYSIS
2   ---------------------------------
3   CURRENT DATE:      11/24/1984
4
5   CRITERIA:                        AGE   PERCENT   HIRE DATE BASE PAY
6                                      0         0       ERROR        0
7
8   OUTPUT BLOCK
9                                                               CONTRIB      CONTRIB
10  NAME               HIRE DATE           AGE     BASE PAY    PERCENT       AMOUNT
11  DELTA              8/ 2/1982            28          400          7           28
12  ECHO               1/ 1/1984            34          500         10           50
13  FOX                7/ 3/1976            38         1000         12          120
14
15
16
17
18
19
20
21  INPUT BLOCK
22                                                              CONTRIB      CONTRIB
23  NAME               HIRE DATE           AGE     BASE PAY    PERCENT       AMOUNT
24  ------------------------------------------------------------------------------
25  ABLE               3/10/1983            24          100          2          N/A
26  BAKER              1/ 1/1984            30          200          0          N/A
27  CHARLES            1/ 1/1980            22          300          5           15
28  DELTA              8/ 2/1982            28          400          7           28
29  ECHO               1/ 1/1984            34          500         10           50
30  FOX                7/ 3/1976            38         1000         12          120
31
32
33
34
35
36
37
38
39
40
```

g. Press C, then enter **D5.E6** and press RETURN.
h. Press E, then press RETURN.
The resulting spreadsheet should match Figure 13.18.
i. Press R to terminate data management.

Figure 13.18 Pension Plan Spreadsheet: Exercise 13-3h

```
    :     A      ::     B     ::  C  ::     D    ::   E   ::     F    :
1   PENSION PLAN ELIGIBILITY ANALYSIS
2   ---------------------------------
3   CURRENT DATE:     11/24/1984
4
5   CRITERIA:                   AGE  PERCENT  HIRE DATE BASE PAY
6                                 0        0      ERROR        0
7
8   OUTPUT BLOCK
9                                                     CONTRIB     CONTRIB
10  NAME              HIRE DATE       AGE    BASE PAY PERCENT      AMOUNT
11  CHARLES           1/ 1/1980        22         300        5         15
12  DELTA             8/ 2/1982        28         400        7         28
13  FOX               7/ 3/1976        38        1000       12        120
14
15
16
17
18
19
20
21  INPUT BLOCK
22                                                    CONTRIB     CONTRIB
23  NAME              HIRE DATE       AGE    BASE PAY PERCENT      AMOUNT
24  ---------------------------------------------------------------------
25  ABLE              3/10/1983        24         100        2        N/A
26  BAKER             1/ 1/1984        30         200        0        N/A
27  CHARLES           1/ 1/1980        22         300        5         15
28  DELTA             8/ 2/1982        28         400        7         28
29  ECHO              1/ 1/1984        34         500       10         50
30  FOX               7/ 3/1976        38        1000       12        120
31
32
33
34
35
36
37
38
39
40
```

CHAPTER 14

Using SuperCalc^3 Command Files

Chapter Overview and Objectives

- Purpose of Command Files
- Creating Command Files
- Executing Command Files

This chapter introduces the concept of command files and how they can be used to save time and eliminate some of the redundancy associated with frequently issued commands.

Purpose of Command Files

You've probably noticed that there is a great deal of repetition of certain spreadsheet commands. A very common sequence of events is:

/Load a spreadsheet.
Make new entries or change existing entries and formats.
/Save the spreadsheet.
/Output the spreadsheet.

SuperCalc^3 provides an alternative to these repetitious tasks through its use of command files. These files are ASCII formatted files with an extension of .XQT. They can contain any valid SuperCalc^3 command. When you issue the /eXecute command, SuperCalc^3 automatically executes all the instructions contained in your command (.XQT) file.

Command files can be as simple or as complex as your imagination. Here's a simple example:

Load a spreadsheet.
Print the spreadsheet.
Quit SuperCalc^3.

Here's a slightly more complicated example:

Load a spreadsheet.
Load one or more additional spreadsheets using the consolidation option.
Print the consolidated spreadsheet.
Save the consolidated spreadsheet.
Quit SuperCalc³.

Here's an example of an even more complex command file:

Load a data entry template.
Interactively pass control between the command file and your keyboard to perform the data entry process.
Print the data entry results.
Save the data entry spreadsheet.
Merge the data entry spreadsheet into another template to perform some calculations.
Print the resulting spreadsheet.
Save the resulting spreadsheet.
Quit SuperCalc³.

The preceding example is useful in an office environment where data entry is done by an unskilled or semi-skilled clerical staff. This approach limits the clerk to specific entries and can substantially reduce accidental updates to the wrong spreadsheets.

Creating Command Files

Command files may be created from within SuperCalc³ or by SuperWriter, EasyWriter, or some other word processor.[1] The main thrust of this section is on using SuperCalc³ to create command files.

The following rules are applicable for creating command files:

- All entries to the command file are made as text in column A.
- Column A must have a width just slightly greater than the longest command. Excessive width affects performance.
- Command entries are made just as they would be keyed during manual operation. Do not include the characters that SuperCalc³ returns through its interactive prompting. Examples of valid entries include:

  Any "Slash" command.

  Any text, repeating text, formula, or textual values entry.

  Note: text entries must have a double set of quotation marks. The first " is to signify the command line as text. The second " is to make a text entry when the command file is executed.

---

1. If you use a word processor, it must be capable of generating an ASCII formatted disk file with an extension of .XQT.

Any = (GoTo) command.
Recalculate command (!).
Window shift command (;).
Suspend command file execution (&).
Any of the following commands to be used in place of the directional arrows and CTRL E, S, D, X commands for scrolling:
^ Move cursor up one row.
< Move cursor left one column.
> Move cursor right one column.
V Move cursor down one row.

Toggle off the borders via/GB prior to writing the command file to disk. Write each command file to disk in two ways:

1. /Save it as .CAL file so you can later /Load it for modification.
2. /Output it using the D option and an extention of .XQT.

Note: The /Output command uses a default extension of .PRN, while the /eXecute command requires the .XQT extension.

SuperCalc³ Restrictions

Since SuperCalc³ is not able to enter control characters into cells, the following command file entries can be made only by a word processor or other text editor.

CTRL D To produce a one-half second delay in the execution. Multiple CTRL Ds may be entered to cause a longer delay.

Printer Control Sequences These are the commands to turn on and off the compressed and boldface print modes. They are unique to your printer.

Other Control Sequences These are scrolling and graphics commands. They are entered as follows:

^A Scroll page left.
^B Jump to the end.
^C Abort the command file execution.
^F Scroll page right.
^I Tab to the start of next cell group.
^N Scroll page down.
^P Scroll page up.
^O Tab to the end of next cell group.
^T View the graph on the video screen.
^V Enter insert mode.
^W Jump to home.
^Y Plot the graph on the attached printer or plotter.

Examples of Creating Command Files

EXAMPLE NO. 1

This first example is designed to load the P&L Statement spreadsheet, print it, then exit SuperCalc³. First, enter /**ZY** to clear memory, then make the following text entries:

Cell	Entry	Explanation
A1	**"/ZY**	Clear any existing spreadsheets from memory.
A2	**"/LPALDEMO,A**	Load the entire P&L spreadsheet.
A3	**"/ODALL,P**	Print the entire spreadsheet in display format.
A4	**"/QY**	Exit SuperCalc³.

Notice that the above entries contain only the actual keystrokes you would make if you were doing this in a live session. Also, it is very important to include the double quotation marks ("), otherwise SuperCalc³ will immediately execute the command you're entering. Remember, the purpose of a .XGT file is a deferred execution of a series of commands.

The next step is to set the width for column A so it just exceeds the length of the longest command. Cell A2 contains the longest command entry, 12 characters. A rule of thumb that allows for future enhancement is to use the next highest multiple of five for the column width. Using this guideline, enter

/FCA,15

then press RETURN. Now the spreadsheet of commands can be put onto disk.

There are two operations in this phase. The first operation is to save it as a .CAL file so it can be loaded for subsequent review or revision. This is done by entering

/SMACRO1,A

The second operation involves suppressing border display and outputting the spreadsheet to disk as a .XQT file. The entries are

/GB or **/ODALL, SB,** then press F2

/ODALL,DMACRO1.XQT

It's important that the .XQT file extension be specified with the /Output command, otherwise you won't be able to execute your command file. Also, the borders could have been turned off prior to the /Save command. They were left on for the /Save because you would turn them back on anyway if you ever /Loaded the spreadsheet to revise it.

The new term "MACRO" is used as part of the filename. This term is commonly used to represent a command that causes the execution of a series of other commands. Use whatever filenames are meaningful to you. Note, however, the similarity between the filename used in /Save and the filename used in /Output. The only difference is the file extension. This technique is not required by SuperCalc³ but it does help you keep better track of your disk files.

EXAMPLE NO. 2

This example is designed to consolidate several P&L Statement spreadsheets, print and save the consolidated result, then exit SuperCalc³.

First, enter **/ZY** to clear memory, then make the following text entries:

Cell	Entry	Explanation
A1	**"/ZY**	Clear any existing spreadsheets from memory.
A2	**"/LPALDEMO,A**	Load the entire P&L spreadsheet.
A3	**"/LPALDEMO,C**	Consolidate the entire P&L spreadsheet with the current memory contents (first consolidation).
A4	**"/LPALDEMO,C**	Consolidate the entire P&L spreadsheet with the current memory contents (second consolidation).
A5	**"/ODALL,P**	Print the entire consolidated spreadsheet in display format.
A6	**"/SCONSOLPL,A**	Save the consolidated result.
A7	**"/QY**	Exit SuperCalc³.

The following entries complete the creation of this example:
/FCA,15 and press RETURN
/SMACRO2,A
/GB or **/ODALL, SB**, then press F2.
/ODALL,DMACRO2.XQT

EXAMPLE NO. 3

This example is designed to load a data entry template, capture employee job code and hours worked, and merge the results into another template to do a series of payroll calculations. The interim and final results are printed and saved. When all commands have been executed, SuperCalc³ is terminated. Of the three command file examples, this one is the most complicated. It's also the most powerful.

As a preliminary step to building this command file, it's necessary to construct two templates. These templates are based on the payroll example illustrated in Chapter 11.

The first template, shown in Figure 14.1, contains the names and numbers of all employees in the organization. In an actual office environment this template would be periodically updated to reflect employee turnover. All cells are protected except D8 through E13. Also, cells D8 through E13 are initially set to zero. The following steps will quickly build this template:

1. Enter the headings in cells A3 through E7.
2. Enter the department numbers and employee names and numbers in cells A8 through C13.

3. Protect all cells by entering
   /PA1:D14
4. Unprotect cells D8 through E13 by entering
   /UD8:E13
5. Set JOB CODE and HOURS WORKED cells to zero. At cell D8 enter 0. Then enter
   /RD8,D9:D13 and press RETURN
   /RE8,E9:E13 and press RETURN
6. Make the following format and global settings:
   Enter **/FD** to call up the User-Defined Format Table.
   Under U8 set **"ZERO AS BLANK"** to **"Y"** and set all other table entries to **"N"** or **0** as appropriate.
   Press F2 to return to your spreadsheet.
   Enter **/FE8:E13,U8** and press RETURN.
   Enter **/GT** to enable cursor tabbing to non-blank cells.
7. Save the template by entering
   /SDETMPLT,A
   The filename DETMPLT represents Data Entry TeMPLaTe

Figure 14.1 Data Entry Template

```
    !  A  !!  B  !!  C  !!  D  !!  E  !!  F  !!  G  !!  H  !
1
2
3   Payroll Report
4   --------------
5   Dept       Employee Employee       Job     Hours
6   No.        No.      Name           Code    Worked
7   ---------------------------------------------------
8   053        1011     Alpha
9   062        1015     Zebra
10  062        1002     Bravo
11  053        1014     Yankee
12  062        2012     Gamma
13  053        3015     Maryjane
14  ---------------------------------------------------
```

The second template, shown in Figure 14.2, is an extension of Figure 14.1. In an actual office environment this template would be periodically updated to reflect additions or deletions to headcount as well as changes in the tax computations. It contains an hourly rate lookup table accessed by job code. It is identical to the payroll illustration in Chapter 11 (see p. 206) except that the department numbers and the employee names and numbers in cells A8 through C13 have been blanked. Also the job codes and hours worked in cells D8 through E13 have been set to zero. The calculation mode is manual. This template has been saved as PRCTMPLT. The filename represents PayRoll Calculation TeMPLaTe.

Figure 14.2 Payroll Calculation Template

	A	B	C	D	E	F	G	H	I	J	K
1											
2											
3	Payroll Report										
4	--------------										
5	Dept	Employee	Employee	Job	Hours	Gross	Federal	Fica	State	City	Net
6	No.	No.	Name	Code	Worked	Pay	Tax	Tax	Tax	Tax	Pay
7	--------	--------	--------	--------	--------	--------	--------	--------	--------	--------	--------
8				0	0	N/A	N/A	N/A	N/A	N/A	N/A
9				0	0	N/A	N/A	N/A	N/A	N/A	N/A
10				0	0	N/A	N/A	N/A	N/A	N/A	N/A
11				0	0	N/A	N/A	N/A	N/A	N/A	N/A
12				0	0	N/A	N/A	N/A	N/A	N/A	N/A
13				0	0	N/A	N/A	N/A	N/A	N/A	N/A
14	--------	--------	--------	--------	--------	--------	--------	--------	--------	--------	--------
15						N/A	N/A	N/A	N/A	N/A	N/A
16											
17											
18	Rate Table			Tax List							
19	--------	--------		--------	--------						
20	Job	Hourly		Tax	Tax						
21	Code	Rate		Name	Rate						
22	--------	--------		--------	--------						
23	1	5.0000		Federal	22.5000%						
24	2	5.5575		Fica	6.7000%						
25	3	5.7550		State	2.4500%						
26	4	6.0000		City	4.3125%						
27	5	6.2500									
28	6	6.5000									
29	7	6.7500									
30	8	7.0000									
31	9	7.5000									
32	10	8.0000									

The following steps are performed to create the command file: First, enter **/ZY** to clear memory, then make the following text entries:

Cell	Entry	Explanation
A1	**"/ZY**	Clear any existing spreadsheets from memory.
A2	**"/LDETMPLT,A**	Load the Data Entry TeMPLaTe.
A3	**"=A1**	Jump to cell A1, positioning the cursor at the beginning of the template.
A4	**"=D8**	Jump to cell D8, positioning the cursor at the cell where data entry is to start.
A5	**"/GM &**	Sets manual calculation mode and interrupts execution for entry of job code and hours worked.
A6	**"/ODALL,P**	Prints the template after data entry is completed.
A7	**"/SDE841010,A**	Saves the data entry spreadsheet.
A8	**"/ZY**	Erases the data entry template.
A9	**"/LPRCTMPLT,A**	Loads the PayRoll Calculation TeMPLaTe.

(continued on next page)

Cell	Entry	Explanation
A10	**"/LDE841010,PA8:E13,A8**	Does a partial load of the data entry spreadsheet.
A11	**"!**	Manually calculates the payroll spreadsheet.
A12	**"/ODALL,P**	Prints the template after payroll calculations are completed.
A13	**"/SPR841010,A**	Saves the payroll spreadsheet.
A14	**"/QY**	Exit SuperCalc³.

The following entries complete the creation of this example:

/FCA,25, then press RETURN

/SMACRO3,A

/GB or **/ODALL, SB**, then press F2

/ODALL,DMACRO3.XQT

The characters 841010 in the filenames of the completed data entry and payroll calculation spreadsheets represent the payroll effective date in yymmdd format. Such a naming convention is a simple but unique way of identifying critical spreadsheets.

Executing Command Files

The execution of command files can be initiated when SuperCalc³ is booted or from within SuperCalc³.

To start a command file execution as soon as booting is completed, specify the name of the command file following the command to start the SuperCalc³ program. When this approach is used, SuperCalc³'s logo screen is bypassed. The entry to do this is

SC3 B:MACRO3.XQT

The file extension can be omitted since only files with an extension are executed. The disk drive identifier must be specified.

Command files can be executed from within SuperCalc³ via the /X command. Entering **/X** results in the following PROMPT and ENTRY line displays

Enter File Name (or <RETURN> for directory)

13>/X(Execute),

Now enter the name of your command file. For example, enter

B:MACRO1.XQT and press RETURN.

No matter which way you start the command file execution, you can now sit back and watch everything happen automatically.

Suspend/Resume Command File Execution

This feature gives you the option of interrupting and resuming the execution of a command file. When an ampersand is encountered in the command file, the following message is displayed in the PROMPT LINE:

Awaiting keyboard entry

The keyboard is unlocked and any data or commands can be entered.

Automatic execution resumes when one of the following occurs:

1. An & is entered from the keyboard.
2. When an entry has been made in the current session to the last unprotected cell of the spreadsheet while /Global Tabs and /Global Next are both toggled on.

During an interruption of command file execution, caution should be exercised regarding which "Slash" commands are used. Avoid using commands such as /Zap and /Quit since they would prematurely terminate the execution. If it's necessary to cancel the execution, use CTRL C. This returns the PROMPT LINE message:

User abort

Examples of Executing Command Files

These examples use the three examples from the section on Creating Command Files.

EXAMPLE NO. 1

From outside SuperCalc³, enter

SC3 B:MACRO1

From inside SuperCalc³, enter

/XMACRO1

See Figure 14.3 for an illustration of the resulting output.

Figure 14.3 /eXecute of MACRO1.XQT: Load and Print

	A	B	C	D	E	F	G
1			Bill's P & L Statement				
2			Fiscal Year 1984				
3		QTR #1	QTR #2	QTR #3	QTR #4	TOTAL	
4		--------	--------	--------	--------	--------	
5	SALES	5000.00	4000.00	4500.00	7500.00	21000.00	
6	COST OF GOODS SOLD	1500.00	1200.00	1350.00	2250.00	6300.00	
7		--------	--------	--------	--------	--------	
8	GROSS MARGIN	3500.00	2800.00	3150.00	5250.00	14700.00	
9							
10	OPERATING EXPENSES						
11	MARKETING	1000.00	1000.00	1000.00	1000.00	4000.00	
12	ADMINISTRATIVE	500.00	400.00	450.00	750.00	2100.00	
13		--------	--------	--------	--------	--------	
14	TOTAL	1500.00	1400.00	1450.00	1750.00	6100.00	
15							
16	PRE-TAX PROFIT	2000.00	1400.00	1700.00	3500.00	8600.00	
17	INCOME TAX	1000.00	700.00	850.00	1750.00	4300.00	
18		--------	--------	--------	--------	--------	
19	NET INCOME	1000.00	700.00	850.00	1750.00	4300.00	
20		========	========	========	========	========	

EXAMPLE NO. 2

From outside SuperCalc³, enter

SC3 B:MACRO2

From inside SuperCalc³, enter

/XMACRO2

See Figure 14.4 for an illustration of the resulting output.

Figure 14.4 /eXecute of MACRO2.XQT: Consolidated Load and Print

	A	B	C	D	E	F	G
1				Bill's P & L Statement			
2				Fiscal Year 1984			
3		QTR #1	QTR #2	QTR #3	QTR #4	TOTAL	
4		--------	--------	--------	--------	--------	
5	SALES	15000.00	12000.00	13500.00	22500.00	63000.00	
6	COST OF GOODS SOLD	4500.00	3600.00	4050.00	6750.00	18900.00	
7		--------	--------	--------	--------	--------	
8	GROSS MARGIN	10500.00	8400.00	9450.00	15750.00	44100.00	
9							
10	OPERATING EXPENSES						
11	MARKETING	3000.00	3000.00	3000.00	3000.00	12000.00	
12	ADMINISTRATIVE	1500.00	1200.00	1350.00	2250.00	6300.00	
13		--------	--------	--------	--------	--------	
14	TOTAL	4500.00	4200.00	4350.00	5250.00	18300.00	
15							
16	PRE-TAX PROFIT	6000.00	4200.00	5100.00	10500.00	25800.00	
17	INCOME TAX	3000.00	2100.00	2550.00	5250.00	12900.00	
18		--------	--------	--------	--------	--------	
19	NET INCOME	3000.00	2100.00	2550.00	5250.00	12900.00	
20		========	========	========	========	========	

EXAMPLE NO. 3

Prior to executing this example, you should use the S option of the /Output command to set your line width to 132 positions and also enter the control codes to set your printer to 17 cpi. An alternative is change the /Output commands in the command file so that they output to disk. Then you can use the SIDEWAYS program to print your payroll reports.

From outside SuperCalc³, enter

SC3 B:MACRO3

From inside SuperCalc³, enter

/XMACRO3

When the data entry template has been loaded, the cursor will position itself at cell D8 and wait for you to make the following entries:

Cell	Entry	Cell	Entry
D8	**10**	E8	**40**
D9	**5**	E9	**55**
D10	**2**	E10	**30**
D11	**3**	E11	**20**
D12	**1**	E12	**60**
D13	**9**	E13	**55**

If your cursor directional indicator is set as →, you will move as follows each time you make an entry and press RETURN:

D8, E8, D9, E9, D10, E10, D11, E11, D12, E12, D13, E13

If your cursor directional indicator is set as ↓, you will move as follows each time you make an entry and press RETURN:

D8, D9, D10, D11, D12, D13, E8, E9, E10, E11, E12, E13

After the data entry is completed, reports like those illustrated in Figure 14.5 and Figure 14.6 are generated.

Figure 14.5 /eXecute of MACRO3.XQT: Completed Data Entry Spreadsheet

	A	B	C	D	E	F	G	H
1								
2								
3	Payroll Report							
4	----------------							
5	Dept	Employee	Employee	Job	Hours			
6	No.	No.	Name	Code	Worked			
7	----------	----------	----------	----------	----------			
8	053	1011	Alpha	10	40			
9	062	1015	Zebra	5	55			
10	062	1002	Bravo	2	30			
11	053	1014	Yankee	3	20			
12	062	2012	Gamma	1	60			
13	053	3015	Maryjane	9	55			
14	----------	----------	----------	----------	----------			

Figure 14.6 /eXecute of MACRO3.XQT: Completed Payroll Spreadsheet

	A	B	C	D	E	F	G	H	I	J	K
1											
2											
3	Payroll Report										
4	----------------										
5	Dept	Employee	Employee	Job	Hours	Gross	Federal	Fica	State	City	Net
6	No.	No.	Name	Code	Worked	Pay	Tax	Tax	Tax	Tax	Pay
7	----------	----------	----------	----------	----------	----------	----------	----------	----------	----------	----------
8	053	1011	Alpha	10	40	320.00	72.00	21.44	7.84	13.80	204.92
9	062	1015	Zebra	5	55	390.63	87.89	26.17	9.57	16.85	250.15
10	062	1002	Bravo	2	30	166.73	37.51	11.17	4.08	7.19	106.78
11	053	1014	Yankee	3	20	115.10	25.90	7.71	2.82	4.96	73.71
12	062	2012	Gamma	1	60	350.00	78.75	23.45	8.58	15.09	224.13
13	053	3015	Maryjane	9	55	468.75	105.47	31.41	11.48	20.21	300.18
14	----------	----------	----------	----------	----------	----------	----------	----------	----------	----------	----------
15						1811.21	407.52	121.35	44.37	78.10	1159.87
16											
17											
18	Rate Table			Tax List							
19	----------	----------		----------	----------						
20	Job	Hourly		Tax	Tax						
21	Code	Rate		Name	Rate						
22	----------	----------		----------	----------						
23	1	5.0000		Federal	22.5000%						
24	2	5.5575		Fica	6.7000%						
25	3	5.7550		State	2.4500%						
26	4	6.0000		City	4.3125%						
27	5	6.2500									
28	6	6.5000									
29	7	6.7500									
30	8	7.0000									
31	9	7.5000									
32	10	8.0000									

Other Suggestions for Command Files

Increased flexibility in command file utilization can be achieved by replacing filenames with the ampersand. This enables you to specify the filename at execution time rather than when you create the command file. For example:

"/L& instead of "/LPRCTMPLT,A
"/S& instead of "/SPR840414,A

In the case of templates, such as you saw in Example No. 3, the TODAY function could be included at the top of the template. This would enable you to easily distinguish one execution from another. This assumes, of course, that the executions were run on different days.

Review Exercises

1. Show the entries to build a command file that loads and prints the Depreciation Spreadsheet from Exercise 11.1.
   a. How would you put this file on disk so it can later be modified?
   b. How would you put this file on disk so it can later be executed?
   c. How would you invoke this command file from inside SuperCalc³?
   d. How would you invoke this command file from outside SuperCalc³?
2. This exercise uses Exercise 11.3 as a starting point:
   a. Build a sales data entry template to capture product code and units sold.
   b. Build a sales calculation template containing formulas to compute sales, commission, and net proceeds. Also include tables for product name, product price, and commission rate.
   c. Create a command file that
      Loads the sales data entry template.
      Allows keyboard entry of product code and units sold.
      Prints out then saves the data entry template.
      Loads the sales calculation template.
      Prints out the sales calculation template.
      Saves the sales calculation template.
   d. Execute the command file.

Answers to Review Exercises

1. The following text entries build the command file

Cell	Entry
A1	**"/ZY**
A2	**"/LEX11-1,A**
A3	**"/ODALL,P**
A4	**"/QY**

The following entry saves the entries as a .CAL file:
/SMACRO-X1,A
The following entries turn off border display and then output the spreadsheet to disk as a .XQT file:
/GB or **/ODALL, SB,** then press F2
/ODALL,DMACRO1.XQT
To execute this file from inside SuperCalc³, enter
/XMACRO-X1.XQT
To execute this file from outside SuperCalc³, enter
SC3 B:MACRO-X1.XQT

2. a. See Figure 14.7.

Figure 14.7 Sales Data Entry Template: Exercise 14-2a

```
    |   A   ||   B    ||   C   ||   D   ||   E   ||   F   ||   G   |
1              Product    Units
2   Seller        Code     Sold
3   ----------------------------
4   Bravo
5   Alpha
6   Yankee
7   Zebra
8   Gamma
9   ----------------------------
```

Protect the following cells:
/PA1:D3
/PA4:A9
Set cells B4 through C8 to zero.
Enter **/FD** to call up the User-Defined Format Table.
Under U8 set **"ZERO AS BLANK"** to **"Y"** and set all other table entries to **"N"** or **"0"** as appropriate.
Press F2 to return to your spreadsheet.
Enter **/FEB4:C8,U8**, then press RETURN.
Enter **/GT** to enable cursor tabbing to non-blank cells.
Save the template by entering:
/SSLSDETPL,A

b. See Figure 14.8 on the next page.

Figure 14.8 Sales Calculation Template: Exercise 14-2b

```
   :  A   ::    B    ::  C   ::    D   ::    E    ::    F   ::    G   :
1               Product   Units                        Net    Product
2  Seller          Code    Sold      Sales Commission Proceeds     Name
3  ------------------------------------------------------------------
4                     0       0        N/A        N/A      N/A      N/A
5                     0       0        N/A        N/A      N/A      N/A
6                     0       0        N/A        N/A      N/A      N/A
7                     0       0        N/A        N/A      N/A      N/A
8                     0       0        N/A        N/A      N/A      N/A
9  ------------------------------------------------------------------
10 Totals           N/A       0        N/A        N/A      N/A      N/A
11
12 Product Name Table           Product Price Table  Commission Table
13      Code       Name               Code   Price       Code    Rate
14 ------------------           -------------------  ----------------
15         1   Columbia                  1    2995          1    .245
16         2     IBM PC                  2    3245          2    .100
17         3  Sperry PC                  3    3119          3    .150
18         4  ZDS Z-150                  4    2800          4    .200
19         5   Compaq +                  5    4995          5    .180
20
```

Save the template by entering
/SSLSRPTPL,A

c. Command file entries:

Cell	Entry
A1	**"/ZY**
A2	**"/LSLSDETPL,A**
A3	**" = A1**
A4	**" = B4**
A5	**"/GM &**
A6	**"/ODALL,P**
A7	**"/SEX14-2A,A**
A8	**"/ZY**
A9	**"/LSLSRPTPL,A**
A10	**"/LEX14-2A,PA4:C8,A4**
A11	**"!**
A12	**"/ODALL,P**
A13	**"/SEX14-2B,A**
A14	**"/QY**

The following entries finish the creation of the command file:
/FCA,25, then press RETURN
/SMACRO-X2,A
/GB or **/ODALL, SB**
/ODALL,DMACRO-X2.XQT

d. Command file execution:
/XMACRO-X2
When this file completes its execution, there will be printed output similar to Figures 14.9 and 14.10.

Figure 14.9 Completed Sales Data Entry Spreadsheet: Exercise 14-2d

	A	B	C	D	E	F	G
1		Product	Units				
2	Seller	Code	Sold				
3	----------	----------	----------				
4	Bravo	2	200				
5	Alpha	1	600				
6	Yankee	4	200				
7	Zebra	3	400				
8	Gamma	5	450				
9	----------	----------	----------				

Figure 14.10 Completed Sales Calculation Spreadsheet: Exercise 14-2d

	A	B	C	D	E	F	G
1		Product	Units			Net	Product
2	Seller	Code	Sold	Sales	Commission	Proceeds	Name
3	----------	----------	----------	----------	----------	----------	----------
4	Bravo	2	200	1,797,000	550,699	2,130,930	Columbia
5	Alpha	1	600	2,247,750	116,820	469,300	Compaq +
6	Yankee	4	200	1,247,600	84,000	310,480	Sperry PC
7	Zebra	3	400	560,000	249,520	1,163,600	ZDS Z-150
8	Gamma	5	450	649,000	179,700	1,246,301	IBM PC
9	----------	----------	----------	----------	----------	----------	----------
10	Totals	N/A	1850	6,501,350	1,180,739	5,320,611	N/A
11							
12	Product Name Table			Product Price Table		Commission Table	
13	Code	Name		Code	Price	Code	Rate
14	----------	----------		----------	----------	----------	----------
15	1	Columbia		1	2995	1	.245
16	2	IBM PC		2	3245	2	.100
17	3	Sperry PC		3	3119	3	.150
18	4	ZDS Z-150		4	2800	4	.200
19	5	Compaq +		5	4995	5	.180
20							

CHAPTER 15

Interfacing SuperCalc^3 with Other Systems

Chapter Overview and Objectives

- SuperData Interchange Utility
- Filenaming Defaults and Cautions
- Interfacing SuperCalc^3 Files with Comma-Separated Value Files
- Interfacing SuperCalc^3 Files with SuperData Interchange Files
- Converting VisiCalc Files to SuperCalc^3 Files
- Converting Lotus 1-2-3 Files to SuperCalc^3 Files

This chapter introduces the concept of information exchange between SuperCalc^3 and other information systems. Novices may have difficulty with this chapter since it assumes a knowledge of other systems in addition to SuperCalc^3. For this reason, they may want to bypass the chapter until they need to interface SuperCalc^3 with another information processor.

For the demonstrations in this chapter, Microsoft GW-BASIC is used as the other system. This language has been selected since vendors usually include some version of it as a standard feature on most microcomputers. It's also one of the most popular and well-known programming languages used on microcomputers.

SuperData Interchange Utility

This utility allows you to do file format conversions to transfer your data between SuperCalc^3 and other systems. It eliminates the redundancy of keystroking data into multiple systems. Here are some popular transfer applications:

- Extracting data from other systems for special analyses within SuperCalc^3.
- Performing data entry functions within SuperCalc^3 and transferring the resulting data files to other systems.

Examples of "other systems" include:

- Microcomputer applications systems—for example, General Ledger or Payroll, written in symbolic languages such as BASIC, COBOL, and Pascal.

- Microcomputer database management systems such as dBASE II and DataStar.
- Other spreadsheet packages such as VisiCalc and LOTUS 1-2-3.
- Communications software that is capable of transferring files to and from mainframe computers. The process of sending a file to another computer is called an upline load, while receiving a file from another computer is called a downline load.

The SuperData Interchange utility is used at operating system level, outside of SuperCalc³. To execute it, enter **SDI** and press RETURN. The SDI utility displays the menu shown in Figure 15.1.

Figure 15.1 SuperData Interchange Menu

```
          Sorcim File Conversion Utility
                 Version :  2.0
          --------------------------------
     These are the File Conversions Available :
A.   SuperCalc                  to Comma Separated Value
B.   Comma Separated Value      to SuperCalc
C.   SuperCalc                  to SuperData Interchange
D.   SuperData Interchange      to SuperCalc
E.   VisiCalc                   to SuperCalc
F.   Lotus 123                  to SuperCalc

X.   Exit from program
     Enter Your choice (A, B, C, D, E, F, or X) ?
```

Menu items A and B show that SuperCalc³ (.CAL) files can be converted to and from Comma Separated Value (.CSV) files. These files contain fields of constants separated by commas. Menu item A generates values only, while menu item B can produce values and formulas. Neither menu item can accommodate format settings. These menu items are generally used by BASIC and Pascal programs and database management systems such as dBASE II and DataStar.

Menu items C and D show that SuperCalc³ (.CAL) files can be converted to and from SuperData Interchange (.SDI) files. Although these files are more complex than Comma Separated Value files, their structure can accommodate both formulas and format settings. They would be used in situations where the other system could not generate Comma Separated Value files or where you wanted the other system to generate a spreadsheet complete with formulas and formats.

Menu item E converts VisiCalc (.VC) files to SuperCalc³ (.CAL) files. Menu item F converts Lotus 1-2-3 (.WKS) files to SuperCalc³ (.CAL) files.

The conversions done by menu items E and F are one-way conversions. The SuperData Interchange does not convert .CAL, .CSV, or .SDI files into .VC or .WKS files.

For menu items other than X, SDI responds with

Enter Source File Name :

After you enter the name of the file to be converted, SDI displays

Enter DESTINATION file name :

When you enter the name of the destination file, SDI displays:

Converting file d:input.ext to d:output.ext

More conversion?(y/n):

where **d:input.ext** represents the drive identifier, filename, and extension of the source file, and **d:output.ext** represents the drive identifier, filename, and extension of the destination file.

Press y if you have more conversions to do. Otherwise press n and you'll be returned to operating system level.

The following message is displayed when the destination file currently exists on the specified or default disk drive:

Enter DESTINATION file name: d:output.ext—File Already Exists!

Is it okay to Overwrite your file (y/n)?

If y is entered, the file on disk is overwritten with the converted data and the following message is displayed:

Converting file d:input.ext to d:output.ext

More conversion?(y/n):

If n is entered, the conversion process is aborted and SDI displays the message

File operation ABORTED on your request

More conversion?(y/n):

Filenaming Defaults and Cautions

The following table illustrates the defaults used by SuperData Interchange for filenames and extensions:

	Source File Defaults		Destination File Defaults	
Menu Item	Filename	Extension	Filename	Extension
A	N/A	.CAL	Source filename	.CSV
B	N/A	.CSV	Source filename	.CAL
C	N/A	.CAL	Source filename	.SDI
D	N/A	.SDI	Source filename	.CAL
E	N/A	.VC	Source filename	.CAL
F	N/A	.WKS	Source filename	.CAL

Do not use the destination file defaults when converting the same file from a .CAL format into either .CSV or .SDI format and then back into .CAL format. If the defaults were used, the destination .CAL file being converted from .CSV or .SDI would have the same name as the original .CAL source file. The destination .CAL file could overwrite and destroy the source .CAL file. This may result in a data loss, formats or formulas, depending on how the initial conversion was done. When doing a "360 degree" conversion, use a different filename on the conversion back into the SuperCalc³ format.

The next two sections provide some application examples on converting an employee time record spreadsheet and interfacing the converted file into some

Payroll programs written in BASIC.[1] These BASIC programs generate output files that SDI converts to .CAL files and are subsequently loaded into SuperCalc³.

Interfacing .CAL Files with .CSV Files

Comma-Separated Value (.CSV) files are ASCII formatted files containing fields of constants separated by commas. The constants may be either numeric values or string values. String constants are the equivalent of text in SuperCalc³ and are enclosed in double quotes.

Each field in a .CSV file represents one spreadsheet cell. Each line in a .CSV file is equivalent to one row in a spreadsheet. Lines in .CSV files end with two special, invisible, ASCII characters—the carriage return and the line feed. These two characters are interpreted by SuperData Interchange to mean the end of a row for the .CAL file being created.

When converting .CAL files to .CSV files, SDI translates all formulas to values. Textual values are converted to string constants as though they were text. Date functions are output as integers representing the modified Julian Date, just as though the JDATE function had been executed.

Figure 15.2 represents a spreadsheet of employee time records, which resides in the file B:EMPHOURS.CAL. The following table defines the spreadsheet.

Column	Data Content
A	Department
B	Employee Number
C	Employee Name
D	Rate Code
E	Hours Worked

Figure 15.2 Employee Time Records in .CAL File Format

	A	B	C	D	E
1	053	1011	Alpha	10	40
2	062	1015	Zebra	5	55
3	062	1002	Bravo	2	30
4	053	1014	Yankee	3	20
5	062	2012	Gamma	1	60
6	053	3015	Maryjane	9	55

To interface this spreadsheet with a payroll system written in BASIC, enter **SDI** at operating system level. When the SDI menu is displayed, enter **A** to convert a SuperCalc³ file to a Comma-Separated Value file.

1. Microsoft GW-BASIC, version 1.0, has been used for these programs. The program syntax may vary for implementations of BASIC developed by other software houses.

When SDI displays the prompt **Enter Source File Name :** you can enter **B:EMPHOURS** and press RETURN. SDI replies with

Enter DESTINATION file name :

Press RETURN to use the defaults. SDI responds with:

Converting B:EMPHOURS.CAL to B:EMPHOURS.CSV

More conversions (y/n)

Enter **n** to terminate SDI.

The external PRINT command can be used to list out the .CSV file created by SDI. The following entry made at operating system level

PRINT B:EMPHOURS.CSV

generates a list similar to Figure 15.3.

Figure 15.3 Employee Time Records in .CSV File Format

```
"053","1011","Alpha",10.0,40.0
"062","1015","Zebra",5.0,55.0
"062","1002","Bravo",2.0,30.0
"053","1014","Yankee",3.0,20.0
"062","2012","Gamma",1.0,60.0
"053","3015","Maryjane",9.0,55.0
```

The next phase is for you to enter BASIC and execute the payroll program, B:PAYPROG1.BAS, shown in Figure 15.4. In Microsoft GW-BASIC, the following steps complete this phase:

BASICA Loads BASIC into memory.

SAVE "B:PAYPROG1.BAS" Saves the payroll program onto the diskette in drive B. This command wouldn't be given until the program has been keyed in.

LLIST Lists the payroll program onto your printer.

RUN Executes the payroll program.

SYSTEM Returns to operating system level.

At the operating system level, the output created by the BASIC program B:PAYPROG1.BAS can be listed using the PRINT command. The entry

PRINT B:PAYROLL.CSV

generates a list similar to Figure 15.5.

The last phase is to convert PAYROLL.CSV into a SuperCalc³ file. Enter **SDI.** When the menu is displayed, select menu item **B.** At the prompt

Enter Source File Name :

enter **B:PAYROLL.CSV** and press RETURN. SDI replies with

Enter Destination file name :

Press RETURN to use the defaults. SDI responds with

Converting B:PAYROLL.CSV to B:PAYROLL.CAL

More conversions (y/n)?

Enter **n** to terminate SDI.

Enter SuperCalc³ and load the converted spreadsheet with the command

/LB:PAYROLL.CAL,A

The spreadsheet displayed will look like Figure 15.6.

Figure 15.4 Listing of BASIC Program PAYPROG1.BAS

```
5 REM    PROGRAM NAME: PAYPROG1.BAS
10 REM PURPOSE  1. LOADS A RATE VECTOR WITH HOURLY RATES
20 REM          2. READS DEPARTMENT, EMPLOYEE NUMBER, NAME, RATE
30 REM             CODE, & HOURS WORKED FROM A COMMA SEPARATED VALUE
40 REM             FILE CREATED BY SDI
50 REM          3. LOOKS UP HOURLY RATE IN THE RATE TABLE USINNG RATE CODE
60 REM             AND CALCULATES GROSS PAY.  "TIME-AND-ONE-HALF" IS ALLOWED
70 REM             FOR HOURS WORKED IN EXCESS OF 40
80 REM          4. CALCULATES THE FOLLOWING TAXES:
90 REM             FEDERAL INCOME TAX, SOCIAL SECURITY (FICA) TAX,
100 REM            STATE INCOME TAX, AND CITY WAGE TAX
110 REM         5. WRITES EMPLOYEE NUMBER, EMPLOYEE NAME, HOURLY RATE,
120 REM            HOURS WORKED, GROSS PAY, AND CALCULATED TAXES TO A
130 REM            COMMA SEPARATED VALUES FILE
140 REM LOAD # OF HOURLY RATES & DIMENSION RATE VECTOR
150 READ TABLEMAX
160 DIM RATE(TABLEMAX)
170 FOR INDEX=1 TO TABLEMAX
180      READ RATE(INDEX)
190 NEXT INDEX
200 REM TAX RATES
210 FIT.RATE = .225
220 FICA.RATE = .067
230 SIT.RATE = .0245
240 CWT.RATE = .043125
250 REM CREATE EMPLOYEE PAYROLL FILE
260 OPEN "INPUT", #1, "B:EMPHOURS.CSV"
270 OPEN "OUTPUT", #2, "B:PAYROLL.CSV"
280 IF EOF(1) THEN CLOSE #1, #2: END
290      INPUT #1, DEPT$, EMPLOYEE.NUMBER$, EMPLOYEE.NAME$, RATE.CODE, HOURS.WRKD
300      IF HOURS.WRKD > 40 THEN PAY.HOURS = (HOURS.WRKD - 40) * 1.5 + 40
         ELSE PAY.HOURS = HOURS.WRKD
310      GROSS.PAY = INT(PAY.HOURS * RATE(RATE.CODE) * 10^2 + .5) / 10^2
320      FIT.TAX = INT(GROSS.PAY * FIT.RATE * 10^2 + .5)/ 10^2
330      FICA.TAX = INT(GROSS.PAY * FICA.RATE * 10^2 + .5) / 10^2
340      SIT.TAX = INT(GROSS.PAY * SIT.RATE * 10^2 + .5) / 10^2
350      CWT.TAX = INT(GROSS.PAY * CWT.RATE * 10^2 + .5) / 10^2
360      WRITE #2, DEPT$, EMPLOYEE.NUMBER$, EMPLOYEE.NAME$, RATE(RATE.CODE),
         HOURS.WRKD, GROSS.PAY, FIT.TAX, FICA.TAX, SIT.TAX, CWT.TAX
370      GOTO 280
380 REM DATA SECTION
390 DATA 10: REM TABLE SIZE
400 DATA 5, 5.5575,5.755,6,6.25: REM RATE TABLE DATA
410 DATA 6.5, 6.75, 7, 7.5, 8  : REM RATE TABLE DATA
420 END
```

Figure 15.5 .CSV File Created by Program PAYPROG1.BAS

```
"053","1011","Alpha",8,40,320,72,21.44,7.84,13.8
"062","1015","Zebra",6.25,55,390.63,87.89,26.17,9.57,16.85
"062","1002","Bravo",5.5575,30,166.73,37.51,11.17,4.08,7.19
"053","1014","Yankee",5.755,20,115.1,25.9,7.71,2.82,4.96
"062","2012","Gamma",5,60,350,78.75,23.45,8.58,15.09
"053","3015","Maryjane",7.5,55,468.75,105.47,31.41,11.48,20.21
```

Figure 15.6 Spreadsheet Converted from PAYROLL.CSV

	A	B	C	D	E	F	G	H	I	J
1	053	1011	Alpha	8	40	320	72	21.44	7.84	13.8
2	062	1015	Zebra	6.25	55	390.63	87.89	26.17	9.57	16.85
3	062	1002	Bravo	5.5575	30	166.73	37.51	11.17	4.08	7.19
4	053	1014	Yankee	5.755	20	115.1	25.9	7.71	2.82	4.96
5	062	2012	Gamma	5	60	350	78.75	23.45	8.58	15.09
6	053	3015	Maryjane	7.5	55	468.75	105.47	31.41	11.48	20.21

Notice that the converted spreadsheet has no headings or totals. Although these could have been generated by the BASIC program after some minor modifications to it, the headings and totals would come across as values. An easier solution is to create a skeletal spreadsheet like the one shown in Figure 15.7.

Figure 15.7 Skeletal Payroll Spreadsheet

```
   :  A  ::  B  ::  C  ::  D  ::  E  ::  F  ::  G  ::  H  ::  I  ::  J  ::  K  ::  L  :
1           Employee Employee   Hourly    Hours    Gross  Federal     Fica    State     City      Net
2  Dept.    Name     Number       Rate   Worked      Pay      Tax      Tax      Tax      Tax      Pay
3  ---------------------------------------------------------------------------------------------------
4                                                                                             .00
5                                                                                             .00
6                                                                                             .00
7                                                                                             .00
8                                                                                             .00
9                                                                                             .00
10 ---------------------------------------------------------------------------------------------------
11 Totals                                     0      .00      .00      .00      .00      .00      .00
```

This skeleton uses the following formats:

Format Command	Explanation
/FCD:K,TR	Right justify text in columns D through K.
/FCD,U1	User-Defined Table Format 1 set to 4 decimal places and applied to column D.
/FCE,I	Display column E as integers.
/FCF:K,$	Display columns F through K as dollars and cents.

The NET PAY entries in column K are built as follows:

In cell K4, enter **F4-SUM(G4:J4)**
/RK4,K5:K9, then press RETURN.

The TOTALS entries in row 11 are built as follows:

In cell E11, enter **SUM(E4:E9)**
/RE11,F11:K11, then press RETURN.

To use the skeleton, load into memory
/LB:PAYSKEL.CAL,A
then do a partial load of the converted payroll spreadsheet:
/LB:PAYROLL.CAL,PA1:J6,A4 and press RETURN.
This will load the entire payroll spreadsheet into the skeleton, starting at cell A4. The result looks like Figure 15.8.

Figure 15.8 Completed Payroll Spreadsheet

```
   :  A  ::  B  ::  C  ::  D  ::  E  ::  F  ::  G  ::  H  ::  I  ::  J  ::  K  ::  L  :
1           Employee Employee   Hourly    Hours    Gross  Federal     Fica    State     City      Net
2  Dept.    Name     Number       Rate   Worked      Pay      Tax      Tax      Tax      Tax      Pay
3  ---------------------------------------------------------------------------------------------------
4  053      1011     Alpha      8.0000       40   320.00    72.00    21.44     7.84    13.80   204.92
5  062      1015     Zebra      6.2500       55   390.63    87.89    26.17     9.57    16.85   250.15
6  062      1002     Bravo      5.5575       30   166.73    37.51    11.17     4.08     7.19   106.78
7  053      1014     Yankee     5.7550       20   115.10    25.90     7.71     2.82     4.96    73.71
8  062      2012     Gamma      5.0000       60   350.00    78.75    23.45     8.58    15.09   224.13
9  053      3015     Maryjane   7.5000       55   468.75   105.47    31.41    11.48    20.21   300.18
10 ---------------------------------------------------------------------------------------------------
11 Totals                                   260  1811.21   407.52   121.35    44.37    78.10  1159.87
```

Interfacing .CAL Files with .SDI Files

SuperData Interchange (.SDI) files are ASCII formatted files. Each .SDI file consists of two sections, a TABLE section and a DATA section.

The TABLE section must be at the top of every .SDI file. It contains formatting specifications. Each TABLE section must have the following minimal entries:

TABLE
0,1
" "

The next series of entries is optionally used to control spreadsheet formatting when the .SDI file is converted to a .CAL file. These entries use the *formatting strings* I, G, E, $, R, L, TR, TL, *, and D, which have exactly the same meanings as the options associated with the /Format command.

Here are the valid formatting entries for the TABLE section:

GDISP-FORMAT Specifies the global display format settings for the spreadsheet. Only one GDISP-FORMAT entry may be specified per .SDI file. The general format for this specification is

GDISP-FORMAT
column width,0
formatting string

A sample specification is

GDISP-FORMAT
9,0
GTL

This globally sets column widths at 9 positions, numeric values use the general, best fit format, and text is left justified.

COL-FORMAT Specifies the format settings to be used for a given column. As many **COL-FORMAT** entries as are necessary may be specified per .SDI file. Note that column references use the range of numbers 1 through 127 rather than the range of letters A through DW. The general format for this specification is

COL-FORMAT
column #,width
formatting string

A sample specification is

COL-FORMAT
4,15
$TR

This sets the width of column D at 15 positions, numeric values use the dollar and cents format, and text is right justified.

ROW-FORMAT Specifies the format settings to be used for a given row. As many **ROW-FORMAT** entries as are necessary may be specified per .SDI file. Note that row references use the range of numbers 1 through 9999. The general format for this specification is

ROW-FORMAT
row #,0
formatting string

A sample specification is

ROW-FORMAT
1,0
TL

This right justifies all text in row 1.

The DATA section immediately follows the TABLE section in the .SDI file. It contains the data definitions from, or for, the spreadsheet file. Each DATA section must start with the following entries:

DATA
0,0
" "
−1,0
BOT

Also, each DATA section must end as follows:

−1,0
EOD

The remainder of the DATA section is structured by row. Within each row, the equivalent of cell entries are made left to right across the row. With one exception, these entries must account for all columns in the row, up to the rightmost column used. Although there can be open space on the right of the last column in a row, there can be no gaps to the left of the last column in a row unless a special entry called an origin specifier is used. Each data entry is a two line entry consisting of three fields:

Line 1: **field #1, field #2**
Line 2: **field #3**

These fields have the following meanings:

Line 1: **type indicator, numeric value**
Line 2: **string value**

The following table defines the valid type indicators. Detailed explanations and illustrations of the DATA section syntax follow the table.

Type Indicator	Definition
0	Numeric Data
1	Text
−1	Data Definition
−2	Origin Specifier
−3	Entry Level Display Formatting
−4	Formula
−5	Repeat Count

Grouped by type indicator, here is valid syntax for the DATA section:

Numeric Data The cell contains a numeric value. The entry structure is
Field 1 = 0
Field 2 = Numeric value
Field 3 = Value indicator
where
V = Valid number. Field 2 contains the decimal number.
NA = Unavailable value for this cell. Use 0 in field 2. This entry is the same as the NA function.
NULL = Unoccupied cell. Use 0 in field 2. This entry is used to fill gaps in the column range.
ERROR = Cell value is in error due to an invalid arithmetic operation. SDI puts 0 in field 2.
Examples:
0,55
V
This assigns the number 55 to the cell.
0,0
NULL
This identifies the cell as unoccupied.

Text The cell contains text. The entry structure is
Field 1 = 1
Field 2 = Type of text, where 0 = regular text, 1 = repeating text.
Field 3 = Text string. When field 2 = 0, this text string may be optionally enclosed in double quotation marks (").
Examples:
1,0
GROSS PAY
This assigns the text string GROSS PAY to the cell.
1,1
–
which assigns the repeating text string – to the cell.

Data Definition There are only two data definitions. One specifies the beginning of a row. The other specifies the end of the file. The entry structure is
Field 1 = −1
Field 2 = 0
Field 3 = Data definition string.
BOT = beginning of row.
EOD = end of file. SDI does not interpret any more data after this entry.
Examples:
−1,0
BOT

Starts a new row.
−1,0
EOD
Ends the DATA section as well as the file.

Origin Specifier This is equivalent to the GoTo (=) command. It indicates the cell where the next data item is to be entered. It avoids excessive NULL entries and is the only permissible way to have gaps between columns. SDI cannot create this entry when going from a .CAL file to a .SDI file, but it does properly translate the entry when going from a .SDI file to a .CAL file. The entry structure is
Field 1 = −2
Field 2 = 0
Field 3 = Cell address. This is specified by the column number, 1 through 127, separated from the row number, 1 through 9999, by a colon.
Examples:
−2,0
1:1
Skips to cell A1.
−2,0
63:254
Skips to cell BK254.
−2,0
4:15
Skips to cell D15.

Entry Level Display Formatting Allows a display format specification for the preceding cell entry. The entry structure is
Field 1 = −3
Field 2 = 0
Field 3 = Formatting string. These are identical to those in the TABLE section.
Examples:
1,0
GROSS PAY
−3,0
TR
Right justifies the preceding text entry.
0,25.1
V
−3,0
$
Displays the preceding numeric entry as dollars and cents.

Formula Specifies a numeric formula for the preceding cell entry. There must be a previous data item or an error results. The

entry structure is
Field 1 = −4
Field 2 = 0
Field 3 = Any valid SuperCalc³ formula. The cell becomes an **ERROR** cell if the formula is not valid.
Example:
−1,0
BOT
0,10
V
0,20
V
0,30
V
0,60
V
−4,0
SUM(A1:C1)
In row 1, the numeric value 60 is defined as the sum of the numeric values 10, 20, and 30. The summed values are located in cells A1, B1, and C1. The formula is located in cell D1.

Repeat Count Specifies the number of times the preceding data item is to be repeated across a row. There must be a previous data item or an error results. This feature is quite useful for padding zeros or NULL values into a spreadsheet section. The entry structure is
Field 1 = −5
Field 2 = Number of times to repeat
Field 3 = R
Examples:
1,0
TAX
−5,3
R
Repeats the text string "TAX" three times for a total of four text entries in the row.
−1,0
BOT
0,0
V
−5,9
R
Loads the row with ten zeroes.

Creating .SDI Files from BASIC: A Simple Example

Figure 15.9 shows the BASIC program PAYPROG2.BAS. This payroll program accesses file EMPHOURS.CSV, which was previously converted by SDI from EMPHOURS.CAL. It then creates a SuperData Interchange file named PAYSD1.SDI.

Figure 15.9 Listing of BASIC Program PAYPROG2.BAS

```
5 REM   PROGRAM NAME: PAYPROG2.BAS
10 REM PURPOSE  1. LOADS A RATE VECTOR WITH HOURLY RATES
20 REM          2. READS DEPARTMENT, EMPLOYEE NUMBER, NAME, RATE
30 REM             CODE, & HOURS WORKED FROM A COMMA SEPARATED VALUE
40 REM             FILE CREATED BY SDI
50 REM          3. LOOKS UP HOURLY RATE IN THE RATE TABLE USINNG RATE CODE
60 REM             AND CALCULATES GROSS PAY.  "TIME-AND-ONE-HALF" IS ALLOWED
70 REM             FOR HOURS WORKED IN EXCESS OF 40
80 REM          4. CALCULATES THE FOLLOWING TAXES:
90 REM             FEDERAL INCOME TAX, SOCIAL SECURITY (FICA) TAX,
100 REM            STATE INCOME TAX, AND CITY WAGE TAX
110 REM         5. WRITES EMPLOYEE NUMBER, EMPLOYEE NAME, HOURLY RATE,
120 REM            HOURS WORKED, GROSS PAY, AND CALCULATED TAXES TO A
130 REM            SUPERDATA INTERCHANGE FILE
140 REM LOAD # OF HOURLY RATES & DIMENSION RATE VECTOR
150 READ TABLEMAX
160 DIM RATE(TABLEMAX)
170 FOR INDEX=1 TO TABLEMAX
180     READ RATE(INDEX)
190 NEXT INDEX
200 REM TAX RATES
210 FIT.RATE = .225
220 FICA.RATE = .067
230 SIT.RATE = .0245
240 CWT.RATE = .043125
250 REM CREATE EMPLOYEE PAYROLL FILE
260 OPEN "INPUT", #1, "B:EMPHOURS.CSV"
270 OPEN "OUTPUT", #2, "B:PAYSD1.SDI"
280 PRINT #2, "TABLE" : PRINT #2, "0,1" : PRINT #2, CHR$(34); CHR$(34)
290 PRINT #2, "DATA"  : PRINT #2, "0,0" : PRINT #2, CHR$(34); CHR$(34)
300 IF EOF(1) THEN CLOSE #1: GOTO 500
310     INPUT #1, DEPT$, EMPLOYEE.NUMBER$, EMPLOYEE.NAME$, RATE.CODE, HOURS.WRKD
320     IF HOURS.WRKD > 40 THEN PAY.HOURS = (HOURS.WRKD - 40) * 1.5 + 40
        ELSE PAY.HOURS = HOURS.WRKD
330     GROSS.PAY = INT(PAY.HOURS * RATE(RATE.CODE) * 10^2 + .5) / 10^2
340     FIT.TAX = INT(GROSS.PAY * FIT.RATE * 10^2 + .5)/ 10^2
350     FICA.TAX = INT(GROSS.PAY * FICA.RATE * 10^2 + .5) / 10^2
360     SIT.TAX = INT(GROSS.PAY * SIT.RATE * 10^2 + .5) / 10^2
370     CWT.TAX = INT(GROSS.PAY * CWT.RATE * 10^2 + .5) / 10^2
380     PRINT #2, "-1,0"                     : PRINT #2, "BOT"
390     PRINT #2,  "1,0"                     : PRINT #2, DEPT$
400     PRINT #2,  "1,0"                     : PRINT #2, EMPLOYEE.NUMBER$
410     PRINT #2,  "1,0"                     : PRINT #2, EMPLOYEE.NAME$
420     PRINT #2,  "0,"; RATE(RATE.CODE)     : PRINT #2, "V"
430     PRINT #2,  "0,"; HOURS.WRKD          : PRINT #2, "V"
440     PRINT #2,  "0,"; GROSS.PAY           : PRINT #2, "V"
450     PRINT #2,  "0,"; FIT.TAX             : PRINT #2, "V"
460     PRINT #2,  "0,"; FICA.TAX            : PRINT #2, "V"
470     PRINT #2,  "0,"; SIT.TAX             : PRINT #2, "V"
480     PRINT #2,  "0,"; CWT.TAX             : PRINT #2, "V"
490     GOTO 300
500 PRINT #2, "-1,0" : PRINT #2, "EOD" : CLOSE #2 : END
510 REM DATA SECTION
520 DATA 10: REM TABLE SIZE
530 DATA 5, 5.5575,5.755,6,6.25: REM RATE TABLE DATA
540 DATA 6.5, 6.75, 7, 7.5, 8  : REM RATE TABLE DATA
550 END
```

This program is functionally similar to PAYPROG1.BAS. It follows the same series of entry and execution steps. The programs differ in that PAYPROG1.BAS uses WRITE # statements, while PAYPROG2.BAS uses PRINT # statements. The WRITE # statement outputs comma-separated values, while the PRINT # statement generates undelimited images—that is, no commas separating the fields and no quotes on text.

In the program, note the additional PRINT # statements necessary to generate the TABLE and DATA sections for the .SDI file. PAYPROG1.BAS required only one statement to output employee payroll information, line 360. PAYPROG2.BAS requires 10 statements to output employee payroll details, lines 380 through 480, plus statements for the section headings, lines 280 and 290, and the end of data, line 500.

Back at system level after running PAYPROG2.BAS, its file output can be listed using the PRINT command. The entry

PRINT B:PAYSD1.SDI

generates a list similar to Figure 15.10.

Figure 15.10 .SDI File Created by Program PAYPROG2.BAS

```
TABLE
0,1
""
DATA
0,0
""
-1,0
BOT
1,0
053
1,0
1011
1,0
Alpha
0, 8
V
0, 40
V
0, 320
V
0, 72
V
0, 21.44
V
0, 7.84
V
0, 13.8
V
-1,0
BOT
1,0
062
1,0
1015
1,0
Zebra
0, 6.25
V
0, 55
V
0, 390.63
V
0, 87.89
V
0, 26.17
V
0, 9.57
V
0, 16.85
V
-1,0
BOT
1,0
062
1,0
1002
1,0
Bravo
0, 5.5575
V
0, 30
V
0, 166.73
V
0, 37.51
V
0, 11.17
V
0, 4.08
V
0, 7.19
V
-1,0
BOT
1,0
053
1,0
1014
1,0
Yankee
0, 5.755
V
0, 20
V
0, 115.1
V
0, 25.9
V
0, 7.71
V
0, 2.82
V
0, 4.96
V
-1,0
BOT
1,0
062
1,0
2012
1,0
Gamma
0, 5
V
0, 60
V
0, 350
V
0, 78.75
V
0, 23.45
V
0, 8.58
V
0, 15.09
V
-1,0
BOT
1,0
053
1,0
3015
1,0
Maryjane
0, 7.5
V
0, 55
V
0, 468.75
V
0, 105.47
V
0, 31.41
V
0, 11.48
V
0, 20.21
V
-1,0
EOD
```

The last phase is to convert PAYSD1.SDI into a SuperCalc³ file. Enter **SDI.** When the menu is displayed, select menu item D. At the prompt

Enter Source File Name :

enter **B:PAYSD1** and press RETURN. SDI replies with

Enter Destination File Name :

Press RETURN to use the defaults. SDI responds with

Converting file B:PAYSD1.SDI to B:PAYSD1.CAL

More conversion?(y/n)

Enter **n** to terminate SDI. Next, enter SuperCalc³ and load the converted spreadsheet with the command

/LB:PAYSD1.CAL,A

The resulting spreadsheet will resemble Figure 15.6, when you loaded **B:PAYROLL.CAL** after converting it from **B:PAYROLL.CSV.** You can also use the previously created skeletal spreadsheet for headings, formats, and SUM functions. Refer to the illustration in Figure 15.7. The construction guidelines are shown at the end of the section on comma-separated value files.

To use the skeleton, load it into memory:

/LB:PAYSKEL.CAL,A

Then do a partial load of the converted payroll spreadsheet:

/LB:PAYSD1.CAL,PA1:J6,A4<RETURN>

This will load the entire payroll spreadsheet into the skeleton, starting at cell A4. Your display will match the spreadsheet shown in Figure 15.8, when you loaded B:PAYROLL.CAL.

Creating .SDI Files from BASIC: A More Complex Example

Figure 15.11 shows the BASIC program PAYPROG3.BAS. This program accesses file EMPHOURS.CSV, similar to PAYPROG2.BAS; but the SuperData Interchange formatted output file it creates, PAYSD2.SDI, is an entire spreadsheet, complete with formats and formulas.

Figure 15.11 Listing of BASIC Program PAYPROG3.BAS

```
5 REM   PROGRAM NAME: PAYPROG3.BAS
10 REM PURPOSE  1. LOADS A RATE VECTOR WITH HOURLY RATES
20 REM          2. READS DEPARTMENT, EMPLOYEE NUMBER, NAME, RATE
30 REM             CODE, & HOURS WORKED FROM A COMMA SEPARATED VALUE
40 REM             FILE CREATED BY SDI
50 REM          3. LOOKS UP HOURLY RATE IN THE RATE TABLE USINNG RATE CODE
60 REM             AND CALCULATES GROSS PAY.  "TIME-AND-ONE-HALF" IS ALLOWED
70 REM             FOR HOURS WORKED IN EXCESS OF 40
80 REM          4. CALCULATES THE FOLLOWING TAXES:
90 REM             FEDERAL INCOME TAX, SOCIAL SECURITY (FICA) TAX,
100 REM            STATE INCOME TAX, AND CITY WAGE TAX
110 REM         5. WRITES EMPLOYEE NUMBER, EMPLOYEE NAME, HOURLY RATE,
120 REM            HOURS WORKED, GROSS PAY, CALCULATED TAXES AND NET PAY
130 REM            TO A SUPERDATA INTERCHANGE FILE
140 REM LOAD # OF HOURLY RATES & DIMENSION RATE VECTOR
150 READ TABLEMAX
160 DIM RATE(TABLEMAX)
170 FOR INDEX=1 TO TABLEMAX
180     READ RATE(INDEX)
190 NEXT INDEX
200 REM TAX RATES
210 FIT.RATE = .225
220 FICA.RATE = .067
```

(continued on next page)

```
230 SIT.RATE = .0245
240 CWT.RATE = .043125
250 REM CREATE EMPLOYEE PAYROLL FILE
260 OPEN "INPUT", #1, "B:EMPHOURS.CSV"
270 OPEN "OUTPUT", #2, "B:PAYSD2.SDI"
280 PRINT #2, "TABLE" : PRINT #2, "0,1" : PRINT #2, CHR$(34); CHR$(34)
290 FOR LOOP = 4 TO 5
300      PRINT #2, "COL-FORMAT" : PRINT #2, STR$(LOOP); ",9" : PRINT #2, "TR"
310 NEXT LOOP
320 FOR LOOP = 6 TO 11
330      PRINT #2, "COL-FORMAT" : PRINT #2, STR$(LOOP); ",9" : PRINT #2, "TR$"
340 NEXT LOOP
350 PRINT #2, "GDISP-FORMAT" : PRINT #2, "9,0" : PRINT #2, "GTL"
360 PRINT #2, "DATA"  : PRINT #2, "0,0" : PRINT #2, CHR$(34); CHR$(34)
370 REM ROW 1 HEADINGS
380 PRINT #2, "-1,0"  : PRINT #2, "BOT"
390 PRINT #2,  "0,0"  : PRINT #2, "NULL"
400 PRINT #2,  "1,0"  : PRINT #2, "EMPLOYEE"
410 PRINT #2,  "1,0"  : PRINT #2, "EMPLOYEE"
420 PRINT #2,  "1,0"  : PRINT #2, "HOURLY"
430 PRINT #2,  "1,0"  : PRINT #2, "HOURS"
440 PRINT #2,  "1,0"  : PRINT #2, "GROSS"
450 PRINT #2,  "1,0"  : PRINT #2, "FEDERAL"
460 PRINT #2,  "1,0"  : PRINT #2, "FICA"
470 PRINT #2,  "1,0"  : PRINT #2, "STATE"
480 PRINT #2,  "1,0"  : PRINT #2, "CITY"
490 PRINT #2,  "1,0"  : PRINT #2, "NET"
500 REM ROW 2 HEADINGS
510 PRINT #2, "-1,0"  : PRINT #2, "BOT"
520 PRINT #2,  "1,0"  : PRINT #2, "DEPT."
530 PRINT #2,  "1,0"  : PRINT #2, "NUMBER"
540 PRINT #2,  "1,0"  : PRINT #2, "NAME"
550 PRINT #2,  "1,0"  : PRINT #2, "RATE"
560 PRINT #2,  "1,0"  : PRINT #2, "WORKED"
570 PRINT #2,  "1,0"  : PRINT #2, "PAY"
580 FOR LOOP = 1 TO 4
590      PRINT #2,  "1,0"  : PRINT #2, "TAX"
600 NEXT LOOP
610 PRINT #2,  "1,0"  : PRINT #2, "PAY"
620 REM ROW 3 UNDERLINES
630 PRINT #2, "-1,0"  : PRINT #2, "BOT"
640 PRINT #2,  "1,1"  : PRINT #2, "-"
650 FOR LOOP = 1 TO 10
660      PRINT #2,  "0,0"  : PRINT #2, "NULL"
670 NEXT LOOP
680 ROW = 4
690 IF EOF(1) THEN CLOSE #1: GOTO 1000
700      INPUT #1, DEPT$, EMPLOYEE.NUMBER$, EMPLOYEE.NAME$, RATE.CODE, HOURS.WRKD
710      IF HOURS.WRKD > 40 THEN PAY.HOURS = (HOURS.WRKD - 40) * 1.5 + 40
         ELSE PAY.HOURS = HOURS.WRKD
720      GROSS.PAY = INT(PAY.HOURS * RATE(RATE.CODE) * 10^2 + .5) / 10^2
730      FIT.TAX = INT(GROSS.PAY * FIT.RATE * 10^2 + .5)/ 10^2
740      FICA.TAX = INT(GROSS.PAY * FICA.RATE * 10^2 + .5) / 10^2
750      SIT.TAX = INT(GROSS.PAY * SIT.RATE * 10^2 + .5) / 10^2
760      CWT.TAX = INT(GROSS.PAY * CWT.RATE * 10^2 + .5) / 10^2
770      NET.PAY = GROSS.PAY -FIT.TAX - FICA.TAX - SIT.TAX - CWT.TAX
780      HOURS.TOTAL = HOURS.TOTAL + HOURS.WRKD
790      GROSS.TOTAL = GROSS.TOTAL + GROSS.PAY
800      FIT.TOTAL = FIT.TOTAL + FIT.TAX
810      FICA.TOTAL = FICA.TOTAL + FICA.TAX
820      SIT.TOTAL = SIT.TOTAL + SIT.TAX
830      CWT.TOTAL = CWT.TOTAL + CWT.TAX
840      NET.TOTAL = NET.TOTAL + NET.TAX
850      PRINT #2, "-1,0"                     : PRINT #2, "BOT"
860      PRINT #2,  "1,0"                     : PRINT #2, DEPT$
870      PRINT #2,  "1,0"                     : PRINT #2, EMPLOYEE.NUMBER$
880      PRINT #2,  "1,0"                     : PRINT #2, EMPLOYEE.NAME$
890      PRINT #2,  "0,"; RATE(RATE.CODE)     : PRINT #2, "V"
900      PRINT #2,  "0,"; HOURS.WRKD          : PRINT #2, "V"
910      PRINT #2,  "0,"; GROSS.PAY           : PRINT #2, "V"
920      PRINT #2,  "0,"; FIT.TAX             : PRINT #2, "V"
930      PRINT #2,  "0,"; FICA.TAX            : PRINT #2, "V"
940      PRINT #2,  "0,"; SIT.TAX             : PRINT #2, "V"
950      PRINT #2,  "0,"; CWT.TAX             : PRINT #2, "V"
960      PRINT #2,  "0,"; NET.PAY             : PRINT #2, "V"
970      PRINT #2,  "-4,0" : ROW$ = RIGHT$(STR$(ROW),1) :
         PRINT #2, "F"; ROW$; "-SUM(G"; ROW$; ":J"; ROW$; ")"
980      ROW = ROW + 1
990      GOTO 690
1000 REM 10 UNDERLINES
1010 PRINT #2, "-1,0" : PRINT #2, "BOT"
1020 PRINT #2,  "1,1" : PRINT #2, "-"
```

(continued on next page)

```
1030 FOR LOOP = 1 TO 10
1040    PRINT #2, "0,0" : PRINT #2, "NULL"
1050 NEXT LOOP
1060 REM 11 TOTALS
1070 PRINT #2, "-1,0"                        : PRINT #2, "BOT"
1080 PRINT #2, "1,0"                         : PRINT #2, "TOTALS"
1090 PRINT #2, "0,0"                         : PRINT #2, "NULL"
1100 PRINT #2, "0,0"                         : PRINT #2, "NULL"
1110 PRINT #2, "1,0"                         : PRINT #2, "N/A"
1120 PRINT #2,  "0," ; HOURS.TOTAL : PRINT #2, "V"
1130 PRINT #2, "-4,0"                        : PRINT #2, "SUM(E4:E9)"
1140 PRINT #2,  "0," ; GROSS.TOTAL : PRINT #2, "V"
1150 PRINT #2, "-4,0"                        : PRINT #2, "SUM(F4:F9)"
1160 PRINT #2,  "0," ;   FIT.TOTAL : PRINT #2, "V"
1170 PRINT #2, "-4,0"                        : PRINT #2, "SUM(G4:G9)"
1180 PRINT #2,  "0," ;  FICA.TOTAL : PRINT #2, "V"
1190 PRINT #2, "-4,0"                        : PRINT #2, "SUM(H4:H9)"
1200 PRINT #2,  "0," ;   SIT.TOTAL : PRINT #2, "V"
1210 PRINT #2, "-4,0"                        : PRINT #2, "SUM(I4:I9)"
1220 PRINT #2,  "0," ;   CWT.TOTAL : PRINT #2, "V"
1230 PRINT #2, "-4,0"                        : PRINT #2, "SUM(J4:J9)"
1240 PRINT #2,  "0," ;   NET.TOTAL : PRINT #2, "V"
1250 PRINT #2, "-4,0"                        : PRINT #2, "SUM(K4:K9)"
1260 PRINT #2, "-1,0"  : PRINT #2, "EOD" :  CLOSE #2 : END
1270 REM DATA SECTION
1280 DATA 10: REM TABLE SIZE
1290 DATA 5, 5.5575,5.755,6,6.25: REM RATE TABLE DATA
1300 DATA 6.5, 6.75, 7, 7.5, 8  : REM RATE TABLE DATA
1310 END
```

As shown in this program, generating such a file requires substantially more statements than PAYPROG2.BAS. It does, however, follow the same series of entry and execution steps used for PAYPROG1.BAS and PAYPROG2.BAS.

Back at system level after running PAYPROG3.BAS, its file output can be listed using the PRINT command. The entry

PRINT B:PAYSD2.SDI

generates a list similar to Figure 15.12.

Figure 15.12 .SDI File Created by Program PAYPROG3.BAS

```
TABLE
0,1
""
COL-FORMAT
 4,9
TR
COL-FORMAT
 5,9
TR
COL-FORMAT
 6,9
TR$
COL-FORMAT
 7,9
TR$
COL-FORMAT
 8,9
TR$
COL-FORMAT
 9,9
TR$
COL-FORMAT
 10,9
TR$
COL-FORMAT
 11,9
TR$
GDISP-FORMAT
9,0
GTL
DATA
0,0
""
-1,0
BOT
0,0
NULL
1,0
EMPLOYEE
1,0
EMPLOYEE
1,0
HOURLY
1,0
HOURS
1,0
GROSS
1,0
FEDERAL
1,0
FICA
1,0
STATE
1,0
CITY
1,0
NET
-1,0
BOT
1,0
DEPT.
1,0
NUMBER
1,0
NAME
1,0
RATE
1,0
WORKED
1,0
PAY
1,0
TAX
1,0
TAX
1,0
TAX
1,0
TAX
1,0
PAY
-1,0
BOT
1,1
-
0,0
NULL
0,0
NULL
0,0
NULL
0,0
NULL
0,0
NULL
0,0
NULL
0,0
NULL
0,0
NULL
0,0
```

(continued on next page)

```
NULL
0,0
NULL
-1,0
BOT
1,0
053
1,0
1011
1,0
Alpha
0, 8
V
0, 40
V
0, 320
V
0, 72
V
0, 21.44
V
0, 7.84
V
0, 13.8
V
0, 204.92
V
-4,0
F4-SUM(G4:J4)
-1,0
BOT
1,0
062
1,0
1015
1,0
Zebra
0, 6.25
V
0, 55
V
0, 390.63
V
0, 87.89
V
0, 26.17
V
0, 9.57
V
0, 16.85
V
0, 250.15
V
-4,0
F5-SUM(G5:J5)
-1,0
BOT
1,0
062
1,0
1002
1,0
Bravo
0, 5.5575
V
0, 30
V
0, 166.73
V
0, 37.51
V
0, 11.17
V
0, 4.08
V
0, 7.19
V
0, 106.78
V
-4,0
F6-SUM(G6:J6)
-1,0
BOT
1,0
053
1,0
1014
1,0
Yankee
0, 5.755
V
0, 20
V
0, 115.1
V
0, 25.9
V
0, 7.71
V
0, 2.82
V
0, 4.96
V
0, 73.71
V
-4,0
F7-SUM(G7:J7)
-1,0
BOT
1,0
062
1,0
2012
1,0
Gamma
0, 5
V
0, 60
V
0, 350
V
0, 78.75
V
0, 23.45
V
0, 8.58
V
0, 15.09
V
0, 224.13
V
-4,0
F8-SUM(G8:J8)
-1,0
BOT
1,0
053
1,0
3015
1,0
Maryjane
0, 7.5
V
0, 55
V
0, 468.75
V
0, 105.47
V
0, 31.41
V
0, 11.48
V
0, 20.21
V
0, 300.18
V
-4,0
F9-SUM(G9:J9)
-1,0
BOT
1,1
-
0,0
NULL
0,0
NULL
0,0
NULL
0,0
NULL
0,0
NULL
0,0
NULL
0,0
NULL
0,0
NULL
0,0
NULL
0,0
NULL
-1,0
BOT
1,0
TOTALS
0,0
NULL
0,0
NULL
1,0
N/A
0, 260
V
-4,0
SUM(E4:E9)
0, 1811.21
V
-4,0
SUM(F4:F9)
0, 407.52
V
-4,0
SUM(G4:G9)
0, 121.35
V
-4,0
SUM(H4:H9)
0, 44.37
V
-4,0
SUM(I4:I9)
0, 78.1
V
-4,0
SUM(J4:J9)
0, 0
V
-4,0
SUM(K4:K9)
-1,0
EOD
```

The last phase is to convert B:PAYSD2.SDI into a SuperCalc³ file using the same sequence of steps that were used to convert B:PAYSD1.SDI.

After the conversion process has been completed, enter SuperCalc³ and load the converted spreadsheet

/LB:PAYSD2.CAL,A

The displayed spreadsheet will match Figure 15.13.

Figure 15.13 Spreadsheet PAYSD2.CAL: Formulas Off

	A	B	C	D	E	F	G	H	I	J	K
1		EMPLOYEE	EMPLOYEE	HOURLY	HOURS	GROSS	FEDERAL	FICA	STATE	CITY	NET
2	DEPT.	NUMBER	NAME	RATE	WORKED	PAY	TAX	TAX	TAX	TAX	PAY
3	-----	-----	-----	-----	-----	-----	-----	-----	-----	-----	-----
4	053	1011	Alpha	8	40	320.00	72.00	21.44	7.84	13.80	204.92
5	062	1015	Zebra	6.25	55	390.63	87.89	26.17	9.57	16.85	250.15
6	062	1002	Bravo	5.5575	30	166.73	37.51	11.17	4.08	7.19	106.78
7	053	1014	Yankee	5.755	20	115.10	25.90	7.71	2.82	4.96	73.71
8	062	2012	Gamma	5	60	350.00	78.75	23.45	8.58	15.09	224.13
9	053	3015	Maryjane	7.5	55	468.75	105.47	31.41	11.48	20.21	300.18
10	-----	-----	-----	-----	-----	-----	-----	-----	-----	-----	-----
11	TOTALS			N/A	260	1811.21	407.52	121.35	44.37	78.10	1159.87

It is not necessary to use the skeletal spreadsheet because the headings, formats, and SUM functions were generated by the BASIC program. Notice in Figure 15.13 that the hourly rates are not uniformly displaying four decimal places. This is because SDI cannot generate a User-Defined Format Table.

If you have any doubts about whether or not the program worked, enter **/GF** to toggle on formulas display. Now the spreadsheet display matches Figure 15.14.

Figure 15.14 Spreadsheet PAYSD2.CAL: Formulas On

	A	B	C	D	E	F	G	H	I	J	K
1		EMPLOYEE	EMPLOYEE	HOURLY	HOURS	GROSS	FEDERAL	FICA	STATE	CITY	NET
2	DEPT.	NUMBER	NAME	RATE	WORKED	PAY	TAX	TAX	TAX	TAX	PAY
3	-----	-----	-----	-----	-----	-----	-----	-----	-----	-----	-----
4	053	1011	Alpha	8	40	320	72	21.44	7.84	13.8	F4-SUM(G4:J4)
5	062	1015	Zebra	6.25	55	390.63	87.89	26.17	9.57	16.85	F5-SUM(G5:J5)
6	062	1002	Bravo	5.5575	30	166.73	37.51	11.17	4.08	7.19	F6-SUM(G6:J6)
7	053	1014	Yankee	5.755	20	115.1	25.9	7.71	2.82	4.96	F7-SUM(G7:J7)
8	062	2012	Gamma	5	60	350	78.75	23.45	8.58	15.09	F8-SUM(G8:J8)
9	053	3015	Maryjane	7.5	55	468.75	105.47	31.41	11.48	20.21	F9-SUM(G9:J9)
10	-----	-----	-----	-----	-----	-----	-----	-----	-----	-----	-----
11	TOTALS			N/A	SUM(E4:E9)	SUM(F4:F9)	SUM(G4:G9)	SUM(H4:H9)	SUM(I4:I9)	SUM(J4:J9)	SUM(K4:K9)

Some Parting Suggestions

As you can tell from the preceding sections, comma-separated value files are substantially easier to generate and access than SuperData Interchange files. Although you may prefer to use .CSV files, the following circumstances may preclude their use:

- The system being interfaced is not capable of inputting or writing comma-separated value files.
- The design criteria of the interface necessitates generation of a spreadsheet in its final form, complete with formats and formulas.

In the second instance, you have no choice but to use files in the SuperData Interchange format. The first case, however, is not so clearcut. If you intend to interface SuperCalc³ with a large mainframe computer, you'll probably find that COBOL is used to process business and commercial data.

COBOL is not automatically capable of creating comma-separated value files in the same sense that BASIC can. However, with the right design and programming, COBOL can produce results that look exactly like a .CSV file from BASIC. You may want to discuss this further with a systems analyst who works on the mainframe. Some hints for this person:

- Use the (COBOL) UNSTRING verb specifying comma as a delimiter when inputting a .CSV file to a COBOL program.
- Use the (COBOL) STRING verb specifying comma as a delimiter when writing a .CSV file from a COBOL program.
- Quotation marks around string values are probably best handled by the INSPECT verb with the REPLACING option.

If you don't understand the above terms, don't worry. Your systems analyst will. A word of advice—when you meet with the analyst, bring a listing of the comma-separated value file. You can easily make one by building a spreadsheet that resembles your desired end product but that contains limited data. After building and saving the spreadsheet, use SDI to convert it to a .CSV file.

Here are some hints for when you need a program to generate a .SDI file and you're not sure how to start.

First, build and save a spreadsheet that resembles your desired end product, but that contains limited data.

Second, use SDI to convert it to an .SDI file. Select menu item C. When SDI prompts you with

Output All or Values (A or V) :

enter **A** if you want formats and formulas put into the resulting .SDI file. Enter **V** if you only want values put into the resulting .SDI file.

Third, use the PRINT command to list out the .SDI file. You can now take this file listing and use it as a model for your program.

Converting .VC Files to .CAL Files

VisiCalc (.VC) files can be converted to SuperCalc³ (.CAL) files.

When converting .VC files to .CAL files, SDI translates most formulas and values as they were entered in VisiCalc. Note the following conversion differences:

- The VisiCalc @CHOOSE function is converted from @CHOOSE(list pointer, value 1, value 2 . . .)
  to
  IF(INT(list pointer) = 1,INT(list pointer)*value 1,
  IF(INT(list pointer) = 2,INT(list pointer)*value 2,). . .)
  If the converted expression has more than 116 characters, **ERROR** results in the .CAL file. If the list pointer is negative, zero, or greater than the number of values in the @CHOOSE function, **0** results in the .CAL file.
- The VisiCalc @AND and @OR functions allow more than two arguments. Since their SuperCalc³ counterparts only permit two arguments, SDI translates them as nested functions. For example:
  @OR(A1>B1,B1>C1,C1>D1)
  is converted as
  OR(OR(A1>B1,B1>C1),C1>D1)
  If the converted expression has more than 116 characters, **ERROR** results in the .CAL file.
- VisiCalc allows parentheses in expressions to be nested nine deep, while SuperCalc³ allows seven. SDI makes the translation when the converted expression does not exceed 116 characters. If the converted expression has more than 116 characters, **ERROR** results in the .CAL file.
- VisiCalc text that exceeds 116 characters is truncated to 116 characters during the conversion.
- VisiCalc formulas that exceed 116 characters cause **ERROR** to result in the .CAL file.
- The VisiCalc formula prefix "+" is stripped from the front of the formula during the conversion. For example:
  +A1+B1
  is converted as
  A1+B1
- VisiCalc formulas evaluate from left to right, ignoring the hierarchy of arithmetic operators. SuperCalc³ formulas use the standard hierarchy of arithmetic operators. VisiCalc evaluates 2 + 4 * 3 as 18, while SuperCalc³ evaluates it as 14.
- VisiCalc repeats text across a single column width. When SDI converts it, the text repeats across the spreadsheet to column DW or a non-blank cell, whichever occurs first.

To convert VisiCalc files to SuperCalc³ files, enter **SDI** at operating system level. When the SDI menu is displayed, enter **E.** Then follow the prompts for source file and destination file.

Converting .WKS Files to .CAL Files

Lotus 1-2-3 (.WKS) files can be converted to SuperCalc³ (.CAL) files.

When converting .WKS files to .CAL files, SDI translates many formulas and values as they were entered in Lotus. Note the following conversion differences:

- Lotus 1-2-3 columns extending beyond column DW are not converted because SuperCalc³ only supports 127 columns.
- Lotus 1-2-3 table functions, @HLOOKUP and @VLOOKUP, can be converted to the SuperCalc³ LOOKUP function when their third argument, the offset, equals 1. For example:

  @VLOOKUP(list pointer, table range,1)

  converts to

  LOOKUP(list pointer, table range)

  These functions are converted to text when the offset is not equal to 1.
- The following Lotus 1-2-3 functions are converted as text:

  @DAVG(input range,offset,criterion range)
  @DCOUNT(input range,offset,criterion range)
  @DMAX(input range,offset,criterion range)
  @DMIN(input range,offset,criterion range)
  @DSTD(input range,offset,criterion range)
  @DSUM(input range,offset,criterion range)
  @DVAR(input range,offset,criterion range)
  @STD(list)
  @VAR(list)
- Formats are translated as follows:

Lotus 1-2-3	SuperCalc³	Comments
0 decimals	Integer	None
2 decimals	$	None
General	General	None
Scientific	Exponential	SuperCalc³ display depends on column width.
Percent	General	Consider using % in User-Defined Format Table.
+/-	*	SuperCalc³ histograms do not plot negative values.

- The Lotus 1-2-3 "TEXT" format produces the same results as the SuperCalc³ /Global, Formula toggle command. It toggles on formula display only when it is a globally set format in Lotus, otherwise it is converted as normal text.
- Lotus 1-2-3 region names are not converted.
- The following Lotus 1-2-3 data base information is not converted:

  Ranges and fields associated with the Data Table command.
  The range associated with the Data Fill command.
  Ranges and fields associated with the Data Distribution command.

The sort range.
The primary sort key.
The secondary sort key range.

- Lotus 1-2-3 printer controls are not converted.
- Only the first nine Lotus 1-2-3 graphs are converted. Any Lotus graphs that reference columns beyond column DW are not converted. TITLES and LEGENDS are converted only if they are cell references.
- Lotus 1-2-3 keystroke macros are converted as normal text. They cannot be directly executed from the resulting .CAL file. The SuperCalc³ /Output command must be used to generate a .XQT file, which can subsequently be executed via the /eXecute command.

To convert Lotus 1-2-3 files to SuperCalc³ files, enter **SDI** at operating system level. When the SDI menu is displayed, enter **F.** Then follow the prompts for source file and destination file.

Review Exercises

These exercises use the following data for a team of bowlers:

Name	Game #1	Game #2	Game #3
Al	240	250	260
Bob	300	300	300
Chuck	175	200	225
Denise	135	155	175
Eileen	100	125	150

Although Exercises 2 and 3 suggest a BASIC program, feel free to use Pascal, COBOL, a database management system, or any other software that can generate the .CSV and .SDI files required by these two exercises.

1. Prepare a spreadsheet skeleton for a team's bowling scores. Provide columnar headings for bowler name; games 1, 2, and 3; total pins and bowling average. For anyone who has never bowled, or at least kept score, the individual bowling average is calculated as the quotient of total pins divided by 3, truncated to an integer. Also provide team totals for the three games plus the team average. The team bowling average is the average of the individual bowling averages, truncated to an integer.
2. Interface a comma-separated values file with SuperCalc³.
   a. Provide a BASIC program to output the above bowling data into a .CSV file.
   b. Use the appropriate system command to list out the file.
   c. Convert the file to a .CAL file.
   d. From within SuperCalc³, merge the converted .CAL file into the bowling skeleton built in Exercise 1.

3. Interface a SuperData Interchange file with SuperCalc³.
   a. Provide a BASIC program to output the above bowling data into a .SDI file.
   b. Use the appropriate system command to list out the file.
   c. Convert the file to a .CAL file.
   d. From within SuperCalc³, merge the converted .CAL file into the bowling skeleton built in Exercise 1.
4. Directly generate a complete spreadsheet from a SuperData Interchange file, then interface it with SuperCalc³.
   a. Provide a BASIC program to output the above bowling data into a .SDI file. This .SDI file must also contain the headings, formats, and formulas used by the bowling skeleton.
   b. Use the appropriate system command to list out the file.
   c. Convert the file to a .CAL file.
   d. From within SuperCalc³, load the converted .CAL file and check your results.

Answers to Review Exercises

1. See Figure 15.15 for a display with formulas toggled on.

Figure 15.15 Bowling Skeleton, Formulas On: Exercise 15-1

```
   :  A   ::     B     ::     C     ::     D     ::     E     ::     F     :
1  Bowler                                             Total         Bowling
2  Name         Game #1     Game #2     Game #3        Pins         Average
3  ------------------------------------------------------------------------
4                                                  SUM(B4.D4)    INT(E4/3)
5                                                  SUM(B5.D5)    INT(E5/3)
6                                                  SUM(B6.D6)    INT(E6/3)
7                                                  SUM(B7.D7)    INT(E7/3)
8                                                  SUM(B8.D8)    INT(E8/3)
9  ------------------------------------------------------------------------
10 Team       SUM(B4.B8)  SUM(C4.C8)  SUM(D4.D8)  SUM(E4.E8) INT(AV(F4.F8))
```

See Figure 15.16 for a display with formulas toggled off.

Figure 15.16 Bowling Skeleton, Formulas Off: Exercise 15-1

```
   :  A   ::     B     ::     C     ::     D     ::     E     ::     F     ::     G     :
1  Bowler                                             Total  Bowling
2  Name         Game #1     Game #2     Game #3        Pins  Average
3  -----------------------------------------------------------------
4                                                         0        0
5                                                         0        0
6                                                         0        0
7                                                         0        0
8                                                         0        0
9  -----------------------------------------------------------------
10 Team               0           0           0           0        0
```

2. a. See the program listing shown in Figure 15.17.

Figure 15.17 Listing of BASIC Program X15PROG1.BAS: Exercise 15-2a

```
10 REM PROGRAM NAME: X15PROG1.BAS
20 OPEN "OUTPUT", #2, "B:BOWLERS.CSV"
30 READ BOWLER$, GAME1, GAME2, GAME3
40       IF BOWLER$ = "DUMMY" THEN CLOSE #2 : END
50       WRITE #2, BOWLER$, GAME1, GAME2, GAME3
60       GOTO 30
9000 REM DATA SECTION
9010 DATA AL,      240, 250, 260 : REM LIVE DATA
9020 DATA BOB,     300, 300, 300 : REM LIVE DATA
9030 DATA CHUCK,   175, 200, 225 : REM LIVE DATA
9040 DATA DENISE,  135, 155, 175 : REM LIVE DATA
9050 DATA EILEEN,  100, 125, 150 : REM LIVE DATA
9060 DATA DUMMY,     0,   0,   0 : DUMMY DATA
9070 END
```

Enter **RUN** from within BASIC to generate the .CSV file, then enter SYSTEM to return to operating system level.

b. The command PRINT B:BOWLERS.CSV produces the listing shown in Figure 15.18.

Figure 15.18 .CSV File Created by Program X15PROG1.BAS: Exercise 15-2b

```
"AL",240,250,260
"BOB",300,300,300
"CHUCK",175,200,225
"DENISE",135,155,175
"EILEEN",100,125,150
```

c. Enter **SDI** to call the file conversion utility.
Select menu item B.
Specify B:BOWLERS.CSV as the Source File Name.
Specify B:BOWLERS.CAL as the Destination File Name.
Enter **n** to exit SDI.

d. Call SuperCalc³.
Enter **/LB:EX15SKEL.CAL,A** to load the skeleton.
Enter **/LB:BOWLERS.CAL,PA1:D5,A4**, then press RETURN to merge the bowling data via partial load.
If you set manual mode via /GM, enter **!** to force a manual recalculation.
See Figure 15.19 for an illustration of the merged spreadsheet.

Figure 15.19 Completed Bowling Spreadsheet: Exercise 15-2d

	A	B	C	D	E	F	G
1	Bowler				Total	Bowling	
2	Name	Game #1	Game #2	Game #3	Pins	Average	
3	------	------	------	------	------	------	
4	AL	240	250	260	750	250	
5	BOB	300	300	300	900	300	
6	CHUCK	175	200	225	600	200	
7	DENISE	135	155	175	465	155	
8	EILEEN	100	125	150	375	125	
9	------	------	------	------	------	------	
10	Team	950	1030	1110	3090	206	

3. a. See the program listing shown in Figure 15.20.

Figure 15.20 Listing of BASIC Program X15PROG2.BAS: Exercise 15-3a

```
10 REM PROGRAM NAME: X15PROG2.BAS
20 OPEN "OUTPUT", #2, "B:BOWLERS1.SDI"
30 PRINT #2, "TABLE" : PRINT #2, "0,1" : PRINT #2, CHR$(34); CHR$(34)
40 PRINT #2,  "DATA" : PRINT #2, "0,0" : PRINT #2, CHR$(34); CHR$(34)
50 READ BOWLER$, GAME1, GAME2, GAME3
60        IF BOWLER$ = "DUMMY" GOTO 130
70        PRINT #2, "-1,0"        : PRINT #2, "BOT"
80        PRINT #2,  "1,0"        : PRINT #2, BOWLER$
90        PRINT #2,  "0,"; GAME1  : PRINT #2, "V"
100       PRINT #2,  "0,"; GAME2  : PRINT #2, "V"
110       PRINT #2,  "0,"; GAME3  : PRINT #2, "V"
120       GOTO 50
130 PRINT #2, "-1,0" : PRINT #2, "EOD" : CLOSE #2 : END
9000 REM DATA SECTION
9010 DATA AL,      240, 250, 260 : REM LIVE DATA
9020 DATA BOB,     300, 300, 300 : REM LIVE DATA
9030 DATA CHUCK,   175, 200, 225 : REM LIVE DATA
9040 DATA DENISE,  135, 155, 175 : REM LIVE DATA
9050 DATA EILEEN,  100, 125, 150 : REM LIVE DATA
9060 DATA DUMMY,     0,   0,   0 : DUMMY DATA
9070 END
```

Enter **RUN** from within BASIC to generate the .SDI file, then enter **SYSTEM** to return to operating system level.

b. The command PRINT B:BOWLERS1.SDI produces the listing shown in Figure 15.21.

Figure 15.21 .SDI File Created by Program X15PROG2.BAS: Exercise 15-3b

```
TABLE
0,1
""
DATA
0,0
""
-1,0
BOT
1,0
AL
0, 240
V
0, 250
V
0, 260
V
-1,0
BOT
1,0
BOB
0, 300
V
0, 300
V
0, 300
V
-1,0
BOT
1,0
CHUCK
0, 175
V
0, 200
V
0, 225
V
-1,0
BOT
1,0
DENISE
0, 135
V
0, 155
V
0, 175
V
-1,0
BOT
1,0
EILEEN
0, 100
V
0, 125
V
0, 150
V
-1,0
EOD
```

c. Enter **SDI** to call the file conversion utility.
Select menu item D.
Specify B:BOWLERS1.SDI as the Source File Name.
Specify B:BOWLERS1.CAL as the Destination File Name.
Enter **n** to exit SDI.

d. Call SuperCalc³.
Enter **/LB:EX15SKEL.CAL,A** to load the skeleton.
Enter **/LB:BOWLERS1.CAL,PA1:D5,A4**, then press RETURN to merge the bowling data via partial load.
If you set manual mode via /GM, enter **!** to force a manual recalculation.
See Figure 15.22 for an illustration of the merged spreadsheet.

Figure 15.22 Completed Bowling Spreadsheet: Exercise 15-3d

	A	B	C	D	E	F	G
1	Bowler				Total	Bowling	
2	Name	Game #1	Game #2	Game #3	Pins	Average	
3	----------	----------	----------	----------	----------	----------	
4	AL	240	250	260	750	250	
5	BOB	300	300	300	900	300	
6	CHUCK	175	200	225	600	200	
7	DENISE	135	155	175	465	155	
8	EILEEN	100	125	150	375	125	
9	----------	----------	----------	----------	----------	----------	
10	Team	950	1030	1110	3090	206	

4. a. See the program listing shown in Figure 15.23.

Figure 15.23 Listing of BASIC Program X15PROG3.BAS: Exercise 15-4a

```
10 REM PROGRAM NAME: X15PROG3.BAS
20 OPEN "OUTPUT", #2, "B:BOWLERS2.SDI"
30 PRINT #2, "TABLE" : PRINT #2, "0,1" : PRINT #2, CHR$(34); CHR$(34)
40 FOR LOOP = 2 TO 6
50      PRINT #2, "COL-FORMAT" : PRINT #2, LOOP; ",9" : PRINT #2, "TR"
60 NEXT LOOP
70 PRINT #2, "GDISP-FORMAT" : PRINT #2, "9,0" : PRINT #2, "GTL"
80 PRINT #2,  "DATA" : PRINT #2, "0,0" : PRINT #2, CHR$(34); CHR$(34)
90 REM ROW 1 HEADINGS
100 PRINT #2, "-1,0" : PRINT #2, "BOT"
110 PRINT #2,  "1,0" : PRINT #2, "BOWLER"
120 PRINT #2,  "0,0" : PRINT #2, "NULL"
130 PRINT #2,  "0,0" : PRINT #2, "NULL"
140 PRINT #2,  "0,0" : PRINT #2, "NULL"
150 PRINT #2,  "1,0" : PRINT #2, "TOTAL"
160 PRINT #2,  "1,0" : PRINT #2, "BOWLING"
170 REM ROW 2 HEADINGS
180 PRINT #2, "-1,0" : PRINT #2, "BOT"
190 PRINT #2,  "1,0" : PRINT #2, "NAME"
200 PRINT #2,  "1,0" : PRINT #2, "GAME #1"
210 PRINT #2,  "1,0" : PRINT #2, "GAME #2"
220 PRINT #2,  "1,0" : PRINT #2, "GAME #3"
230 PRINT #2,  "1,0" : PRINT #2, "PINS"
240 PRINT #2,  "1,0" : PRINT #2, "AVERAGE"
250 REM ROW 3 UNDERLINES
260 PRINT #2, "-1,0" : PRINT #2, "BOT"
270 PRINT #2,  "1,1" : PRINT #2, "-"
280 FOR LOOP = 1 TO 5
290      PRINT #2, "0,0" : PRINT #2, "NULL"
300 NEXT LOOP
310 PRINT #2,  "1,0" : PRINT #2, " "
320 ROW = 4
330 READ BOWLER$, GAME1, GAME2, GAME3
340      IF BOWLER$ = "DUMMY" GOTO 560
350      BOWLER.PINS = GAME1 + GAME2 + GAME3
360      BOWLER.AVG = INT(BOWLER.PINS / 3)
370      GAME1.TOTAL = GAME1.TOTAL + GAME1
380      GAME2.TOTAL = GAME2.TOTAL + GAME2
390      GAME3.TOTAL = GAME3.TOTAL + GAME3
400      TEAM.PINS = TEAM.PINS + BOWLER.PINS
410      TEAM.AVG = INT(TEAM.PINS / 3)
420      PRINT #2, "-1,0"         : PRINT #2, "BOT"
430      PRINT #2,  "1,0"         : PRINT #2, BOWLER$
440      PRINT #2,  "0,"; GAME1   : PRINT #2, "V"
450      PRINT #2,  "0,"; GAME2   : PRINT #2, "V"
460      PRINT #2,  "0,"; GAME3   : PRINT #2, "V"
470      PRINT #2,  "0,"; BOWLER.PINS : PRINT #2, "V"
480      PRINT #2, "-4,0"
490      ROW$ = RIGHT$(STR$(ROW),1)
500      PRINT #2, "SUM(B"; ROW$; ":D"; ROW$; ")"
510      PRINT #2,  "0,"; BOWLER.AVG : PRINT #2, "V"
520      PRINT #2, "-4,0"
530      PRINT #2, "INT(E"; ROW$; "/3)"
540      ROW = ROW + 1
550      GOTO 330
560 REM ROW 9 UNDERLINES
570 PRINT #2, "-1,0" : PRINT #2, "BOT"
580 PRINT #2, "1,1" : PRINT #2, "-"
590 FOR LOOP = 1 TO 5
600      PRINT #2, "0,0" : PRINT #2, "NULL"
```

(continued on next page)

```
610 NEXT LOOP
620 PRINT #2, "1,0" : PRINT #2, " "
630 REM ROW 10 TOTALS
640 PRINT #2, "-1,0"                 : PRINT #2, "BOT"
650 PRINT #2,  "1,0"                 : PRINT #2, "TEAM"
660 PRINT #2,  "0,"; GAME1.TOTAL : PRINT #2, "V"
670 PRINT #2,  "-4,0"                : PRINT #2, "SUM(B4:B8)"
680 PRINT #2,  "0,"; GAME2.TOTAL : PRINT #2, "V"
690 PRINT #2,  "-4,0"                : PRINT #2, "SUM(C4:C8)"
700 PRINT #2,  "0,"; GAME3.TOTAL : PRINT #2, "V"
710 PRINT #2,  "-4,0"                : PRINT #2, "SUM(D4:D8)"
720 PRINT #2,  "0,"; TEAM.PINS   : PRINT #2, "V"
730 PRINT #2,  "-4,0"                : PRINT #2, "SUM(E4:E8)"
740 PRINT #2,  "0,"; TEAM.AVG    : PRINT #2, "V"
750 PRINT #2,  "-4,0"                : PRINT #2, "INT(AV(F4:F8))"
760 PRINT #2, "-1,0" : PRINT #2, "EOD" : CLOSE #2 : END
9000 REM DATA SECTION
9010 DATA AL,      240, 250, 260 : REM LIVE DATA
9020 DATA BOB,     300, 300, 300 : REM LIVE DATA
9030 DATA CHUCK,   175, 200, 225 : REM LIVE DATA
9040 DATA DENISE,  135, 155, 175 : REM LIVE DATA
9050 DATA EILEEN,  100, 125, 150 : REM LIVE DATA
9060 DATA DUMMY,     0,   0,   0 : DUMMY DATA
9070 END
```

Enter **RUN** from within BASIC to generate the .SDI file, then enter **SYSTEM** to return to operating system level.

b. The command PRINT B:BOWLERS2.SDI produces the listing shown in Figure 15.24

Figure 15.24 .SDI File Created by Program X15PROG3.BAS: Exercise 15-4b

```
TABLE
0,1
""
COL-FORMAT
 2 ,9
TR
COL-FORMAT
 3 ,9
TR
COL-FORMAT
 4 ,9
TR
COL-FORMAT
 5 ,9
TR
COL-FORMAT
 6 ,9
TR
GDISP-FORMAT
9,0
GTL
DATA
0,0
""
-1,0
BOT
1,0
BOWLER
0,0
NULL
0,0
NULL
0,0
NULL
1,0
TOTAL
1,0
BOWLING
-1,0
BOT
1,0
NAME
1,0
GAME #1
1,0
GAME #2
1,0
GAME #3
1,0
PINS
1,0
AVERAGE
-1,0
BOT
1,1
-
0,0
NULL
0,0
NULL
0,0
NULL
0,0
NULL
0,0
NULL
1,0

-1,0
BOT
1,0
AL
0, 240
V
0, 250
V
0, 260
V
0, 750
V
-4,0
SUM(B4:D4)
0, 250
V
-4,0
INT(E4/3)
-1,0
BOT
1,0
BOB
0, 300
V
0, 300
V
0, 300
V
0, 900
V
-4,0
SUM(B5:D5)
0, 300
V
-4,0
INT(E5/3)
-1,0
BOT
1,0
CHUCK
0, 175
V
0, 200
V
0, 225
V
0, 600
V
-4,0
SUM(B6:D6)
0, 200
V
-4,0
INT(E6/3)
-1,0
BOT
1,0
DENISE
0, 135
V
0, 155
V
0, 175
V
```

(continued on next page)

```
0, 465
V
-4,0
SUM(B7:D7)
0, 155
V
-4,0
INT(E7/3)
-1,0
BOT
1,0
EILEEN
0, 100
V
0, 125
V
0, 150
V
0, 375
V
-4,0
SUM(B8:D8)
0, 125
V
-4,0
INT(E8/3)
-1,0
BOT
1,1
-
0,0
NULL
0,0
NULL
0,0
NULL
0,0
NULL
0,0
NULL
1,0

-1,0
BOT
1,0
TEAM
0, 950
V
-4,0
SUM(B4:B8)
0, 1030
V
-4,0
SUM(C4:C8)
0, 1110
V
-4,0
SUM(D4:D8)
0, 3090
V
-4,0
SUM(E4:E8)
0, 1030
V
-4,0
INT(AV(F4:F8))
-1,0
EOD
```

d. Call SuperCalc³.
Enter **/LB:BOWLERS2.CAL,A** to load the converted spreadsheet. See Figure 15.25 for a display with formulas toggled on.

Figure 15.25 Spreadsheet BOWLERS2.CAL: Formulas On

```
   :  A    ::      B      ::      C      ::      D      ::       E      ::         F       :
1  BOWLER                                                      TOTAL           BOWLING
2  NAME           GAME #1       GAME #2       GAME #3           PINS           AVERAGE
3  --------------------------------------------------------------------------------------
4  AL                 240           250           260     SUM(B4:D4)         INT(E4/3)
5  BOB                300           300           300     SUM(B5:D5)         INT(E5/3)
6  CHUCK              175           200           225     SUM(B6:D6)         INT(E6/3)
7  DENISE             135           155           175     SUM(B7:D7)         INT(E7/3)
8  EILEEN             100           125           150     SUM(B8:D8)         INT(E8/3)
9  --------------------------------------------------------------------------------------
10 TEAM        SUM(B4:B8)    SUM(C4:C8)    SUM(D4:D8)     SUM(E4:E8)    INT(AV(F4:F8))
```

See Figure 15.26 for a display with formulas toggled off.

Figure 15.26 Spreadsheet BOWLERS2.CAL: Formulas Off

```
   :  A    ::    B    ::    C    ::    D    ::   E   ::    F    ::    G    :
1  BOWLER                                        TOTAL  BOWLING
2  NAME        GAME #1   GAME #2   GAME #3       PINS  AVERAGE
3  -----------------------------------------------------------
4  AL              240       250       260        750      250
5  BOB             300       300       300        900      300
6  CHUCK           175       200       225        600      200
7  DENISE          135       155       175        465      155
8  EILEEN          100       125       150        375      125
9  -----------------------------------------------------------
10 TEAM            950      1030      1110       3090      206
```

SECTION FOUR

Business Applications

CHAPTER 16

SuperCalc[3] Business Applications

Chapter Overview and Objectives

- An Income Tax Application
- A Capital Budgeting Application
- A Statement of Net Worth Application
- A Mortgage Amortization Application
- A System for Planning and Analyzing the Profitability of Operations
- Constructing Your Own Templates

This chapter presents a series of models that demonstrate the applicability of SuperCalc[3] for personal and business financial information needs. Each model is shown twice, once blank and once with sample data.

The chapter is intended to synthesize many of the SuperCalc[3] features covered in previous chapters. Try to customize the models to fit your specific needs and use them as a springboard to more advanced applications.

Optional disks, containing all the models shown in the chapter, are available from the publisher. These disks contain the blank template and the completed sample application. See Appendix A for a cross reference between filenames and figure numbers, as well as a contents listing of the completed templates.

The disks also contain the Microsoft BASIC programs and the associated input files used in Chapter 15 to demonstrate interfacing SuperCalc[3] with other systems. If you don't have the companion disks, you can build the models using the contents output shown in Appendix A.

The models contained in the section titled A System for Planning and Analyzing the Profitability of Operations make very heavy use of command files. You may want to review the concepts and syntax of command files as well as the /eXecute command in Chapter 14 before going into this particular section.

An Income Tax Application

Each year, most people file a federal income tax return. Many of them use the forms shown in parts A and B of Figure 16.1 and in Figure 16.2.

Figure 16.1A U.S. Individual Income Tax Return, Form 1040

Form **1040** Department of the Treasury—Internal Revenue Servic
U.S. Individual Income Tax Return **1984** (0)

For the year January 1-December 31, 1984, or other tax year beginning , 1984, ending , 19 OMB No. 1545-0074

Use IRS label. Otherwise, please print or type.

Your first name and initial (if joint return, also give spouse's name and initial)	Last name	**Your social security number**
Present home address (Number and street, including apartment number, or rural route)		**Spouse's social security number**
City, town or post office, State, and ZIP code	Your occupation	
	Spouse's occupation	

Presidential Election Campaign ▶ Do you want $1 to go to this fund? . . . . Yes No
If joint return, does your spouse want $1 to go to this fund?. . Yes No
Note: *Checking "Yes" will not change your tax or reduce your refund.*

For Privacy Act and Paperwork Reduction Act Notice, see Instructions.

Filing Status

Check only one box.

1 ☐ Single
2 ☐ Married filing joint return (even if only one had income)
3 ☐ Married filing separate return. Enter spouse's social security no. above and full name here.
4 ☐ Head of household (with qualifying person). (See page 5 of Instructions.) If the qualifying person is your unmarried child but not your dependent, write child's name here.
5 ☐ Qualifying widow(er) with dependent child (Year spouse died ▶ 19). (See page 6 of Instructions.)

Exemptions

Always check the box labeled Yourself. Check other boxes if they apply.

6a ☐ Yourself ☐ 65 or over ☐ Blind
b ☐ Spouse ☐ 65 or over ☐ Blind
Enter number of boxes checked on 6a and b ▶ ☐
c First names of your dependent children who lived with you
Enter number of children listed on 6c ▶ ☐

d Other dependents: (1) Name	(2) Relationship	(3) Number of months lived in your home	(4) Did dependent have income of $1,000 or more?	(5) Did you provide more than one-half of dependent's support?

Enter number of other dependents ▶ ☐
Add numbers entered in boxes above ▶ ☐

e Total number of exemptions claimed (also complete line 36). . . . .

Income

Please attach Copy B of your Forms W-2, W-2G, and W-2P here.

If you do not have a W-2, see page 4 of Instructions.

7 Wages, salaries, tips, etc. 7
8 Interest income *(also attach Schedule B if over $400)* 8
9a Dividends *(also attach Schedule B if over $400)* ______ , 9b Exclusion ______
c Subtract line 9b from line 9a and enter the result 9c
10 Refunds of State and local income taxes, from the worksheet on page 9 of Instructions *(do not enter an amount unless you itemized deductions for those taxes in an earlier year—see page 9)* 10
11 Alimony received 11
12 Business income or (loss) *(attach Schedule C)* 12
13 Capital gain or (loss) *(attach Schedule D)* 13
14 40% of capital gain distributions not reported on line 13 (see page 9 of Instructions) . . . 14
15 Supplemental gains or (losses) *(attach Form 4797)* 15
16 Fully taxable pensions, IRA distributions, and annuities not reported on line 17 16
17a Other pensions and annuities, including rollovers. Total received 17a
b Taxable amount, if any, from the worksheet on page 10 of Instructions 17b
18 Rents, royalties, partnerships, estates, trusts, etc. *(attach Schedule E)* 18
19 Farm income or (loss) *(attach Schedule F)* 19
20a Unemployment compensation (insurance). Total received . . . 20a
b Taxable amount, if any, from the worksheet on page 10 of Instructions 20b
21a Social security benefits. (see page 10 of Instructions) . . . 21a
b Taxable amount, if any, from the worksheet on page 11 of Instructions 21b
22 Other income (state nature and source—see page 11 of Instructions) 22
23 Add lines 7 through 22. This is your **total income** . . . . ▶ 23

Please attach check or money order here.

Adjustments to Income

(See Instructions on page 11.)

24 Moving expense *(attach Form 3903 or 3903F)* 24
25 Employee business expenses *(attach Form 2106)* 25
26a IRA deduction, from the worksheet on page 12 . . . . . . 26a
b Enter here IRA payments you made in 1985 that are included in line 26a above ▶
27 Payments to a Keogh *(H.R. 10)* retirement plan 27
28 Penalty on early withdrawal of savings 28
29 Alimony paid 29
30 Deduction for a married couple when both work *(attach Schedule W)* 30
31 Add lines 24 through 30. These are your **total adjustments** . . . . ▶ 31

Adjusted Gross Income

32 Subtract line 31 from line 23. *This is your* **adjusted gross income.** *If this line is less than $10,000, see "Earned Income Credit" (line 59) on page 16 of Instructions. If you want IRS to figure your tax, see page 12 of Instructions.* . . . . ▶ 32

Figure 16.1B U.S. Individual Income Tax Return, Form 1040

Form 1040 (1984) Page 2

Tax Computation

(See Instructions on page 13.)

33	Amount from line 32 (adjusted gross income)	33	
34a	If you itemize, attach Schedule A (Form 1040) and enter the amount from Schedule A, line 26	34a	
	Caution: If you have unearned income and can be claimed as a dependent on your parent's return, check here ▶ ☐ and see page 13 of the Instructions. Also see page 13 if: • You are married filing a separate return and your spouse itemizes deductions, OR • You file Form 4563, OR • You are a dual-status alien.		
34b	If you do not itemize deductions, and you have charitable contributions, complete the worksheet on page 14. Then enter the allowable part of your contributions here	34b	
35	Subtract line 34a or 34b, whichever applies, from line 33	35	
36	Multiply $1,000 by the total number of exemptions claimed on Form 1040, line 6e	36	
37	Taxable Income. Subtract line 36 from line 35	37	
38	Tax. Enter tax here and check if from ☐ Tax Table, ☐ Tax Rate Schedule X, Y, or Z, or ☐ Schedule G	38	
39	Additional Taxes. (See page 14 of Instructions.) Enter here and check if from ☐ Form 4970, ☐ Form 4972, or ☐ Form 5544	39	
40	Add lines 38 and 39. Enter the total ▶	40	

Credits

(See Instructions on page 14.)

41	Credit for child and dependent care expenses *(attach Form 2441)*	41		
42	Credit for the elderly and the permanently and totally disabled *(attach Schedule R)*	42		
43	Residential energy credit *(attach Form 5695)*	43		
44	Partial credit for political contributions for which you have receipts	44		
45	Add lines 41 through 44. These are your total personal credits		45	
46	Subtract line 45 from 40. Enter the result (but not less than zero)		46	
47	Foreign tax credit *(attach Form 1116)*	47		
48	General business credit. Check if from ☐ Form 3800, ☐ Form 3468, ☐ Form 5884, ☐ Form 6478	48		
49	Add lines 47 and 48. These are your total business and other credits		49	
50	Subtract line 49 from 46. Enter the result (but not less than zero). ▶		50	

Other Taxes

(Including Advance EIC Payments)

51	Self-employment tax *(attach Schedule SE)*	51	
52	Alternative minimum tax *(attach Form 6251)*	52	
53	Tax from recapture of investment credit *(attach Form 4255)*	53	
54	Social security tax on tip income not reported to employer *(attach Form 4137)*	54	
55	Tax on an IRA *(attach Form 5329)*	55	
56	Add lines 50 through 55. This is your **total tax** ▶	56	

Payments

Attach Forms W-2, W-2G, and W-2P to front.

57	Federal income tax withheld	57		
58	1984 estimated tax payments and amount applied from 1983 return	58		
59	Earned income credit. If line 33 is under $10,000, see page 16	59		
60	Amount paid with Form 4868	60		
61	Excess social security tax and RRTA tax withheld (two or more employers)	61		
62	Credit for Federal tax on gasoline and special fuels *(attach Form 4136)*	62		
63	Regulated Investment Company credit *(attach Form 2439)*	63		
64	Add lines 57 through 63. These are your **total payments** ▶		64	

Refund or Amount You Owe

65	If line 64 is larger than line 56, enter amount **OVERPAID** ▶		65	
66	Amount of line 65 to be **REFUNDED TO YOU** ▶		66	
67	Amount of line 65 to be applied to your 1985 estimated tax ▶	67		
68	If line 56 is larger than line 64, enter **AMOUNT YOU OWE.** Attach check or money order for full amount payable to "Internal Revenue Service." Write your social security number and "1984 Form 1040" on it ▶ (Check ▶ ☐ if Form 2210 (2210F) is attached. See page 17 of Instructions.) $		68	

Please Sign Here

Under penalties of perjury, I declare that I have examined this return and accompanying schedules and statements, and to the best of my knowledge and belief, they are true, correct, and complete. Declaration of preparer (other than taxpayer) is based on all information of which preparer has any knowledge.

▶ Your signature | Date | ▶ Spouse's signature (if filing jointly, BOTH must sign)

Paid Preparer's Use Only

Preparer's signature ▶	Date	Check if self-employed ☐	Preparer's social security no.
Firm's name (or yours, if self-employed) and address ▶		E.I. No.	
		ZIP code	

☆ U.S. G.P.O. 1984-423-075 23-188-5979

Figure 16.2 Schedule A, Itemized Deductions

SCHEDULES A&B (Form 1040)
Department of the Treasury Internal Revenue Service (O)

Schedule A—Itemized Deductions
(Schedule B is on back)
▶ Attach to Form 1040. ▶ See Instructions for Schedules A and B (Form 1040).

OMB No. 1545-0074
1984
07

Name(s) as shown on Form 1040 | Your social security number

Medical and Dental Expenses (Do not include expenses reimbursed or paid by others.) (See Instructions on page 19)	1	Prescription medicines and drugs; and insulin	1
	2 a	Doctors, dentists, nurses, hospitals, insurance premiums you paid for medical and dental care, etc.	2a
	b	Transportation and lodging	2b
	c	Other (list—include hearing aids, dentures, eyeglasses, etc.) ▶	2c
	3	Add lines 1 through 2c, and write the total here	3
	4	Multiply the amount on Form 1040, line 33, by 5% (.05)	4
	5	Subtract line 4 from line 3. If zero or less, write -0-. **Total** medical and dental ▶	5
Taxes You Paid (See Instructions on page 20)	6	State and local income taxes	6
	7	Real estate taxes	7
	8 a	General sales tax (see sales tax tables in instruction booklet)	8a
	b	General sales tax on motor vehicles	8b
	9	Other taxes (list—include personal property taxes) ▶	9
	10	Add the amounts on lines 6 through 9. Write the total here. **Total** taxes ▶	10
Interest You Paid (See Instructions on page 20)	11 a	Home mortgage interest you paid to financial institutions	11a
	b	Home mortgage interest you paid to individuals (show that person's name and address) ▶	11b
	12	Total credit card and charge account interest you paid	12
	13	Other interest you paid (list) ▶	13
	14	Add the amounts on lines 11a through 13. Write the total here. **Total** interest ▶	14
Contributions You Made (See Instructions on page 20)	15 a	Cash contributions. (If you gave $3,000 or more to any one organization, report those contributions on line 15b.)	15a
	b	Cash contributions totaling $3,000 or more to any one organization. (Show to whom you gave and how much you gave.) ▶	15b
	16	Other than cash (attach required statement)	16
	17	Carryover from prior year	17
	18	Add the amounts on lines 15a through 17. Write the total here. **Total** contributions ▶	18
Casualty and Theft Losses	19	Total casualty or theft loss(es). (You must attach Form 4684 or similar statement.) (see page 21 of Instructions) ▶	19
Miscellaneous Deductions (See Instructions on page 21)	20	Union and professional dues	20
	21	Tax return preparation fee	21
	22	Other (list type and amount) ▶	22
	23	Add the amounts on lines 20 through 22. Write the total here. **Total** miscellaneous ▶	23
Summary of Itemized Deductions (See Instructions on page 22)	24	Add the amounts on lines 5, 10, 14, 18, 19, and 23. Write your answer here.	24
	25	If you checked Form 1040 { Filing Status box 2 or 5, write $3,400; Filing Status box 1 or 4, write $2,300; Filing Status box 3, write $1,700 }	25
	26	Subtract line 25 from line 24. Write your answer here and on Form 1040, line 34a. (If line 25 is more than line 24, see the Instructions for line 26 on page 22.) ▶	26

For Paperwork Reduction Act Notice, see Form 1040 Instructions. Schedule A (Form 1040) 1984

These forms involve many tedious and interdependent computations. Occasionally, an omitted item necessitates recalculating all or most of the tax return. The template shown in Figures 16.3 and 16.4 removes the tedium associated with annual tax filing.[1] Figure 16.3 is equivalent to Form 1040 and Schedule A. Figure 16.4 contains Tax Rate Schedules X, Y, and Z.

1. These tax examples reflect federal requirements for the filing of 1984 returns. There may be variations in subsequent years.

Figure 16.3 IRS Form 1040: Template

```
    :         A          ::  B  ::  C  ::  D  ::  E  ::  F  ::  G  ::  H  :
 1  IRS FORM 1040: 1984
 2  NAME:
 3  ADDRESS:
 4
 5
 6  YOUR SOCIAL SECURITY NUMBER
 7  SPOUSE'S SOCIAL SECURITY NUMBER
 8
 9  YOUR OCCUPATION
10  SPOUSE'S OCCUPATION
11
12  FILING STATUS:                                   0
13                                              1: SINGLE
14                                              2: MARRIED, FILING JOINTLY
15                                              3: MARRIED, FILING SEPARATELY
16                                              4: HEAD OF HOUSEHOLD
17                                              5: QUALIFYING WIDOW(ER)
18
19  NO. OF EXEMPTIONS:                               0
20
21  WAGES & SALARIES                                          .00
22  INTEREST INCOME                                           .00
23  DIVIDEND INCOME                                .00
24  DIVIDEND EXCLUSION                          100.00
25  REPORTABLE DIVIDENDS                                      .00
26  STATE & LOCAL TAX REFUNDS FROM PRIOR YEARS                .00
27  ALIMONY RECEIVED                                          .00
28  BUSINESS INCOME OR (LOSS)                                 .00
29  CAPITAL GAIN OR (LOSS)                                    .00
30  40% OF CAPITAL GAIN DISTRIBUTIONS NOT REPORTED ABOVE      .00
31  SUPPLEMENTAL GAIN OR (LOSS)                               .00
32  FULLY TAXABLE PENSIONS & IRA DISTRIBUTIONS                .00
33  OTHER PENSIONS & ANNUITIES, INCLUDING ROLLOVERS           .00
34  RENTS & ROYALTIES                                         .00
35  FARM INCOME OR (LOSS)                                     .00
36  UNEMPLOYMENT COMPENSATION                                 .00
37  SOCIAL SECURITY BENEFITS                                  .00
38  OTHER INCOME
39                                                            .00
40                                                      ---------
41     TOTAL GROSS INCOME                                                  .00
42
43  ADJUSTMENTS TO INCOME
44   MOVING EXPENSES                                          .00
45   EMPLOYEE BUSINESS EXPENSES                               .00
46   IRA DEDUCTION                                            .00
47   KEOUGH PLAN PAYMENTS                                     .00
48   PENALTY ON EARLY WITHDRAWAL OF SAVINGS                   .00
49   ALIMONY PAID                                             .00
50   DEDUCTION FOR A MARRIED COUPLE WHEN BOTH WORK            .00
51                                                      ---------
52  TOTAL ADJUSTMENTS                                                      .00
53                                                                   ---------
54  ADJUSTED GROSS INCOME                                                  .00
55  LESS: NET ITEMIZED DEDUCTIONS                             .00
56  LESS: CHARITABLE DEDUCTIONS IF NOT ITEMIZING              .00
57                                                      ---------
58  SUB TOTAL                                                              .00
59  MULTIPLY EXEMPTIONS BY $1,000                                          .00
60                                                                   ---------
61  TAXABLE INCOME                                                         .00
62
63  TAX PER SCHEDULES X, Y, Z                                              N/A
64  ADDITIONAL TAXES FORM 4970, 4972, OR 5544                              .00
65                                                                   ---------
66     TOTAL                                                               N/A
67
68  PERSONAL CREDITS
69   CREDIT FOR CHILD & DEPENDENT CARE                        .00
70   CREDIT FOR THE ELDERLY & PERMANENTLY DISABLED            .00
71   RESIDENTIAL ENERGY                                       .00
```

(continued on next page)

```
  POLITICAL CONTRIBUTIONS, PARTIAL CREDIT                   .00
                                                      ---------
    TOTAL PERSONAL CREDITS                                                  .00
                                                                      ---------
    TAX BALANCE AFTER PERSONAL CREDITS                                      N/A
 BUSINESS CREDITS
  FOREIGN TAX CREDIT                                        .00
  GENERAL BUSINESS CREDIT                                   .00
                                                      ---------
    TOTAL BUSINESS CREDITS                                                  .00
                                                                      ---------
    TAX BALANCE AFTER BUSINESS CREDITS                                      N/A

 OTHER TAXES
  SELF-EMPLOYMENT TAX                                       .00
  ALTERNATIVE MINIMUM TAX                                   .00
  INVESTMENT CREDIT RECAPTURE                               .00
  SOCIAL SECURITY TIP INCOME                                .00
  TAX ON IRA                                                .00
                                                      ---------
 TOTAL TAXES                                                                .00

 PAYMENTS
  FEDERAL INCOME TAX WITHHELD                               .00
  ESTIMATED TAX PAYMENTS                                    .00
  EARNED INCOME CREDIT                                      .00
  AMOUNT PAID FORM 4868                                     .00
  EXCESS SOCIAL SECURITY TAX                                .00
  TAX CREDIT ON SPECIAL FUELS                               .00
  REGULATED INVESTMENT COMPANY CREDIT                       .00
                                                      ---------
  TOTAL PAYMENTS                                                            .00

TAXES OVERPAID                                                              .00
TAXES DUE                                                                   N/A


IRS SCHEDULE A: 1984

MEDICAL & DENTAL EXPENSES
-------------------------
MEDICINES & DRUGS                                           .00
DRS, HOSPTLS, INSURANCE                                     .00
TRANSPORTATION & LODGING                                    .00
OTHER
                                                            .00
                                                            .00
                                                      ---------
SUBTOTAL                                                    .00
5% AGI                                                      .00
                                                      ---------
MEDICAL DEDUCTION                                                     .00

TAXES
-----
 STATE INCOME TAX                                 .00
 CITY WAGE TAX                                    .00
                                          ---------
STATE & LOCAL                                               .00
REAL ESTATE                                                 .00
SALES TAX - TABLES                                          .00
SALES TAX - AUTOS                                           .00
OTHER
 TOWNSHIP OCCUPATION TAX                                    .00
 COUNTY PERSONAL PROPERTY TAX                               .00
                                                      ---------
TOTAL TAXES                                                           .00

INTEREST EXPENSE
----------------
HOME MORTGAGE INTEREST TO FINANCIAL INSTITUTIONS            .00
HOME MORTGAGE INTEREST TO INDIVIDUALS                       .00
CREDIT CARDS & CHARGE ACCOUNTS                              .00
```

(continued on next page)

```
145 OTHER
146                                                        .00
147                                                        .00
148                                                        .00
149                                                        .00
150                                                  ---------
151 TOTAL INTEREST                                                      .00
152
153 CONTRIBUTIONS
154 -------------
155 CASH                                                   .00
156 NON-CASH                                               .00
157 PRIOR YEAR CARRYOVER                                   .00
158                                                  ---------
159 TOTAL CONTRIBUTIONS                                                 .00
160
161 MISCELLANEOUS
162 -------------
163 UNION & PROFESSIONAL DUES                              .00
164 TAX RETURN PREPARATION FEES                            .00
165 OTHER
166                                                        .00
167                                                        .00
168                                                        .00
169                                                        .00
170                                                        .00
171                                                        .00
172                                                  ---------
173 TOTAL MISCELLANEOUS                                                 .00
174
175 TOTAL ITEMIZED DEDUCTIONS                                                    .00
176 LESS: STANDARD DEDUCTION                                                     .00
177                                                                        ---------
178 NET ITEMIZED DEDUCTIONS                                                      .00
179
180
```

Figure 16.4 Tax Rate Schedules X, Y, and Z: Template

```
    |  J  ||  K  ||  L  ||  M  ||  N  ||  O  ||  P  ||  Q  |
1
2   1984 TAX RATE SCHEDULES
3
4   ENTER TAXABLE INCOME (FORM 1040 LINE 37):                  .00
5
6           BASE TAX                                           N/A
7           EXCESS INCOME                              N/A
8           TAX ON EXCESS INCOME                               N/A
9           BASE TAX                                     ---------
10          INCOME TAX LIABILITY                               N/A
11                                                       =========
12
13
14  SCHEDULE X: SINGLE TAX PAYERS
15  -----------------------------
16  BASE INCOME BRACKET                                   TAX RATE
17     TAXABLE INCOME         TABLE     BASE TAX      TABLE  ON EXCESS
18      NOT LESS THAN        POINTERS     AMOUNT     POINTERS   INCOME
19
20          0        0              0          0          0        0%
21      2,300    2,300          2,300          0      2,300       11%
22      3,400    3,400          3,400        121      3,400       12%
23      4,400    4,400          4,400        241      4,400       14%
24      6,500    6,500          6,500        535      6,500       15%
25      8,500    8,500          8,500        835      8,500       16%
26     10,800   10,800         10,800      1,203     10,800       18%
27     12,900   12,900         12,900      1,581     12,900       20%
28     15,000   15,000         15,000      2,001     15,000       23%
```

(continued on next page)

```
    18,200   18,200          18,200      2,737           18,200      26%
    23,500   23,500          23,500      4,115           23,500      30%
    28,800   28,800          28,800      5,705           28,800      34%
    34,100   34,100          34,100      7,507           34,100      38%
    41,500   41,500          41,500     10,319           41,500      42%
    55,300   55,300          55,300     16,115           55,300      48%
    81,800   81,800          81,800     28,835           81,800      50%

SCHEDULE Y: MARRIED TAX PAYERS FILING JOINTLY AND QUALIFYING WIDOW(ER)S
----------------------------------------------------------------------
BASE INCOME BRACKET                                             TAX RATE
   TAXABLE INCOME          TABLE       BASE TAX       TABLE    ON EXCESS
    NOT LESS THAN          POINTERS      AMOUNT       POINTERS    INCOME

         0        0               0          0                0       0%
     3,400    3,400           3,400          0            3,400      11%
     5,500    5,500           5,500        231            5,500      12%
     7,600    7,600           7,600        483            7,600      14%
    11,900   11,900          11,900      1,065           11,900      16%
    16,000   16,000          16,000      1,741           16,000      18%
    20,200   20,200          20,200      2,497           20,200      22%
    24,600   24,600          24,600      3,465           24,600      25%
    29,900   29,900          29,900      4,790           29,900      28%
    35,200   35,200          35,200      6,274           35,200      33%
    45,800   45,800          45,800      9,772           45,800      38%
    60,000   60,000          60,000     15,168           60,000      42%
    85,600   85,600          85,600     25,920           85,600      45%
   109,400  109,400         109,400     36,630          109,400      49%
   162,400  162,400         162,400     62,600          109,400      50%

SCHEDULE Y: MARRIED TAX PAYERS FILING SEPARATELY
------------------------------------------------
BASE INCOME BRACKET                                             TAX RATE
   TAXABLE INCOME          TABLE       BASE TAX       TABLE    ON EXCESS
    NOT LESS THAN          POINTERS      AMOUNT       POINTERS    INCOME

         0        0               0        .00                0       0%
     1,700    1,700           1,700        .00            1,700      11%
     2,750    2,750           2,750     115.50            2,750      12%
     3,800    3,800           3,800     241.50            3,800      14%
     5,950    5,950           5,950     542.50            5,950      16%
     8,000    8,000           8,000     870.50            8,000      18%
    10,100   10,100          10,100   1,248.50           10,100      22%
    12,300   12,300          12,300   1,732.50           12.300      25%
    14,950   14,950          14,950   2,395.00           14,950      28%
    17,600   17,600          17,600   3,137.00           17,600      33%
    22,900   22,900          22,900   4,886.00           22,900      38%
    30,000   30,000          30,000   7,584.00           30,000      42%
    42,800   42,800          42,800  12,960.00           42,800      45%
    54,700   54,700          54,700  18,315.00           54,700      49%
    81,200   81,200          81,200  31,300.00           81,200      50%

SCHEDULE Z: HEADS OF HOUSEHOLD
------------------------------
BASE INCOME BRACKET                                             TAX RATE
   TAXABLE INCOME          TABLE       BASE TAX       TABLE    ON EXCESS
    NOT LESS THAN          POINTERS      AMOUNT       POINTERS    INCOME

         0        0               0          0                0       0%
     2,300    2,300           2,300          0            2,300      11%
     4,400    4,400           4,400        231            4,400      12%
     6,500    6,500           6,500        483            6,500      14%
     8,700    8,700           8,700        791            8,700      17%
    11,800   11,800          11,800      1,318           11,800      18%
    15,000   15,000          15,000      1,894           15,000      20%
    18,200   18,200          18,200      2,534           18,200      24%
    23,500   23,500          23,500      3,806           23,500      28%
    28,800   28,800          28,800      5,290           28,800      32%
    34,100   34,100          34,100      6,986           34,100      35%
    44,700   44,700          44,700     10,696           44,700      42%
    60,600   60,600          60,600     17,374           60,600      45%
    81,800   81,800          81,800     26,914           81,800      48%
   108,300  108,300         108,300     39,634          108,300      50%
```

The following hypothetical tax data produced the results shown in Figures 16.5 and 16.6 (see pp. 334-337).

Taxpayer Name:	John Doe
Taxpayer Address:	943 Cactus Court Maple Glen, PA 19038
Taxpayer Social Security No.:	123-45-6789
Marital Status:	Married. This determines the Filing Status of 2, entered in cell D12.
Spouse Name:	Jane Doe
Spouse Address:	Same as taxpayer
Spouse Social Security No.:	234-99-9876

Exemption and Dependent Information

Taxpayer date of birth: 10/10/1916 (extra exemption for over 65).

Spouse date of birth: 05/24/1918 (extra exemption for over 65).

Note: Mrs. Doe has been blind since birth, which gives her another exemption. The Does have 3 non-working, teenage children living at home. The children are fully supported by their parents. Mr. Doe is the sole support of his family. This is the basis for the entry of 8 in cell D19.

Income Information

John Doe is a systems consultant for Mainframe Computers, Inc., Suburbia, PA. He earned wages of $37,800 there in 1984. Federal Income Tax Withholding amounted to $4,500 and social security (FICA) withholding amounted to $2,532.60. John also teaches computer science in the evening division at Germantown University in Philadelphia. He earned $8,500 there in 1984. Federal Income Tax Withholding amounted to $500 and social security (FICA) withholding amounted to $569.50. He drives 15 miles from his primary place of employment to his teaching job. This trip is made twice a week for the 38 weeks covered by the Spring, Summer, and Fall terms.

The social security (FICA) tax is limited to $2,532.60. Employees with two jobs may be eligible for a refund if their FICA withholdings have exceeded $2,532.60. See 1040 line 61. This information is the basis for the following entries:

cell E21: **37800 + 8500**
cell E45: **2*38*15*0.205**
cell E99: **IF(E21>37800,ROUND(6.7%E21,2) − 2532.60,2)**
cell D127: **ROUND(2.45%G54,2)**
cell D128: **ROUND(4.3125%8500,2)**
cell E95: **4500 + 500**

During the year, John made two stock purchases:
75 shares @ $36.50 per share
100 shares @ $44.50 per share

On 12/30/84, John sold all his shares @ $43.75 each and incurred brokerage fees of $200 on the sale. The net gain from these transactions is reported on line 13 of Form 1040. This information is the basis for the cell E29 entry of

(175*43.75) − 200 − (75*36.50 + 100*44.50)

John contracted with a major New York publisher to write a book about electronic spreadsheets. He got a royalty advance of $5,000 in 1984.

John and his wife received $100 in dividends from their stock shares.

The Does received $1,200 in interest from their passbook savings and money market accounts.

John earned $100 of other income doing a partnership tax return for his cousin's business.

Adjustments to Income

Expenses of traveling from the primary place of employment to a second job are deductible as a business expense (1040 line 24) at the rate of $0.205 per mile. See cell E45 in Figure A.1 (page 376).

John paid $3,000 in alimony to his first wife.

John paid $2,250 into IRA accounts for himself and his current wife.

The Does prematurely redeemed a Certificate of Deposit (CD) and were subject to an early redemption penalty of $250.

Expense Deduction Information

Medical

The Does spent $200 on medicines and drugs that was not covered by medical insurance. Their medical insurance premiums amounted to $500. Their plan pays 85% of covered expenses after an annual family deductible of $300. John and his family had covered expenses of $12,500. They also had the following non-covered expenses:

Eyeglasses for John and child #1	$150
Hearing aid for John	450
Dental care	850
Eye examinations	80

They traveled 2,400 miles during 1984 to secure medical services. Their medical transportation deduction is calculated at the rate of 9 cents per mile. This information is the basis for the following entries:

cell E113: **200**

cell E114: **ROUND(300+15%12200+500+850+80,2)**

cell E115: **ROUND(2400*0.09,2)**

State and Local Taxes

The Pennsylvania Income Tax rate is 2.45% on the Adjusted Gross Income. See cell D127 in Figure B.1. The Philadelphia City Wage Tax rate is 4.3125% on John's teaching income earned in Philadelphia. See cell D128 in Figure A.1.

The Does paid real estate taxes of $1,500. They paid a county personal property tax of $50. John paid an occupational privilege of $10 to the township where he works full time.

John bought a new car in 1984 and paid sales taxes of $300. The Optional State Sales Tax Tables, contained in the Form 1040 instruction booklet, were used to determine the Pennsylvania sales tax deduction.

Interest Expense

The Does paid interest as follows:

Home mortgage held by the bank	$6,532.89
Credit card purchases	653.58
Auto loan #1	425.53
Auto loan #2	482.92
Student loan	53.98
Home improvement loan	317.46

Charitable Contributions

John gave $1,500 to his church and school and donated old clothes worth $300 to Goodwill.

Miscellaneous

John spent $50 in 1984 to have his 1983 tax return prepared. He subscribes to *Byte, Creative Computing,* and *Personal Computing*. These subscriptions cost $66. John incurred business telephone expenses of $300.

John has an Apple II computer system and elected to take the following deductions:

1. Second year depreciation on the capitalized basis of $4,000.
2. Fully expense new hardware acquired in 1984:

Printer	$500
1200 baud modem	500

3. Supplies expense for 1984:

Disks	$100
Printer ribbons	30
Repairs & parts	50

Assets placed in service after 01-01-82 must be depreciated under the Accelerated Cost Recovery System (ACRS). Under ACRS, computer systems have a depreciable life of 5 years and are depreciated as follows:

year #1 depreciation expense = 15% of basis
year #2 depreciation expense = 22% of basis
year #3 depreciation expense = 21% of basis
year #4 depreciation expense = 21% of basis
year #5 depreciation expense = 21% of basis

Assets up to $5,000 may be fully expensed in the year of acquisition if they are used for business purposes.

This information is the basis for the cell E171 entry of

ROUND(22%4000+500+500,2)

The tax liability shown in cell G63 is determined through a lookup of the tax rate schedules contained in cells J1 through Q101 of the template. The parameters used for this are the Filing Status, cell D12, and the Taxable Income, cell G61. Although this template uses Schedules X, Y, and Z for computational efficiency, IRS regulations require most taxpayers to use the tax tables contained in the Form 1040 instruction booklet. The tax rate lookup and automated tax calculation can be overridden by using only cells A1 through G178. The tax liability can be gotten from the tax tables in the Form 1040 instruction booklet, then entered in cell G63.

Figure 16.5 IRS Form 1040: Completed Spreadsheet

```
   :            A            :: B ::  C :: D :: E :: F ::   G  :: H :
 1  IRS FORM 1040: 1984
 2  NAME:                    John & Jane Doe
 3  ADDRESS:                 943 Cactus Court
 4                           Maple Glen, PA 19038
 5
 6  YOUR SOCIAL SECURITY NUMBER         123-45-6789
 7  SPOUSE'S SOCIAL SECURITY NUMBER     234-99-9876
 8
 9  YOUR OCCUPATION          Systems Consultant
10  SPOUSE'S OCCUPATION      Housewife
11
12  FILING STATUS:                                   2
13                                            1: SINGLE
14                                            2: MARRIED, FILING JOINTLY
15                                            3: MARRIED, FILING SEPARATELY
16                                            4: HEAD OF HOUSEHOLD
17                                            5: QUALIFYING WIDOW(ER)
18
19  NO. OF EXEMPTIONS:                               8
20
21  WAGES & SALARIES                                  46,300.00
22  INTEREST INCOME                                    1,200.00
23  DIVIDE[illegible]                          100.00
24  DIVID[illegible]                           200.00
25  REPOR[illegible]                                        .00
26  STATE & [illegible]NDS FROM PRIOR YEARS                 .00
27  ALIMONY RECEIV[illegible]                               .00
28  BUSINESS INCOME OR (LOSS)                               .00
29  CAPITAL GAIN OR (LOSS)                               268.75
30  40% OF CAPITAL GAIN DISTRIBUTIONS NOT REPORTED ABOVE    .00
31  SUPPLEMENTAL GAIN OR (LOSS)                             .00
32  FULLY TAXABLE PENSIONS & IRA DISTRIBUTIONS              .00
33  OTHER PENSIONS & ANNUITIES, INCLUDING ROLLOVERS         .00
34  RENTS & ROYALTIES                                  5,000.00
35  FARM INCOME OR (LOSS)                                   .00
36  UNEMPLOYMENT COMPENSATION                               .00
37  SOCIAL SECURITY BENEFITS                                .00
38  OTHER INCOME
39     Partnership tax return preparation                100.00
40                                                    ---------
41     TOTAL GROSS INCOME                                           52,868.75
42
43  ADJUSTMENTS TO INCOME
44   MOVING EXPENSES                                        .00
45   EMPLOYEE BUSINESS EXPENSES                          233.70
46   IRA DEDUCTION                                     2,250.00
47   KEOUGH PLAN PAYMENTS                                   .00
48   PENALTY ON EARLY WITHDRAWAL OF SAVINGS              250.00
49   ALIMONY PAID                                      3,000.00
50   DEDUCTION FOR A MARRIED COUPLE WHEN BOTH WORK          .00
51                                                    ---------
52  TOTAL ADJUSTMENTS                                                5,733.70
53                                                                  ---------
54  ADJUSTED GROSS INCOME                                           47,135.05
55  LESS: NET ITEMIZED DEDUCTIONS                     15,288.98
56  LESS: CHARITABLE DEDUCTIONS IF NOT ITEMIZING            .00
57                                                    ---------
58  SUB TOTAL                                                       31,846.07
59  MULTIPLY EXEMPTIONS BY $1,000                                    8,000.00
60                                                                  ---------
61  TAXABLE INCOME                                                  23,846.07
62
63  TAX PER SCHEDULES X, Y, Z                                        3,299.14
64  ADDITIONAL TAXES FORM 4970, 4972, OR 5544                             .00
65                                                                  ---------
66     TOTAL                                                         3,299.14
67
68  PERSONAL CREDITS
69   CREDIT FOR CHILD & DEPENDENT CARE                      .00
70   CREDIT FOR THE ELDERLY & PERMANENTLY DISABLED          .00
71   RESIDENTIAL ENERGY                                     .00
72   POLITICAL CONTRIBUTIONS, PARTIAL CREDIT                .00
```

(continued on next page)

```
73                                                          ---------
74    TOTAL PERSONAL CREDITS                                                                .00
75                                                                                    ---------
76    TAX BALANCE AFTER PERSONAL CREDITS                                               3,299.14
77  BUSINESS CREDITS
78   FOREIGN TAX CREDIT                                           .00
79   GENERAL BUSINESS CREDIT                                      .00
80                                                          ---------
81    TOTAL BUSINESS CREDITS                                                                .00
82                                                                                    ---------
83    TAX BALANCE AFTER BUSINESS CREDITS                                               3,299.14
84
85  OTHER TAXES
86   SELF-EMPLOYMENT TAX                                          .00
87   ALTERNATIVE MINIMUM TAX                                      .00
88   INVESTMENT CREDIT RECAPTURE                                  .00
89   SOCIAL SECURITY TIP INCOME                                   .00
90   TAX ON IRA                                                   .00
91                                                          ---------
92  TOTAL TAXES                                                                        3,299.14
93
94  PAYMENTS
95   FEDERAL INCOME TAX WITHHELD                             5,000.00
96   ESTIMATED TAX PAYMENTS                                       .00
97   EARNED INCOME CREDIT                                         .00
98   AMOUNT PAID FORM 4868                                        .00
99   EXCESS SOCIAL SECURITY TAX                                569.50
100  TAX CREDIT ON SPECIAL FUELS                                  .00
101  REGULATED INVESTMENT COMPANY CREDIT                          .00
102                                                         ---------
103  TOTAL PAYMENTS                                                                    5,569.50
104
105 TAXES OVERPAID                                                                     2,270.36
106 TAXES DUE                                                                               N/A
107
108
109 IRS SCHEDULE A: 1984
110
111 MEDICAL & DENTAL EXPENSES
112 -------------------------
113 MEDICINES & DRUGS                                          200.00
114 DRS, HOSPTLS, INSURANCE                                  3,560.00
115 TRANSPORTATION & LODGING                                   216.00
116 OTHER
117  Eye glasses                                               150.00
118  Hearing aid                                               450.00
119                                                         ---------
120 SUBTOTAL                                                 4,576.00
121 5% AGI                                                   2,356.75
122                                                         ---------
123 MEDICAL DEDUCTION                                                      2,219.25
124
125 TAXES
126 -----
127  STATE INCOME TAX                             1,154.81
128  CITY WAGE TAX                                  366.56
129                                              ---------
130 STATE & LOCAL                                            1,521.37
131 REAL ESTATE                                              1,500.00
132 SALES TAX - TABLES                                         346.00
133 SALES TAX - AUTOS                                          300.00
134 OTHER
135  TOWNSHIP OCCUPATION TAX                                    10.00
136  COUNTY PERSONAL PROPERTY TAX                               50.00
137                                                         ---------
138 TOTAL TAXES                                                            3,727.37
139
140 INTEREST EXPENSE
141 ----------------
142 HOME MORTGAGE INTEREST TO FINANCIAL INSTITUTIONS         6,532.89
143 HOME MORTGAGE INTEREST TO INDIVIDUALS                         .00
144 CREDIT CARDS & CHARGE ACCOUNTS                             653.58
145 OTHER
```

(continued on next page)

```
146  Auto loan #1                                   425.53
147  Auto loan #2                                   482.92
148  Student loan                                    53.98
149  Home improvement loan                          317.46
150                                              ---------
151 TOTAL INTEREST                                          8,466.36
152
153 CONTRIBUTIONS
154 -------------
155 CASH                                          1,500.00
156 NON-CASH                                        300.00
157 PRIOR YEAR CARRYOVER                               .00
158                                              ---------
159 TOTAL CONTRIBUTIONS                                     1,800.00
160
161 MISCELLANEOUS
162 -------------
163 UNION & PROFESSIONAL DUES                          .00
164 TAX RETURN PREPARATION FEES                      50.00
165 OTHER
166  Professional journals                           66.00
167  Business telephone                             300.00
168  Floppy disks                                   100.00
169  Printer ribbons                                 30.00
170  Computer repairs & parts                        50.00
171  Computer system depreciation                 1,880.00
172                                              ---------
173 TOTAL MISCELLANEOUS                                     2,476.00
174
175 TOTAL ITEMIZED DEDUCTIONS                                          18,600.98
176 LESS: STANDARD DEDUCTION                                            3,400.00
177                                                                    ---------
178 NET ITEMIZED DEDUCTIONS                                            15,200.98
```

Figure 16.6 Tax Rate Schedules X, Y, and Z: Completed Spreadsheet

```
    ¦ J ¦¦ K ¦¦ L ¦¦ M ¦¦   N   ¦¦ O ¦¦ P ¦¦    Q   ¦
1
2   1984 TAX RATE SCHEDULES
3
4   ENTER TAXABLE INCOME (FORM 1040 LINE 37):               23,846.07
5
6          BASE TAX                                          2,497.00
7          EXCESS INCOME                           3646.07
8          TAX ON EXCESS INCOME                                802.14
9          BASE TAX                                      ------------
10         INCOME TAX LIABILITY                              3,299.14
11                                                       ============
12
13
14  SCHEDULE X: SINGLE TAX PAYERS
15  -----------------------------
16  BASE INCOME BRACKET                                      TAX RATE
17     TAXABLE INCOME       TABLE      BASE TAX      TABLE  ON EXCESS
18     NOT LESS THAN      POINTERS      AMOUNT     POINTERS    INCOME
19
20          0       0            0           0           0        0%
21      2,300   2,300        2,300           0       2,300       11%
22      3,400   3,400        3,400         121       3,400       12%
23      4,400   4,400        4,400         241       4,400       14%
24      6,500   6,500        6,500         535       6,500       15%
25      8,500   8,500        8,500         835       8,500       16%
26     10,800  10,800       10,800       1,203      10,800       18%
```

(continued on next page)

```
27    12,900  12,900         12,900     1,581        12,900        20%
28    15,000  15,000         15,000     2,001        15,000        23%
29    18,200  18,200         18,200     2,737        18,200        26%
30    23,500  23,500         23,500     4,115        23,500        30%
31    28,800  28,800         28,800     5,705        28,800        34%
32    34,100  34,100         34,100     7,507        34,100        38%
33    41,500  41,500         41,500    10,319        41,500        42%
34    55,300  55,300         55,300    16,115        55,300        48%
35    81,800  81,800         81,800    28,835        81,800        50%
36
37  SCHEDULE Y: MARRIED TAX PAYERS FILING JOINTLY AND QUALIFYING WIDOW(ER)S
38  ------------------------------------------------------------------------
39  BASE INCOME BRACKET                                           TAX RATE
40     TAXABLE INCOME        TABLE     BASE TAX       TABLE     ON EXCESS
41      NOT LESS THAN      POINTERS     AMOUNT      POINTERS      INCOME
42
43         0       0              0         0             0         0%
44     3,400   3,400          3,400         0         3,400        11%
45     5,500   5,500          5,500       231         5,500        12%
46     7,600   7,600          7,600       483         7,600        14%
47    11,900  11,900         11,900     1,085        11,900        16%
48    16,000  16,000         16,000     1,741        16,000        18%
49    20,200  20,200         20,200     2,497        20,200        22%
50    24,600  24,600         24,600     3,465        24,600        25%
51    29,900  29,900         29,900     4,790        29,900        28%
52    35,200  35,200         35,200     6,274        35,200        33%
53    45,800  45,800         45,800     9,772        45,800        38%
54    60,000  60,000         60,000    15,168        60,000        42%
55    85,600  85,600         85,600    25,920        85,600        45%
56   109,400 109,400        109,400    36,630       109,400        49%
57   162,400 162,400        162,400    62,600       109,400        50%
58
59  SCHEDULE Y: MARRIED TAX PAYERS FILING SEPARATELY
60  ------------------------------------------------
61  BASE INCOME BRACKET                                           TAX RATE
62     TAXABLE INCOME        TABLE     BASE TAX       TABLE     ON EXCESS
63      NOT LESS THAN      POINTERS     AMOUNT      POINTERS      INCOME
64
65         0       0              0       .00             0         0%
66     1,700   1,700          1,700       .00         1,700        11%
67     2,750   2,750          2,750    115.50         2,750        12%
68     3,800   3,800          3,800    241.50         3,800        14%
69     5,950   5,950          5,950    542.50         5,950        16%
70     8,000   8,000          8,000    870.50         8,000        18%
71    10,100  10,100         10,100  1,248.50        10,100        22%
72    12,300  12,300         12,300  1,732.50        12,300        25%
73    14,950  14,950         14,950  2,395.00        14,950        28%
74    17,600  17,600         17,600  3,137.00        17,600        33%
75    22,900  22,900         22,900  4,886.00        22,900        38%
76    30,000  30,000         30,000  7,584.00        30,000        42%
77    42,800  42,800         42,800 12,960.00        42,800        45%
78    54,700  54,700         54,700 18,315.00        54,700        49%
79    81,200  81,200         81,200 31,300.00        81,200        50%
80
81  SCHEDULE Z: HEADS OF HOUSEHOLD
82  ------------------------------
83  BASE INCOME BRACKET                                           TAX RATE
84     TAXABLE INCOME        TABLE     BASE TAX       TABLE     ON EXCESS
85      NOT LESS THAN      POINTERS     AMOUNT      POINTERS      INCOME
86
87         0       0              0         0             0         0%
88     2,300   2,300          2,300         0         2,300        11%
89     4,400   4,400          4,400       231         4,400        12%
90     6,500   6,500          6,500       483         6,500        14%
91     8,700   8,700          8,700       791         8,700        17%
92    11,800  11,800         11,800     1,318        11,800        18%
93    15,000  15,000         15,000     1,894        15,000        20%
94    18,200  18,200         18,200     2,534        18,200        24%
95    23,500  23,500         23,500     3,806        23,500        28%
96    28,800  28,800         28,800     5,290        28,800        32%
97    34,100  34,100         34,100     6,986        34,100        35%
98    44,700  44,700         44,700    10,696        44,700        42%
99    60,600  60,600         60,600    17,374        60,600        45%
100   81,800  81,800         81,800    26,914        81,800        48%
101  108,300 108,300        108,300    39,634       108,300        50%
```

A Capital Budgeting Application

In many business organizations, capital acquisitions such as plant machinery and office equipment must be financially justified. This justification process is called cost-benefit analysis. It involves comparing a proposed asset's acquisition and operating costs against the estimated savings the asset is expected to generate.

Such a study also takes into consideration the time-value of money. Cash inflows, savings, and cash outflows for future periods are discounted to present period dollars. The sum of the initial cash outlay plus the future periodic net cash flows is the net present value for the proposed asset. The acceptance or rejection of the proposal hinges on whether or not the net present value is zero or greater. Although the net present value represents the bottom line of the investment decision, its reliability is directly dependent upon the accuracy of the cash flow projections. Figure 16.7 shows a capital budgeting template structured for equipment investment decisions.

Figure 16.7 Capital Budgeting: Template

```
     :           A          ::    B    ::    C    ::    D    ::    E    ::    F    :
1    CAPITAL BUDGETING: COST-BENEFIT ANALYSIS
2    ----------------------------------------
3    PROPOSED ASSET                                    DISCOUNT RATE:           .000000
4    COMPONENT                            COST
5    -----------------------------------------
6                                            0
7                                            0
8                                            0
9                                            0
10                                           0
11                                           0
12   -----------------------------------------
13       TOTAL                               0
14
15   PERIODIC CASH INFLOWS          YEAR #1   YEAR #2   YEAR #3   YEAR #4   YEAR #5
16   ----------------------------------------------------------------------------
17   LABOR SAVINGS                        0         0         0         0         0
18   DEPRECIATION                         0         0         0         0         0
19   ----------------------------------------------------------------------------
20     TOTAL                              0         0         0         0         0
21
22   PERIODIC CASH OUTFLOWS         YEAR #1   YEAR #2   YEAR #3   YEAR #4   YEAR #5
23   ----------------------------------------------------------------------------
24   SUPPLIES                             0         0         0         0         0
25   INSURANCE                            0         0         0         0         0
26   MAINTENANCE                          0         0         0         0         0
27   ELECTRICITY                          0         0         0         0         0
28   ----------------------------------------------------------------------------
29     TOTAL                              0         0         0         0         0
30
31   NET PRESENT VALUE                         DISCOUNT       NET   DISCNTED
32   COMPUTATIONS                   PERIODS     FACTORS     FLOWS      FLOWS
33                             ----------------------------------------------
34                                        0    1.000000         0          0
35                                        1    1.000000         0          0
36                                        2    1.000000         0          0
37                                        3    1.000000         0          0
38                                        4    1.000000         0          0
39                                        5    1.000000         0          0
40                                                               -------
41   MANUALLY COMPUTED NPV                                                 0
42                                                               =======
43
44   NPV FUNCTION                                                          0
45                                                               =======
46
47
48   RECOMMENDATION:
49   PROJECT SHOULD BE          ACCEPTED
50
51   INTERNAL RATE OF RETURN                                           ERROR
```

The financial data shown below presents a hypothetical case for the proposed acquisition of a Zenith Data Systems Personal Computer:

	Cost
ZDS ZF-151-52	$2,795
Memory Expansion to 640K	650
Dot-matrix printer	450
Daisy-wheel printer	3,000
10MB fixed disk	3,000
1200 baud modem	500

Other assumptions:

a. 15% discount rate over 5 years.

b. Cash inflows (savings):

Labor Savings:	year 1 $5,000
	year 2 $7,000
	year 3 $10,000
	year 4 $12,000
	year 5 $14,000
Depreciation:	year 1 15% of cost
	year 2 22% of cost
	year 3 21% of cost
	year 4 21% of cost
	year 5 21% of cost

c. Cash outflows (expenses):

Annual supplies costs:

30 boxes of invoices	@ $30
10 boxes of stock paper	@ $20
10 boxes of checks	@ $10
1,000 diskettes	@ $ 3

Insurance $300 per year

Electricity $500 per year

Maintenance:	year 1 $150
	year 2 $200
	year 3 $250
	year 4 $300
	year 5 $350

d. Periodic net cash flow = cash inflow for the period − cash outflow for the period

The spreadsheet in Figure 16.8 contains the results of the cost-benefit analysis with a net present value of $8,944.

In some situations, management may be more interested in the rate of return on investment rather than the absolute number expressed by the net present value. The desired relative value is called the internal rate of return. It is the discount rate that sets the net present value to zero. The entry in cell E51 of

ROUND(IRR(F3,D34:D39),6)

calculates an internal rate of return of 38.0978%.

Figure 16.8 Capital Budgeting: Completed Spreadsheet

```
    :              A               ::    B   ::     C    ::     D    ::     E    ::     F    :
1   CAPITAL BUDGETING: COST-BENEFIT ANALYSIS
2   ----------------------------------------------
3   PROPOSED ASSET                                      DISCOUNT RATE:                .150000
4   COMPONENT                            COST
5   ----------------------------------------
6   ZDS ZF-151-52                       2,795
7   MEMORY EXPANSION: 640K                650
8   DOT MATRIX PRINTER                    450
9   DAISY WHEEL PRINTER                 3,000
10  10MB FIXED DISK                     3,000
11  1200 BAUD MODEM                       500
12  ----------------------------------------
13      TOTAL                          10,395
14
15  PERIODIC CASH INFLOWS             YEAR #1    YEAR #2    YEAR #3    YEAR #4    YEAR #5
16  ---------------------------------------------------------------------------------------
17  LABOR SAVINGS                       5,000      7,000     10,000     12,000     14,000
18  DEPRECIATION                        1,559      2,287      2,183      2,183      2,183
19  ---------------------------------------------------------------------------------------
20     TOTAL                            6,559      9,287     12,183     14,183     16,183
21
22  PERIODIC CASH OUTFLOWS            YEAR #1    YEAR #2    YEAR #3    YEAR #4    YEAR #5
23  ---------------------------------------------------------------------------------------
24  SUPPLIES                            4,200      4,200      4,200      4,200      4,200
25  INSURANCE                             300        300        300        300        300
26  MAINTENANCE                           150        200        250        300        350
27  ELECTRICITY                           500        500        500        500        500
28  ---------------------------------------------------------------------------------------
29     TOTAL                            5,150      5,200      5,250      5,300      5,350
30
31  NET PRESENT VALUE                            DISCOUNT        NET   DISCNTED
32  COMPUTATIONS                      PERIODS     FACTORS      FLOWS      FLOWS
33                                ---------------------------------------------
34                                          0  1.000000    -10,395    -10,395
35                                          1   .869565      1,409      1,225
36                                          2   .756144      4,087      3,090
37                                          3   .657516      6,933      4,559
38                                          4   .571753      8,883      5,079
39                                          5   .497177     10,833      5,386
40                                                                    -------
41  MANUALLY COMPUTED NPV                                               8,944
42                                                                    =======
43
44  NPV FUNCTION                                                        8,944
45                                                                    =======
46
47
48  RECOMMENDATION:
49  PROJECT SHOULD BE              ACCEPTED
50
51  INTERNAL RATE OF RETURN                                          38.0978%
```

A Statement of Net Worth Application

Credit applications must be submitted for home mortgage, auto, or charge card loans. Although the depth of disclosure varies with the type of loan and the amount of the principal, all credit applications request information on assets and liabilities. Implicitly, they also provide information on the applicant's net worth, which is simply the difference between assets and liabilities.

An automated statement of net worth eliminates tedium and redundancy from the credit application process. It's much easier to write "see attached statement of net worth" on a credit application than it is to laboriously fill in the blanks. Also, implementing the statement of net worth in a SuperCalc[3] spreadsheet allows easy updating as your circumstances change.

The grouping of assets within the statement is based on the liquidity of the asset—that is, the speed with which the asset can be converted to cash. Here are some general examples:

Cash: Bank checking and savings accounts, pension funds, and credit unions.

Receivables: Anything owed to you in payment for goods or services.

Marketable Securities: Stocks, bonds, certificates of deposit, and cash surrender value of insurance policies.

Physical Personal Property: Automobiles, personal computers, and furniture and appliances.

Real Property: Primary dwelling, secondary dwelling, and rental property.

Liabilities represent amounts owed to creditors. Some common examples: Home mortgages, auto loans, school loans, charge accounts, and other loans.

Liabilities do not include such things as insurance premiums and utility bills. These items are really monthly operating expenses and are not handled by the statement of net worth.

Figure 16.9 shows a template for a statement of net worth. Rows can be easily inserted to provide additional assets or liabilities. After a few insertions, however, the entire spreadsheet may not fit on one printed page. If this happens, consider printing the assets on the first page and the liabilities and net worth on the next. The headings shown in rows 1 through 4 of the template should be duplicated so they print at the top of the second page. This method produces output that looks neater and much more professional than several lines overflowing onto the second page.

Figure 16.10 shows a completed example of the statement of net worth. Notice that cell E38, the amount associated with TOTAL ASSETS, equals cell E55, the amount associated with TOTAL LIABILITIES & NET WORTH. These cells must always be equal. If they're not, there is an error in the spreadsheet.

The personal income tax application, shown earlier, illustrates a static example of a spreadsheet since it only addresses one year. Unless the IRS audits your tax return, you can usually forget about the spreadsheet once you've submitted your return and either paid the tax due or received your refund. The statement of net worth, on the other hand, is dynamic in nature because the financial circumstances for most individuals are constantly chang-

Figure 16.9 Statement of Net Worth: Template

	A	B	C	D	E
1		YOUR NAME			
2		STATEMENT OF NET WORTH			
3		AS OF DATE			
4		------------------------------			
5	ASSETS				
6	CASH				
7		BANK ACCOUNTS			
8		CHECKING	.00		
9		MONEY MARKET	.00		
10		PASSBOOK #1	.00		
11		PASSBOOK #2	.00		
12			---------		
13		TOTAL CASH IN BANK		.00	
14		PENSION PLANS			
15		PLAN #1	.00		
16		PLAN #2	.00		
17			---------		
18		TOTAL PENSION PLANS		.00	
19		OTHER FUNDS			
20		OTHER #1	.00		
21		OTHER #2	.00		
22			---------		
23		TOTAL OTHER FUNDS		.00	
24				---------	
25		TOTAL CASH			.00
26	RECEIVABLES				
27			.00		
28			---------		
29		TOTAL RECEIVABLES			.00
30	AUTOMOBILES				
31		YEAR & MODEL AUTO #1		.00	
32		YEAR & MODEL AUTO #2		.00	
33				---------	
34		TOTAL AUTOMOBILES			.00
35	REAL ESTATE				
36		PROPERTY LOCATION			.00
37					------------
38	TOTAL ASSETS				.00
39					============
40					
41	LIABILITIES & NET WORTH				
42	LIABILITIES				
43		MORTGAGE:		.00	
44		AUTO:		.00	
45		CHARGE ACCOUNTS:		.00	
46				.00	
47				.00	
48				.00	
49		OTHER:		.00	
50				.00	
51				---------	
52	TOTAL LIABILITIES				.00
53	NET WORTH				.00
54					------------
55	TOTAL LIABILITIES & NET WORTH				.00
56					============

ing. Each month the outstanding balances on mortgages and other loans decrease as payments are made. Similarly, the balances of pension plans and credit union accounts increase as monthly or weekly payroll contributions are made. Furthermore, depending on the volatility of your cash flows, there may be significant fluctuations in the balances of your bank accounts.

Therefore, this type of spreadsheet should be updated monthly if it is to contain meaningful and relevant information.

Figure 16.10 Statement of Net Worth: Completed Spreadsheet

```
   :  A  ::               B               ::     C    ::     D    ::      E     :
 1                  JOHN & JANE DOE
 2              STATEMENT OF NET WORTH
 3              AS OF DECEMBER 31, 1984
 4        -------------------------------
 5  ASSETS
 6    CASH
 7            HOME-TOWNE SAVINGS BANK ACCOUNTS
 8               01-123456 JOINT CHECKING          1,005.67
 9               02-234567 JOINT MONEY MARKET      9,498.38
10               03-345678 JOHN PASSBOOK             175.50
11               04-456789 JANE PASSBOOK             217.99
12                                                ---------
13                 TOTAL CASH IN BANK                          10,897.54
14            PENSION PLANS
15               MAINFRAME COMPUTERS, INC.         6,497.81
16               GERMANTOWN UNIVERSITY             1,733.03
17                                                ---------
18                 TOTAL PENSION PLANS                          8,230.84
19            OTHER FUNDS
20               EMPLOYEE STOCK PURCHASE PLAN      1,592.38
21               CREDIT UNION                      1,250.00
22                                                ---------
23                 TOTAL OTHER FUNDS                            2,842.38
24                                                             ---------
25            TOTAL CASH                                                     21,970.76
26    RECEIVABLES
27                  PUBLISHER'S ROYALTY ADVANCE    5,000.00
28                                                ---------
29                 TOTAL RECEIVABLES                                          5,000.00
30    AUTOMOBILES
31            1983 NISSAN SENTRA 4 DOOR                         7,163.58
32            1981 DATSUN 210 STATION WAGON                     4,500.00
33                                                             ---------
34                 TOTAL AUTOMOBILES                                         11,663.58
35    REAL ESTATE
36            943 CACTUS COURT, MAPLE GLEN PA                                89,000.00
37                                                                        ------------
38  TOTAL ASSETS                                                            127,634.34
39                                                                        ============
40
41  LIABILITIES & NET WORTH
42  LIABILITIES
43            MORTGAGE: LOCAL SAVINGS & LOAN                   46,000.00
44            AUTO: HOME-TOWNE SAVINGS BANK                     3,511.11
45            CHARGE ACCOUNTS: VISA                             1,692.52
46                             SEARS                              802.92
47                                                                   .00
48                                                                   .00
49            OTHER: NDSL STUDENT LOAN                            292.96
50                                                                   .00
51                                                             ---------
52  TOTAL LIABILITIES                                                        52,299.51
53  NET WORTH                                                                75,334.83
54                                                                        ------------
55  TOTAL LIABILITIES & NET WORTH                                           127,634.34
56                                                                        ============
```

A Mortgage Amortization Application

Computing periodic payments for loans and mortgages was covered with financial functions in Chapter 9. There are times, however, when this calculation provides inadequate information. One of the most comprehensive tools used in the analysis of debt repayment is the mortgage amortization schedule. This analytical device computes the monthly payment for a given principal, interest rate, and loan term, and shows how the payment is split between principal and interest on a declining principal balance.

The template shown in Figure 16.11 is designed to calculate 48 payment periods at a time, adequate for many automobile and other personal loans. Loan terms with more than 48 periods are handled by a series of manual recalculations. Each time ! is pressed, amortization computations are made for an additional 48 periods. This is done until the amortization is calculated for the last period in the loan. The global settings /GM and /GI1 control these calculations. Furthermore, all cells are protected except for cells C3, C4, and C6. Also, /GT is toggled on, so the protected cells are skipped.

Figure 16.11 Mortgage Amortization: Template

```
     !     A     !!     B     !!     C     !!     D     !!     E     !!     F     !
1    MORTGAGE PAYMENT AND AMORTIZATION SCHEDULE                   PAGE             1
2    -------------------------------------------
3    MORTGAGE PRINCIPAL                     .00<--Enter Principal, e.g.: 48100
4    ANNUAL INTEREST RATE                .0000%<--Enter Rate, e.g.: 0.09
5*   MONTHLY INTEREST RATE               .0000%
6    NUMBER OF YEARS                          0<--Enter Term in years, e.g.: 30
7    NUMBER OF MONTHS                         0
8    MONTHLY PAYMENT                      ERROR
9
10   MORTGAGE AMORTIZATION SCHEDULE
11          MONTH     INTEREST   PRINCIPAL   PRINCIPAL       FINAL
12         NUMBER      PAYMENT     PAYMENT     BALANCE     PAYMENT
13              1
14              2
15              3
16              4
17              5
18              6
19              7
20              8
21              9
22             10
23             11
24             12
25             13
26             14
27             15
28             16
29             17
30             18
31             19
32             20
33             21
34             22
35             23
36             24
37             25
38             26
39             27
40             28
41             29
42             30
43             31
44             32
45             33
46             34
47             35
48             36
49             37
50             38
51             39
52             40
53             41
54             42
55             43
56             44
57             45
58             46
59             47
60             48
```

To use the template, make the following entries, then press !

Enter principal amount in cell C3
Enter annual interest rate in cell C4
Enter mortgage term in years in cell C6

Figure 16.12 illustrates the amortization schedule for a $48,100, 9%, 30-year mortgage. The command /ODALL,P is entered after a 48-period amortization calculation. The page length has been set to 65.

Figure 16.12 Mortgage Amortization: Completed Spreadsheet

```
    :     A     ::     B     ::     C     ::     D     ::     E     ::     F     :
1   MORTGAGE PAYMENT AND AMORTIZATION SCHEDULE                      PAGE           1
2   ----------------------------------------
3   MORTGAGE PRINCIPAL          48,100.00<--Enter Principal, e.g.: 48100
4   ANNUAL INTEREST RATE          9.0000%<--Enter Rate, e.g.: 0.09
5   MONTHLY INTEREST RATE          .7500%
6   NUMBER OF YEARS                     30<--Enter Term in years, e.g.: 30
7   NUMBER OF MONTHS                   360
8   MONTHLY PAYMENT                 387.02
9
10  MORTGAGE AMORTIZATION SCHEDULE
11          MONTH     INTEREST   PRINCIPAL    PRINCIPAL        FINAL
12         NUMBER      PAYMENT     PAYMENT      BALANCE      PAYMENT
13              1       360.75       26.27    48,073.73
14              2       360.55       26.47    48,047.26
15              3       360.35       26.67    48,020.59
16              4       360.15       26.87    47,993.72
17              5       359.95       27.07    47,966.65
18              6       359.75       27.27    47,939.38
19              7       359.55       27.47    47,911.91
20              8       359.34       27.68    47,884.23
21              9       359.13       27.89    47,856.34
22             10       358.92       28.10    47,828.24
23             11       358.71       28.31    47,799.93
24             12       358.50       28.52    47,771.41
25             13       358.29       28.73    47,742.68
26             14       358.07       28.95    47,713.73
27             15       357.85       29.17    47,684.56
28             16       357.63       29.39    47,655.17
29             17       357.41       29.61    47,625.56
30             18       357.19       29.83    47,595.73
31             19       356.97       30.05    47,565.68
32             20       356.74       30.28    47,535.40
33             21       356.52       30.50    47,504.90
34             22       356.29       30.73    47,474.17
35             23       356.06       30.96    47,443.21
36             24       355.82       31.20    47,412.01
37             25       355.59       31.43    47,380.58
38             26       355.35       31.67    47,348.91
39             27       355.12       31.90    47,317.01
40             28       354.88       32.14    47,284.87
41             29       354.64       32.38    47,252.49
42             30       354.39       32.63    47,219.86
43             31       354.15       32.87    47,186.99
44             32       353.90       33.12    47,153.87
45             33       353.65       33.37    47,120.50
46             34       353.40       33.62    47,086.88
47             35       353.15       33.87    47,053.01
48             36       352.90       34.12    47,018.89
49             37       352.64       34.38    46,984.51
50             38       352.38       34.64    46,949.87
51             39       352.12       34.90    46,914.97
52             40       351.86       35.16    46,879.81
53             41       351.60       35.42    46,844.39
54             42       351.33       35.69    46,808.70
55             43       351.07       35.95    46,772.75
56             44       350.80       36.22    46,736.53
57             45       350.52       36.50    46,700.03
58             46       350.25       36.77    46,663.26
59             47       349.97       37.05    46,626.21
60             48       349.70       37.32    46,588.89
```

(continued on next page)

	A	B	C	D	E	F
1	MORTGAGE PAYMENT AND AMORTIZATION SCHEDULE				PAGE	2
2	--					
3	MORTGAGE PRINCIPAL		48,100.00<--Enter Principal, e.g.: 48100			
4	ANNUAL INTEREST RATE		9.0000%<--Enter Rate, e.g.: 0.09			
5	MONTHLY INTEREST RATE		.7500%			
6	NUMBER OF YEARS		30<--Enter Term in years, e.g.: 30			
7	NUMBER OF MONTHS		360			
8	MONTHLY PAYMENT		387.02			
9						
10	MORTGAGE AMORTIZATION SCHEDULE					
11	MONTH	INTEREST	PRINCIPAL	PRINCIPAL	FINAL	
12	NUMBER	PAYMENT	PAYMENT	BALANCE	PAYMENT	
13	49	349.42	37.60	46,551.29		
14	50	349.13	37.89	46,513.40		
15	51	348.85	38.17	46,475.23		
16	52	348.56	38.46	46,436.77		
17	53	348.28	38.74	46,398.03		
18	54	347.99	39.03	46,359.00		
19	55	347.69	39.33	46,319.67		
20	56	347.40	39.62	46,280.05		
21	57	347.10	39.92	46,240.13		
22	58	346.80	40.22	46,199.91		
23	59	346.50	40.52	46,159.39		
24	60	346.20	40.82	46,118.57		
25	61	345.89	41.13	46,077.44		
26	62	345.58	41.44	46,036.00		
27	63	345.27	41.75	45,994.25		
28	64	344.96	42.06	45,952.19		
29	65	344.64	42.38	45,909.81		
30	66	344.32	42.70	45,867.11		
31	67	344.00	43.02	45,824.09		
32	68	343.68	43.34	45,780.75		
33	69	343.36	43.66	45,737.09		
34	70	343.03	43.99	45,693.10		
35	71	342.70	44.32	45,648.78		
36	72	342.37	44.65	45,604.13		
37	73	342.03	44.99	45,559.14		
38	74	341.69	45.33	45,513.81		
39	75	341.35	45.67	45,468.14		
40	76	341.01	46.01	45,422.13		
41	77	340.67	46.35	45,375.78		
42	78	340.32	46.70	45,329.08		
43	79	339.97	47.05	45,282.03		
44	80	339.62	47.40	45,234.63		
45	81	339.26	47.76	45,186.87		
46	82	338.90	48.12	45,138.75		
47	83	338.54	48.48	45,090.27		
48	84	338.18	48.84	45,041.43		
49	85	337.81	49.21	44,992.22		
50	86	337.44	49.58	44,942.64		
51	87	337.07	49.95	44,892.69		
52	88	336.70	50.32	44,842.37		
53	89	336.32	50.70	44,791.67		
54	90	335.94	51.08	44,740.59		
55	91	335.55	51.47	44,689.12		
56	92	335.17	51.85	44,637.27		
57	93	334.78	52.24	44,585.03		
58	94	334.39	52.63	44,532.40		
59	95	333.99	53.03	44,479.37		
60	96	333.60	53.42	44,425.95		

(continued on next page)

```
     |     A     ||     B     ||     C     ||     D     ||     E     ||     F     |
1    MORTGAGE PAYMENT AND AMORTIZATION SCHEDULE                 PAGE            3
2    ----------------------------------------
3    MORTGAGE PRINCIPAL              48,100.00<--Enter Principal, e.g.: 48100
4    ANNUAL INTEREST RATE              9.0000%<--Enter Rate, e.g.: 0.09
5    MONTHLY INTEREST RATE              .7500%
6    NUMBER OF YEARS                         30<--Enter Term in years, e.g.: 30
7    NUMBER OF MONTHS                       360
8    MONTHLY PAYMENT                     387.02
9
10   MORTGAGE AMORTIZATION SCHEDULE
11          MONTH     INTEREST    PRINCIPAL    PRINCIPAL        FINAL
12         NUMBER      PAYMENT      PAYMENT      BALANCE      PAYMENT
13             97       333.19        53.83    44,372.12
14             98       332.79        54.23    44,317.89
15             99       332.38        54.64    44,263.25
16            100       331.97        55.05    44,208.20
17            101       331.56        55.46    44,152.74
18            102       331.15        55.87    44,096.87
19            103       330.73        56.29    44,040.58
20            104       330.30        56.72    43,983.86
21            105       329.88        57.14    43,926.72
22            106       329.45        57.57    43,869.15
23            107       329.02        58.00    43,811.15
24            108       328.58        58.44    43,752.71
25            109       328.15        58.87    43,693.84
26            110       327.70        59.32    43,634.52
27            111       327.26        59.76    43,574.76
28            112       326.81        60.21    43,514.55
29            113       326.36        60.66    43,453.89
30            114       325.90        61.12    43,392.77
31            115       325.45        61.57    43,331.20
32            116       324.98        62.04    43,269.16
33            117       324.52        62.50    43,206.66
34            118       324.05        62.97    43,143.69
35            119       323.58        63.44    43,080.25
36            120       323.10        63.92    43,016.33
37            121       322.62        64.40    42,951.93
38            122       322.14        64.88    42,887.05
39            123       321.65        65.37    42,821.68
40            124       321.16        65.86    42,75[illegible].82
41            125       320.67        66.35    42,689.47
42            126       320.17        66.85    42,622.62
43            127       319.67        67.35    42,555.27
44            128       319.16        67.86    42,487.41
45            129       318.66        68.36    42,419.05
46            130       318.14        68.88    42,350.17
47            131       317.63        69.39    42,280.78
48            132       317.11        69.91    42,210.87
49            133       316.58        70.44    42,140.43
50            134       316.05        70.97    42,069.46
51            135       315.52        71.50    41,997.96
52            136       314.98        72.04    41,925.92
53            137       314.44        72.58    41,853.34
54            138       313.90        73.12    41,780.22
55            139       313.35        73.67    41,706.55
56            140       312.80        74.22    41,632.33
57            141       312.24        74.78    41,557.55
58            142       311.68        75.34    41,482.21
59            143       311.12        75.90    41,406.31
60            144       310.55        76.47    41,329.84
```

(continued on next page)

	A	B	C	D	E	F
1	MORTGAGE PAYMENT AND AMORTIZATION SCHEDULE				PAGE	4
2	--					
3	MORTGAGE PRINCIPAL		48,100.00<--Enter Principal, e.g.: 48100			
4	ANNUAL INTEREST RATE		9.0000%<--Enter Rate, e.g.: 0.09			
5	MONTHLY INTEREST RATE		.7500%			
6	NUMBER OF YEARS		30<--Enter Term in years, e.g.: 30			
7	NUMBER OF MONTHS		360			
8	MONTHLY PAYMENT		387.02			
9						
10	MORTGAGE AMORTIZATION SCHEDULE					
11	MONTH	INTEREST	PRINCIPAL	PRINCIPAL	FINAL	
12	NUMBER	PAYMENT	PAYMENT	BALANCE	PAYMENT	
13	145	309.97	77.05	41,252.79		
14	146	309.40	77.62	41,175.17		
15	147	308.81	78.21	41,096.96		
16	148	308.23	78.79	41,018.17		
17	149	307.64	79.38	40,938.79		
18	150	307.04	79.98	40,858.81		
19	151	306.44	80.58	40,778.23		
20	152	305.84	81.18	40,697.05		
21	153	305.23	81.79	40,615.26		
22	154	304.61	82.41	40,532.85		
23	155	304.00	83.02	40,449.83		
24	156	303.37	83.65	40,366.18		
25	157	302.75	84.27	40,281.91		
26	158	302.11	84.91	40,197.00		
27	159	301.48	85.54	40,111.46		
28	160	300.84	86.18	40,025.28		
29	161	300.19	86.83	39,938.45		
30	162	299.54	87.48	39,850.97		
31	163	298.88	88.14	39,762.83		
32	164	298.22	88.80	39,674.03		
33	165	297.56	89.46	39,584.57		
34	166	296.88	90.14	39,494.43		
35	167	296.21	90.81	39,403.62		
36	168	295.53	91.49	39,312.13		
37	169	294.84	92.18	39,219.95		
38	170	294.15	92.87	39,127.08		
39	171	293.45	93.57	39,033.51		
40	172	292.75	94.27	38,939.24		
41	173	292.04	94.98	38,844.26		
42	174	291.33	95.69	38,748.57		
43	175	290.61	96.41	38,652.16		
44	176	289.89	97.13	38,555.03		
45	177	289.16	97.86	38,457.17		
46	178	288.43	98.59	38,358.58		
47	179	287.69	99.33	38,259.25		
48	180	286.94	100.08	38,159.17		
49	181	286.19	100.83	38,058.34		
50	182	285.44	101.58	37,956.76		
51	183	284.68	102.34	37,854.42		
52	184	283.91	103.11	37,751.31		
53	185	283.13	103.89	37,647.42		
54	186	282.36	104.66	37,542.76		
55	187	281.57	105.45	37,437.31		
56	188	280.78	106.24	37,331.07		
57	189	279.98	107.04	37,224.03		
58	190	279.18	107.84	37,116.19		
59	191	278.37	108.65	37,007.54		
60	192	277.56	109.46	36,898.08		

(continued on next page)

```
    |    A    ||    B    ||    C    ||    D    ||    E    ||    F    |
 1  MORTGAGE PAYMENT AND AMORTIZATION SCHEDULE                  PAGE          5
 2  ------------------------------------------
 3  MORTGAGE PRINCIPAL              48,100.00<--Enter Principal, e.g.: 48100
 4  ANNUAL INTEREST RATE              9.0000%<--Enter Rate, e.g.: 0.09
 5  MONTHLY INTEREST RATE               .7500%
 6  NUMBER OF YEARS                         30<--Enter Term in years, e.g.: 30
 7  NUMBER OF MONTHS                       360
 8  MONTHLY PAYMENT                     387.02
 9
10  MORTGAGE AMORTIZATION SCHEDULE
11          MONTH     INTEREST   PRINCIPAL    PRINCIPAL       FINAL
12         NUMBER      PAYMENT     PAYMENT      BALANCE     PAYMENT
13            193       276.74      110.28    36,787.80
14            194       275.91      111.11    36,676.69
15            195       275.08      111.94    36,564.75
16            196       274.24      112.78    36,451.97
17            197       273.39      113.63    36,338.34
18            198       272.54      114.48    36,223.86
19            199       271.68      115.34    36,108.52
20            200       270.81      116.21    35,992.31
21            201       269.94      117.08    35,875.23
22            202       269.06      117.96    35,757.27
23            203       268.18      118.84    35,638.43
24            204       267.29      119.73    35,518.70
25            205       266.39      120.63    35,398.07
26            206       265.49      121.53    35,276.54
27            207       264.57      122.45    35,154.09
28            208       263.66      123.36    35,030.73
29            209       262.73      124.29    34,906.44
30            210       261.80      125.22    34,781.22
31            211       260.86      126.16    34,655.06
32            212       259.91      127.11    34,527.95
33            213       258.96      128.06    34,399.89
34            214       258.00      129.02    34,270.87
35            215       257.03      129.99    34,140.88
36            216       256.06      130.96    34,009.92
37            217       255.07      131.95    33,877.97
38            218       254.08      132.94    33,745.03
39            219       253.09      133.93    33,611.10
40            220       252.08      134.94    33,476.16
41            221       251.07      135.95    33,340.21
42            222       250.05      136.97    33,203.24
43            223       249.02      138.00    33,065.24
44            224       247.99      139.03    32,926.21
45            225       246.95      140.07    32,786.14
46            226       245.90      141.12    32,645.02
47            227       244.84      142.18    32,502.84
48            228       243.77      143.25    32,359.59
49            229       242.70      144.32    32,215.27
50            230       241.61      145.41    32,069.86
51            231       240.52      146.50    31,923.36
52            232       239.43      147.59    31,775.77
53            233       238.32      148.70    31,627.07
54            234       237.20      149.82    31,477.25
55            235       236.08      150.94    31,326.31
56            236       234.95      152.07    31,174.24
57            237       233.81      153.21    31,021.03
58            238       232.66      154.36    30,866.67
59            239       231.50      155.52    30,711.15
60            240       230.33      156.69    30,554.46
```

(continued on next page)

```
     !    A    !!    B    !!    C    !!    D    !!    E    !!    F    !
1    MORTGAGE PAYMENT AND AMORTIZATION SCHEDULE              PAGE        6
2    ------------------------------------------
3    MORTGAGE PRINCIPAL            48,100.00<--Enter Principal, e.g.: 48100
4    ANNUAL INTEREST RATE             9.0000%<--Enter Rate, e.g.: 0.09
5    MONTHLY INTEREST RATE            .7500%
6    NUMBER OF YEARS                      30<--Enter Term in years, e.g.: 30
7    NUMBER OF MONTHS                    360
8    MONTHLY PAYMENT                  387.02
9
10   MORTGAGE AMORTIZATION SCHEDULE
11            MONTH     INTEREST    PRINCIPAL    PRINCIPAL           FINAL
12           NUMBER      PAYMENT      PAYMENT      BALANCE         PAYMENT
13              241       229.16       157.86    30,396.60
14              242       227.97       159.05    30,237.55
15              243       226.78       160.24    30,077.31
16              244       225.58       161.44    29,915.87
17              245       224.37       162.65    29,753.22
18              246       223.15       163.87    29,589.35
19              247       221.92       165.10    29,424.25
20              248       220.68       166.34    29,257.91
21              249       219.43       167.59    29,090.32
22              250       218.18       168.84    28,921.48
23              251       216.91       170.11    28,751.37
24              252       215.64       171.38    28,579.99
25              253       214.35       172.67    28,407.32
26              254       213.05       173.97    28,233.35
27              255       211.75       175.27    28,058.08
28              256       210.44       176.58    27,881.50
29              257       209.11       177.91    27,703.59
30              258       207.78       179.24    27,524.35
31              259       206.43       180.59    27,343.76
32              260       205.08       181.94    27,161.82
33              261       203.71       183.31    26,978.51
34              262       202.34       184.68    26,793.83
35              263       200.95       186.07    26,607.76
36              264       199.56       187.46    26,420.30
37              265       198.15       188.87    26,231.43
38              266       196.74       190.28    26,041.15
39              267       195.31       191.71    25,849.44
40              268       193.87       193.15    25,656.29
41              269       192.42       194.60    25,461.69
42              270       190.96       196.06    25,265.63
43              271       189.49       197.53    25,068.10
44              272       188.01       199.01    24,869.09
45              273       186.52       200.50    24,668.59
46              274       185.01       202.01    24,466.58
47              275       183.50       203.52    24,263.06
48              276       181.97       205.05    24,058.01
49              277       180.44       206.58    23,851.43
50              278       178.89       208.13    23,643.30
51              279       177.32       209.70    23,433.60
52              280       175.75       211.27    23,222.33
53              281       174.17       212.85    23,009.48
54              282       172.57       214.45    22,795.03
55              283       170.96       216.06    22,578.97
56              284       169.34       217.68    22,361.29
57              285       167.71       219.31    22,141.98
58              286       166.06       220.96    21,921.02
59              287       164.41       222.61    21,698.41
60              288       162.74       224.28    21,474.13
```

(continued on next page)

```
   !    A    !!    B    !!    C    !!    D    !!    E    !!    F    !
 1  MORTGAGE PAYMENT AND AMORTIZATION SCHEDULE                 PAGE         7
 2  ------------------------------------------
 3  MORTGAGE PRINCIPAL          48,100.00<--Enter Principal, e.g.: 48100
 4  ANNUAL INTEREST RATE          9.0000%<--Enter Rate, e.g.: 0.09
 5  MONTHLY INTEREST RATE          .7500%
 6  NUMBER OF YEARS                    30<--Enter Term in years, e.g.: 30
 7  NUMBER OF MONTHS                  360
 8  MONTHLY PAYMENT                387.02
 9
10  MORTGAGE AMORTIZATION SCHEDULE
11         MONTH   INTEREST  PRINCIPAL   PRINCIPAL      FINAL
12        NUMBER    PAYMENT    PAYMENT     BALANCE    PAYMENT
13           289     161.06     225.96   21,248.17
14           290     159.36     227.66   21,020.51
15           291     157.65     229.37   20,791.14
16           292     155.93     231.09   20,560.05
17           293     154.20     232.82   20,327.23
18           294     152.45     234.57   20,092.66
19           295     150.69     236.33   19,856.33
20           296     148.92     238.10   19,618.23
21           297     147.14     239.88   19,378.35
22           298     145.34     241.68   19,136.67
23           299     143.53     243.49   18,893.18
24           300     141.70     245.32   18,647.86
25           301     139.86     247.16   18,400.70
26           302     138.01     249.01   18,151.69
27           303     136.14     250.88   17,900.81
28           304     134.26     252.76   17,648.05
29           305     132.36     254.66   17,393.39
30           306     130.45     256.57   17,136.82
31           307     128.53     258.49   16,878.33
32           308     126.59     260.43   16,617.90
33           309     124.63     262.39   16,355.51
34           310     122.67     264.35   16,091.16
35           311     120.68     266.34   15,824.82
36           312     118.69     268.33   15,556.49
37           313     116.67     270.35   15,286.14
38           314     114.65     272.37   15,013.77
39           315     112.60     274.42   14,739.35
40           316     110.55     276.47   14,462.88
41           317     108.47     278.55   14,184.33
42           318     106.38     280.64   13,903.69
43           319     104.28     282.74   13,620.95
44           320     102.16     284.86   13,336.09
45           321     100.02     287.00   13,049.09
46           322      97.87     289.15   12,759.94
47           323      95.70     291.32   12,468.62
48           324      93.51     293.51   12,175.11
49           325      91.31     295.71   11,879.40
50           326      89.10     297.92   11,581.48
51           327      86.86     300.16   11,281.32
52           328      84.61     302.41   10,978.91
53           329      82.34     304.68   10,674.23
54           330      80.06     306.96   10,367.27
55           331      77.75     309.27   10,058.00
56           332      75.44     311.58    9,746.42
57           333      73.10     313.92    9,432.50
58           334      70.74     316.28    9,116.22
59           335      68.37     318.65    8,797.57
60           336      65.98     321.04    8,476.53
```

(continued on next page)

	A	B	C	D	E	F
1	MORTGAGE PAYMENT AND AMORTIZATION SCHEDULE				PAGE	8
2	--					
3	MORTGAGE PRINCIPAL		48,100.00	<--Enter Principal, e.g.: 48100		
4	ANNUAL INTEREST RATE		9.0000%	<--Enter Rate, e.g.: 0.09		
5	MONTHLY INTEREST RATE		.7500%			
6	NUMBER OF YEARS		30	<--Enter Term in years, e.g.: 30		
7	NUMBER OF MONTHS		360			
8	MONTHLY PAYMENT		387.02			
9						
10	MORTGAGE AMORTIZATION SCHEDULE					
11	MONTH	INTEREST	PRINCIPAL	PRINCIPAL	FINAL	
12	NUMBER	PAYMENT	PAYMENT	BALANCE	PAYMENT	
13	337	63.57	323.45	8,153.08		
14	338	61.15	325.87	7,827.21		
15	339	58.70	328.32	7,498.89		
16	340	56.24	330.78	7,168.11		
17	341	53.76	333.26	6,834.85		
18	342	51.26	335.76	6,499.09		
19	343	48.74	338.28	6,160.81		
20	344	46.21	340.81	5,820.00		
21	345	43.65	343.37	5,476.63		
22	346	41.07	345.95	5,130.68		
23	347	38.48	348.54	4,782.14		
24	348	35.87	351.15	4,430.99		
25	349	33.23	353.79	4,077.20		
26	350	30.58	356.44	3,720.76		
27	351	27.91	359.11	3,361.65		
28	352	25.21	361.81	2,999.84		
29	353	22.50	364.52	2,635.32		
30	354	19.76	367.26	2,268.06		
31	355	17.01	370.01	1,898.05		
32	356	14.24	372.78	1,525.27		
33	357	11.44	375.58	1,149.69		
34	358	8.62	378.40	771.29		
35	359	5.78	381.24	390.05		
36	360	2.93	384.09	5.96	392.98	
37	361					
38	362					
39	363					
40	364					
41	365					
42	366					
43	367					
44	368					
45	369					
46	370					
47	371					
48	372					
49	373					
50	374					
51	375					
52	376					
53	377					
54	378					
55	379					
56	380					
57	381					
58	382					
59	383					
60	384					

Conditional logic—i.e., IF function—reuses rows 13 through 60 for each 48-period increment. Although mortgages with very long terms can be processed, the number of rows in the spreadsheet never exceeds 60. The spreadsheet can be reset by entering **0** in cell C3 and pressing ! twice.

One use for an amortization schedule is to identify the outstanding loan balance at any time so that it can be reported in a statement of net worth.

A System for Planning and Analyzing the Profitability of Operations

Due to the reporting regulations of federal, state, and local taxing authorities, all business organizations are required to submit annual Profit and Loss Statements. This statement reports income and expenses associated with an organization's intended business operations—i.e., operating income and expenses. It also reports any income and expenses arising from non-operating, non-routine, or extraordinary circumstances.

The thrust of this section is on the routine operating aspects of an organization's P&L.

The first few chapters of this book used a very simple P&L Statement to demonstrate the elementary features of SuperCalc³. The P&L used in this section is much more realistic. Its structure is typical for small and medium-sized distribution and retail organizations. Throughout this section the example P&L is called a Statement of Operations because it doesn't deal with any income and expenses beyond the normal scope of operations.

The template shown in Figure 16.13 illustrates the basic framework for the Statement of Operations. The template uses 17 columns to capture financial data. Columns B through M represent the 12 months of the fiscal year. Month numbers have been used instead of month names to accommodate fiscal years not coincident with calendar years.

Columns N through Q contain quarterly totals. Column R is the total for the year.

Figure 16.13 Statement of Operations: Template Printed Via SIDEWAYS Utility

:	A	B	C	D	E	F	G	H	I	J	K	L	M	N	O	P	Q	R
1		COMPANY NAME																
2		STATEMENT OF OPERATIONS																
3		(ACTUAL, PLANNED, OR VARIANCE)																
4		FOR THE PERIOD ENDING MM/DD/YY																
5																		
6		MONTH	MONTH	MONTH	MONTH	MONTH	MONTH	MONTH	MONTH	MONTH	MONTH	MONTH	MONTH	1ST	2ND	3RD	4TH	Y-T-D
7	CLASSIFICATION	1	2	3	4	5	6	7	8	9	10	11	12	QUARTER	QUARTER	QUARTER	QUARTER	TOTAL
8	-------	-------	-------	-------	-------	-------	-------	-------	-------	-------	-------	-------	-------	-------	-------	-------	-------	-------
9	SALES													0	0	0	0	0
10	-------	-------	-------	-------	-------	-------	-------	-------	-------	-------	-------	-------	-------	-------	-------	-------	-------	-------
11	COST OF GOODS SOLD:																	
12	BEGINNING INVENTORY													0	0	0	0	0
13	PURCHASES													0	0	0	0	0
14	ENDING INVENTORY													0	0	0	0	0
15		-------	-------	-------	-------	-------	-------	-------	-------	-------	-------	-------	-------	-------	-------	-------	-------	-------
16	COST OF GOODS SOLD	0	0	0	0	0	0	0	0	0	0	0	0	0	0	0	0	0
17	-------	-------	-------	-------	-------	-------	-------	-------	-------	-------	-------	-------	-------	-------	-------	-------	-------	-------
18	GROSS PROFIT	0	0	0	0	0	0	0	0	0	0	0	0	0	0	0	0	0
19	-------	-------	-------	-------	-------	-------	-------	-------	-------	-------	-------	-------	-------	-------	-------	-------	-------	-------
20	OPERATING EXPENSES:																	
21	SALARIES & WAGES													0	0	0	0	0
22	FRINGE BENEFITS													0	0	0	0	0
23	FICA TAX													0	0	0	0	0
24	FED'L UNEMPLOYMENT INSUR													0	0	0	0	0
25	STATE UNEMPLOYMENT INSUR													0	0	0	0	0
26	BUILDING RENT													0	0	0	0	0
27	COMPUTER RENT													0	0	0	0	0
28	DEPRECIATION													0	0	0	0	0
29	OFFICE SUPPLIES													0	0	0	0	0
30	EQUIPMENT MAINTENANCE													0	0	0	0	0
31	TELEPHONE													0	0	0	0	0
32	ELECTRICITY													0	0	0	0	0
33	HEAT													0	0	0	0	0
34	ADVERTISING													0	0	0	0	0
35	POSTAGE & FREIGHT													0	0	0	0	0
36	SALES PROMOTIONS													0	0	0	0	0
37	PROFESSIONAL MEMBERSHIPS													0	0	0	0	0
38	SUBSCRIPTIONS													0	0	0	0	0
39	EQUIPMENT INSURANCE													0	0	0	0	0
40		-------	-------	-------	-------	-------	-------	-------	-------	-------	-------	-------	-------	-------	-------	-------	-------	-------
41	TOTAL EXPENSES	0	0	0	0	0	0	0	0	0	0	0	0	0	0	0	0	0
42	-------	-------	-------	-------	-------	-------	-------	-------	-------	-------	-------	-------	-------	-------	-------	-------	-------	-------
43	PRE-TAX PROFIT	0	0	0	0	0	0	0	0	0	0	0	0	0	0	0	0	0
44	FEDERAL TAXES													0	0	0	0	0
45	STATE TAXES													0	0	0	0	0
46		-------	-------	-------	-------	-------	-------	-------	-------	-------	-------	-------	-------	-------	-------	-------	-------	-------
47	NET INCOME	0	0	0	0	0	0	0	0	0	0	0	0	0	0	0	0	0
48		=======	=======	=======	=======	=======	=======	=======	=======	=======	=======	=======	=======	=======	=======	=======	=======	=======

This total is generated as follows:

1. /ODALL,SW255 and press F2.
   Note: This sets the width for the /Output command at 255 positions. This width is used in step #2 when the .PRN file is generated.
2. /ODALL,DTMPEXPEN.PRN and press RETURN.
3. /QY
4. SIDEWAYS

Figure 16.14 shows the SIDEWAYS options menu and the settings used to produce Figure 16.13.

Figure 16.14 SIDEWAYS Utility Option Selection Menu

```
                         S I D E W A Y S  version 2.02

Printer selected:    C.Itoh Prowriter

Vertical form size (inches):    11.00
Horizontal form size (inches):   8.00

Double strike:                     ON
Character font:                NORMAL           5 x 11 dot matrix

Character spacing (dots):           1            12.00 characters per inch
Line spacing (dots):                1             6.66 lines per inch

Left margin (inches):            0.25
Top margin (inches):             0.25
Bottom margin (inches):          0.25               50 lines per page

Starting page:                      1
Enter name of print file:   B:TMPEXPEN.PRN
Directory:     A:\

F1 for HELP                                                    F10 to exit
```

Figure 16.15 shows a command file that prints the template one fiscal quarter at a time and then prints a quarterly summary.

Figure 16.15 Macro to Print Statement of Operations Template by Quarter

```
     :     A      :
1    /ZY
2    /LB:TMPEXPEN,A
3    /FCE:M,0
4    /FCO:Q,0
5    /ODA1:R50,P
6    /FCB:R,9
7    /FCB:D,0
8    /FCH:N,0
9    /FCP:Q,0
10   /ODA1:R50,P
11   /FCB:R,9
12   /FCB:G,0
13   /FCK:O,0
14   /FCQ,0
15   /ODA1:R50,P
16   /FCB:R,9
17   /FCB:J,0
18   /FCN:P,0
19   /ODA1:R50,P
20   /FCB:R,9
21   /FCB:M,0
22   /ODA1:R50,P
23   /FCB:R,9
```

Entering **/XPLMACR01.XQT** executes the command file and produces the results shown in Figures 16.16 through 16.20.

Figure 16.16 Statement of Operations Template: First Quarter

```
    :           A            ::   B   ::   C   ::   D   ::   N   ::   R   :
1                            COMPANY NAME
2                            STATEMENT OF OPERATIONS
3                            (ACTUAL, PLANNED, OR VARIANCE)
4                            FOR THE PERIOD ENDING MM/DD/YY
5
6                                MONTH     MONTH     MONTH       1ST    Y-T-D
7   CLASSIFICATION                   1         2         3   QUARTER    TOTAL
8   ------------------------------------------------------------------------
9   SALES                                                          0        0
10  ------------------------------------------------------------------------
11  COST OF GOODS SOLD:
12   BEGINNING INVENTORY                                           0        0
13   PURCHASES                                                     0        0
14   ENDING INVENTORY                                              0        0
15                            -------- -------- -------- -------- --------
16     COST OF GOODS SOLD            0         0         0         0        0
17  ------------------------------------------------------------------------
18  GROSS PROFIT                     0         0         0         0        0
19  ------------------------------------------------------------------------
20  OPERATING EXPENSES:
21   SALARIES & WAGES                                              0        0
22   FRINGE BENEFITS                                               0        0
23   FICA TAX                                                      0        0
24   FED'L UNEMPLOYMENT INSUR                                      0        0
25   STATE UNEMPLOYMENT INSUR                                      0        0
26   BUILDING RENT                                                 0        0
27   COMPUTER RENT                                                 0        0
28   DEPRECIATION                                                  0        0
29   OFFICE SUPPLIES                                               0        0
30   EQUIPMENT MAINTENANCE                                         0        0
31   TELEPHONE                                                     0        0
32   ELECTRICITY                                                   0        0
33   HEAT                                                          0        0
34   ADVERTISING                                                   0        0
35   POSTAGE & FREIGHT                                             0        0
36   SALES PROMOTIONS                                              0        0
37   PROFESSIONAL MEMBERSHIPS                                      0        0
38   SUBSCRIPTIONS                                                 0        0
39   EQUIPMENT INSURANCE                                           0        0
40                            -------- -------- -------- -------- --------
41     TOTAL EXPENSES                0         0         0         0        0
42  ------------------------------------------------------------------------
43  PRE-TAX PROFIT                   0         0         0         0        0
44  FEDERAL TAXES                                                  0        0
45  STATE TAXES                                                    0        0
46                            -------- -------- -------- -------- --------
47  NET INCOME                       0         0         0         0        0
48                            ======== ======== ======== ======== ========
49
50
```

Figure 16.17 Statement of Operations Template: Second Quarter

	A	E	F	G	O	R
1		COMPANY NAME				
2		STATEMENT OF OPERATIONS				
3		(ACTUAL, PLANNED, OR VARIANCE)				
4		FOR THE PERIOD ENDING MM/DD/YY				
5						
6		MONTH	MONTH	MONTH	2ND	Y-T-D
7	CLASSIFICATION	4	5	6	QUARTER	TOTAL
8	----------------------	--------	--------	--------	--------	--------
9	SALES				0	0
10	----------------------	--------	--------	--------	--------	--------
11	COST OF GOODS SOLD:					
12	BEGINNING INVENTORY				0	0
13	PURCHASES				0	0
14	ENDING INVENTORY				0	0
15		--------	--------	--------	--------	--------
16	COST OF GOODS SOLD	0	0	0	0	0
17	----------------------	--------	--------	--------	--------	--------
18	GROSS PROFIT	0	0	0	0	0
19	----------------------	--------	--------	--------	--------	--------
20	OPERATING EXPENSES:					
21	SALARIES & WAGES				0	0
22	FRINGE BENEFITS				0	0
23	FICA TAX				0	0
24	FED'L UNEMPLOYMENT INSUR				0	0
25	STATE UNEMPLOYMENT INSUR				0	0
26	BUILDING RENT				0	0
27	COMPUTER RENT				0	0
28	DEPRECIATION				0	0
29	OFFICE SUPPLIES				0	0
30	EQUIPMENT MAINTENANCE				0	0
31	TELEPHONE				0	0
32	ELECTRICITY				0	0
33	HEAT				0	0
34	ADVERTISING				0	0
35	POSTAGE & FREIGHT				0	0
36	SALES PROMOTIONS				0	0
37	PROFESSIONAL MEMBERSHIPS				0	0
38	SUBSCRIPTIONS				0	0
39	EQUIPMENT INSURANCE				0	0
40		--------	--------	--------	--------	--------
41	TOTAL EXPENSES	0	0	0	0	0
42	----------------------	--------	--------	--------	--------	--------
43	PRE-TAX PROFIT	0	0	0	0	0
44	FEDERAL TAXES				0	0
45	STATE TAXES				0	0
46		--------	--------	--------	--------	--------
47	NET INCOME	0	0	0	0	0
48		========	========	========	========	========
49						
50						

Figure 16.18 Statement of Operations Template: Third Quarter

	A	H	I	J	P	R
1		COMPANY NAME				
2		STATEMENT OF OPERATIONS				
3		(ACTUAL, PLANNED, OR VARIANCE)				
4		FOR THE PERIOD ENDING MM/DD/YY				
5						
6		MONTH	MONTH	MONTH	3RD	Y-T-D
7	CLASSIFICATION	7	8	9	QUARTER	TOTAL
8	----------------------	--------	--------	--------	--------	--------
9	SALES				0	0
10	----------------------	--------	--------	--------	--------	--------
11	COST OF GOODS SOLD:					
12	BEGINNING INVENTORY				0	0
13	PURCHASES				0	0
14	ENDING INVENTORY				0	0
15		--------	--------	--------	--------	--------
16	COST OF GOODS SOLD	0	0	0	0	0
17	----------------------	--------	--------	--------	--------	--------
18	GROSS PROFIT	0	0	0	0	0
19	----------------------	--------	--------	--------	--------	--------
20	OPERATING EXPENSES:					
21	SALARIES & WAGES				0	0
22	FRINGE BENEFITS				0	0
23	FICA TAX				0	0

(continued on next page)

```
24   FED'L UNEMPLOYMENT INSUR                                        0        0
25   STATE UNEMPLOYMENT INSUR                                        0        0
26   BUILDING RENT                                                   0        0
27   COMPUTER RENT                                                   0        0
28   DEPRECIATION                                                    0        0
29   OFFICE SUPPLIES                                                 0        0
30   EQUIPMENT MAINTENANCE                                           0        0
31   TELEPHONE                                                       0        0
32   ELECTRICITY                                                     0        0
33   HEAT                                                            0        0
34   ADVERTISING                                                     0        0
35   POSTAGE & FREIGHT                                               0        0
36   SALES PROMOTIONS                                                0        0
37   PROFESSIONAL MEMBERSHIPS                                        0        0
38   SUBSCRIPTIONS                                                   0        0
39   EQUIPMENT INSURANCE                                             0        0
40                              -------- -------- -------- -------- --------
41     TOTAL EXPENSES                  0        0        0        0        0
42  -------------------------------------------------------------------------
43  PRE-TAX PROFIT                     0        0        0        0        0
44  FEDERAL TAXES                                                 0        0
45  STATE TAXES                                                   0        0
46                              -------- -------- -------- -------- --------
47  NET INCOME                         0        0        0        0        0
48                              ======== ======== ======== ======== ========
49
50
```

Figure 16.19 Statement of Operations Template: Fourth Quarter

```
    :           A             ::    K   ::    L   ::    M   ::    Q   ::    R   :
1                               COMPANY NAME
2                               STATEMENT OF OPERATIONS
3                               (ACTUAL, PLANNED, OR VARIANCE)
4                               FOR THE PERIOD ENDING MM/DD/YY
5
6                                   MONTH     MONTH     MONTH       4TH     Y-T-D
7   CLASSIFICATION                     10        11        12   QUARTER     TOTAL
8   --------------------------------------------------------------------------
9   SALES                                                             0        0
10  --------------------------------------------------------------------------
11  COST OF GOODS SOLD:
12   BEGINNING INVENTORY                                              0        0
13   PURCHASES                                                        0        0
14   ENDING INVENTORY                                                 0        0
15                              -------- -------- -------- -------- --------
16     COST OF GOODS SOLD              0        0        0        0        0
17  --------------------------------------------------------------------------
18  GROSS PROFIT                       0        0        0        0        0
19  --------------------------------------------------------------------------
20  OPERATING EXPENSES:
21   SALARIES & WAGES                                                 0        0
22   FRINGE BENEFITS                                                  0        0
23   FICA TAX                                                         0        0
24   FED'L UNEMPLOYMENT INSUR                                         0        0
25   STATE UNEMPLOYMENT INSUR                                         0        0
26   BUILDING RENT                                                    0        0
27   COMPUTER RENT                                                    0        0
28   DEPRECIATION                                                     0        0
29   OFFICE SUPPLIES                                                  0        0
30   EQUIPMENT MAINTENANCE                                            0        0
31   TELEPHONE                                                        0        0
32   ELECTRICITY                                                      0        0
33   HEAT                                                             0        0
34   ADVERTISING                                                      0        0
35   POSTAGE & FREIGHT                                                0        0
36   SALES PROMOTIONS                                                 0        0
37   PROFESSIONAL MEMBERSHIPS                                         0        0
38   SUBSCRIPTIONS                                                    0        0
39   EQUIPMENT INSURANCE                                              0        0
40                              -------- -------- -------- -------- --------
41     TOTAL EXPENSES                  0        0        0        0        0
42  --------------------------------------------------------------------------
43  PRE-TAX PROFIT                     0        0        0        0        0
44  FEDERAL TAXES                                                     0        0
45  STATE TAXES                                                       0        0
46                              -------- -------- -------- -------- --------
47  NET INCOME                         0        0        0        0        0
48                              ======== ======== ======== ======== ========
49
50
```

Figure 16.20 Statement of Operations Template: Quarterly Summary

```
   :           A              :: N  ::  O  ::  P  ::  Q  ::  R  :
1                             COMPANY NAME
2                             STATEMENT OF OPERATIONS
3                             (ACTUAL, PLANNED, OR VARIANCE)
4                             FOR THE PERIOD ENDING MM/DD/YY
5
6                                   1ST      2ND      3RD      4TH     Y-T-D
7  CLASSIFICATION                QUARTER  QUARTER  QUARTER  QUARTER    TOTAL
8  ------------------------------------------------------------------------
9  SALES                              0        0        0        0        0
10 ------------------------------------------------------------------------
11 COST OF GOODS SOLD:
12  BEGINNING INVENTORY               0        0        0        0        0
13  PURCHASES                         0        0        0        0        0
14  ENDING INVENTORY                  0        0        0        0        0
15                              -------- -------- -------- -------- --------
16     COST OF GOODS SOLD             0        0        0        0        0
17 ------------------------------------------------------------------------
18 GROSS PROFIT                       0        0        0        0        0
19 ------------------------------------------------------------------------
20 OPERATING EXPENSES:
21  SALARIES & WAGES                  0        0        0        0        0
22  FRINGE BENEFITS                   0        0        0        0        0
23  FICA TAX                          0        0        0        0        0
24  FED'L UNEMPLOYMENT INSUR          0        0        0        0        0
25  STATE UNEMPLOYMENT INSUR          0        0        0        0        0
26  BUILDING RENT                     0        0        0        0        0
27  COMPUTER RENT                     0        0        0        0        0
28  DEPRECIATION                      0        0        0        0        0
29  OFFICE SUPPLIES                   0        0        0        0        0
30  EQUIPMENT MAINTENANCE             0        0        0        0        0
31  TELEPHONE                         0        0        0        0        0
32  ELECTRICITY                       0        0        0        0        0
33  HEAT                              0        0        0        0        0
34  ADVERTISING                       0        0        0        0        0
35  POSTAGE & FREIGHT                 0        0        0        0        0
36  SALES PROMOTIONS                  0        0        0        0        0
37  PROFESSIONAL MEMBERSHIPS          0        0        0        0        0
38  SUBSCRIPTIONS                     0        0        0        0        0
39  EQUIPMENT INSURANCE               0        0        0        0        0
40                              -------- -------- -------- -------- --------
41     TOTAL EXPENSES                 0        0        0        0        0
42 ------------------------------------------------------------------------
43 PRE-TAX PROFIT                     0        0        0        0        0
44 FEDERAL TAXES                      0        0        0        0        0
45 STATE TAXES                        0        0        0        0        0
46                              -------- -------- -------- -------- --------
47 NET INCOME                         0        0        0        0        0
48                              ======== ======== ======== ======== ========
49
50
```

Remember, once a command file has been constructed, the borders must be toggled off. Column A must be wide enough so that none of the commands overflow into column B, otherwise they will be truncated at execution time. The command file spreadsheet is then put onto disk via the /Output command.

Many organizations formulate elaborate forecasts of expected operating results across the fiscal year. Sometimes these forecasts are called profit plans, sometimes they're called operating budgets. One of the models provided in this section illustrates this planning tool. It incorporates the assumptions shown in the following table.

Classification	Month #1	Months 2–12
Sales	$3,000,000	compounded @ 10%
Beginning Inventory	350,000	prior month ending
Purchases	1,200,000	compounded @ 12%
Ending Inventory	125,000	compounded @ 2.5%
Salaries & Wages	100,000	compounded @ 8%
Fringe Benefits	20% of wages	same as month #1
FICA Tax	6.7% of wages	same as month #1
Fed'l Unemployment	3.4% of wages	same as month #1
State Unemployment	2% of wages	same as month #1
Building Rent	5,000	same as month #1
Computer Rent	2,000	same as month #1
Depreciation	12,000	compounded @ 8%
Office Supplies	1,000	compounded @ 8%
Equipment Maintenance	1,000	compounded @ 8%
Telephone	2,000	compounded @ 8%
Electricity	2,000	compounded @ 8%
Heat	2,000	compounded @ 8%
Advertising	25,000	compounded @ 8%
Postage & Freight	21,000	compounded @ 8%
Sales Promotions	15,000	compounded @ 8%
Professional Memberships	1,000	same as month #1
Subscriptions	1,000	same as month #1
Equipment Insurance	4,100	compounded @ 8%

The above assumptions are entered into the template, which is saved as a budget data spreadsheet. Throughout the data entry process, the /Replicate command can be used to accelerate the speed of entry.

Figure 16.21 shows a command file that prints the budget spreadsheet one fiscal quarter at a time and then prints a quarterly budget summary.

Figure 16.21 **Macro to Print Statement of Operations (Planned) Spreadsheet by Quarter**

```
   :     A     :
/ZY
/LB:BUDOPSTA,A
/FCE:M,0
/FCO:Q,0
/ODA1:R50,P
/FCB:R,9
/FCB:D,0
/FCH:N,0
/FCP:Q,0
/ODA1:R50,P
/FCB:R,9
/FCB:G,0
/FCK:O,0
/FCQ,0
/ODA1:R50,P
/FCB:R,9
/FCB:J,0
/FCN:P,0
/ODA1:R50,P
/FCB:R,9
/FCB:M,0
/ODA1:R50,P
/FCB:R,9
```

Entering **/XPLMACR02.XQT** executes the command file and produces the results shown in Figures 16.22 through 16.26.

Figure 16.22 Statement of Operations (Planned): First Quarter

```
    !          A            !!   B    !!   C    !!   D    !!   N    !!   R    !
1                             BILL & CONNIE'S ELECTRONIC COTTAGE
2                             STATEMENT OF OPERATIONS
3                             (PLANNED)
4                             FOR THE PERIOD ENDING 12/31/84
5
6                                 MONTH     MONTH     MONTH      1ST     Y-T-D
7   CLASSIFICATION                    1         2         3  QUARTER     TOTAL
8   ------------------------------------------------------------------------
9   SALES                       3000000   3300000   3630000  9930000  64152850
10  ------------------------------------------------------------------------
11  COST OF GOODS SOLD:
12   BEGINNING INVENTORY         350000    125000    128125   350000    350000
13   PURCHASES                  1200000   1344000   1505280  4049280  28959771
14   ENDING INVENTORY            125000    128125    131328   131328    164011
15                             --------  --------  --------  --------  --------
16     COST OF GOODS SOLD       1425000   1340875   1502077  4267952  29145760
17  ------------------------------------------------------------------------
18  GROSS PROFIT                1575000   1959125   2127923  5662048  35007090
19  ------------------------------------------------------------------------
20  OPERATING EXPENSES:
21   SALARIES & WAGES            100000    108000    116640   324640   1897720
22   FRINGE BENEFITS              20000     21600     23328    64928    379545
23   FICA TAX                      6700      7236      7815    21751    127147
24   FED'L UNEMPLOYMENT INSUR      3400      3672      3966    11038     64523
25   STATE UNEMPLOYMENT INSUR      2000      2160      2333     6493     37955
26   BUILDING RENT                 5000      5000      5000    15000     60000
27   COMPUTER RENT                 2000      2000      2000     6000     24000
28   DEPRECIATION                 12000     12960     13997    38957    227727
29   OFFICE SUPPLIES               1000      1080      1166     3246     18976
30   EQUIPMENT MAINTENANCE         1000      1080      1166     3246     18976
31   TELEPHONE                     2000      2160      2333     6493     37965
32   ELECTRICITY                   2000      2160      2333     6493     37965
33   HEAT                          2000      2160      2333     6493     37965
34   ADVERTISING                  25000     27000     29160    81160    474432
35   POSTAGE & FREIGHT            21000     22680     24494    68174    398517
36   SALES PROMOTIONS             15000     16200     17496    48696    284665
37   PROFESSIONAL MEMBERSHIPS      1000      1000      1000     3000     12000
38   SUBSCRIPTIONS                 1000      1000      1000     3000     12000
39   EQUIPMENT INSURANCE           4100      4428      4782    13310     77802
40                             --------  --------  --------  --------  --------
41     TOTAL EXPENSES            226200    243576    262342   732118   4229880
42  ------------------------------------------------------------------------
43  PRE-TAX PROFIT              1348800   1715549   1865581  4929930  30777210
44  FEDERAL TAXES                674400    857775    932791  2464966  15388608
45  STATE TAXES                  161856    205866    223870   591592   3693267
46                             --------  --------  --------  --------  --------
47  NET INCOME                   512544    651908    708920  1873372  11695335
48                             ========  ========  ========  ========  ========
49
50
```

Figure 16.23 Statement of Operations (Planned): Second Quarter

BILL & CONNIE'S ELECTRONIC COTTAGE
STATEMENT OF OPERATIONS
(PLANNED)
FOR THE PERIOD ENDING 12/31/84

	A	E	F	G	O	R
6		MONTH	MONTH	MONTH	2ND	Y-T-D
7	CLASSIFICATION	4	5	6	QUARTER	TOTAL
9	SALES	3993000	4392300	4831530	13216830	64152850
11	COST OF GOODS SOLD:					
12	BEGINNING INVENTORY	131328	134611	137976	131328	350000
13	PURCHASES	1685914	1888224	2114811	5688949	28959771
14	ENDING INVENTORY	134611	137976	141425	141425	164011
16	COST OF GOODS SOLD	1682631	1884859	2111362	5678852	29145760
18	GROSS PROFIT	2310369	2507441	2720168	7537978	35007090
20	OPERATING EXPENSES:					
21	SALARIES & WAGES	125971	136049	146933	408953	1897720
22	FRINGE BENEFITS	25194	27210	29387	81791	379545
23	FICA TAX	8440	9115	9845	27400	127147
24	FED'L UNEMPLOYMENT INSUR	4283	4626	4996	13905	64523
25	STATE UNEMPLOYMENT INSUR	2519	2721	2939	8179	37955
26	BUILDING RENT	5000	5000	5000	15000	60000
27	COMPUTER RENT	2000	2000	2000	6000	24000
28	DEPRECIATION	15117	16326	17632	49075	227727
29	OFFICE SUPPLIES	1259	1360	1469	4088	18976
30	EQUIPMENT MAINTENANCE	1259	1360	1469	4088	18976
31	TELEPHONE	2520	2722	2940	8182	37965
32	ELECTRICITY	2520	2722	2940	8182	37965
33	HEAT	2520	2722	2940	8182	37965
34	ADVERTISING	31493	34012	36733	102238	474432
35	POSTAGE & FREIGHT	26454	28570	30856	85880	398517
36	SALES PROMOTIONS	18896	20408	22041	61345	284665
37	PROFESSIONAL MEMBERSHIPS	1000	1000	1000	3000	12000
38	SUBSCRIPTIONS	1000	1000	1000	3000	12000
39	EQUIPMENT INSURANCE	5165	5578	6024	16767	77802
41	TOTAL EXPENSES	282610	304501	328144	915255	4229880
43	PRE-TAX PROFIT	2027759	2202940	2392024	6622723	30777210
44	FEDERAL TAXES	1013880	1101470	1196012	3311362	15388608
45	STATE TAXES	243331	264353	287043	794727	3693267
47	NET INCOME	770548	837117	908969	2516634	11695335

Figure 16.24 Statement of Operations (Planned): Third Quarter

BILL & CONNIE'S ELECTRONIC COTTAGE
STATEMENT OF OPERATIONS
(PLANNED)
FOR THE PERIOD ENDING 12/31/84

	A	H	I	J	P	R
6		MONTH	MONTH	MONTH	3RD	Y-T-D
7	CLASSIFICATION	7	8	9	QUARTER	TOTAL
9	SALES	5314683	5846151	6430766	17591600	64152850
11	COST OF GOODS SOLD:					
12	BEGINNING INVENTORY	141425	144961	148585	141425	350000
13	PURCHASES	2368588	2652819	2971157	7992564	28959771
14	ENDING INVENTORY	144961	148585	152300	152300	164011
16	COST OF GOODS SOLD	2365052	2649195	2967442	7981689	29145760
18	GROSS PROFIT	2949631	3196956	3463324	9609911	35007090
20	OPERATING EXPENSES:					
21	SALARIES & WAGES	158688	171383	185094	515165	1897720
22	FRINGE BENEFITS	31738	34277	37019	103034	379545
23	FICA TAX	10632	11483	12401	34516	127147
24	FED'L UNEMPLOYMENT INSUR	5395	5827	6293	17515	64523
25	STATE UNEMPLOYMENT INSUR	3174	3428	3702	10304	37955

(continued on next page)

26	BUILDING RENT	5000	5000	5000	15000	60000
27	COMPUTER RENT	2000	2000	2000	6000	24000
28	DEPRECIATION	19043	20566	22211	61820	227727
29	OFFICE SUPPLIES	1587	1714	1851	5152	18976
30	EQUIPMENT MAINTENANCE	1587	1714	1851	5152	18976
31	TELEPHONE	3175	3429	3703	10307	37965
32	ELECTRICITY	3175	3429	3703	10307	37965
33	HEAT	3175	3429	3703	10307	37965
34	ADVERTISING	39672	42846	46274	128792	474432
35	POSTAGE & FREIGHT	33324	35990	38869	108183	398517
36	SALES PROMOTIONS	23804	25708	27765	77277	284665
37	PROFESSIONAL MEMBERSHIPS	1000	1000	1000	3000	12000
38	SUBSCRIPTIONS	1000	1000	1000	3000	12000
39	EQUIPMENT INSURANCE	6506	7026	7588	21120	77802
40		--------	--------	--------	--------	--------
41	TOTAL EXPENSES	353675	381249	411027	1145951	4229880
42	----------------------------	--------	--------	--------	--------	--------
43	PRE-TAX PROFIT	2595956	2815707	3052297	8463960	30777210
44	FEDERAL TAXES	1297978	1407854	1526149	4231981	15388608
45	STATE TAXES	311515	337885	366276	1015676	3693267
46		--------	--------	--------	--------	--------
47	NET INCOME	986463	1069968	1159872	3216303	11695335
48		========	========	========	========	========
49						
50						

Figure 16.25 Statement of Operations (Planned): Fourth Quarter

	A	K	L	M	Q	R
1		BILL & CONNIE'S ELECTRONIC COTTAGE				
2		STATEMENT OF OPERATIONS				
3		(PLANNED)				
4		FOR THE PERIOD ENDING 12/31/84				
5						
6		MONTH	MONTH	MONTH	4TH	Y-T-D
7	CLASSIFICATION	10	11	12	QUARTER	TOTAL
8	----------------------------	--------	--------	--------	--------	--------
9	SALES	7073843	7781227	8559350	23414420	64152850
10	----------------------------	--------	--------	--------	--------	--------
11	COST OF GOODS SOLD:					
12	BEGINNING INVENTORY	152300	156108	160011	152300	350000
13	PURCHASES	3327696	3727020	4174262	11228978	28959771
14	ENDING INVENTORY	156108	160011	164011	164011	164011
15		--------	--------	--------	--------	--------
16	COST OF GOODS SOLD	3323888	3723117	4170262	11217267	29145760
17	----------------------------	--------	--------	--------	--------	--------
18	GROSS PROFIT	3749955	4058110	4389088	12197153	35007090
19	----------------------------	--------	--------	--------	--------	--------
20	OPERATING EXPENSES:					
21	SALARIES & WAGES	199902	215894	233166	648962	1897720
22	FRINGE BENEFITS	39980	43179	46633	129792	379545
23	FICA TAX	13393	14465	15622	43480	127147
24	FED'L UNEMPLOYMENT INSUR	6797	7340	7928	22065	64523
25	STATE UNEMPLOYMENT INSUR	3998	4318	4663	12979	37955
26	BUILDING RENT	5000	5000	5000	15000	60000
27	COMPUTER RENT	2000	2000	2000	6000	24000
28	DEPRECIATION	23988	25907	27980	77875	227727
29	OFFICE SUPPLIES	1999	2159	2332	6490	18976
30	EQUIPMENT MAINTENANCE	1999	2159	2332	6490	18976
31	TELEPHONE	3999	4319	4665	12983	37965
32	ELECTRICITY	3999	4319	4665	12983	37965
33	HEAT	3999	4319	4665	12983	37965
34	ADVERTISING	49976	53974	58292	162242	474432
35	POSTAGE & FREIGHT	41979	45337	48964	136280	398517
36	SALES PROMOTIONS	29986	32385	34976	97347	284665
37	PROFESSIONAL MEMBERSHIPS	1000	1000	1000	3000	12000
38	SUBSCRIPTIONS	1000	1000	1000	3000	12000
39	EQUIPMENT INSURANCE	8195	8851	9559	26605	77802
40		--------	--------	--------	--------	--------
41	TOTAL EXPENSES	443189	477925	515442	1436556	4229880
42	----------------------------	--------	--------	--------	--------	--------
43	PRE-TAX PROFIT	3306766	3580185	3873646	10760597	30777210
44	FEDERAL TAXES	1653383	1790093	1936823	5380299	15388608
45	STATE TAXES	396812	429622	464838	1291272	3693267
46		--------	--------	--------	--------	--------
47	NET INCOME	1256571	1360470	1471985	4089026	11695335
48		========	========	========	========	========
49						
50						

Figure 16.26 Statement of Operations (Planned): Quarterly Summary

	A	N	O	P	Q	R
1		BILL & CONNIE'S ELECTRONIC COTTAGE				
2		STATEMENT OF OPERATIONS				
3		(PLANNED)				
4		FOR THE PERIOD ENDING 12/31/84				
5						
6		1ST	2ND	3RD	4TH	Y-T-D
7	CLASSIFICATION	QUARTER	QUARTER	QUARTER	QUARTER	TOTAL
8	----------------------	--------	--------	--------	--------	--------
9	SALES	9930000	13216830	17591600	23414420	64152850
10	----------------------	--------	--------	--------	--------	--------
11	COST OF GOODS SOLD:					
12	BEGINNING INVENTORY	350000	131328	141425	152300	350000
13	PURCHASES	4049280	5688949	7992564	11228978	28959771
14	ENDING INVENTORY	131328	141425	152300	164011	164011
15		--------	--------	--------	--------	--------
16	COST OF GOODS SOLD	4267952	5678852	7981689	11217267	29145760
17	----------------------	--------	--------	--------	--------	--------
18	GROSS PROFIT	5662048	7537978	9609911	12197153	35007090
19	----------------------	--------	--------	--------	--------	--------
20	OPERATING EXPENSES:					
21	SALARIES & WAGES	324640	408953	515165	648962	1897720
22	FRINGE BENEFITS	64928	81791	103034	129792	379545
23	FICA TAX	21751	27400	34516	43480	127147
24	FED'L UNEMPLOYMENT INSUR	11038	13905	17515	22065	64523
25	STATE UNEMPLOYMENT INSUR	6493	8179	10304	12979	37955
26	BUILDING RENT	15000	15000	15000	15000	60000
27	COMPUTER RENT	6000	6000	6000	6000	24000
28	DEPRECIATION	38957	49075	61820	77875	227727
29	OFFICE SUPPLIES	3246	4088	5152	6490	18976
30	EQUIPMENT MAINTENANCE	3246	4088	5152	6490	18976
31	TELEPHONE	6493	8182	10307	12983	37965
32	ELECTRICITY	6493	8182	10307	12983	37965
33	HEAT	6493	8182	10307	12983	37965
34	ADVERTISING	81160	102238	128792	162242	474432
35	POSTAGE & FREIGHT	68174	85880	108183	136280	398517
36	SALES PROMOTIONS	48696	61345	77277	97347	284665
37	PROFESSIONAL MEMBERSHIPS	3000	3000	3000	3000	12000
38	SUBSCRIPTIONS	3000	3000	3000	3000	12000
39	EQUIPMENT INSURANCE	13310	16767	21120	26605	77802
40		--------	--------	--------	--------	--------
41	TOTAL EXPENSES	732118	915255	1145951	1436556	4229880
42	----------------------	--------	--------	--------	--------	--------
43	PRE-TAX PROFIT	4929930	6622723	8463960	10760597	30777210
44	FEDERAL TAXES	2464966	3311362	4231981	5380299	15388608
45	STATE TAXES	591592	794727	1015676	1291272	3693267
46		--------	--------	--------	--------	--------
47	NET INCOME	1873372	2516634	3216303	4089026	11695335
48		========	========	========	========	========
49						
50						

At the beginning of the fiscal year, the actual results of operations for month #1 are entered into the template. The template is then saved as an actual data spreadsheet. As the fiscal year progresses, the monthly operating results are entered into the actual data spreadsheet.

Periodically, financial analysts compare the actual results of operations against the planned results. The difference between plan and actual is called the variance, and the process of analyzing the difference is called variance analysis. From an income perspective—i.e., sales, gross profit, pre-tax profit, and net income—a favorable variance exists when actual amounts exceed plan amounts. Conversely, an unfavorable variance exists when plan amounts exceed actual amounts. From an expense viewpoint—i.e., cost of goods sold, operating expenses, and income taxes—there is a favorable variance when plan amounts are greater than actual amounts. On the other hand, there is an unfavorable variance when actual amounts are greater than plan amounts.

An analysis of the specific circumstances indicates whether the variance is due to poor planning or to events that could not be reasonably foreseen at the time the plan was formulated.

Figure 16.27 shows a command file that prints the first quarter actual results, calculates the variance through a partial load of the first quarter budget data using the consolidating subtraction, and then prints the first quarter variance.

Figure 16.27 Macro to Print First Quarter Actual and Variance from Plan

```
      :            A            :
1     /ZY
2     /LB:ACTOPSTA,A
3     /FCE:M,0
4     /FCO:Q,0
5     /ODA1:R50,P
6     =B3
7     &
8     /LB:BUDOPSTA,PB9:D47,B9,-
9     !
10    /ODA1:R50,P
```

Entering **/XPLMACR03.XQT** executes the command file and produces the results shown in Figures 16.28 and 16.29.

Figure 16.28 Statement of Operations (Actual): First Quarter

```
      :            A            :: B   :: C   :: D   :: N   :: R   :
1                                 BILL & CONNIE'S ELECTRONIC COTTAGE
2                                 STATEMENT OF OPERATIONS
3                                 (ACTUAL)
4                                 FOR THE PERIOD ENDING 06/30/84
5
6                                    MONTH    MONTH    MONTH      1ST      Y-T-D
7     CLASSIFICATION                     1        2        3  QUARTER     TOTAL
8     ------------------------------------------------------------------------
9     SALES                        1500000  3000000  4000000  8500000   8500000
10    ------------------------------------------------------------------------
11    COST OF GOODS SOLD:
12     BEGINNING INVENTORY          475000    75000   135123   475000    475000
13     PURCHASES                   1200000  1234000  1305765  3739765   3739765
14     ENDING INVENTORY              75000   135123   145875   145875    145875
15                                --------  -------- -------- --------  --------
16       COST OF GOODS SOLD        1600000  1173877  1295013  4068890   4068890
17    ------------------------------------------------------------------------
18    GROSS PROFIT                 -100000  1826123  2704987  4431110   4431110
19    ------------------------------------------------------------------------
20    OPERATING EXPENSES:
21     SALARIES & WAGES             103000   112000   135875   350875    350875
22     FRINGE BENEFITS               20600    22400    27175    70175     70175
23     FICA TAX                       6901     7504     9104    23509     23509
24     FED'L UNEMPLOYMENT INSUR       3502     3808     4620    11930     11930
25     STATE UNEMPLOYMENT INSUR       2060     2240     2718     7018      7018
```

(continued on next page)

26	BUILDING RENT	5000	5000	5000	15000	15000
27	COMPUTER RENT	2000	2000	2000	6000	6000
28	DEPRECIATION	12000	12960	13997	38957	38957
29	OFFICE SUPPLIES	1100	1000	1200	3300	3300
30	EQUIPMENT MAINTENANCE	1050	995	1160	3205	3205
31	TELEPHONE	2100	2200	2400	6700	6700
32	ELECTRICITY	2100	2200	2400	6700	6700
33	HEAT	2100	2200	2400	6700	6700
34	ADVERTISING	24500	27750	30000	82250	82250
35	POSTAGE & FREIGHT	19500	23500	26500	69500	69500
36	SALES PROMOTIONS	16200	17500	18575	52275	52275
37	PROFESSIONAL MEMBERSHIPS	585	695	1035	2315	2315
38	SUBSCRIPTIONS	985	1015	1035	3035	3035
39	EQUIPMENT INSURANCE	4500	4500	4500	13500	13500
40		--------	--------	--------	--------	--------
41	TOTAL EXPENSES	229783	251467	291694	772944	772944
42	--------------------------	--------	--------	--------	--------	--------
43	PRE-TAX PROFIT	-329783	1574656	2413293	3658166	3658166
44	FEDERAL TAXES	-164892	787328	1206647	1829083	1829083
45	STATE TAXES	-39574	188959	289595	438980	438980
46		--------	--------	--------	--------	--------
47	NET INCOME	-125317	598369	917051	1390103	1390103
48		========	========	========	========	========
49						
50						

Figure 16.29 Statement of Operations (Variance): First Quarter

	A	B	C	D	N	R
1		BILL & CONNIE'S ELECTRONIC COTTAGE				
2		STATEMENT OF OPERATIONS				
3		(VARIANCE)				
4		FOR THE PERIOD ENDING 06/30/84				
5						
6		MONTH	MONTH	MONTH	1ST	Y-T-D
7	CLASSIFICATION	1	2	3	QUARTER	TOTAL
8	--------------------------	--------	--------	--------	--------	--------
9	SALES	-1500000	-300000	370000	-1430000	-1430000
10	--------------------------	--------	--------	--------	--------	--------
11	COST OF GOODS SOLD:					
12	BEGINNING INVENTORY	125000	-50000	6998	125000	125000
13	PURCHASES	0	-110000	-199515	-309515	-309515
14	ENDING INVENTORY	-50000	6998	14547	14547	14547
15		--------	--------	--------	--------	--------
16	COST OF GOODS SOLD	175000	-166998	-207064	-199062	-199062
17	--------------------------	--------	--------	--------	--------	--------
18	GROSS PROFIT	-1675000	-133[illegible]	577064	-1230938	-1230938
19	--------------------------	--------	--------	--------	--------	--------
20	OPERATING EXPENSES:					
21	SALARIES & WAGES	3000	4000	19235	26235	26235
22	FRINGE BENEFITS	600	800	3847	5247	5247
23	FICA TAX	201	268	1289	1758	1758
24	FED'L UNEMPLOYMENT INSUR	102	136	654	892	892
25	STATE UNEMPLOYMENT INSUR	60	80	385	525	525
26	BUILDING RENT	0	0	0	0	0
27	COMPUTER RENT	0	0	0	0	0
28	DEPRECIATION	0	0	0	0	0
29	OFFICE SUPPLIES	100	-80	34	54	54
30	EQUIPMENT MAINTENANCE	50	-85	-6	-41	-41
31	TELEPHONE	100	40	67	207	207
32	ELECTRICITY	100	40	67	207	207
33	HEAT	100	40	67	207	207
34	ADVERTISING	-500	750	840	1090	1090
35	POSTAGE & FREIGHT	-1500	820	2006	1326	1326
36	SALES PROMOTIONS	1200	1300	1079	3579	3579
37	PROFESSIONAL MEMBERSHIPS	-415	-305	35	-685	-685
38	SUBSCRIPTIONS	-15	15	35	35	35
39	EQUIPMENT INSURANCE	400	72	-282	190	190
40		--------	--------	--------	--------	--------
41	TOTAL EXPENSES	3583	7891	29352	40826	40826
42	--------------------------	--------	--------	--------	--------	--------
43	PRE-TAX PROFIT	-1678583	-140893	547712	-1271764	-1271764
44	FEDERAL TAXES	-839292	-70447	273856	-635883	-635883
45	STATE TAXES	-201430	-16907	65725	-152612	-152612
46		--------	--------	--------	--------	--------
47	NET INCOME	-637861	-53539	208131	-483269	-483269
48		========	========	========	========	========
49						
50						

Some managements reforecast their operating plan to reflect actual results from the prior quarter. This allows management to make interim adjustments to planned results for future quarters based on the actual results of previous quarters.

Figure 16.30 shows a command file that updates the first quarter actual results into the budget spreadsheet, then prints the reforecast spreadsheet one quarter at a time followed by a quarterly summary.

Figure 16.30 **Macro to Reforecast Remainder of Fiscal Year Based on First Quarter Results**

```
        :           A           :
1       /ZY
2       /LB:BUDOPSTA,A
3       /LB:ACTOPSTA,PB9:D47,B9
4       /FCE:M,0
5       /FCO:Q,0
6       =B3
7       &
8       !
9       /ODA1:R50,P
10      /FCB:R,9
11      /FCB:D,0
12      /FCH:N,0
13      /FCP:Q,0
14      /ODA1:R50,P
15      /FCB:R,9
16      /FCB:G,0
17      /FCK:O,0
18      /FCQ,0
19      /ODA1:R50,P
20      /FCB:R,9
21      /FCB:J,0
22      /FCN:P,0
23      /ODA1:R50,P
24      /FCB:R,9
25      /FCB:M,0
26      /ODA1:R50,P
27      /FCB:R,9
```

Entering **/XPLMACR04.XQT** executes the command file and produces the results shown in Figures 16.31 through 16.35.

Figure 16.31 Statement of Operations (Reforecast): First Quarter

	A	B	C	D	N	R
1		BILL & CONNIE'S ELECTRONIC COTTAGE				
2		STATEMENT OF OPERATIONS				
3		1ST QUARTER REFORECAST OF PLAN				
4		FOR THE PERIOD ENDING 12/31/84				
5						
6		MONTH	MONTH	MONTH	1ST	Y-T-D
7	CLASSIFICATION	1	2	3	QUARTER	TOTAL
8	----------	--------	--------	--------	--------	--------
9	SALES	1500000	3000000	4000000	8500000	68249698
10	----------	--------	--------	--------	--------	--------
11	COST OF GOODS SOLD:					
12	BEGINNING INVENTORY	475000	75000	135123	475000	475000
13	PURCHASES	1200000	1234000	1305765	3739765	25348533
14	ENDING INVENTORY	75000	135123	145875	145875	182177
15		--------	--------	--------	--------	--------
16	COST OF GOODS SOLD	1600000	1173877	1295013	4068890	25641356
17	----------	--------	--------	--------	--------	--------
18	GROSS PROFIT	-100000	1826123	2704987	4431110	42608342
19	----------	--------	--------	--------	--------	--------
20	OPERATING EXPENSES:					
21	SALARIES & WAGES	103000	112000	135875	350875	2183369
22	FRINGE BENEFITS	20600	22400	27175	70175	436673
23	FICA TAX	6901	7504	9104	23509	146284
24	FED'L UNEMPLOYMENT INSUR	3502	3808	4620	11930	74234
25	STATE UNEMPLOYMENT INSUR	2060	2240	2718	7018	43667
26	BUILDING RENT	5000	5000	5000	15000	60000
27	COMPUTER RENT	2000	2000	2000	6000	24000
28	DEPRECIATION	12000	12960	13997	38957	227727
29	OFFICE SUPPLIES	1100	1000	1200	3300	19489
30	EQUIPMENT MAINTENANCE	1050	995	1160	3205	18845
31	TELEPHONE	2100	2200	2400	6700	39065
32	ELECTRICITY	2100	2200	2400	6700	39065
33	HEAT	2100	2200	2400	6700	39065
34	ADVERTISING	24500	27750	30000	82250	486838
35	POSTAGE & FREIGHT	19500	23500	26500	69500	426899
36	SALES PROMOTIONS	16200	17500	18575	52275	302787
37	PROFESSIONAL MEMBERSHIPS	585	695	1035	2315	11315
38	SUBSCRIPTIONS	985	1015	1035	3035	12035
39	EQUIPMENT INSURANCE	4500	4500	4500	13500	74195
40		--------	--------	--------	--------	--------
41	TOTAL EXPENSES	229783	251467	291694	772944	4665552
42	----------	--------	--------	--------	--------	--------
43	PRE-TAX PROFIT	-329783	1574656	2413293	3658166	37942790
44	FEDERAL TAXES	-164892	787328	1206647	1829083	18971398
45	STATE TAXES	-39574	188959	289595	438980	4553135
46		--------	--------	--------	--------	--------
47	NET INCOME	-125317	598369	917051	1390103	14418257
48		========	========	========	========	========
49						
50						

Figure 16.32 Statement of Operations (Reforecast): Second Quarter

	A	E	F	G	O	R
1		BILL & CONNIE'S ELECTRONIC COTTAGE				
2		STATEMENT OF OPERATIONS				
3		1ST QUARTER REFORECAST OF PLAN				
4		FOR THE PERIOD ENDING 12/31/84				
5						
6		MONTH	MONTH	MONTH	2ND	Y-T-D
7	CLASSIFICATION	4	5	6	QUARTER	TOTAL
8	----------	--------	--------	--------	--------	--------
9	SALES	4400000	4840000	5324000	14564000	68249698
10	----------	--------	--------	--------	--------	--------
11	COST OF GOODS SOLD:					
12	BEGINNING INVENTORY	145875	149522	153260	145875	475000
13	PURCHASES	1462457	1637952	1834506	4934915	25348533
14	ENDING INVENTORY	149522	153260	157092	157092	182177
15		--------	--------	--------	--------	--------
16	COST OF GOODS SOLD	1458810	1634214	1830674	4923698	25641356
17	----------	--------	--------	--------	--------	--------
18	GROSS PROFIT	2941190	3205786	3493326	9640302	42608342
19	----------	--------	--------	--------	--------	--------
20	OPERATING EXPENSES:					
21	SALARIES & WAGES	146745	158485	171164	476394	2183369
22	FRINGE BENEFITS	29349	31697	34233	95279	436673
23	FICA TAX	9832	10618	11468	31918	146284
24	FED'L UNEMPLOYMENT INSUR	4989	5388	5820	16197	74234

(continued on next page)

25	STATE UNEMPLOYMENT INSUR	2935	3170	3423	9528	43667
26	BUILDING RENT	5000	5000	5000	15000	60000
27	COMPUTER RENT	2000	2000	2000	6000	24000
28	DEPRECIATION	15117	16326	17632	49075	227727
29	OFFICE SUPPLIES	1296	1400	1512	4208	19489
30	EQUIPMENT MAINTENANCE	1253	1353	1461	4067	18845
31	TELEPHONE	2592	2799	3023	8414	39065
32	ELECTRICITY	2592	2799	3023	8414	39065
33	HEAT	2592	2799	3023	8414	39065
34	ADVERTISING	32400	34992	37791	105183	486838
35	POSTAGE & FREIGHT	28620	30910	33383	92913	426899
36	SALES PROMOTIONS	20061	21666	23399	65126	302787
37	PROFESSIONAL MEMBERSHIPS	1000	1000	1000	3000	11315
38	SUBSCRIPTIONS	1000	1000	1000	3000	12035
39	EQUIPMENT INSURANCE	4860	5249	5669	15778	74195
40		--------	--------	--------	--------	--------
41	TOTAL EXPENSES	314233	338651	365024	1017908	4665552
42	--------------------------------	--------	--------	--------	--------	--------
43	PRE-TAX PROFIT	2626957	2867135	3128302	8622394	37942790
44	FEDERAL TAXES	1313479	1433568	1564151	4311198	18971398
45	STATE TAXES	315235	344056	375396	1034687	4553135
46		--------	--------	--------	--------	--------
47	NET INCOME	998243	1089511	1188755	3276509	14418257
48		========	=======	=======	========	========
49						
50						

Figure 16.33 Statement of Operations (Reforecast): Third Quarter

BILL & [illegible]NNIE'S ELECTRONIC COTTAGE
STATEMENT OF OPERATIONS
1ST QUARTER REFORECAST OF PLAN
FOR THE PE[illegible]D ENDING 12/31/84

	A	H	I	J	P	R
1						
2						
3						
4						
5						
6		MONTH	MONTH	MONTH	3RD	Y-T-D
7	CLASSIFICATION	7	8	9	QUARTER	TOTAL
8	--------------------------------	--------	--------	--------	--------	--------
9	SALES	5856400	6442040	7086244	19384684	68249698
10	--------------------------------	--------	--------	--------	--------	--------
11	COST OF GOODS SOLD:					
12	BEGINNING INVENTORY	157092	161019	165044	157092	475000
13	PURCHASES	2054647	2301205	2577350	6933202	25348533
14	ENDING INVENTORY	161019	165044	169170	169170	182177
15		--------	--------	--------	--------	--------
16	COST OF GOODS SOLD	2050720	2297180	2573224	6921124	25641356
17	--------------------------------	--------	--------	--------	--------	--------
18	GROSS PROFIT	3805680	4144860	4513020	12463560	42608342
19	--------------------------------	--------	--------	--------	--------	--------
20	OPERATING EXPENSES:					
21	SALARIES & WAGES	184857	199646	215618	600121	2183369
22	FRINGE BENEFITS	36971	39929	43124	120024	436673
23	FICA TAX	12385	13376	14446	40207	146284
24	FED'L UNEMPLOYMENT INSUR	6285	6788	7331	20404	74234
25	STATE UNEMPLOYMENT INSUR	3697	3993	4312	12002	43667
26	BUILDING RENT	5000	5000	5000	15000	60000
27	COMPUTER RENT	2000	2000	2000	6000	24000
28	DEPRECIATION	19043	20566	22211	61820	227727
29	OFFICE SUPPLIES	1633	1764	1905	5302	19489
30	EQUIPMENT MAINTENANCE	1578	1704	1840	5122	18845
31	TELEPHONE	3265	3526	3808	10599	39065
32	ELECTRICITY	3265	3526	3808	10599	39065
33	HEAT	3265	3526	3808	10599	39065
34	ADVERTISING	40814	44079	47605	132498	486838
35	POSTAGE & FREIGHT	36054	38938	42053	117045	426899
36	SALES PROMOTIONS	25271	27293	29476	82040	302787
37	PROFESSIONAL MEMBERSHIPS	1000	1000	1000	3000	11315
38	SUBSCRIPTIONS	1000	1000	1000	3000	12035
39	EQUIPMENT INSURANCE	6123	6613	7142	19878	74195
40		--------	--------	--------	--------	--------
41	TOTAL EXPENSES	393506	424267	457487	1275260	4665552
42	--------------------------------	--------	--------	--------	--------	--------
43	PRE-TAX PROFIT	3412174	3720593	4055533	11188300	37942790
44	FEDERAL TAXES	1706087	1860297	2027767	5594151	18971398
45	STATE TAXES	409461	446471	486664	1342596	4553135
46		--------	--------	--------	--------	--------
47	NET INCOME	1296626	1413825	1541102	4251553	14418257
48		========	========	========	========	========
49						
50						

Figure 16.34 Statement of Operations (Reforecast): Fourth Quarter

	A	K	L	M	Q	R
1		BILL & CONNIE'S ELECTRONIC COTTAGE				
2		STATEMENT OF OPERATIONS				
3		1ST QUARTER REFORECAST OF PLAN				
4		FOR THE PERIOD ENDING 12/31/84				
5						
6		MONTH	MONTH	MONTH	4TH	Y-T-D
7	CLASSIFICATION	10	11	12	QUARTER	TOTAL
8	--------	--------	--------	--------	--------	--------
9	SALES	7794868	8574355	9431791	25801014	68249698
10	--------	--------	--------	--------	--------	--------
11	COST OF GOODS SOLD:					
12	BEGINNING INVENTORY	169170	173399	177734	169170	475000
13	PURCHASES	2886632	3233028	3620991	9740651	25348533
14	ENDING INVENTORY	173399	177734	182177	182177	182177
15		--------	--------	--------	--------	--------
16	COST OF GOODS SOLD	2882403	3228693	3616548	9727644	25641356
17	--------	--------	--------	--------	--------	--------
18	GROSS PROFIT	4912465	5345662	5815243	16073370	42608342
19	--------	--------	--------	--------	--------	--------
20	OPERATING EXPENSES:					
21	SALARIES & WAGES	232867	251496	271616	755979	2183369
22	FRINGE BENEFITS	46573	50299	54323	151195	436673
23	FICA TAX	15602	16850	18198	50650	146284
24	FED'L UNEMPLOYMENT INSUR	7917	8551	9235	25703	74234
25	STATE UNEMPLOYMENT INSUR	4657	5030	5432	15119	43667
26	BUILDING RENT	5000	5000	5000	15000	60000
27	COMPUTER RENT	2000	2000	2000	6000	24000
28	DEPRECIATION	23988	25907	27980	77875	227727
29	OFFICE SUPPLIES	2057	2222	2400	6679	19489
30	EQUIPMENT MAINTENANCE	1987	2146	2318	6451	18845
31	TELEPHONE	4113	4442	4797	13352	39065
32	ELECTRICITY	4113	4442	4797	13352	39065
33	HEAT	4113	4442	4797	13352	39065
34	ADVERTISING	51413	55526	59968	166907	486838
35	POSTAGE & FREIGHT	45417	49050	52974	147441	426899
36	SALES PROMOTIONS	31834	34381	37131	103346	302787
37	PROFESSIONAL MEMBERSHIPS	1000	1000	1000	3000	11315
38	SUBSCRIPTIONS	1000	1000	1000	3000	12035
39	EQUIPMENT INSURANCE	7713	8330	8996	25039	74195
40		--------	--------	--------	--------	--------
41	TOTAL EXPENSES	493364	532114	573962	1599440	4665552
42	--------	--------	--------	--------	--------	--------
43	PRE-TAX PROFIT	4419101	4813548	5241281	14473930	37942790
44	FEDERAL TAXES	2209551	2406774	2620641	7236966	18971398
45	STATE TAXES	530292	577626	628954	1736872	4553135
46		--------	--------	--------	--------	--------
47	NET INCOME	1679258	1829148	1991686	5500092	14418257
48		========	========	========	========	========
49						
50						

Figure 16.35 Statement of Operations (Reforecast): Quarterly Summary

	A	N	O	P	Q	R
1		BILL & CONNIE'S ELECTRONIC COTTAGE				
2		STATEMENT OF OPERATIONS				
3		1ST QUARTER REFORECAST OF PLAN				
4		FOR THE PERIOD ENDING 12/31/84				
5						
6		1ST	2ND	3RD	4TH	Y-T-D
7	CLASSIFICATION	QUARTER	QUARTER	QUARTER	QUARTER	TOTAL
8	--------	--------	--------	--------	--------	--------
9	SALES	8500000	14564000	19384684	25801014	68249698
10	--------	--------	--------	--------	--------	--------
11	COST OF GOODS SOLD:					
12	BEGINNING INVENTORY	475000	145875	157092	169170	475000
13	PURCHASES	3739765	4934915	6933202	9740651	25348533
14	ENDING INVENTORY	145875	157092	169170	182177	182177
15		--------	--------	--------	--------	--------
16	COST OF GOODS SOLD	4068890	4923698	6921124	9727644	25641356
17	--------	--------	--------	--------	--------	--------
18	GROSS PROFIT	4431110	9640302	12463560	16073370	42608342
19	--------	--------	--------	--------	--------	--------
20	OPERATING EXPENSES:					

(continued on next page)

21	SALARIES & WAGES	350875	476394	600121	755979	2183369
22	FRINGE BENEFITS	70175	95279	120024	151195	436673
23	FICA TAX	23509	31918	40207	50650	146284
24	FED'L UNEMPLOYMENT INSUR	11930	16197	20404	25703	74234
25	STATE UNEMPLOYMENT INSUR	7018	9528	12002	15119	43667
26	BUILDING RENT	15000	15000	15000	15000	60000
27	COMPUTER RENT	6000	6000	6000	6000	24000
28	DEPRECIATION	38957	49075	61820	77875	227727
29	OFFICE SUPPLIES	3300	4208	5302	6679	19489
30	EQUIPMENT MAINTENANCE	3205	4067	5122	6451	18845
31	TELEPHONE	6700	8414	10599	13352	39065
32	ELECTRICITY	6700	8414	10599	13352	39065
33	HEAT	6700	8414	10599	13352	39065
34	ADVERTISING	82250	105183	132498	166907	486838
35	POSTAGE & FREIGHT	69500	92913	117045	147441	426899
36	SALES PROMOTIONS	52275	65126	82040	103346	302787
37	PROFESSIONAL MEMBERSHIPS	2315	3000	3000	3000	11315
38	SUBSCRIPTIONS	3035	3000	3000	3000	12035
39	EQUIPMENT INSURANCE	13500	15778	19878	25039	74195
40		--------	--------	--------	--------	--------
41	TOTAL EXPENSES	772944	1017908	1275260	1599440	4665552
42	----------------------------------	--------	--------	--------	--------	--------
43	PRE-TAX PROFIT	3658166	8622394	11188300	14473930	37942790
44	FEDERAL TAXES	1829083	4311198	5594151	7236966	18971398
45	STATE TAXES	438980	1034687	1342596	1736872	4553135
46		--------	--------	--------	--------	--------
47	NET INCOME	1390103	3276509	4251553	5500092	14418257
48		========	========	========	========	========
49						
50						

Constructing Your Own Templates

There are two ways to construct a template—build one from an existing spreadsheet or design one from scratch.

Building a template from an existing spreadsheet is the easier of the two. In this situation you have a spreadsheet containing headings, formulas, and numeric data. You want to remove the numbers from the spreadsheet but leave the headings and formulas intact. Here's the procedure:

1. /Load the source spreadsheet.
2. /GF to toggle on formula display
3. Change all numeric values to zero. The /Replicate command will expedite matters.
4. /GF to toggle off formula display
5. /Save the template. Put something in the filename that identifies the spreadsheet as a template. Examples are TMPL, TMP, TPL, or just T.

You have just seen how to build a template from an existing spreadsheet. This technique is particularly useful for converting spreadsheets built by friends or business associates.

Although designing a spreadsheet from scratch is more complicated than converting an existing spreadsheet, the finished product generally brings with it a sense of achievement. This is particularly important to beginning spreadsheet users. As with everything else associated with computers, the key to success is having a logical and organized approach. The following guidelines provide some suggestions about how to approach your design project.

First, know your application. If you don't understand what you want to do, you'll never succeed in developing a spreadsheet for it. If you intend to design a spreadsheet to handle an income statement, you must understand the principles of accounting as they relate to profit and loss.

Second, sketch out on paper the general framework of the template. This includes determining the approximate number of rows and columns involved. Also included is the definition of margin and column headings. The headings for columns A through R in the Statement of Operations spreadsheet were determined at this point. The definition was also made here for the margin headings in cells A9 through A47 and the underlines.

Third, still using paper and pencil, identify the formulas to be used. It's better to express them using the nomenclature of the application rather than cell references. Keep things system independent at this point so that associates can review your design rather than addressing systems issues.

Consider the Statement of Operations example. The following formulas are based on general accounting principles and are applicable to the downward progression in all columns of the spreadsheet:

Cost of Goods Sold = Beginning Inventory + Purchases − Beginning Inventory
Gross Profit = Sales − Costs of Goods Sold
Total Expenses = Sum of all Operating Expenses
Pre-Tax Profit = Gross Profit − Total Expenses
Net Income = Pre-Tax Profit − Taxes on Income

Summation across rows in this example has been defined as:

1st Quarter = Month #1 + Month #2 + Month #3
2nd Quarter = Month #4 + Month #5 + Month #6
3rd Quarter = Month #7 + Month #8 + Month #9
4th Quarter = Month #10 + Month #11 + Month #12
Y-T-D Total = 1st Quarter + 2nd Quarter + 3rd Quarter + 4th Quarter

Fourth, turn on your computer and key in the design you've just sketched out. You'll probably find you want to make some formatting changes. The most likely ones are increasing some of the column widths and setting some of the column headings as right justification of text. Save the template as soon as you've completed entering it. Don't turn off your machine because you're not finished.

Fifth, and most important, test the template. Make up some data that is low in volume and magnitude—i.e., the size of the numbers themselves. Compute the results with an adding machine or hand-held calculator. Next, key the test data into your spreadsheet and compare these results against your manual computations. If the results are identical, you're finished. If they're not identical, check your spreadsheet formulas for an error. It's also possible you made a manual computation error, so you might have to recalculate those results if you can't find any problems in the spreadsheet.

The test data used for the Statement of Operations template covered the entire first quarter.

As you develop templates, keep them on disks by themselves so you don't have to worry about accidentally writing over them after you've used the template to build a spreadsheet of live data.

APPENDIX A

SuperCalc³ Applications File Cross Reference and Contents Output

Filename and Figure Cross Reference

Figure	Filename	Figure	Filename
Chap 14	MACRO3.CAL	16.14	TMPEXPEN.PRN
Chap 14	MACRO3.XQT	16.15	PLMACRO1.CAL
14.1	DETMPLT.CAL		PLMACRO1.XQT
14.2	PRCTMPLT.CAL	16.16	TMPEXPEN.CAL
15.2	EMPHOURS.CAL	16.17	TMPEXPEN.CAL
15.3	EMPHOURS.CSV	16.18	TMPEXPEN.CAL
15.4	PAYPROG1.BAS	16.19	TMPEXPEN.CAL
15.7	PAYSKEL.CAL	16.20	TMPEXPEN.CAL
15.9	PAYPROG2.BAS	16.21	PLMACRO2.CAL
15.11	PAYPROG3.BAS		PLMACRO2.XQT
15.16	X15SKEL.CAL	16.22	BUDOPSTA.CAL
15.17	X15PROG1.BAS	16.23	BUDOPSTA.CAL
15.18	BOWLERS.CSV	16.24	BUDOPSTA.CAL
15.20	X15PROG2.BAS	16.25	BUDOPSTA.CAL
15.23	X15PROG3.BAS	16.26	BUDOPSTA.CAL
16.3	IRS84-TP.CAL	16.27	PLMACRO3.CAL
16.4	IRS84-TP.CAL		PLMACRO3.XQT
16.5	IRS84-DA.CAL	16.28	ACTOPSTA.CAL
16.6	IRS84-DA.CAL	16.29	VAROPSTA.CAL
16.7	TPCAPBUD.CAL	16.30	PLMACRO4.CAL
16.8	DACAPBUD.CAL		PLMACRO4.XQT
16.9	TMPWORTH.CAL	16.31	REFOPSTA.CAL
16.10	DATWORTH.CAL	16.32	REFOPSTA.CAL
16.11	TMPLMORT.CAL	16.33	REFOPSTA.CAL
16.12	DATAMORT.CAL	16.34	REFOPSTA.CAL
16.13	TMPEXPEN.CAL	16.35	REFOPSTA.CAL

Contents Output from Chapter 16

Figure A.1 Contents Output of Figures 16.5 and 16.6

```
SuperCalc ver.  2.00
IRS FORM 1040: 1984
A1       = "IRS FORM 1040: 1984
A2       = "NAME:
B2       = "John & Jane Doe
J2       = "1984 TAX RATE SCHEDULES
A3       = "ADDRESS:
B3       = "943 Cactus Court
B4       = "Maple Glen, PA 19038
J4       = "ENTER TAXABLE INCOME (FORM 1040 LINE 37):
Q4 3     = 661
A6       = "YOUR SOCIAL SECURITY NUMBER
C6       = "123-45-6789
K6       = "BASE TAX
N6 H     = IF(OR(D12=2,D12=5),LOOKUP(Q4,M43.M57),
           IF(D12=1,LOOKUP(Q4,M20.M35),NA))
O6 H     = IF(D12=3,LOOKUP(Q4,M65.M79),IF(D12=4,
           LOOKUP(Q4,M87.M101),NA))
P6       =
Q6 3     = IF(ISNA(N6),O6,N6)
A7       = "SPOUSE'S SOCIAL SECURITY NUMBER
C7       = "234-99-9876
K7       = "EXCESS INCOME
N7 H     = IF(OR(D12=2,D12=5),Q4-LOOKUP(Q4,J43.J57),
           IF(D12=1,Q4-LOOKUP(Q4,J20.J35),NA))
O7 H     = IF(D12=3,Q4-LOOKUP(Q4,J65.J79),IF(D12=4,
           Q4-LOOKUP(Q4,J87.J101),NA))
P7       = IF(ISNA(N7),O7,N7)
Q7       =
K8       = "TAX ON EXCESS INCOME
N8 H     = IF(OR(D12=2,D12=5),P7*LOOKUP(Q4,P43.P57),
           IF(D12=1,P7*LOOKUP(Q4,P20.P35),NA))
O8 H     = IF(D12=3,P7*LOOKUP(Q4,P65.P79),IF(D12=4,
           P7*LOOKUP(Q4,P87.P101),NA))
P8       =
Q8       = ROUND(IF(ISNA(N8),O8,N8),2)
A9       = "YOUR OCCUPATION
B9       = "Systems Consultant
K9       = "BASE TAX
Q9 3     = "------------
A10      = "SPOUSE'S OCCUPATION
B10      = "Housewife
K10      = "INCOME TAX LIABILITY
Q10 3    = SUM(Q6:Q8)
Q11      = "============
A12      = "FILING STATUS:
D12 I    = 2
D13      = "1: SINGLE
D14      = "2: MARRIED, FILING JOINTLY
J14      = "SCHEDULE X: SINGLE TAX PAYERS
D15      = "3: MARRIED, FILING SEPARATELY
J15      = "------------------------------
D16      = "4: HEAD OF HOUSEHOLD
J16      = "BASE INCOME BRACKET
Q16 TR   = "TAX RATE
D17      = "5: QUALIFYING WIDOW(ER)
J17      = "    TAXABLE INCOME
M17      = "TABLE
N17 TR   = "BASE TAX
P17      = "TABLE
Q17 TR   = "ON EXCESS
J18      = "     NOT LESS THAN
M18      = "POINTERS
N18 TR   = "AMOUNT
P18      = "POINTERS
Q18 TR   = "INCOME
A19      = "NO. OF EXEMPTIONS:
D19 I    = 8
J20 1    = 0
K20 1    = 0
M20 1    = 0
N20 1    = 0
P20 1    = 0
Q20 2    = 0
A21      = "WAGES & SALARIES
E21      = 37800+8500
J21 1    = 2300
K21 1    = 2300
M21 1    = 2300
N21 1    = 0
P21 1    = 2300
Q21 2    = .11
A22      = "INTEREST INCOME
E22      = 1200
J22 1    = 3400
K22 1    = 3400
M22 1    = 3400
N22 1    = 121
P22 1    = 3400
Q22 2    = .12
A23      = "DIVIDEND INCOME
D23      = 100
J23 1    = 4400
K23 1    = 4400
M23 1    = 4400
N23 1    = 241
P23 1    = 4400
Q23 2    = .14
A24      = "DIVIDEND EXCLUSION
D24      = IF(D12=2,200,100)
J24 1    = 6500
```

```
K24 1    = 6500
M24 1    = 6500
N24 1    = 535
P24 1    = 6500
Q24 2    = .15
A25      = "REPORTABLE DIVIDENDS
E25      = IF(A23-A24(0,0,A23-A24)
J25 1    = 8500
K25 1    = 8500
M25 1    = 8500
N25 1    = 835
P25 1    = 8500
Q25 2    = .16
A26      = "STATE & LOCAL TAX REFUNDS FROM PRIOR
           YEARS
E26      = 0
J26 1    = 10800
K26 1    = 10800
M26 1    = 10800
N26 1    = 1203
P26 1    = 10800
Q26 2    = .18
A27      = "ALIMONY RECEIVED
E27      = 0
J27 1    = 12900
K27 1    = 12900
M27 1    = 12900
N27 1    = 1581
P27 1    = 12900
Q27 2    = .20
A28      = "BUSINESS INCOME OR (LOSS)
E28      = 0
J28 1    = 15000
K28 1    = 15000
M28 1    = 15000
N28 1    = 2001
P28 1    = 15000
Q28 2    = .23
A29      = "CAPITAL GAIN OR (LOSS)
E29      = (175*43.75)-200-(75*36.50+100*44.50)
J29 1    = 18200
K29 1    = 18200
M29 1    = 18200
N29 1    = 2737
P29 1    = 18200
Q29 2    = .26
A30      = "40% OF CAPITAL GAIN DISTRIBUTIONS NOT
           REPORTED ABOVE
E30      = 0
J30 1    = 23500
K30 1    = 23500
M30 1    = 23500
N30 1    = 4115
P30 1    = 23500
Q30 2    = .30
A31      = "SUPPLEMENTAL GAIN OR (LOSS)
E31      = 0
J31 1    = 28800
K31 1    = 28800
M31 1    = 28800
N31 1    = 5705
P31 1    = 28800
Q31 2    = .34
A32      = "FULLY TAXABLE PENSIONS & IRA
           DISTRIBUTIONS
E32      = 0
J32 1    = 34100
K32 1    = 34100
M32 1    = 34100
N32 1    = 7507
P32 1    = 34100
Q32 2    = .38
A33      = "OTHER PENSIONS & ANNUITIES, INCLUDING
           ROLLOVERS
E33      = 0
J33 1    = 41500
K33 1    = 41500
M33 1    = 41500
N33 1    = 10319
P33 1    = 41500
Q33 2    = .42
A34      = "RENTS & ROYALTIES
E34      = 5000
J34 1    = 55300
K34 1    = 55300
M34 1    = 55300
N34 1    = 16115
P34 1    = 55300
Q34 2    = .48
A35      = "FARM INCOME OR (LOSS)
E35      = 0
J35 1    = 81800
K35 1    = 81800
L35 1    =
M35 1    = 81800
N35 1    = 28835
O35 1    =
P35 1    = 81800
Q35 2    = .50
A36      = "UNEMPLOYMENT COMPENSATION
E36      = 0
A37      = "SOCIAL SECURITY BENEFITS
E37      = 0
J37      = "SCHEDULE Y: MARRIED TAX PAYERS FILING
           JOINTLY AND QUALIFYING WIDOW(ER)S
A38      = "OTHER INCOME
J38      = "-----------------------------------------
           -----------------------------------
A39      = "   Partnership tax return preparation
E39      = 100
J39      = "BASE INCOME BRACKET
Q39 TR   = "TAX RATE
E40 TR   = "--------
J40      = "    TAXABLE INCOME
M40      = "TABLE
N40 TR   = "BASE TAX
P40      = "TABLE
Q40 TR   = "ON EXCESS
```

```
A41        = "   TOTAL GROSS INCOME
G41        = SUM(E20:E40)
J41        = "      NOT LESS THAN
M41        = "POINTERS
N41 TR     = "AMOUNT
P41        = "POINTERS
Q41 TR     = "INCOME
A43        = "ADJUSTMENTS TO INCOME
J43 1      = 0
K43 1      = 0
M43 1      = 0
N43 1      = 0
P43 1      = 0
Q43 2      = 0
A44        = " MOVING EXPENSES
E44        = 0
J44 1      = 3400
K44 1      = 3400
M44 1      = 3400
N44 1      = 0
P44 1      = 3400
Q44 2      = .11
A45        = " EMPLOYEE BUSINESS EXPENSES
E45        = 2*38*15*0.205
J45 1      = 5500
K45 1      = 5500
M45 1      = 5500
N45 1      = 231
P45 1      = 5500
Q45 2      = .12
A46        = " IRA DEDUCTION
E46        = 2250
J46 1      = 7600
K46 1      = 7600
M46 1      = 7600
N46 1      = 483
P46 1      = 7600
Q46 2      = .14
A47        = " KEOUGH PLAN PAYMENTS
E47        = 0
J47 1      = 11900
K47 1      = 11900
M47 1      = 11900
N47 1      = 1085
P47 1      = 11900
Q47 2      = .16
A48        = " PENALTY ON EARLY WITHDRAWAL OF SAVINGS
E48        = 250
J48 1      = 16000
K48 1      = 16000
M48 1      = 16000
N48 1      = 1741
P48 1      = 16000
Q48 2      = .18
A49        = " ALIMONY PAID
E49        = 3000
J49 1      = 20200
K49 1      = 20200
M49 1      = 20200
N49 1      = 2497
P49 1      = 20200
Q49 2      = .22
A50        = " DEDUCTION FOR A MARRIED COUPLE WHEN
             BOTH WORK
E50        = 0
J50 1      = 24600
K50 1      = 24600
M50 1      = 24600
N50 1      = 3465
P50 1      = 24600
Q50 2      = .25
E51 TR     = "---------
J51 1      = 29900
K51 1      = 29900
M51 1      = 29900
N51 1      = 4790
P51 1      = 29900
Q51 2      = .28
A52        = "TOTAL ADJUSTMENTS
G52        = SUM(E43:E51)
J52 1      = 35200
K52 1      = 35200
M52 1      = 35200
N52 1      = 6274
P52 1      = 35200
Q52 2      = .33
G53 TR     = "---------
J53 1      = 45800
K53 1      = 45800
M53 1      = 45800
N53 1      = 9772
P53 1      = 45800
Q53 2      = .38
A54        = "ADJUSTED GROSS INCOME
G54        = G41-G52
J54 1      = 60000
K54 1      = 60000
M54 1      = 60000
N54 1      = 15168
P54 1      = 60000
Q54 2      = .42
A55        = "LESS: NET ITEMIZED DEDUCTIONS
E55        = G178
J55 1      = 85600
K55 1      = 85600
M55 1      = 85600
N55 1      = 25920
P55 1      = 85600
Q55 2      = .45
A56        = "LESS: CHARITABLE DEDUCTIONS IF NOT
             ITEMIZING
E56        = 0
J56 1      = 109400
K56 1      = 109400
M56 1      = 109400
N56 1      = 36630
P56 1      = 109400
Q56 2      = .49
```

```
E57 TR    = "---------
J57 1     = 162400
K57 1     = 162400
M57 1     = 162400
N57 1     = 62600
P57 1     = 109400
Q57 2     = .50
A58       = "SUB TOTAL
G58       = IF(E55)0,G54-E55,G54-E56)
A59       = "MULTIPLY EXEMPTIONS BY $1,000
G59       = D19*1000
J59       = "SCHEDULE Y: MARRIED TAX PAYERS FILING
            SEPARATELY
G60 TR    = "---------
J60       = "-------------------------------------
            ----------
A61       = "TAXABLE INCOME
G61       = G58-G59
J61       = "BASE INCOME BRACKET
Q61 TR    = "TAX RATE
J62       = "   TAXABLE INCOME
M62       = "TABLE
N62 TR    = "BASE TAX
P62       = "TABLE
Q62 TR    = "ON EXCESS
A63       = "TAX PER SCHEDULES X, Y, Z
G63       = Q10
J63       = "     NOT LESS THAN
M63       = "POINTERS
N63 TR    = "AMOUNT
P63       = "POINTERS
Q63 TR    = "INCOME
A64       = "ADDITIONAL TAXES FORM 4970, 4972, OR
            5544
G64       = 0
G65 TR    = "---------
J65 1     = 0
K65 1     = 0
M65 1     = 0
N65 4     = 0
P65 1     = 0
Q65 2     = 0
A66       = "  TOTAL
G66       = G63+G64
J66 1     = 1700
K66 1     = 1700
M66 1     = 1700
N66 4     = 0
P66 1     = 1700
Q66 2     = .11
J67 1     = 2750
K67 1     = 2750
M67 1     = 2750
N67 4     = 115.50
P67 1     = 2750
Q67 2     = .12
A68       = "PERSONAL CREDITS
J68 1     = 3800
K68 1     = 3800
M68 1     = 3800
N68 4     = 241.5
P68 1     = 3800
Q68 2     = .14
A69       = " CREDIT FOR CHILD & DEPENDENT CARE
E69       = 0
J69 1     = 5950
K69 1     = 5950
M69 1     = 5950
N69 4     = 542.5
P69 1     = 5950
Q69 2     = .16
A70       = " CREDIT FOR THE ELDERLY & PERMANENTLY
            DISABLED
E70       = 0
J70 1     = 8000
K70 1     = 8000
M70 1     = 8000
N70 4     = 870.5
P70 1     = 8000
Q70 2     = .18
A71       = " RESIDENTIAL ENERGY
E71       = 0
J71 1     = 10100
K71 1     = 10100
M71 1     = 10100
N71 4     = 1248.5
P71 1     = 10100
Q71 2     = .22
A72       = " POLITICAL CONTRIBUTIONS, PARTIAL
            CREDIT
E72       = 0
J72 1     = 12300
K72 1     = 12300
M72 1     = 12300
N72 4     = 1732.5
P72 1     = 12300
Q72 2     = .25
E73 TR    = "---------
J73 1     = 14950
K73 1     = 14950
M73 1     = 14950
N73 4     = 2395
P73 1     = 14950
Q73 2     = .28
A74       = "  TOTAL PERSONAL CREDITS
G74       = SUM(E69:E74)
J74 1     = 17600
K74 1     = 17600
M74 1     = 17600
N74 4     = 3137
P74 1     = 17600
Q74 2     = .33
G75 TR    = "---------
J75 1     = 22900
K75 1     = 22900
M75 1     = 22900
N75 4     = 4886
P75 1     = 22900
Q75 2     = .38
A76       = "   TAX BALANCE AFTER PERSONAL CREDITS
```

```
G76        = G66-G74
J76 1      = 30000
K76 1      = 30000
M76 1      = 30000
N76 4      = 7584
P76 1      = 30000
Q76 2      = .42
A77        = "BUSINESS CREDITS
J77 1      = 42800
K77 1      = 42800
M77 1      = 42800
N77 4      = 12960
P77 1      = 42800
Q77 2      = .45
A78        = " FOREIGN TAX CREDIT
E78        = 0
J78 1      = 54700
K78 1      = 54700
M78 1      = 54700
N78 4      = 18315
P78 1      = 54700
Q78 2      = .49
A79        = " GENERAL BUSINESS CREDIT
E79        = 0
J79 1      = 81200
K79 1      = 81200
L79 1      =
M79 1      = 81200
N79 4      = 31300
O79 1      =
P79 1      = 81200
Q79 2      = .50
E80 TR     = "---------
A81        = "   TOTAL BUSINESS CREDITS
G81        = SUM(E77:E80)
J81        = "SCHEDULE Z: HEADS OF HOUSEHOLD
G82 TR     = "---------
J82        = "------------------------------
A83        = "   TAX BALANCE AFTER BUSINESS CREDITS
G83        = G76-G81
J83        = "BASE INCOME BRACKET
Q83 TR     = "TAX RATE
J84        = "     TAXABLE INCOME
M84        = "TABLE
N84 TR     = "BASE TAX
P84        = "TABLE
Q84 TR     = "ON EXCESS
A85        = "OTHER TAXES
J85        = "       NOT LESS THAN
M85        = "POINTERS
N85 TR     = "AMOUNT
P85        = "POINTERS
Q85 TR     = "INCOME
A86        = " SELF-EMPLOYMENT TAX
E86        = 0
A87        = " ALTERNATIVE MINIMUM TAX
E87        = 0
J87 1      = 0
K87 1      = 0
M87 1      = 0
N87 1      = 0
P87 1      = 0
Q87 2      = 0
A88        = " INVESTMENT CREDIT RECAPTURE
E88        = 0
J88 1      = 2300
K88 1      = 2300
M88 1      = 2300
N88 1      = 0
P88 1      = 2300
Q88 2      = .11
A89        = " SOCIAL SECURITY TIP INCOME
E89        = 0
J89 1      = 4400
K89 1      = 4400
M89 1      = 4400
N89 1      = 231
P89 1      = 4400
Q89 2      = .12
A90        = " TAX ON IRA
E90        = 0
J90 1      = 6500
K90 1      = 6500
M90 1      = 6500
N90 1      = 483
P90 1      = 6500
Q90 2      = .14
E91 TR     = "---------
J91 1      = 8700
K91 1      = 8700
M91 1      = 8700
N91 1      = 791
P91 1      = 8700
Q91 2      = .17
A92        = "TOTAL TAXES
G92        = SUM(G83,E85:E91)
J92 1      = 11800
K92 1      = 11800
M92 1      = 11800
N92 1      = 1318
P92 1      = 11800
Q92 2      = .18
J93 1      = 15000
K93 1      = 15000
M93 1      = 15000
N93 1      = 1894
P93 1      = 15000
Q93 2      = .20
A94        = "PAYMENTS
J94 1      = 18200
K94 1      = 18200
M94 1      = 18200
N94 1      = 2534
P94 1      = 18200
Q94 2      = .24
A95        = " FEDERAL INCOME TAX WITHHELD
E95        = 4500+500
J95 1      = 23500
```

```
K95 1     = 23500
M95 1     = 23500
N95 1     = 3806
P95 1     = 23500
Q95 2     = .28
A96       = " ESTIMATED TAX PAYMENTS
E96       = 0
J96 1     = 28800
K96 1     = 28800
M96 1     = 28800
N96 1     = 5290
P96 1     = 28800
Q96 2     = .32
A97       = " EARNED INCOME CREDIT
E97       = 0
J97 1     = 34100
K97 1     = 34100
M97 1     = 34100
N97 1     = 6986
P97 1     = 34100
Q97 2     = .35
A98       = " AMOUNT PAID FORM 4868
E98       = 0
J98 1     = 44700
K98 1     = 44700
M98 1     = 44700
N98 1     = 10696
P98 1     = 44700
Q98 2     = .42
A99       = " EXCESS SOCIAL SECURITY TAX
E99       = IF(E21)37800,ROUND(6.7*E21,2)-2532.60,0)
J99 1     = 60600
K99 1     = 60600
M99 1     = 60600
N99 1     = 17374
P99 1     = 60600
Q99 2     = .45
A100      = " TAX CREDIT ON SPECIAL FUELS
E100      = 0
J100 1    = 81800
K100 1    = 81800
M100 1    = 81800
N100 1    = 26914
P100 1    = 81800
Q100 2    = .48
A101      = " REGULATED INVESTMENT COMPANY CREDIT
E101      = 0
J101 1    = 108300
K101 1    = 108300
L101 1    =
M101 1    = 108300
N101 1    = 39634
O101 1    =
P101 1    = 108300
Q101 2    = .5
E102 TR   = "---------
A103      = " TOTAL PAYMENTS
G103      = SUM(E94:E102)
A105      = "TAXES OVERPAID
G105      = IF(G92-G103(=0,ABS(G92-G103),NA)
A106      = "TAXES DUE
G106      = IF(G92-G103)0,G92-G103,NA)
A109      = "IRS SCHEDULE A: 1984
A111      = "MEDICAL & DENTAL EXPENSES
A112      = "-------------------------
A113      = "MEDICINES & DRUGS
E113      = 200
A114      = "DRS, HOSPTLS, INSURANCE
E114      = ROUND(300+15*12200+500+850+80,2)
A115      = "TRANSPORTATION & LODGING
E115      = ROUND(2400*0.09,2)
A116      = "OTHER
A117      = " Eye glasses
E117      = 150
A118      = " Hearing aid
E118      = 450
C119 TR   =
D119 TR   =
E119 TR   = "---------
F119 TR   =
A120      = "SUBTOTAL
C120 TR   =
D120 TR   =
E120 TR   = SUM(E113:E119)
F120 TR   =
A121      = "5% AGI
C121 TR   =
D121 TR   =
E121 TR   = ROUND(.05*G54,2)
F121 TR   =
C122 TR   =
D122 TR   =
E122 TR   = "---------
F122 TR   =
A123      = "MEDICAL DEDUCTION
C123 TR   =
D123 TR   =
F123 TR   = IF(E120-E121(0,0,E120-E121)
C124 TR   =
D124 TR   =
F124 TR   =
A125      = "TAXES
C125 TR   =
D125 TR   =
F125 TR   =
A126      = "-----
C126 TR   =
D126 TR   =
F126 TR   =
A127      = " STATE INCOME TAX
C127 TR   =
D127 TR   = ROUND(2.45*G54,2)
F127 TR   =
A128      = " CITY WAGE TAX
C128 TR   =
D128 TR   = ROUND(4.3125*8500,2)
F128 TR   =
C129 TR   =
```

```
D129 TR    = "---------
E129 TR    =
A130       = "STATE & LOCAL
C130 TR    =
D130 TR    =
E130 TR    = SUM(D127:D128)
F130 TR    =
A131       = "REAL ESTATE
C131 TR    =
D131 TR    =
E131 TR    = 1500
F131 TR    =
A132       = "SALES TAX - TABLES
C132 TR    =
D132 TR    =
E132 TR    = 346
F132 TR    =
A133       = "SALES TAX - AUTOS
C133 TR    =
E133 TR    = 300
F133 TR    =
A134       = "OTHER
C134 TR    =
E134 TR    =
F134 TR    =
A135       = " TOWNSHIP OCCUPATION TAX
C135 TR    =
E135 TR    = 10
F135 TR    =
A136       = " COUNTY PERSONAL PROPERTY TAX
C136 TR    =
D136 TR    =
E136 TR    = 50
F136 TR    =
C137 TR    =
D137 TR    =
E137 TR    = "---------
F137 TR    =
A138       = "TOTAL TAXES
C138 TR    =
D138 TR    =
F138 TR    = SUM(E130:E137)
A140       = "INTEREST EXPENSE
C140 TR    =
D140 TR    =
E140 TR    =
F140 TR    =
A141       = "---------------
C141 TR    =
D141 TR    =
F141 TR    =
A142       = "HOME MORTGAGE INTEREST TO FINANCIAL
             INSTITUTIONS
E142 TR    = 6532.89
F142 TR    =
A143       = "HOME MORTGAGE INTEREST TO INDIVIDUALS
D143 TR    =
E143 TR    = 0
F143 TR    =
A144       = "CREDIT CARDS & CHARGE ACCOUNTS
C144 TR    =
D144 TR    =
E144 TR    = 653.58
A145       = "OTHER
C145 TR    =
D145 TR    =
E145 TR    =
F145 TR    =
A146       = " Auto loan #1
C146 TR    =
D146 TR    =
E146 TR    = 425.53
F146 TR    =
A147       = " Auto loan #2
C147 TR    =
D147 TR    =
E147 TR    = 482.92
F147 TR    =
A148       = " Student loan
C148 TR    =
D148 TR    =
E148 TR    = 53.98
F148 TR    =
A149       = " Home improvement loan
C149 TR    =
D149 TR    =
E149 TR    = 317.46
F149 TR    =
C150 TR    =
D150 TR    =
E150 TR    = "---------
F150 TR    =
A151       = "TOTAL INTEREST
C151 TR    =
D151 TR    =
E151 TR    =
F151 TR    = SUM(E142:E150)
C152 TR    =
D152 TR    =
F152 TR    =
A153       = "CONTRIBUTIONS
C153 TR    =
D153 TR    =
F153 TR    =
A154       = "------------
C154 TR    =
D154 TR    =
F154 TR    =
A155       = "CASH
C155 TR    =
D155 TR    =
E155 TR    = 1500
F155 TR    =
A156       = "NON-CASH
C156 TR    =
D156 TR    =
E156 TR    = 300
F156 TR    =
```

```
A157        = "PRIOR YEAR CARRYOVER
C157 TR     =
D157 TR     =
E157 TR     = 0
C158 TR     =
D158 TR     =
E158 TR     = "---------
F158 TR     =
A159        = "TOTAL CONTRIBUTIONS
C159 TR     =
D159 TR     =
E159 TR     =
F159 TR     = SUM(E155:E158)
C160 TR     =
D160 TR     =
E160 TR     =
F160 TR     =
A161        = "MISCELLANEOUS
C161 TR     =
D161 TR     =
F161 TR     =
A162        = "-------------
A163        = "UNION & PROFESSIONAL DUES
C163 TR     =
D163 TR     =
E163 TR     = 0
F163 TR     =
A164        = "TAX RETURN PREPARATION FEES
C164 TR     =
D164 TR     =
E164 TR     = 50
F164 TR     =
A165        = "OTHER
C165 TR     =
D165 TR     =
F165 TR     =
A166        = " Professional journals
C166 TR     =
D166 TR     =
E166 TR     = 66
A167        = " Business telephone
C167 TR     =
D167 TR     =
E167 TR     = 300
F167 TR     =
A168        = " Floppy disks
C168 TR     =
D168 TR     =
E168 TR     = 100
F168 TR     =
A169        = " Printer ribbons
C169 TR     =
D169 TR     =
E169 TR     = 30
F169 TR     =
A170        = " Computer repairs & parts
C170 TR     =
D170 TR     =
E170 TR     = 50
F170 TR     =
A171        = " Computer system depreciation
C171 TR     =
D171 TR     =
E171 TR     = ROUND(22%4000+500+500,2)
F171 TR     =
C172 TR     =
D172 TR     =
E172 TR     = "---------
F172 TR     =
A173        = "TOTAL MISCELLANEOUS
C173 TR     =
D173 TR     =
F173 TR     = SUM(E163:E172)
C174 TR     =
D174 TR     =
A175        = "TOTAL ITEMIZED DEDUCTIONS
C175 TR     =
D175 TR     =
F175 TR     =
G175        = SUM(F123:F173)
A176        = "LESS: STANDARD DEDUCTION
C176 TR     =
D176 TR     =
G176        = IF(D12=1,2300,IF(D12=2,3400,IF(D12=3,
              1700,IF(D12=4,2300,IF(D12=5,3400,0)))))
C177 TR     =
D177 TR     =
G177 TR     = "---------
A178        = "NET ITEMIZED DEDUCTIONS
C178 TR     =
D178 TR     =
G178        = G175-G176
C179 TR     =
D179 TR     =
C180 TR     =
```

Figure A.2 User-Defined Format Table for Figures 16.5 and 16.6

```
                User-defined formats
                1 2 3 4 5 6 7 8

Floating $      N N N N Y Y Y Y

Embedded Commas Y Y Y Y Y Y Y Y

Minus in ( )    N N N N N N N N

Zero as Blank   N N N N N N N N

%               N Y N N N N N N

Decimal Places  0 0 2 2 2 2 2 2

Scaling factor  0 0 0 0 0 0 0 0


F2 to return to spreadsheet.


 A1           Text="IRS FORM 1040: 1984
Y(es) or N(o) ?
 15>/Format,Define
F1 = Help; F2 = Cancel; F9 = Plot; F10 = View          CAPS
```

Figure A.3 Contents Output of Figure 16.8

```
SuperCalc ver.  2.00
CAPITAL BUDGETING: COST-BENEFIT ANALYSIS
A1        = "CAPITAL BUDGETING: COST-BENEFIT ANALYSIS
A2        = "----------------------------------------
D2        = "
A3        = "PROPOSED ASSET
D3 TL     = "DISCOUNT RATE:
F3 1      = .15
A4        = "COMPONENT
B4        = "COST
A5        = '-
C5        = "
A6        = "ZDS ZF-151-52
B6 3      = 2795
C6 3      =
D6 3      =
E6 3      =
F6 3      =
A7        = "MEMORY EXPANSION: 640K
B7 3      = 650
C7 3      =
D7 3      =
E7 3      =
F7 3      =
A8        = "DOT MATRIX PRINTER
B8 3      = 450
C8 3      =
D8 3      =
E8 3      =
F8 3      =
A9        = "DAISY WHEEL PRINTER
B9 3      = 3000
C9 3      =
D9 3      =
E9 3      =
F9 3      =
A10       = "10MB FIXED DISK
B10 3     = 3000
C10 3     =
D10 3     =
E10 3     =
F10 3     =
A11       = "1200 BAUD MODEM
B11 3     = 500
C11 3     =
D11 3     =
E11 3     =
F11 3     =
A12       = '-
C12 3     = "
D12 3     =
E12 3     =
```

```
F12 3      =
A13        = "    TOTAL
B13 3      = SUM(B6:B11)
C13 3      =
D13 3      =
E13 3      =
F13 3      =
B14 3      =
C14 3      =
D14 3      =
E14 3      =
F14 3      =
A15        = "PERIODIC CASH INFLOWS
B15 3      = "YEAR #1
C15 3      = "YEAR #2
D15 3      = "YEAR #3
E15 3      = "YEAR #4
F15 3      = "YEAR #5
A16        = '-
G16        = "
A17        = "LABOR SAVINGS
B17 3      = 5000
C17 3      = 7000
D17 3      = 10000
E17 3      = 12000
F17 3      = 14000
A18        = "DEPRECIATION
B18 3      = ROUND(B13*.15,0)
C18 3      = ROUND(B13*.22,0)
D18 3      = ROUND(B13*.21,0)
E18 3      = ROUND(B13*.21,0)
F18 3      = ROUND(B13*.21,0)
A19        = '-
G19        = "
A20        = "    TOTAL
B20 3      = SUM(B17:B18)
C20 3      = SUM(C17:C18)
D20 3      = SUM(D17:D18)
E20 3      = SUM(E17:E18)
F20 3      = SUM(F17:F18)
B21 3      =
C21 3      =
D21 3      =
E21 3      =
F21 3      =
A22        = "PERIODIC CASH OUTFLOWS
B22 3      = "YEAR #1
C22 3      = "YEAR #2
D22 3      = "YEAR #3
E22 3      = "YEAR #4
F22 3      = "YEAR #5
A23        = '-
G23        = "
A24        = "SUPPLIES
B24 3      = 30*30+10*20+10*10+1000*3
C24 3      = 30*30+10*20+10*10+1000*3
D24 3      = 30*30+10*20+10*10+1000*3
E24 3      = 30*30+10*20+10*10+1000*3
F24 3      = 30*30+10*20+10*10+1000*3
A25        = "INSURANCE
B25 3      = 300
C25 3      = 300
D25 3      = 300
E25 3      = 300
F25 3      = 300
A26        = "MAINTENANCE
B26 3      = 150
C26 3      = 200
D26 3      = 250
E26 3      = 300
F26 3      = 350
A27        = "ELECTRICITY
B27 3      = 500
C27 3      = 500
D27 3      = 500
E27 3      = 500
F27 3      = 500
A28        = '-
G28        = "
A29        = "    TOTAL
B29 3      = SUM(B24:B27)
C29 3      = SUM(C24:C27)
D29 3      = SUM(D24:D27)
E29 3      = SUM(E24:E27)
F29 3      = SUM(F24:F27)
A31        = "NET PRESENT VALUE
C31        = "DISCOUNT
D31        = "NET
E31        = "DISCNTED
A32        = "COMPUTATIONS
B32        = "PERIODS
C32        = "FACTORS
D32        = "FLOWS
E32        = "FLOWS
B33 TL     = '-
F33        = "
B34        = 0
C34 1      = ROUND(1/((1+F3)^B34),6)
D34 3      = -B13
E34 3      = ROUND(C34*D34,0)
B35        = 1
C35 1      = ROUND(1/((1+F3)^B35),6)
D35 3      = B20-B29
E35 3      = ROUND(C35*D35,0)
B36        = 2
C36 1      = ROUND(1/((1+F3)^B36),6)
D36 3      = C20-C29
E36 3      = ROUND(C36*D36,0)
B37        = 3
C37 1      = ROUND(1/((1+F3)^B37),6)
D37 3      = D20-D29
E37 3      = ROUND(C37*D37,0)
B38        = 4
C38 1      = ROUND(1/((1+F3)^B38),6)
D38 3      = E20-E29
E38 3      = ROUND(C38*D38,0)
```

```
B39        = 5
C39 1      = ROUND(1/((1+F3)^B39),6)
D39 3      = F20-F29
E39 3      = ROUND(C39*D39,0)
E40        = "  -------
A41        = "MANUALLY COMPUTED NPV
E41 3      = SUM(E34:E39)
E42 3      = "  =======
E43 3      =
A44        = "NPV FUNCTION
E44 3      = ROUND(NPV(F3,D35:D39),0)+D34
E45        = "  =======
A48        = "RECOMMENDATION:
A49        = "PROJECT SHOULD BE
B49        = IF(E44)=0,("ACCEPTED"),("REJECTED"))
A51        = "INTERNAL RATE OF RETURN
E51 2      = ROUND(IRR(F3,D34:D39),6)
```

Figure A.4 User-Defined Format Table for Figure 16.8

```
                    User-defined formats
                    1 2 3 4 5 6 7 8

Floating $          N N N Y Y Y Y Y

Embedded Commas     N N Y Y Y Y Y Y

Minus in ( )        N N N N N N N N

Zero as Blank       N N N N N N N N

%                   N Y N N N N N N

Decimal Places      6 4 0 2 2 2 2 2

Scaling factor      0 0 0 0 0 0 0 0


F2 to return to spreadsheet.


 E51    2      Form=ROUND(IRR(F3,D34:D39),6)
Y(es) or N(o) ?
 15)/Format,Define
F1 = Help; F2 = Cancel; F9 = Plot; F10 = View          CAPS
```

Figure A.5 Contents Output of Figure 16.10

```
SuperCalc ver.  2.00

B1 TC      = "          JOHN & JANE DOE
B2 TC      = "       STATEMENT OF NET WORTH
B3 TC      = "       AS OF DECEMBER 31, 1984
B4 TC      = " ------------------------------
A5         = "ASSETS
A6         = "  CASH
B7         = "HOME-TOWNE SAVINGS BANK ACCOUNTS
B8         = "   01-123456 JOINT CHECKING
C8 1       = 1005.67
D8 1       =
E8 1       =
B9         = "   02-234567 JOINT MONEY MARKET
C9 1       = 9498.38
D9 1       =
E9 1       =
B10        = "   03-345678 JOHN PASSBOOK
C10 1      = 175.5
D10 1      =
E10 1      =
B11        = "   04-456789 JANE PASSBOOK
C11 1      = 217.99
D11 1      =
E11 1      =
C12 1TR    = "---------
```

```
D12 1     =
E12 1     =
B13       = "     TOTAL CASH IN BANK
C13 1     =
D13 1     = SUM(C8:C11)
E13 1     =
B14       = "PENSION PLANS
C14 1     =
D14 1     =
E14 1     =
B15       = "   MAINFRAME COMPUTERS, INC.
C15 1     = 6497.81
D15 1     =
E15 1     =
B16       = "   GERMANTOWN UNIVERSITY
C16 1     = 1733.03
D16 1     =
E16 1     =
C17 1TR   = "---------
D17 1     =
E17 1     =
B18       = "     TOTAL PENSION PLANS
C18 1     =
D18 1     = SUM(C15:C16)
E18 1     =
B19       = "OTHER FUNDS
C19 1     =
D19 1     =
E19 1     =
B20       = "   EMPLOYEE STOCK PURCHASE PLAN
C20 1     = 1592.38
D20 1     =
E20 1     =
B21       = "   CREDIT UNION
C21 1     = 1250
D21 1     =
E21 1     =
C22 1TR   = "---------
D22 1     =
E22 1     =
B23       = "     TOTAL OTHER FUNDS
C23 1     =
D23 1     = SUM(C20:C21)
E23 1     =
C24 1     =
D24 1     = "---------
E24 1     =
B25       = "TOTAL CASH
C25 1     =
D25 1     =
E25 1     = SUM(D13:D25)
A26       = "  RECEIVABLES
C26 1     =
D26 1     =
E26 1     =
B27       = "      PUBLISHER'S ROYALTY ADVANCE
C27 1     = 5000
D27 1     =
E27 1     =
C28 1TR   = "---------
D28 1     =
E28 1     =
B29       = "     TOTAL RECEIVABLES
C29 1     =
D29 1     =
E29 1     = C27
A30       = "  AUTOMOBILES
C30 1     =
D30 1     =
E30 1     =
B31       = "1983 NISSAN SENTRA 4 DOOR
C31 1     =
D31 1     = 7163.58
E31 1     =
B32       = "1981 DATSUN 210 STATION WAGON
C32 1     =
D32 1     = 4500
E32 1     =
C33 1     =
D33 1     = "---------
E33 1     =
B34       = "     TOTAL AUTOMOBILES
C34 1     =
D34 1     =
E34 1     = SUM(D31:D32)
A35       = "  REAL ESTATE
C35 1     =
D35 1     =
E35 1     =
B36       = "943 CACTUS COURT, MAPLE GLEN PA
C36 1     =
D36 1     =
E36 1     = 89000
C37 1     =
D37 1     =
E37 1     = "----------
A38       = "TOTAL ASSETS
C38 1     =
D38 1     =
E38 1     = SUM(E25:E36)
C39 1     =
D39 1     =
E39 1     = "==========
C40 1     =
D40 1     =
E40 1     =
A41       = "LIABILITIES & NET WORTH
C41 1     =
D41 1     =
E41 1     =
A42       = "LIABILITIES
C42 1     =
D42 1     =
E42 1     =
B43       = "MORTGAGE: LOCAL SAVINGS & LOAN
C43 1     =
D43 1     = 46000
```

```
E43 1      =
B44        = "AUTO: HOME-TOWNE SAVINGS BANK
C44 1      =
D44 1      = 3511.11
E44 1      =
B45        = "CHARGE ACCOUNTS: VISA
C45 1      =
D45 1      = 1874.52-182
E45 1      =
B46        = "                   SEARS
C46 1      =
D46 1      = 843.92-41
E46 1      =
C47 1      =
D47 1      = 0
E47 1      =
C48 1      =
D48 1      = 0
E48 1      =
B49        = "OTHER: NDSL STUDENT LOAN
C49 1      =
D49 1      = 292.96
E49 1      =
C50 1      =
D50 1      = 0
E50 1      =
C51 1      =
D51 1      = "---------
E51 1      =
A52        = "TOTAL LIABILITIES
C52 1      =
D52 1      =
E52 1      = SUM(D43:D50)
A53        = "NET WORTH
C53 1      =
D53 1      =
E53 1      = E38-E52
C54 1      =
D54 1      =
E54 1      = "-----------
A55        = "TOTAL LIABILITIES & NET WORTH
C55 1      =
D55 1      =
E55 1      = E52+E53
C56 1      =
D56 1      =
E56 1      = "===========
```

Figure A.6 User-Defined Format Table for Figure 16.10

```
                     User-defined formats
                     1  2  3  4  5  6  7  8

Floating $           N  Y  Y  Y  Y  Y  Y  Y

Embedded Commas      Y  Y  Y  Y  Y  Y  Y  Y

Minus in ( )         N  N  N  N  N  N  N  N

Zero as Blank        N  N  N  N  N  N  N  N

%                    N  N  N  N  N  N  N  N

Decimal Places       2  2  2  2  2  2  2  2

Scaling factor       0  0  0  0  0  0  0  0


F2 to return to spreadsheet.


 E1
Y(es) or N(o) ?
 15)/Format,Define
F1 = Help; F2 = Cancel; F9 = Plot; F10 = View              CAPS
```

Figure A.7 Contents Output of Figure 16.12

```
SuperCalc ver.  2.00
MORTGAGE PAYMENT AND AMORTIZATION SCHEDULE
A1       P= "MORTGAGE PAYMENT AND AMORTIZATION
            SCHEDULE
E1 TR    P= "PAGE
F1       P= IF(D60<0.01,1,F1+1)
A2       P= "-------------------------------------
            -----
A3       P= "MORTGAGE PRINCIPAL
C3 4      = 48100
D3       P= "<--Enter Principal, e.g.: 48100
A4       P= "ANNUAL INTEREST RATE
C4 2      = .09
D4       P= "<--Enter Rate, e.g.: 0.09
A5       P= "MONTHLY INTEREST RATE
C5 2     P= ROUND(C4/12,6)
A6       P= "NUMBER OF YEARS
C6        = 30
D6       P= "<--Enter Term in years, e.g.: 30
A7       P= "NUMBER OF MONTHS
C7       P= C6*12
A8       P= "MONTHLY PAYMENT
C8 1     P= ROUND((C3*C5)/(1-1/(1+C5)^C7),2)
A10      P= "MORTGAGE AMORTIZATION SCHEDULE
A11 TR   P= "MONTH
B11 TR   P= "INTEREST
C11 TR   P= "PRINCIPAL
D11 TR   P= "PRINCIPAL
E11 TR   P= "FINAL
A12 TR   P= "NUMBER
B12 TR   P= "PAYMENT
C12 TR   P= "PAYMENT
D12 TR   P= "BALANCE
E12 TR   P= "PAYMENT
A13 3    P= IF(D60<=0,1,A60+1)
B13 1    P= ROUND(IF(A13=1,C5*C3,IF(A13>C7,0,
            C5*D60)),2)
C13 1    P= IF(A13>C7,0,C8-B13)
D13 1    P= IF(A13=1,C3-C13,IF(A13>C7,0,D60-C13))
E13 1    P= IF(A13=C7,B13+C13+D13,0)
A14 3    P= A13+1
B14 1    P= IF(A14>C7,0,ROUND(D13*C5,2))
C14 1    P= IF(A14>C7,0,C8-B14)
D14 1    P= IF(A14>C7,0,D13-C14)
E14 1    P= IF(A14=C7,B14+C14+D14,0)
A15 3    P= A14+1
B15 1    P= IF(A15>C7,0,ROUND(D14*C5,2))
C15 1    P= IF(A15>C7,0,C8-B15)
D15 1    P= IF(A15>C7,0,D14-C15)
E15 1    P= IF(A15=C7,B15+C15+D15,0)
A16 3    P= A15+1
B16 1    P= IF(A16>C7,0,ROUND(D15*C5,2))
C16 1    P= IF(A16>C7,0,C8-B16)
D16 1    P= IF(A16>C7,0,D15-C16)
E16 1    P= IF(A16=C7,B16+C16+D16,0)
A17 3    P= A16+1
B17 1    P= IF(A17>C7,0,ROUND(D16*C5,2))
C17 1    P= IF(A17>C7,0,C8-B17)
D17 1    P= IF(A17>C7,0,D16-C17)
E17 1    P= IF(A17=C7,B17+C17+D17,0)
A18 3    P= A17+1
B18 1    P= IF(A18>C7,0,ROUND(D17*C5,2))
C18 1    P= IF(A18>C7,0,C8-B18)
D18 1    P= IF(A18>C7,0,D17-C18)
E18 1    P= IF(A18=C7,B18+C18+D18,0)
A19 3    P= A18+1
B19 1    P= IF(A19>C7,0,ROUND(D18*C5,2))
C19 1    P= IF(A19>C7,0,C8-B19)
D19 1    P= IF(A19>C7,0,D18-C19)
E19 1    P= IF(A19=C7,B19+C19+D19,0)
A20 3    P= A19+1
B20 1    P= IF(A20>C7,0,ROUND(D19*C5,2))
C20 1    P= IF(A20>C7,0,C8-B20)
D20 1    P= IF(A20>C7,0,D19-C20)
E20 1    P= IF(A20=C7,B20+C20+D20,0)
A21 3    P= A20+1
B21 1    P= IF(A21>C7,0,ROUND(D20*C5,2))
C21 1    P= IF(A21>C7,0,C8-B21)
D21 1    P= IF(A21>C7,0,D20-C21)
E21 1    P= IF(A21=C7,B21+C21+D21,0)
A22 3    P= A21+1
B22 1    P= IF(A22>C7,0,ROUND(D21*C5,2))
C22 1    P= IF(A22>C7,0,C8-B22)
D22 1    P= IF(A22>C7,0,D21-C22)
E22 1    P= IF(A22=C7,B22+C22+D22,0)
A23 3    P= A22+1
B23 1    P= IF(A23>C7,0,ROUND(D22*C5,2))
C23 1    P= IF(A23>C7,0,C8-B23)
D23 1    P= IF(A23>C7,0,D22-C23)
E23 1    P= IF(A23=C7,B23+C23+D23,0)
A24 3    P= A23+1
B24 1    P= IF(A24>C7,0,ROUND(D23*C5,2))
C24 1    P= IF(A24>C7,0,C8-B24)
D24 1    P= IF(A24>C7,0,D23-C24)
E24 1    P= IF(A24=C7,B24+C24+D24,0)
A25 3    P= A24+1
B25 1    P= IF(A25>C7,0,ROUND(D24*C5,2))
C25 1    P= IF(A25>C7,0,C8-B25)
D25 1    P= IF(A25>C7,0,D24-C25)
E25 1    P= IF(A25=C7,B25+C25+D25,0)
A26 3    P= A25+1
B26 1    P= IF(A26>C7,0,ROUND(D25*C5,2))
C26 1    P= IF(A26>C7,0,C8-B26)
D26 1    P= IF(A26>C7,0,D25-C26)
E26 1    P= IF(A26=C7,B26+C26+D26,0)
A27 3    P= A26+1
B27 1    P= IF(A27>C7,0,ROUND(D26*C5,2))
C27 1    P= IF(A27>C7,0,C8-B27)
D27 1    P= IF(A27>C7,0,D26-C27)
E27 1    P= IF(A27=C7,B27+C27+D27,0)
A28 3    P= A27+1
B28 1    P= IF(A28>C7,0,ROUND(D27*C5,2))
C28 1    P= IF(A28>C7,0,C8-B28)
```

```
D28 1      P= IF(A28)C7,0,D27-C28)
E28 1      P= IF(A28=C7,B28+C28+D28,0)
A29 3      P= A28+1
B29 1      P= IF(A29)C7,0,ROUND(D28*C5,2))
C29 1      P= IF(A29)C7,0,C8-B29)
D29 1      P= IF(A29)C7,0,D28-C29)
E29 1      P= IF(A29=C7,B29+C29+D29,0)
A30 3      P= A29+1
B30 1      P= IF(A30)C7,0,ROUND(D29*C5,2))
C30 1      P= IF(A30)C7,0,C8-B30)
D30 1      P= IF(A30)C7,0,D29-C30)
E30 1      P= IF(A30=C7,B30+C30+D30,0)
A31 3      P= A30+1
B31 1      P= IF(A31)C7,0,ROUND(D30*C5,2))
C31 1      P= IF(A31)C7,0,C8-B31)
D31 1      P= IF(A31)C7,0,D30-C31)
E31 1      P= IF(A31=C7,B31+C31+D31,0)
A32 3      P= A31+1
B32 1      P= IF(A32)C7,0,ROUND(D31*C5,2))
C32 1      P= IF(A32)C7,0,C8-B32)
D32 1      P= IF(A32)C7,0,D31-C32)
E32 1      P= IF(A32=C7,B32+C32+D32,0)
A33 3      P= A32+1
B33 1      P= IF(A33)C7,0,ROUND(D32*C5,2))
C33 1      P= IF(A33)C7,0,C8-B33)
D33 1      P= IF(A33)C7,0,D32-C33)
E33 1      P= IF(A33=C7,B33+C33+D33,0)
A34 3      P= A33+1
B34 1      P= IF(A34)C7,0,ROUND(D33*C5,2))
C34 1      P= IF(A34)C7,0,C8-B34)
D34 1      P= IF(A34)C7,0,D33-C34)
E34 1      P= IF(A34=C7,B34+C34+D34,0)
A35 3      P= A34+1
B35 1      P= IF(A35)C7,0,ROUND(D34*C5,2))
C35 1      P= IF(A35)C7,0,C8-B35)
D35 1      P= IF(A35)C7,0,D34-C35)
E35 1      P= IF(A35=C7,B35+C35+D35,0)
A36 3      P= A35+1
B36 1      P= IF(A36)C7,0,ROUND(D35*C5,2))
C36 1      P= IF(A36)C7,0,C8-B36)
D36 1      P= IF(A36)C7,0,D35-C36)
E36 1      P= IF(A36=C7,B36+C36+D36,0)
A37 3      P= A36+1
B37 1      P= IF(A37)C7,0,ROUND(D36*C5,2))
C37 1      P= IF(A37)C7,0,C8-B37)
D37 1      P= IF(A37)C7,0,D36-C37)
E37 1      P= IF(A37=C7,B37+C37+D37,0)
A38 3      P= A37+1
B38 1      P= IF(A38)C7,0,ROUND(D37*C5,2))
C38 1      P= IF(A38)C7,0,C8-B38)
D38 1      P= IF(A38)C7,0,D37-C38)
E38 1      P= IF(A38=C7,B38+C38+D38,0)
A39 3      P= A38+1
B39 1      P= IF(A39)C7,0,ROUND(D38*C5,2))
C39 1      P= IF(A39)C7,0,C8-B39)
D39 1      P= IF(A39)C7,0,D38-C39)
E39 1      P= IF(A39=C7,B39+C39+D39,0)
A40 3      P= A39+1
B40 1      P= IF(A40)C7,0,ROUND(D39*C5,2))
C40 1      P= IF(A40)C7,0,C8-B40)
D40 1      P= IF(A40)C7,0,D39-C40)
E40 1      P= IF(A40=C7,B40+C40+D40,0)
A41 3      P= A40+1
B41 1      P= IF(A41)C7,0,ROUND(D40*C5,2))
C41 1      P= IF(A41)C7,0,C8-B41)
D41 1      P= IF(A41)C7,0,D40-C41)
E41 1      P= IF(A41=C7,B41+C41+D41,0)
A42 3      P= A41+1
B42 1      P= IF(A42)C7,0,ROUND(D41*C5,2))
C42 1      P= IF(A42)C7,0,C8-B42)
D42 1      P= IF(A42)C7,0,D41-C42)
E42 1      P= IF(A42=C7,B42+C42+D42,0)
A43 3      P= A42+1
B43 1      P= IF(A43)C7,0,ROUND(D42*C5,2))
C43 1      P= IF(A43)C7,0,C8-B43)
D43 1      P= IF(A43)C7,0,D42-C43)
E43 1      P= IF(A43=C7,B43+C43+D43,0)
A44 3      P= A43+1
B44 1      P= IF(A44)C7,0,ROUND(D43*C5,2))
C44 1      P= IF(A44)C7,0,C8-B44)
D44 1      P= IF(A44)C7,0,D43-C44)
E44 1      P= IF(A44=C7,B44+C44+D44,0)
A45 3      P= A44+1
B45 1      P= IF(A45)C7,0,ROUND(D44*C5,2))
C45 1      P= IF(A45)C7,0,C8-B45)
D45 1      P= IF(A45)C7,0,D44-C45)
E45 1      P= IF(A45=C7,B45+C45+D45,0)
A46 3      P= A45+1
B46 1      P= IF(A46)C7,0,ROUND(D45*C5,2))
C46 1      P= IF(A46)C7,0,C8-B46)
D46 1      P= IF(A46)C7,0,D45-C46)
E46 1      P= IF(A46=C7,B46+C46+D46,0)
A47 3      P= A46+1
B47 1      P= IF(A47)C7,0,ROUND(D46*C5,2))
C47 1      P= IF(A47)C7,0,C8-B47)
D47 1      P= IF(A47)C7,0,D46-C47)
E47 1      P= IF(A47=C7,B47+C47+D47,0)
A48 3      P= A47+1
B48 1      P= IF(A48)C7,0,ROUND(D47*C5,2))
C48 1      P= IF(A48)C7,0,C8-B48)
D48 1      P= IF(A48)C7,0,D47-C48)
E48 1      P= IF(A48=C7,B48+C48+D48,0)
A49 3      P= A48+1
B49 1      P= IF(A49)C7,0,ROUND(D48*C5,2))
C49 1      P= IF(A49)C7,0,C8-B49)
D49 1      P= IF(A49)C7,0,D48-C49)
E49 1      P= IF(A49=C7,B49+C49+D49,0)
A50 3      P= A49+1
B50 1      P= IF(A50)C7,0,ROUND(D49*C5,2))
C50 1      P= IF(A50)C7,0,C8-B50)
D50 1      P= IF(A50)C7,0,D49-C50)
E50 1      P= IF(A50=C7,B50+C50+D50,0)
A51 3      P= A50+1
B51 1      P= IF(A51)C7,0,ROUND(D50*C5,2))
C51 1      P= IF(A51)C7,0,C8-B51)
D51 1      P= IF(A51)C7,0,D50-C51)
E51 1      P= IF(A51=C7,B51+C51+D51,0)
A52 3      P= A51+1
```

```
B52 1    P= IF(A52)C7,0,ROUND(D51*C5,2))
C52 1    P= IF(A52)C7,0,C8-B52)
D52 1    P= IF(A52)C7,0,D51-C52)
E52 1    P= IF(A52=C7,B52+C52+D52,0)
A53 3    P= A52+1
B53 1    P= IF(A53)C7,0,ROUND(D52*C5,2))
C53 1    P= IF(A53)C7,0,C8-B53)
D53 1    P= IF(A53)C7,0,D52-C53)
E53 1    P= IF(A53=C7,B53+C53+D53,0)
A54 3    P= A53+1
B54 1    P= IF(A54)C7,0,ROUND(D53*C5,2))
C54 1    P= IF(A54)C7,0,C8-B54)
D54 1    P= IF(A54)C7,0,D53-C54)
E54 1    P= IF(A54=C7,B54+C54+D54,0)
A55 3    P= A54+1
B55 1    P= IF(A55)C7,0,ROUND(D54*C5,2))
C55 1    P= IF(A55)C7,0,C8-B55)
D55 1    P= IF(A55)C7,0,D54-C55)
E55 1    P= IF(A55=C7,B55+C55+D55,0)
A56 3    P= A55+1
B56 1    P= IF(A56)C7,0,ROUND(D55*C5,2))
C56 1    P= IF(A56)C7,0,C8-B56)
D56 1    P= IF(A56)C7,0,D55-C56)
E56 1    P= IF(A56=C7,B56+C56+D56,0)
A57 3    P= A56+1
B57 1    P= IF(A57)C7,0,ROUND(D56*C5,2))
C57 1    P= IF(A57)C7,0,C8-B57)
D57 1    P= IF(A57)C7,0,D56-C57)
E57 1    P= IF(A57=C7,B57+C57+D57,0)
A58 3    P= A57+1
B58 1    P= IF(A58)C7,0,ROUND(D57*C5,2))
C58 1    P= IF(A58)C7,0,C8-B58)
D58 1    P= IF(A58)C7,0,D57-C58)
E58 1    P= IF(A58=C7,B58+C58+D58,0)
A59 3    P= A58+1
B59 1    P= IF(A59)C7,0,ROUND(D58*C5,2))
C59 1    P= IF(A59)C7,0,C8-B59)
D59 1    P= IF(A59)C7,0,D58-C59)
E59 1    P= IF(A59=C7,B59+C59+D59,0)
A60 3    P= A59+1
B60 1    P= IF(A60)C7,0,ROUND(D59*C5,2))
C60 1    P= IF(A60)C7,0,C8-B60)
D60 1    P= IF(C3=0,0,IF(A60)C7,0,D59-C60))
E60 1    P= IF(A60=C7,B60+C60+D60,0)
```

Figure A.8 User-Defined Format Table for Figure 16.12

```
                    User-defined formats
                    1  2  3  4  5  6  7  8

Floating $          N  N  N  N  Y  Y  Y  Y

Embedded Commas     Y  N  N  Y  Y  Y  Y  Y

Minus in ( )        N  N  N  N  N  N  N  N

Zero as Blank       Y  N  Y  N  N  N  N  N

%                   N  Y  N  N  N  N  N  N

Decimal Places      2  4  0  2  2  2  2  2

Scaling factor      0  0  0  0  0  0  0  0


F2 to return to spreadsheet.


 C6             Form=30
Y(es) or N(o) ?
 15)/Format,Define
F1 = Help; F2 = Cancel; F9 = Plot; F10 = View              CAPS
```

Figure A.9 Contents Output of Figures 16.22 through 16.26

```
SuperCalc ver.  2.00

B1 TL     = "BILL & CONNIE'S ELECTRONIC COTTAGE
B2 TL     = "STATEMENT OF OPERATIONS
B3 TL     = "(PLANNED)
B4 TL     = "FOR THE PERIOD ENDING 12/31/84
B6        = "MONTH
C6        = "MONTH
D6        = "MONTH
E6        = "MONTH
F6        = "MONTH
G6        = "MONTH
H6        = "MONTH
I6        = "MONTH
J6        = "MONTH
K6        = "MONTH
L6        = "MONTH
M6        = "MONTH
N6        = "  1ST
O6        = "  2ND
P6        = "  3RD
Q6        = "  4TH
R6        = "Y-T-D
A7        = "CLASSIFICATION
B7        = "  1
C7        = "  2
D7        = "  3
E7        = "  4
F7        = "  5
G7        = "  6
H7        = "  7
I7        = "  8
J7        = "  9
K7        = " 10
L7        = " 11
M7        = " 12
N7        = "QUARTER
O7        = "QUARTER
P7        = "QUARTER
Q7        = "QUARTER
R7        = "TOTAL
A8        = '-
S8        = "
A9        = "SALES
B9        = 3000000
C9        = ROUND(1.1*B9,0)
D9        = ROUND(1.1*C9,0)
E9        = ROUND(1.1*D9,0)
F9        = ROUND(1.1*E9,0)
G9        = ROUND(1.1*F9,0)
H9        = ROUND(1.1*G9,0)
I9        = ROUND(1.1*H9,0)
J9        = ROUND(1.1*I9,0)
K9        = ROUND(1.1*J9,0)
L9        = ROUND(1.1*K9,0)
M9        = ROUND(1.1*L9,0)
N9        = SUM(B9:D9)
O9        = SUM(E9:G9)
P9        = SUM(H9:J9)
Q9        = SUM(K9:M9)
R9        = SUM(N9:Q9)
A10       = '-
S10       = "
A11       = "COST OF GOODS SOLD:
A12       = " BEGINNING INVENTORY
B12       = 350000
C12       = B14
D12       = C14
E12       = D14
F12       = E14
G12       = F14
H12       = G14
I12       = H14
J12       = I14
K12       = J14
L12       = K14
M12       = L14
N12       = B12
O12       = E12
P12       = H12
Q12       = K12
R12       = B12
A13       = " PURCHASES
B13       = 1200000
C13       = ROUND(1.12*B13,0)
D13       = ROUND(1.12*C13,0)
E13       = ROUND(1.12*D13,0)
F13       = ROUND(1.12*E13,0)
G13       = ROUND(1.12*F13,0)
H13       = ROUND(1.12*G13,0)
I13       = ROUND(1.12*H13,0)
J13       = ROUND(1.12*I13,0)
K13       = ROUND(1.12*J13,0)
L13       = ROUND(1.12*K13,0)
M13       = ROUND(1.12*L13,0)
N13       = SUM(B13:D13)
O13       = SUM(E13:G13)
P13       = SUM(H13:J13)
Q13       = SUM(K13:M13)
R13       = SUM(N13:Q13)
A14       = " ENDING INVENTORY
B14       = 125000
C14       = ROUND(1.025*B14,0)
D14       = ROUND(1.025*C14,0)
E14       = ROUND(1.025*D14,0)
F14       = ROUND(1.025*E14,0)
G14       = ROUND(1.025*F14,0)
H14       = ROUND(1.025*G14,0)
I14       = ROUND(1.025*H14,0)
J14       = ROUND(1.025*I14,0)
K14       = ROUND(1.025*J14,0)
L14       = ROUND(1.025*K14,0)
M14       = ROUND(1.025*L14,0)
N14       = D14
```

```
O14    = G14
P14    = J14
Q14    = M14
R14    = IF(NOT(Q14=0),Q14,IF(NOT(P14=0),P14,
         IF(NOT(O14=0),O14,N14)))
B15    = "--------
C15    = "--------
D15    = "--------
E15    = "--------
F15    = "--------
G15    = "--------
H15    = "--------
I15    = "--------
J15    = "--------
K15    = "--------
L15    = "--------
M15    = "--------
N15    = "--------
O15    = "--------
P15    = "--------
Q15    = "--------
R15    = "--------
A16    = "   COST OF GOODS SOLD
B16    = B12+B13-B14
C16    = C12+C13-C14
D16    = D12+D13-D14
E16    = E12+E13-E14
F16    = F12+F13-F14
G16    = G12+G13-G14
H16    = H12+H13-H14
I16    = I12+I13-I14
J16    = J12+J13-J14
K16    = K12+K13-K14
L16    = L12+L13-L14
M16    = M12+M13-M14
N16    = N12+N13-N14
O16    = O12+O13-O14
P16    = P12+P13-P14
Q16    = Q12+Q13-Q14
R16    = R12+R13-R14
A17    = '-
S17    = "
A18    = "GROSS PROFIT
B18    = B9-B16
C18    = C9-C16
D18    = D9-D16
E18    = E9-E16
F18    = F9-F16
G18    = G9-G16
H18    = H9-H16
I18    = I9-I16
J18    = J9-J16
K18    = K9-K16
L18    = L9-L16
M18    = M9-M16
N18    = N9-N16
O18    = O9-O16
P18    = P9-P16
Q18    = Q9-Q16
R18    = R9-R16
A19    = '-
S19    = "
A20    = "OPERATING EXPENSES:
A21    = " SALARIES & WAGES
B21    = 100000
C21    = ROUND(1.08*B21,0)
D21    = ROUND(1.08*C21,0)
E21    = ROUND(1.08*D21,0)
F21    = ROUND(1.08*E21,0)
G21    = ROUND(1.08*F21,0)
H21    = ROUND(1.08*G21,0)
I21    = ROUND(1.08*H21,0)
J21    = ROUND(1.08*I21,0)
K21    = ROUND(1.08*J21,0)
L21    = ROUND(1.08*K21,0)
M21    = ROUND(1.08*L21,0)
N21    = SUM(B21:D21)
O21    = SUM(E21:G21)
P21    = SUM(H21:J21)
Q21    = SUM(K21:M21)
R21    = SUM(N21:Q21)
A22    = " FRINGE BENEFITS
B22    = ROUND(20%B21,0)
C22    = ROUND(20%C21,0)
D22    = ROUND(20%D21,0)
E22    = ROUND(20%E21,0)
F22    = ROUND(20%F21,0)
G22    = ROUND(20%G21,0)
H22    = ROUND(20%H21,0)
I22    = ROUND(20%I21,0)
J22    = ROUND(20%J21,0)
K22    = ROUND(20%K21,0)
L22    = ROUND(20%L21,0)
M22    = ROUND(20%M21,0)
N22    = SUM(B22:D22)
O22    = SUM(E22:G22)
P22    = SUM(H22:J22)
Q22    = SUM(K22:M22)
R22    = SUM(N22:Q22)
A23    = " FICA TAX
B23    = ROUND(6.7%B21,0)
C23    = ROUND(6.7%C21,0)
D23    = ROUND(6.7%D21,0)
E23    = ROUND(6.7%E21,0)
F23    = ROUND(6.7%F21,0)
G23    = ROUND(6.7%G21,0)
H23    = ROUND(6.7%H21,0)
I23    = ROUND(6.7%I21,0)
J23    = ROUND(6.7%J21,0)
K23    = ROUND(6.7%K21,0)
L23    = ROUND(6.7%L21,0)
M23    = ROUND(6.7%M21,0)
N23    = SUM(B23:D23)
O23    = SUM(E23:G23)
P23    = SUM(H23:J23)
Q23    = SUM(K23:M23)
R23    = SUM(N23:Q23)
A24    = " FED'L UNEMPLOYMENT INSUR
B24    = ROUND(3.4%B21,0)
C24    = ROUND(3.4%C21,0)
```

```
D24         = ROUND(3.4%D21,0)
E24         = ROUND(3.4%E21,0)
F24         = ROUND(3.4%F21,0)
G24         = ROUND(3.4%G21,0)
H24         = ROUND(3.4%H21,0)
I24         = ROUND(3.4%I21,0)
J24         = ROUND(3.4%J21,0)
K24         = ROUND(3.4%K21,0)
L24         = ROUND(3.4%L21,0)
M24         = ROUND(3.4%M21,0)
N24         = SUM(B24:D24)
O24         = SUM(E24:G24)
P24         = SUM(H24:J24)
Q24         = SUM(K24:M24)
R24         = SUM(N24:Q24)
A25         = " STATE UNEMPLOYMENT INSUR
B25         = ROUND(2%B21,0)
C25         = ROUND(2%C21,0)
D25         = ROUND(2%D21,0)
E25         = ROUND(2%E21,0)
F25         = ROUND(2%F21,0)
G25         = ROUND(2%G21,0)
H25         = ROUND(2%H21,0)
I25         = ROUND(2%I21,0)
J25         = ROUND(2%J21,0)
K25         = ROUND(2%K21,0)
L25         = ROUND(2%L21,0)
M25         = ROUND(2%M21,0)
N25         = SUM(B25:D25)
O25         = SUM(E25:G25)
P25         = SUM(H25:J25)
Q25         = SUM(K25:M25)
R25         = SUM(N25:Q25)
A26         = " BUILDING RENT
B26         = 5000
C26         = 5000
D26         = 5000
E26         = 5000
F26         = 5000
G26         = 5000
H26         = 5000
I26         = 5000
J26         = 5000
K26         = 5000
L26         = 5000
M26         = 5000
N26         = SUM(B26:D26)
O26         = SUM(E26:G26)
P26         = SUM(H26:J26)
Q26         = SUM(K26:M26)
R26         = SUM(N26:Q26)
A27         = " COMPUTER RENT
B27         = 2000
C27         = 2000
D27         = 2000
E27         = 2000
F27         = 2000
G27         = 2000
H27         = 2000
I27         = 2000
J27         = 2000
K27         = 2000
L27         = 2000
M27         = 2000
N27         = SUM(B27:D27)
O27         = SUM(E27:G27)
P27         = SUM(H27:J27)
Q27         = SUM(K27:M27)
R27         = SUM(N27:Q27)
A28         = " DEPRECIATION
B28         = 12000
C28         = ROUND(1.08*B28,0)
D28         = ROUND(1.08*C28,0)
E28         = ROUND(1.08*D28,0)
F28         = ROUND(1.08*E28,0)
G28         = ROUND(1.08*F28,0)
H28         = ROUND(1.08*G28,0)
I28         = ROUND(1.08*H28,0)
J28         = ROUND(1.08*I28,0)
K28         = ROUND(1.08*J28,0)
L28         = ROUND(1.08*K28,0)
M28         = ROUND(1.08*L28,0)
N28         = SUM(B28:D28)
O28         = SUM(E28:G28)
P28         = SUM(H28:J28)
Q28         = SUM(K28:M28)
R28         = SUM(N28:Q28)
A29         = " OFFICE SUPPLIES
B29         = 1000
C29         = ROUND(1.08*B29,0)
D29         = ROUND(1.08*C29,0)
E29         = ROUND(1.08*D29,0)
F29         = ROUND(1.08*E29,0)
G29         = ROUND(1.08*F29,0)
H29         = ROUND(1.08*G29,0)
I29         = ROUND(1.08*H29,0)
J29         = ROUND(1.08*I29,0)
K29         = ROUND(1.08*J29,0)
L29         = ROUND(1.08*K29,0)
M29         = ROUND(1.08*L29,0)
N29         = SUM(B29:D29)
O29         = SUM(E29:G29)
P29         = SUM(H29:J29)
Q29         = SUM(K29:M29)
R29         = SUM(N29:Q29)
A30         = " EQUIPMENT MAINTENANCE
B30         = 1000
C30         = ROUND(1.08*B30,0)
D30         = ROUND(1.08*C30,0)
E30         = ROUND(1.08*D30,0)
F30         = ROUND(1.08*E30,0)
G30         = ROUND(1.08*F30,0)
H30         = ROUND(1.08*G30,0)
I30         = ROUND(1.08*H30,0)
J30         = ROUND(1.08*I30,0)
K30         = ROUND(1.08*J30,0)
L30         = ROUND(1.08*K30,0)
M30         = ROUND(1.08*L30,0)
N30         = SUM(B30:D30)
O30         = SUM(E30:G30)
P30         = SUM(H30:J30)
```

```
Q30     = SUM(K30:M30)
R30     = SUM(N30:Q30)
A31     = " TELEPHONE
B31     = 2000
C31     = ROUND(1.08*B31,0)
D31     = ROUND(1.08*C31,0)
E31     = ROUND(1.08*D31,0)
F31     = ROUND(1.08*E31,0)
G31     = ROUND(1.08*F31,0)
H31     = ROUND(1.08*G31,0)
I31     = ROUND(1.08*H31,0)
J31     = ROUND(1.08*I31,0)
K31     = ROUND(1.08*J31,0)
L31     = ROUND(1.08*K31,0)
M31     = ROUND(1.08*L31,0)
N31     = SUM(B31:D31)
O31     = SUM(E31:G31)
P31     = SUM(H31:J31)
Q31     = SUM(K31:M31)
R31     = SUM(N31:Q31)
A32     = " ELECTRICITY
B32     = 2000
C32     = ROUND(1.08*B32,0)
D32     = ROUND(1.08*C32,0)
E32     = ROUND(1.08*D32,0)
F32     = ROUND(1.08*E32,0)
G32     = ROUND(1.08*F32,0)
H32     = ROUND(1.08*G32,0)
I32     = ROUND(1.08*H32,0)
J32     = ROUND(1.08*I32,0)
K32     = ROUND(1.08*J32,0)
L32     = ROUND(1.08*K32,0)
M32     = ROUND(1.08*L32,0)
N32     = SUM(B32:D32)
O32     = SUM(E32:G32)
P32     = SUM(H32:J32)
Q32     = SUM(K32:M32)
R32     = SUM(N32:Q32)
A33     = " HEAT
B33     = 2000
C33     = ROUND(1.08*B33,0)
D33     = ROUND(1.08*C33,0)
E33     = ROUND(1.08*D33,0)
F33     = ROUND(1.08*E33,0)
G33     = ROUND(1.08*F33,0)
H33     = ROUND(1.08*G33,0)
I33     = ROUND(1.08*H33,0)
J33     = ROUND(1.08*I33,0)
K33     = ROUND(1.08*J33,0)
L33     = ROUND(1.08*K33,0)
M33     = ROUND(1.08*L33,0)
N33     = SUM(B33:D33)
O33     = SUM(E33:G33)
P33     = SUM(H33:J33)
Q33     = SUM(K33:M33)
R33     = SUM(N33:Q33)
A34     = " ADVERTISING
B34     = 25000
C34     = ROUND(1.08*B34,0)
D34     = ROUND(1.08*C34,0)
E34     = ROUND(1.08*D34,0)
F34     = ROUND(1.08*E34,0)
G34     = ROUND(1.08*F34,0)
H34     = ROUND(1.08*G34,0)
I34     = ROUND(1.08*H34,0)
J34     = ROUND(1.08*I34,0)
K34     = ROUND(1.08*J34,0)
L34     = ROUND(1.08*K34,0)
M34     = ROUND(1.08*L34,0)
N34     = SUM(B34:D34)
O34     = SUM(E34:G34)
P34     = SUM(H34:J34)
Q34     = SUM(K34:M34)
R34     = SUM(N34:Q34)
A35     = " POSTAGE & FREIGHT
B35     = 21000
C35     = ROUND(1.08*B35,0)
D35     = ROUND(1.08*C35,0)
E35     = ROUND(1.08*D35,0)
F35     = ROUND(1.08*E35,0)
G35     = ROUND(1.08*F35,0)
H35     = ROUND(1.08*G35,0)
I35     = ROUND(1.08*H35,0)
J35     = ROUND(1.08*I35,0)
K35     = ROUND(1.08*J35,0)
L35     = ROUND(1.08*K35,0)
M35     = ROUND(1.08*L35,0)
N35     = SUM(B35:D35)
O35     = SUM(E35:G35)
P35     = SUM(H35:J35)
Q35     = SUM(K35:M35)
R35     = SUM(N35:Q35)
A36     = " SALES PROMOTIONS
B36     = 15000
C36     = ROUND(1.08*B36,0)
D36     = ROUND(1.08*C36,0)
E36     = ROUND(1.08*D36,0)
F36     = ROUND(1.08*E36,0)
G36     = ROUND(1.08*F36,0)
H36     = ROUND(1.08*G36,0)
I36     = ROUND(1.08*H36,0)
J36     = ROUND(1.08*I36,0)
K36     = ROUND(1.08*J36,0)
L36     = ROUND(1.08*K36,0)
M36     = ROUND(1.08*L36,0)
N36     = SUM(B36:D36)
O36     = SUM(E36:G36)
P36     = SUM(H36:J36)
Q36     = SUM(K36:M36)
R36     = SUM(N36:Q36)
A37     = " PROFESSIONAL MEMBERSHIPS
B37     = 1000
C37     = 1000
D37     = 1000
E37     = 1000
F37     = 1000
G37     = 1000
H37     = 1000
```

```
I37     = 1000
J37     = 1000
K37     = 1000
L37     = 1000
M37     = 1000
N37     = SUM(B37:D37)
O37     = SUM(E37:G37)
P37     = SUM(H37:J37)
Q37     = SUM(K37:M37)
R37     = SUM(N37:Q37)
A38     = " SUBSCRIPTIONS
B38     = 1000
C38     = 1000
D38     = 1000
E38     = 1000
F38     = 1000
G38     = 1000
H38     = 1000
I38     = 1000
J38     = 1000
K38     = 1000
L38     = 1000
M38     = 1000
N38     = SUM(B38:D38)
O38     = SUM(E38:G38)
P38     = SUM(H38:J38)
Q38     = SUM(K38:M38)
R38     = SUM(N38:Q38)
A39     = " EQUIPMENT INSURANCE
B39     = 4100
C39     = ROUND(1.08*B39,0)
D39     = ROUND(1.08*C39,0)
E39     = ROUND(1.08*D39,0)
F39     = ROUND(1.08*E39,0)
G39     = ROUND(1.08*F39,0)
H39     = ROUND(1.08*G39,0)
I39     = ROUND(1.08*H39,0)
J39     = ROUND(1.08*I39,0)
K39     = ROUND(1.08*J39,0)
L39     = ROUND(1.08*K39,0)
M39     = ROUND(1.08*L39,0)
N39     = SUM(B39:D39)
O39     = SUM(E39:G39)
P39     = SUM(H39:J39)
Q39     = SUM(K39:M39)
R39     = SUM(N39:Q39)
B40     = "--------
C40     = "--------
D40     = "--------
E40     = "--------
F40     = "--------
G40     = "--------
H40     = "--------
I40     = "--------
J40     = "--------
K40     = "--------
L40     = "--------
M40     = "--------
N40     = "--------
O40     = "--------
P40     = "--------
Q40     = "--------
R40     = "--------
A41     = "   TOTAL EXPENSES
B41     = SUM(B21:B39)
C41     = SUM(C21:C39)
D41     = SUM(D21:D39)
E41     = SUM(E21:E39)
F41     = SUM(F21:F39)
G41     = SUM(G21:G39)
H41     = SUM(H21:H39)
I41     = SUM(I21:I39)
J41     = SUM(J21:J39)
K41     = SUM(K21:K39)
L41     = SUM(L21:L39)
M41     = SUM(M21:M39)
N41     = SUM(N21:N39)
O41     = SUM(O21:O39)
P41     = SUM(P21:P39)
Q41     = SUM(Q21:Q39)
R41     = SUM(R21:R39)
A42     = '-
S42     = "
A43     = "PRE-TAX PROFIT
B43     = B18-B41
C43     = C18-C41
D43     = D18-D41
E43     = E18-E41
F43     = F18-F41
G43     = G18-G41
H43     = H18-H41
I43     = I18-I41
J43     = J18-J41
K43     = K18-K41
L43     = L18-L41
M43     = M18-M41
N43     = N18-N41
O43     = O18-O41
P43     = P18-P41
Q43     = Q18-Q41
R43     = R18-R41
A44     = "FEDERAL TAXES
B44     = ROUND(50%B43,0)
C44     = ROUND(50%C43,0)
D44     = ROUND(50%D43,0)
E44     = ROUND(50%E43,0)
F44     = ROUND(50%F43,0)
G44     = ROUND(50%G43,0)
H44     = ROUND(50%H43,0)
I44     = ROUND(50%I43,0)
J44     = ROUND(50%J43,0)
K44     = ROUND(50%K43,0)
L44     = ROUND(50%L43,0)
M44     = ROUND(50%M43,0)
N44     = SUM(B44:D44)
O44     = SUM(E44:G44)
P44     = SUM(H44:J44)
Q44     = SUM(K44:M44)
```

```
R44      = SUM(N44:Q44)
A45      = "STATE TAXES
B45      = ROUND(12%B43,0)
C45      = ROUND(12%C43,0)
D45      = ROUND(12%D43,0)
E45      = ROUND(12%E43,0)
F45      = ROUND(12%F43,0)
G45      = ROUND(12%G43,0)
H45      = ROUND(12%H43,0)
I45      = ROUND(12%I43,0)
J45      = ROUND(12%J43,0)
K45      = ROUND(12%K43,0)
L45      = ROUND(12%L43,0)
M45      = ROUND(12%M43,0)
N45      = SUM(B45:D45)
O45      = SUM(E45:G45)
P45      = SUM(H45:J45)
Q45      = SUM(K45:M45)
R45      = SUM(N45:Q45)
B46      = "--------
C46      = "--------
D46      = "--------
E46      = "--------
F46      = "--------
G46      = "--------
H46      = "--------
I46      = "--------
J46      = "--------
K46      = "--------
L46      = "--------
M46      = "--------
N46      = "--------
O46      = "--------
P46      = "--------
Q46      = "--------
R46      = "--------
A47      = "NET INCOME
B47      = B43-B44-B45
C47      = C43-C44-C45
D47      = D43-D44-D45
E47      = E43-E44-E45
F47      = F43-F44-F45
G47      = G43-G44-G45
H47      = H43-H44-H45
I47      = I43-I44-I45
J47      = J43-J44-J45
K47      = K43-K44-K45
L47      = L43-L44-L45
M47      = M43-M44-M45
N47      = N43-N44-N45
O47      = O43-O44-O45
P47      = P43-P44-P45
Q47      = Q43-Q44-Q45
R47      = R43-R44-R45
B48      = "========
C48      = "========
D48      = "========
E48      = "========
F48      = "========
G48      = "========
H48      = "========
I48      = "========
J48      = "========
K48      = "========
L48      = "========
M48      = "========
N48      = "========
O48      = "========
P48      = "========
Q48      = "========
R48      = "========
```

Figure A.10 User-Defined Format Table for Figures 16.22 through 16.26

```
                    User-defined formats
                   1  2  3  4  5  6  7  8

Floating $         Y  Y  Y  Y  Y  Y  Y  Y

Embedded Commas    Y  Y  Y  Y  Y  Y  Y  Y

Minus in ( )       N  N  N  N  N  N  N  N

Zero as Blank      N  N  N  N  N  N  N  N

%                  N  N  N  N  N  N  N  N

Decimal Places     2  2  2  2  2  2  2  2

Scaling factor     0  0  0  0  0  0  0  0


F2 to return to spreadsheet.


R14          Form=IF(NOT(Q14=0),Q14,IF(NOT(P14=0),P14,IF(NOT(O14=0),O14,N14))
Y(es) or N(o) ?
 15)/Format,Define
F1 = Help; F2 = Cancel; F9 = Plot; F10 = View              CAPS
```

Contents Output from Chapter 12

Figure A.11 Contents Output of Figure 12.15

```
SuperCalc ver.  2.00
Information Systems Department
A1        = "Information Systems Department
A2        = "Fiscal Year 1985
A3        = "Salary Budget
B5        = "Annual
C5        = "Biweekly
E5        = "Biweekly
F5        = "Annual
B6        = "Salary
C6        = "Salary
D6        = "Salary
E6        = "Salary
F6        = "Salary
G6        = "Jul 84
H6        = "Aug 84
I6        = "Sep 84
J6        = "Oct 84
K6        = "Nov 84
L6        = "Dec 84
M6        = "Jan 85
N6        = "Feb 85
O6        = "Mar 85
P6        = "Apr 85
Q6        = "May 85
R6        = "Jun 85
A7        = "Employee
B7        = "Before
C7        = "Before
D7        = "Increase
E7        = "After
F7        = "After
G7        = "Weeks =
H7        = "Weeks =
I7        = "Weeks =
J7        = "Weeks =
K7        = "Weeks =
L7        = "Weeks =
M7        = "Weeks =
N7        = "Weeks =
O7        = "Weeks =
P7        = "Weeks =
Q7        = "Weeks =
R7        = "Weeks =
S7        = "Total
A8        = "Name
B8        = "Raise
C8        = "Raise
D8        = "Percent
E8        = "Raise
F8        = "Raise
G8        = 4
H8        = 5
I8        = 4
J8        = 4
K8        = 5
L8        = 4
M8        = 4
N8        = 4
O8        = 5
P8        = 4
Q8        = 5
R8        = 4
S8        = SUM(G8.R8)
A9        = '-
T9        = "
A10        = "Arthur
B10        = 48048
C10        = B10/26
D10        = 12
E10        = ROUND((100+D10)%C10,0)
F10        = E10*26
G10        = C10/2*G8
H10        = C10/2*H8
I10        = C10/2*I8
J10        = C10/2*J8
K10        = C10/2*K8
L10           = C10/2*L8
M10           = C10/2*M8
N10           = C10/2*N8
O10           = E10/2*O8
P10           = E10/2*P8
Q10           = E10/2*Q8
R10           = E10/2*R8
S10           = SUM(G10:R10)
A11           = "Bernadette
B11           = 28028
C11           = B11/26
D11           = 10
E11           = ROUND((100+D11)%C11,0)
F11           = E11*26
G11           = C11/2*G8
H11           = C11/2*H8
I11           = C11/2*I8
J11           = C11/2*J8
K11           = C11/2*K8
L11           = C11/2*L8
M11           = C11/2*M8
N11           = C11/2*N8
O11           = C11/2*O8
P11           = C11/2*P8
Q11           = C11/2*Q8
R11           = C11/2*R8
S11           = SUM(G11:R11)
A12           = "Cynthia
B12           = 32500
C12           = B12/26
D12           = 9
E12           = ROUND((100+D12)%C12,0)
F12           = E12*26
G12           = C12/2*G8
H12           = C12/2*H8
I12           = C12/2*I8
J12           = C12/2*J8
K12           = E12/2*K8
L12           = E12/2*L8
M12           = E12/2*M8
N12           = E12/2*N8
O12           = E12/2*O8
P12           = E12/2*P8
Q12           = E12/2*Q8
R12           = E12/2*R8
S12           = SUM(G12:R12)
A13           = "David
B13           = 27300
C13           = B13/26
D13           = 9
E13           = ROUND((100+D13)%C13,0)
F13           = E13*26
G13           = C13/2*G8
H13           = ROUND(C13/2*H8,0)
I13           = C13/2*I8
J13           = C13/2*J8
K13           = ROUND(C13/2*K8,0)
L13           = C13/2*L8
M13           = C13/2*M8
N13           = C13/2*N8
O13           = ROUND(C13/2*O8,0)
P13           = C13/2*P8
Q13           = ROUND(C13/2*Q8,0)
R13           = E13/2*R8
S13           = SUM(G13:R13)
A14           = "Edward
B14           = 18512
C14           = B14/26
D14           = 10
E14           = ROUND((100+D14)%C14,0)
F14           = E14*26
G14           = C14/2*G8
H14           = C14/2*H8
I14           = C14/2*I8
J14           = C14/2*J8
K14           = C14/2*K8
L14           = C14/2*L8
```

```
M14        = C14/2*M8
N14        = C14/2*N8
O14        = C14/2*O8
P14        = C14/2*P8
Q14        = C14/2*Q8
R14        = C14/2*R8
S14        = SUM(G14:R14)
A15        = '-
T15        = "
A16        = "Total
B16        = SUM(B10.B14)
C16        = SUM(C10.C14)
D16        = AV(D10.D14)
E16        = SUM(E10.E14)
F16        = SUM(F10.F14)
G16        = SUM(G10.G14)
H16        = SUM(H10.H14)
I16        = SUM(I10.I14)
J16        = SUM(J10.J14)
K16        = SUM(K10.K14)
L16        = SUM(L10.L14)
M16        = SUM(M10.M14)
N16        = SUM(N10.N14)
O16        = SUM(O10.O14)
P16        = SUM(P10.P14)
Q16        = SUM(Q10.Q14)
R16        = SUM(R10.R14)
S16        = SUM(S10.S14)
```

Figure A.12 User-Defined Format Table for Figure 12.15

```
                  User-defined formats
                  1  2  3  4  5  6  7  8

Floating $        N  N  Y  Y  Y  Y  Y  Y

Embedded Commas   Y  Y  Y  Y  Y  Y  Y  Y

Minus in ( )      Y  N  N  N  N  N  N  N

Zero as Blank     N  N  N  N  N  N  N  N

%                 N  N  N  N  N  N  N  N

Decimal Places    0  0  2  2  2  2  2  2

Scaling factor    0  0  0  0  0  0  0  0

F2 to return to spreadsheet.


 D9
Y(es) or N(o) ?
 15)/Format,Define
F1 = Help; F2 = Cancel; F9 = Plot; F10 = View
```

APPENDIX B

SIDEWAYS Printing Utility

This utility allows you to print spreadsheets up to 255 positions wide without breaking the rows onto a second page.

Installing SIDEWAYS

The first task is to configure SIDEWAYS for your printer. Insert the UTIL disk into drive A, enter **SIDEINS** and press RETURN. Your screen will display a menu like the one shown in Figure B.1.

Figure B.1 SIDEWAYS Utility Installation Menu

```
You now have the following printer installed:
        IBM Graphics Printer


Which of these printers do you use?

1.   IBM Graphics Printer
2.   Epson Printer
3.   IDS Prism, 460, or 560 (Dataproducts P-80/132)
4.   Okidata Printer
5.   C.Itoh Prowriter Printer
6.   Printronix MVP 150B Printer
7.   Texas Instruments Printer
8.   Mannesmann Talley Printer
9.   Anadex 9000 Series Printer
10.  Hewlett Packard Model 2225 Printer

Enter a number between 1 and 10, or 0 to cancel ...
```

Enter the number that identifies your printer and press RETURN. The installation process doesn't have to be repeated unless you change printers. If your printer isn't shown, consult your printer manual. You may find your printer is compatible with one of those shown on the menu. If your printer isn't compatible, you won't be able to use this utility.

Using SIDEWAYS

Any ASCII formatted file can be printed using the SIDEWAYS utility. This includes all files created via the SuperCalc[3] /Output command. The files created by the /Save command are in a special compressed binary format and cannot be printed by this utility.

To invoke this utility, enter **SIDEWAYS** and press RETURN. You'll be presented with an option selection menu. The menu default settings for the IBM Graphics Printer are shown in Figure B.2.

Figure B.2 SIDEWAYS Utility Option Selection Menu with Defaults

```
                        S I D E W A Y S  version 2.02

Printer selected:         IBM Graphics

Vertical form size (inches):    11.00
Horizontal form size (inches):   8.00

Double strike:                     ON
Character font:                NORMAL            5 x 15 dot matrix

Character spacing (dots):           1             12.00 characters per inch
Line spacing (dots):                1              7.50 lines per inch

Left margin (inches):            0.00
Top margin (inches):             0.00
Bottom margin (inches):          0.00                60 lines per page

Starting page:                      1
Enter name of print file:  b:
Directory:    A:\

F1 for HELP                                                    F10 to exit
```

The menu is used as follows:

↑ and ↓ Scroll from one menu selection item to another.

any key Scrolls through the range of selections for the following options:
- Horizontal form size
- Double strike
- Character font

→ Scrolls through the disk directory showing the names of all .PRN files on the specified drive.

RETURN Enters a parameter for the following options:
- Vertical form size
- Character spacing
- Line spacing
- Left margin
- Top margin
- Bottom margin
- Starting page
- Name of print file
- Directory

F2 or ESC Cancels a selection and restores the previous setting.

BACKSPACE Deletes the last character typed.

F9 Saves the current options to disk.

F10 Terminates SIDEWAYS.

The menu items and their settings are defined as follows:

Vertical form size The distance between the perforations at the top and bottom of the page. The standard form size is 11 inches. If your paper is nonstandard, measure it and enter the results in this field.

Horizontal form size The distance between the tear-away right and left perforated margins. The setting toggles between 8.00 and 13.20.

Double strike Lets you select a heavier print density. The setting toggles between on and off.

Character font Lets you toggle between six font styles:

Font	Dot Matrix	Characters per Inch	Lines per Inch
Normal	5 × 11	12.00	5.71
Large	7 × 11	8.00	6.15
Extra Large	7 × 12	8.00	5.33
Tiny	4 × 9	14.40	7.27
Very Small	4 × 11	14.40	6.15
Small	5 × 9	12.00	7.27

Font selections automatically change the character spacing and line spacing parameters.

Character spacing Valid entries and their resulting characters per inch (CPI) are:

Entry	CPI
1	12.00
2	10.28
3	9.00
4	8.00
5	7.20
6	6.54
7	6.00
8	5.53
9	5.14

Line spacing Valid entries and their resulting lines per inch (LPI) are:

Entry	LPI	Lines per Page
1	8.00	64
2	7.27	58
3	6.66	53
4	6.15	49
5	5.71	46
6	5.33	43
7	5.00	40
8	4.70	38
9	4.44	36

Left margin Defines the open space in inches between the physical top-of-form and the leftmost column of SIDEWAYS printed output.

Top margin Defines the open space in inches between the physical right edge and the first line of SIDEWAYS printed output.

Bottom margin Defines the open space in inches between the physical left edge and the last line of SIDEWAYS printed output.

Starting page Identifies the page where printing is to commence.

Name of print file Both ambiguous and unambiguous filenames may be used. Also, you can enter only the drive name, then use the → key to scroll through the disk directory. When you find the desired filename, press RETURN.

Directory This allows you to specify the subdirectory on a hard disk.

The SIDEWAYS menu is bypassed when the name of the file to be printed is specified immediately following SIDEWAYS, for example:
SIDEWAYS: B:FILENAME.EXT

Index